# EDUCATION OF THE GIFTED
# AND TALENTED

# EDUCATION OF THE GIFTED AND TALENTED

## FIFTH EDITION

**GARY A. DAVIS**
*University of Wisconsin*

**SYLVIA B. RIMM**
*Case Western Reserve University School of Medicine and the
Family Achievement Clinic, Cleveland, Ohio*

Boston   New York   San Francisco
Mexico City   Montreal   Toronto   London   Madrid   Munich   Paris
Hong Kong   Singapore   Tokyo   Cape Town   Sydney

Executive Editor: Virginia Lanigan
Editorial Assistant: Robert Champagne
Production Administrator: Joe Sweeney
Editorial-Production Service: Walsh & Associates, Inc.
Composition and Prepress Buyer: Linda Cox
Manufacturing Buyer: Andrew Turso
Cover Administrator: Kristina Mose-Libon
Electronic Composition: Publishers' Design and Production Services, Inc.

For related titles and support materials, visit our online catalog at www.ablongman.com.

Library of Congress Cataloging-in-Publication Data

Davis, Gary A., 1938–
    Education of the gifted and talented / Gary A. Davis, Sylvia B.
Rimm. — 5th ed.
        p. cm.
Includes bibliographical references and index.
    ISBN 0-205-38850-7
    1. Gifted children—Education—United States. I. Rimm, Sylvia B.,
1935–  II. Title.

    LC3993.9.D38   2003
    371.95—dc21                                    2003041819

Printed in the United States of America

10   9   8   7                         08   07   06

*To Bonnie, Dot, R.C., Emily, Merle,*
*and the memory of Dan and Al*

*To Buck, Ilonna, David, Eric, and Sara*

# CONTENTS

*To provide programs to help meet the psychological, social, educational, and career needs of gifted and talented students.*

*To help students become capable of intelligent choice, independent learning, problem solving, and self-initiated action.*

*To strengthen skills and abilities in problem solving, creative thinking, communication, independent study, and research.*

*To reinforce individual interests.*

*To bring capable and motivated students together for support and intellectual stimulation.*

*To maximize learning and individual development—while minimizing boredom, confusion, and frustration.*

*In sum, to help gifted students realize their potential and their contributions to self and society.*

These are the goals of educational programs for gifted and talented students, and these are the purposes of this book. Gifted and talented students have special needs and special problems. They also have special, sometimes immense, talent to lend to society. We owe it to them to help cultivate their abilities. We owe it to society to help prepare tomorrow's leaders and professional talent. Such students are a tremendous natural resource, one that must not be squandered.

In the mid-1970s, interest in accommodating the educational needs of gifted and talented children began its climb to higher levels and with greater public awareness than ever before. Federal statements, definitions, and funds appeared. States passed legislation that formalized the existence and needs of gifted students and often provided funds for state directors, teachers, and programs. Cities and districts hired gifted program directors and teacher-coordinators who designed and implemented identification, acceleration, and enrichment plans. In many schools and classrooms where help from the outside did not

appear, enthusiastic teachers planned challenging and beneficial projects and activities for gifted students in their classes.

Although the ball was still rolling, in the mid-1980s the gifted movement began an uncertain step backward. As we will see in Chapter 1, the problem was a reborn commitment to *equity*—helping troubled students become more average—in the form of the detracking reform movement. Some school districts trashed their gifted programs along with their tracking and some grouping plans. While the concepts of detracking (to promote equity) and providing for high ability students (to promote excellence) are not necessarily incompatible, many educators perceived gifted programs as a type of tracking and pitched the baby with the bath water.

A second and smaller backward step has been the cooperative learning style of teaching. Cooperative learning groups certainly supply academic and social benefits for most children, but usually not for gifted ones. Gifted students need advanced academic work; challenging independent projects that develop creativity, thinking skills, and habits of independent work; and grouping with gifted peers to accommodate their educational and social needs. They should not be required to work at a too-slow pace or serve as teachers to others in the group.

A third factor that is taking its toll of gifted programs is simply the economy. When the going gets tough, gifted programs—viewed by critics as elitist luxuries for "students who don't need help" or even "welfare for the rich"—are among the first to go.

Although some damage continues, gifted education is recovering nicely. In many schools and districts it is healthier than ever. At least three visible occurrences aided the survival and even growth of gifted education. First, some schools and districts mostly ignored the reform movement and steamed ahead with differentiated instruction for gifted students. Research shows that such resilience is most likely if two disarmingly simple features are present: enthusiastic teachers and administrators and/or state legislation that requires gifted services.

A second fact, documented by Kulik (2003), is simply that despite the reform movement, grouping based on ability or achievement remains alive and well at all educational levels. Special classes in high school (e.g., for advanced math or art) and grouping in the elementary school (especially for math and reading) continues in nearly every individual school.

A third strength, partly a response to the reform movement, and under the *talent development* banner, is the move toward improving education for *all* students—including high-ability ones. For example, high-level activities such as thinking skills and creativity are brought into the regular classroom, and strategies for identifying gifted students are becoming more liberal. Renzulli's Schoolwide Enrichment Model (described in Chapter 7) exemplifies this trend.

Changes to this fifth edition of *Education of the Gifted and Talented* consist largely of updating views, happenings, and research findings. One new and insightful topic is the research by Rimm and her two daughters, Sara Rimm-Kaufman and Ilonna Rimm, in which they explored childhoods, family and career patterns, sources of motivation and resilience, and life satisfactions of over 1,000 extraordinarily successful career women. While this topic is discussed mainly in Chapter 14 dealing with underachievement of females, her research findings are relevant to, and are mentioned in, many topics in many chapters. Chapter 12 includes an expanded section on gifted education in rural areas, a topic of increasing focus. And two completely new—and overdue—topics appear in Chapter 17 on counseling the gifted. First, we discuss problems and fears of gay students, along with steps schools can take to make the educational environment more civilized and safe and to reduce homophobia, including among the teaching staff. Nonaction can be life-threatening. Another new topic is suicide. While gifted students may not commit suicide more often than others, we discuss common traits of and pressures on gifted students that can dispose them to suicide; warning signs of suicidal thoughts; and school suicide prevention measures. With suicide, non-action is even more life-threatening.

The authors with to thank Joanne Riedl for her ever-helpful contributions, Allyn and Bacon editor Virginia Lanigan for her help and encouragement, the many families with gifted children who supplied real-life examples, and Rimm's remarkable professional women for their many insights into the nurturing of future successful females. We are also grateful to the following reviewers of this edition for their time and input: Amy P. Dietrich, University of Memphis; Sally M. Reis, University of Connecticut; and Michael F. Shaughnessy, Eastern New Mexico University. Finally, we are grateful to our families for their encouragement, support, and experiences that helped enrich out text.

# CHAPTER 1

# GIFTED EDUCATION
## MATCHING INSTRUCTION WITH NEEDS

*The mismatch between gifted youth and the curriculum they are forced to study most of the time is nothing short of an American tragedy. The human waste in terms of both student and faculty time is inestimable, and this waste can be found in both rich schools and poor, and even in schools that have well established programs for the gifted.*
Joseph Renzulli (1991, pp. 75–76)

Tens of thousands of gifted and talented children and adolescents are sitting in their classrooms—their abilities unrecognized, their needs unmet. Some are bored, patiently waiting for peers to learn skills and concepts that they had mastered one or two years earlier. Some find school intolerable, feigning illness or creating other excuses to avoid the trivia. Many develop poor study habits from the slow pace and lack of challenge. Some feel pressured to hide their keen talents and skills from uninterested and unsympathetic peers. Some give up on school entirely, dropping out as soon as they are legally able. Some educators call it a "quiet crisis" (Ross, 1993, 1997).

Other gifted students tolerate school but satisfy their intellectual, creative, and artistic needs outside the formal system. The lucky ones have parents who will sponsor their dance or music lessons, chemistry kits and telescopes, art supplies, frequent trips to the library, and home computers. The less fortunate ones make do as best they can, silently paying a price for a predicament they may not understand and that others choose to ignore. That price is lost academic growth, lost creative potential, and sometimes lost enthusiasm for educational success and eventual professional achievement and substantial contributions to society.

Some educators—and many parents of non-gifted students—are not swayed by the proposition that unrecognized and unsupported talent is wasted talent. A common reaction is, "Those kids will make it on their own," or "Give the extra help to kids who really need it!" The argument is that providing special services for highly able or talented students is "elitist"—giving to the "haves" and ignoring the "have-nots"—and therefore unfair and undemocratic. Other criticisms are the costs of additional teachers and other resources, and the idea that pullout programs or special classes remove good role models from the regular classroom. Many teachers feel that students should adjust to the curriculum, rather than the other way around (Coleman & Cross, 2000).

Naming the problem "sounds of silence," Sternberg (1996) itemized dismal ways in which society reacts to the needs of the gifted. Specifically, federal funding is almost absent. There are no laws to protect the rights of the gifted, in contrast with laws protecting minorities and women. As Sternberg noted, gifted programs tend to be the last installed and the first to be axed. Disgruntled parents register their gifted children in private schools. Grade inflation and pass-fail courses reward minimal work, leading gifted students to become listless and bored.

Sternberg reiterated some reasons behind the "sounds of silence." Some see the programs as "welfare for the rich." Average children are the majority, and their parents prefer not to support other parents' "pointy-headed" bright children. Besides, don't gifted children possess great potential without special support? Some critics of gifted programs believe that gifted students are inherently selfish, and that parents of the gifted at PTA meetings are "the loudest and least deserving."

Sternberg stressed altering our attitudes and our behavior. Gifted children are indeed our most valuable natural resource. We must recognize multiple forms of giftedness. We must recognize alternative learning styles, thinking styles, and patterns of abilities and coordinate instruction with these. Programs need to be expanded and evaluated. And to remove sounds of silence, everyone—parents, teachers, administrators, and others—must be educated.

Now some criticisms of gifted education include a strong spark of conscience-rending truth. In fact, white middle-class and Asian students tend to be overrepresented in gifted and talented (G/T) programs, while African American, Hispanic, and poor students are underrepresented. The problem is drawing strong attention to identification strategies, with a move toward multiple and culturally fair identification criteria (Chapter 4); to broadened conceptions of intelligence and giftedness (later in Chapter 1); and even to G/T program evaluation in the sense of assessing effects on students *not* in the program, other teachers, administrators, and the larger community (Borland, 2003).

Our "love-hate" relationship with gifted education has been noted by Gallagher (1997, 2003), Colangelo and Davis (2003), and others. We admire and applaud the individual who rises from a humble background to high educational and career success. At the same time, as a nation we are committed to equality.

The educational pendulum swings back and forth between strong concern for *excellence* and a zeal for *equity*; that is, for helping bright and creative students develop their capabilities and realize their potential contributions to society, or for helping below-average and troubled students reach minimum academic standards. While inter-

est in the gifted has mushroomed worldwide since the mid-1970s, the pendulum is swinging forcefully back to equity. Programs for the gifted are being terminated because they are not "politically correct," as well as because of budget cutting, because of too-few supportive teachers and administrators, and because gifted education is not mandated by the particular state (Purcell, 1995).

Especially, the anti-tracking/anti-ability grouping movement and the companion dilemma of cooperative learning have inflicted damage on G/T programs and on gifted children themselves. Gifted education leader Joseph Renzulli (1992) expressed his perception of this "quiet crisis" by stating that for many people "the word *gifted* has become the worst [type of] ethnic, gender slur word."

Of course, America and the world need both equity *and* excellence. Many students need special help. The rights of slower learners, students with physical or psychological disabilities, and students with language and cultural differences are vehemently defended, and they should be. However, a good argument can be made that gifted students also have rights and that these rights are often ignored. Just as with other exceptional students, students with gifts and talents also deserve an education commensurate with their capabilities. It is unfair to them to ignore, or worse, to prevent the development of their special skills and abilities and to depress their educational aspirations and eventual career achievements. Our democratic system promises each person—regardless of racial, cultural, or economic background and regardless of sex or condition that is disabling—the opportunity to develop as an individual as far as that person's talents and motivation will permit. This guarantee seems to promise that opportunities and training will be provided to help gifted and talented students realize their innate potential.

To those who argue that gifted students will "make it on their own," sensible replies are that (a) they should not be held back and required to succeed in spite of a frustrating educational system, and (b) some do not make it on their own.

Rimm (1997), for example, cited research showing that 10 to 20 percent of high school dropouts are in the tested gifted range. Almost invariably, gifted dropouts are underachievers, talented students who are unguided, uncounseled, and unchallenged (Rimm, 1995d, 2003; Whitmore, 1980). The widely cited *A Nation at Risk* report by the National Commission on Excellence in Education (1983) reported that "over half the population of gifted students do not match their tested ability with comparable achievement in school."

It is not only the gifted students themselves who benefit from specific programs that recognize and cultivate their talents. Teachers involved with gifted students learn to stimulate creative, artistic, and scientific thinking, and they learn to help students understand themselves, develop good self-concepts, and value educational and career accomplishments. In short, teachers of the gifted become better teachers, and their skills benefit "regular" students as well. Society also reaps a profit. Realistically, it is only today's gifted and talented students who will become tomorrow's political leaders, medical researchers, artists, writers, innovative engineers, and business entrepreneurs. Indeed, it is difficult to propose that this essential talent be left to fend for itself— if it can—instead of being valued, identified, and cultivated. Tomorrow's promise is in today's schools, and it must not be ignored.

## HISTORY OF GIFTEDNESS AND GIFTED EDUCATION

### Giftedness over the Centuries

Whether a person is judged "gifted" depends upon the values of the culture. General academic skills or talents in more specific aesthetic, scientific, economic, or athletic areas have not always been judged as desirable "gifts."

In ancient Sparta, for example, military skills were so exclusively valued that all boys beginning at age seven received schooling and training in the arts of combat and warfare. Babies with physical defects, or who otherwise were of questionable value, were flung off a cliff (Meyer, 1965).

In Athens, social position and gender determined opportunities. Upper-class free Greeks sent their boys to private schools that taught reading, writing, arithmetic, history, literature, the arts, and physical fitness. Sophists were hired to teach young men mathematics, logic, rhetoric, politics, grammar, general culture, and "disputation." Apparently, only Plato's Academy charged no fees and selected both young men and women based on intelligence and physical stamina, not social class.

Roman education emphasized architecture, engineering, law, and administration. Both boys and girls attended first-level (elementary) schools and some girls attended second-level (grammar) schools, but higher education was restricted to boys. Rome valued mother and family, however, and some gifted women emerged who greatly affected Roman society, most notably Cornelia, Roman matron and mother of statesmen Gaius and Tiberius Gracchus.

Early China, beginning with the Tang Dynasty in A.D. 618, valued gifted children and youth, sending child prodigies to the imperial court, where their gifts were both recognized and cultivated. China anticipated several principles of modern G/T education. They accepted a multiple-talent concept of giftedness, valuing literary ability, leadership, imagination, and originality, and such intellectual and perceptual abilities as reading speed, memory, reasoning, and perceptual sensitivity (Tsuin-chen, 1961). They also recognized (a) apparently precocious youth who grow up to be average adults, (b) seemingly average youth whose gifts emerge later, and (c) true child prodigies, whose gifts and talents are apparent throughout their lives. Importantly, and attributed to Confucius about 500 B.C., they recognized that education should be available to all children, but they should be educated differently according to their abilities.

In Japan, birth again determined opportunities. During the Tokugawa Society period, 1604–1868 (Anderson, 1975), Samurai children received training in Confucian classics, martial arts, history, composition, calligraphy, moral values, and etiquette. Commoners conveniently were taught loyalty, obedience, humility, and diligence. A few scholars established private academies for intellectually gifted children, both Samurai and common.

Aesthetics influenced Renaissance Europe, which valued and produced remarkable art, architecture, and literature. Strong governments sought out and rewarded the creatively gifted, for example, Michelangelo, Da Vinci, Boccaccio, Bernini, and Dante.

### Giftedness in America

In early America, concern for the education of gifted and talented children was not great. Some gifted youth were accommodated in the sense that attending secondary school and college was based both on academic achievement and the ability to pay the fees (Newland, 1976).

With compulsory attendance laws, schooling became available to all, but special services for gifted children were sparse (Abraham, 1976; Greenlaw & McIntosh, 1988; Heck, 1953; Witty, 1967, 1971). A few bright spots:

- In 1870 St. Louis initiated tracking, which allowed some students to accelerate through the first eight grades in fewer than eight years.
- In 1884 Woburn, Massachusetts, created the "Double Tillage Plan," a form of grade-skipping in which bright children attended the first semester of first grade, then switched directly into the second semester of second grade.
- In 1886 schools in Elizabeth, New Jersey, began a multiple-tracking system that permitted gifted learners to progress at a faster pace.
- In 1891 Cambridge, Massachusetts, schools developed a "double-track" plan; also, special tutors taught students capable of even more highly accelerated work.
- Around 1900, some "rapid progress" classes appeared that telescoped three years of school work into two.
- In 1901 Worcester, Massachusetts, opened the first special school for gifted children.
- In 1916 "opportunity classes" (special classes) were created for gifted children in Los Angeles and Cincinnati.
- By about 1920 approximately two-thirds of all larger cities had created some type of program for gifted students; for example, special classes were begun in 1919 in Urbana, Illinois, and in 1922 in Manhattan and Cleveland.

In the 1920s and into the 1930s interest in gifted education dwindled, apparently for two good reasons. Dean Worcester (Getzels, 1977, pp. 263–264) referred to the 1920s as "the age of the common man" and "the age of mediocrity," a time when "the idea was to have everybody just as near alike as they could be." Administrators had no interest in helping any student achieve beyond the standard; the focus was on *equity*. The second reason was the Great Depression, which reduced most people's concern to mere survival. Providing special opportunities for gifted children was low on the totem pole.

### Giftedness in Europe

In contrast with the United States, tracking and ability grouping (streaming) have not been as contentious in Europe (Passow, 1997). On the surface, not much was said about "the gifted." However, the structure of the European national school systems was openly geared to identifying and educating the most intellectually able. Ability grouping, particularly, has been a traditional way to identify able learners and channel their education.

In England, the strong class-consciousness that has pervaded British society, which includes resentment of inherited (unearned) wealth and titles, led to an egalitarian reluctance to spend scarce educational funds to help gifted students, who seemed already advantaged. Not until the late 1990s did gifted education gain momentum in England (Gross, 2003).

## CONTEMPORARY HISTORY OF GIFTED EDUCATION

Recent history underlying today's strong interest in gifted education begins with capsule stories of the contributions of Francis Galton, Alfred Binet, Lewis Terman, and Leta Hollingworth, followed by the impact of Russia's Sputnik, a look at the gifted movement in America and worldwide, the National Research Center on the Gifted and Talented, the anti-grouping educational reform movement, and the cooperative learning dilemma.

### Hereditary Genius: Sir Francis Galton

The English scientist Sir Francis Galton (1822–1911), a younger cousin of Charles Darwin, is credited with the earliest significant research and writing devoted to intelligence testing. Galton believed that intelligence was related to the keenness of one's senses; for example, vision, audition, smell, touch, and reaction time. His efforts to measure intelligence therefore involved such tests as those of visual and auditory acuity, tactile sensitivity, and reaction time. Impressed by cousin Charles's *Origin of the Species,* Galton reasoned that evolution would favor persons with keen senses—persons who could more easily detect food sources or sense approaching danger. Therefore, he concluded that one's sensory ability— that is, intelligence—is due to natural selection and heredity. The hereditary basis of intelligence seemed to be confirmed by his observations— reported in his most famous book, *Hereditary Genius* (Galton, 1869)—that distinguished persons seemed to come from succeeding generations of distinguished families. Galton initially overlooked the fact that members of distinguished, aristocratic families also inherit a superior environment, wealth, privilege, and opportunity— incidentals that make it easier to become distinguished.

Galton's emphasis on the high heritability of

intelligence is today shared by leading intelligence researchers (e.g., Gottfredson, 1997a, 2003; Plomin, DeFries, McClearn, & McGuffin, 2001).

### Roots of Modern Intelligence Tests: Alfred Binet

Modern intelligence tests have their roots in France, in the 1890s. Alfred Binet, aided by T. Simon, was hired by government officials in Paris to devise a test to identify which (dull) children would not benefit from regular classes and therefore should be placed in special classes to receive special training. Someone had perceptively noticed that teachers' judgments of student ability sometimes were biased by such traits as docility, neatness, and social skills. Some children were placed in schools for the retarded because they were too quiet, too aggressive, or had problems with speech, hearing, or vision. A direct test of intelligence was badly needed.

Binet tried a number of tests that failed. It seemed that normal students and dull students were not particularly different in (a) hand-squeezing strength, (b) hand speed in moving 50 cm (almost 20 inches), (c) the amount of pressure on the forehead that causes pain, (d) detecting differences in hand-held weights, or (e) reaction time to sounds or in naming colors. When he measured the ability to pay attention, memory, judgment, reasoning, and comprehension, he began to obtain results. The tests would separate children judged by teachers to differ in intelligence (Binet & Simon, 1905a, 1905b).

One of Binet's significant contributions was the notion of *mental age*—the concept that children grow in intelligence, and that any given child may be at the proper stage intellectually for his or her years, or else measurably ahead or behind. A related notion is that at any given age level, children who learn the most do so partly because of greater intelligence.

In 1890 noted American psychologist James McKeen Cattell had called for the development of tests that would measure mental ability (Stanley, 1978a); his request was at least partly responsible for the immediate favorable reception to Binet's tests in America. In 1910, Goddard described the use of Binet's methods to measure the intelligence of 400 "feebleminded" New Jersey children and in 1911 summarized his evaluation of two thousand normal children. The transition from using the Binet tests with below-average children to employing them with normal and above-average children thus was complete and successful.

### Lewis Terman: The Stanford-Binet Test, His Gifted Children Studies

Stanford psychologist Lewis Madison Terman made two historically significant contributions to gifted education that have earned him the title of father of the gifted education movement. First, Terman supervised the modification and Americanization of the Binet-Simon tests, producing in 1916 the forerunner of all American intelligence tests, the *Stanford-Binet Intelligence Scale*.

Terman's second contribution was his identification and longitudinal study of 1528 gifted children, published in the *Genetic Studies of Genius* series (Burks, Jensen, & Terman, 1930; Terman, 1925; Terman & Oden, 1947, 1959; see Shurkin, 1992). In 1922 Terman and his colleagues identified 1000 children with Stanford-Binet IQ scores above 135 (most were above 140), the upper one percent. By 1928 he added another 528. Of the 1528, 856 were boys, 672 were girls. The average age was 12 years. All gifted and most comparison children were from major California cities: Los Angeles, San Francisco, Oakland, Berkeley, and Alameda. They had been initially identified by teachers as highly intelligent. Tests, questionnaires, and interviews in at least nine major contacts (field studies or mailings) in 1922, 1927–28, 1936, 1939–40, 1945, 1950, 1955, 1960, and 1972) traced their physical, psychological, social, and professional development for a half-century (e.g., Oden, 1968). The earliest research involved parents, teachers, medical records, and even anthropometric (head) measurements. Terman died

in 1956. His work was continued by others, for example, Anne H. Barbee, Melita Oden, Pauline S. Sears, and Robert R. Sears.

Regarding his subject sample, in comparison with the populations of the California urban centers at the time, there were twice as many children of Jewish descent than would be expected, but fewer children of African American or Hispanic American parents. Chinese American children were not sampled at all because they attended special Asian schools at the time. Note also that the effects of heredity versus environment were hopelessly tangled in Terman's subjects. Most parents of these bright children generally were better educated and had higher-status occupations, and so their children grew up in advantaged circumstances.

Terman's high IQ children—called "Termites" in gifted education circles—were superior in virtually every quality examined. As we will see in Chapter 2, they not only were better students, they were psychologically, socially, and even physically healthier than the average. Terman observed that the myth of brilliant students being weak, unattractive, or emotionally unstable was simply not true as a predominant trend.

Some other noteworthy conclusions related to the Terman studies are these:

• While in elementary and secondary school, those who were allowed to accelerate according to their intellectual potential were more successful. Those not permitted to accelerate developed poor work habits that sometimes wrecked college careers.

• Differences between the most and least successful gifted men indicated that family values and parents' education were major factors. For example, 50 percent of the parents of Terman's "most productive" group were college graduates, but only 15 percent of the parents of the "least productive" group had college degrees.

• On the downside, and with benefit of hindsight, restricting the identification of "genius" or "giftedness" to high IQ scores is severely limiting; artistic and creative genius and genius in a single area were ignored.

• As another negative, Terman's conclusions regarding the mental and social health of his bright children swayed educators for many decades to ignore the sometimes desperate counseling needs of gifted children (Chapter 17).

## Leta Hollingworth: "Nurturant Mother" of Gifted Education

According to Stanley (1978a), Galton was the grandfather of the gifted-child movement, Binet the midwife, Terman the father, and Columbia University's profoundly gifted Leta Hollingworth the nurturant mother. Her pioneering efforts began in 1916, when she encountered an 8-year-old boy who tested 187 IQ on the new Stanford-Binet scale. Said Hollingworth (1942, p. xii), "I perceived the clear and flawless working of his mind against a contrasting background of thousands of dull and foolish minds. It was an unforgettable observation." Indeed, the observation changed the direction of her career and life (Delisle, 1992).

Hollingworth's efforts supporting gifted children and gifted education in the New York area included literally inventing strategies to identify, teach, and counsel gifted children. Space will not permit an adequate summary of this remarkable woman's accomplishments and contributions. See Klein (2000) for a brief but more adequate overview.

In 1922, at New York City Public School 165, with help from school teachers and the Columbia University Teachers College faculty and administrators, Hollingworth studied and personally taught 50 students divided into two classes, one with an average IQ of 165 and the other with an average IQ of 145. Children spent about half of their school hours working on the regular curriculum, the other half on enrichment activities. These included conversational French, history of civilization, social science, algebra, nutrition, music, dramatics, chess, writing biographies, and physi-

cal education, plus field trips to the Museum of Natural History and the Metropolitan Museum of Art. Classroom resources included a typewriter, a mimeograph machine, a microscope, hand lenses, a carpenter's bench, and work tables (Gray & Hollingworth, 1931; Klein, 2000). She spent 18 years at P.S. 165.

A 1936 study took place at Speyer Elementary School (P.S. 500). The Speyer project included 225 students, 25 per class, representing 23 nationalities from all five New York City boroughs. There were 50 gifted students (two "Terman Classes") and 175 students with IQs in the 75–90 range (seven "Binet Classes"). The Terman students interacted daily with the Binet students in such activities as student council, physical education, a Girl Scout troop, a boy's basketball team, the school newspaper, field trips to factories and museums, and recess—which fostered tolerance for individual differences.

The curriculum for the high-IQ Terman students, which earned worldwide attention, included "a rich background of ideas . . . education for initiative and originality . . . [based] upon sound and exhaustive knowledge . . . [and] evolution of culture" (Hollingworth, 1938, p. 297–298). Remarkably, homework was not required and reading was not taught because most students could read before they entered school.

Addressing more general issues, Hollingworth believed that the top 1 percent (IQ 130 to 180) are gifted; gifted children become gifted adults; early identification is essential in order to provide optimal educational experiences; and schools should use multiple identification criteria. Hollingworth's identification procedure included individual IQ tests, interviews with parents and the child, teacher and principal nominations, and a review of each child's social and emotional maturity.

Further, "proper training does not consist in 'pushing' the child on [too] rapidly . . . nor does it consist in 'holding him back' and compelling him to become a drifter and a wastrel of time. The most rational policy . . . is to provide extra work for the bright, in line with their intellectual interests. . . . A good plan is to combine this enrichment with a moderate degree of rapid progress through school" (Hollingworth, 1929, p. 375).

Importantly, Hollingworth observed that children of IQ 140 waste about half their time in school, and children of IQ 170 waste practically all of their time (Hollingworth, 1939). Few of today's gifted educators would disagree.

Hollingworth made early contributions to counseling the gifted, or as she put it, to their "emotional education." Unlike Terman's overemphasis on the mental health of bright children, Hollingworth (1942) underscored that highly intelligent children also are highly *vulnerable*. Social and emotional problems emerge because intellectual development outstrips the child's age and physical development. Especially, the child's advanced vocabulary, interests, and preferences for games with complicated rules will alienate average children. Hollingworth sought to help gifted children understand that less talented students could be friends and, in many circumstances, even mentors.

Many adults do not understand precocity, observed Hollingworth. They may tease a child about his or her knowledge, or a teacher may prevent a child from exploring advanced resources. The combination of adult ignorance with childhood knowledge causes problems for the precocious child. Many gifted children become apathetic in schools that ignore their intellectual needs, and may develop negative attitudes toward authority figures.

Hollingworth's experiences with gifted children are summarized in two books, *Gifted Children: Their Nature and Nurture* (Hollingworth, 1926) and *Children Above 180 IQ Stanford-Binet: Origin and Development* (Hollingworth, 1942). One noteworthy 1931 quote is: "It is the business of education to consider all forms of giftedness in pupils in reference to how unusual individuals may be trained for their own welfare and that of society at large" (Passow, 1981).

Hollingworth also was an early advocate for women's rights. She died in 1939.

## Sputnik: The Russians Are Gaining! The Russians Are Gaining!

Our last significant historical event to predate the 1970s resurgence of interest in gifted education is the launching in 1957 of the Russian satellite Sputnik. To many, the launch of Sputnik was a glaring and shocking technological defeat—Russia's scientific minds had outperformed ours (Tannenbaum, 1979). Suddenly, reports criticizing American education and, particularly, its ignoring of gifted children became popular. For example, a 1950 Educational Policies Commission had noted that mentally superior children were being neglected, which would produce losses in the arts, sciences, and professions. In a book entitled *Educational Wastelands,* Bestor (1953) charged that "know-nothing educationists" had created schools that provided "meager intellectual nourishment or inspiration," particularly for bored gifted students.

Tannenbaum (1979) referred to the aftermath of Sputnik as a "total talent mobilization." Gifted students were identified. Acceleration and ability grouping were installed. Academic course work was telescoped (condensed). College courses were offered in high school. Foreign languages were taught to elementary school children. New math and science curricula were developed. Funds, public and private, were earmarked for training in science and technology. In high school there was a new awareness of and concern for high scholastic standards and career mindedness. Bright and talented students were expected to take tough courses to "fulfill their potential, and submit their developed abilities for service to the nation" (Tannenbaum, 1979).

While Sputnik itself was a great success, the keen interest in educating gifted and talented students fizzled in about five years. The awareness and concern were rekindled in the mid 1970s.

## Gifted Education in the Twenty-First Century

By 1990, the U.S. government and all 50 states had enacted legislation and many states had allocated funds. Many teachers and administrators nationwide and across Canada had become more and more committed to gifted education. Most large school systems and many small ones had initiated programs and services for gifted children. Researchers, teachers, materials writers, and others continue to write articles, books, tests, and new materials for teaching computer skills, math, art, science, communication skills, learning-how-to-learn skills, values, leadership, and creativity and other thinking skills. Counseling has become increasingly recognized as an essential program component. Enthusiasm among many educators—and certainly among parents of children who are gifted—remains high.

The gifted movement also is worldwide, although some countries are just beginning to make some sort of special provisions for their high-ability students (Persson, Joswig, & Balogh, 2000). For example, a few European countries do not allow enrichment or special classes, but they permit grade-skipping—which, incidentally, requires not one whit of special facilities, funds, or teacher training. Some European countries offer no gifted education options whatever, but do sponsor competitions in math, computing, physics, and the arts (e.g., painting, writing, filmmaking); some countries provide special schools only for music, art, or sports; some routinely assume that classroom differentiation of instruction by teachers is all that is needed for faster learners; some are just now beginning to offer special classes for high-ability learners; some are adopting Gardner's multiple-intelligences model (explained later in this chapter) to accommodate bright and talented students in the regular classroom; some leave gifted education programs to the discretion of individual schools; and worst of all, some simply count on gifted children always to be resilient—and somehow to manage whatever their circumstances (Persson, Joswig, & Balogh, 2000).

Gifted programs of various types—and with various degrees of teacher training and commitment and support by administrators—presently are offered in Australia, Austria, Belgium, Brazil, Bulgaria, mainland China, Columbia, Croatia, the Dominican Republic, Egypt, England, Finland, France, Germany, Guam, Hong Kong, Hungary, India, Indonesia, Iraq, Israel, Japan, Korea, Latvia, Mexico, Micronesia, the Netherlands, the Philippines, Poland, Portugal, Romania, Russia, Saudi Arabia, Scotland, Singapore, Slovakia, Slovenia, South Africa, Spain, Sweden, Switzerland, Taiwan, the Ukraine, and Wales (Gross, 2003; Passow, 1997; Persson, Joswig, & Balogh, 2000; Sisk, 1990).

## Comments from the *National Excellence* Report

The 1993 U.S. Department of Education report *National Excellence: A Case for Developing America's Talent* (Ross, 1993) is a breath of fresh air for educators of gifted students. The report, whose first chapter is entitled, "A Quiet Crisis in Educating Talented Students," flies smack in the face of the powerful and seemingly anti-gifted educational reform movement aimed at abolishing tracking and grouping students according to ability (discussed later in this chapter). Some highlights of the report are:

• The United States is squandering one of its most precious resources—the gifts and talents of many of its students. These youngsters are not challenged to do their best work. They perform poorly in comparison with top students in other countries.
• America relies on its top-performing students to provide leadership in science, math, writing, politics, dance, art, business, history, health, and other human pursuits.
• Most gifted and talented students spend their school days without attention to their special learning needs; teachers make few if any provisions for gifted students.
• In elementary school, gifted students already have mastered 35 to 50 percent of the curriculum to be offered before they begin the school year.

Some report recommendations are:

• Content standards, curriculum, and assessment practices must challenge all students, including those who are gifted and talented.

• Communities and schools must provide more and better opportunities for top students to learn advanced material and move at their own pace. Flexible learning opportunities must be available inside and outside the school building.

• Opportunities, support, and high-level learning experiences must be made available for disadvantaged and minority children with outstanding talents.

• Teachers must receive better training in how to teach high-level curricula. They need to provide instruction that sufficiently challenges all students. This will benefit children at every academic level.

There is indeed a quiet crisis in American schools.

### The Bell Curve and Recent IQ Conclusions

Herrnstein and Murray's (1994) *The Bell Curve* appears to present a strong gift to gifted education. The authors support programs for the gifted because these high IQ persons supply our professional leadership. However, Sternberg, Callahan, Burns, Gubbins, Purcell, Reis, Renzulli, and Westberg (1995; see also Richert, 2003; Rogers, 1996) made these points regarding the "meanspirited and prejudiced" authors. First, Herrnstein and Murray's definition of *giftedness* (high IQ scores) ignores modern conceptions such as those of Gardner, Sternberg, Renzulli, and even the federal multiple-talent definition. Second, correlations (e.g., between IQ and life success) do not necessarily imply causation, that is, that a high IQ causes life success. Third, Herrnstein and Murray stress group and racial differences in IQ, for example, that whites, Asians, and especially Jewish people, on average, produce higher IQ scores. They pay little attention to the necessity of a favorable social and physical environment. Fourth, *The Bell Curve* largely ignores the modifiability of tested IQ scores, for example, with Feuerstein's *Instrumental Enrichment* program (see Chapter 11). Finally, the central danger, conclude Sternberg et al., is that in the IQ meritocracy described in *The Bell Curve,* low performance on an IQ test

shades into low valuation as a human being, a position with which thoughtful people disagree.

It feels good to criticize a politically incorrect book for its apparent racism, "classism," occasional faulty logic, and for maligning traditional American values of initiative and hard work. However, intelligence researchers and scholars have recently presented polite in-your-face arguments—based on decades of twin and sibling studies—that essentially conclude, "life is a long train of activities that constantly requires . . . learning, thinking, problem-solving, and decision making . . . in short, the exercise of *g*" (general intelligence; Gottfredson, 2003, p. 35). Further, whether we like it and whether it appears elitist, racist, unfair, and/or undemocratic, basic intelligence, which is best measured by IQ tests, "is the best single predictor—and a better one than social class background" (Gottfredson, p. 35), of school achievement, years of education, occupational level, performance in job training, performance on the job, social competence, child abuse, delinquency, crime, poverty, accident proneness, death from auto accidents, dropping out of school, having a child out of wedlock, smoking during pregnancy, health problems and Medicare claims, and getting a divorce within five years of marriage (Gottfredson, in press, 1997b; Tannenbaum, 2003). The predictions are valid for all American subpopulations (Gottfredson, 2003).

While such research conclusions have indeed placed many fair-minded scholars in an uncomfortable dilemma, others remain stolidly in their initial and smug pro-IQ or anti-IQ positions.

On the bright side, other factors do substantially affect life outcomes, for example, favorable family circumstances, practice and experience, persistence, special talents, physical capabilities, and a winning personality (Tannenbaum, 2003).

### NATIONAL RESEARCH CENTER ON THE GIFTED AND TALENTED

Joseph Renzulli's manifold contributions to gifted education appear in many chapters. A major brainchild is his National Research Center on the

Gifted and Talented (NRC/GT). The purpose of NRC/GT is to conduct "consumer-oriented" research on key problems in gifted education, and thereby influence educational practices and policies. It is a collaborative effort among Renzulli's University of Connecticut, Yale University, and the Universities of Georgia and Virginia; 54 state and territorial departments of education; over 260 public and private schools that represent diverse ethnic, socioeconomic, and demographic differences; 200 content area consultants; and "stakeholders" representing professional organizations, parent groups, businesses, federal agencies, and state and local legislators and boards of education.

Some challenges are to (1) establish fair identification instruments and practices; (2) identify effective programming practices; (3) examine giftedness in special populations; (4) examine the evaluation of gifted programs; (5) evaluate different staff development techniques; (6) study standards for teacher certification in gifted education; (7) apply a theory-based approach (the Schoolwide Enrichment Model, Chapter 7) to identification, teaching, and program evaluation; (8) study methods and effects of *compacting*—the elimination of already mastered material; (9) describe financial, administrative, and staff training activities for schools that serve students from various ethnic, socioeconomic, handicapped, and geographic groups; and (10) disseminate information about these practices and issues to educators, policymakers, and parents.

Some products include the *NRC/GT Newsletter*, which summarizes, for example, exemplary elementary school programs (Delcourt, 1994), planning gifted programs (Gubbins, 1999), evaluating gifted programs (Gubbins, 1998), professional development in gifted education (Gubbins, 2000; Westberg et al., 1998), and free summer programs for gifted and talented teenagers (McCoach, 1999). The NRC/GT also distributes one-sheet *Practitioner's Guides* that encapsulate, for example, "What Parents [and Teachers] Need To Know About ..." gifted young children; gifted adolescents; attention deficit hyperactivity disorder (ADHD); creativity; acceleration; early read-

ers; television viewing; and more. Videotapes are available that describe, among other things, teaching thinking skills, curricular options, and curriculum compacting.

Perhaps most importantly, 50- to 150-page research reports (including library research) present information on such subjects as grouping, cooperative learning, gifted children's self-concepts, parenting young gifted children, state policies, curriculum compacting, recruiting and retaining African American students, developing mathematical talent, gifted students with learning disabilities, cluster grouping gifted students (Chapter 6), perfectionism (having neurotically high standards; Chapters 13, 14, and 17), ADHD, using Gardner's multiple intelligences model (described later in this chapter), and evaluating identification instruments.

Their best-known—and most depressing—project was a national survey of ongoing classroom practices for gifted students. The Classroom Practices Study (Archambault & Hallmark, 1992; Westberg, Dobyns, & Salvin, 1992) surveyed 7000 teachers to discover "a very disturbing picture ... teachers make only minor modifications in regular classrooms to meet the needs of gifted and talented students." About half of the teachers had no training in gifted education, and about half did not identify gifted students in their classes. Over half of the schools did not permit acceleration. There were essentially no opportunities for students to work on advanced projects, work in enrichment centers, engage in self-directed learning with advanced curriculum, work at a higher grade level, or work with other gifted students.

All teachers of the gifted or program developers should become acquainted with the insights, guidelines, problem solutions, and material pioneered by the NRC/GT. NRC/GT is funded by the Jacob K. Javits Gifted and Talented Students Education Act of 1988, Office of Educational Research and Improvement, U.S. Department of Education (National Research Center on the Gifted and Talented, 362 Fairfield Road, U-7, Storrs, CT 06269-2007; www.gifted.uconn.edu).

## EDUCATIONAL REFORM AND ABILITY GROUPING

Since the mid-1980s a reform movement has aimed at abolishing ability grouping. The move is toward *heterogeneous* (ability) grouping, and away from *homogeneous* (ability) grouping. For gifted children, the consequences are bad. The movement includes eliminating separate classes for faster and slower students at both elementary and secondary levels. It includes abolishing special classes for the gifted and usually gifted programs themselves.

Reis (Reis et al., 1992) referred to the trend as a "national hysteria." Renzulli (1995) called grouping the "single biggest issue in gifted education." Renzulli (1991) reminded us that with heterogeneous grouping "bright kids learn nothing new until January."

The most common target of critics is *between-class grouping,* also called *tracking, XYZ grouping,* or *homogeneous grouping,* in which, for example, low, average, and high ability students are placed in three different classes at each grade. Two other common forms of ability grouping are *cross-grade grouping* and *within-class grouping.* Cross-grade grouping, or the *Joplin Plan,* means placing students for part of their day in the next higher grade, usually for reading, math, or science (Kulik, 2003; Kulik and Kulik, 1997; Schatz, 1990).

Within-class grouping includes separating students in each class for small-group instruction, usually based on reading or math ability. Within-class grouping also includes cooperative learning, in which two to four students interact to master material or produce a group answer to a problem; skill groups, in which small groups work on specific skills (e.g., math or reading); groups created to complete projects of various types; and peer teaching (Schatz, 1990).

The most influential spokespersons have been Jeanie Oakes (1985; Goodlad & Oakes, 1988), author of *Keeping Track,* and Sapon-Shevin (1994). Oakes (1985) argued several core points. First, she claims that tracking is *ineffective*—students learn less and they lose motivation and self-esteem. Second, she alleges that the practice is *discriminatory* and racist because too many minority children are in slow tracks. Third, she asserts that tracking is *unfair in principle*; it is simply wrong to deny access to deeper academic content and opportunities based on ability.

Gifted education leader James Gallagher (2000) suggested that some attacks on gifted education are because it is so good—gifted students usually do have smaller classes, more enthusiastic teachers, more individualization, and a richer curriculum. Such features could benefit all students. Perhaps it is not surprising that the American public finds at least some of Oakes's arguments compelling, and the detracking, degrouping movement remains with us.

Gifted education and gifted students are in deep trouble without grouping practices, some of which have been used effectively for over a century. Most G/T program designs place capable students in part-time or full-time *special classes* for enriched or accelerated work; in weekly or more frequent *pullout* or *resource room* groups for independent projects or other skill-development activities; in small *cluster groups* in one classroom at each grade for advanced learning activities and projects; in *talent, interest,* or *project* groups (Schatz, 1990); in higher grades for part of the day (*cross-grade grouping*); or in *school-within-a-school* plans, in which gifted students attend academic classes with other gifted students, nonacademic classes with regular students.

What does research say about ability grouping? Kulik (1992a, 1992b, 2003; Kulik and Kulik, 1997) conducted meta-analyses on 51 controlled studies of between-class grouping. Results of meta-analyses are reported in *effect size,* which is the difference between two groups in standard deviation units. Effect sizes may be interpreted as follows (Kulik, 1992b):

.10 to .35 = small difference
.35 to .70 = moderate difference
Above .70 = large difference

For practical purposes, effect sizes larger than

about .30 (a difference of approximately three months achievement) indicate a practically significant difference between an experimental condition (e.g., ability grouping) versus its control (e.g., heterogeneous classes).

The Kuliks' (e.g., 2003) conclusions favor grouping gifted kids, if not all kids. First of all, Kulik (1992a) reminds us of the highly successful effects of grouping mathematically talented adolescents for acceleration in summer or college programs. Such students make phenomenal gains in math achievement (e.g., Lupkowski-Shoplik, Benbow, Assouline, & Brody, 2003; Stanley, 1991a).

Kulik (1992b) reported that students grouped in lower- and middle-level tracks learn the same amount as equivalent pupils do in mixed classes. However, "Students in the top classes in XYZ programs outperform equivalent pupils from mixed classes" (p. vii). Kulik (1992b) also found a worthwhile achievement advantage with two types of grouping likely to be used in gifted programs. With part-time *cross-grade grouping,* the overall achievement advantage of homogeneously grouped versus heterogeneous classes was reflected in an effect size of about 0.30. *Within-class grouping* (to teach arithmetic) produced an overall achievement advantage effect size of about 0.35; low-, medium-, and especially high-ability students benefited, with effect sizes of 0.20, 0.15, and 0.40, respectively. *An important conclusion of the Kuliks is that the achievement of low-ability students has not been harmed by homogeneous grouping.*

Analyzing 13 research syntheses, including those of the Kuliks, Rogers (1991) noted that grouping for enrichment, either within the class or in a resource room (pullout program), produces substantial gains in academic achievement, creativity, and other thinking skills.

Rogers (1991) noted that the higher achievement of gifted students likely is due to a combination of higher ability, interested teachers, and "the willingness of gifted students to learn while in a classroom with other interested, high-ability learners." Table 1.1 summarizes effect sizes across the 13 syntheses for various grouping practices currently used with gifted students. The data strongly support the practice of grouping gifted students.

But what about self-esteem? According to "stigma theory" grouping should cause slow-track students to label themselves "dummies" and lower their self-expectations (e.g., Oakes, 1985). Perhaps so; but self-concepts also are shaped by successes and failures that occur when interacting with others of higher or lower ability. In mixed-ability classes less able students observe others learning faster and see themselves as the last to understand. Such day-after-day comparisons can devastate self-concepts (Kulik, 1992a).

Many teachers are aware of the blossoming effect that occurs for some average- and low-ability children when the gifted leave for pullout enrichment activities or are removed altogether for special classes (Feldhusen, 1989b). Said one student, "When Bill (the gifted one) went out to work with other gifted kids, the rest of us were like the moon and the stars—that's when we finally got a chance to shine" (Fiedler, Lange, & Winebrenner, 1993).

Kulik (2003) noted that the self-concepts of low- and medium-ability students tend to be *higher* when ability grouped than in heterogeneous classes. However, high-ability students, when grouped (and competing) with others of high ability, seem to be "taken down a peg"; their self-concepts are slightly slower—perhaps an appropriate dose of humility.

Rogers's (1991) and Kulik's (1992a, 1992b, 2003) conclusions regarding the detracking movement take the form of guidelines that are combined in Inset 1.1.

Finally, some optimistic news. Perhaps the damage from the detracking, degrouping, heterogeneous classes movement is not as extensive as many assume. Based on surveys of grouping/ tracking by ability or skill at all elementary and secondary levels, Kulik (2003; see also Gamoran & Weinstein, 1998; Loveless, 1999; Rees, Argys, & Brewer, 1996) concluded that (1) almost all elementary and secondary schools in America still

**TABLE 1.1** Effect Sizes for Acceleration and Enrichment Options Used in Gifted Programs

| Option | Effect Size |
| --- | --- |
| **Options in Which Grouping Is Central** | |
| Pullout Programs (Enrichment; Curriculum Extension) | .65 |
| Ability-Grouped Enriched Classes | .33 |
| Cross-grade Grouping (Reading, Math) | .45 |
| Nongraded Classes | .38 |
| Regrouping for Specific Instruction (Reading, Math) | .34 |
| Advanced Placement Programs | .29 |
| Cluster Grouping (within regular class) | .62 |
| Special Classes for Gifted | .33 |
| Cooperative Learning (three methods) | 0, .38, .30 |
| **More Individualized Options; Grouping Is Less Central** | |
| Early Entrance to School | .36 |
| Subject Acceleration | .49 |
| Curriculum Compacting (Compression) | .45 |
| Grade Skipping | .78 |
| Concurrent Enrollment (e.g., in junior and senior high school) | .36 |
| Credit by Examination | .75 |
| Grade Telescoping (e.g., 4 years of high school into 3) | .56 |
| Mentorships | .42 |

Adapted from Rogers, 1992.

use ability or skill grouping for some classes, and (2) most children are grouped by ability or skill either within their class or in separate classrooms for some or all of their work. Faster and slower students are segregated most often in high school and least often in elementary school. Within-class grouping (especially for reading or math) continues to be widely used in elementary schools—even in schools with highly reform-conscious administrators. See Inset 1.2.

**COOPERATIVE LEARNING**

Cooperative learning is students working together and helping each other learn, typically in groups of two to four. Often, groups are composed of a mixture of ability levels. For example, a four-student group might include two average students, a mainstreamed student with a learning disability or retardation, and a fast-learning student. Members of the group can all receive the same grade, based on group accomplishment, or members of the group can be graded separately, based on their specific contributions and achievements. Cooperative learning has proven remarkably effective, leading some experts (and teachers) to recommend it as the primary instructional method, especially for teaching reading, writing, and math (Slavin, Madden, & Stevens, 1990).

The benefits of cooperative learning, if only half correct, justify its flourishing popularity—with all but gifted students. Both motivation and

**INSET 1.1** _____

## Guidelines about Grouping the Gifted

Based on reviews of research syntheses, Rogers (1992) and Kulik (1992) summarized their conclusions relating to ability grouping in these guidelines.

- *Schools should resist calls for the wholesale elimination of ability grouping* (Kulik; Rogers). Some grouping programs help students a great deal. Programs for gifted students are beneficial. Also, slow, average, and bright students benefit from grouping programs that adjust the curriculum to aptitude levels of the groups, specifically, cross-grade grouping and within-class grouping.
- *Benefits are slight from programs that group children by ability, but prescribe common curricular experiences for all ability groups* (Kulik). Schools should not expect student achievement to change dramatically by either eliminating or initiating such programs.
- *Students who are academically or intellectually gifted should spend the majority of their school day with others of similar ability and interests* (Rogers). Such grouping (e.g., in special classes, special schools) has produced marked academic achievement gains as well as improved attitudes.
- *When full-time gifted programs are not available, gifted students might be offered cluster-grouping or cross-grade instructional grouping according to their individual proficiencies in school subjects* (Rogers).
- *Gifted students, individually or in groups, should be offered acceleration-based options* (Kulik; Rogers). Highly talented youngsters profit greatly from work in programs of accelerated work.
- *Mixed-ability cooperative learning plans should be used sparingly for gifted students* (Rogers). Cooperative learning might be used with the gifted for developing social skills. Research thus far indicates that—for gifted students—cooperative learning seems to produce fewer academic benefits than grouping plans.

achievement run higher. Group discussions promote cognitive growth and thinking skills (e.g., examining others' ideas, asking good questions, avoiding hasty decisions, viewing situations in new ways; John-Steiner, 2000). Group interaction helps children construct knowledge. Students learn to communicate clearly, check for understanding, and resolve conflicts constructively. Self-confidence and self-esteem improve. Social and teamwork skills improve, including those of mainstreamed students. The classroom climate improves, with decreased classroom management problems. Surveying third-grade teachers, Mc-Manus and Gettinger (1996) found widespread and daily use of cooperative groups.

But cooperative learning works against the educational needs of gifted students. The reasons are simple but important. Gifted students:

- Often prefer not to work in cooperative groups—they can learn faster alone (Robinson, 1997, 2003)
- Often must assume the role of junior teacher
- May get stuck doing most of the work for their group
- Miss opportunities for accelerated or enriched work that matches their abilities, for example, with other gifted students
- For these reasons, lose academic interest and motivation

**INSET 1.2** _____

## A Bicycle Ride: Why We Need Grouping

Rimm (1992c) assembled her thoughts on ability grouping by comparing the issue to bike riding with her husband and youngest daughter—both of whom needed a faster pace and longer ride to obtain a suitable fitness experience. Thinking analogically about children of varying abilities in the same classroom, she imagined not three but 23 bike riders and posed the following questions. As you read, think first about your answer to each biking question, then think of the answer as though you were a student in a classroom:

1. Was the main purpose of our biking social or physical fitness? (While social fitness is important, the primary purpose of school is not social but educational fitness.)
2. Would it have been possible for us to all meet our social and physical fitness goals with the same activity? (We cannot meet all students' social and educational fitness needs with the same activities; they can be better met with grouping for some parts of the curriculum and not grouping for others.)
3. How would my husband and daughter have felt if I asked them to slow their pace for me or spend most of their time teaching me to bike better? (Students who need more challenge may resent teachers and other students who slow their learning process. They feel bored in class and tend to feel superior to other kids if they spend their time teaching instead of learning.)
4. How would I feel about myself if the more able bikers were to spend most of their time teaching me or slowing down to wait for me? (Slower students hesitate to ask questions or to volunteer and discuss if they feel they are slowing other students. Believing they are slowing others is not good for self-esteem.)
5. Would the better bikers enjoy biking with persons of similar skills, strength, and endurance? (Very capable students enjoy learning with intellectual peers and often miss the stimulation when peers are unavailable.)
6. How could I feel good about my physical fitness activity even though I was slowest? (All children experience satisfaction in learning if they feel they are making progress. Setting and reaching personal goals is important for children at all levels.)
7. How would I feel if an outsider insisted that I keep up with the faster bikers? (Children feel pressured if they are rushed beyond their capacity.)
8. How would I feel if others did not see the value of my physical fitness activity for me? (Children who are not viewed as achieving by parents and teachers do not feel good about themselves. All students should experience a sense of accomplishment and "worth-whileness" of effort.)
9. How would I feel if my fitness and strength improved, but I was forced to continue to ride at my same speed and distance? (It is important to show children paths for movement between groups, particularly upward mobility through effort.)

A bike ride provides physical fitness only when all riders are encouraged to exercise to their abilities.

## Motivation and Engagement

Not surprisingly, some students in cooperative groups are highly engaged while others are more passive. Robinson (2003) described three common and interrelated problems that affect gifted students: the *social loafing, free-rider,* and *sucker* effects.

Social loafing is just that. Passive and less capable students simply let the bright kids do the work, and then share in a nice group grade. Further, the larger the group, the more individuals are willing to let others perform the work or assume responsibility.

Recent eye-opening research has discovered that two-person groups—dyads—produce greater individual learning than other cooperative group sizes. The results are best when a high-achieving student is paired with a low-achieving student (Fuchs et al., 2000; Robinson, 2003), and less dramatic if a medium-achiever is paired with a low-achiever. Either way, it's difficult to loaf in a group of two.

With the free-rider effect, a group member may not contribute if he or she does not see a need to do so. That is, other members are willing to do the work, and rewards are based on group, not individual, performance. For example, completing one worksheet or creating one group product invites free riding (Slavin, 1992). The lowest achiever is not always the free rider. If the group is evaluated on the best score, high-ability members work harder; if evaluation is based on the lowest score, low-ability members work harder (Robinson, 2003).

The sucker effect occurs when high-achieving group members get tired of being taken advantage of by free riders—and they quit working. They don't like being "played for a sucker." Kerr (1983) found that college students sometimes preferred to fail rather than carry a free rider and be a sucker. With gifted students, the sucker effect can severely depress school performance, especially if the bright student is unable to (1) motivate others to help or (2) switch to another group (Robinson, 2003; Robinson & Clinkenbeard, 1993).

On the positive side, at least two developments in recent years favor gifted learners. First, cooperative learning researchers and advocates are paying increased attention to the roles, learning needs, and dynamics of high ability students in cooperative groups. It's hardly surprising to hear that high-ability students are more productive when they are grouped together (Fuchs et al., 1998; Webb, Nemer, Chizhik, & Sugrue, 1998). As an example of cooperative-learning dynamics, Webb and Palinscar (1996) found that when a low-, medium-, and high-ability student are grouped together, the high ability student usually tutors the low-ability student while the medium-ability student is left out. They concluded that medium-ability students, as well as high-ability students, learn better if grouped homogeneously. As a second recent trend, while the traditional focus has been on basic skill development, cooperative learning advocates are beginning to recommend using more complex tasks, which promote both higher-level thinking skills and higher achievement (Barron, 2000; Fuchs et al., 2000; Robinson, 2003).

## DEFINITIONS OF GIFTEDNESS

Defining *gifted* and *talented* is both an important and a complicated matter. First, the particular definition adopted by a school district will guide the identification process and thus determine who is selected for the special services of a gifted program. Second, there is danger that one's definition and consequent identification methods will discriminate against such special populations as poor, minority, disabled, underachieving, and even female students. Third, one's definition of gifts and talents is also tied to programming practices; opportunities should be available for different types of gifts and talents. Fourth, the labeling effect of defining a student as "gifted" can have both positive and adverse effects, for example, raising self-esteem and self-expectations on one hand, but sometimes alienating peers, peers' parents, and siblings, on the other.

There is no one definition of "gifted," "talented," or "giftedness" that is universally accepted. Common usage of the terms even by experts is ambiguous and inconsistent. For example, it is acceptable to use the terms interchangeably, as when we describe the same person as either a "gifted artist" or a "talented artist." For convenience, your authors and others use the single word *gifted* to abbreviate *gifted and talented*.

Some writers and the general public see *talent* and *giftedness* on a continuum, with giftedness at the upper end. Noted Cox (1986), we speak of talented musicians, writers, and scientists and the few who are truly gifted, but no one reverses this usage.

Related to this continuum definition, many programs include students who barely meet the established criteria, along with one or two others who are extraordinarily brilliant or astonishingly talented in a particular area. No accepted label distinguishes between these two visible groups, although "extremely gifted" or "low-incidence gifted" are used, along with the tongue-in-cheek "severely gifted," "profoundly gifted," or "exotically gifted."

June Cox (Cox, Daniel, and Boston, 1985) avoids the term *gifted,* preferring *able learners.* Renzulli (1994; Renzulli and Reis, 1997) prefers the phrase "gifted behaviors," which can be developed in certain students at certain times and in certain circumstances. They argue that the title of "gifted" should not be bestowed on children as a result of the identification process. For the same reason, many prefer the phrase "potentially gifted."

## Formal Federal Definitions of Gifted and Talented

Any discussion of definitions of *gifted* and *talented* must begin with the original U.S. Office of Education (now the Department of Education) definition of gifted and talented (Marland, 1972):

Gifted and talented children are those identified by professionally qualified persons who by virtue of outstanding abilities are capable of high performance. These are children who require differentiated educational programs and services beyond those normally provided by the regular school program in order to realize their contribution to self and society.

Children capable of high performance include those with demonstrated achievement and/or potential in any of the following areas:

1. General intellectual ability
2. Specific academic aptitude
3. Creative or productive thinking
4. Leadership ability
5. Visual and performing arts
6. Psychomotor ability

The federal definition is thoughtful and appealing. It recognizes not only high general intelligence, but gifts in specific academic areas and in the arts. It further calls attention to creative, leadership, and psychomotor gifts and talents. It recognizes that gifted and talented students require "differentiated educational programs and services beyond those normally provided," thus justifying the development of gifted programs. It recognizes the two fundamental aims of gifted programs: To help individual gifted and talented students develop their high potential and to provide society with educated professionals who are creative leaders and problem solvers. By including "demonstrated achievement and/or potential ability" it takes underachieving students into consideration. As we will see in Chapter 4, many specific identification strategies are based on the categories of the federal definition.

In 1978 the U.S. Congress revised Marland's definition to read as follows. The gifted and talented are:

children and, whenever applicable, youth who are identified at the pre-school, elementary, or secondary level as possessing demonstrated or potential abilities that give evidence of high performance capability in areas such as intellectual, creative, specific academic or leadership ability or in the performing and visual arts, and who by reason thereof require services or activities not ordinarily provided by the school (U.S. Congress, Educational Amendment of 1978 [P.L. 95–561, IX (A)]).

In 1988 an even shorter version reads:

The term "gifted and talented students" means children and youth who give evidence of high performance capability in areas such as intellectual, creative, artistic, or leadership capacity, or in specific academic fields, and who require services or activities not ordinarily provided by the school in order to fully develop such capabilities (P.L. 100–297, Sec. 4103. Definitions).

The 1993 "quiet crisis" report presented this definition, which in the new millennium still "reflect today's knowledge and thinking" (p. 3):

Children and youth with outstanding talent perform or show the potential for performing at remarkably high levels of accomplishment when compared with others of their age, experience, or environment. These children and youth exhibit high performance capability in intellectual, creative, and/or artistic areas, possess an unusual leadership capacity, or excel in specific academic fields. They require services of activities not ordinarily provided by the schools. Outstanding talents are present in children and youth from all cultural groups, across all economic strata, and in all areas of human endeavor.

The main difference between the 1972 version and the three later statements is that psychomotor ability was excluded. The reason for this change is that artistic psychomotor ability talents (for example, dancing, mime) could be included under performing arts, and athletically gifted students typically are well-provided for outside of G/T programs. In fact, athletic programs may be seen as almost ideal gifted programs: Special teachers (coaches) are hired; expensive equipment and space are provided; training is partly individualized; students meet with others like themselves; they encourage and reward each other for doing their best; and students even travel to other schools to meet and compete with other talented individuals and teams. Not much was lost by dropping "psychomotor ability" from Congress's definition.

British Columbia funds 2 percent of its school population who are identified as gifted according to the following definition (British Columbia Ministry of Education Special Education Services, 1995). Note that this definition resembles the U.S. definitions, but acknowledges "multipotentiality" (high ability in several areas; Chapter 17), unusually intense motivation and persistence in a particular area (Chapter 2), and the possibility of also having a physical or learning disability (Chapter 15):

A student is considered gifted when she/he possesses demonstrated or potential abilities that give evidence of exceptionally high capability with respect to intellect, creativity, or the skills associated with specific disciplines. Students who are gifted often demonstrate outstanding abilities in more than one area. They may demonstrate extraordinary intensity of focus in their particular areas of talent or interest. However, they may also have accompanying disabilities and should not be expected to have strengths in all areas of intellectual functioning.

Because of its official status, a 1990 survey showed that most states had adopted an exact or modified version of a federal definition, usually the well-known 1972 one (Cassidy & Hossler, 1992). A more recent state-by-state survey by Stevens and Karnes (2000) indicated that 29 states had modified their definitions. Space will not permit a complete report of which state definitions include which of 14 areas of giftedness (see Stevens & Karnes; also Table 1.2), but some highlights are these. Three states now include underrepresented groups in their new definition (FL, MI, NC). Two states include just one characteristic of giftedness,

**TABLE 1.2**  Areas of Giftedness in State Definitions of Gifted and Talented

| Areas of Giftedness | Number of States (of 50) that Include this Area |
| --- | --- |
| Superior intellect | 39 |
| High achievement/high performance | 33 |
| Specific academic ability | 33 |
| Advanced potential | 25 |
| Creative, artistic abilities | 20 |
| Visual and performing arts | 19 |
| Leadership | 18 |
| Advanced learning ability | 6 |
| Psychomotor | 3 |
| Exceptional production | 2 |
| Practical arts | 1 |
| Motivation/task commitment | 1 |
| Critical thinking | 1 |
| Vocational | 0 |

Based on data from Stevens and Karnes (2000).

specific academic ability (NV) or demonstrated achievement (ND). Two states added creative and artistic ability (GA, MS), two added leadership (MS, RI), and one added industrial arts (RI). One state added specific academic areas (GA), another state dropped specific categories of giftedness (WY). And five states no longer have a state definition of giftedness (MN, MA, NH, NJ, SD).

### EXPLANATIONS AND INTERPRETATIONS OF GIFTEDNESS AND INTELLIGENCE

Apart from the formal federal and British Columbia definitions, there are many other conceptions, explanations, interpretations, and definitions of *giftedness* and *intelligence*.

### Five Categories of Definitions

Stankowski (1978) outlined five categories of definitions of *gifts* and *talents*. All but the first category continue to guide the identification process.

First, *after-the-fact* definitions emphasize prominence in one of the professions—consistent and outstanding achievements in a valuable area.

Second, *IQ* definitions set a point on the IQ scale, and persons scoring above that point are classed as *gifted*. Terman's Stanford-Binet cutoff of 135 is a classic example. The practice remains popular despite its glaring shortcomings of (1) ignoring creative and artistic gifts, (2) ignoring gifts in particular areas, (3) discriminating against disadvantaged students, and (4) branding motivated and creative students who score 1 point below the cutoff as "not gifted."

Third, *percentage* definitions set a fixed proportion of the school (or district) as "gifted," based on ability scores or grades. The percentage may be a restrictive 1 to 5 percent or a generous 15 to 20 percent. A misguided assumption is that "five percent of our children are gifted!" Nature is not so helpful. Like most human characteristics, abilities are distributed according to a bell-shaped curve, and any cutoff point is arbitrary.

Fourth, *talent* definitions focus on students who are outstanding in art, music, math, science, or other specific aesthetic or academic areas.

Fifth, *creativity* definitions stress the significance of superior creative abilities. Curiously, while every G/T programs seeks to increase creative growth, some states do not consider creativity to be an acceptable selection criteria (Torrance, 1984; look again at Table 1.2).

### Renzulli's Three-Ring Model

Based upon descriptions of creatively productive persons, primarily adults who have made valuable contributions to society, Renzulli (1986; also Renzulli and Reis, 2003) argues that

> Gifted behavior . . . reflects an interaction among three basic clusters of human traits— these clusters being above average (but not necessarily high) general and/or specific ability, high levels of task commitment (motivation), and high levels of creativity. Gifted and talented children are those possessing or capable of developing this composite set of traits and applying them to any potentially valuable area of human performance (Figure 1.1).

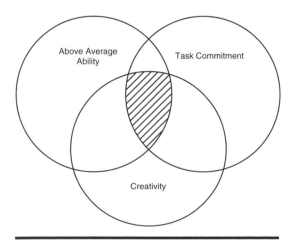

**FIGURE 1.1.**  Renzulli's three-ring model. Reprinted by permission of the author.

The combination of the three are "brought to bear" on general and specific performance areas, resulting in gifted behaviors.

Some gifted program coordinators or teachers mistakenly use Renzulli's three-ring model as a guide for selecting only children who are high in all three characteristics. As we will see in Chapter 4 on identification, Renzulli outlines a reasonable identification plan that is not tied strictly to possessing a strong combination of all three traits. For example, a teacher may nominate a student based on a high IQ score, despite the student's record of unmotivated underachievement; or a teacher may nominate a student based on observed creativity or strong motivation, but without IQ information.

### General Gifts and Specific Talents: Gagné's DMTG Model

Gagné's (2000, 2003) Differentiated Model of Giftedness and Talent (DMGT) makes a definite distinction between *gifts* and *talents*. Here, gifts (general aptitudes) are untrained natural abilities. Talents (specific skills) are learned capabilities. Four types of innate gifts are intellectual (e.g., reasoning, judgment), creative (e.g., inventiveness, imagination), socioaffective (e.g., perceptiveness, empathy, tact), and sensorimotor (e.g., auditory, coordination). He also identifies seven categories (fields) of talents: academics, arts, business, leisure (e.g., games), social action (e.g., public office), sports, and technology. Personal factors that influence talent development are physical characteristics, motivation (e.g., needs, values), volition (e.g., will-power, effort), self-management (e.g., work habits), and personality (e.g., temperament, adaptability). Environment influences include one's milieu (e.g., physical, cultural), persons (teachers, parents, peers), provisions (e.g., services, activities), and events (encounters, awards). Talent development also is affected by chance factors, such as one's family environment, a school gifted program, or a bad athletic accident.

## Tannenbaum's Who, What, and How of Giftedness

Tannenbaum (2003) addressed the problem of defining *giftedness* with a taxonomy that answers *who, what,* and *how* questions. One can be a producer of thoughts creatively or proficiently; a producer of tangibles creatively or proficiently; a performer of staged artistry creatively or proficiently; or a performer of human services creatively or proficiently. Table 1.3 summarizes his model with examples of each category. Tannenbaum noted that gifted and talented students will show advanced learning and creativity—that is, *promise*—but high-level creativity and productivity is almost always an adult phenomena. He lists five interweaving factors that contribute to eventual demonstrated giftedness: (1) A superior general intellect, (2) strong special aptitudes, (3) supportive nonintellective (e.g., personality) traits, (4) a challenging and supportive environment, and, like Gagné, (5) chance, "the smile of good fortune at critical periods of life."

## Taylor's Multiple-Talent Totem Poles

Calvin Taylor's (1978, 1986, 1988) *multiple-talent totem pole* concept does not define "gifts and talents." Rather, it raises our awareness that the majority of students will possess special skills or talents of some type. Taylor's (1978) original six talents (academic, creative, planning, communicating, forecasting, decision making) were expanded into the nine talents in Figure 1.2. The second through sixth talents (productive thinking, communicating, forecasting, decision making, planning) were called "thinking talents" that contribute to creativity and problem solving. The final three (implementing, human relations, discerning opportunities) are essential for getting ideas into action.

How do we define gifted and talented? Who should be selected to participate in a gifted education program? Different children would be chosen depending upon which talent is emphasized.

## Gardner's Theory of Multiple Intelligences

"Intelligence is too important to be left to the intelligence testers," said Gardner (1999, p. 3), criticizing the severe limitation of single IQ scores. In his original theory of multiple intelligences (MI theory; Gardner, 1983, 1993, 1999), Gardner described seven types of intelligence, and more recently added an eighth. (See Inset 1.3 for

**TABLE 1.3**    Examples of Tannenbaum's Eight Categories of Gifted Persons

| Category | Examples |
| --- | --- |
| Producers of thoughts creatively | Novelists, artists, composers |
| Producers of thoughts proficiently | Mathematicians, computer programmers, editors |
| Producers of tangibles creatively | Inventors, architects, design engineers |
| Producers of tangibles proficiently | Diamond cutters, machinists, art forgers |
| Performers of staged artistry creatively | Musicians, conductors, dancers, poetry readers, and actors, who interpret and "breathe life" into others' works |
| Performers of staged artistry proficiently | Musicians, conductors, dancers, and the like, who faithfully translate and reproduce the works of others |
| Performers of human services creatively | Innovative teachers, political leaders, and researchers in medicine, education, and the social sciences |
| Performers of human services proficiently | Successful teachers, physicians, and administrators who follow guidelines and procedures faithfully and successfully |

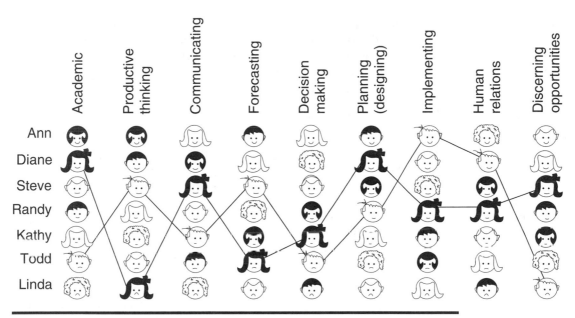

**FIGURE 1.2**  Taylor's multiple-talent totem poles, extended version.
Copyright © 1984, Calvin W. Taylor. Reprinted by permission.

---

INSET **1.3** _____

## What Qualifies as an Intelligence in MI Theory?

Gardner's rationale for the existence of his eight intelligences includes eight sources of scientific or rational evidence. "I consider the establishment of these criteria to be one of the enduring contributions of multiple intelligences theory" (Gardner, 1999, p. 41).

- *Brain injury* often disrupts functioning in one area of intelligence but not in others.
- *Evolutionary history* suggests that to survive, *Homo sapiens* had to move about effectively (spatial intelligence), discern the motives of others (interpersonal intelligence), and classify animals and vegetation (naturalist intelligence).
- Each intelligence possesses a *unique set of core operations,* for example, those in language, mathematics, music, biological taxonomies, and body movement.
- Each intelligence can be encoded in a *separate symbol system*—for example, linguistic, mathematical, musical, pictorial.
- Each intelligence has a *unique developmental history*—unique experience that leads to expertise.
- *Idiot savants and prodigies* have demonstrated phenomenal strengths in one area of intelligence—usually math, music, or art—while being severely deficient in the others.
- The intelligences *tend not to interfere with one another* if performed simultaneously.
- Research shows *low intercorrelations* among many of the intelligences.

Gardner's criteria for independent intelligences.) A central point is that academics traditionally recognizes only linguistic and logical-mathematical types of intelligence—as represented in IQ scores—and educators undervalue or ignore students with strengths in Gardner's other forms of intelligence. His intelligences may be viewed as intellectual gifts "with only loose and nonpredictable relations with one another" (1999, p. 32). A person thus may be gifted in one or several of the intelligence areas, but not in others.

Like Gardner, we can ignore his students' tongue-in-cheek recommendations for cooking intelligence, humor intelligence, and sexual intelligence. As a brief overview, the original seven plus his eighth intelligences are:

**1.** *Linguistic* (verbal) intelligence, which includes verbal comprehension, syntax, semantics, and written and oral expression. A novelist or lawyer would require linguistic intelligence.

**2.** *Logical-mathematical* intelligence, which includes inductive and deductive reasoning and computing, as required by a mathematician or physicist.

Note that linguistic and logical-mathematical intelligence are the two fundamental competencies measured by traditional intelligence tests and are most valued in school settings (von Károlyi, Ramos-Ford, & Gardner, 2003).

**3.** *Spatial* intelligence, the capacity to represent and manipulate three-dimensional configurations, as needed by an architect, engineer, interior decorator, sculptor, or chess player.

**4.** *Musical* intelligence, which includes such abilities as pitch discrimination; sensitivity to rhythm, texture, and timbre; the ability to hear and perform themes in music; and in its most integrated form, music composition.

**5.** *Bodily-kinesthetic* intelligence, the ability to use all or part of one's body to perform a task or fashion a product. It would be present to a high degree in a dancer, athlete, or mime.

**6.** *Interpersonal* intelligence, including the ability to understand the actions and motivations of others and to act sensibly and productively based on that knowledge. Counselors, teachers, politicians, and evangelists need this ability.

**7.** *Intrapersonal* intelligence, which is a person's understanding of one's own cognitive strengths and weaknesses, thinking styles, feelings, emotions—and intelligences. As one of Ramos-Ford and Gardner's (1997) examples, a child exemplifying high intrapersonal intelligence might remark, "Drawing is my favorite activity, even though I don't draw as well as I want to" (p. 57).

**8.** Gardner (1999) considered the possibility of a spiritual, moral, existential, and naturalist intelligence. Of these, only *naturalist* intelligence met most of his eight criteria (Inset 1.3). A person strong in naturalist intelligence possesses extensive knowledge of the living world and its taxonomies, and is highly capable in recognizing and classifying plants and animals.

While Gardner (1999) felt that *existential intelligence*—the capacity to deal with such cosmic concerns as the significance of life, the meaning of death, the ultimate fate of physical and psychological worlds, love of another person, total immersion in a work of art—"may well be admissible" (p. 64) and is "attractive" (p. 66), he decided not to add existential intelligence to his list. On later reflection, he curiously resolved the matter by pronouncing existential intelligence to be one-half of an intelligence (Gardner, 2000). The Dalai Lama and Gandhi would score high.

MI theory is attractive to teachers, especially teachers of the gifted. It has strong intuitive appeal, it is uncomplicated, and it definitely alters how students are perceived and taught. One straightforward approach is to look for strengths in each area, then plan activities to help develop those abilities. Lazear (1991), for example, outlined activities to strengthen each of the original seven intelligences (see Table 1.4).

The catchphrase "MI classrooms" includes even more involved efforts to incorporate MI theory (Callahan et al., 1995b; Fasko, 2001; Krechevsky & Seidel, 1998; Maker, Nielson, &

**TABLE 1.4**   Ways to Strengthen Multiple Intelligences

| Type of Intelligence | Teaching Suggestion |
| --- | --- |
| Linguistic | General learning and vocabulary |
| Logical-Mathematical | Inductive, deductive, scientific reasoning |
| Spatial | Forming and manipulating mental images, spatial relationships exercises |
| Musical | Raising awareness of sounds, tone qualities, musical structures |
| Bodily-Kinesthetic | Movement control exercises |
| Interpersonal | Working in groups, raising awareness of nonverbal communication |
| Intrapersonal | Raising awareness of feelings, metacognition (thinking about thinking) |

Adapted from Lazear (1991).

Rogers, 1994; Reid & Romanoff, 1997; Willard-Holt & Holt, 1997). As some examples:

- Creating a classroom environment that values all MI intelligences
- Teaching skills and information aimed at different intelligences, and using multiple symbol systems
- Flexibly teaching subject matter in several different ways, including working with students' individual MI strengths
- Using process activities that integrate multiple intelligences with thinking skills
- Using interest centers to illustrate multiple intelligences and help students explore their own strengths
- Helping students develop projects based on interests and different intelligences
- Using a variety of content that is abstract and broad to stimulate students' intelligences
- Infusing arts into the curriculum
- Allowing students to express their learning with creative and personal products

What are the effects of MI classrooms on teaching G/T students? Of course, Gardner's eye-opening model draws attention to individual differences in the creative domains of musical, spatial, and bodily-kinesthetic intelligence, as well as social/interpersonal and intrapersonal (self-understanding) intelligence. Callahan and colleagues (1995) found that teachers were enthusiastic in their MI-based Project START. Also, students' self-concepts improved—they liked school, felt they were good at school, and attendance increased. Language skills and standardized test scores also improved.

With any major innovation, criticisms are quick and sometimes accurate. Several authors have noted the "fadlike" nature of MI theory (e.g., Callahan et al., 1995b). Some see an appealing egalitarian flavor—all kids may be gifted (e.g., Delisle, 1996)—although Gardner (1997) does not agree. Callahan et al. (1995b) found no benefit to gifted students in an MI classroom. White and Breen (1998)—labeling MI theory "edutainment"—wondered if the "intelligences" are intelligences or abilities, and if the intelligences remain constant throughout one's life span. Gottfredson (2003) noted that Gardner's interpersonal and intrapersonal "intelligence" may be personality factors, not abilities. Finally, some have criticized Gardner for his mostly intuitive—not psychometric and experimental—identification of his intelligences.

### Emotional Intelligence?

Gardner (1999) rejected the idea of an *emotional intelligence* (ED), considering it a "separate sphere of values and social policy" (p. 69). He also decided that emotional intelligence is simply a special combination of interpersonal and intrapersonal intelligences. However, many others accept emotional intelligence as real and extremely important, although they seem not to agree on exactly what it is.

Silverman (1983a) described an emotionally gifted student as being unusually concerned with, for example, the meaning of existence and of being human, and with having more loving and caring relationships. In large agreement, Piechowski (1997, 2003) related emotional intelligence— whose high end is *emotional giftedness*—to high empathy, a strong sense of moral justice (ideals, beliefs), a lively imagination, overexcitability, high sensuality, and intensely positive and negative emotional feelings. "To be emotionally gifted is to *dare* to act on one's awareness of what is happening with others by alleviating lack and emotional distress, opposing unfairness, and fighting injustice" (Piechowski, 2003, p. 405).

According to *Emotional Intelligence* author Goleman (1995), emotional intelligence is the capability to control emotional impulse, to understand another person's feelings, and to handle relationships well. Goleman emphasized that good emotional balance and management will influence how sensibly we behave and how successful we become.

Mayer, Perkins, Caruso, and Salovey (2001; Salovey & Sluyter, 1997) argue that high emotional intelligence helps people make better social and life choices—and therefore is worth teaching. Their version of emotional intelligence includes the abilities to (1) perceive emotions, (2) use emotions to assist thought, (3) understand emotions and emotional knowledge, and (4) regulate emotions to promote emotional and intellectual growth. Mayer and colleagues created two tests, the Multifactor Emotional Intelligence Scale (MEIS) and the adolescent MEIS-A, to measure these abilities.

At present, while emotional intelligence seems important and overlaps considerably with attitudes and character education considerations (Chapter 8), it keeps a low profile.

## Sternberg's Triarchic Theory

Sternberg (1997a, 2003) agrees that intellectual giftedness cannot be represented by a single IQ number and identified three main kinds of intelligence. *Analytic giftedness* is the academic talent measured by typical intelligence tests, particularly analytical reasoning and reading comprehension. Sternberg's example is Alice, who scored high on intelligence tests, earned high grades, and her teachers knew she was smart. However, she was not good at producing innovative ideas of her own. *Synthetic giftedness* refers to creativity, insightfulness, intuition, or the ability to cope with novelty. Such persons may not earn the highest IQ scores, but ultimately may make the greatest contributions to society. Sternberg's Barbara was not as strong as Alice in analytic thinking, but was enormously creative in finding innovative ideas. *Practical giftedness* involves applying analytic and/or synthetic abilities successfully to everyday, pragmatic situations. Celia, for example, could enter a new environment, figure out what one must do to succeed, and then do it.

Most people possess some blend of the three skills. Further, the blend can change over time as intelligence is developed in various directions. Said Sternberg (2003), a central part of giftedness is coordinating the three abilities and knowing when to use which one. Giftedness is viewed as a well-managed balance of the three abilities, and a gifted person is thus a good "mental self-manager."

In 2000, Sternberg modified his triarchic theory to include *wisdom* as a subtype of practical intelligence. Wisdom centers on concern for the needs and welfare of others. High wisdom usually takes the form of good advice to others and to oneself. Sternberg used Gandhi, Mother Theresa, Martin Luther King, Jr., and Nelson Mandela as examples of persons high in practical wisdom. While all four would score high in practical "getting the job done" intelligence, so would Osama bin Laden and other successful terrorists and tyrants, who are devoid of Sternberg's empathic and humanistic wisdom.

Regarding developing student wisdom, Sternberg made these recommendations:

1. Give students problems requiring wise thinking, such as ethical and moral dilemmas.
2. Help students think in terms of a "common good" when solving these problems.
3. Help students balance their own interests with the interests of others when solving these problems.
4. Provide examples of wise thinking from the past.
5. Model wisdom using good and bad examples of your own past decisions and behavior, and show students you value wise thinking.
6. Encourage students to think wisely—for the common good—outside the classroom.

## Sternberg's Implicit Theory of Giftedness

Beyond the above formal or explicit theories of giftedness, Sternberg (1995) described an *implicit* theory that summarizes "what we mean by *giftedness . . .* people's conception of giftedness" (p. 88–89). The theory specifies five necessary and sufficient conditions that gifted persons have in common:

1. *Excellence.* A gifted person must be extremely good at something.
2. *Rarity.* He or she must possess a high level of an attribute that is uncommon relative to peers.
3. *Productivity.* The superior trait must (potentially) lead to productivity.
4. *Demonstrability.* The trait also must be demonstrable through one or more valid tests.
5. *Value.* The superior performance must be in an area that is valued by society.

Such implicit theories, noted Sternberg, are relative to the culture because they are based on the values of that culture. Importantly, such values, and implicit theories, guide the identification of gifted persons as well as suggest content for gifted educational programs.

## A Hierarchy of Intelligence Abilities

Carroll (1993; Gottfredson, 2003) described a three-level, pyramid-shaped model of intelligence (see Table 1.5). At the top (I) is basic intelligence, or *g*, by itself. The middle level (II) consists of broad, general abilities, all of which are related to and statistically correlated with *g*. The bottom tier includes myriads of specific abilities, many unidentified, that are related to one or more intermediate, more general types of intelligence. Gottfredson reasoned that Gardner's eight intelligences and Sternberg's triarchic categorization would fall in the middle level of this pyramid, indicating that all are related to basic intelligence.

**TABLE 1.5**   The Three-Level Hierarchy of Intelligence

| I. | Top Level: (General Ability) | *g* | | | |
|---|---|---|---|---|---|
| II. | Middle Level: (Broad Factors) | Verbal | Spatial | Memory | Other |
| III. | Bottom Level: (Specific Abilities) | Reading decoding, listening ability, language comprehension, visualization, visual memory, memory span, associative memory, maintaining rhythm, quantitative reasoning, expressional fluency, and others | | | |

From Carroll (1993). See also Gottfredson (2003).

## Thinking Dispositions

As we know, strong intellectual abilities do not guarantee high achievement or life success. Ritchart (2001) proposed that we look at *thinking dispositions* that comprise *intellectual character.* His dispositions are "characteristics that animate, motivate, and direct abilities toward . . . better and more powerful thinking" (pp. 146–147). After reviewing numerous lists, Ritchart decided upon three core categories: *Creative thinking* dispositions include imaginativeness, openness to new ideas, adventurousness, curiosity, inquisitiveness, and others; *reflective thinking* dispositions include awareness of one's beliefs, metacognition (awareness of one's own thinking), being well informed, seeking truth, seeking alternatives, and others; and *critical thinking* dispositions include planning, thinking strategically, being skeptical, having intellectual integrity, seeking reasons and alternatives, and others.

Intelligence and intelligent behavior are indeed more complicated than a high IQ score.

## Gifted Education? Talent Development?

Some leaders in gifted education have recommended that the term *gifted education* be replaced by *talent development* (e.g., Renzulli & Reis, 1997; Treffinger, 1995b; Treffinger & Feldhusen, 1996). In a sense, the talent development focus is a response to the detracking movement, with its stress on heterogeneous classes and quality education for all. Talent development emphasizes, first, that the focus be on developing the talents and capabilities of all students—including "high-end learners"—for example, in academic, artistic, vocational, and personal-social areas (Feldhusen, 1992). Second, talent identification must be broader than using IQ and achievement scores; Treffinger (1995b) suggested profiling students' talents. Third, programming must become more varied to accommodate individual characteristics and needs. A final benefit is that the talent development orientation eliminates the awkwardness of the words "gifted" and, by exclusion, "not gifted."

Renzulli and Reis's (1997) schoolwide enrichment model (Chapter 7) is an excellent example of a talent development approach that presents thinking skill activities and other enrichment in the regular classroom to all students, while also accommodating the needs of bright and motivated students.

As a final comment on the definition challenge, we repeat that there is no one final and agreed-upon definition of *gifted* and *talented,* and for any given program the specific instruments and decision criteria will actually define who is gifted and talented, that is, who receives the special training and who does not.

## SUMMARY

Despite increased public awareness of gifted education, many gifted students remain ignored in school. Critics claim that gifted programs are elitist—welfare for the rich. Sternberg's "sounds of silence" include little federal funding and no laws to protect rights of the gifted.

We admire gifted people, but we also are committed to equality—a love-hate relationship. The public alternates between an interest in excellence and the desire for equity. The detracking movement stresses equity at the expense of gifted students.

Gifted students, like students with disabilities, deserve an education consistent with their needs and abilities. Society benefits from helping gifted students become professionals.

Ancient Sparta defined giftedness in military terms. Athenian boys attended private schools and were taught by sophists. In Rome, boys and girls attended first-level schools, but higher education was for boys only.

Renaissance Europe rewarded its gifted artists, architects, and writers with wealth and honor.

China's seventh-century Tang dynasty brought child prodigies to the imperial court. They accepted a multiple-talent conception of giftedness, recognized that talents must be nurtured, and believed children should be educated according to their abilities.

Into the late 1800s, Japan provided high level education only for Samurai children. A few private academies accepted gifted children regardless of birth.

In early America, children needed ability and wealth to attend secondary school and college. From about 1870 to the Depression years, some schools, especially in large cities, initiated tracking, grade-skipping, telescoping, and special classes. "Age of mediocrity" thinking emphasized equity (1920s, 1930s).

The educational systems of England and Europe have long used tracking, which is less contentious there than in North America. In England, education for gifted students has been slowed by resentment of traditional unearned privilege.

Sir Francis Galton produced the first significant research and writing on intelligence. He believed that intelligence was related to keen senses, and so his "intelligence tests" evaluated sensory acuity and reaction time. His book *Hereditary Genius* argued for a hereditary basis of intelligence.

Alfred Binet in Paris developed the first successful intelligence test. He created the concept of *mental age.*

Lewis M. Terman Americanized the Binet tests, creating in 1916 the Stanford-Binet Intelligence Scale. In the 1920s he identified over 1500 high-intelligence children, who have been tracked and studied into the 1980s. Contradicting then-popular conceptions, the "Termites" were psychologically, socially, and physically healthier than average persons. Terman noted that acceleration is valuable and that family values are crucial to adult success.

Leta Hollingworth emphasized that bright students waste much time in regular classes. In the 1920s and 1930s she developed G/T counseling programs and imaginative G/T curriculum. She taught gifted and below-average students, the former identified with multiple criteria, and authored two significant books on gifted children.

The launching of Sputnik in 1957 triggered an American effort to improve education, particularly in science and for gifted students. Enthusiasm faded after about five years.

In the mid 1970s a new and continuing national and worldwide gifted education movement began, one that in the United States includes federal and state legislation, special funds, and high commitment by many educators.

The 1993 National Excellence report drew strong attention to the plight of America's ignored gifted students—future leaders—especially with its catchy and accurate "quiet crisis" phrase.

Herrnstein and Murray's *The Bell Curve* is criticized for ignoring modern conceptions of intellectual giftedness, assuming causation from IQ-success correlations, for seemingly equating IQ with personal value, and for racist conclusions. However, some intelligence researchers recently concede that, like it or not, tested IQ relates to many important life outcomes, such as education, career level, and crime. Other factors, such as favorable family circumstances and persistence, also influence success.

Renzulli's National Research Center on the Gifted and Talented is a nationwide "consumer-oriented" effort to clarify key problems and practices, for example, identification, programming, and special populations. One study concluded that little is being done for gifted students in most classrooms.

The anti-tracking movement assumes that ability grouping practices are ineffective, unfair, and discriminatory. Not only fast-track classes but also some gifted programs are being abandoned. Research indicates that achievement of slow- and middle-track students is no different in heterogeneous classes compared with ability-grouped classes; part-time cross-grade grouping and within-class grouping raise achievement for all students; self-esteem of low-ability students is lower in heterogeneous classes; and gifted students benefit tremendously from grouping with gifted peers for advanced work.

In 2003, Kulik reported that, despite the detracking movement, grouping is alive and well in almost all elementary and especially in secondary schools.

For the majority of students, cooperative learning groups produce improvements in achievement, motivation, cognitive growth, and social and communication skills. However, it prevents gifted students from engaging in more beneficial educational experiences. Three interrelated problems in cooperative learning groups, which directly affect gifted students, are the social loafing, free-rider, and sucker effects. With dyads, these problems are substantially lessened. Two recent trends are (1) attending to the needs of gifted students, and (2) using more complex tasks, which develop higher-level thinking skills.

Defining *gifted* and *talented* is important because one's definition influences the selection of students for G/T programs and may prevent poor, minority, disabled, underachieving, and female gifted students from participating.

There are no universally accepted definitions of *gifted* and *talented*. The terms may be used interchangeably. Some see talented and gifted on a continuum, with gifted at the upper end. Extraordinary students have been labeled "low-incidence" gifted or "severely" or "profoundly" gifted.

Cox avoids the term *gifted,* preferring *able learners.* Renzulli prefers the phrase *gifted behaviors.*

The 1972 U.S.O.E. definition is cited in many state and district G/T plans. A multitalent definition, it includes the six categories of (1) general intellectual ability, (2) specific academic aptitude, (3) creativity, (4) leadership, (5) visual and performing art ability, and (6) psychomotor skills. The statement recognizes the need for differentiated educational programs and cites the two basic goals of gifted education: helping capable students realize their potential and providing society with high-level talent. The 1978 and 1988 revisions and the 1993 "quiet crisis" report dropped psychomotor skills. A similar British Columbia definition acknowledges multipotentiality, intense motivation, and the possibility of being gifted while having a disability.

Stankowski's five categories are after-the-fact, IQ, percentage, talent, and creativity definitions.

Renzulli's three-ring model emphasizes above-average ability, high task commitment (motiva-

tion), and high creativity, which are characteristics of creatively productive adults.

Gagné's DMGT model proposes that *gifts* should refer to natural abilities and *talents* to learned performances. The model assumes that environmental and intrapersonal catalysts (e.g., one's milieu; motivation) helps or hinders talent development.

Tannenbaum's eight-category model of giftedness assumes that one can be creative or proficient in producing thoughts, producing tangibles, performing staged artistry, or performing human services.

Taylor's multiple-talent totem pole model raises the possibility that most students possess special gifts and talents, if we look carefully enough.

Gardner's eight intelligences—an alternative to using a single IQ number to describe student ability—are linguistic, logical-mathematical, spatial, musical, bodily-kinesthetic, interpersonal, intrapersonal, and his newest, naturalist intelligence. Many "MI classrooms" have appeared, which value all intelligences, teach skills and information aimed at different intelligences, and more. MI theory is criticized for being a fad.

Others promote the concepts of emotional intelligence and emotional giftedness. Some scholars relate emotional intelligence to having existential concerns and being a caring, moral person. Others relate emotional intelligence to the ability to control emotions, perceive and understand others' emotions, and handle relationships well.

Sternberg's triarchic theory emphasizes three categories of intellectual gifts: analytic, synthetic, and practical giftedness. He recently included *wisdom*—concern for the welfare of others—as a subtype of practical giftedness, since highly visible but evil persons are devoid of humanistic wisdom in accomplishing their goals.

Sternberg's work with implicit theories of giftedness indicate that we define as *gifted* people whose behavior shows excellence, rarity, productivity, demonstrability, and value.

Gottfredson described a three-level pyramid describing intelligence, with *g* at the top, broad abilities in the middle, and many specific abilities at the base.

Richart argued that "intellectual character" includes dispositions, especially creative thinking, reflective thinking, and critical thinking dispositions.

Many leaders are recommending that the label *talent development* replace *gifted education*. It implies broader identification and programming for all students, including gifted and talented ones, and the elimination of the unpleasant "gifted" versus "non-gifted."

# CHAPTER 2

# CHARACTERISTICS
# OF GIFTED STUDENTS

*[From a letter to the Duke University Talent Identification Program (TIP).]*
For the first time, we were challenged in the classroom. We found out
there were many students as bright as—and even brighter than—we
were. . . . We found other people who were like us—students who loved
to learn and try new, difficult things.
Two former TIP students (Pfeiffer, 2000, p. 11)

The topic of characteristics of the gifted overlaps directly with every other topic and chapter in this book, all of which focus on gifted children, their unique characteristics, and how to identify and provide personal and educational services for them. Gifted children differ from one another not only in size, shape, and color, but in cognitive and language abilities, interests, learning styles, motivation and energy levels, personalities, mental health and self-concepts, habits and behavior, background and experience, and any other mental, physical, or experiential characteristic that one cares to look for. They differ also in their patterns of educational needs.

Most of the descriptions that follow are "usual" characteristics, traits that have appeared and reappeared in studies of gifted children and adults. All traits will not and cannot apply to each and every gifted and talented student.

As a summary overview, Table 2.1 presents a collection of descriptors from a number of sources (Campbell & Verna, n.d.; Frasier, 1993; Colangelo & Assouline, 2000; Coleman & Cross, 2000; Han & Marvin, 2000; Perleth, Lehwald, & Browder, 1993; Silverman, 1997; and others). (Characteristics and problems of gifted and talented minority, female, economically disadvantaged, and underachieving students, plus personal and career

counseling concerns and topics will be discussed in later chapters.)

## THE TERMAN STUDIES

One of the most frequently cited findings of Terman's (1925) landmark project was the fact his 1528 students not only were more intelligent, they were better adjusted psychologically and socially, and were even physically healthier than the average person. Just a few decades before, Cesare Lombroso (1895), naming specific famous persons, claimed that "signs of degeneration in men of genius" included stuttering, short stature, general emaciation, sickly color, rickets (leading to club-footedness, lameness, or a hunched back), baldness, amnesia/forgetfulness, sterility, and that awful symptom of brain degeneration—left-handedness. Lombroso's proclamation was well known and widely accepted; it made a lot of average people feel better about being average. Terman's scientific data trashed the myth that brilliant students are predominantly weak, unattractive, and emotionally unstable. They not only were well-adjusted in childhood but in adulthood reported greater personal adjustment, emotional stability, self-esteem, professional success, and personal contentment (Sears, 1979; Terman and Oden,

**TABLE 2.1**   Recurrent Characteristics of Students Who Are Gifted

| Positive Characteristics | Negative Characteristics |
| --- | --- |
| Unusual alertness in infancy and later | Uneven mental development |
| Early and rapid learning | Interpersonal difficulties, due |
| Rapid language development as a child | often to intellectual |
| Superior language ability—verbally fluent, large vocabulary, | differences |
| complex grammar | Underachievement, especially in |
| Enjoyment of learning | uninteresting areas |
| Academic superiority, large knowledge base, sought out as | Nonconformity, sometimes in |
| a resource | disturbing directions |
| Superior analytic ability | Perfectionism, which can be |
| Keen observation | extreme |
| Efficient, high-capacity memory | Excessive self-criticism |
| Superior reasoning, problem-solving | Self-doubt, poor self-image |
| Thinking that is abstract, complex, logical, insightful | Variable frustration and anger |
| Insightful, sees "big picture," recognizes patterns, connects topics | Depression |
| Manipulates symbol systems | |
| Uses high-level thinking skills, efficient strategies | |
| Extrapolates knowledge to new situations, goes beyond what | |
| is taught | |
| Expanded awareness, greater self-awareness | |
| Greater metacognition (understanding own thinking) | |
| Advanced interests | |
| Needs for logic and accuracy | |
| Wide interests, interested in new topics | |
| High curiosity, explores how and why | |
| Multiple capabilities (multipotentiality) | |
| High career ambitions | |
| Overexcitability | |
| Emotional intensity and sensitivity | |
| High alertness and attention | |
| High intellectual and physical activity level | |
| High motivation, concentrates, perseveres, persists, task-oriented | |
| Active—shares information, directs, leads, offers help, eager to be | |
| involved | |
| Strong empathy, moral thinking, sense of justice, honesty, | |
| intellectual honesty | |
| Aware of social issues | |
| High concentration, long attention span | |
| Strong internal control | |
| Independent, self-directed, works alone | |
| Inquisitive, asks questions | |
| Excellent sense of humor | |
| Imaginative, creative, solves problems | |
| Preference for novelty | |
| Reflectiveness | |
| Good self-concept—usually | |

1947, 1959). They showed a below-average incidence of suicide and mental illness.

Terman and Oden (1947) summarized the main characteristics of the gifted children as follows:

> The average member of our group is a slightly better physical specimen than the average child. . . .
>
> For the fields of subject matter covered in our tests, the superiority of gifted over unselected children was greater in reading, language usage, arithmetical reasoning, science, literature and the arts. In arithmetical computation, spelling and factual information about history and civics, the superiority of the gifted was somewhat less marked. . . .
>
> The interests of gifted children are many-sided and spontaneous, they learn to read easily and read more and better books than the average child. At the same time, they make numerous collections, cultivate many kinds of hobbies, and acquire far more knowledge of plays and games than the average child. . . .
>
> As compared with unselected children, they are less inclined to boast or to overstate their knowledge; they are more trustworthy when under temptation to cheat; their character preferences and social attitudes are more wholesome, and they score higher in a test of emotional stability. . . .
>
> The deviation of the gifted subjects from the generality is in the upward direction for nearly all traits. There is no law of compensation whereby the intellectual superiority of the gifted tends to be offset by inferiorities along nonintellectual lines.

As a few health-related details, compared with other children, Terman's students weighed more at birth, learned to walk a month earlier, and learned to talk three and one-half months earlier. They were taller, heavier, and healthier—with better breathing capacity, superior nutritional status, fewer headaches, and less general weakness. However, the relationship between giftedness and health is muddied by a third related factor of socioeconomic level.

The superior mental and physical characteristics continued into adulthood. Oden (1968) wrote "all the evidence indicates that with few exceptions the superior child becomes the superior adult" (p. 50). Terman (1954) earlier had noted, "So far, no one has developed post-adolescent stupidity!"

While high IQ was common to all, Terman's gifted persons differed among themselves in many ways; they were a heterogeneous group. One important difference was adult productivity. When they were children, the most productive adults had been rated by parents and teachers as higher in self-confidence, leadership, sensitivity to approval, perseverance, desire to excel, and "force of character." They rated themselves as higher in persistence, goal-directedness, and self-confidence.

As a caution, the descriptions of Terman's gifted children present them as near-perfect children. However, there was a serious bias in their selection. The 1528 children were identified from a larger group of children who first were nominated by their teachers as "gifted." We know that teachers will identify as "gifted" those children who are pleasant, well-behaved, prompt, conforming, high-achieving, attractive, neat, and popular and who wear expensive clothes and speak standard English (e.g., Good and Weinstein, 1986; Keneal, 1991; LeTendre, 1991). Perhaps it is not surprising that Terman could describe his students' physical and mental health in such glowing language. His conclusions would not necessarily apply, for example, to students who are artistically or creatively gifted, who are bright underachievers, or who are intelligent but rebellious, irritating, or otherwise undesirable.

It is significant that two Nobel Prize winners, Luis Alvarez and William B. Shockley, were excluded from the Terman study because their IQ scores were not sufficiently high (Hermann and Stanley, 1983).

## TRAITS OF INTELLECTUALLY GIFTED CHILDREN

Let's examine more closely what it means to be "intellectually gifted."

## Precocious Language and Thought

The overriding trait—indeed, the definition—of intellectually gifted students is that they are developmentally advanced in language and thought. VanTassel-Baska (2003) named *precocity* as the first of just three characteristics relevant to G/T curriculum planning (the other two characteristics were *intensity* and *complexity*). Binet similarly described intelligent students as having a *higher mental age,* compared with their chronological age. Silverman (1993a, 1993b, 2002, 2003) and others refer to intellectual giftedness as *asynchronous* development characterized by advanced cognitive abilities. Simply put, gifted students' mental development outstrips their chronological (physical) development. Their intelligence test performance matches that of older children.

Some young gifted children begin talking at 7 months. Other bright children do not begin talking early—but progress rapidly once they do begin. Gross (1992a) quoted the mother of one high-IQ boy: "Once he decided he was going to talk he went from single words to complete sentences with incredible speed . . . and there were very few pronunciation errors" (p. 115).

Some gifted children draw recognizable pictures or use elaborate language at age 2½, or begin reading by age 3 and read fluently at 4 (Jackson, 1988, 2003). You may recall that Hollingworth did not teach reading to her gifted students because they could read before entering school.

Not all gifted children learn to read early or quickly. Albert Einstein did not learn until he was 8, and one after another of Picasso's reading tutors quit in despair.

The advanced language ability of the intellectually gifted child includes a superior comprehension skill. Therefore, the intellectually gifted child usually acquires a large working vocabulary and a large store of information about many topics. The child may grasp complex and abstract concepts and relationships that normally are learned at an older age.

The intellectually gifted child also may begin writing at a precocious age. This talent will result from some combination of teaching by parents, older siblings, or preschool teachers, added to the child's strong drive and mental readiness to imitate and learn.

## Logical Thinking

Compared with the average child, the thinking processes of the gifted child are quick and logical, two traits that can disturb impatient parents and teachers. Combined with a natural curiosity and an urge to learn, the precocious child can be forever asking questions, wanting to know, and wanting to know "Why?" Their bear-trap logic may not accept an abrupt "Because!" or any other incomplete or illogical response. In light of their swift and logical thinking, it is no surprise that questioning ability, a good understanding of cause-and-effect relationships, convergent problem solving, persistence, and insight frequently are cited as traits of gifted children.

## Early Math, Art, and Music

For many gifted children, advanced mathematical, musical, and artistic abilities also appear early, paralleling the verbal and conceptual skills. The mathematically precocious child may be counting by fives and tens and adding and subtracting two-digit numbers by kindergarten. The child may explain with surprisingly good reasoning his or her own special way of deducing or calculating a mathematical solution. For example, one such second-grade child concluded, "There must be numbers below zero because temperatures can go below zero."

At a young age, artistically precocious children differ dramatically from other children in their seemingly instinctive art skill. Winner and Martino (2000, 2003) noted that artistically gifted children learn to draw at an earlier age than average, they learn rapidly, they have superior visual memories, they are obsessively motivated to develop their artistic ability, and they learn virtually on their own, solving problems (e.g., perspective, necessary distortions) in idiosyncratic and creative ways. They even see the world differently—less in terms of concepts than shapes and visual surface features.

Musical giftedness may appear at age 1 or 2—earlier than in any other skill domain (Winner & Martino, 2000). One clue is that the very young child is enthralled by musical sounds. Seventy percent of great violinists were prodigies as young children. At age 4 Mozart composed a harpsichord concerto, and at age 7 Yehudi Menuhin performed with symphonies. Solo violinist Pamela Frank remembers, "I loved music. I'd get chills and tears in my eyes—even when I was three and four years old. These images have never left me" (Rimm & Rimm-Kaufman, 2001).

A core music ability is sensitivity to, and an innate understanding of, music structure—tonality, key, harmony, and rhythm—and the ability to hear expressive properties (timbre, loudness, articulation, phrasing). Such sensitivity, combined with a strong "musical memory," allows the prodigy to remember music, play it back vocally or with an instrument, and even transpose and improvise with the music.

Incidentally, a young child's slower-developing motor ability may stand in the way of some accomplishments. For example, some children may not be able to write numbers or letters, illustrate their ideas, or play a musical instrument because of immature eye-hand coordination.

## Motivation, Persistence, Advanced Interests

One of the single most recurrent traits of productive gifted students and eminent adults is high motivation and persistence. A main reason that some of Terman's students became successful and some did not was differences in their motivation, due in large part to family values (Terman and Oden, 1959). Even with gifted nursery-school to second-grade children, Burk (1980) found that persistence was related to both achievement and personal adjustment.

The high motivation and urge to learn found in many gifted children, combined with their curios-

ity and their advanced comprehension and logical abilities, can lead to surprisingly advanced accomplishments. One group of gifted elementary students in Manitowish Waters, Wisconsin, conducted an environmental impact study that led the State Highway Department to move a section of a proposed freeway.

## AFFECTIVE CHARACTERISTICS

### Social Skills, Personal Adjustment, Self-Concepts

A common comparison—indeed, a classic conflict—is the reported high mental health of Terman's subjects, as both students and adults, versus Leta Hollingworth's forceful descriptions of troubled gifted children who are too different and too smart to fit in, and therefore are in desperate need of "emotional education" (counseling). We already noted one explanation: Perhaps biased teachers had preselected only well-adjusted children for Terman's research. Another key to the controversy is *level* of giftedness. Hollingworth (1942) noted that students with IQs in the 140–160 range tend to be successful, have friends, and be well-adjusted. But above IQ 180, they are too different and social adjustment is difficult. A young woman counseled by Rimm had an IQ score of 193. She finally found appropriate mental peers at a summer program at MIT before her senior year in high school, and anticipated a new social life at MIT with great relief. She would no longer carry the "geek" label. She would no longer be alone.

Unfortunately, research on the personal adjustment of gifted students rarely includes students with IQs above 180 (Norman, Ramsay, Roberts, & Martray, 2000). Rather, the "highly gifted" experimental samples typically are equivalent in IQ to Hollingworth's well-adjusted middle group, roughly IQ 130–150. Consequently, many studies that compare "highly gifted," "moderately gifted," and average students (e.g., Gallucci, Middleton, & Kline, 1999a, 1999b; Garland & Zigler, 1999; Richardson & Benbow, 1990; Sayler & Brookshire, 1996) report good psychological and social adjustment that is unrelated to level of giftedness.

For example, Norman, Ramsay, Roberts, and Martray (2000) took a close look at the social status (popular, average, rejected) of "highly gifted" students (IQs over 130) and "moderately gifted" students (everybody else) in a summer program for gifted students age 12 to 16. There were no differences in average social status between the two groups, either in dormitory or classroom settings. But if gifted peers rejected a gifted student in the classroom, that student probably also was rejected in the dorm, and vice versa. In short, factors other than giftedness—namely, disruptiveness or shyness—influenced social rejection.

In agreement with Hollingworth, Gross (1993a, 2000) showed clearly damaging effects of a too-high IQ. She studied 15 Australian children with extraordinarily high IQ scores: All scored over IQ 160, three scored over 200. Their social self-esteem scores on the Coopersmith Self-Esteem Inventory (Coopersmith, 1981) were significantly below the average for age mates. They were fully aware that peers disliked and rejected them.

Colangelo and Kelly (1983) discovered that gifted students' self-concepts depend on which "self" the researcher is looking at ("academic self" or "social self"). The authors compared scores on the Tennessee Self-Concept Scale of gifted students, regular students, and students with learning problems in grades 7, 8, and 9. For the *overall* scale, gifted students scored significantly higher than regular students, who in turn scored higher than students with learning problems. However, on closer examination the gifted students scored significantly higher only on the *academic self* subscale; on the *social self* subscale the gifted students scored about the same as the other students.

Regarding gender, Loeb and Jay (1987) found that upper elementary gifted girls had a more positive self-concept and higher internal locus of control than nongifted girls. Said Loeb and Jay, their high classroom success was consistent with "a positive sense of self and feelings of control over their life space." However, there were no dif-

ferences between gifted and nongifted boys in self-concept or locus of control.

In high school, however, Kelly and Colangelo (1984) found the reverse. Gifted adolescent boys had better overall self-concepts than nongifted boys, but there were no differences in self-concepts between gifted and nongifted adolescent girls. High school norms appear to support a masculine, aggressive achievement style, thus supporting a positive self-image for males. The high school female, however, may experience conflict over her role as a gifted achiever versus her emerging identity as a woman, and her self-concept suffers.

A study of 85 seventh- and ninth-grade students in a summer program in math, computers, business, and engineering asked students, "What's it like to be gifted?" (Kunkel, Chapa, Patterson, and Walling, 1995). Responses were classified as positive or negative, individual or social. In the category of positive individual aspects of giftedness the authors found *intellectual superiority* (e.g., good grades, competing well), *skillfullness* (e.g., being talented and creative), and *self-satisfaction* (e.g., feeling happy and proud). Negative individual qualities included *estrangement* (e.g., feeling different or embarrassed) and *conformity* (e.g., feeling bored). Some positive social benefits were *social superiority* (e.g., special classes, being the best in school) and *respect from others* (e.g., students praise me, ask for my help). Negative social aspects of giftedness included one problem: *social stress* (e.g., people think I'm a snob, make fun of me, make me wish I wasn't smart).

One affective problem peculiar to extremely bright students is their emotional excitability and high sensitivity, which we will describe more fully in Chapter 17. For example, due to high energy they tend to talk rapidly and compulsively, and may become workaholics. They have sprightly imaginations and sensual experiences that are "more alive." Their emotional reactions are more intensely joyful but also more fearful and depressed. They develop steadfast values, with strong concerns for right and wrong (Piechowski, 1997).

As a general rule, gifted students are as well or better adjusted than regular students and have better self-concepts and greater overall self-actualization (Pufal-Struzik, 1999). Giftedness clearly is an advantage, one that conveys both academic and personal benefits.

However, the tendency for healthy adjustment must not blind educators to frequent turbulent problems and strong needs for counseling. Common problems, some noted in Table 2.1, include social rejection, leading to feelings of aloneness, differentness, even "weirdness"; depression (with suicide in rare cases); boredom, apathy, and frustration toward an indifferent school; compulsive and neurotic perfectionism; feelings of stress; neurotic concern that one must be superior in all activities; sibling difficulties; and even eating disorders in adolescence (Neihart, 1999b). Hollingworth (1942) recommended that counseling be part of all gifted programs, a widely accepted idea (e.g., Colangelo, 2003; Colangelo & Assouline, 2000; Silverman, 1993a, 1993b; see Chapter 17).

## Independence, Self-Confidence, Internal Control

An important set of personality characteristics of the gifted child relates to his or her typically high level of self-confidence and independence. Such an attitude is a natural outgrowth of years of favorable comparisons with less-able peers; of glowing feedback and evaluations from parents, teachers, peers, and siblings; and from the child's clear history of success in school.

The concept of high *internal control* describes the confident children or adolescents who feel responsible for their successes and failures and who feel in control of their destinies. The child with high internal control is likely to use errors and failures constructively; he or she learns from mistakes. Importantly, the internally controlled child usually attributes failure to lack of effort, not lack of ability, and so a failure is a momentary setback that motivates the student to "try harder next time."

In contrast, the *externally controlled* child is more likely to attribute success or failure to luck, chance, easy or difficult tasks, generous or unfair teachers, lack of sleep, a sick cat, and so on. The "external" child also is less likely to try harder after failure—since he or she does not accept responsibility for the outcome in the first place.

Their generally higher levels of internal control and personal responsibility often lead gifted students to set high goals for themselves. When these goals are not met, the natural outcome is disappointment, frustration, and feelings of incompetence, ineptness, or stupidity. Parents and teachers are frequently mystified by displays of frustration and self-criticism by students who are obviously extraordinarily capable and talented. The frustration occurs not because the students are comparing their own performances with those of others, but with their own high expectations and perfectionism.

## Preferred Styles of Learning, Instruction, Thinking, and Expression

*Learning styles* refers to students' preferred physical and sociopsychological conditions and preferred teaching/learning methods (Dunn & Griggs, 1988; Griggs & Dunn, 1984). The overlapping concept of *instructional styles* also refers to teaching/learning methods (Renzulli & Reis, 1997). *Thinking styles* refers to how one intellectually responds to situations and problems (Dai & Feldhusen, 1999; Sternberg & Grigorenko, 1993). *Expression Style* is one's preferred mode of response.

A classic instrument for assessing learning styles is the Dunn, Dunn, and Price (1981) Learning Styles Inventory (LSI). The LSI assesses learning preferences in these areas: *environmental* (light, sound, temperature, design), *emotional* (motivation, persistence, responsibility, need for structure or options), *sociological* (self, peer, team, adult, varied), *physical* (time of day, need for intake, mobility), and *psychological* (global/analytical, left/right, impulsive/reflective).

It is not surprising that gifted students' preferred learning styles match their frequent characteristics of high motivation, persistence, self-confidence, independence, and high internal control. Griggs and Dunn (1984; Griggs, 1984) concluded that gifted students tend to be independent self-motivated learners more than teacher-motivated. They need and enjoy learning tasks that are unstructured and flexible, rather than the highly structured tasks needed by less able students. They prefer active participant approaches to learning, rather than spectator approaches. They can learn through varied sensory channels, including visual, auditory, tactile, and kinesthetic. They generally are more responsible, prefer a quieter learning environment, and prefer to learn alone or with other gifted students.

Renzulli and Reis (1997) took a broad view of style preferences that includes four subcategories: *instructional style preferences, learning environment preferences, thinking styles preferences,* and *expression style preferences.* In increasing order, they report gifted students' instructional style preferences as lecture (tied with drill and recitation, or "drill-and-kill," according to Renzulli, 1995), discussion, demonstration, small group discussion, peer tutoring, cooperative learning, field trips, learning centers, learning games, electronic learning, simulations/role playing, projects, mentorships (internships, apprenticeships), and independent study.

Renzulli and Reis (1997) noted that gifted students differ in learning environment preferences, and the teacher should ask "Which does the young person prefer?" (p. 81). They acknowledged variations among gifted students in preferred *interpersonal combinations* (self-, peer-, adult-oriented, or combined) and *physical combinations* (e.g., sound, heat, light, room design, mobility, time of day, food intake, seating) of learning environments.

Thinking styles preferences includes Sternberg's (e.g., 2003) triarchic categories of *analytic, synthetic,* and *practical* giftedness (Chapter 1), along with Sternberg's (1997b; Grigorenko & Sternberg, 1997; Sternberg & Grigorenko, 1993) *legislative* (e.g., creates own rules, does things in own way), *executive* (e.g., carries out plans, fol-

lows rules), and *judicial* (e.g., compares and evaluates ideas, rules, procedures).

Finally, expression style preferences includes written, oral, manipulative, discussion, display, dramatization, artistic, graphic, commercial, or service types of demonstrations of learning.

In regard to thinking styles, or "how individuals apply [intellectual abilities] in adapting to the demands of the environment" (Dai & Feldhusen, 1999, p. 302), probably all thinking styles are tied closely to personality traits. Also, as with learning styles, gifted students can be most successful if their thinking styles are coordinated with their learning tasks (Sternberg, 1997b; Sternberg & Grigorenko, 1993). Dai and Feldhusen noted that gifted adolescent students are diverse in thinking styles, despite similar profiles of abilities and academic achievement. Interestingly, teachers tend to favorably evaluate students whose thinking style matches their own (Grigorenko & Sternberg, 1997).

Dai and Feldhusen (1999) and Sternberg and Grigorenko (1993) mentioned several familiar two-part thinking styles, for example, *liberal* and *conservative* and preferring to *work alone* versus *work with others.* Perhaps the best-known two-part thinking style is *creative* thinking versus *convergent* thinking. Sternberg's (1997b) legislative function (creating ideas and rules) versus executive/judicial functions (following rules, evaluating ideas) reflects this distinction. Kirton (1976) used the phrases *innovative* versus *adaptive* thinking. As personality correlates, according to Kirton innovators may seem undisciplined, impractical, and able to do routine work for only short bursts. In contrast, adaptors tend to be precise, efficient, conforming, highly accurate in long spells of work; may show self-doubt; and rarely challenge authority. Simonton (1996) used the terms *creative expertise* versus *received expertise.* As we saw in Chapter 1, Tannenbaum (2003) described gifted persons who produce ideas, tangibles, or performances *creatively* or *proficiently.* Renzulli (1986) distinguished between *creative-productive giftedness* (developing original ideas and products) and *schoolhouse giftedness* (adeptness at learning school material, taking tests, earning high grades—and getting admitted to G/T programs).

## Superior Humor

The superior sense of humor of most gifted children would seem to follow quite naturally from their abilities to think quickly and see relationships, and from their general confidence and social adeptness. The humor will appear in art, creative writing, and other areas as well as in social interaction.

Gross (2000) recounted a preschool teacher who asked young Steven to assist in picking up empty fruit juice cups: "Can you pass that cup, please?" Steven placed the cup on the floor and solemnly paced back and forth in front of it. His IQ tested at 158 and he adored puns and wordplay—in this case, alternative definitions of "pass." Another true story describes a young gifted child who locked his mother out of the house. When she yelled at him, "Open the door!" he walked into the kitchen with a grin and opened the refrigerator.

## High Moral Thinking and Empathy

As a general trend, gifted students are more sensitive to values and moral issues and they intuitively understand why certain behavior is "good" and other behavior is "bad." Piaget and Inhelder (1969) explain that developmentally advanced children are less egocentric; that is, they are able to view a situation from another person's point of view. Therefore, gifted students are more likely to acknowledge the rights and feelings of others.

Gifted children and youth are likely to develop, refine, and internalize a system of values and a keen sense of fair play and justice at a relatively early age. Not only is the child likely to be more fair, empathic, and honest, but he or she will evaluate others according to the same standards. It follows that gifted students are less likely to show antisocial or other behavior problems in school.

Gifted students, especially the brightest ones, may develop an interest in social issues, particularly those in which his or her sense of reason and justice seems to be violated. Teachers or parents may find themselves embroiled in serious discussions with gifted children about why adults litter streets and highways with beer cans and burger wrappers, why politicians cut benefits and programs for the elderly and poor, and why parents voted against enlarging the crowded school building. Hollingworth (1942, p. 281) described a 6-year-old boy of 187 IQ who "wept bitterly after reading how the North taxed the South after the Civil War."

Hollingworth also described one not-so-moral tendency. She noted that most of her very bright students engaged in "benign chicanery." That is, the children used their intelligence to get their own way with less intelligent peers or to avoid disagreeable academic or other tasks. Because such talent could be helpful in the adult world, Hollingworth helped them to be aware of when they were taking advantage of their ability (Delisle, 1992).

In the Gross (1993a) study of very high IQ Australian children mentioned earlier, eight children ages 10 to 13 took a test of moral judgment. Their moral and ethical sense resembled that of high school or college students.

Be cautioned: Despite their high mental ability and high capacity for moral thought, "benign chicanery" may progress to delinquency and crime, where the talents of bright and clever students are quickly rewarded (money, status) by misconduct-oriented peers.

## CHARACTERISTICS OF THE CREATIVELY GIFTED

### Creativity and Intelligence: The Threshold Concept

The student who is highly intelligent may or may not be creatively gifted as well. Getzels and Jackson (1962) and Wallach and Kogan (1965) contrasted highly intelligent versus highly creative students, confirming that the two traits are indeed *not* the same. Of interest to teachers, Getzels and Jackson reported that highly creative and highly intelligent students did equally well in course work—but teachers preferred the highly intelligent students!

On the other hand, there is good evidence that creativity and intelligence are related. The resolution to this apparent inconsistency—creativity *is* versus *is not* related to intelligence—lies in the *threshold* concept: A base level of intelligence usually is essential for creative productivity; above that threshold (about IQ 120) there is virtually no relationship between measured intelligence and creativity (MacKinnon, 1978). For example, Walberg, Williams, and Zeiser (2003) noted that high intelligence is less important to adult creative eminence than other psychological traits and conditions (e.g., perseverance, stimulating social environments, and luck). Particularly, as we will see, creative persons must be independent and confident, motivated and energetic, and dare to make changes, challenge traditions, make waves, bend rules, and sometimes fail in the process.

*An important implication of distinguishing between intellectual and creative giftedness is that if students are selected for a gifted program based upon scores in the top 1 to 5 percent in intelligence, the majority of creative students will be missed.* Another implication is that when asked to identify "gifted" students, as we noted earlier in this chapter, many teachers will quickly nominate the well-behaved, conforming, neat, and dutiful "teacher pleasers," rather than less conforming students who are highly creative and more unconventional. Also, in many classes (for example, math or science in the middle school) the special talents of the creatively gifted may not be required. Creative students therefore will be less visible and less likely to be nominated as "gifted" than highly intelligent students.

Ultimately, the achievements and contributions to society of many highly creative students will surpass those of brighter, conforming grade-getters.

## Personality and Cognitive Characteristics

There is a recurrent group of personality and cognitive traits that appear again and again in descriptions of the creative person (e.g., Barron, 1969, 1988; Costa, 2003; Csikszentmihalyi & Wolfe, 2000; MacKinnon, 1962, 1978; Simonton, 1988, 2003; Tardif & Sternberg, 1988; Torrance, 1981a, 1984, 1988; Walberg, Williams, & Zeiser, 2003). Again, not all characteristics will apply to all creative people. However, most traits square well with our intuitive understanding of a creative person. Recurrent traits are listed in the left column of Table 2.2. Some common near-synonyms are listed in the right column.

Two personality characteristics are especially worth emphasizing. First, every creatively productive person of any age shows high *energy* and *motivation*. Such persons have been described as impulsive, overactive (even hyperactive), enthusiastic, excitable, spontaneous, persistent, persevering, adventurous, willing to work beyond assigned tasks, and having high drive for accomplishment and recognition (Davis, 1999).

The other noteworthy, and related, trait is *risk-taking*, sometimes described as not being afraid to try something new, not minding the consequences of being different, having courage, exposing oneself to hostility, rejecting limits imposed by others, gambling on failure, and being willing to make a fool of oneself. Failing and looking like an idiot are not particularly appealing. Indeed, fear of failure and fear of rejection are emotional barriers to creative thinking (Davis, 1999). If one tries new ideas, one will often fail. As IBM founder Thomas J. Watson once said, "The way to succeed is to double your failure rate" (von Oech, 1983, p. 93).

But creative people are complex. Depending on their phase of thinking or other circumstances, they may be gregarious or hermitlike, extroverted or introverted, arrogant or humble, masculine or

**TABLE 2.2**   Characteristics Related to Creativity

| Positive Traits | Approximate Synonyms |
| --- | --- |
| Original | Imaginative, resourceful, flexible, unconventional, thinks metaphorically, challenges assumptions, asks "what if?," irritated and bored by the obvious, avoids perceptual set |
| Aware of creativeness | Creativity conscious, values originality, values own creativity |
| Independent | Self-confident, individualistic, nonconforming, sets own rules, unconcerned with impressing others, resists societal demands |
| Risk-taking | Not afraid to be different or try something new, willing to cope with hostility, willing to cope with failure |
| Motivated | Energetic, adventurous, sensation seeking, enthusiastic, excitable, spontaneous, impulsive, intrinsically motivated, perseveres, works beyond assigned tasks |
| Curious | Questions norms and assumptions, experiments, inquisitive, wide interests, asks "why?," is a problem-finder |
| Sense of humor | Playful, plays with ideas, childlike freshness in thinking |
| Attracted to complexity | Attracted to novelty, asymmetry, the mysterious, theoretical and abstract problems; is a complex person; tolerant of ambiguity, disorder, incongruity |
| Artistic | Artistic and aesthetic interests, attracted to beauty and order |
| Open-minded | Receptive to new ideas, other viewpoints, new experiences, and growth; liberal, altruistic |
| Needs alone time | Reflective, introspective, internally preoccupied, sensitive, may be withdrawn, likes to work alone |
| Intuitive | Perceptive, sees relationships, finds order in chaos, uses all senses in observing |
| Intelligent | Verbally fluent, articulate, logical, good decision maker, detects gaps in knowledge, visualizes |

feminine, or warm and sensitive or cold and aloof (Csikszentmihalyi & Wolfe, 2000).

## Other Traits and Some Negative Traits

Torrance (1981b) itemized additional traits that might help the teacher or parent recognize and understand creative students:

- Likes to work by himself or herself
- Is a "what if?" person
- Sees relationships
- Is full of ideas
- High verbal, conversational fluency
- Constructs, builds, rebuilds
- Copes with several ideas at once
- Irritated and bored by the routine and obvious
- Goes beyond assigned tasks
- Enjoys telling about his or her discoveries or inventions
- Finds ways of doing things differently from standard procedures
- Is not afraid to try something new
- Does not mind consequences of appearing different

So far, the creative personality looks pretty good. However, creative children, adolescents, and adults may show habits and dispositions that will upset normal parents, teachers, or administrators, as well as other students. Some "negative" traits are itemized in Table 2.3. Such characteristics may stem from a creative student's confidence, independence, persistence, curiosity, unconventionality, interest in novelty, and humor.

When stubborn Sammy or independent Elissa shows some of these upsetting characteristics, the teacher or parent might consider the possibility that the symptoms are part of a larger picture of original, energetic creativeness that may need rechanneling into constructive outlets.

True creativity is the product not only of personality traits that predispose a person to think creatively but a constellation of creative abilities as well. Important creative abilities and ideas for strengthening them will be described in Chapters 10 and 11.

**TABLE 2.3** Negative Traits of Some Creative Persons

| |
|---|
| Overactive physically and mentally |
| Temperamental, emotional |
| Indifferent to conventions and courtesies |
| Question rules, laws, and authority |
| Stubborn |
| Resists domination |
| Egocentric, intolerant, tactless |
| Rebellious, uncooperative |
| Capricious, careless, disorderly |
| Arrogant, cynical, sarcastic |
| Impatient, demanding |
| Absentminded, forgetful, mind wanders |
| Argumentative, argues that everyone else is wrong |
| Sloppy and disorganized with details and unimportant matters |

Primarily from Smith (1966), Tardif and Sternberg (1988), and Torrance (1962).

## CHARACTERISTICS OF HISTORICALLY EMINENT PERSONS

### Herbert Walberg's Studies of Eminent Men, Eminent Women, and High School Artists and Scientists

Walberg (1982; Walberg et al., 1981; Walberg, Williams, & Zeiser, 2003) reviewed childhood traits of over 200 eminent people from artistic, scientific, religious, and political domains born between the 14th and 20th centuries. The following traits were common to virtually all of these gifted and visibly productive men and women.

- Versatility
- Concentration
- Perseverance
- Superior communication skills
- At least moderately high intelligence

In addition, the majority were rated as:

- Ethical
- Sensitive
- Optimistic
- Magnetic and popular

In childhood they were exposed to stimulating family, educational, and cultural conditions. About 80 percent were successful in school and liked it. About 90 percent were given considerable autonomy in their school years, although 70 percent also were guided by clear parental expectations. Many showed outstanding early accomplishments.

Turning to Walberg's study of 771 high school students, he identified three groups: (1) students who won competitive awards in science, (2) students who won awards in the arts, and (3) average classmates. The *scientist* and *artist* groups showed a number of traits in common. According to self-reports, students in both groups:

- Visited libraries for nonschool reading, had greater numbers of books at home, and found books more interesting than people(!)
- Had early strong interests in mechanical and scientific objects as well as the arts
- Were interested in work with fine detail

- Were persistent in carrying things through
- Liked school, studied hard, and completed their work faster than classmates
- Felt more creative, curious, and expressive than others; and believed it is important to be creative
- Selected creativity, rather than wealth and power, as the "best characteristic to develop in life"
- Indicated they were brighter and quicker to understand than their friends
- Attached great importance to money and expected to earn higher salaries than the average; expected to earn graduate degrees

The gifted scientists and artists differed in many respects. The scientists were more concerned with things and ideas rather than with people and feelings. For example, the science award winners reported more difficulty making friends after changing schools and they did not date much. The scientists also were more persistent; they tended to complete work regardless of problems or distractions. They were more "bookish" and less involved in school activities. While the scientists valued their intelligence more highly than creativity, the artists valued their creativity more highly. The scientists made more detailed plans regarding their future education and were more concerned about future job security. The artists leaned toward "letting fate take its course."

Walberg and his colleagues itemized important traits of intelligent and creatively productive eminent adults and contemporary youth. But he was not the first to study personal, family, and environment traits of eminent persons; see Insets 2.1 and 2.2.

## When Does Giftedness Become Genius?: Dean Simonton

Consider this dilemma. Simonton (2003) noted that, ideally, Terman's (1925) gifted children should have become eminent adults and, vice versa, Cox's (1926) eminent adults should have been gifted children. But some of Terman's high IQ children were "misfits and failures," and "many

**INSET 2.1** _____

### Studies of Eminent Persons: Catharine Cox

The Stanford University Press *Genetic Studies of Genius* consisted of five volumes. Only volume 2, by Catharine Cox (1926), was not devoted to Lewis Terman's high IQ subjects as students and adults. Cox, a colleague of Terman, took an approach to understanding traits of gifted persons that was quite the reverse of her famous cohort. Instead of beginning with bright children and tracking their accomplishments, she began by identifying 282 eminent persons and then examined their biographical and personal records. The findings related to intelligence are most enlightening. Cox estimated their IQ scores to range from 100 to 200, with an average of 159. However, many estimated IQs were rather modest: Thirteen IQ scores fell between 100 and 110, 30 between 110 and 120, and 30 between 120 and 130. Extraordinary innate brilliance helped but was not essential. Cox concluded that individuals who achieve eminence are likely to (1) be born of intelligent parents and raised in advantaged circumstances, (2) show precocious childhood traits and behavior that indicate unusually superior intelligence, and significantly (3) be "characterized not only by high intellectual traits, but also by persistence of motive and effort, confidence in their abilities, and great strength and force of character."

---

of the 301 geniuses in her [Cox's] sample would not have qualified for inclusion in Terman's study" (Simonton, p. 358). Simonton puzzled out some of the often subtle circumstances that help explain this apparent peculiarity.

First of all, one's IQ can be too high. A brilliant person may "talk over the heads" of important persons and be dismissed as too "high brow" or "eccentric." If high achievement requires appealing to the masses, said Simonton (1985), an IQ around 119 is optimal.

Also, as we saw in Gardner's MI theory, there are intelligences other than IQ. In fact, while many of Terman's Termites became doctors, pro-

**INSET 2.2** _____

### Studies of Eminent Adults: The Goertzels

In two studies, the Goertzels (Goertzel and Goertzel, 1962; Goertzel, Goertzel, and Goertzel, 1978) reviewed the family backgrounds and personal lives of some 700 adults who had achieved eminence via highly creative achievements that made a strong impact on society. A composite picture, based on recurrent traits and behavior, runs as follows:

> The eminent man or woman is likely to be the firstborn or only child in a middle-class family. . . . In these families there are rows of books on shelves, and parental expectations are high for all children. . . .
>
> Children who become eminent love learning but dislike school and school teachers who try to confine them to a curriculum not designed for individual needs. They respond well to being tutored or to being left alone, and they like to go to special schools such as those that train actors, dancers, musicians, and artists.
>
> . . . They are more self-directed, less motivated in wanting to please than are their peers or siblings. They need and manage to find periods of isolation when they have freedom to think, to read, to write, to experiment, to paint, to play an instrument, or to explore the countryside. Sometimes this freedom can be obtained only by real or feigned illnesses; a sympathetic parent may respond to the child's need to have long free periods of concentrated effort. . . .
>
> They treasure their uniqueness and find it hard to be conforming, in dress, behavior, and other ways. (Goertzel, Goertzel, and Goertzel, 1978, pp. 336–338)

The Goertzel and Goertzel (1962) study of 400 eminent adults revealed two consistent family characteristics across all talent areas. First, all the parents were highly energetic and goal-directed. Second, almost all the families displayed an intense and intrinsic love for learning and achievement that was not simply attached to materialistic goals.

---

fessors, and scientists, few become artists, composers, or world leaders, requiring forms of intelligence not measured by Terman's Stanford-Binet Intelligence Scale. Further, "drive and determination could more than compensate for a less than stratospheric IQ" (Simonton, 2003, p. 359). Creative ability—Sternberg's synthetic giftedness—and its many companion personality traits are other important characteristics.

As we will see in Chapter 9, a touch of psychopathology—virtually absent in Terman's subjects—is extremely common in biographies of creatively eminent achievers, especially artists and writers.

Genius apparently is both born and made. First-born children were overrepresented in Terman's (1925) high IQ sample and in other researchers' samples of child prodigies, successful politicians, successful women (Rimm, Rimm-Kaufman, & Rimm, 1999), and eminent scientists (Feldman, 1991). But later borns are more likely to become great artists, writers (Simonton, 2003), or psychologists (Rimm et al., 1999).

Traumatic childhood events, such as economic hardship or the early loss of a parent, characterize many persons who became eminent in science or, especially, the arts. Said Simonton, to achieve eminence, one's childhood cannot be too happy. We should caution, as did Simonton, that the development of child prodigies virtually always requires supportive parents and a favorable environment (e.g., Morelock & Feldman, 2003).

Finally, the role of formal education and academic performance in attaining eminence may be surprising—too much and too high are bad. There is virtually no correlation between earning high college grades/honors and achieving eminence in one's field. Said Simonton (2003), the ideal amount of education peaks "somewhere in the last half of undergraduate training" (p. 365).

## A Termite Who Made It: Ancel Keys

Ancel Keys made the cover of both *Time* and *Life* magazines (Shurkin, 1992). When identified by Terman, he was 18 years old and in high school, which he didn't much like, and even dropped out for a semester to shovel bat guano in an Arizona cave. At the University of California, Berkeley, he majored in chemistry and "earned loose change by beating his classmates at bridge" (p. 133). Before graduating, he signed on as an oiler for a ship bound for China.

Returning to Berkeley, he graduated in economics in two years and went to work at Woolworth's as a management trainee. He was "bored silly." Back at Berkeley, he completed a second major in biology, then a Ph.D. in 1928 with lots of training in physiology, biology, and zoology.

He went to Cambridge University as a fellow of the Rockefeller Foundation, studied physiology, and somehow received a second Ph.D. "with no examination, no thesis, and no cost" (Shurkin, 1992, p. 135).

Back in America, Keys took a job at the Harvard Fatigue Laboratory. He decided to explore the effects of high altitude on the human body, so he went to Chile to climb the Andes—accompanied, fortunately, by 10 others who knew how to climb. With two Peruvians, they set up camp at 20,000 feet and conducted blood, lung, body temperature, and pulse rate tests despite the 50-below zero temperature. One scientist turned blue and passed out, but recovered at 17,000 feet.

From Harvard, Keys joined the Mayo Clinic (which doubled his salary), then joined the Department of Physiology in the University of Minnesota Medical School.

World War II made him famous. The War Department wanted him to develop high-nutrition, pocket-size emergency rations, resulting in the famous K-rations (yes, "K" stands for "Keys").

With 36 conscientious objectors as guinea pigs, he also studied effects of starvation and the best way to rehabilitate the undernourished, resulting in the two-volume *Biology of Human Starvation*. He discovered that all aspects of their life were affected—dreams and behavior, weakness, weariness, apathy, and "no more sexual feeling than a sick oyster" (p. 249). Recovery was not rapid or complete, and food *increased* depression.

After the war, Keys examined causes of heart attack. Of 27 executives who had heart attacks in his study, *all* had cholesterol counts over 240. He also knew that, under German occupation and deprived of a fatty diet, the Dutch and Scandinavians saw a decrease in heart attacks. And that in Naples, Italy, only rich persons had heart attacks—everybody else ate lots of pasta, olive oil, and wine, but no butter or milk. And that people in Finland slathered butter on big slabs of cheese and died of heart attacks even faster than Americans. Ancel Keys was the first to clarify matters and get the message to the public. The "Keys equation" predicts cholesterol level from the quantity of fatty acids in our diet.

Keys's crowning achievement was his Seven Countries Study—still in progress after over 40 years. He monitored the diets and heart attacks of nearly 13,000 men aged 40 to 59. In 1960 he and his wife, Margaret, published the best-seller *Eat Well and Stay Well*, which put him on the cover of *Time* magazine. He upped his warning: Americans eat too much, especially eggs, dairy products, and marbled meat, leading to cancer, heart disease, and diabetes.

"His work is now considered part of medical wisdom" (Shurkin, p. 251).

Quiz: How many abilities and personality traits of creative people and creative scientists can you detect in this brief sketch?

---

While lawyers, doctors, and scientists must possess higher degrees, artistic creators and other unconventional achievers can succeed at high levels with just a little college education.

Incidentally, as an example of one of Terman's kids who *did* succeed at a high level (there were others; see Shurkin, 1992), see Inset 2.3.

## Parental Support, Communities of Support, and Intense Individualized Instruction: Lauren Sosniak and Benjamin Bloom

Bloom and Sosniak (1981; Bloom, 1985; Sosniak, 1997, 2003) examined the home environment and the early training of exceptional, accomplished pianists, sculptors, swimmers, tennis players, mathematicians, and research neurologists, whose talents roughly represented artistic, motoric, and cognitive skill areas. They discovered that the home environments and the gifted persons' parents were almost entirely responsible for nurturing the children's early interests and developing their child's skills to extraordinary levels. The remarkably talented individuals in the Bloom and Sosniak sample "typically did *not* show unusual promise at the start" (Sosniak, 2003, p. 247). Sosniak quoted Bloom as confessing, "We were looking for exceptional kids and what we found were exceptional conditions" (p. 247).

Almost always, one or both parents had a strong interest in the particular talent and were themselves above average in the skill. In every case the parents strongly supported the children, encouraging and rewarding their interests, talents, and efforts. Importantly, the talented parent or parents served as role models, exemplifying the personality and lifestyle of the highly talented person.

Initially, parents themselves provided the necessary training and supervision of practice. However, at some point each child switched to a professional instructor. In many cases parental support was so strong that the family would move to another location to be closer to an outstanding teacher or better facilities. The single student often would be the central concern of the devoted instructor. During this time the student's dedication to the talent area would grow strong— which explains his or her willingness to spend approximately fifteen hours per week in lessons and practice.

Importantly, these students learned to handle failures constructively. That is, failures were learning experiences used to pinpoint problems to be solved and new skills to be mastered. In con-trast, according to Bloom (1985), among "talent dropouts" failures led to feelings of inadequacy and quitting.

Bloom (1985) contrasted the development of talent with traditional educational philosophy and methods. First, in the early years of home instruction talent development is informal, exploratory, and similar to play; the school setting is serious, formal, and on a set schedule. Second, with talent development instruction is totally individualized, with praise and rewards based completely on individualized objectives and standards. School learning, of course, is group oriented. Third, the purpose of school is to provide all students with a broad basic education, and strong specialization is not encouraged. In talent development, the student and teacher focus on moving the learner to higher and higher levels of accomplishment in just one specialized area. Fourth, for many students school learning is seen as devoid of meaning, something to be tolerated. In contrast, the purposes and meaning in talent development are clear, which inspires the dedication and hard work.

As reflected in the title of a recent article, "Developing Talent: Time, Task, and Context," Sosniak (2003) stressed that developing exceptional abilities takes a lot of time. Concert pianists worked about 17 years for international recognition; swimmers trained about 15 years before earning a spot on the Olympic team.

Regarding Sosniak's *context,* her key concept is the development of *communities of practice*— groups of people who share a focus on the particular talent, work in that area, and are anxious to support the aspiring youth. Families are the first communities of practice. For example, music was expressly valued, every day, in the homes of later accomplished pianists; sports were valued in the homes of future Olympic swimmers. The reverse combinations never happened.

Regarding communities of practice outside the home, pianists took lessons from local music teachers, and swimmers took lessons at the "Y" and joined swim clubs. Young scientists had friends with whom they studied their area and/or conducted experiments, typically with youth science sets. Other strongly supportive communities of practice include music performances and competitions, art shows, math or science clubs, and summer camps associated with a talent area. People in these groups introduce the young person to recordings, books, magazines, and other resources in the talent area. They help shape interests and educational and training needs. And critically, they introduce youth to expert models in an area and resources for support and inspiration.

Finally, in Sosniak's (2003) words, "We appear to be looking for the wrong things, in the wrong ways. . . . We are quite confident that extraordinary levels of accomplishment are possible for individuals who do not necessarily show early promise" (p. 247). A thought-provoking view indeed.

### Child Prodigies, Extraordinary IQ, Available Knowledge, and Coincidence: David Feldman and Martha Morelock

Morelock (2000) and Morelock and Feldman (2003) studied and described *child prodigies* and *children of extraordinarily high IQ.* A *prodigy* is defined as a young person who performs at the level of a highly trained adult. Similar to Cox's (1926) eminent adults (Inset 2.1), child prodigies usually show high but not extraordinary IQ scores. Nearly always, their prodigious ability is limited to a specific domain, as reflected in Morelock and Feldman's descriptions of a remarkable violinist and a pianist, both of whom had poor hand coordination in folding and cutting paper. As other prodigy examples, Morelock and Feldman (1997) named chess player Bobby Fischer, who became a grand master by age 15, and Wolfgang Amadeus Mozart, who composed mature works by age 10.

Feldman (1991, 1994) had also studied six prodigies since 1975—two chess players, a young mathematician, a musician-composer, a writer, and an "omnibus prodigy who showed prodigious achievement in a number of areas, but who eventually focused on music composition and perfor-

mance" (Morelock and Feldman, 1997, p. 448). All six were performing in their chosen field at the level of an adult professional before age 10.

Feldman attributed such amazing youthful accomplishment to a coincidence of *individual, environmental,* and *historical* forces, which he dubbed the *co-incidence theory* (Feldman, 1991, 1994). The *individual* component of this coincidence is the rare prodigies themselves, described as highly intelligent, developmentally advanced, and biologically "preorganized" with giftedness in a certain domain. *Environmental* factors include the existence of a highly evolved field of knowledge that can be taught to the precocious child. *Historical* factors include, for example, the value society attaches to a domain.

As an example, Mozart was clearly precocious and musically gifted. He also grew up in an environment where music was composed and played, and he was exposed to the values and lifestyles of musicians. He also received considerable personal instruction, based on an existing body of knowledge.

Based on the biographies, observations, and studies of prodigies, Morelock and Feldman (1997, 2003) itemized conclusions regarding the prodigies and their teachers:

- The children possessed extraordinary native ability.
- The children were born into families that recognized, valued, and fostered that ability.
- The children received instruction from master teachers who possessed superior knowledge of a domain and its history, and who imparted that knowledge in ways that engaged interested and sustained commitment.
- The children showed strong inner-directedness and a passionate commitment to their field; they derived a strong sense of joy from their achievements.

Concerning high-IQ children, Morelock (1995, 1996, 1997; Morelock & Feldman, 1993, 2003) studied the personality and family backgrounds of eight children, all of whom scored above IQ

180, six well above IQ 200. One 200+ boy gradu-ated from college at age 10; another at age 8 scored 760 out of 800 on the mathematics section of the SAT, the highest score ever recorded at that early age.[1] A third boy at age 5 read *A Brief History of Time,* by Stephen Hawking, concerning the origins of the universe. Addressing a suitable problem for a bright 5-year-old, he promptly figured out how Santa Claus could use black holes to (1) become thin enough to descend chimneys, and (2) have adequate time to visit every child on earth (Morelock, 1997, 2000).

Virtually all of the extremely high IQ children were first born. Interestingly, siblings tended to describe themselves in terms of what they could *do,* for example, in dancing, art, or creative (toy) constructions. The high-IQ sibling was the "thinker" and "talker."

Morelock (2000; Morelock & Feldman, 2003) endorsed Silverman's (e.g., 1997) concept of *asynchronous development.* An IQ score estimates the degree to which children's cognitive development is "in synch" with their physical, social, and emotional development. In one case described by Morelock (2000; Morelock & Feldman, 2003), 4-year-old "Jennie" (tested IQ = 176) experienced intense existential questioning and strong emotional turmoil (e.g., regarding her own mortality). Said Morelock (2000, p. 68), "Her advanced cognitive capacities . . . left her emotionally defenseless in the face of her own reason."

Finally, in addition to prodigies and high-IQ children, Morelock and Feldman (1997, 2003) described a third type of precocity that teachers of the gifted are unlikely to encounter—persons with *savant syndrome,* originally called *idiot savants.* Such persons are severely retarded, perhaps autistic, but nonetheless demonstrate astounding gifts in limited areas (see Inset 2.4)

---

[1]The SAT—Scholastic Aptitude Test—is taken by college-bound high school seniors, just 1% of whom score 750 or higher.

## CHARACTERISTICS OF TEACHERS OF THE GIFTED

*Good teachers of the gifted should be gifted themselves,* which aids understanding, empathy, and communication. Beyond this primary qualification, many experts have proposed other characteristics of effective teachers of the gifted. Most characteristics would apply to all good teachers. The summary in Table 2.4 draws heavily from Feldhusen (1997) and Croft (2003), who themselves found good suggestions in other sources.

Regarding competencies and teacher preparation, Feldhusen (1997a) argued that it is more productive to focus on competencies, skills, and knowledge than on personal traits. He also cautioned also that competencies needed to teach gifted math and science students will be different than those needed to teach gifted art, music, or literature students. Nonetheless, Feldhusen presented the core results of two particularly commendable surveys of G/T teacher competencies by Hultgren and Seeley (1982) and Nelson and Prindle (1992). These appear in Table 2.5.

Finally, if you ask gifted students themselves what they believe are prerequisite characteristics in teachers of the gifted, you might get answers like those reported by Lewis (1982; see Inset 2.5).

## SUMMARY

Identifying characteristics of gifted students is important because it helps teachers and parents recognize and understand gifted children. Even though all children differ in physical, intellectual, affective, and behavioral traits, some characteristics of gifted and talented students recur frequently in the research literature.

Terman's gifted children were better adjusted as children and adults. Compared with other children, they were better achievers and learned more easily, had more hobbies, read more books, were more trustworthy, and were healthier and better "physical specimens." The traits continued into adulthood. The most productive of the group were

## The Strange Case of Savant Syndrome

Persons with savant syndrome are a fascinating and seemingly impossible phenomenon. These are persons with severe mental disabilities (retardation, autism, or schizophrenia) who display spectacular islands of ability in narrow areas. Savant brilliance occurs in art and mechanical ability, but the highest levels are almost always found in mathematics ("lightning calculating"), music (consistently piano), and memory (Morelock and Feldman, 1993, 1997, 2003; Treffert, 1989).

The original term *idiot savant* was coined in 1887 by J. Langdon Down of London. However, they are neither "idiots" nor "savants." While *idiocy* used to be defined as IQ scores between 0 and 20, idiot savants typically score between 40 and 70 (Treffert, 1989). Further, *savant* is the French word for "person of learning"—hardly the correct description of these unique people. The phenomenon is six times more common in males than females; it can be either congenital or acquired by a normal person after an accident; and the skills can appear and disappear in sudden and unexplained ways (Treffert, 1989).

While persons with savant syndrome have an immediate and intuitive access to the underlying structural rules of a domain, they are restricted by those rules—they are not flexible and creative. For example, musical performances are said to be imitative, shallow, and lacking in subtlety and emotional expressiveness.

George and Charles were identical twin "calendar calculators." At the age of nine they could answer questions like "On what day of the week was your third birthday?" or "In the year 31,275, on what day of the week will June 6th fall?" Given a date, these twins could name the day of the week over a span of 80,000 years, 40,000 forward or 40,000 backward. They swapped 20-digit prime numbers for amusement, and they could remember up to 30 digits. Incredibly, they could neither add nor count to 30; their tested IQ scores were between 40 and 50.*

Leslie Lemke was blind almost from birth, palsied, and mentally handicapped. At age $5\frac{1}{2}$ he could repeat verbatim a whole day's conversation while impersonating each speaker's voice. He is most famous for his musical precocity; in fact, he gave concerts. He was introduced to the piano at the age of 7 and began playing by ear. By age 8 he also played the ukulele, the concertina, the xylophone, the accordion, and the bongo drums, and at age 9 the chord organ. He required help in dressing and feeding himself, however.

The "miracle" of Leslie began at age 14, when at 3:00 in the morning his parents heard him playing Tchaikovsky's Piano Concerto No. 1, the theme song in a movie they had seen earlier and which Leslie had heard only once (Treffert, 1989). After hearing a 45-minute opera once, Leslie can transpose the music to the piano and sing the entire score in its original foreign language. He seems never to forget his music; his repertoire includes thousands of pieces.

Perhaps the most credible explanation of savant syndrome is that of Treffert (1989), who suggested simply that injury to the left hemisphere of the brain (language and analytic thought) produces compensatory growth in the right hemisphere (music and spatial/mathematical abilities). Further, injury to the cerebral cortex causes memory functions to shift to more primitive brain areas, causing memory to become habitual, emotionless, and involuntary—essentially a conditioned reflex. Treffert concedes, however, that such extreme alterations in brain function cannot explain the savants' seemingly intuitive access to the structural rules of domains such as mathematics or music.

*For further information on George and Charles and other fascinating cases, see D. J. Hamblin's article in *Life,* March 18, 1966, pp. 106–108.

**TABLE 2.4**  Exemplary Teachers of the Gifted: Characteristics

*Exemplary Teachers of the Gifted:*

Are highly intelligent

Are enthusiastic about giftedness, talent, and learning

Are aware of gifted students' needs

Are energetic, ready to do extra work, and ready to experiment

Are patient, sensitive, respectful, and empathic; they understand and see matters
from students' points of view

Recognize individual differences, including personal self-images and personal
integrity

Accept responsibility for individual children

Create a vibrant, warm, safe, and democratic learning environment

Are less judgmental and critical; have confidence in gifted students

Align more closely with gifted students than do more formal teachers

Are imaginative, innovative, flexible, and open to change

Have cultural and intellectual interests and broad general knowledge

Are honest, fair, and objective

Are mature, experienced, and self-confident

Are willing to learn with and from students; are "perennial students" themselves

Seek new solutions through continued learning

Have control over their personal lives

Can work closely with other members of gifted staff, students, parents, and other
professionals

Can communicate the needs of gifted children and muster support for the gifted
program

Adapted from Feldhusen (1997), Croft (2003), and other sources.

high in confidence, leadership, goal-directedness, and desire to excel. The selection of Terman's group was biased due to their initial nomination by teachers prior to testing.

Bright children are developmentally advanced in language and thought. Early, rapidly improving speech reflects a growing conceptual ability and knowledge base. They may learn to read early, sometimes teaching themselves. Comprehension, retention, vocabulary, stored information, and logical abilities also are usually superior.

Writing, math, music, and artistic abilities appear early.

Motivation and persistence are common and are important for later adult success. Gifted students' high motivation and curiosity lead to advanced interests.

Gifted students frequently show superior affective characteristics, such as lower anxiety and depression and better self-concepts. However, some G/T children will suffer from social inadequacies, anxieties, and depression. Students with IQ scores above 145 may have special difficulty relating to peers, said Hollingworth. Very bright students can also be highly excitable and sensitive.

Research on self-concepts is complicated by age, gender, level of giftedness, and which "self" is studied. For example, gifted students have higher academic than social self-concepts. Also,

**TABLE 2.5**   Exemplary Teachers of the Gifted: Competencies

*Exemplary Teachers of the Gifted:*

Have knowledge of the nature and needs of the gifted

Can identify gifted and talented students

Can select or develop methods and materials for use with gifted students

Are well prepared, well-organized, "on their toes," well-grounded in the subject matter, ready for creative questions

Are skilled in teaching higher-level thinking skills, including creativity and problem solving

Are skilled in questioning for higher-level thinking

Focus on process as well as product

Can facilitate independent research and other projects

Can direct individualized learning

Can teach students to evaluate for themselves

Guide and facilitate learning, but do not coerce

Can work with culturally different gifted and talented students

Are skilled in counseling gifted and talented students

Help develop students' self-concepts

Can present educational and career options

Are skilled in group processes; teaching groups

Motivate students to strive for high achievement, successful accomplishments, and general excellence

Can conduct inservices for other teachers regarding G/T philosophy and methods

Adapted from Feldhusen (1997) and others.

compared with nongifted females, gifted females may have better self-concepts in elementary school than when they become adolescents, and vice versa for males.

The gifted student's history of success usually leads to high independence, self-confidence, and feelings of internal control. However, high self-expectations can lead to frustration.

Gifted students tend to have an independent, self-motivated learning style. They usually prefer unstructured and participant learning activities. Two popular inventories for assessing learning styles are the Dunn, Dunn, and Price LSI and the Renzulli and Smith LSI.

Thinking styles—for example, divergent and convergent thinking—describe how one responds to situations.

Intellectually gifted students intuitively comprehend values and moral issues and are less egocentric, thus able to empathize with the rights, feelings, and problems of others. They usually are more honest and trustworthy, although some may be delinquent. Values and a sense of fairness and justice develop early, leading to consistency in attitudes and behavior and an interest in social issues.

Creativity and intelligence are different traits. They are moderately correlated, but above a threshold IQ (about 120) the correlation disappears. If students are selected for G/T programs based on IQ scores, most creative students will be missed. Teachers often select "teacher pleasers" for gifted programs. Highly creative students, who may be less visible than highly intelligent

INSET 2.5 _____

### What Do Gifted Students Say about Teachers of the Gifted?*

"The difference between a normal teacher and a gifted teacher is that a gifted teacher is very much like her kids."

"A gifted teacher needs to be more than a normal teacher. She needs more talent and imagination."

"Other teachers teach us things. Gifted teachers teach us how to think about things."

"We need teachers who help us, not haunt us."

"It's easy to know what you want in a teacher—it's hard to know how to get it."

*From Lewis (1982), reprinted by permission of *Gifted Child Today.*

students, may ultimately make greater contributions to society.

The creative personality includes high self-confidence, independence, risk taking, high energy, adventurousness, creativity consciousness, playfulness and humor, idealism, attraction to the complex and mysterious, tolerance for ambiguity, needs for alone time, and artistic and aesthetic interests—and perhaps stubbornness, absentmindedness, or other "negative" traits.

Torrance suggested that creative students prefer working alone, see relationships, go beyond assigned tasks, and are imaginative, flexible, highly verbal, persistent, and irritated by the routine and obvious.

A background of creative activities is an unsurprising biographical characteristic. Less expected ones include having younger or older friends, having had an imaginary playmate, and involvement in theater.

Walberg's study of eminent persons indicated that virtually all, both men and women, possessed versatility, perseverance, superior communication skills, high ethics, personal magnetism, a stimu-

lating early environment, and at least moderately high intelligence. His high school art and science award winners showed confidence, early interests in art and science, much nonschool reading, persistence, and a liking for school. Unlike his artists, Walberg's scientists valued intelligence more than creativity.

Simonton examined why many "Termites" did not become eminent, and why Cox's eminent persons were not all extraordinarily brilliant. Important traits included *not* being too brilliant or educated, and being first-born, highly motivated, and often experiencing childhood trauma.

Studying gifted pianists, swimmers, mathematicians, and others, Bloom and Sosniak concluded that home and parental influences were critical to high levels of talent development. Parents supported the child and modeled the appropriate personality, values, and lifestyle. All instruction was individualized. Student (and teacher) motivation and dedication ran high. Compared with traditional schooling, talent development is informal, individualized, specialized, and more meaningful. High-level talent development takes many years. A key concept is Sosniak's *communities of support.*

Morelock and Feldman examined child prodigies, children of extraordinarily high IQ, and persons with savant syndrome. Prodigies seem mentally "preorganized" in an area. They have high but not always outstanding intelligence. Feldman's co-incidence theory stressed the combination of individual, environmental, and historical factors. Morelock studied eight children above IQ 180 who showed remarkable accomplishments. They endorsed the concept of *asynchronous development.*

Teachers of the gifted should also be gifted. They have such traits as high enthusiasm, empathy, broad knowledge, maturity, and willingness to work with other staff. Competencies include knowledge of the gifted, and the abilities to teach higher-level thinking skills, direct research and individualized learning, counsel gifted students, and more.

# CHAPTER 3

# PROGRAM PLANNING

*We must create an openness to fly, to be challenged, to grow for . . .
gifted and talented children.*
John F. Feldhusen (1992, p. 49)

The complexity of plans to help meet the educational needs of gifted and talented children can range from (1) a single teacher who provides extra study materials to students who finish assignments quickly; (2) to individual teachers who compact curriculum to supply extra time for bright students to work at learning centers or with other projects; (3) to part-time acceleration to a higher grade; (4) to grade skipping; (5) to "cluster grouping" all gifted students at each grade level in a single classroom for special services; (6) to schoolwide plans to accommodate gifted students in every regular classroom; (7) to district-wide pullout programs, in which a traveling coordinator teaches gifted students in each school for one afternoon per week; (8) to part-time special gifted classes; (9) to full-time special gifted classes at every grade level; (10) to special schools for the gifted. (These and other acceleration, enrichment, and grouping plans and curriculum models will be elaborated in Chapters 5, 6, and 7.) As Gallagher (2000) noted, differentiating the curriculum for gifted students "can refer to changes . . . in *content,* in *skills,* in *learning environments,* and even in *technology*" (p. 7). Many issues and considerations indeed.

As a preliminary thought, five interrelated concepts should underlie any thoughtful adjustments or programs for gifted and talented students: *challenge, choice, interest, enjoyment,* and *personal meaning* (Gentry & Ferriss, 1999). These combine to motivate students, promote excellence, and help students develop habits of lifelong learning. *Challenge* is increased by including high-level content and high-level thinking skills in classroom curriculum and student projects. Giving students *choices* of academic curricula and research problems in which they are *interested* leads to feelings of ownership and increased motivation and achievement. *Enjoyment* stems from allowing students to do what they like to do, and from challenging tasks that lead to feelings of accomplishment. *Personal meaning* is increased when students engage in self-selected, self-directed learning and research experiences—the students "want to be there and work together for a commonly agreed upon purpose" (Gentry & Ferriss, 1999, p. 317).

A common criticism of gifted programs is simply: "Wouldn't that be good for all students?" The answer is yes and no. In fact, some traditionally gifted activities such as creativity and other thinking skills are being brought into the regular classroom for all students. At the same time, some activities and experiences are uniquely suited to bright students with keen interests and high motivation. While a field trip could indeed benefit all students, as described in Chapter 6, follow-up reports and projects for gifted students would be at a higher level than most students could handle. Gifted students are expected to understand and create in greater depth than other kids. If the answer is an unqualified "yes," it's not a good gifted program.

This chapter will look first at four global areas in program planning. The main body of the chapter will examine 16 more specific areas of program planning. A brief section on curriculum considerations includes some curriculum principles that align with characteristics of gifted students. We then turn to not-uncommon attitudes and views of school board members and "other teachers," with suggestions for improving negative attitudes. The next section surveys common criticisms, issues, and problems—several of which seem built in to some programs—that can lead to the disappearance of gifted programs. Some alterations and solutions are suggested. Finally, active parents of gifted students sometimes differ strongly with their school district about what their gifted children need and deserve, and so we will look briefly at a new area in gifted education—recurrent legal issues and how to proceed with them.

## MAIN COMPONENTS OF PROGRAM PLANNING

There are four traditional components to planning any gifted program that may be elaborated as *why, who, what, where, when,* and *how* questions (e.g., Treffinger, 1986).

(1) *Program philosophy and goals.* A school gifted committee (consisting perhaps of several teachers, an administrator, a school counselor, one or more parents, and in secondary programs, one or more students) will consider such basic questions as: What is our attitude toward gifted children? Why are we doing this? What are our goals and objectives? What do we wish to accomplish? *Can we prepare a defensible statement of philosophy and goals?*

(2) *Definition and identification.* What exactly do we mean by "gifted and talented"? Who will the program be for? Which grades? Which students? What about minority representation? Gifted students with disabilities? How will we identify gifted students—that is, how will "gifted and talented" be operationally defined in our school's program?

(3) *Instruction. Students:* What are gifted students' needs? How can we best meet these needs? *Programs:* What forms of grouping, acceleration, and enrichment should we use? What options do

we have for our gifted program? Which produce the best results? Which are cost effective? Which programs can be used within strict heterogeneous classes? *Personnel:* Who should be on the G/T committee? Who will design, coordinate, and oversee the program? Who will teach the students? What inservice training and site visits do we need for teachers of the gifted? For all teachers? *Location:* Where will we do this? In the regular class? In special classes? At a district resource center? In a special school? How will we use community resources and professionals? *Time considerations:* When will the G/T services take place? When students finish regular assignments? When regular assignments are "compacted" to free up time for special projects (see Chapter 7)? On Wednesday afternoon? All day, every day? After school? Saturdays? Summers? When can we implement our plan? Can we formulate timelines? For identification? For initiating the instructional program(s)?

(4) *Program evaluation.* How will we evaluate gains in students' knowledge and high-level cognitive skills? In student and parent satisfaction? How can we evaluate progress and make adjustments and improvements during the school year? At the end of May, how will we evaluate program success? How will we evaluate the effectiveness of each instructional activity and each of the component materials, lessons, and teaching/learning activities and strategies? (See Inset 3.1.)

## PROGRAM PLANNING: SIXTEEN AREAS

Sixteen problem areas in program planning relate to the four main components—program philosophy and goals, definition and identification, instruction, and program evaluation—and to the *why, who, what, where, when,* and *how* questions. The 16 areas are not sequential in the one-at-a-time sense. Many will be dealt with simultaneously in planning a G/T program. Some areas are major ones, dealing, for example, with whether there will be a program at all and, if so, the directions the program will take and the students who will be served. Other problem areas are lesser

INSET 3.1 _____

## Dear School People: What Are You Doing for our Bright Child?

Gifted education leader Donald Treffinger and colleague Marion Sortore (Treffinger & Sortore, 1992a, 1992b) itemized "tough questions" that a thoughtful program planner should ponder. (We have inserted the apparent issue in parentheses.) In slightly altered form:

**1.** How does our child learn best? How does your school program take into account students' characteristics and learning styles? (*Student differences, learning styles*)

**2.** In what areas (academic and general) does our child display strengths and special interests? What provisions do you make for these to be expressed and developed in school? (*Student strengths, interests*)

**3.** What specific provisions are made for students to learn at their own rate or pace, rather than being limited to a rigid, "lock-step" curriculum? That is, what provisions are made to insure that students receive instruction that is suited to their *real* instructional needs? (*Needs for acceleration*)

**4.** What provisions are made for advanced content or courses for students whose achievement warrants them? How are the students' needs determined and reviewed? (*Acceleration; students' educational/counseling needs*)

**5.** What enrichment opportunities are offered that are not merely "busywork" or "more of the same" assignments? (*Enrichment*)

**6.** How do you help students to become aware of their own best talents and interests and to appreciate those of others as well? (*Counseling; self-understanding; empathy*)

**7.** How do teachers provide opportunities for students to learn and apply critical and creative thinking and problem-solving skills? (*Creativity, thinking skills*)

**8.** How do you help students learn to plan and investigate everyday real problems, rather than contrived, textbook exercises? How do they create and share the products or results of those investigations? (*True problems; audiences*)

**9.** What specific steps do you take to insure that learning is exciting and original, rather than boring and repetitious? (*Motivation, interest*)

**10.** What provisions are made to create opportunities for students to explore a variety of motivating and challenging topics outside the regular curriculum? (*Challenges outside of school*)

**11.** How do you provide opportunities for students to interact regularly with others who share similar talents and interests? (*Working with other gifted students; social support and friendships*)

**12.** How do you help students learn to set goals, plan projects, locate and use resources, create products, and evaluate their work? (*Goal setting, planning, evaluation—thinking skills*)

**13.** How do you use community resources and mentors to extend students' learning in areas of special talents and interests? (*Community resources, mentors*)

**14.** What resources and materials are available to expose students to the newest ideas and developments in many fields and to the people whose work creates those ideas. (*New ideas and innovators*)

**15.** How do you help students to consider future career possibilities and to cope with rapid change in our world. (*Career counseling; futuristic thinking*)

**16.** In what ways do faculty members inspire students to ask probing questions, examine many viewpoints, and use criteria to make and justify decisions? (*Critical thinking, decision making*)

**17.** What provisions do you make to help students feel comfortable and confident in expressing and dealing with their personal and academic goals and concerns? (*Personal, educational, career counseling*)

**18.** How do you insure that our children are challenged to work toward their full potential and "at the edge of their ability," rather than permitting them to drift along "on cruise control"? (*Challenging, interesting, motivating learning tasks*)

**19.** How does the school program help students to learn social or interpersonal skills without sacrificing their individuality. (*Social skills*)

**20.** Have you asked me about my child? (*Communication with parents*)

**TABLE 3.1**   Sixteen Areas in Program Planning

1. Needs assessment
2. Preliminary staff education
3. Philosophy, rational, goals, objectives, and a written program plan
4. Types of gifts and talents to be provided for and estimated enrollment
5. Identification methods and specific criteria
6. Specific provisions for identifying female, underachieving, disabled, culturally different, and economically disadvantaged gifted students
7. Staff responsibilities and assignments
8. School psychologists, counselors, and other support services
9. The detracking reform movement and acceleration and enrichment plans
10. Organizational and administrative design
11. Transportation needs
12. Community resources: professionals and organizations
13. In-service workshops, training, and visits
14. Budgetary needs and allocations
15. Developing social capital: students who care
16. Program evaluation

managerial and administrative matters necessary for smooth program operation. As an overview, the problem areas are listed in Table 3.1.

## 1. Needs Assessment

A *needs assessment* aims at determining the discrepancy between the current status of gifted education in the school or district and the desired status. There are three excellent sources of information regarding school and district needs for a G/T program and specific student needs: *parents* of gifted and talented students, gifted *students* themselves, and *teachers* and *administrators* who have become gifted conscious. First, many parents of gifted students have been frustrated by and vocal about the lack of specific services for their children. Exasperated parents register these types of complaints: "My third-grade daughter has a

Stanford-Binet IQ of 145, but the teacher says she can't help because the superintendent is opposed to special programs for the 'haves,' and current rules do not permit skipping a grade." "My son obviously is gifted and does wonderful and creative things at home, but in school he has become bored and lazy, and I am afraid his talent and enthusiasm are going to waste."

Second, many upper elementary and older gifted students can explain their strong special interests. Their curiosity and high energy levels also may be visible. Would they like to learn advanced computer programming? Would they like a special Saturday science or drama class? Would they be able to handle math, reading, or social studies at a higher grade level? Would they like to spend time with a professional artist, executive, or medical researcher? Would they be interested in a three-week summer education program at State University? You bet they would.

Third, another confirmation of the need for G/T programming may come from teachers and administrators who attend conferences or take courses that address the characteristics, needs, and problems of gifted children. With their newly found awareness, and despite emphases on equity, they may take an enthusiastic leadership role in helping document district needs and initiating programs for gifted students.

The need for a G/T program and specific student needs may be documented formally or informally, briefly or extensively depending on the size and formality of the school district and the type and source of the available information or evidence. If a school board or district administration prefers a formal and objective documentation of needs, a needs-assessment questionnaire may be distributed to parents, teachers, and perhaps students. Such a questionnaire should include two main components: (1) perceptions of what needs to be provided in the community, and (2) opinions regarding the extent to which current school programs are meeting these needs. The questionnaire will quantify the desire for differentiated educational services, the preferred directions for the services, and the extent of support. One example of a needs-assessment questionnaire appears in Table 3.2.

Gifted children and parents of gifted children are minorities in the community, so one cannot expect landslide majority support for such programs. Therefore, the criteria for deciding that programs are needed should only be "sufficient" support, not necessarily strong majority support.

After a need for special services is confirmed (formally or informally), a committee of teachers, administrators, and parents can meet to discuss possible directions for gifted programs. The fifteen problem areas may provide topics for discussion. Eventually, a formal steering committee will be organized, usually appointed (on request) by a district administrator or school principal, to make concrete plans with a definite timetable. In the elementary school, the steering committee might be composed of a district coordinator; teachers from the lower, middle, and upper grades; administrators at the school and district levels; one or two school board members; the school librarian; a school psychologist or counselor; and parents. At the secondary level, it may be helpful to have some gifted secondary students on the committee; they may be able to provide important insights into the kinds of challenges that, in their experience, have been effective, ineffective, or absent.

If a program already exists and improvement is the goal, a needs assessment will consider such matters as: What are the gaps in the current program? Given "what is," "what might be?" and "where should we be?" (VanTassel-Baska, 1988). Do our classroom teaching units, activities, and resources align with our district-wide planned objectives? If not, what can be adjusted?

## 2. Preliminary Staff Education

The goal of building a gifted education program cannot wait for several teachers and administrators to take one or two college courses in gifted education. Teachers must educate themselves and each other in the essential basics—preferably before they all make some uninformed assumptions and mistakes.

Part of a preliminary education will include becoming acquainted with the present status of gifted education in your school, district, city, and even state. One might ask such questions as:

1. What is being done at the present time?
2. What kinds of G/T services are needed?
3. Do other schools in the area have programs? What exactly are they doing?
4. What do school board members and the district superintendent think about special programs for gifted students?
5. Do existing district policies allow students to enter kindergarten early? Skip a grade? What screening procedures are in effect? What are the criteria?
6. Is there a written district policy? A district G/T coordinator? A state G/T director?
7. What exactly does the state legislation on educating gifted children say?
8. Are other teachers interested and supportive? Are they willing to assume responsibility for the work? Is the principal enthusiastic? What about the district superintendent?
9. Can high school students take college courses in person or by correspondence? Are Advanced Placement courses available? International Baccalaureate programs (described briefly in Chapter 5)?
10. Are parents or parent groups becoming restless about their ignored children?

Some of these questions can be answered with a few phone calls. Others will require lengthier exploration and thought.

People seriously interested in gifted education must acquaint themselves with any written district policies or position statements. They should read any state legislation and state plan on behalf of gifted students. The *state legislation* will at the very least (1) define *gifted and talented,* (2) endorse the concept of differentiated educational experiences, and sometimes (not always) (3) allocate funds for developing and maintaining programs. A *state plan,* which is formally accepted by the superintendent or the state board of education, will also define *gifted and talented* and

**TABLE 3.2**   Needs-Assessment Questionnaire

Please rate the statements below in two ways. The first rating relates to the strength of a particular program as you see it in the school. The second rating refers to the way you think the program should be. Program need will be determined by subtracting Rating 1 from Rating 2. For programs that are presently weak but are determined to be strong, important preferences will be set as first priorities.

Rate 1 if you STRONGLY DISAGREE with the statement.
Rate 2 if you DISAGREE SOMEWHAT with the statement.
Rate 3 if you are UNDECIDED.
Rate 4 if you AGREE SOMEWHAT with the statement.
Rate 5 if you STRONGLY AGREE with the statement.

|  | *NOW* | *FUTURE* |
|---|---|---|
| 1. In general, the needs of gifted children in the school district are being met. | 1 2 3 4 5 | 1 2 3 4 5 |
| 2. The attitude of most teachers toward the gifted child is positive and helpful. | 1 2 3 4 5 | 1 2 3 4 5 |
| 3. The program provides individualization of curriculum for gifted children. | 1 2 3 4 5 | 1 2 3 4 5 |
| 4. Special enrichment opportunities are provided for gifted children. | 1 2 3 4 5 | 1 2 3 4 5 |
| 5. Classes that teach creative and critical thinking are available. | 1 2 3 4 5 | 1 2 3 4 5 |
| 6. The school has appropriate guidelines for determining early entrance to kindergarten. | 1 2 3 4 5 | 1 2 3 4 5 |
| 7. The school has appropriate guidelines for determining subject or grade skipping. | 1 2 3 4 5 | 1 2 3 4 5 |
| 8. The school provides for the needs of the underachieving gifted child. | 1 2 3 4 5 | 1 2 3 4 5 |
| 9. The special social-emotional needs of gifted children are being addressed. | 1 2 3 4 5 | 1 2 3 4 5 |
| 10. The special needs of the highly creative child are being met. | 1 2 3 4 5 | 1 2 3 4 5 |
| 11. The school provides for the needs of gifted and talented girls. | 1 2 3 4 5 | 1 2 3 4 5 |
| 12. The school provides for the needs of gifted and talented minority children. | 1 2 3 4 5 | 1 2 3 4 5 |
| 13. The school includes parents in the planning and guiding of gifted and talented children. | 1 2 3 4 5 | 1 2 3 4 5 |
| 14. Teacher-education opportunities in the area of gifted and talented are provided for the teaching staff. | 1 2 3 4 5 | 1 2 3 4 5 |
| 15. The administration supports education of the gifted and talented. | 1 2 3 4 5 | 1 2 3 4 5 |

endorse providing G/T services and programs. The state plan may further itemize specific objectives related to program development, and usually will itemize training services and resources that may be used to meet those objectives.

Many state and local educational organizations sponsor one- or two-day conferences and workshops usually led by one or more experienced leaders in gifted education or related areas. For one- or two-hour workshops, chances are good that a nearby college or a state education office can suggest speakers to address specific topics in gifted education.

National and state conferences are immensely informative, for example, those sponsored by the National Association for Gifted Children (NAGC), the Council for Exceptional Children, and by state parent groups and state educational associations. Speakers at national and state conferences will describe the workings of their programs; the pros and cons of their own identification, acceleration, and enrichment strategies; and how they coped with some of the same problems the reader will face. Several journals and magazines also are devoted to the education of gifted, talented, and creative students, especially the *Gifted Child Quarterly, Gifted Child Today, Roeper Review, Journal for the Education of the Gifted, Advanced Development Journal,* and the *Journal of Secondary Gifted Education.*

A highly enlightening staff activity is visiting schools with successful programs. By speaking directly with involved teachers one will get an inside look at how plans are implemented and how problems are dealt with. One will also gain valuable insights into what works and what does not, tips that will help avoid common pitfalls.

### 3. Philosophy, Rationale, Goals, Objectives, and a Written Program Plan

A brief statement of philosophy and goals is essential because everyone—parents, teachers, administrators, the local school board—will want to know exactly what the program entails and why. The written philosophy and rationale should include the reasons for the program, which is a position statement explaining why the program is necessary, plus general and, if desired, specific program objectives.

A sample of the possible contents of a philosophy and goals statement appears in Appendix 3.1 at the end of this chapter. Read it now. Also, a state plan, if one exists, undoubtedly will include a statement of philosophy and objectives that can be modified to fit a specific program. A one-page philosophy statement for a small Wisconsin city appears in Inset 3.2.

If a statement of philosophy and goals is expanded, it can serve as a written plan for a program. A written program plan should present sufficient detail to answer any question that anyone could ask about a proposed program. The written plan usually is built around:

**1.** A definition of gifts and talents. For example, a federal definition often is used.

**2.** Philosophy and goals. This section explains why a program is necessary. Itemizing the cognitive and affective goals can be brief and general, or more lengthy and specific.

**3.** Screening and identification methods. This section describes the information used—test scores, grades, teacher nominations, teacher ratings, self-nominations, and so on—and how the various sources of information will be combined in making selection decisions. The identification section should also comment on provisions for identifying culturally different, economically disadvantaged, underachieving, and gifted students with disabilities. Selection information will be scrutinized by everyone reading your plan, especially any state or federal funding agency.

**4.** Instructional programming strategies. This section outlines the curriculum model (if any) on which the program is built. Also included are the specific grouping, acceleration, and enrichment plans, along with the necessary organizational changes; subject areas of concentration and planned activities; and the use of community resources (e.g., universities, museums, and busi-

## A Philosophy of Gifted and Talented Education

The Watertown, Wisconsin, Public School System is committed to an education program that recognizes individual student differences. Embodied in this commitment is a responsibility to talented and gifted students to help them maximize their high potential.

Gifted children differ from others in learning ability: they learn faster, have wider interests, remember more, and think with greater depth about what they learn. An education program can be designed that will more adequately meet the needs of the gifted student.

A program for gifted students should provide a comprehensively planned curriculum that utilizes within discipline and/or cross-disciplinary studies. These studies should allow for both vertical (acceleration) and horizontal (breadth and depth in a topic) movement that is educationally relevant. The program should stress higher-level thinking skills such as inquiring skills, problem solving, and creative thinking. In addition, development of self-direction, risk-taking, curiosity, imagination, and interpersonal relations should be emphasized. The program framework will allow for individual projects and peer-group interaction.

The long-range goals of this program are self-actualization for the gifted person and the development of a sense of responsibility to self, school, and society.

Watertown, Wisconsin, School District, 1980. Reprinted by permission.

---

nesses for visitations; professionals who can serve as mentors).

**5.** Program evaluation and modification. This section outlines specific evaluation plans, both of the *formative* type, which provides continuous feedback regarding the ongoing methods and activities, and the final *summative,* did-we-succeed type at the end of the unit, the semester, or most likely, the year.

A written program plan may deal with any of the 16 points discussed in this section and itemized in Table 3.1.

## 4. Types of Gifts and Talents to Provide for and Estimated Enrollment

The problem of specifying types of gifts and talents to be accommodated is intimately related to the identification problem—defining who will be "in" the program—and it relates closely to proposed program plans. Some relevant questions and considerations are: Will the program serve only bright, intellectually gifted students? Or will a multidimensional definition of gifts and talents be used, providing special opportunities to students with specific academic talents, scientific talents, creative talents, communication (speaking, writing) talents, artistic and musical talents, and others?

As for the size of your gifted population, Stanley's (e.g., Benbow and Lubinski, 1997) original *Studies of Mathematically Precocious Youth* program catered to students in the top one percent in math ability. In contrast, Renzulli and Reis's (1997, 2003) increasingly popular Schoolwide Enrichment Model identifies 15 to 20 percent of the school population for a *talent pool.* These students individually revolve in and out of a resource room to work on special projects. A common size for a single "pullout" or other special class is about 5 percent of the school population.

If grade-skipping, taking advanced classes, or some other acceleration strategy is to be part of the plan, then fixing a number or percentage of "in" students is not as sensible as setting criteria that can qualify *any number* of students for the acceleration. For example, standardized achievement test scores, probably already on file, are one good basis for decision making. But be warned: Due to random score variability, a single cutoff score should never be rigidly used to exclude students who are close to the magical cutoff number. Selection should be flexible and include subjective judgments as well as test scores.

## 5. Identification Methods and Specific Criteria

Issues and methods related to identifying gifted and talented students are sufficiently complex to merit a chapter of their own—a highly condensed one at that (Chapter 4). For now, we will simply mention (or repeat) a few basic considerations.

**1.** Identification methods must be consistent with one's definition of gifted and talented students. Unfortunately, it is common for a stated plan to endorse the federal multiple-talent definition, but then use only IQ scores for the actual selection procedure. Note that the identification methods define exactly *who* is "gifted and talented" for any given program.

**2.** Identification methods must be coordinated with the type of program(s) one plans to implement. For example, intelligence test scores, reading and math abilities, and teacher nominations might be appropriate for selecting students for grade-skipping. Math ability would be critical for participation in an accelerated math program. If a program accommodates many types of gifts and talents, a variety of ability, achievement, creativity, and interest information will be appropriate, again, including both test scores and subjective evidence.

**3.** Identification methods must be defensible to the community. Parents will ask why one child was selected for a program while another (theirs) was not. Selection decisions must be clearly justifiable. Some identification methods are intelligence tests, standardized achievement tests (particularly reading and math), and creativity tests and inventories; inventories assessing interests, hobbies, special needs, and past special opportunities; teacher ratings of various characteristics (for example, academic talent, abstract thinking, creativity, motivation, leadership, organizing ability, and visual or performing arts talents); parent ratings and inventories, peer ratings of various characteristics, and self ratings; and work samples and products (for example, in art, music, or science). An advantage of the talent pool approach, men-

tioned above, is that larger numbers of students can be included, selection and admission to the program are flexible, and complaints about exclusiveness and elitism are reduced. More will be said about the Schoolwide Enrichment Model later in this chapter and especially in Chapter 7.

## 6. Specific Provisions for Identifying Female, Underachieving, Disabled, Culturally Different, and Economically Disadvantaged Gifted Students

We mentioned earlier that not only males and females must be fairly represented but also economically disadvantaged, minority, and students with physical handicaps and learning disabilities. The problem is not that these students have no gifts and talents; it is that educators too often do not look to these populations for G/T students.

Identification measures themselves tend not to identify culturally different and minority students. As Richert (2003) observed, "The more measures that are used and combined inappropriately, the more likely it becomes that disadvantaged students (poor, minority, creative, and others) . . . will be excluded" (p. 149). Efforts to represent all student groups in the G/T program are essential.

Gifted underachievers may be even less visible than gifted minority or poor students or students with disabilities. For underachieving students, their lost talent development is a personal crisis for them and a lost natural resource for humankind. More than one underachieving gifted student has become motivated toward higher educational and career achievement by the specific attention of teachers in gifted programs, by individual and family therapy, and, ironically, by acceleration or special opportunities such as Future Problem Solving (Chapter 6; Rimm, 1997; Rimm & Lovance, 1992a, 1992b).

## 7. Staff Responsibilities and Assignments

There is a large difference between the passive acceptance or even hearty endorsement of a new gifted program versus the willingness to roll up one's sleeves and do the work. It is an essential preliminary problem to decide just who will assume responsibility for what and when.

It is not unusual to include some accountability checks, for example, by setting deadlines for obtaining information, preparing reports, purchasing tests or materials, conferring with administrators, and so forth. Scheduled weekly or biweekly meetings also have the effect of establishing accountability—getting things done.

## 8. School Psychologists, Counselors, and Other Support Services

A successful program for gifted and talented students will involve experts and professionals beyond the immediate teaching staff. The school psychologist, counselors, the district or state coordinator, and outside consultants all will play important roles.

Few school psychologists have taken coursework in gifted education. If the school psychologist is not an expert in G/T education (some are, some are not), his or her main contribution probably will be the administration and interpretation of tests. Individual intelligence tests, mainly the Stanford-Binet and the WISC-III, require a trained administrator. The psychologist also might administer individual achievement tests and interpret interest or personality inventories, such as the *Kuder Preference Record,* to help secondary students better understand themselves, their possible career directions, and the educational preparation necessary for various career alternatives. The school psychologist also might supervise the administration of group achievement or group intelligence tests. In addition, many school psychologists are able to work with underachieving gifted students and their parents, or with gifted students with other problems.

School counselors also may or may not have expertise in gifted education. If not, the elementary school counselor will be involved in helping students cope with academic difficulties and with personal problems. The counselor also can help educate parents of gifted children regarding the child's particular talents, academic strengths and weaknesses, and personal difficulties. Importantly, the counselor can help specify the parents' role; for example, the counselor can recommend participation in the school's gifted program (many parents are reluctant) and can recommend valuable summer programs such as science, art, music, language, or computer camps and workshops. It is important that counselors learn about the characteristics and special needs of gifted children. Without such additional background, they may make shortsighted and inappropriate recommendations, for example, by stressing social adjustment and conformity instead of achievement and uniqueness.

A counselor acquainted with the field of gifted education probably will understand recurrent emotional as well as intellectual characteristics of gifted students; be sensitive to value conflicts of poor and minority students (e.g., high educational and professional aspirations that alienate friends and parents); assist the gifted student with academic progress; and when appropriate communicate a gifted students' problems and needs to other school staff (Colangelo, 2003; Landrum, 1987; VanTassel-Baska, 1983b). In private sessions counselors can help gifted students, for example, (1) understand differences and similarities between themselves and others, (2) learn to get along with others, (3) understand their abilities, (4) understand that they may not be superior in everything, (5) develop good self-concepts, (6) set realistic goals, and (7) become self-directed and responsible for their behavior. At the secondary level counselors can address career interests and prerequisite educational needs and deal with *multipotentiality,* the tendency for some gifted students to have many career interests and matching strong abilities.

Counseling with groups of gifted students can aid self-awareness and self concepts, for example, with discussion questions such as "How is being gifted an advantage for you? How is it a disadvantage?" (Colangelo, 2003, p. 378). (Chapter 17 is devoted entirely to understanding and counseling gifted students.)

Planning a gifted program frequently involves a series of consultants, for example, state or district coordinators, university instructors with relevant experience or knowledge, professional G/T consultants or workshop leaders, or experienced teacher-coordinators from other locations. These consultants can present workshops for the entire school staff, perhaps dealing with methods of identification, alternative instructional models and strategies, program evaluation methods, problems of gifted girls, or other topics. Particularly, some G/T teachers might describe in colorful detail the workings and problems of their own successful program.

You also may work with consultants on a one-to-one basis, outlining strategies for:

- Obtaining funds
- Preparing written statements
- Selecting goals and objectives
- Designing relevant acceleration and enrichment activities
- Installing a particular program model, such as the Schoolwide Enrichment Model
- Selecting or creating nomination forms, rating forms, or questionnaires for identification
- Insuring proper representation of different student groups
- Designing program evaluation procedures
- Selecting or creating instruments for program evaluation
- Promoting good public relations

## 9. The Detracking Reform Movement and Acceleration and Enrichment Plans

In Chapter 1 we sketched briefly the detracking, anti-grouping educational reform movement that may or may not complicate planning for gifted students. In a survey of educational policy makers, Subotnik (1998) discovered that several anti-grouping leaders were strongly in favor of providing a suitable education for gifted students; they just didn't like visible grouping arrangements—such as special classes and pullout programs—that announce to everyone, "I'm gifted, but you're not" and "They're gifted, but gosh darn, I guess I'm not!" Thus one program consideration today is whether a gifted program can take the form of a highly visible grouping plan, or whether enrichment and acceleration must take place in the individual, mixed-ability classroom. See Inset 3.3 for a description of a successful school plan for accelerating and enriching gifted students in a regular, mixed-ability classroom.

Issues, details, and recommendations regarding acceleration (for example, grade-skipping, advanced classes) and enrichment (for example, resource room or Saturday programs) are elaborated in Chapters 5, 6, and 7. For now, we will just emphasize that specific instructional plans must be designed to produce sensible, defensible, and valuable educational benefits. While this recommendation may sound obvious and trivial, as Renzulli and his colleagues (e.g., Renzulli, 1994; Renzulli and Reis, 1985) have repeated, far too many programs entertain the children with fun-and-games time fillers and interest-getters, with little attention to worthwhile, theory-based goals. For inspiration regarding valuable goals and activities, you may review the philosophy and goals ideas in Appendix 3.1 and the Curriculum for the Gifted section (Table 5.1) at the beginning of Chapter 5. Aligning specific classroom activities with higher-level program goals—scope and sequence concerns—will be reemphasized later in this chapter. For now, some examples of high-level goals that guide specific acceleration and enrichment plans are:

- High achievement; advanced academic skills and content
- Complex, abstract, theoretical thinking
- Creative, critical, evaluative thinking; other thinking skills
- Scientific research skills
- Library research skills
- Computer research skills
- Communication (speaking, writing) skills, including creative writing
- Career-related content

## Program Planning in Heterogeneous Classes: The Mustard Seed Project

Responding to reform trends toward heterogeneous grouping, the Mustard Seed Project (Johnson, Haensley, Ryser, & Ford, 2002) was a two-year effort to train teachers to differentiate curricula for gifted students (many of whom were poor) in the regular classroom in mostly rural schools. The project included eight elementary schools and 17 "mentor teachers," who were trained by project staff to teach and guide 74 "cohort teachers." Twenty-two training units included such topics as learner differences, differentiated curriculum, assessment, managing the learning environment, learning strategies, teacher facilitation, acceleration, mentoring, peer coaching, collaboration, support, and change.

As program planning considerations: (1) The project involved important stakeholders; thus the team at each school included the principal, the mentor teacher, between 5 and 14 cohort teachers, two community representatives (always parent volunteers with a child in the school), and, of course, project staff. (2) Mentor and cohort teachers were enthusiastic volunteers who wanted to adapt to student differences. (3) The teachers possessed a "people orientation," good communication skills, confidence and flexibility, a love of learning, a sense of humor, and a commitment to project ideas and goals. (4) The professional development itself included exposure to various G/T learning strategies (e.g., teacher-directed instruction, games, self-paced instruction, reading, audiovisual instruction, role-playing, and problem solving) so that teachers could learn by doing. (5) To accommodate the teachers' own styles and preferences, they had a choice of the types (and degrees) of changes they would use in their own classrooms. (6) The principal supplied essential financial support, for example, for staff development activities requiring substitute teachers, for preparation time, and for teaching materials.

The training and desired teaching changes fell into four categories. First, changes in *content,* for example, might include teaching for creativity and thinking skills, integrating multiple disciplines, focusing on broad themes and authentic methods, or even allowing students to select content based on interests and ability levels. Second, changes in *rate* might include allowing early finishers to work on a related learning task, testing for content mastery at various times, and/or providing in-depth study (acceleration, enrichment). Third, *environment* changes could include allowing student interaction (so they can learn from each other), providing learning centers, and even letting students use the community as a "learning center." The fourth type of desired change was in *preference,* in which teachers provided various learning tasks and allowed students to choose how to respond, or even allowed students to choose both the learning task and the mode of response.

Virtually all teachers made changes favoring the education of able students. While teachers made changes in all four areas described above, most changes were in *preference* and *environment.* The teachers moved from tightly teacher-controlled classes (some with desks in rows and columns) with no provisions for the gifted, to providing acceleration, enrichment, and self-selected in-depth studies for capable students. Most teachers created learning centers.

Some important factors that contributed to positive change included the staff development activities (summer and school year), clear vision and leadership by Mustard Seed staff, positive attitudes—even excitement—by teachers and principals, teachers' freedom to choose goals (degrees and types of changes), and mutual support among teachers (who served as models for each other).

Some negative factors included nonproject teachers who resented changes made by others, and rigid and unsupportive central office administrators. Teachers reported that change was inhibited by current school organization (departmentalization), lack of resources, lack of time, unsupportive coworkers, and weak administrative support (e.g., by replacement principals or superintendents).

- College preparatory content
- Self-awareness, affective, and humanistic principles

Each of the curriculum models outlined in Chapter 7 usually serves as the basis for planning specific acceleration and enrichment activities.

## 10. Organizational and Administrative Design

Most G/T plans require some administrative reshuffling of the school organization and budget to provide the necessary time, space, facilities, and inservice training, and coordinate the G/T activities with the rest of the school schedule. If the program is district-wide or city-wide, the planning will take place partly, not entirely, at these higher levels. In addition, any program for gifted and talented students will require considerable recordkeeping by those directly involved—particularly the teacher or teacher-coordinator, although secretaries can carry some of the burden.

For example, acceleration plans as straightforward as grade-skipping or taking college or correspondence courses will require that new types of records be created and that student progress be monitored. A more complicated acceleration plan such as telescoping (for example, condensing three years of math or science into two) will require not only a teacher, a classroom, and a time slot, but complete coordination with the rest of the school course offerings and organization, along with keeping records of student participation and success.

Enrichment plans also require attention to organizational and administrative matters. A Wednesday pullout program will require at the very least a teacher-coordinator and a resource room, plus such miscellaneous supplies and equipment as resource books, workbooks, chemistry and biology supplies, calculators, computers, art supplies, perhaps a 35mm camera and a videocam, and so forth. Other enrichment plans, such as Saturday classes, extra classes, field trips, and mentoring programs, will also require attention to organizational, administrative, and managerial matters of staff, space, scheduling, budget, transportation, materials, and record keeping.

If a plan is district-wide or city-wide, particularly when special schools for the gifted and talented are created or Saturday or summer programs are planned, the organizational and administrative planning clearly is more involved. It is not unusual for large metropolitan areas to have several full-time G/T personnel in the central office to help plan and manage city-wide programs. However, regardless of the size and type of program, a local school staff member must be designated as having administrative responsibility for the G/T program in that school. A designated responsible person—at whose desk the buck stops—is essential.

## 11. Transportation Needs

Transportation plans may be simple and relatively minor, but they cannot be ignored. Transportation problems and costs must be considered for students who attend special schools, take college courses, or travel to schools with special resource-room programs. Transportation must also be considered for field trips, mentoring programs, after-school projects and clubs, summer programs, and Saturday programs.

## 12. Community Resources: Professionals and Organizations

Community resources, namely professional people and organizations, will be invaluable in at least three types of instructional plans and programs for the gifted: mentoring plans, enrichment-oriented field trips, and career education. At either the elementary or secondary level, potentially valuable community resources should be reviewed and itemized.

Mentoring plans involve the placing of gifted students with a community professional for usually a few hours each week. The professional could be in any area of the arts, science, or business. There is no substitute for the values, attitudes, skills, job requirements, and knowledge of daily routines and life-styles acquired by gifted students in such a personal educational experience.

While mentoring plans are used almost entirely at the secondary level, community resources for field trips and career education are useful with any age group. Some possibilities for field trips are art galleries and museums; university art, science, and engineering laboratories; police and government facilities; manufacturing plants; and so forth. Engineering and computer departments enjoy showing off their latest robots.

Do not forget that *all* students—not just the gifted—profit from field trips in increased knowledge, better school attitudes, and perhaps raised aspirations.

Capitalizing on community resources for career education also can involve inviting professionals to make presentations to the class—to all students. If a field trip or class presentation is not relevant to the needs of all students, small groups or even individuals can visit with a professional and receive a guided tour of his or her organization. To ensure an educational benefit, the plans for such a trip must include specific questions to be answered. Follow-up activities can include discussions and/or the preparation of written or oral reports on the experience.

### 13. In-Service Workshops, Training, and Visits

Initially, workshops should be at an *awareness* level. Introductory exposures should (1) attempt to improve attitudes of teachers who believe that gifted children do not require special services, and (2) heighten the interest and commitment of all teachers and staff. Some good awareness topics are characteristics and needs of gifted students, general approaches—programs and strategies—designed to meet these needs, and how G/T activities are related to other aspects of the curriculum.

Next in order should be in-service training dealing with the *identification* of gifted children and the teacher's role in this process. A good understanding of the selection tests, criteria, and weighting procedures—and the role of subjective judgment—may prevent problems later. For example, teachers should understand why Johnny, a highly creative "B" student, should be included in the program even if his tested IQ is not over 125.

The choice of other topics will vary according to the direction of the G/T program. If acceleration strategies are planned, teachers must understand both the reasons behind these strategies and the specific procedures for conducting the acceleration. If a pullout enrichment program is used, all teachers should understand the curriculum of that program and how they can help their own students' participation. They also must help resolve a traditional dilemma: the extent to which their students will be expected to make up missed work while in the resource room.

Some additional important in-service topics are:

- Identifying and teaching poor, minority, economically disadvantaged, and underachieving gifted students
- Program goals and objectives, and coordinating classroom activities to meet these goals
- Program models and prototypes
- Role expectations of school staff
- Instructional strategies and teaching skills in specific content areas and with particular age groups
- Understanding and teaching creative students
- Helping students understand and cope successfully with competition
- Strategies and materials for teaching creativity and thinking skills to gifted students and all students
- Counseling needs of gifted children and adolescents
- Understanding and coping with perfectionism in students
- Evaluating the gifted program and making changes and modifications
- The detracking, anti-ability grouping movement and the critical need to group gifted students (Kulik, 2003)

- Cooperative learning and gifted students (Robinson, 2003)
- Parent-school relationships

From a survey, Tomlinson (1986), found that teachers were most interested in obtaining information concerning methods and techniques for use with gifted students at their particular grade level and/or in their subject area. Further, teachers strongly preferred group participation and hands-on experience—working through types of activities that could be used immediately with their gifted students—rather than "lecture only" approaches.

As noted in Item 2 an excellent source of inspiration for planning or improving a G/T program is visiting other successful programs. It is best to visit several types of programs. These may include special schools for gifted and talented students along with schools with resource-room or pullout programs, special classes, Saturday programs, mentoring plans, telescoping plans, or whatever else you might be considering for your own school. Do not be surprised if the visits help you decide what *not* to do. You can speak with teachers regarding such matters as:

- What they are doing and how they are doing it
- Who the target students are and how they were identified
- What the students are specifically supposed to get out of the program (goals and objectives)
- Their perceptions (and evidence) of the success of their program
- The difficulties they experienced and how they were resolved
- The sorts of resistance they encountered from other teachers, administrators, parents, or the community

You also might speak with the gifted and talented students in various types of programs. How do they like school? Do they like the program? What are their problems? How could the program be improved?

## 14. Budgetary Needs and Allocations

Many programs operate on a shoestring, using part of the regular school budget to purchase special workbooks, art supplies, or other inexpensive items. It can be done. However, to plan a proper program one should consider expenses related to some or all of the following:

- A full-time or part-time teacher/coordinator—or several, in a larger district
- Physical facilities
- Texts and workbooks
- Special equipment and supplies
- Computers
- Transportation costs
- Tests and inventories
- Secretarial services
- Office supplies
- Duplicating expenses
- Consultant and in-service training expenses
- Travel to visit other programs
- Travel to state and national conferences
- Services of psychologists and counselors
- Evaluation expenses (a consultant; purchasing or constructing tests, rating scales, or questionnaires)

Budgetary matters must be considered at the time you are planning the various identification strategies, instructional program alternatives, and needed evaluation data. From the outset, one should be concerned with cost-benefit matters. Some programs clearly cost more than others, and priorities may have to be modified in light of the available dollars. However, with creative cost-cutting, many goals can be achieved relatively economically, without a large loss in interest value or educational benefit.

One happy acceleration idea is that grade acceleration costs nothing, beyond paperwork. Grade skipping can provide a more suitable academic challenge, with the benefit of associating with peers who are closer in intellectual ability. (Criteria for selecting students for grade-skipping are discussed in Chapter 5.)

Finally, a search for federal, state, or private

funding will be worthwhile. Even though funding may be scarce for "a program for gifted and talented students," requesting funds for a specific category of persons or subject matter—such as disabled or minority gifted, computer literacy, math and science, or arts and humanities—can improve one's chances for an award or grant. Local service organizations, medical and health organizations, or local businesses or industries may be willing to provide small amounts of designated funding. Usually, a newspaper story or other publicity can be arranged to reward such contributions. Note too that chances for a financial commitment by the school district will be improved if administrators recognize that funds from other sources also are forthcoming.

## 15. Developing Social Capital: Students Who Care

Renzulli (2003) argued strongly that gifted education should do more than help bright students become educated, professionally successful, and financially comfortable. Rather, gifted education should include the development of *social capital:* "intangible assets that address the collective needs and problems of others" (p. 77). Both the economic and the social capital of a nation "can result in greater prosperity and physical and mental health as well as a society that honors freedom, happiness, justice, civic participation, and the dignity of a diverse population" (p. 77). Program planning for gifted students, then, should include (1) raising students' awareness that they can and should develop positive human concerns, preferably by involving them with socially relevant activities, and (2) training in leadership, which underlies a willingness to take action. Renzulli's University of Connecticut social capital project, Operation Houndstooth, focuses on developing the six characteristics of optimism, moral courage and integrity, a passion for a topic or discipline, sensitivity to human concerns (empathy, altruism), physical/mental energy (charisma, curiosity), and vision/sense of destiny. He recommends that we promote these capa-

bilities and virtues, which aim at replacing self-interest and consumerism with a social conscience—and the sooner the better. (Social capital and character education are discussed further in Chapter 8.)

## 16. Program Evaluation

The evaluation of gifted programs is an important and complex topic that will be discussed in Chapter 18. For now, the reader should keep in mind that good evaluation information has a direct bearing on (1) the survival and continuation of the program, (2) the continuation or improvement of budgetary allocations, and (3) the modification and improvement of the program. Evaluation is indeed important and should be part of the program planning from the beginning. *Every* aspect of the program—the staff, the materials, the identification procedures, the acceleration, enrichment, and grouping activities, and each and every goal and objective—can be evaluated regarding its effectiveness in contributing to program success.

As mentioned in Item 3, evaluation is of two types—first, a *formative,* ongoing process aimed at continuous modification and improvement of the program; second, a *summative,* final assessment of the overall success of the program. Both are necessary. Evaluation can be aimed at determining how well students' needs and goals were met; evaluation also is sometimes directed at assessing how well the program plan was carried out.

In a thought-provoking article, Borland (2003) recommended a broader view of program evaluation. He recommended that we evaluate not only program success, but its effects on factors and stakeholders external to the program, namely, other students, other teachers, the school district, and the larger community, plus budgetary effects on other programs.

### THE VIEW FROM THE SCHOOL BOARD

The main function of the district school board is to help set policy governing both school administration and school programs. Because board members are either elected directly by the community or appointed by elected officials, they are accountable to the public. Whether or not school board members support gifted education therefore may be a political question ("What will my constituency think?") as well as an educational issue. The scope of a gifted program—the grades served, categories of gifted children, diversity of program activities, and the types of support services—will be affected by the support and funding of school board members.

Programs for gifted and talented students, by definition, are directed at a minority of children and adolescents. Therefore, teachers and parents must convince board members that even though gifted children are a minority, their educational needs are genuine. How can educators and parents encourage board members to maintain a quality gifted program in a school district? The following are some suggestions for fostering support:

***Keep board members educated and aware.***   Before board members voted for that gifted program, parents probably attended meetings and, in a positive way, showed interest in gifted education. When the G/T program is in place, that communication process must continue. Teachers or coordinators may make yearly presentations on program progress. If an oral presentation is not feasible, a short written report is helpful.

***Keep board members involved.***   One or two board members should be included on each district or school G/T steering committee. Board members can be invited to in-service meetings, parent meetings, or student performances and shows. They also may be invited to speak at local or state parent meetings or other educational meetings.

***Help board members to be accountable.***   For board members to justify continued support and funding for gifted programs, they absolutely must be assured that the program is achieving its objectives. Educators therefore must keep board mem-

bers informed of the effectiveness and accomplishments of the G/T program.

There also may be pressure on board members to jump on the detracking bandwagon and, in the process, eliminate grouping opportunities for gifted students and the gifted program itself. They must be reminded that the issues are separate— that tracking plans can be changed (if necessary) without trashing G/T programs, and that the very real academic, social, and personal needs of the gifted require grouping.

***Encourage school boards to have a written policy.***   Board policy is a formalization of philosophy and should be incorporated into a formal policy manual. The written policy becomes the basis by which the school administration and teaching staff can justify decisions favorable to gifted education. An example of a written school board policy is shown in Inset 3.4.

***Be patient, but not too patient.***   Board members need time to gather support and plan resources for a comprehensive gifted program. Furthermore, they logically must view the gifted program in relation to the total needs of the district. At the same time, however, parents and educators must not permit board members to forget or indefinitely postpone the needs of gifted children, regardless of the stresses of educational problems and too-small budgets.

***Remember that all board members should be encouraged to support gifted education.***   On any school board there always will be a variety of viewpoints on gifted education. Some members will be active supporters, and it may be tempting to believe that they alone can keep programs going. It is necessary, however, to also focus one's attention on those less-willing potential supporters, those who require further convincing. Note their doubts and questions and make a special effort to personally give them the information they need to convince them that gifted education truly is legitimate, important, and a widespread national, even international movement. Even if

INSET 3.4 _____

## A Sample School Board Policy

The Board of Education and professional staff members are dedicated to developing a comprehensive program for the identification and education of the gifted and talented child. Empathy and understanding are of paramount importance for all personnel having contact with such a child and are basic to achievement of the district goals.

The gifted and talented child is an individual who, by virtue of outstanding abilities, is capable of high performance. This child possesses demonstrated or potential intellectual or specific academic abilities, leadership capabilities, creativity, or talent in the performing or visual arts. This child may need educational services beyond those being provided by the regular school program in order to realize his or her potential.

To provide a comprehensive program for the gifted and talented child, the board recognizes that:

**1.** Early identification of the gifted and talented child is necessary to maximize the opportunities for the child's own self-realization. This shall be accomplished through the application of several criteria.
**2.** The educational program should provide for continuity and overlap among the elementary, junior high, and high school levels. The program should specify long-range goals for the district, with major emphasis on differentiated curriculum and programming.
**3.** The objectives of the educational program shall be to meet the gifted and talented child's needs, whether they be intellectual, social, physical, or emotional.
**4.** Active parental involvement is viewed as an integral and crucial ingredient of a quality gifted and talented program. Every effort should be made to foster parental involvement in all aspects of their child's educational program.
**5.** Qualified instructional and administrative personnel with appropriate knowledge, training, and experience are required to implement an effective program of education for the gifted and talented.
**6.** The achievement of a quality gifted and talented educational program demands the presence of a competent ancillary support staff, particularly for the early identification of the gifted or talented child.
**7.** The administration of the gifted and talented program shall provide leadership and coordination in developing and maintaining a comprehensive district K–12 program.
**8.** The placement and progress of the gifted or talented child will be continually evaluated and documented, with periodic progress reports issued to the parents of the child.

they cannot be converted into strong supporters, the strength of their opposition might at least be reduced.

***Help board members be answerable to their public.*** Board members will be asked by constituents why they support gifted education. They also will be given reasons why they should *not* help gifted students (e.g., "They don't need

help!"). In raising their awareness of the needs of the gifted, give board members the information they will require to justify to their constituents the existence and funding of special programs for the gifted. The issues they will need to debate may not always seem reasonable, but they nonetheless must be prepared with answers. Some issues to which board members often must respond appear in Inset 3.5.

INSET 3.5 _____

## Some Questions School Board Members Must Answer

**1.** *Isn't gifted education elitist?*
RESPONSE: Gifted education only provides appropriate education for children who need a special challenge. These children come from all neighborhoods and economic backgrounds. Children from poor families often need G/T education the most because their families are unable to provide enrichment opportunities for them. Also, minority and poor parents often do no have high educational and career expectations for their children. If we are to keep our country a place where people can achieve regardless of their economic background, gifted education can help us.

**2.** *We have special programs for the low-ability child and the high-ability child—but what about the average child?*
RESPONSE: Most educational programs are geared to the needs of the average child. In a real sense, most money is now spent on the average child. We agree that the average child should never be short-changed in the educational process, but neither should the gifted child.

**3.** *Aren't all children really gifted, so don't we need to provide for all their gifts?*
RESPONSE: In a sense, yes, all children do have special gifts and talents. Some may play basketball or soccer well, others have marvelous personal charm. The purpose of a gifted and talented program is to help develop students' strong academic and creative needs that are not met in the regular program. For example, a math whiz in the regular classroom is rarely provided with advanced math instruction. Young creative writers or poets do not have special opportunities to help develop their unique talents. These students may be bored, and their talents are not challenged or strengthened. When we find special gifts and talents, we must provide opportunities to develop them.

**4.** *Why should we spend more money for kids who will make it anyway?*
RESPONSE: While many gifted kids will "make it anyway," it is nonetheless unfair to hold them back and make them succeed in spite of the system.

More importantly, many gifted children do not "make it anyway." Their lost talent is both a personal tragedy for them and a loss to society. Studies of high school dropouts have found that between 9 and 20 percent are in the gifted IQ range—certainly many more than one would expect, and certainly a waste.

Schools often turn off gifted children because they do not provide appropriate challenges. Further, when children become bored they sometimes use their creative energy and their giftedness in inappropriate, antisocial, and even destructive ways. They need special help and guidance.

**5.** *Can we afford to pay for more special education?*
RESPONSE: Gifted programs can be very inexpensive, compared to all other kinds of special education. Also, we save money in the long run by investing small amounts to help make school more meaningful. This small investment helps insure us against larger problems that can be more costly—for example, bored, apathetic, or even antisocial students, to say nothing of lost talent development.

**6.** *What do the rest of the kids get out of it?*
RESPONSE: Teachers who become involved in gifted education learn to stimulate creative development, to use questions effectively, to foster good self-concepts and humanistic attitudes, to individualize instruction, and other valuable concepts and skills. Much of this can be—and is—applied in the regular classroom. They become better teachers, and this benefits other children as well.

Also, when there are gifted programs in a school, it becomes apparent to all that excellence is rewarded and valued. When excellence is valued more children become motivated to achieve, and we sometimes discover giftedness where we might not have expected to find it. For example, if there is peer pressure not to achieve, some students will hide their abilities and talents. Gifted programs encourage these children to achieve, too. So while providing for the special needs of gifted children, we also encourage hard work and excellence in our schools for all children.

*Support school board members who support gifted education.* When school board members visibly endorse a program, they need to know the public "out there" is supporting them. Be vocal in expressing your appreciation to board members who assist with the education you believe in. You also can help them in their campaigns, both formally and informally (e.g., by telling your friends what a fine job you believe a board member is doing). Keeping supporters of gifted education in office will help them to provide appropriate educational opportunities in your community.

## PERSPECTIVES OF OTHER TEACHERS

Not all teachers agree that gifted students truly need special services. In fact, some are downright antagonistic. However, with time and exposure some indifferent teachers come to understand the issues and concerns and will become more receptive to gifted programming. Others will never change, and progifted teachers simply have to work around them.

What are their concerns? Some will have the same reservations expressed to school board members (see Inset 3.5); others will express different problems. For example:

• Some teachers will object to their brightest students leaving their classes. They miss the contributions these students make and their visibility as good role models.
• Some will argue that they already are challenging the gifted children in their classrooms (sometimes they are, more often they are not; Archambault et al., 1993).
• Some will complain that the gifted program requires additional work, and they are already overworked.
• Some believe that the gifted child is somehow "getting out of " required work and will individually penalize those children by requiring makeup work or even "busy work."
• If they teach a section of gifted students, some teachers will penalize them by grading on a nor-

mal curve, ignoring the fact that the students were preselected. A few might delight in awarding gifted children Cs and Ds to somehow prove the students are *not* gifted.
• Some may quote Jeannie Oakes (1985) regarding questionable benefits of ability grouping, citing damaging effects on the self-concepts of other students. Others may quote *The Hurried Child* (Elkind, 1981), a book that describes harm caused by pushing children beyond a natural developmental pace.
• Some negative teachers may subtly attempt to sabotage the gifted program.

There is no secret psychological strategy to elicit the cooperation and support of every teacher. One should, however, be ready for antigifted attacks and not take them personally. If one remains positive there is a better chance of gaining converts and allies. For example, you can listen to their arguments and try to explain the unmet educational needs of gifted children. Negative teachers can be encouraged to take a course in gifted education or to attend a conference with you. Lend them this book. Make the assumption that they *do* care about *all* children and that with a better understanding of the issue they may develop a sincere concern for gifted children as a mistreated minority.

Fortunately, in most school districts there will be more allies than enemies. There will be many teachers and administrators who enthusiastically support the program and contribute time and ideas. There will be many who enjoy the new challenge of gifted education and the excitement of seeing new enthusiasm in energetic and talented children. Without these supporters, being a teacher of the gifted would be lonely indeed.

## CURRICULUM CONSIDERATIONS

Several guides and assumptions underlie recent curriculum theory in gifted education (Maker & Nielson, 1996; C. A. Tomlinson, personal communication, May 18, 2002; VanTassel-Baska, 2000, 2003):

• *All* students should experience high-quality, engaging, intellectually challenging curriculum that meets their present and future academic needs.

• Such curriculum will not only develop the abilities of gifted students, it will also help identify advanced potential in other students.

• The needs of gifted students are different than those of others. Curriculum must be adapted or designed to accommodate these needs.

• As gifted students move toward expertise in a discipline, the level of intellectual demand provided for the student should escalate in accordance with his or her individual growth.

• All high-quality curriculum should contain key components or "organizers" that make the material meaningful for learners.

• Appropriate curriculum activities for gifted students cut across these areas: cognitive (e.g., their precocity), affective (e.g., their motivational intensity), and social (e.g., their need for intellectual peers).

• Gifted students require curriculum that is both enriched and accelerated.

• For maximum effect, curriculum experiences for gifted students should be carefully planned, implemented, and evaluated.

Two thoughtful curriculum models accommodate most of these suggestions. First, VanTassel-Baska's (2003) Integrated Curriculum Model (ICM) underlies her three curriculum programs for gifted learners in language arts, science, and social studies. (Space will not permit an adequate elaboration of VanTassel's thoughtful and involved model. See VanTassel-Baska, 1994, 1995, 2003; VanTassel-Baska, Bass, Reis, Poland, & Avery, 1998; VanTassel-Baska & Little, in press; and VanTassel-Baska, Zuo, Avery, & Little, in press.) The core principles of the ICM that differentiate learning for gifted students include: (1) presenting advanced content (e.g., advanced literature), (2) eliciting higher-order thinking and processing (e.g., reasoning, problem-based learning), and (3) focusing on important issues, themes, and ideas in the curriculum area (e.g., systems, change, cause and effect).

Second, the Parallel Curriculum Model (PCM; C. A. Tomlinson, personal communication, May 18, 2002), sponsored by the NAGC, emphasizes four parallel principles that teachers can follow to help gifted students explore and understand a discipline. The *Core Curriculum* notion emphasizes teaching central concepts and principles of a discipline. The *Curriculum of Connections* stresses helping students connect core concepts within and across disciplines, times, places, and cultures. The *Curriculum of Practice* emphasizes helping students to understand and use key concepts and skills much as a practitioner in the discipline would understand and use them. The *Curriculum of Identity* invites students to use information about a discipline not only as a way to understand the discipline itself, but also as means of clarifying their own ways of seeing, organizing, and relating to the world. The four "parallels" may be used singly or in combination to develop sound units or courses of study for individuals or groups. The parallels help insure increasing intellectual demand for advanced and advancing learners.

In designing curriculum, VanTassel-Baska's ICM and Tomlinson's PCM help answer such key questions as: How important are certain concepts and skills? How broadly (or briefly) should various skills and concepts be covered? How much time will be needed with a topic to reach an appropriate level of depth? What critical new content should be covered? How can we organize learning experiences at suitable abstract levels to accommodate the capacities of gifted learners? What content and processes should appear at different points in a comprehensive curriculum plan?

## THE DEATH OF GIFTED PROGRAMS

In addition to the detracking movement, many other concerns have led to the demise of gifted programs. Hickey (1990), Mosley (1982), and Starko (1990) identified numerous problems that alienate other teachers, perhaps administrators, and certainly parents of average and troubled learners:

- The program looks like a fun-and-games waste of time.
- Other teachers are led to believe that your students are motivated, easy to teach, and receive marvelous opportunities unavailable to regular students—while they struggle with slow learners, at-risk students, and perhaps students with disabilities.
- Parents are led to believe that upper-crust children receive opportunities that their children cannot have.
- Students not selected are resentful and have poor self-concepts.
- Students not selected are deprived of opportunities to develop leadership.
- All parents want the best teachers for their children.
- Wouldn't these activities be good for all children?
- Program participants become arrogant and snobbish.
- There is too much pressure on G/T students; levels of competition are unhealthy.
- Gifted students develop unhealthy levels of perfectionism.
- Some G/T students "level off" in the program and no longer seem superior.
- Class routines are disrupted by pulling out gifted kids, forcing regular teachers to deal with whether critical skills are missed.
- Gifted students' contributions to class are lost. As noted earlier, many teachers like gifted students in their classes; they serve as good student models and are available to help others.
- There is too much reliance on IQ scores for selection; identification can be restrictive.
- G/T students sometimes are isolated and provided with expensive equipment, materials, and field trips—making charges of elitism easy to defend.
- Teachers believe that the focus should shift to less capable students—who are the clear majority.
- The program creates problems of content repetition in the next grades.

- G/T teachers do not communicate with regular teachers about the program.
- Regular teachers are untrained in gifted education—unaware of the needs of gifted students and appropriate curriculum for them.
- Many teachers believe the needs of gifted students can be met in heterogeneous classes (e.g., through individualization, technology, team teaching).
- The program appears to be a reward for polite, cooperative, high-achieving children with good attitudes; it is a status symbol.
- Junior and senior high school students seem successful without having participated in a special elementary program.

Starko (1990) also reported positive comments about their gifted program:

- It is good academic stimulation and good preparation for later academic work.
- It eliminates boredom.
- Bright students receive opportunities to follow their interests.
- There is a sense of community among gifted students.
- There are good effects on social and emotional maturity.
- There are greater opportunities, for example, for learning French and being creative.

Renzulli (1995) drew partly from an outspoken critic of gifted education, Sapon-Shevin (1994), to itemize common criticisms of gifted education as well as to outline solutions. Some criticisms of gifted education were these:

- Gifted students sometimes are presented as "superior to all other kids in every way."
- Gifted programs are guilty of both racism and elitism.
- Gifted programs are deemed an expensive hoax.
- Gifted children tend to have aggressive parents (to get them into the program).
- Taxpayers help a small minority with money that could be used for the unexceptional

majority—gifted students are supported at regular children's expense. Some consider investment in programs for the gifted "welfare for the rich."

Factors that support gifted program survival are (1) good state "economic health" plus state mandates for gifted education (Purcell, 1995), and (2) enthusiastic support for gifted education by teachers, the principal, and hopefully the district superintendent. Without strong support at the state, school administration, and teacher level, a sound gifted program is unlikely to materialize and survive, despite protests by parents of bright students.

*As the reader may suspect, the dilemma is that many G/T programs are guilty of many of the charges leveled by Hickey (1990), Mosley (1982), Starko (1990), and Sapon-Shevin (1994). Some problems are built-in to the program design.*

One problem recognized by Renzulli (1995; Renzulli & Reis, 1997), Feldhusen (1992), Treffinger (1995b), and others is the label "gifted." Renzulli recommended changing the orientation from labeling the *students* to labeling the *service;* we change from "gifted/not gifted" to the *development* of giftedness and gifted behavior. This orientation includes providing services to all children, for example, by giving training in higher-order thinking skills and creativity in the regular classroom. Of course, noted Renzulli, we have truly remarkable kids in every class—kids who need and deserve an appropriate education. We therefore must focus on the full range of talents, the education of all children. But *equity* must include the cheerful acknowledgment of differences. In regard to special, high-level learning experiences and activities for gifted children, the question should be "Can everyone do it?" the answer should be "no."

## LEGAL ISSUES IN GIFTED EDUCATION

The growth of gifted education is reflected in the development of a spanking new topic: legal issues in gifted education. Of course, disgruntled parents have taken legal action on behalf of their gifted children for many years. Only recently, however, have legal problems and recommended actions coalesced into a coherent topic, thanks to the efforts of Frances Karnes and Ronald Marquardt (2003; Karnes, Troxclair, & Marquardt, 1997) at the University of Southern Mississippi, where in 1994 they created the Legal Issues Network.

Legal difficulties, some more common than others, evolve around these categories of problems: early admission to school; the provision of programs or appropriate instruction; racial balance in gifted programs; the awarding of high school credits toward graduation to students who take advanced courses prior to high school; transferring of students to districts that offer more suitable programs; legal status of certification in gifted education (e.g., when applying for a G/T teaching job or when staff positions are cut); transportation to sites that provide appropriate instruction; tort liability (e.g., for injury on a field trip); fraud and misrepresentation (e.g., by a private school claiming to accommodate the gifted); and home schooling (e.g., whether home-schooled children are entitled to participate in public school gifted or other programs).

Karnes and Marquardt offer the following advice to anyone considering legal action. Conflicts can be settled at any level from informal discussions to supreme court decisions. The best solution, however, is to resolve the problem at the lowest level possible, because as the complainant proceeds up the ladder, costs and delays expand exponentially. Said Karnes and Marquardt, the typical ladder starts with informal negotiation and proceeds to mediation, due process, state court, and even federal court.

As Russo, Harris, and Ford (1996) noted, "supporters see gifted education as a *right,* the unaffected see it as a *privilege,* and opponents see it as *superflous*" (p. 182).

## SUMMARY

Plans for differentiating the curriculum for gifted learners vary greatly in type and complexity. Planning should consider challenge, choice, interest, enjoyment, and personal meaning for students.

Four traditional components of a gifted program are (1) philosophy and goals, (2) definition and identification, (3) instruction (with attention to students' needs, type of program, personnel, location, and timelines), and (4) program evaluation.

Sixteen problem areas in program planning are:

**1.** A needs assessment aims at determining the discrepancy between the current and the desired state of gifted education in the district. Three sources of information are gifted students, their parents, and teachers and administrators. Because gifted students are a minority, only sufficient (not majority) support is needed. To make concrete plans, a steering committee will be necessary.

**2.** Preliminary staff education will include determining the present status of gifted education in the area; becoming acquainted with state legislation and state plans; attending local, state, and national G/T conferences; and visiting schools with successful programs.

**3.** A written statement of philosophy, rationale, and goals should explain the reasons for and the goals and objectives of a program. The statement can be expanded into a written program plan, which includes a definition of gifts and talents, identification methods, instructional program strategies and activities, program evaluation, and any other of the 16 points in this list.

**4.** Types of gifts and talents to be accommodated must be specified, a matter related to one's definition of giftedness. Regarding numbers, while some programs are highly restrictive (e.g., SMPY), the talent pool approach accepts many students.

**5.** Identification methods and criteria must be consistent with one's definition of giftedness and coordinated with the type of program being planned. The methods must be defensible, yet both objective and subjective.

**6.** Identification methods must include plans for locating gifted female, culturally different, economically disadvantaged, and underachieving students, and students with a disability.

**7.** Staff responsibilities and accountability checks (such as monthly meetings or reports) must be planned.

**8.** Support staff and services will include school psychologists and counselors, district and perhaps state coordinators, and consultants. Counseling services are essential.

**9.** Program plans should include both acceleration and enrichment alternatives. There are many specifics to select from. They should aim at defensible goals and objectives, namely, the development of high level skills and knowledge. Planning might have to accommodate the detracking reform movement.

**10.** The organizational and administrative design, including space allocations, record keeping, modifications to the budget, and more, must be considered. Much planning is usually at the district level.

**11.** Transportation needs cannot be ignored.

**12.** Community professionals and organizations can supply enriching field trips for all students or for small groups of G/T students, mentorships, and career education.

**13.** In-service workshops begin with general awareness information and proceed to the identification of the gifted or talented child and then other matters. Workshop content should be directly applicable (e.g., methods, techniques), perhaps including hands-on activities. Visits to several types of programs are valuable.

**14.** Budgetary needs and cost-effectiveness must be considered from the outset. Some programs operate on almost nothing; others pay for teacher-coordinators plus plenty of materials and equipment. Grade acceleration is basically free. Federal, state, or private funds often can be obtained.

**15.** Beyond helping gifted students to become more professionally successful, program planners might wish to develop "social capital." That is, a program can raise gifted students' awareness of the needs of others, increase empathy, and convince them they can and should take action to help. Leadership training is central.

**16.** Program evaluation is important for survival and expansion. Every component of the program can be evaluated. Formative evaluations are continuous ones aimed at modification and improvement. Summative evaluations evaluate overall success. A broader view of program evaluation includes looking at effects on other students and school staff, as well as the school budget.

School board members must be convinced that G/T students have important unmet needs. Suggestions for fostering support include keeping board members educated and involved, helping them be accountable, and changing the attitudes of nonsupportive members.

For various reasons, many teachers may not support a G/T program in a given school. One should attempt to alter their attitudes in a more positive and helpful direction.

Recent curriculum theory confirms that educational needs of gifted students are indeed different. Cognitive, affective, and social needs should be considered. Program planning should include both enrichment and acceleration. VanTassel-Baska's ICM includes advanced content, higher-level thinking skills, and a focus on central content ideas. Tomlinson's PCM also includes teaching central concept and principles, helping students connect core concepts across disciplines, and helping students understand and use concepts and skills as a practitioner would.

Some reasons for the death of gifted programs include, in addition to the detracking movement: "fun-and-games" activities; teachers and parents believing (rightfully) that other students are deprived of high-quality opportunities; separating G/T teachers and students from the rest of the school program; no training for G/T teachers; resentfulness of students not selected; snobbishness; restrictive identification methods (particularly, overreliance on IQ scores); high pressure on students in the program; and the program appearing to be a reward for high achievement and cooperation.

Reasons that programs survive include good state economic health, state mandates for gifted education, and enthusiastic support by teachers and administrators.

Legal issues, perhaps related to providing appropriate G/T services, racial balance, or the legal status of certification, are best resolved at the lowest level (e.g., informal negotiation) before proceeding to higher levels (e.g., state or federal court).

## APPENDIX 3.1    IDEAS FOR STATEMENTS OF PHILOSOPHY, RATIONALE, AND OBJECTIVES

To provide gifted and talented students with an educational environment that will provide the greatest possible development of their abilities, thus enabling them to realize their contributions to self and society.

"The gifted and talented represent a group of students whose learning style and thinking dimensions demand experiences which are outside the educational mainstream . . . (we need) an education commensurate with each child's ability to learn" (Kaplan, 1974).

To provide programs designed to help meet the psychological, social, educational, and career needs of gifted and talented students.

To assist students in becoming individuals who are able to take self-initiated action and accept responsibility for that action, and who are capable of intelligent choice, independent learning, and problem solving.

To meet the special needs of minority gifted children.

To develop a functional procedure for identifying gifted and talented students in the school in order that they may express and develop their gifts or talents.

To provide a program that will stimulate individual interests and develop individual abilities in academic and/or talent areas.

To provide the superior learner with new and highly challenging learning experiences that are not ordinarily included in the regular classroom curriculum.

To provide opportunities that will develop self-awareness, personal strengths, and social responsibilities beyond those in the regular school program.

To provide gifted children with the opportunity to explore personal interests through independent study and community involvement.

To foster high-level thinking and self-development processes, resulting in a more complete, productive individual who is challenged by the school environment.

To provide a learning atmosphere that will enable the gifted child to develop his or her potential and exceptional abilities, particularly in the areas of decision making, planning, performing, reasoning, creating, and communicating.

To provide experiences that develop the higher operations of analyzing, synthesizing, divergent production, and evaluation.

To provide activities and experiences that stimulate critical thinking, comprehension, competency, and creativity.

To enable those students desiring to do so to prepare for advanced placement.

To encourage cross-discipline exploration.

To include strong components of basic skills, career awareness, sex-equity, and multiethnic experiences.

To develop an ability to transfer information to humanistic goals.

To develop intrinsic motivation.

To provide experiences that guide a student toward independence.

To provide gifted and talented students with a positive self-concept.

To foster awareness of self and others.

To develop problem-solving abilities and creative thinking skills; develop research skills; strengthen individual interests; develop independent study skills; exercise communication skills in the humanities (visual, oral, and written); receive intellectual stimulation from contact with other highly motivated students; expand their learning activities to include resources available in the entire community area.

"The good of any program for the gifted should be to provide meaningful experiences in the most efficient and effective way in order to maximize learning and individual development and to minimize boredom, confusion, and frustration" (Fox, 1979).

# CHAPTER 4

# IDENTIFYING GIFTED AND TALENTED STUDENTS

*Giftedness cannot possibly be captured by a single number. Unless we examine multiple sources of giftedness, we risk missing identification of large numbers of gifted individuals.*
Robert Sternberg (2003)

There probably are as many different strategies and policies for identifying gifted and talented students as there are programs. In the words of Feldhusen, Hoover, and Sayler (1990), "The ideal identification system has not been developed."

For example, some programs will base identification entirely upon intelligence test scores, either admitting all students who score above a certain cutoff, or else selecting the top 3 to 5 percent regardless of the particular scores. According to Cassidy and Johnson (1986), one state defines giftedness as the "top 3 percent" in intellectual ability; another as scoring two standard deviations above the mean (top 2.28 percent) in intellectual development; a third state allows for artistic and other forms of giftedness, but absolutely requires that "Persons shall be assigned to a program for the gifted when they have an IQ score of 130 or higher."

The various Talent Search programs (see Lupkowski-Shoplik, Benbow, Assouline, & Brody, 2003; discussed in Chapter 5), primarily for seventh-grade students, have almost exclusively used scores on the Scholastic Aptitude Test-Mathematics (SAT-M), the Scholastic Aptitude Test-Verbal (SAT-V), and sometimes the American College Testing Program (ACT) as the sole admissions criteria. (In 1994 the SAT-M and the SAT-V were replaced by the single Scholastic Assessment Test I [SAT I], which still produces a mathematics and a verbal ability score.)

Other programs take a multidimensional approach. As a common but minor modification of the strict IQ/academic ability criterion, teachers may review IQ scores, achievement scores, and grades to nominate students for a G/T program. Other multidimensional approaches will identify students who seem high in any one of a number of criteria, particularly the five components of the U.S. Department of Education definition: general intellectual ability, specific academic talent, creativity, leadership, or talent in the visual or performing arts. Many states have adopted definitions of giftedness—which are supposed to guide identification—that are based on a five-part federal definition. As we will see later in this chapter, the Gifted Evaluation Scale (McCarney & Anderson, n.d.) uses teacher ratings to directly evaluate the five Department of Education talents.

As still another multidimensional variation, Renzulli and others (Renzulli et al., 2001; Kolo, 1999) have developed checklists and rating scales that evaluate various personality and intellectual characteristics of giftedness. Final decisions normally combine checklist or rating scores with other information.

Also as we will see later, Maker (1996) and her colleague Sarouphim (1999, 2000, 2001) concluded that student problem-solving ability underlies most definitions of intelligence and creativity, that is, giftedness. Their DISCOVER identification procedure evaluates the ability to solve problems and think creatively, and seems remarkably culturally fair.

According to Cramer (1991), a panel of 29 G/T experts agreed that, among a list of 12 issues, identification is priority number one.

## THOUGHTS AND ISSUES IN IDENTIFICATION

Current thinking on the centrality and challenge of identification is reflected in these statements and recommendations (Callahan, 1993a; Callahan, et al., 1995a; Han & Marvin, 2000).

- Adopt a clearly defined but broadened conception of giftedness.
- Avoid using a single cut-off score.
- Recognize intelligence as multifaceted (e.g., Gardner, 1983, 1999; Sternberg, 1988a, 1988b, 1997a).
- Accept multiple manifestations of giftedness.
- Use multiple alternative criteria—not multiple required hurdles—from several different sources.
- Use separate instruments or procedures for different areas of giftedness; be sure tests (including ratings and nominations) are reliable and valid.
- Promote inclusiveness rather than exclusiveness.
- Include authentic assessments (e.g., portfolios, examples of work) and performance-based procedures (e.g., evaluation tasks that elicit problem solving and creativity).
- Be aware that giftedness may appear in different forms in different cultural or socio-economic groups.
- Base identification on students' educational needs—not on program quotas, numbers, or slots.
- Repeat assessments over time to identify additional gifted students.
- Use identification data to enhance understanding of students.
- Assume strong links between identification and instruction.
- Promote collaborative efforts among teachers, with administrators, and with the community.
- Develop early and continuous procedures to evaluate the identification process.
- Be prepared to work within the general education (detracking) reform movement.

### Multiple Criteria

As Frasier (1997) summarized the issue, "multiple criteria provide educators with a defensible and logical way to be inclusive in their search for various types and expressions of potential for gifted performance, [yet] restrictive enough so that decisions made about students with extraordinary ability are exclusive enough to be meaningful" (p. A-4).[1] Frasier also noted that multiple-criteria information can guide program and curriculum development, counseling activities, and the evaluation of the program's effects on individual students.

A core reason for multiple criteria is to identify more minority and poor students, who are overlooked when one or two restrictive criteria (IQ and/or achievement scores) are used. The underrepresentation problem has plagued gifted education for decades.[2]

As an example of a multiple-criteria approach, in 1991 the state of Georgia defined giftedness according to a single IQ score (Krisel, 1997). But with help from Renzulli's NRC/GT, eight school districts explored the use of multiple criteria to obtain "a rich profile of students' strengths and interests" (p. A-1), and especially to identify gifted minority students. Based on observational and performance information, teachers showed that they could readily identify children—from every cultural and economic background—who showed traits, aptitudes, and behaviors associated with giftedness.

---

[1]The December 1997 issue of *Roeper Review* included a special section that reviewed the value of using multiple identification criteria, instead of just an ability score.

[2]The entire December 2002 issue of *Roeper Review* was devoted to discussions of problems and solutions.

Convinced of the fairness of using multiple criteria, in 1994 Georgia legislators passed a bill requiring multiple-criteria identification, which the governor signed into law (HB 1768). The changes were these: Eligibility includes meeting criteria in any three of four areas—mental ability, achievement, creativity, and motivation. More specifically: (1) intellectual ability above the 96th percentile; (2) standardized achievement test scores above the 90th percentile on the total battery, or just reading, or math, or a superior performance on a student-generated product or performance; (3) creativity scores above the 90th percentile on a creativity test or a creative characteristics rating scale, or superior evaluations of a creative product or performance; and (4) motivation, as reflected in a GPA above 3.5, or a score above the 90th percentile on a motivational characteristics scale, or ratings above the 90th percentile on a student-generated product or performance.

Multiple-criteria—or "multiple-hurdle"—approaches can be restrictive. Matthews (1995) described a rural Southwest elementary school with these state guidelines: a gifted child must have a measured IQ score (verbal or nonverbal) at least two standard deviations above the mean (top 2.28 percent) on an intelligence test approved by the State Board. *In addition,* a child must score above the 95th percentile on a standardized achievement test (approved by the state board), *or* show outstanding creativity (as defined in state regulations), *or* show outstanding critical thinking or problem-solving ability (as defined in state regulations). On the upside, in this particular rural school—known for its excellent and enthusiastic principal and teachers, and its excellent regular and gifted programs—bright and energetic children who did not meet the rigid state definition were admitted anyway.

## Pros and Cons of Formal Identification Methods

In her article "The Case Against Formal Identification," Davidson (1986) expressed strong frustration with formal testing, rating, and nomination procedures, including the use of point systems and cutoffs. Said Davidson, such procedures do not allow students actually to demonstrate their abilities in areas in which they are interested and talented (see Inset 4.1). Davidson noted that a student with a tested IQ of 110 may show greater giftedness in the sense of originality and thought-provoking ideas and answers than a student with a tested IQ of 140—who will be selected for the program. Even creativity tests do not measure every aspect of a child's creativeness, noted Davidson; and peer, parent, and teacher nominations can be biased in favor of popular, English-speaking, middle-class students.

Davidson's three-step solution—designed to not exclude truly gifted children—included, first, setting a liberal selection quota of about 15 to 20 percent of the school, in accord with Renzulli's (Renzulli and Reis, 1997, 2003) talent pool philosophy. Second, students who score in the 90th percentile or above on intelligence, achievement, or creativity tests (according to local norms) have clear needs and should automatically be placed in the program. Third, and most importantly, Davidson recommended the increased use of *informal* parent and teacher nominations, based on observations of creativity, critical thinking, problem solving, or motivation.

## Top 3 to 5 Percent or a Liberal Talent Pool Approach

The traditional method for selecting students for participation in a G/T program is this: Each fall a school screening committee reviews data from many sources for each potential candidate, for example, ability and achievement scores and nominations. The top 3 to 5 percent are selected and labeled *gifted*—and the identification process is ended for the year.

More and more, districts and individual schools are adopting Renzulli's *talent pool* strategy, part of the *Schoolwide Enrichment Model* (Renzulli and Reis, 1997, 2003; see Chapter 7). It is the most popular programming model in the United States, Canada, and the world (Renzulli,

**INSET 4.1** _____

## The Case Against Formal Identification

The following is a condensation of a spoof by Karen Davidson (1986) that illustrates how formal testing and identification measures could inadvertently exclude truly gifted students from programs for the gifted and talented.

> John loved to run and he was very good at it. He always ran the four miles down country roads from school to home. In early September John's school began a formal identification process to select students for the cross-country team.
>
> With the peer nomination procedure, few of his fellow students had ever seen him run, and so he was nominated just once and received one point. Teachers nominated the students with the flashy jogging pants—the ones who looked like runners. One teacher saw John chase a dog and thought he was fast, and nominated him—one more point. With parent nominations, John's dad thought cross-country teams were silly, but John got two points because his dad knew he was fast.
>
> On the *California Standardized Test of Running Skills*, a written test, John scored at the 56th percentile because he did not know such terms as "hitting the wall" and "pacing yourself." Other students had taken running lessons and scored above the 90th percentile. John earned one point.
>
> A test of running ability partly evaluated knowledge of famous runners and muscles used in running. When John finally had a chance to run, the teacher evaluated only his form and style. He earned two more points.
>
> John's total score in the identification procedure was seven points. With a cutoff of 15, he wasn't even close.

The moral of the story is this: "Many students who would profit from enrichment and from differentiated programs are not identified; formal identification procedures do not allow them to demonstrate their abilities in the areas in which they are most interested and able" (Davidson, 1986).

---

1987), and for good reason. With the talent pool approach, a generous and flexible 15 to 20 percent of the school population is identified according to ability, achievement, or rating or nomination information, including self-selection and including suitability for a particular gifted program. In professional communities with large numbers of high-ability students, the talent pool may consist of 25 percent or, in extraordinary neighborhoods, even 100 percent of the student body. From the talent pool, some students—high in motivation and creativity—self-select an intensive research, literary, artistic, or other creative project.

The main identification-related attractions of the talent pool approach are that, most importantly, (1) more students receive the opportunity

ties, resources, and encouragement provided in special programs—the door remains open to many children whose gifts and talents simply are not measured by tests nor easily recognized by teachers. As Renzulli (e.g., 1986) has stressed repeatedly, society's most creative contributors are not always found in the top 3 to 5 percent. Further, with a restrictive criterion some talented students who are potential dropouts will be overlooked and not receive critical educational assistance, particularly counseling (Renzulli & Park, 2000). In addition, with the talent pool solution, (2) teachers remain concerned with identifying students for independent projects throughout the school year, not just in September; (3) charges of elitism are reduced; and (4) the difficult problem of deciding "who is and is not admissible" becomes a nonproblem. When in doubt, admit.

Renzulli's thoughtful recommendations for identifying talent pool candidates by using many criteria will be presented later in this chapter.

### Disadvantaged, Minority, Disabled, Female, and Underachieving Students

The identification of gifted and talented minority, economically disadvantaged, and culturally different students is an especially sensitive problem (e.g., Ford, 2003; Richert, 2003). Too often, administrators claim they have "none of those children in our school." Teachers, too, are guilty of this oversight. LeRose (1977), for example, reported, "Martin Jenkins, who has conducted more studies of high IQ African American children than any one else, has commented on how frequently children with IQs above 150 have not been spotted as outstanding by their teachers."

Culturally different learners do tend to score, on average, about one standard deviation (15 points) lower than middle-class students on standardized intelligence tests (Gottfredson, 2003). We repeat, "on average." Many minority children will score extremely high in both verbal and nonverbal measures of intelligence. Nonetheless, if IQ testing is part of the selection battery, there frequently is a built-in bias against minority and economically disadvantaged children. And if the school population includes minority and culturally different students (for example, African American, Hispanic American, Native American, Native Hawaiian, Vietnamese, immigrant), it will not be acceptable to produce a list of White children of middle-class professional people.

Issues related to minority and culturally different students will be explored in more detail in Chapter 12, along with suggestions for identification and programming (see also Ford, 1994a, 1996, 2003). For now, we emphasize that a multidimensional approach to identification is essential for identifying gifted and talented minority students—a procedure that looks beyond IQ scores. Also, a *quota* system is one frequently

used solution to the problem of ensuring racial, gender, geographical, or economic balance in G/T programs (Gallagher, 1991a, 1991b; LeRose, 1978; Smith, LeRose, and Clasen, 1991). For example, if a school contains 30 percent African American children, the G/T program also would contain 30 percent African American children. One problem with the quota system is that minority students who meet the same high criterion as others in the program might be wrongly assumed to have met only the lowered cutoff (Frasier, 1997; Frasier & Passow, 1994).

Richert (1997, 2003) described a relatively simple method that resembles a quota system and that assures equitable minority and gender participation. Local norms are created for each subgroup of students for each data source, for example, ability scores, achievement scores, and various nominations (e.g., for creativity). "Data from different sources should be used independently, and any one source should be sufficient to include a student in a program. . . . Students should qualify for a program by scoring high on any of several measures" (Richert, 1997, p. 82). She uses self-nominations by asking students to express their level of interest in various program options, thus avoiding the difficulty of underachievers who would never nominate themselves as "gifted." For her Project APOGEE, Richert (1997) selected a full 20 to 25 percent of students for the program—with whopping increases in G/T participation of 500 percent with culturally diverse students, 600 percent with poor students, and 800 percent with males who were poor and culturally diverse.

To increase participation by minority and poor students, Gallagher (1997) and Maker and Schiever (1989) recommended using not only multiple criteria, but case study information for each child.

Often we overlook gifted students among the ranks of those who are physically or psychologically disabled (for example, learning disabled). Do not be shocked when ten-year-old Joe Smith, whose dyslexia prevents him from reading or writing normally, is nominated as an intellectually or artistically gifted child. Albert Einstein, Thomas

Edison, Nelson Rockefeller, Pablo Picasso, and other "slow learners" had the same problems.

Regarding girls, we should be aware in our identification activities that if math scores, science grades, or computer expertise are criteria, girls can be discriminated against. Girls also may be more conforming, less aggressive, and less success-oriented than boys, which can influence nominations.

Virtually by definition, an underachieving student will not have high grades, whether or not he or she is capable of scoring high on standardized ability and achievement tests. Sometimes an unchallenged, perhaps bored gifted student will underachieve. He or she usually will not be selected for a gifted program—which is exactly what the student needs. For now, we should simply be aware that many bright and creative students are among the ranks of underachievers, and we should look for them. (Chapter 13 elaborates on underachievement.)

### Biases in Ratings and Nominations

As noted earlier, there is an understandable tendency for teachers to favor students who are cooperative, smiling, and anxious to please; who do their work well, neatly, and on time; and who absolutely never talk back. While "teacher pleasers" are a pleasure to work with, they may or may not be the most gifted and talented students in the class. However, they have a high likelihood of being perceived as gifted and being nominated for participation in special programs. Even if teachers rate students on specific qualities such as academic talent, leadership, motivation, or even creativity, teacher pleasers still are likely to be selected. The extremely bright or the creative, curious, and questioning students, who may be stubborn, rule-breaking, egotistical, or otherwise high in nuisance value, may not be the teachers' favorites, but they sometimes are the most gifted.

### Test Reliability and Validity

Reliability refers to the accuracy or consistency of a test, inventory, rating scale, or other selection procedure. There are three main types of test reliability, all on a scale of 0 to 1.0 (or –1.0, for inversely related characteristics such as stupidity and college grades). *Internal* reliability reflects the degree to which all items on a test (or subscale) measure the same characteristics, for example, motivation. *Test-retest* reliability is the correlation between scores on the same test retaken by the same persons. *Alternate forms* reliability is the correlation between scores on two forms of the same test, again taken by the same persons. All three types of reliability, as reported in test manuals, directly indicate the accuracy of a test. As a rule, a test with more items will be more reliable than one with fewer items. A fourth type, *inter-rater* reliability, applies when two or more teachers or other evaluators rate the same student on the same scale or characteristic. We also can speak informally of Ms. Garcia being a reliable (accurate) identifier of giftedness, while Mr. Jones is horribly unreliable in his ratings. Test reliability above about .80 is good; reliability around .60 is not terrific, but common. If test reliability is low, as reported in the test manual, the test cannot be accurate and decisions based on those test results will not be accurate.

*Validity* is the degree to which a test or inventory actually measures what it is supposed to measure. Does the motivation, creativity, or leadership test truly measure these traits or abilities? Does the "total giftedness" score truly identify gifted students? Evidence for reliability and validity normally appears in manuals accompanying published tests and inventories. Ideally, validity coefficients should be above .60, and the higher the better. Using several identification criteria will help compensate for a single test or rating scale measure that has borderline validity.

When considering tests, questionnaires, rating scales, and nomination procedures for identifying gifted and talented students, one always must consider both the reliability and the validity of the test or procedure. Sometimes, "face validity"—the degree to which a test simply looks like it measures what it is supposed to measure—will be the only information one has to go on.

## Political Problems in Identification

In the real world of schools, identification of giftedness is surrounded by political and personal problems that go beyond reliability and validity. Teachers and administrators must be prepared for controversies that surround identification. The criticisms one can expect will include everything from "Why isn't my child in the program?" to "Don't you dare identify my child as gifted." School board members may complain that teachers' children appear to be favored; teachers may note that offspring of administrators and board members are being selected. Some will call the selection process discriminatory and elitist; others will say it favors disadvantaged children.

## NATIONAL REPORT ON IDENTIFICATION

In 1982, Susanne Richert, James Alvino, and Rebecca McDonnel completed the *National Report on Identification: Assessment and Recommendations for Comprehensive Identification of Gifted and Talented Youth,* a study commissioned by the U.S. Department of Education (Richert, 1985, 1991b, 1997). The study focused on such issues as definitions adopted, principles of identification, identification instruments and procedures, and practices that screen out gifted students.

The multidimensional U.S. Department of Education definition (Chapter 1) was endorsed because it "attempts to be comprehensive in order to be applicable in many settings . . . (and) it has the legitimacy of national law behind it" (Richert, 1985).

Some principles that should underlie identification are:

1. *Advocacy.* Identification should be designed in the best interests of all students.
2. *Defensibility.* Procedures should be based on the best available research and recommendations.
3. *Equity.* Procedures should guarantee that no one is overlooked (e.g., disadvantaged children).
4. *Pluralism.* The broadest defensible definition of giftedness should be adopted.
5. *Comprehensiveness.* As many gifted learners as possible should be identified and served.

Some common but questionable practices include:

1. Despite the common adoption of the broad U.S. Department of Education definition, identification tends to focus only on high achieving students by using intelligence tests, achievement tests, grades, and teacher nominations.
2. Local districts tend to seek and find white, middle-class academic achievers. Minority groups such as African Americans, Hispanic Americans, and Native Americans are underrepresented by 30 to 70 percent.
3. Multiple criteria often are added together in statistically unsound ways, producing a quantitative score that obscures important indicators of high potential.

Based on these principles and problems, some recommendations were:

1. Because giftedness has many dimensions—abilities, personality factors, and environment—measures that go beyond academic achievement must be used to find students whose abilities are not indicated by tests and school performance. Both informal and formal data must be used validly.
2. Subjective procedures such as rating scales, checklists, and nominations are a legitimate part of the identification process, especially in the early nomination stage. Rating scale and checklist items should include "negative" and unexpected characteristics indicated by research.
3. Data from multiple measures, such as formal tests and informal checklists, should not be combined because their purposes and results are different.

## IDENTIFICATION METHODS

Of course, high intelligence remains a central concept in giftedness. At the same time, the growing use of multiple criteria recognizes that *giftedness* extends beyond an IQ number. Most educators realize that the language and content of ability and achievement tests are biased against culturally and economically deprived students. Gross (1999) noted that in Australia educators are keenly aware that achievement and ability testing can be racist or elitist; many teachers prefer to use their own judgment of student giftedness. Also, such characteristics as high motivation (persistence, zeal, "blazing drive"; Simonton, 2003; Torrance, 1995) and innate talents (e.g., art or music; Winner & Martino, 2000, 2003) are logically part of "giftedness."

Nonetheless, restrictive procedures persist. For example, a year 2000 research article in the *Gifted Child Quarterly* stated: "Gifted eligibility followed state guidelines, which included an intelligence quotient of 120 or greater on an individually administered IQ test." As noted by Han and Marvin (2000), rapid growth in the literature on identification is not paralleled by quick changes in educational practices.

### Intelligence Tests

The bottom-line instruments for confirming suspected high intelligence are individual intelligence tests, particularly the Wechsler Intelligence Scales for Children and the Stanford-Binet Intelligence Scale. Every school psychologist is qualified to administer and interpret either of these.

*Stanford-Binet Intelligence Scale.*  The newest, 1986 Stanford-Binet Intelligence Scale—Fourth Edition is not recommended for gifted children, despite its advantage of producing four "standard age scores" (think of them as IQ scores) in the areas of *verbal reasoning, quantitative reasoning, visual/abstract reasoning,* and *short-term memory,* along with its composite standard age (IQ) score. A big problem is that the upper limit of the fourth edition is lower (about IQ 164) than the previous edition, Form LM; therefore, extraordinary intellectual talent (e.g., IQ 180) will be missed. Form LM produces one IQ score that may be in the ozone: For elementary children there is virtually no ceiling.

A related yet more important complication is that the fourth edition produces IQ scores for gifted children that run about 13.5 points lower than Form LM, according to developers Thorndike, Hagen, and Sattler (1986). Kluever and Green (1990) found one child with a Form LM IQ of 160, but a fourth edition IQ of 110(!); two others showed Form LM IQ scores of 144 and 160, but fourth edition IQs of 112 and 121, respectively. It's difficult to be gifted when tested with the Stanford-Binet, fourth edition.

*Wechsler Intelligence Scale for Children.*  Many school psychologists have used the Wechsler Intelligence Scale for Children-Revised (WISC-R), designed for children age 6 to 16, which produces a *Verbal* IQ score and a *Performance* (nonverbal) IQ score, along with the combined Full-Scale IQ score. Therefore, a student with strong spatial or mechanical gifts can be identified, not just the verbally gifted.

In one study, Hollinger and Kosek (1986) found that a full 35 percent of their sample of gifted students (N = 26, age 6 to 15) produced significantly discrepant *verbal* versus *performance* IQ scores—they were much more outstanding in one area than the other. Further, 85 percent of the gifted students showed individual subtest scores that deviated significantly from their own average *Verbal* or *Performance* score. Examination of subtest patterns provides insights into individual students' cognitive functioning, noted Hollinger and Kosek.

The WISC-III appeared in 1991 (Wechsler, 1991). As before, the *Verbal* and *Performance* IQ scores combine into a *Full-Scale* IQ, and all three produce IQ scores with a mean of 100 and a standard deviation of 15. Like previous editions, the WISC-III was standardized with samples of White, African American, Hispanic American, Puerto Rican American, American Indian, and Asian American students represented in about the same proportions as they appear in the American population.

The WISC tests show two problems. First, the highest possible score on the Wechsler tests is 155. Second, the renorming of the WISC-III in

1991 generally shifted IQ scores down about five points. At the high end of the distribution, where gifted children score, WISC-III scores run about 8 or 9 points lower than WISC-R scores. Therefore, while WISC-III IQ scores cannot be fairly compared to WISC-R scores for any students, the differential is even more pronounced for gifted students.

### Ben

*Second-grader Ben complained to his parents of a lack of challenge at school. The teacher reported that Ben was careless in his work and needed to pay attention to detail. Ben's parents reported their concern to the school and also brought him to Rimm's Family Achievement Clinic for an evaluation. Unaware that the school psychologist had recently tested Ben with the WISC-R, the clinic gave Ben the WISC-III and the Peabody Individual Achievement Test-Revised. Ben's full-scale WISC-III IQ score was 128, yet his achievement test scores were 99+ percentile for all achievement subtests. A conversation with the school psychologist revealed that Ben's WISC-R score was 139, a full 11 points higher than his WISC-III score. In light of the high WISC-R score, Ben was placed in a self-contained classroom for gifted students. The lower WISC-III IQ score would not have allowed Ben special programming.*

Generally, intelligence test scores may be used to bring curriculum more in line with gifted students' abilities. Tests with low ceilings or depressed individual scores may underestimate a child's acceleration needs. The Stanford-Binet (Form LM), despite being outdated, is the only test that discriminates well for highly gifted children.

*Group Intelligence Tests.* IQ scores from group intelligence tests are useful for identifying gifted students because they continue to be administered routinely in many school systems, and so scores may be in the office file. Some of the better-known group intelligence tests are the Cognitive Abilities Test, the SRA Primary Mental Abilities Tests, the Henmon-Nelson Test of Mental Ability, the Otis-Lennon Mental Ability Test, the School and College Ability Test (SCAT), and

the Kuhlman-Anderson Intelligence Tests. However, despite their comparatively low cost and convenient group administration, consider these shortcomings: Group tests tend to be less reliable and less valid than individual tests. Children who are not motivated will produce lower IQ scores than their informally observed ability would indicate. Group tests are mainly verbal and are highly correlated with actual school achievement; therefore, they are biased against children who are nonverbally gifted (or who speak a subcultural dialect). Because most group tests were designed to discriminate in the midsection of the bell curve, they tend to be unreliable at high IQ levels; a few chance errors may substantially lower a bright student's IQ score. Speed is an important factor in group tests, since all are timed. This is not true of individual intelligence tests.

In view of these problems, one may question the value of group intelligence tests. However, children who score high on these tests virtually always will be capable and certainly should be included in a G/T program.

As mentioned at the outset of this chapter, the SAT-Math and the SAT-Verbal tests were replaced in 1994 by the Scholastic Assessment Test I (SAT I), which produces both a math and a verbal score. The SAT I normally is taken by college-bound high school seniors; scores are used by colleges mainly for admissions decisions. In gifted education, the SAT I (or sometimes the ACT Assessment or the Spatial Test Battery) normally are taken only by seventh-grade students interested in participating in a Talent Search program (see Chapter 5). Currently, about 150,000 students take the SAT each year; talent search programs cover the entire United States. Based on research with adolescents who scored above 700 on the SAT-M or above 630 on the SAT-V—the 1 in 10,000 range—Benbow and Minor (1990) concluded that mathematically talented and verbally talented students represent two distinctly different forms of intellectual giftedness. Further, Lupkowski-Shoplik and Swiatek (1999) found that "The SAT is an excellent predictor of students' [academic] achievements through high school and beyond" (p. 266).

In Chapter 5 we will briefly review the relatively new extension of talent search programs to the elementary school (Assouline & Lupkowski-Shoplik, 1997; Lupkowski-Shoplik, Benbow, Assouline, & Brody, 2003). As with the seventh-grade talent search, elementary students in grades three through six are also evaluated with above-level tests. One ability test is the lower level of the Secondary School Admission Test (SSAT), which is designed for students in grades five through seven. The SSAT produces quantitative, verbal, and reading comprehension scores. Another above-level ability test is the eighth-grade PLUS Academic Abilities Assessment, which is used with Talent Search students in grades five and six. The PLUS produces verbal and quantitative scores.

A big plus for intelligence tests, group or individual, is that they may identify underachieving students, students whose grades and classroom performance give no hint of the students' true—and unused—potential. In the negative column, a continuing problem is that if undue weight is given to intelligence test scores, students with other legitimate gifts and talents will be missed—particularly creative students, but also students with gifts in one special academic or aesthetic area, such as art, music, computers, mathematics, or social studies.

Finally, Gross (1999) cautions that testing—ability or achievement—is unstable in childhood years, and may or may not predict later academic success. In the middle years of school, however, "The most effective method of identifying highly gifted children . . . is through standardized tests of ability and achievement" (p. 213).

## Achievement Tests

Specific academic talent is an important category of giftedness. An excellent indicator of academic talent is standardized achievement tests, such as the Iowa Tests of Basic Skills, the Stanford Achievement Tests, the Metropolitan Achievement Tests, the SRA Achievement Series, the California Test of Basic Skills, and the Sequential Tests of Educational Progress (STEP). Other good indicators of specific academic talent are teacher-made achievement tests and school grades.

Standardized tests produce scores based upon national norms (for example, grade-equivalent, percentile, or stanine scores). Consider this advantage. A teacher in an upper-middle-class neighborhood may be accustomed to very bright students who learn quickly. He or she may not realize that compared with national norms, there are many talented and high-potential students in the class who should be participating in the district's G/T program. On the other hand, a teacher accustomed to working with slow learners may believe that a particular student is unusually able when, relative to a national comparison, the student is just slightly above average.

Two important problems should be considered relative to standardized achievement test scores. The first concerns the *grade-equivalent* score. "Grade equivalent" refers to the average score earned by children at a particular grade level on a particular test—not to the grade level at which a specific gifted child can function well in the classroom. Experienced teachers, administrators, and psychologists, as well as parents, make the faulty assumption that if a gifted fourth-grade child performs at the eighth-grade level on, say, a math achievement test, he or she could be moved into an eighth-grade classroom and perform successfully. Not so. While certainly a good math student, this child probably lacks many skills of the average eighth grader. The score is misleading and should be used only as an indication that the child needs special challenge. Further diagnostic testing would determine the child's specific mathematics skills and other skill levels.

The second problem relates to the *low ceiling* score of typical achievement tests. For very able children, most achievement tests are not sufficiently difficult to measure their high ability, knowledge, and skill levels. A considerable number of capable students will score above the 95th percentile; they "top out." It sometimes is incorrectly assumed that all of these children are equally talented and need a similar skill development program. In fact, after diagnostic testing with more difficult tests, a wide range of skill levels will be found. (Of course, an obvious solution is to give high-potential children higher-level achievement tests in the first place.) One example of this problem comes from Stanley's (1991a) SMPY program in which seventh and eighth graders who are selected to take the SAT-M must have performed above the 95th percentile on a group achievement test. The SAT-M scores for this group of "similar" children varied between 200 and 800 on this more difficult test.

## Creativity Tests

In some classes and with some creativity-conscious teachers, it may be easily apparent which students are highly creative and which are not. Creativity tests can be used to confirm a teacher's suspicions about the creativeness of one or more students. The tests also may be used to identify creative students whose unique talents are not visible in classrooms.

It is important to emphasize that creativity tests are not perfect. Especially, scores from a single creativity test might be quite misleading in the sense that a student who, in fact, does extraordinarily creative work in an art or science area could produce a strictly average creativity score. Validity coefficients of published creativity tests typically range from about 0.25 to 0.40, which is not high. Creativity is a complex ability that can take innumerable forms. It is extremely difficult to measure creativity accurately (e.g., Davis, 1998, 2003b). Your authors have repeatedly emphasized that data from creativity tests—including their own—must be combined with other information to make valid decisions regarding creativeness (e.g., Rimm and Davis, 1976). Using two criteria of creativeness is recommended (Davis, 1998, 2003b). For example, a student who scores high on a creativity test and is rated as "highly creative" by a teacher is virtually certain to be a bona fide creative person.

Teachers who have the opportunity to observe creative ideas and products can be asked to rate students' creativeness. For example, art teachers or teachers who supervise original science projects, creative writing, or drama activities are in good position to identify creative talent. Evaluating students' creative products is an excellent indicator of creative potential (Davis, 1998, 2003b).

As for creativity tests themselves, there are two main categories: divergent thinking tests and inventories that assess personality and biographical traits (Davis, 1998, 2003b). Divergent thinking tests require students to think of all the ideas they can for open-ended problems, such as listing unusual uses for a newspaper or a brick, imagining consequences of an unlikely event ("What would happen if people had an eye in the back of their head?"), or asking as many questions as possible about an object or event. Such tests are scored at least for ideational fluency (the number of ideas produced) and originality (uniqueness of the ideas).

The Torrance Tests of Creative Thinking (Torrance, 1966) are the most widely used divergent-thinking tests (see Inset 4.2). They include verbal and nonverbal (figural) subtests and are scored for *fluency, flexibility* (number of different categories of ideas or approaches to the problem), *originality,* and, with the figural tests, *elaboration* (number of additional details and embellishments). Torrance and Ball (1984) developed a "streamlined" scoring procedure for the figural tests that produces 18 measures of creative characteristics and is said to expedite scoring.

The Test for Creative Thinking—Drawing Production (TCT-DP; Urban & Jellen, 1993) is a more recent divergent thinking test. The TCT-DP most resembles a figural divergent thinking test, but the scoring is unique and the test appears to evaluate a combination of creative abilities and creative personality dispositions. Briefly, the test involves a single 6-inch square frame within which are five "figural fragments," a 90-degree angle, a half-circle, a squiggly line, a dot, and a short dotted line. Outside the square frame lies a sixth fragment, a small square with one open side. A single student or groups of students of any age are asked to embellish the "incomplete" drawing. Administration requires 15 minutes or less, and scoring requires 1 to 2 minutes—after considerable

INSET 4.2

## Torrance Tests of Creative Thinking

The *Torrance Tests of Creative Thinking* (Torrance, 1966) measure creative abilities of *fluency* (number of ideas), *flexibility* (number of different types or categories of ideas), *originality* (uniqueness), and *elaboration* (number of embellishments). Exercises similar to Torrance's subtests are presented below. Spend a few minutes on each one. Are you fluent? Flexible? Original? Are you high in elaboration? The "streamlined" scoring procedure produces 18 measures of creative characteristics (Torrance and Ball, 1984).

**Directions:** Make a meaningful picture out of each of the nonsense forms below.

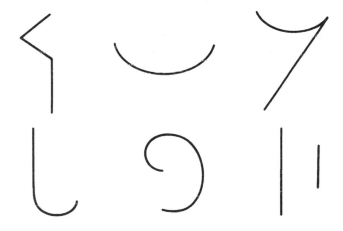

**Directions:** List as many unusual uses as you can for discarded rubber tires.

_____   _____
_____   _____
_____   _____
_____   _____
_____   _____
_____   _____
_____   _____
_____   _____
_____   _____
_____   _____

practice. A 1990 evaluation of the test in Poland led the researchers to recommend that the TCT-DP be used as an official screening instrument in Poland for identifying gifted and creative students (Urban, 1993). As a sample of the 11 scores, test-takers receive points for unconventionality, breaking away from two-dimensionality, adding new elements, humor or emotional expressiveness, producing a theme, and breaking boundaries.

Other divergent thinking batteries are the Guilford (1967) tests, the Wallach and Kogan (1965) tests, the Getzels and Jackson (1962) tests, and for preschool children Torrance's (1982) Thinking Creatively in Action and Movement.

In view of their extensive development and evaluation, and the standard administration and scoring procedures, the Torrance tests are the recommended divergent thinking battery. If money is a problem, the Wallach and Kogan tests and the Getzels and Jackson tests apparently may be used without charge. In the negative column, the administration and scoring of any divergent thinking test are very time-consuming. Further, only one aspect of overall problem solving is evaluated, the divergent thinking stage. (See Davis, 1998, for descriptions of other published creativity tests.)

As for inventories that assess personality and biographical information, the authors—without bias or prejudice—recommend their own PRIDE, GIFT, GIFFI I and GIFFI II instruments (Rimm and Davis, 1983). There is a stereotype of personality traits and biographical characteristics that appears again and again in studies of creative people of all ages (for example, curiosity, humor, risk taking, and a history of creative activities; see Chapter 2).

PRIDE (Preschool and Primary Interest Descriptor; Rimm, 1982) is a preschool/kindergarten inventory that parents fill out. GIFT (Group Inventory for Finding [Creative] Talent) consists of yes–no items in lower-, middle-, and upper-elementary school forms. GIFFI I and II (Group Inventory for Finding Interests) are in a rating scale form designed for junior and senior high school students, respectively. These tests have been validated in seven different countries and with many student populations, including minority, learning disabled, and gifted. The tests produce subscale scores (for example, confidence, imagination, many interests) that can be used to help understand and guide gifted children. They also are available in Spanish (see Appendix 4.2).

Inventories that assess a student's background of creative activities seem to be a face-valid indicator of creative potential—the relationship between past, present, and future creativity is quite logical (Davis, 1998; Holland, 1961; Plucker, 1999). Does the elementary child constantly make or build things? Does he or she have wide interests, unusual hobbies, unique collections? Does the child have unusual experience or talent in art, poetry, creative writing, handicrafts, music, dance, computer programming, or a science area? Perhaps you have a "photography kid" or a child who knows more about Picasso, Wynton Marsalis, DNA, or Russian cosmonauts than do the teachers. Having had an imaginary playmate is a remarkably good predictor of current and future creativeness (Davis, 1998; Somers & Yawkey, 1984).

In the last three pages of *Guiding Creative Talent,* Torrance (1962) presented a checklist of 100 creative activities entitled *Things Done on Your Own,* covering language arts, science, social studies, art, and other fields. Students are asked to check "things you have done on your own," not things required in school. As a sample:

- Kept a collection of my writings
- Played word games with other boys and girls
- Made up an original dance
- Developed a design for jewelry (or cloth)
- Explored a cave
- Read a science magazine
- Made a wild flower collection
- Planned an experiment
- Kept a daily record of weather
- Organized or helped to organize a club
- Drew up plans for an invention, apparatus, or the like
- Made up a recipe for some kind of food dish

It also would not be difficult to create a self-report inventory, or one to be completed by parents, that asks about a student's past or present strong interests or hobbies. For example:

Describe any hobbies, collections, or strong interests that you [your child may] have had. For example, have you [has your child] been really interested in reptiles, writing poetry or stories, magic tricks, theater, computers, Egypt, dinosaurs, collections, science, art, handicrafts, or music? Other hobbies or collections? If so, list them.

A few statements indicating outstanding past creative involvement likely will float to the top.

## Teacher Nominations

Teacher nominations may be very informal ("Say, we're starting a new gifted program, be thinking about one or two kids you want in it!") or quite formal, involving rating forms or checklists that will be objectively scored. Teacher nomination definitely is one of the most common identification methods, yet it can be troublesome. We already noted a tendency for some teachers to favor those well-dressed, cooperative, nondisabled, and English-speaking "teacher pleasers" who do work neatly, on time, and with no smarting off. Bright underachievers will be overlooked, along with bright disruptive students and unconventional creative ones.

In Australia, Gross (1999) discovered that in the early childhood years teacher nomination is the *least* effective method for identifying giftedness. As in America, teacher nomination is susceptible to class and culture bias: Nominees are likely to be middle class and from the dominant culture.

Some reliability and validity difficulties can be overcome by better acquainting teachers with characteristics of gifted students and by training them to rate and identify G/T candidates. We also recommend that teachers get to know students well before nominating them.

Teachers, schools, or school districts may de-velop their own nomination forms to help teachers synthesize grades, ability scores, achievement scores (especially in reading and math), parent or peer nominations, or observations of creativity, motivation, leadership, or other abilities and skills pertinent to the particular G/T program. A sample teacher nomination form, designed by Renzulli to help structure the nomination of students for Schoolwide Enrichment Model programs, appears in Appendix 4.1 at the end of this chapter. The form includes spaces for reporting scores on the Scales for Rating Behavioral Characteristics of Superior Students (SRBCSS). (The SRBCSS and other examples of rating scales, essentially structured teacher nomination forms, are presented later in this chapter.)

## Parent Nominations

No one knows children and adolescents better than their own parents. For example, only parents will know that a child spoke in sentences at age two, taught himself or herself to read at age four, and drew the solar system, composed melodies, produced creative art, and asked about reasons for the Middle East strife at age five. Unfortunately, parent nominations are not used as much as they should be.

Martinson (1974) suggested a one-page letter to parents that explains that the teacher is interested in planning appropriate educational experiences for their child and would the parent please provide information pertaining to:

1. The child's special interests and hobbies
2. Recent books he or she has enjoyed or read
3. Special interests other than reading
4. Unusual accomplishments, past or present
5. Special talents
6. Special opportunities the child has had
7. Preferred activities when alone
8. Relationships with others
9. Special problems and/or needs

Another nomination rating form appears in Appendix 4.3. This form evaluates precocious cognitive development (items 1–5, 9, 20), creativity (items 6, 8, 10–13), leadership (item 14), motor coordination (item 16), energy and persistence (items 7, 15, 19), and other characteristics of gifted and creative children.

## Peer Nominations

Peers are very good at naming gifted and talented classmates. They are especially helpful in identifying minority or rural gifted students, or those who are culturally different, disadvantaged, or have a disability. Children know who's who. For several years have watched Miguel and Kirsten finish their math first, read the best, and answer the most confusing questions correctly. They know about Miguel's and Kirsten's wealth of information, their spelling prowess, their original ideas, and their scientific and artistic projects in and out of school.

As a caution, young children in kindergarten through third grade may have difficulty evaluating peers' capabilities (Banbury & Wellington, 1989). For example, too many lower elementary children *smart* means *fast,* and peers who skip parts of the assignment or otherwise do fast but poor work may earn peer recognition as "smart" (Rimm, 1991b).

One consideration in developing a peer nomination form or strategy is *style*—questions can be *direct, disguised,* or take a *game* format. All three types ask class members to name peers with special characteristics. As an example of a direct approach, a nomination form can simply ask:

Who is the smartest kid in class?
Who is best at math?
Who is the best reader?
Who has the best memory?
Who always finishes his or her work first?
Who has the most unusual ideas?
Who tells great stories?
Who could invent the most games with a box of stuff?

As a similar direct approach, Callahan and colleagues (1995a) described a 10-item modification of Udall's (1987) Peer Referral Form that evaluates general intelligence, learning speed, motivation/task commitment, and creativity in art, music, language, and play. Students in grades four to six are asked to write down just one name (or no name), list either a girl or a boy, and reuse the same name if they wish. The nomination form simply asks, for example, "Who is smart in school?," "Who learns quickly?," "If you need help at school (or at home with a project), who would you ask?," "Who gets interested in a project, spends extra time working, and takes pride in their work?," and "Who is good at making up dances (or stories, games, pictures)?"

Another direct nomination form appears in Appendix 4.4.

As an example of a disguised nomination form (Jenkins, 1979), a form entitled "Let's Make Believe" asks children to imagine they are stranded on a deserted island and name which classmate is the best *organizer* (leader, gets others to do things), *fixer* (improves or makes things better), *artist* (makes pretty things or makes up good stories), *inventor* (invents/discovers), *judge* (helps settle arguments), or *entertainer* (acts, tells jokes, sings). A variation asks children to imagine that a spaceship with friendly aliens has landed and they are visiting class:

Who probably will ask the aliens the most unusual questions?

Who probably will remember the most details about the aliens' visit?

The game mode described by Banbury and Wellington (1989) took the form of a "Guess Who?" game. Following a brief description of a characteristic, students would name someone who fits: "I am thinking of one member of this class who has a great memory. Who do you think it is?" "I am thinking of one of your classmates who always comes up with unusual ideas. Who do you think it might be?"

Finally, Davidson (1986) suggested that students above the lowest primary grades may nominate each other with a form that simply says:

*I believe* _____ *should be placed in the gifted program because I have observed the following behaviors:* _____ .

Said Davidson, "This type of nomination eliminates the possibility that a student may be excluded simply because some unique abilities may not be included on a standardized nomination form."

Students tend to nominate friends. If you construct your own peer nomination form, be sure to include instructions to "Pick someone whom you think is the best choice, and not just a friend." Also, inform students, "You may write a name more than once." To solicit self-nominations as well as peer nominations, add, "You may write your own name if you feel you are the best choice."

### Self-Nominations

Some self-motivated students have strong artistic, creative, scientific, or other interests and talents, and they want to participate in a special program—but nobody asks them. Teachers may be unaware of the talent, creativity, and high motivation. A self-nomination form used in Charlottesville, Virginia, instructs students, "Check the area(s) in which you think you have special abilities or talents and tell why you think you have special abilities or talents in these areas." The 12 areas were general intellectual ability, math, science, social studies, language arts, reading, art, music, drama, dance, creativity, and leadership.

Self-nomination is especially recommended at the junior and senior high school levels, where peer pressures may cause youths to mask their special talents. Renzulli (1987) stated that in high school self-nomination is the *only* identification strategy he uses or recommends.

### Product Evaluations

A good index of academic, artistic, creative, or scientific talent is simply the quality of work the student has done or is doing. Art teachers are in a unique position to evaluate artistic talent and creativity. Other teachers also may have an opportunity to evaluate the quality of students' poetry, science projects, electronic or computer projects, dramatic talent, photography, unusual hobbies, and so on.

Usually, product evaluations are quite informal; the product may obviously reflect high creativity, science ability, writing skill, analysis or synthesis talent, and so on. However, if a more structured and objective product rating form is desired, Appendix 4.5 presents a form developed and used by the State of Michigan Education Department. It is helpful to use more than one rater, since teacher variation (inter-rater reliability) should be considered.

### Rating Scales

We already have seen several rating scales in conjunction with teacher-, parent-, peer-, and self-nomination procedures and product evaluations. Renzulli et al. (2001) developed a set of ten rating scale instruments, used by teachers, entitled *Scales for Rating Behavioral Characteristics of Superior Students* (SRBCSS). The four most widely used scales evaluate intellectual ability (learning), creativity, motivation, and leadership and are reproduced in Appendix 4.6. Others assess artistic, musical, dramatic, and planning characteristics, as well as communication-precision and communication-expressiveness.

The Gifted Evaluation Scale (GES) is used by teachers familiar with students to evaluate capabilities in each of the five categories of the federal definition of giftedness. According to McCarney and Anderson (n.d.), the GES assesses information "easily observed and documented." The 48-item test requires approximately 15 minutes. The GES supplies measures of intellectual ability, creativity, specific academic ability, leadership, and ability in the performing or visual arts. A motivation scale also is available. A technical manual supplies various types of reliability, validity, and other statistical information. For each student, one can obtain a profile of the five scores, reported as standard scores based on the national standardization sample (2,121 students), as well as a total score and a percentile score. There are separate norms for males and females.

Rimm's (1986) Achievement Identification Measure (AIM), filled out by parents, consists of

77 rating-scale items designed to identify under-achievement. It is, in essence, a measure of student academic motivation. The Group Achievement Identification Measure (GAIM; Rimm, 1987a) is virtually identical except that it is administered directly to students. A third instrument, Achievement Identification Measure-Teacher Observation (AIM-TO; Rimm, 1988a), is used by teachers to measure the same construct. All three instruments produce subscale scores of *Competition, Responsibility, Self-Control, Achievement Communication,* and *Respect.*

### Baldwin Identification Matrix

The *Baldwin Identification Matrix* (Baldwin, 1985) is intended to make identification of minority students more equitable. As shown in Table 4.1 it summarizes scores and ratings on a variety of criteria. Standardized intelligence and achievement test data are used for rating intelligence, reading, and math (Items 1.1–1.4). The Renzulli et al. (2001) Scales for Rating Behavioral Characteristics of Superior Students (Appendix 4.5) are used for evaluating *learning, motivation, creativity,* and *leadership* (Items 1.5, 2.1, 5.1, 6.1). The Matrix entries are added to produce a single total score, allowing students to be easily ranked. In addition to the handy total score, the Baldwin Matrix provides a profile of strengths and weaknesses for each student.

The main disadvantage of the Baldwin Matrix, and other identification systems based on total points, is that students who might be extremely talented in just one or two areas are likely to produce mediocre total scores and will be quickly excluded. We recommend flexibility in using the *Baldwin Identification Matrix.*

### Frasier Talent Assessment Profile (F-TAP)

Like the *Baldwin Identification Matrix,* the *Frasier Talent Assessment Profile* (F-TAP; Frasier, 1994, 1997) seeks to make assessment fair to disadvantaged and minority groups. The F-TAP is based on 10 characteristics of gifted persons: high moti-vation, special interests, communication talent, problem solving, memory, inquiry, insight, reasoning, imagination/creativity, and humor. The first component is the *Panning for Gold* observation form, on which teachers record student information pertaining to the 10 traits of giftedness, along with any recommendations, for example, for further assessment. The F-TAP includes a column for recording objective and subjective data that can be represented in numbers (e.g., standardized ability and achievement scores) and a column for recording performance data that cannot be represented in numbers (e.g., observational and referral information, self-perceptions, language proficiency, additional aptitude/achievement information, and awards). Finally, a committee synthesizes and evaluates this information to produce an educational plan that includes suitable program and curriculum options, counseling options, and projected goals and outcomes. (For further details, see Frasier, 1994; also see our Chapter 12, Figure 12.2.)

### ASSESSMENT OF GARDNER'S EIGHT OR NINE INTELLIGENCES

Chapter 1 reviewed Gardner's multiple-intelligence theory, which suggested not one or two but eight types of intelligence: *linguistic, logical-mathematical, spatial, musical, bodily-kinesthetic, interpersonal, intrapersonal,* and *naturalistic.* At this writing, *existential* is under consideration (von Károlyi, Ramos-Ford, & Gardner, 2003).

Gardner (1999) noted that multiple-choice and short-answer tests cannot identify several of his intelligences—for example, intrapersonal (self-understanding) and bodily-kinesthetic intelligence. Rather, a profile of intelligences can be assessed by observing student interactions with materials and ideas in intelligence areas. Gardner described his Project Spectrum classrooms, for students age four to seven, which are stocked with materials that elicit different intelligences, such as artistic and musical materials, specimens of nature, board games, plus areas for building, dance, and exercise. He concluded, "For most children, unfet-

**TABLE 4.1**   Sample Form for Baldwin Identification Matrix

| Area | Assessment Items | M* | S* | Ratings | | | | | | No* | RS* | Area Score (RS/N) |
|---|---|---|---|---|---|---|---|---|---|---|---|---|
| | | | | 5 | 4 | 3 | 2 | 1 | b-na | | | |
| Cognitive | 1.1 General IQ Binet | 44.1 | 150 | | | 3 | | | | | | |
| | 1.2 Stanford Reading | 11.1 | 7 | | | 3 | | | | | | |
| | 1.3 Math | 11.1 | 8 | | 4 | | | | | | | |
| | 1.4 Reading | 11.2 | 91 | | 4 | | | | | | | |
| | 1.5 Renz-Learning | 22.2 | 28 | | 4 | | | | | | | |
| | Total Cognitive | | | 0 | 12 | 6 | 0 | 0 | 0 | 5 | 18 | 3.6 |
| Psychosocial | 2.1 Renz-Leadership | 22.4 | 29 | | | | | 1 | | | | |
| | 2.2 Supplemental | 33.5 | 4 | | 4 | | | | | | | |
| | 2.3 Peer Nomination | 33.5 | 3 | | | 3 | | | | | | |
| | 2.4 | | | | | | | | | | | |
| | 2.5 | | | | | | | | | | | |
| | Total Psychosocial | | | 0 | 4 | 3 | 0 | 1 | 0 | 3 | 8 | 2.7 |
| Creative Prods | 3.1 Art Products | 33.6 | 7 | | | 3 | | | | | | |
| | 3.2 Musical Performance | 33.6 | 8 | | 4 | | | | | | | |
| | 3.3 Supplemental | 33.5 | 4 | | 4 | | | | | | | |
| | 3.4 | | | | | | | | | | | |
| | 3.5 | | | | | | | | | | | |
| | Total Creative Products | | | 0 | 8 | 3 | 0 | 0 | 0 | 3 | 11 | 3.7 |
| Psychomotor | 4.1 School Assessment | 33.5 | 4 | | 4 | | | | | | | |
| | 4.2 Supplemental | 33.5 | 5 | 5 | | | | | | | | |
| | 4.3 | | | | | | | | | | | |
| | 4.4 | | | | | | | | | | | |
| | 4.5 | | | | | | | | | | | |
| | Total Psychomotor | | | 5 | 4 | 0 | 0 | 0 | 0 | 2 | 9 | 4.5 |
| Motivation | 5.1 Renz Motivation | 22.1 | 29 | | | 3 | | | | | | |
| | 5.2 Supplemental | 33.5 | 3 | | | 3 | | | | | | |
| | 5.3 | | | | | | | | | | | |
| | 5.4 | | | | | | | | | | | |
| | 5.5 | | | | | | | | | | | |
| | Total Motivation | | | 0 | 0 | 6 | 0 | 0 | 0 | 2 | 6 | 3 |
| Creative Press | 6.1 Renz Creativity | 22.3 | 29 | | | 3 | | | | | | |
| | 6.2 TTC Creativity | 11.2 | 85% | | 4 | | | | | | | |
| | 6.3 | | | | | | | | | | | |
| | 6.4 | | | | | | | | | | | |
| | 6.5 | | | | | | | | | | | |
| | Total Creative Process | | | 0 | 4 | 3 | 0 | 0 | 0 | 2 | 7 | 3.5 |
| Matrix Totals | Maximum Points for this Matrix | | | | | | | | | | | 30 |
| | Student Total | | | | | | | | | | | 21 |

M* — Mode of Score Code
S* — Score
No* — Number of Items
RS* — Raw Score

tered exploration in a Spectrum classroom or in a children's museum is enough to give a rough-and-ready picture of their intelligences at a given moment in their lives. Nothing more is needed" (Gardner, 1999, p. 137).

As three assessment cautions, Gardner (1999) warns not to confuse students' *interest* (e.g., in sports) with their *ability* (e.g., in math). Also, he noted an MI "assessment mentality" tendency to permanently categorize children, for example, "Terrell's a spatial," "Dinah's linguistic," "Carlos is not at all musical," or "Gracie's interpersonally challenged." Finally, Gardner warns that students' daily routines will dramatically alter profiles of intelligences, such as by taking Suzuki violin lessons.

## Maker's DISCOVER Process

Aiming at "leveling the playing field" for minority students, Maker's (1996; see also Sarouphim, 1999, 2000, 2001) performance-based identification process entitled DISCOVER evaluates "the ability to solve complex problems in effective, efficient, elegant, and economical ways" (p. 44).

Drawing on Gardner's theory of multiple intelligences, five activities evaluate spatial, linguistic, and logical-mathematical intelligences. Spatial intelligence is evaluated with Pablo cardboard pieces and Tangrams, both of which require students to create geometric shapes. Linguistic intelligence is evaluated with storytelling (using toys as props) and story writing (or drawing, for kindergartners). With spatial and linguistic activities, observers look for originality, complexity, and cause-and-effect relationships. Logical-mathematical intelligence is assessed with 12 math problems and Tangrams. With the math problems, observers note the use of strategies and flexible and original thinking.

With each activity for each student, observers record specific behaviors and add relevant comments. They also rate the student's overall problem solving ability as *unknown, maybe, probably,* or *definitely*. A student given a rating of *definitely* in two or more of the five activities is placed in a program for gifted students, or may be tested further. Throughout, the emphasis is on effective, efficient, and creative problem solving.

DISCOVER does indeed identify gifted minority children. In validity studies, Sarouphim (1999) found close relationships between activities on the DISCOVER and corresponding activities on the WISC-R and Raven's Progressive Matrices (a measure of intelligence using geometric patterns). Perhaps best of all, DISCOVER identified a full 23 percent of the 257 minority (Navajo and Mexican American) children as gifted (Sarouphim, 2001). On the downside, according to Sarouphim (2000), administering DISCOVER to groups of five students requires about two and a half hours.

## TRIARCHIC ABILITIES TEST

In Chapter 1 we also described briefly Sternberg's (1998c, 2003) triarchic theory of intelligence, consisting of *analytic, creative,* and *practical* intelligence. This expanded view of intelligence includes the Triarchic Abilities Test (TAT), a set of tests in three domains (verbal, quantitative, figural) and two response modes (multiple-choice and essay). The test thus is comprised of a set of nine multiple-choice subtests, each consisting of four items (total = 36 items), plus three essay items, one each for *analytic, creative,* and *practical* intelligence.

As a sample of three items from the nine multiple-choice subtests:

**Analytic-Verbal:** Students see a novel word embedded in a paragraph and must infer its meaning.

**Practical-Quantitative:** Students solve everyday math problems (e.g., buying tickets for a ball game).

**Creative-Figural:** Subjects are presented with a figural series that involve one or more transformations. They then apply the rule to a new figural series.

In the essay items, the *analytic* problem requires students to analyze the advantages and disadvantages of having security guards in a school building. In the *creative* problem students describe how they would produce an ideal school system. The *practical* problem requires students to name a problem in their life, then state three feasible solutions for it.

The Triarchic Abilities Test provides seven subscores: analytic, synthetic, and practical abilities; automatization; and verbal, quantitative, and figural processing.

## A MULTIDIMENSIONAL CULTURE-FAIR ASSESSMENT STRATEGY

Clasen, Middleton, and Connel (1994) described a nontraditional, largely performance-based multidimensional assessment to identify gifted sixth-grade minority and majority students in three urban Midwest schools. With 433 students (70 percent minority), Clasen and colleagues focused on the domains of problem solving and art, plus peer and teacher nominations.

Brainstorming problems asked for solutions to a home problem (the child you are babysitting disappears) or a school problem (excessive truancy). "What are all the things you could do to solve this problem? Include clever and unusual ideas" (p. 29). The top-scoring 5 percent qualified as gifted.

The art task asked students to draw a picture that included a person, house, tree, and animal. Scoring followed a curriculum guideline that describes seven levels of art ability, with substages in the top four levels for finer discrimination. Again, the top 5 percent were included in the gifted pool.

With their peer nomination strategy, students named the "best" student in their class in 25 areas, for example, problem solving, art, and "helpfulness" (which shows problem solving and leadership). The top 5 percent in number of nominations—and not identified by the problem solving or art tasks—were added to the talent pool. Finally, teachers were asked to nominate three "top" minority students with strong talent in a variety of academic and nonacademic areas, including art and problem solving. Students named by two or more teachers were deemed gifted.

The Clasen and colleagues procedure identified 24 percent of the students, 51 males and 53 females, as having gifts in art or problem solving. Perhaps most importantly, the problem solving, art, and peer nomination procedures *identified minority and majority gifted students in proportion to their numbers in the schools*.

## TALENT POOL IDENTIFICATION PLAN: RENZULLI

With the talent pool approach, the intent is to be inclusive, to "cast a wide net" that includes many kinds of gifts and talents. Renzulli and Reis (1997) outlined a five-step procedure.

***Step 1.*** *Test Score Nominations.* About half of the talent pool can be selected via standardized intelligence and/or achievement tests. Students who score above the 92nd percentile are admitted without further evaluation.

***Step 2.*** *Teacher Nominations.* After being advised of students who are admitted via Step 1 (test scores), in Step 2 teachers nominate additional students who display other worthy characteristics—particularly high creativity, high motivation, unusual interests or talents, or special areas of superior performance or potential.

***Step 3.*** *Alternate Pathways.* Alternate pathways to the talent pool include many of the identification options described in this chapter: self-nominations, parent nominations, peer nominations, creativity test results, product evaluations, "and virtually any other procedure that might lead to initial consideration by a screening committee" (p. 60). Admission is not automatic in Step 3, but depends upon the decision of the screening committee, which interviews students, teachers, and parents and examines all previous school records. Sometimes admission is on a trial basis.

***Step 4.*** *Special Nominations (Safety Valve No. 1).* To avoid biases of current teachers, the list of all students nominated is circulated to all teachers. The purpose is to allow previous-year teachers to nominate students who are not on the list. The procedure also allows resource teachers to make recommendations based on their enrichment experiences in the regular classroom, for example, students who seem unusually creative or to have unusual strengths in a special area.

***Step 5.*** *Action Information Nominations (Safety Valve No. 2).* Part of the Schoolwide Enrichment Model includes *Action Information Messages,* which usually are used to describe talent pool students who are extremely interested or excited about a topic, area of study, or idea and wish to pursue it as an independent project. Action Information also may be used to nominate non-talent pool students for projects and thus for inclusion in the talent pool. Such nominations are reviewed by the screening committee.

As some advantages of Renzulli's talent pool approach: More students have an opportunity to participate; identification is flexible and multi-dimensional; identification continues all year; motivated students self-select; uninterested, unsuccessful students do not waste resource room time and facilities; charges of elitism are reduced or eliminated; the need for painful, hard-and-fast decisions (for example, based on cutoff scores or a 3–5 percent criterion) is eliminated; and silly situations in which, due to altered identification criteria, last year's gifted student is "not gifted this year" are eliminated. There is much to be said for such a plan.

## IDENTIFYING GIFTED PRESCHOOLERS

Burns, Mathews, and Mason (1990) described a three-step solution to the challenge of identifying intellectually gifted preschoolers in Louisiana, a state that offers publicly funded preschool programs for gifted children. Similar plans could be used by any individual or district seeking to develop and promote programs for gifted preschoolers.

The first phase aimed at informing parents and preschool teachers about characteristics of preschool giftedness and the availability of the public programs. This was accomplished by a blitz of feature articles in newspapers and local magazines, TV interviews on morning talk shows and evening news shows, and presentations at parent and church organizations.

Phase two was a general screening, accomplished by a Gifted Preschool Screening Packet that included a parent questionnaire and a teacher questionnaire (if the child was in a preschool), along with a brochure and application form. The questionnaires asked parents or teachers to rate the child on 45 different behaviors—some of which were and some of which were not characteristic of gifted preschoolers—and to "describe additional exceptional behaviors displayed by the child."

The third phase was an individualized screening, first with the Hess School Readiness Scale (Hess, 1975), a test similar to the Stanford-Binet. If the child survived this hurdle (IQ = 120 or higher), he or she was given the Stanford-Binet itself plus tests of math and reading. (Louisiana's stringent criterion for placement in a public preschool gifted program is an IQ score that is three standard deviations above the mean, *or* two and one-half standard deviations plus scores in the 98–99th percentile in reading *and* math.)

While few school systems offer public preschool programs for the gifted, the Burns, Mathews, and Mason (1990) guides can help solve the sticky problem of selecting intellectually gifted 3- to 5-year-old children.

## IDENTIFYING GIFTED SECONDARY STUDENTS

As gifted children move into middle and high school, their talents become increasingly differentiated. The problem is not knowing whether they are gifted, but *how* they are gifted and what the areas of talent are.

Colangelo and colleagues (1996) described the PLAN inventory developed by the American College Testing Program. PLAN is taken by tenth-grade students to help them prepare a suitable high school program. The test measures high-level thinking skills, specifically, problem solving, grasping implied meanings, drawing inferences, evaluating ideas, and making judgments in the areas of English, reading, mathematics, and science reasoning. Colangelo and colleagues primarily explored gender, ethnicity, and career choices. However, their criterion of *perfect* scores on at least one subtest of PLAN indicates that PLAN can indeed be used to identify "exceptional academic performance."

Feldhusen, Hoover, and Sayler (1990; Feldhusen, 1997) developed identification procedures and rating scales designed specifically to identify gifted and talented youth in middle and high school. The Purdue Academic Rating Scales (PARS) and Purdue Vocational Rating Scales

(PVRS) allow teachers to assess specific information suitable for secondary program selection and placement.

There are five academic scales (PARS; math, science, English, social studies, and foreign languages) and four vocational scales (PVRS; agriculture, business and office, home economics, and trade and industrial). All scales contain 15 five-point rating-scale items. Space does not permit total reproduction of the scales, but sample items appear in Table 4.2.

As general identification recommendations, Feldhusen, Hoover, and Sayler advised, for example, (1) using their scales in conjunction with other information (e.g., ability scores, direct observation, student self-assessment, information from parents); (2) training teachers in the interpretation of the scales in relation to student behavior; (3) obtaining ratings of students by several teachers; and (4) watching out for the halo effect—the tendency to bias ratings in line with overall attitudes toward the student.

As a final consideration, and as suggested by Renzulli (1987), in high school many students already have developed specific interests and motivations. Therefore, self-selection for a special class or program is more important than in earlier grades.

## RECOMMENDATIONS FROM THE NATIONAL REPORT ON IDENTIFICATION AND NRC/GT

The *National Report on Identification* (Richert, 1985, 1997, 2003; Richert, Alvino, and McDonnel, 1982), mentioned earlier, included an alphabetized list of over 60 tests, rating scales, checklists, and inventories (Table 4.3). The table includes (1) categories of giftedness assessed by each instrument, (2) appropriateness for advantaged and disadvantaged children, (3) suitable age range, and (4) appropriate stage for their use (i.e., for nominating/identifying gifted students, assessing their abilities, or evaluating their skill development).

As another source of mainly paper-and-pencil tests, rating scales, and checklists, Callahan and colleagues (1995a) reviewed and evaluated the usefulness, appropriateness, reliability, and validity of 73 possible identification instruments, along with the suitable age group. (Reliability, validity, and other information for each test are available from the National Research Center on the Gifted and Talented at the University of Connecticut, Storrs.) Table 4.4 itemizes the categories ("gifted constructs") of the tests, along with some specific tests suggested by them. Descriptions and sources of most of the tests can be obtained from the Internet or the NRC/GT.

## COMMENT

The identification procedure clearly is a crucial part of any G/T program. The procedures themselves define who is "gifted." Most programs are moving toward multiple selection criteria and flexible procedures that use both objective test scores and subjective evaluations and nominations. Identification must be flexible. A major sin is enforcing a rigid IQ cutoff score—a student with an IQ of 130 is included, but a more creative and energetic student with an IQ of only 129 is not. A low test score or a teacher-student personality conflict should not eliminate an obviously gifted student from a needed program. Also, selection methods should be teacher friendly—understandable and require little time.

## SUMMARY

There are many strategies for identifying gifted and talented students for programs. While some programs stress only intelligence (aptitude) scores, a multidimensional assessment is recommended.

Some highlights of current thinking on identification include adopting a broad definition of giftedness, recognizing multiple forms of intelligence, using multiple criteria, promoting inclusiveness (not exclusiveness), including authentic assessments, being aware of cultural differences in "giftedness," basing identification on student needs (not quotas), assuming links between identification and instruction, and promoting collaboration with administrators and the public.

**TABLE 4.2**  Sample Items from the Purdue Academic Rating Scales and the Purdue Vocational Rating Scales

---

*From Purdue Academic Rating Scales*

---

**Mathematics**
1. Generalizes mathematical relationships, relates concepts in various applications.
2. Learns math concepts and processes faster than other students.

**Science**
1. Has science hobbies, is a collector, likes gadgets.
2. Understands scientific method, able to formulate hypotheses and conduct experiments carefully.

**English**
1. Motivated to write even when writing is not assigned; writes stories, poems, or plays; keeps a journal or diary.
2. Has a good sense of humor; uses and understands satire, puns, and second meanings.

**Social Studies**
1. Reads widely on social issues from a variety of books, magazines, or newspapers.
2. Skilled in analyzing topics, finding the underlying problem, questioning, investigating.

**Foreign Language**
1. Learns new vocabulary words and grammatical concepts rapidly.
2. Shows curiosity and inquisitiveness when introduced to new grammatical or cultural concepts.

---

*From Purdue Vocational Rating Scales*

---

**Agriculture**
1. Exhibits leadership in shop activities/organizations.
2. Comes up with good, high-level ideas for projects or for agricultural problems.

**Business and Office**
1. Shows creativity in solving problems or designing reports.
2. Is viewed by other students as showing talent in business and office classes.

**Home Economics**
1. Learns and applies new skills, techniques, or methods rapidly and easily.
2. Is enthusiastic in all or most class activities.

**Trade and Industrial**
1. Shows good manual skills in use of tools and equipment.
2. Seems to have a lot of ideas.

**TABLE 4.3**  Alphabetical Listing of Instruments and Recommendations for Use

| INSTRUMENT | General Intellectual | Specific Academic | Creativity | Leadership | Visual and Performing Arts | Advantaged | Disadvantaged | Early Childhood | Grades 4-8 | High School to Adult | K-12 | Nomination | Assessment | Evaluation |
|---|---|---|---|---|---|---|---|---|---|---|---|---|---|---|
| A.S.S.E.T.S. | + | + | + |   | + | + |   | + | + |   |   | + | + |   |
| Barron-Welsh Art Scale |   |   |   | + | + |   | + | + | + | + | + | + |   |   |
| Biographical Inventory-Form U |   | + | + | + | + | + |   | + | + |   |   |   | + |   |
| California Achievement Tests |   | + |   |   | + |   |   |   | + | + | + |   |   |   |
| California Psychological Inventory |   |   |   |   | + |   |   | + | + |   |   | + |   |   |
| Cartoon Conservation Scales | + |   |   |   | + | + | + | + |   |   |   | + | + |   |
| Lattell Culture Fair Intelligence Series | + |   |   |   | + | + | + | + |   |   |   | + |   |   |
| CIRCUS | + | + |   |   | + | + | + | + |   |   |   | + | + |   |
| Cognitive Abilities Test | + |   |   |   | + |   | + | + | + |   |   | + | + |   |
| Columbia Mental Maturity Scale | + |   |   |   | + | + | + | + | + |   |   | + |   |   |
| Comprehensive Tests of Basic Skills |   | + |   |   | + |   |   |   | + | + | + |   |   |   |
| Cornell Critical Thinking Tests |   |   |   |   | + |   |   |   | + |   |   | + | + | + |
| Creativity Assessment Packet |   |   | + |   | + |   | + | + | + |   |   | + |   |   |
| Creativity Tests for Children |   |   | + |   | + |   |   | + | + |   |   | + |   |   |
| Design Judgement Test |   |   |   | + | + |   |   | + | + |   |   | + |   |   |
| Differential Aptitude Tests | + | + |   |   | + |   |   | + | + |   |   | + | + | + |
| Early School Personality Questionnaire |   |   |   |   | + | + |   | + |   |   |   | + |   |   |
| Gifted and Talented Screening Form | + | + | + | + | + | + |   | + | + | + |   | + |   |   |
| Goodenough-Harris Drawing Test | + |   |   |   | + | + | + | + | + | + |   | + |   |   |
| Group Inventory for Finding Creative Talent (G.I.F.T.) |   |   | + |   | + |   | + | + | + |   |   | + | + |   |
| Group Inventory for Finding Interests (G.I.F.F.I.) |   |   | + |   | + |   |   |   | + |   |   | + | + |   |
| Guilford-Holley L Inventory |   |   |   |   | + |   |   |   | + |   |   | + |   |   |
| GuilFord-Zimmerman Aptitude Survey | + |   |   |   | + |   |   |   | + |   |   | + |   |   |
| Henmon-Nelson Tests of Mental Ability | + | + |   |   | + |   |   |   | + | + | + |   |   |   |
| High School Personality Questionnaire |   |   |   |   | + |   |   | + | + |   |   | + |   |   |
| Horn Art Aptitude Inventory |   |   |   | + | + | + |   |   | + |   |   | + |   |   |
| Iowa Tests of Basic Skills |   | + |   |   | + |   | + | + | + |   |   | + | + |   |
| Kaufman — ABC | + | + |   |   | + | + |   | + |   |   |   | + | + |   |
| Khatena-Torrance Creative Perception Inventory |   |   | + |   | + |   |   | + | + |   |   | + | + |   |
| Lorge-Thorndike Intelligence Tests | + |   |   |   | + |   | + | + | + |   |   | + |   |   |
| Maier Art Judgement Tests |   |   |   | + | + |   |   | + | + |   |   | + |   |   |
| Metropolitan Achievement Tests |   | + |   |   | + |   |   |   |   |   |   | + | + |   |
| Multi-Dimensional Screening Device | + | + | + | + | + | + |   |   |   |   |   | + |   |   |
| Musical Aptitude Profile |   |   |   | + | + | + |   | + | + | + |   | + | + |   |
| Otis-Lennon Mental Ability Test | + |   |   |   |   | + |   |   |   |   |   | + | + |   |

(*continued*)

**TABLE 4.3    (Continued)**

Column groups: **CATEGORY** = General Intellectual, Specific Academic, Creativity, Leadership, Visual and Performing Arts · **POPULATION** = Advantaged, Disadvantaged · **AGE** = Early Childhood, High School to Adult, Grades 4-8, K-12 · **ID STAGE** = Nomination, Assessment, Evaluation

| INSTRUMENT | General Intellectual | Specific Academic | Creativity | Leadership | Visual and Performing Arts | Advantaged | Disadvantaged | Early Childhood | High School to Adult | Grades 4-8 | K-12 | Nomination | Assessment | Evaluation |
|---|---|---|---|---|---|---|---|---|---|---|---|---|---|---|
| Peabody Individual Achievement Test | | + | | | | + | | | | | + | + | | |
| Pennsylvania Assessment of Creative Tendency | | | + | | | + | | + | + | | | + | | |
| Piers-Harris Children's Self-Concept Scale | | | | | | + | | + | + | | | + | | |
| Preschool Talent Checklist | + | + | + | + | + | + | + | + | | | | + | | |
| Primary Measure of Music Audiation | | | | + | + | + | + | | | | | + | | |
| Progressive Matrices — Advanced | + | | | | | + | | | | + | | + | | |
| Progressive Matrices — Standard | + | | | | | + | | | | | | + | | |
| Remote Associates Test | | | | | | + | | + | | | | + | + | |
| Ross Test of Higher Cognitive Processes | + | | | | | + | | + | | | | + | + | + |
| Scales for Rating Behavioral Characteristics of Superior Students | + | | + | + | + | + | + | | | + | | + | | |
| Seashore Measure of Musical Talents | | | | + | + | + | | + | + | | | + | | |
| The Self-Concept and Motivation Inventory (SCAMIN) | | | | | + | + | + | + | + | | | + | | |
| Sequential Tests of Educational Progress (STEP) | | + | | | | + | + | + | + | | | + | + | + |
| Short Form Test of Academic Aptitude | + | + | | | | + | + | + | + | | | + | | |
| Slosson Intelligence Test | + | | | | | + | + | + | + | | | + | | |
| SOI Gifted Screening Form | | + | + | | + | + | + | + | + | | | + | + | |
| SOI Learning Abilities Test | | + | + | | + | + | + | + | + | | | + | + | |
| SRA Achievement Series | | + | | | | + | | | | | + | + | + | |
| Stallings' Environmentally Based Screen | + | | | | | | | + | + | | | + | | |
| Stanford Achievement Test | | + | | | | + | | + | + | + | | + | + | |
| Stanford-Binet Intelligence Scale | + | | | | | + | | + | + | + | | + | | |
| System of Multicultural Pluralistic Assessment (SOMPA) | + | | | | | | + | + | | | | + | | |
| Tennessee Self-Concept Scale | | | | | | + | | + | + | | | + | | |
| Test of Creative Potential | | | + | | | + | + | + | | | | + | + | + |
| Tests of Achievement and Proficiency | | + | | | | + | | | | | | + | + | |
| Torrance Test of Creative Thinking — Verbal | | | + | | | + | | + | | | | | | |
| Torrance Test of Creative Thinking | | | + | | | + | | + | | | + | + | + | |
| Torrance Test of Creative Thinking — Figural | | | | | | | | | | | + | + | + | |
| Vane Kindergarten Test | + | + | | | | + | | | | | | + | + | |
| Watson-Glaser Critical Thinking Appraisal | + | | | | | + | | + | + | | | + | + | + |
| Wechsler Intelligence Scale for Children Revised (WISC-R) | + | | | | | + | + | + | + | | | + | | |
| Weschler Preschool and Primary Scale of Intelligence | + | | | | | + | | + | | | | + | | |

Reprinted by permission of Dr. E. Susanne Richert, Education Information and Resource Center, Sewell, NJ and *Roeper Review*.

**TABLE 4.4**   Gifted Constructs and Sample Tests

| Gifted Construct | Sample Tests |
| --- | --- |
| General academic ability | California Achievement Test (CAT), Kaufman Assessment Battery |
| Specific academic ability | Gifted Evaluation Scale, Woodcock Reading Mastery Test |
| General intellectual ability | CAT, WISC-R, Woodcock Reading Mastery Test-Revised |
| Nonverbal intelligence/ability | Raven's Standard Progressive Matrices, Matrix Analogies Test |
| Information processing | Cognitive Abilities Test |
| Perception/judgment and perceptive reasoning | Myers-Briggs Type Indicator, Ravens Colored Progressive Matrices |
| Science ability/scientific aptitude | CAT, Comprehensive Test of Basic Skills |
| Creativity: | |
| Ideation | Torrance Tests of Creative Thinking (TTCT), Group Inventory for Finding Talent (GIFT), Group Inventory for Finding Interests (GIFFI), Scales for Rating the Behavior Characteristics of Superior Students (SRBCSS)—Creativity. |
| Problem solving | Cornell Critical Thinking Tests, TTCT, GIFT, GIFFI |
| Products | TTCT, WISC-R, GIFT, GIFFI |
| Traits and behaviors | GIFT, GIFFI, SRBCSS |
| General | SRBCSS—Creativity, Raven's Standard Matrices |
| Other problem solving | Raven's Colored Progressive Matrices |
| Math/logical ability | CAT, WISC-R, Peabody Individual Achievement Test |
| Verbal/linguistic ability | CAT, Diagnostic Reading Scales, Gates-MacGinite |
| Reading comprehension | Gilmore Oral Reading Test |
| Social science ability | CAT, Slossen Intelligence Test |
| Psychomotor/bodily-kinesthetic | Cognitive Abilities Test |
| Task commitment/motivation | SRBCSS-Motivation, Raven's Standard Matrices, Self-Concept and Motivation |
| Inter/intrapersonal ability/ leadership, psychosocial ability | Gifted Evaluation Scale, Leadership Skills Inventory, Personality Research Form |
| Artistic ability | Slossen Intelligence Test |
| Acting ability | Scales for Rating the Behavior Characteristics of Superior Students (SRBCSS)—Dramatics |
| Dance ability | SRBCSS—Artistic, TTCT |
| Other performing arts ability | Gifted Evaluation Scale, SRBCSS—Dramatics |
| Painting/drawing | SRBCSS—Artistic, Gifted Evaluation Scale, GIFT, GIFFI, TTCT |
| Sculpting ability | SRBCSS—Artistic, TTCT |
| Photographic ability | SRBCSS—Artistic, TTCT |
| Other visual arts ability | SRBCSS—Dramatics, TTCT, Gifted Evaluation Scale |
| Music ability—general | Primary Measures of Music Audiation, GIFT, GIFFI |
| Music ability (composition, instrumental, or vocal) | Cognitive Abilities Test, TTCT, Watson-Glaser Critical Thinking Appraisal |
| Clinical maladjustment (!) | Self-Perception Inventory |

Adapted from Callahan et al., 1995a.

Using multiple identification criteria promotes inclusiveness by identifying multiple types of gifts and talents. The strategy will identify more minority, poor, and underachieving students. "Multiple hurdle' approaches, however, are restrictive.

Davidson argued against formal identification systems involving tests, ratings, and nominations, including point systems and cutoff scores. She recommended, especially, the increased use of informal parent and teacher nominations based on observations.

Another issue concerns the annual selection of 3 to 5 percent versus a more flexible and generous 15 to 20 percent talent pool approach.

Multidimensional criteria and a quota system will insure representation of disadvantaged and minority students. To insure equitable representation, Richert recommended creating local norms for each subgroup of students for each data source, then selecting the same top percentage from each subgroup. Gifted students who underachieve or have a disability must not be overlooked. Girls may be discriminated against if math, science, and computer skills are weighted heavily.

Teachers may favor "teacher pleasers," ignoring more gifted students with less agreeable habits.

Reliability refers to the accuracy of a test (or procedure) or the test-retest consistency. Validity is the degree to which the instrument measures what it is supposed to measure.

"Political" problems occur when parents complain of their child's nonselection (or selection) for a gifted program, or when the children of teachers, administrators, or board members are favored.

The 1982 *National Report on Identification* endorsed the U.S. Department of Education multidimensional definition of giftedness. It recommended that identification procedures be equitable, designed in the best interests of all students, and designed to identify as many gifted learners as possible. The report identified questionable practices such as limiting selection to high-achieving students. The report recommended using both formal and informal procedures.

The Stanford-Binet Form LM, which produces a single IQ score, is preferred over the newer fourth edition, which has a reduced upper limit and IQ scores tend to be lower.

The WISC-R and the newer WISC-III produce Verbal, Performance, and Full-Scale IQ scores. Both tests have an upper limit; and IQ scores run lower for the WISC-III.

Group intelligence tests are useful but suffer from lower reliability and validity, lower ceilings, and high verbal content.

The SAT I (and occasionally the ACT Assessment or the Spatial Test Battery) are used to identify bright seventh graders for Talent Search programs. The newer elementary Talent Search programs use the SSAT or the PLUS tests of academic ability.

Any intelligence (aptitude) test will help identify underachieving students. Undue weight on intelligence scores will exclude students with other gifts. Ability tests may be unstable in childhood years, but highly accurate in the middle years of schooling.

Achievement tests are good indicators of specific academic talent. However, they tend to have relatively low ceilings and therefore will not discriminate among gifted students who "top out." Grade equivalent scores do not mean that the student belongs in the grade indicated by the score.

Creativity tests may identify creative talent that is not otherwise visible. Among divergent thinking tests, the Torrance Tests of Creativity seem most useful. With personality/biographical inventories, the GIFT, GIFFI, and PRIDE tests work quite well. Assessments of actual creative activities may be a face-valid reflection of creative capability. Using two criteria of creativeness is recommended.

Teacher nomination is the most common identification method, but may be subject to "teacher pleaser" bias. Teachers may be trained regarding characteristics of giftedness. Nomination forms are helpful.

Parents can provide valuable and valid information for identification. However, parents may exaggerate or underestimate their child's abilities.

Peer nominations also are valuable and may be

especially helpful in identifying minority, disabled, and rural gifted students. Three considerations are the characteristic you wish evaluated, grade level, and the style of the nomination questions (direct, disguised, or game). Warning: Students may pick friends.

Self-nominations are highly recommended, especially at the high school level.

Product evaluations may be informal or use structured evaluation forms.

Renzulli's most widely used rating scales allow a teacher to rate intellectual ability, creativity, motivation, and leadership.

The Gifted Evaluation Scale focuses on the five categories of the federal definition of giftedness, plus motivation.

Rimm's AIM and GAIM may be used to identify underachievement patterns.

The *Baldwin Identification Matrix* summarizes scores and ratings on a variety of criteria, combining them into a single total score. Such a procedure risks overlooking students with strength in one or a few categories.

Frasier's F-TAP is based on 10 traits of gifted students, summarized in her *Panning for Gold* component and the F-TAP profile, which includes objective and subjective data.

Gardner recommends informally evaluating his eight intelligences, for example, while observing students in a children's museum.

Maker's DISCOVER is a performance-based evaluation that defines giftedness as problem solving. Five tests evaluate Gardner's spatial, logical-mathematical, and linguistic intelligences: Pablo, Tangrams, storytelling, story writing, and math problems. Research with Navajo and Mexican-American children identified 23 percent as gifted.

Sternberg created a battery that includes multiple-choice and essay questions to evaluate his analytic, creative, and practical types of intelligence.

Clasen, Middleton, and Connel created a culture-fair assessment strategy that used brainstorming, an art task, peer nominations, and teacher nominations. They identified minority and majority students in proportion to their numbers in the school.

Renzulli's talent pool identification plan features five steps: (1) test score nominations (to identify 50 percent of the talent pool), (2) teacher nominations, (3) alternate pathways (e.g., self, parent, or peer nominations, creativity tests, etc.), and two "safety valves" of (4) special nominations by previous and other teachers, and (5) action information nominations. Some advantages are that more students participate, identification is multidimensional, students can self-select, and charges of elitism are reduced.

A three-step model for identifying gifted preschoolers included raising parents' and preschool teachers' awareness of characteristics of preschool giftedness, a general screening, and intelligence testing.

PLAN, which evaluates high-level thinking skills, was introduced by American College Testing to permit tenth graders to plan their high school program. While Colangelo et al. explored other goals, they concluded that PLAN can be used to identify exceptional academic performers.

Feldhusen's strategy for evaluation at the secondary level included his *Purdue Academic Rating Scales* and his *Purdue Vocational Rating Scales,* which are more specific than lower-level, general scales. The scales should be used with other information, and teachers should be trained in their use.

In high school, self-selection is more important than in earlier grades.

The *National Report on Identification* includes a list of sixty instruments, with specifications for each test of the categories of giftedness assessed, appropriateness for advantaged and disadvantaged children, suitable age range, and appropriate stage in the G/T program.

Callahan et al. (1995a) evaluated 73 possible identification instruments.

Identification procedures are critical. In every program, they define who is and is not "gifted." Identification should be flexible and fair, which is aided by multiple identification criteria.

## APPENDIX 4.1     TEACHER NOMINATION FORM

1.  Student _____ Teacher _____

2.  Date of Referral _____ School _____

3.  Grade _____ Date of Birth _____

4.  Average Grades for Current School Year

    Language Arts _____

    Social Studies _____

    Arithmetic _____

    Science _____

5.  Parent Nomination (Check if appropriate): _____

6.  SRBCSS Scale Total _____ 1. _____ 2. _____ 3. _____ 4. _____

7.  Why do you think this student should be included in the Talent Pool? (You may wish to list examples of ideas, projects, creative endeavors, etc.)

    _____

    _____

    _____

    _____

    _____

### INTERESTS

Please indicate the areas of interest that the student has displayed in your class this year. If you've noticed other specific topics (interest in dinosaurs, computers, etc.), please note this in the column entitled "Other."

|  | HIGH | AVERAGE | LOW |  | HIGH | AVERAGE | LOW |
|---|---|---|---|---|---|---|---|
| Fine Arts/Crafts |  |  |  | Music |  |  |  |
| Science |  |  |  | Drama |  |  |  |
| Creative Writing |  |  |  | Mathematics |  |  |  |
| Social Studies |  |  |  | Language Arts |  |  |  |
| Psychomotor |  |  |  | Other |  |  |  |

### CURRICULAR STRENGTH AREAS

Please indicate the curricular areas in which the student has demonstrated proficiency and could possibly be considered for curriculum compacting.

Language Arts _____     Mathematics _____

Science _____     Social Science _____

Reprinted by permission of J.S. Renzulli.

**APPENDIX 4.2   SPANISH EDITION OF RIMM'S (1976)
GIFT CREATIVITY INVENTORY**

# PRENDA

## PRUEBA POR ENCONTRAR
## DADIVOSA HABILIDAD

Lee cada frase en las páginas siguientes. Pon un círculo alrededor de SÍ al lado de cada frase, si estás de acuerdo; o alrededor de NO, si no estás de acuerdo. Si no estás seguro o si crees que algunas veces estás de acuerdo, haz un círculo alrededor de la contestación que esté más cerca de la manera en que tú piensas. Esta prueba no tiene contestaciones correctas o incorrectas. Queremos saber sólo como tú piensas, qué crees tú de ciertas cosas, y qué te gusta hacer.

1. A mí me gusta componer mis propias canciones.    SÍ    NO
   (I like to make up my own songs.)

2. A mí me gusta pasear solo.    SÍ    NO
   (I like to take walks alone.)

3. A mi madre o a mi padre le gusta jugar conmigo.    SÍ    NO
   (My mom or dad likes to play with me.)

4. Me gusta hacer muchas preguntas.    SÍ    NO
   (I ask a lot of questions.)

5. Es una pérdida de tiempo hacer cuentos.    SÍ    NO
   (Making up stories is a waste of time.)

6. A mí me gusta tener solamente uno o dos amigos.    SÍ    NO
   (I like to have only one or two friends.)

7. A mí me gusta oîr historias de la vida de otros países.    SÍ    NO
   (I like to hear stories about life in other countries.)

8. Algunas veces está bien cambiar las reglas de un juego.    SÍ    NO
   (It's all right to sometimes change the rules of a game.)

9. Tengo algunas ideas muy buenas.    SÍ    NO
   (I have some really good ideas.)

10. A mí me gusta pintar retratos.    SÍ    NO
    (I like to paint pictures.)

P. 1 of Elementary Level Grades 3–4. Complete test is 34 items.

**APPENDIX 4.3   SAMPLE PARENT NOMINATION FORM AT THE EARLY CHILDHOOD LEVEL**

Name of Student _____ Age _____

Address _____ School_____ Grade ___

Parent's Name _____

Instructions:  In relationship to the typical child in your neighborhood, please circle a number for each item which best describes your child: 5—has this trait to a high degree; 4—has this trait more than the typical child; 3—compares with the typical child; 2—has this trait less than the typical child; 1—lacks this trait.

1.  Has advanced vocabulary, expresses himself or herself well ........................................ 5  4  3  2  1

2.  Thinks quickly ...................................... 5  4  3  2  1

3.  Recalls facts easily ................................ 5  4  3  2  1

4.  Wants to know how things work ....................... 5  4  3  2  1

5.  Is reading (before he/she started kindergarten) ..... 5  4  3  2  1

6.  Puts unrelated ideas together in new and different ways .................................................. 5  4  3  2  1

7.  Becomes bored easily ................................ 5  4  3  2  1

8.  Asks reasons why — questions almost everything ...... 5  4  3  2  1

9.  Likes "grown-up" things and to be with older people   5  4  3  2  1

10.  Has a great deal of curiosity ...................... 5  4  3  2  1

11.  Is adventurous ..................................... 5  4  3  2  1

12.  Has a good sense of humor .......................... 5  4  3  2  1

13.  Is impulsive, acts before he/she thinks ............ 5  4  3  2  1

14.  Tends to dominate others if given the chance ....... 5  4  3  2  1

15.  Is persistent, sticks to a task ................... 5  4  3  2  1

16.  Has good physical coordination and body control ... 5  4  3  2  1

17.  Is independent and self-sufficient in looking after himself/herself ............................... 5  4  3  2  1

18.  Is aware of his/her surroundings and what is going on around him/her .................................... 5  4  3  2  1

19.  Has a long attention span .......................... 5  4  3  2  1

20.  Wanted to do things for himself/herself early — example:  dressing and feeding himself/herself .... 5  4  3  2  1

Developed by the Staff of the Gifted and Talented Section, Division of Exceptional Children, North Carolina Department of Public Instruction. This instrument is part of an identification model developed by Cornelia Tongue and Charmian Sperling, 1976. Reprinted by permission.

**APPENDIX 4.4   WHO'S WHO—PEER NOMINATION FORM**

Think about your classmates. Everyone is different! Read the questions below. In each space write the name of a classmate who best fits the description. You may write a name more than once and you may write your own name where you feel it fits.

1. If you were forming a committee to work on a project, whom would you choose to lead it?
   Language arts _____     Math _____
   Science _____     Social Studies _____
   Art _____     Other _____

2. If you need somebody to help you with your homework, which one of your classmates would you ask?
   _____

3. If your class was on a trip and became separated from the teacher, which one of your classmates would lead you back safely?
   _____

4. Whose stories do you enjoy listening to?
   _____

5. Who is the most exciting person in class?
   _____

6. Who has the best ideas for games and activities in and out of school?
   _____

7. Who is the best problem solver?
   _____

8. Who is the best person to tell a story to?
   _____

9. Who is the best reader?
   _____

10. Who is the best writer?
    _____

11. Who likes to try new things?
    _____

12. Who uses good judgment?
    _____

13. Who would be a good friend?
    _____

14. Who has a good imagination?
    _____

15. Who has many interests?
    _____

Name _____
School _____
Date _____

From Eisenberg and Epstein (1982). Reprinted by permission.

## APPENDIX 4.5   STUDENT PRODUCT ASSESSMENT FORM

Name(s) _____     Date _____

School _____     District _____

Teacher _____     Grade _____

Product (Title and/or Brief Description) _____

_____

Number of Months Student(s) worked on Product _____

| FACTORS | RATING | NOT APPLICABLE |
|---|---|---|
| **1.** Early Statement of Purpose | _____ | _____ |
| **2.** Problem Focusing | _____ | _____ |
| **3.** Level of Resources | _____ | _____ |
| **4.** Diversity of Resources | _____ | _____ |
| **5.** Appropriateness of Resources | _____ | _____ |
| **6.** Logic, Sequence, and Transition | _____ | _____ |
| **7.** Action Orientation | _____ | _____ |
| **8.** Audience | _____ | _____ |
| **9.** Overall Assessment | _____ | |
|    **A.** Originality of the Idea | _____ | |
|    **B.** Achieved Objectives Stated in Plan | _____ | |
|    **C.** Achieved Familiarity with Subject | _____ | |
|    **D.** Quality Beyond Age/Grade Level | _____ | |
|    **E.** Care, Attention to Detail, etc. | _____ | |
|    **F.** Time, Effort, Energy | _____ | |
|    **G.** Origional Contribution | _____ | |

Comments _____

Person completing this form _____

| Rating Scales | Items 1–8 | Items 9A–9G |
|---|---|---|
| | **1**—To a limited extent | **1**—Poor |
| | **3**—Somewhat | **2**—Below average |
| | **5**—To a great extent | **3**—Average |
| | | **4**—Above average |
| | | **5**—Outstanding |

**APPENDIX 4.6   SCALES FOR RATING BEHAVIORAL CHARACTERISTICS OF SUPERIOR STUDENTS**

Name_____   Date_____

School_____   Grade_____ Age_____
                                                    Yrs.   Mos.
Teacher or person completing this form_____

How long have you known this child?  _____months

DIRECTIONS:  These scales are designed to obtain teacher estimates of a student's characteristics in the areas of learning, motivation, crea- tivity, and leadership.  The items are derived from the research li- terature dealing with characteristics of gifted and creative persons. It should be pointed out that a considerable amount of individual dif- ferences can be found within this population; therefore, the profiles are likely to vary a great deal.  Each item in the scales should be considered separately and should reflect the degree to which you have observed the presence or absence of each characteristic.  Since the four dimensions of the instrument represent relatively different sets of behaviors, <u>the scores obtained from the separate scales should not be summed to yield a total score</u>.  Please read the statements carefully and place an X in the appropriate place according to the following scale of values.

1. If you have <u>seldom</u> or <u>never</u> observed this characteristic
2. If you have observed this characteristic <u>occasionally</u>
3. If you have observed this characteristic to a <u>considerable</u> degree
4. If you have observed this characteristic <u>almost all of the time</u>

Space has been provided following each item for your comments.

SCORING:  Separate scores for each of the four dimensions may be obtained as follows:

<u>Add</u> the total number of Xs in each column to obtain the "Column Total."
<u>Multiply</u> the Column Total by the "Weight" for each column to obtain the "Weighted Column Total."
<u>Sum</u> the Weighted Column Totals across to obtain the "Score" for each dimension of the scale.
<u>Enter</u> the Scores below.

            Learning Characteristics    _____
      Motivational Characteristics    _____
         Creativity Characteristics    _____
         Leadership Characteristics    _____

Reprinted by permission of Creative Learning Press.                    (*continued*)

**APPENDIX 4.6    (Continued)**

PART I:   LEARNING CHARACTERISTICS

| | 1* | 2 | 3 | 4 |
|---|---|---|---|---|
| 1.  Has unusually advanced vocabulary for age or grade level; uses terms in a meaningful way; has verbal behavior characterized by "richness" of expression, elaboration, and fluency. | | | | |
| 2.  Possesses a large storehouse of information about a variety of topics (beyond the usual interests of youngsters his or her age). | | | | |
| 3.  Has quick mastery and recall of factual information. | | | | |
| 4.  Has rapid insight into cause-effect relationships; tries to discover the how and why of things; asks many provocative questions (as distinct from information or factual questions); wants to know what makes things (or people) "tick." | | | | |
| 5.  Has a ready grasp of underlying principles and can quickly make valid generalizations about events, people, or things; looks for similarities and differences in events, people, and things. | | | | |
| 6.  Is a keen and alert observer; usually "sees more" or "gets more" out of a story, film, etc., than others. | | | | |
| 7.  Reads a great deal on his or her own; usually prefers adult-level books; does not avoid difficult material; may show a preference for biography, autobiography, encyclopedias, and atlases. | | | | |
| 8.  Tries to understand complicated material by separating it into its respective parts; reasons things out for himself or herself; sees logical and common sense answers. | | | | |
| Column Total | | | | |
| Weight | 1 | 2 | 3 | 4 |
| Weighted Column Total | | | | |
| TOTAL | | | | |

_____

\* 1—Seldom or never
 2—Occasionally
 3—Considerably
 4—Almost always

**APPENDIX 4.6**   **(Continued)**

PART II:  MOTIVATIONAL CHARACTERISTICS

|  | 1 | 2 | 3 | 4 |
|---|---|---|---|---|

1. Becomes absorbed and truly involved in certain topics or problems; is persistent in seeking task completion. (It is some-times difficult to get him or her to move on to another topic.)

2. Is easily bored with routine tasks.

3. Needs little external motivation to follow through in work that initially excites him or her.

4. Strives toward perfection; is self-critical; is not easily satisfied with his or her own speed or products.

5. Prefers to work independently; requires little direction from teachers.

6. Is interested in many "adult" problems such as religion, politics, sex, race — more than usual for age level.

7. Often is self-assertive (sometimes even aggressive); stubborn in his or her beliefs.

8. Likes to organize and bring structure to things, people, and situations.

9. Is quite concerned with right and wrong, good and bad; often evaluates and passes judgment on events, people, and things.

| | 1 | 2 | 3 | 4 |
|---|---|---|---|---|
| Column Total | | | | |
| Weight | 1 | 2 | 3 | 4 |
| Weighted Column Total | | | | |
| TOTAL | | | | |

**APPENDIX 4.6   (Continued)**

| PART III:   CREATIVITY CHARACTERISTICS | 1 | 2 | 3 | 4 |
|---|---|---|---|---|
| 1. Displays a great deal of curiosity about many things; is constantly asking questions about anything and everything. | | | | |
| 2. Generates a large number of ideas or solutions to problems and questions; often offers unusual ("way out"), unique, clever responses. | | | | |
| 3. Is uninhibited in expressing opinion; is sometimes radical and spirited in disagreement; is tenacious. | | | | |
| 4. Is a high risk taker; is adventurous and speculative. | | | | |
| 5. Displays a good deal of intellectual playfulness; fantasizes; imagines ("I wonder what would happen if ..."); manipulates ideas (i.e., changes, elaborates upon them); is often concerned with adapting, improving, and modifying institutions, objects, and systems. | | | | |
| 6. Displays a keen sense of humor and sees humor in situations that may not appear to be humorous to others. | | | | |
| 7. Is unusually aware of his or her impulses and more open to the irrational in himself or herself (freer expression of feminine interest for boys, greater than usual amount of independence for girls); shows emotional sensitivity. | | | | |
| 8. Is sensitive to beauty; attends to aesthetic characteristics of things. | | | | |
| 9. Is nonconforming; accepts disorder; is not interested in details; is individualistic; does not fear being different. | | | | |
| 10. Criticizes constructively; is unwilling to accept authoritarian pronouncements without critical examination. | | | | |
| Column Total | | | | |
| Weight | 1 | 2 | 3 | 4 |
| Weighted Column Total | | | | |
| TOTAL | | | | |

**APPENDIX 4.6   (Continued)**

| PART IV:   LEADERSHIP CHARACTERISTICS | 1 | 2 | 3 | 4 |
|---|---|---|---|---|
| 1.  Carries responsibility well; can be counted on to do what he or she has promised and usually does it well. | | | | |
| 2.  Is self-confident with children his or her own age as well as adults; seems comfortable when asked to show his or her work to the class. | | | | |
| 3.  Seems to be well-liked by classmates. | | | | |
| 4.  Is cooperative with teacher and classmates; tends to avoid bickering and is generally easy to get along with. | | | | |
| 5.  Can express himself or herself well; has good verbal facility and is usually well understood. | | | | |
| 6.  Adapts readily to new situations; is flexible in thought and action and does not seem disturbed when the normal routine is changed. | | | | |
| 7.  Seems to enjoy being around other people; is sociable and prefers not to be alone. | | | | |
| 8.  Tends to dominate others when they are around; generally directs the activity in which he or she is involved. | | | | |
| 9.  Participates in most social activities connected with the school; can be counted on to be there if anyone is. | | | | |
| 10.  Excels in athletic activities; is well-coordinated and enjoys all sorts of athletic games. | | | | |
| Column Total | | | | |
| Weight | 1 | 2 | 3 | 4 |
| Weighted Column Total | | | | |
| TOTAL | | | | |

# CHAPTER 5

# ACCELERATION

*The pacing of educational programs must be responsive to the capacities and knowledge of individual children.*
Camilla P. Benbow (1991, p. 157)

*Gifted and talented students, like all students, have the right to a continuity of educational experience that meets their present and future academic needs.*
Joyce VanTassel-Baska (2003, p. 174)

This and many of the following chapters describe strategies and models that guide programming decisions, teaching strategies, and curriculum content. To provide a framework for "what to do with gifted and talented kids," Table 5.1 summarizes suggestions for program content based upon student needs. These were integrated from the lists prepared by Feldhusen, Hansen, and Kennedy (1989), Ganapole (1989), Kaplan, (1974), Pyryt (2003), Renzulli (2003), Smith (1990), VanTassel-Baska (2003), Winebrenner (2001), Davis (1998), and Davis and Rimm (1985). The table includes suggestions for acceleration, enrichment, and counseling. Read through Table 5.1 before proceeding. You likely will refer back to this table as you read the following chapters.

There are many types of programs and services designed to fit the needs summarized in Table 5.1, while at the same time accommodating the level of interest, commitment, and resources of the particular school or district. Programs may differ in (1) the categories of students served, (2) program goals, (3) the general program models(s) followed, (4) acceleration plans, (5) enrichment plans, (6) grouping and organizational arrangements, (7) instructional or delivery strategy used, (8) community professionals and resources involved, and (9) program level (classroom, school, district, state, or national; Fox, 1979).

## Overview

We will divide programming into four topics. This chapter will summarize characteristics, advantages, disadvantages, and recommendations related to a number of *acceleration* strategies. Chapter 6 will focus on *enrichment* and *grouping* options. Chapter 7 will summarize several main *curriculum models*. The topics are interrelated in the sense that grouping is for the purpose of enrichment or acceleration; enrichment and acceleration invariably include elements of the other; and program models prescribe the kinds of learning activities and grouping needed for enrichment and/or acceleration opportunities. Together, these four topics help clarify what can be done in successful programs and provide ideas for how to do it.

## ACCELERATION VERSUS ENRICHMENT

One issue pertains to the definitions of and relationships between *acceleration* and *enrichment,* a matter that some see as a passionate controversy. For example, Stanley and Benbow (1986) referred to most kinds of enrichment as "busywork and irrelevant." In contrast, Frost (1981) pointed out that enrichment "implies a supplementation of the depth, breadth, or intensity of content and

**TABLE 5.1**   Curriculum for the Gifted

1. Maximum achievement in basic skills
   A. Learning activities at an appropriate level and pace
   B. Advanced content or skills; extension of depth or breadth of the content
   C. Based on student needs and readiness, not grade-level appropriateness
   D. Oral communication skills; sharing ideas verbally and in depth
   E. Study skills, report writing, outlining
2. Content beyond the prescribed curriculum
   A. Extends or replaces traditional curriculum, not just "more work"
   B. Content related to broad-based issues, themes, and problems
   C. Resources beyond the designated grade-level—materials, equipment, information (not just books)
   D. Learning that is interrelated with other areas, not "separate entity learning"
3. Exposure to a variety of fields of study
   A. Opportunity for in-depth study of major ideas, problems, and themes from multiple disciplines
   B. New disciplines; interrelatedness of disciplines; connections of major ideas and concepts within and between disciplines
   C. Various occupations—the arts, professions
   D. Access to and stimulation of reading
4. Student-selected content
   A. Based on student interests and needs
   B. In-depth learning of a self-selected topic within an area of study
   C. Freedom to select from a wide range of materials and resources
   D. Opportunity to pursue areas of inquiry as far as personal interest dictates
5. High content complexity
   A. Working with abstract ideas and theories that require reflective, evaluative, critical, and creative thinking
   B. Working with concepts and generalizations, not just names, dates, facts, and figures
   C. Applying learning, not just parroting it
   D. Developing products that challenge existing ideas and produce "new" ideas
   E. Developing products that use new techniques, materials, and forms
   F. Exposure to varied ideas, topics, issues, and skills at rates appropriate to individual capabilities
6. Experience in creative thinking and problem solving (see Chapters 10 and 11)
   A. Opportunities for creative expression and creative products
   B. Creative writing that stresses free flow of ideas and developing values
   C. Involvement in art and drama; literature enrichment
   D. Learning creative attitudes and awarenesses
   E. Responding to open-ended problems and tasks
   F. Understanding creative people, processes, techniques
   G. Strengthening fluency, flexibility, originality, visualization, analogical thinking, problem finding, and other creative abilities
   H. Discovery and inquiry skills
   I. Freedom to solve problems in diverse ways
   J. Reconceptualizing existing knowledge; generating new knowledge

*(continued)*

**TABLE 5.1** (Continued)

K. Futuristic thinking
L. Learning things as they should be or could be, not only as they are
7. Development of thinking skills (see Chapter 11)
  A. Independent, self-directed study skills
  B. Library skills
  C. Research/scientific skills and methods
  D. Bloom's higher-level skills: application, analysis, synthesis, evaluation
  E. Critical thinking, in the sense of evaluating biases, credibility, logic, consistency; critical reading and listening skills
  F. Decision making, planning, organizing
  G. Developing expert processing strategies—skills and techniques of a professional in a given field
8. Development of computer skills
  A. Keyboard and word processing skills
  B. Finding enrichment and acceleration information on the Internet
  C. Using email and the Internet for correspondence with mentors and models
9. Affective development
  A. Developing self-awareness and self-understanding; accepting one's capabilities, interests, and needs
  B. Recognizing and using one's abilities
  C. Appreciating likenesses and differences between oneself and others
  D. Relating intellectually, artistically, and effectively with other gifted, talented, creative students
  E. Moral and ethical thinking; humanitarian attitudes; building "social capital"— creating values and norms geared toward the greater public good
10. Development of motivation
  A. Independent thinking and work
  B. Becoming self-directed, disciplined in learning
  C. Achievement motivation; internal locus of control; high-level educational and career aspirations

---

process as appropriate to the students' abilities and needs . . . [and is the prevailing practice because] . . . of the diversity in meeting student needs."

### Defining Acceleration and Enrichment

On the surface, the distinction between acceleration and enrichment seems simple enough. Acceleration implies moving faster through academic content, which typically includes offering standard curriculum to students at a younger-than-usual age. Enrichment refers to richer and more varied educational experiences, a curriculum that is modified to provide greater depth and breadth than is generally provided. Both acceleration and enrichment accommodate the high abilities and individual needs of gifted students, both lead to greater knowledge and skills, and both help develop creativity and other thinking skills.

Looking closely, the terms *acceleration* and *enrichment* are in fact used in overlapping and ambiguous ways. Note that any enrichment experience will involve greater depth or new topics, which in a sense are advanced or accelerated compared with the regular curriculum. It is common and acceptable for teachers and others to refer to any variety of advanced subject matter as "acceleration."

We will use a rule-of-thumb definition (suggested by Fox, 1979) that permits a reasonably clear distinction between acceleration plans versus enrichment plans: Any strategy that results in advanced placement or credit may be titled *acceleration*; strategies that supplement or go beyond standard grade-level work but do not result in advanced placement or credit (that is, anything else) may be called *enrichment*. Thus the special foreign language, math, or science material taught in elementary school and the special high school drama or photography class that does not result in advanced credit or standing would be enrichment. However, if a four-year-old is admitted early to kindergarten, another elementary student skips third grade, a junior high school algebra class condenses three years work into two, or a high school student "tests out of a course," earns college credit, or enters college early, these are acceleration. See Inset 5.1.

---

**INSET 5.1**

### Benefits of Acceleration: Academic, Psychological, and Social

Karen Rogers (1991) evaluated academic, psychological, and social effects of acceleration at elementary and secondary levels with a "best evidence synthesis" (meta-analysis) of the results of 314 studies that evaluated these 12 procedures:

| | |
|---|---|
| Early entrance | Grade skipping |
| Non-graded classes | Curriculum compacting |
| Grade telescoping | Concurrent enrollment (e.g., in high |
| Subject acceleration |    school and college) |
| Mentorships | Advanced Placement (AP) courses |
| Credit by examination | Early admission to college |
| Combinations of two options | |

Two blanket conclusions were that "No form of acceleration led to decreases in any area of performance—academic, social, or emotional" and "There appear to be generally positive academic effects for most forms of acceleration."

Her criterion of a "practically significant" academic benefit was an achievement advantage of accelerated students of at least one-third year over non-accelerated control students. All acceleration strategies produced a significant academic benefit, except concurrent enrollment, AP courses (nearly significant), and combinations of two options. Further, significant academic benefits occurred at all four grade levels, primary (grades K–2), intermediate (3–6), junior high (7–9), and senior high (10–12).

None of the accelerative options damaged either socialization or psychological adjustment. In fact, grade skipping and credit by examination *aided* social relations as well as academic achievement; and concurrent enrollment and mentorships *aided* psychological adjustment in the form of improved self-concepts.

Rogers recommended these acceleration options as the most beneficial at different age levels:

*Elementary children*: Early entrance, grade skipping, nongraded classes, and curriculum compacting.

*Junior high students*: Grade skipping, grade telescoping, concurrent enrollment, subject acceleration, and curriculum compacting.

*Senior high students*: Concurrent enrollment, subject acceleration, AP classes, mentorships, credit by examination, and early admission to college

Any well-rounded, coherent and long-range gifted and talented program will provide both enrichment and acceleration opportunities. Gifted students should be permitted to work at their own rapid pace, accelerating through and out of primary and secondary schools. They also should have opportunities for greater variety in content, greater depth, and the development of affective, creative, scientific, and other high-level skills, that is, enrichment.

## EARLY ADMISSION TO KINDERGARTEN OR FIRST GRADE

Early admission to kindergarten or first grade is an acceleration strategy that accommodates gifted children's high energy, enthusiasm, curiosity, imagination, and their intellectual needs to investigate, observe, and examine (Feldhusen, 1992). Without it, the gifted child will underachieve. Also, early admission is the least administratively disruptive option for gifted children, it avoids discontinuities in the curriculum, and it presents a relatively easy way to "match the child to the system" (Robinson and Weimer, 1991, p. 29). Nonetheless, teachers, principals, and school psychologists express these kinds of concerns about any form of elementary school acceleration (McClusky, Baker, & Masey, 1996; Robinson and Weimer, 1991; Southern, Jones, and Fiscus, 1989):

- Accelerated children will be socially immature—they will not socialize well with older children, will have fewer friends, and will not be happy.
- They will be deprived of necessary childhood experiences.
- They will be involved in fewer extracurricular activities.
- Acceleration will make excessive academic demands, cause stress, and lead to problems of early burnout, rebelliousness, and/or emotional maladjustment.
- Achievement will be low; accelerated children will not do well because of increased academic competition.

- They will miss leadership experiences and not develop leadership skills.
- They will become conceited and arrogant.
- Parents of excluded children will be angry.
- Some parents push their children into early kindergarten admission, whether or not they are ready.

Regarding the latter point, in two remarkable attempts to smuggle children into kindergarten, one parent used white-out and a photocopier to change her child's birth certificate. Another forged a letter—on stolen doctor's stationery—recommending that the child be admitted (McClusky, Baker, & Massey, 1996).

With the critical stipulation that children must be carefully evaluated regarding cognitive, social/emotional, and physical readiness, research supports early admission to kindergarten or first grade. In an early study, Reynolds (1962) compared 550 early entrants with 4000 regular classmates. On average, in elementary school the early entrants performed better academically than their older grade-mates. Hobson (1979) confirmed that their superiority continued through high school, they participated in more extracurricular activities, earned significantly more graduation awards, and were more like to be admitted to college. McClusky, Baker, and Massey (1996) described a Manitoba, Canada, policy of admitting kindergarten children who miss the December 31 cutoff date by one or two months. After parents apply, clinicians evaluate the child's cognitive skills, learning readiness, receptive/expressive language, and the child's interactions and behavior. The authors evaluated the academic success of 54 early admission students of various ages (some were still in school, others had completed college). The academic performance of 80 percent was rated "excellent" or "acceptable"; 20 percent were rated "poor." They recommended a flexible school entry policy for children who need it.

Many other studies of acceleration (or "grouping" with older students) show that the vast majority of early-entering precocious children—who are carefully selected for readiness—adjust at least as well as nonaccelerated gifted control children. Further, their achievement not only is equal to that of others in their grade, it typically is superior (Feldhusen, 1992; Gross, 1999; Kulik, 2003; Proctor, Black, & Feldhusen, 1986; Robinson & Weimer, 1991; see Inset 5.1).

Teachers' negative experiences usually stem from accelerated children who were too immature to function well in their classes. The problem sometimes is that these children were not carefully screened.

One difficulty relates to the finding that highly gifted children often have more social difficulties than other gifted children (e.g., Hollingworth, 1942). However, it is these children who have the greatest need for early admission to kindergarten. Kindergarten and first-grade teachers should allow time for adjustment. Also, highly verbal gifted children may be unaccustomed to sharing adult attention and thus may appear troublesome and immature whether or not they are entered early (Rimm, 1990b). Here is an example:

### Robert

*Robert, an only child, was highly gifted and very verbal. His parents took the advice of the school to hold him back for a year because of his young age and their perception that Robert was immature. Robert waited a year and entered as one of the oldest in his class.*

*Robert brought two backpacks to school for each show and tell. He had learned so much and wanted to share so much. When he was not called on as frequently as he would have liked, he clowned and disrupted the class. Lack of challenge continued to be a problem, although with therapeutic help for Robert, his parents, and teachers Robert's behavior problems disappeared. He was subject accelerated in reading in first grade, but Robert knew he was also ahead in math. The school was not eager to move him ahead because of his earlier behavior problems. Finally, Robert was allowed to skip fourth grade; he was placed with age mates. There will be more need for challenge, but it is obvious to his parents and teachers that this is a better fit for Robert. He likely will need further subject or grade acceleration.*

If Robert had entered school as youngest in his class, his behavior problems likely would have been blamed on his young age. It took time before the problems were correctly associated with his lack of challenge.

How can a school district resolve the differences between the results of multiple research projects and typical teacher impressions? An early admission policy that gives careful consideration to the following variables is likely to select gifted children who will succeed despite their younger age.

***Intellectual Precocity.*** An individual intelligence test score of 130 or more is recommended for early admission (Feldhusen, 1992).

***Eye-hand Coordination.*** Tests of eye-hand coordination should suggest at least average perceptual-motor skill, since problems in this area may put unnecessary stress on the early entrant who must cut, paste, draw, write, and so on.

***Reading and Arithmetic Readiness.*** Reading is the skill most critical to early school success. Test scores should show clear readiness to read. Many gifted children are able to read prior to school entrance. Feldhusen (1992) recommended that for early admission to first grade, the child should demonstrate both reading comprehension and arithmetic reasoning at or above the level of second semester of first grade.

***Social and Emotional Maturity.*** The child should not have serious adjustment problems. Ideally, the child would have adapted readily to preschool experiences, adapted to other group activities, and/or have friends in the grade he or she wishes to enter (Feldhusen, 1992). Development should be evenly advanced in all domains, although uneven development—making decision-making difficult—actually is more common (Robinson & Weimer, 1991). Observations by a psychologist can be helpful in determining school social adjustment.

Perceptions of immaturity may be misleading and biased by the often-held assumption that small children and young children automatically are immature. Here are two examples:

### Timmy

*Based on her observations of his immaturity, Timmy's nursery school teacher recommended that he wait an extra year before entering kindergarten as a young kindergartener. Timmy already was reading beyond first-grade level and doing math beyond second-grade level. The school psychologist tested and found him to be in the very superior range of ability.*

*Timmy's parents asked what the symptoms of his immaturity were. His small size was given as one indicator, and his inability to sit still during story time was another.*

*At the recommendation of the psychologist, Timmy's dad asked him to work hard at sitting still during story hour each day and to report his progress to him each day. After two weeks, Timmy's parents called the teacher who commented on Timmy's jump in maturity.*

*Both of Timmy's parents are small and both have high energy. One specific change in Timmy's behavior made a difference in the teacher's perception of his maturity. He now is in fourth grade and has made excellent adjustment, although he continues to require further academic challenge. He also continues to be short for his age and undoubtedly will never become a professional basketball player.*

### David

*David was tested for early entrance to kindergarten. Academic and intelligence testing showed him to be beyond readiness for first grade. The teacher observed him as shy and somewhat of a loner and thus recommended he not be entered early. Despite the teacher's recommendations, David entered kindergarten.*

*All teachers have indicated excellent adjustment for David. They also comment on his quiet personality. In fifth grade at the time of this writing, David searches for challenge and loves learning. He expresses himself well and has a few good friends. An extra year of nursery school likely would not have changed his quiet personality.*

**Health.**   A child who has a history of good health is more likely to attend school regularly and concentrate on classwork. Frequent health problems combined with a young age may put too much stress on even a very gifted child.

**Gender.**   Although each child must be considered individually, males do mature later than females. Because physical maturity is a consideration, it is not unusual or necessarily unfair for girls to be favored for early admission. At the same time, there is absolutely no research that suggests boys are less successful at early admission or grade skipping.

**School of Entrance.**   The average IQ in some schools may be 120 or 125, while in others the average may be 100 or less. Thus an early-entering child's intellectual ability should be considered relative to the school population. If the school has many very bright children, its regular fare is likely to provide adequate challenge. The gifted child therefore may do just as well by waiting to enter with same-age children.

The openness and flexibility of the school system also are important. If administrators and teachers are opposed, an early entrance may set the child up for failure. A cooperative spirit of partnership among teachers, counselors, and parents will increase success (Robinson & Weimer, 1991).

**The Receiving Teacher.**   Ideally, the child's teacher should favor early admission and be willing to help the child adjust; the child does not need a pessimistic or hostile teacher (Feldhusen, 1992). However, the child should not be forced to wait because of the teacher's early attitudes. Most initially pessimistic teachers change their attitude if a child truly shows readiness.

**Family Values.**   The child who is permitted to enter school early needs the support of a family that values education and academic achievement. For example, if success in team sports is an important family goal, there is high risk of stress for the undersized accelerated boy.

In sum, early entrance to kindergarten or first grade definitely is recommended for gifted children who are carefully screened according to the above criteria. If parents are considering early kindergarten admission for their precocious child, teachers and principals might recommend that they enroll the child in a quality nursery school. The nursery school will provide parents and educators an opportunity to observe the child's social and cognitive adjustment in a school setting. The experience also will foster further skill development and will acquaint the child with social and academic classroom routines. With extraordinarily bright children, Gross (1999) recommended that early entrance to kindergarten or first grade should include some form of ability or achievement grouping. Finally, note that admitting a child early to either kindergarten or first grade is not a rigid, unchangeable decision. In fact, noted Feldhusen (1992, p. 47), "All cases of early admission should be on a trial basis." While Feldhusen recommends a trial period of 6 weeks, Rimm (1992b) found that some children required as much as a semester for a completely smooth adjustment. All students she recommended for early entrance, based on careful screening, adjusted smoothly.

## GRADE-SKIPPING

Grade-skipping is the traditional method of accelerating precocious elementary school students. It requires no special materials or facilities, no G/T coordinator, not even a G/T program. In fact, it is extraordinarily cost-effective in moving the gifted or talented child through and out of the school system ahead of schedule. Grade-skipping may be initiated by parents who are aware that their child is one or two years ahead of the rest of the class, bored with school, and impatient with his or her peers, or by a teacher who makes the same observation. Grade-skipping or "double promotion" usually takes place in the lowest elementary grades, but sometimes in advanced grades. Some gifted children skip two or three grades (occasionally more) and enter college at age 15 or 16. Parents become quite frustrated if their district does not permit grade-skipping; many districts do not.

There are at least two major concerns regarding grade-skipping. The first is the problem of missing critical basic skills. Many teachers feel that if a child is not taught an important math or reading skill, he or she will be at a great disadvantage in later grades. They frequently predict that the child (1) will not be able to maintain good grades, (2) will see himself or herself as less capable, and therefore (3) will lose school motivation. It is true that some skills are absolutely critical to the learning of later skills, and their absence could place stress on the student. However, many gifted students have acquired knowledge and skills far ahead of their grade levels, learned either independently or from an interested parent or older sibling. That is, the "missing skills" may not be missing at all. As a precaution, a series of diagnostic tests for the grade to be skipped can identify missing skills, and the motivated gifted child typically can learn these quickly, either working independently or with the help of interested adults.

The second concern—social adjustment to peers—is even more common. Parents and teachers may be familiar with a gifted child who skipped a grade and experienced social problems or maladjustment. Once again we find a conflict between research conclusions and what many teachers, administrators, and parents claim. The current research-based consensus is that in most cases gifted students are quite comfortable with their *intellectual* peers—older students—and suffer no noticeable maladjustment or neuroses (Benbow & Lubinski, 1997; Feldhusen, 1992; Kulik and Kulik, 1984; Rimm, 1991a, 1992b; Southern and Jones, 1991, 1992; VanTassel-Baska, 1986).

For example, among Terman's gifted children, those who had been accelerated one or two years made *better* adjustments than those who were not (Terman and Oden, 1947). Brody and Benbow (1987) found that accelerated high school students did as well or better than the others in all areas of achievement, had higher career aspirations, and attended more select colleges. There were no differences in social or emotional adjustment. Said Brody and Benbow, "This study did not reveal any harmful effects as a result of acceleration."

VanTassel-Baska (1986) noted these benefits of all forms of academic acceleration. Accelerated gifted students:

- Improve in motivation, confidence, and scholarship.
- Do not develop habits of mental laziness.
- Complete their professional training earlier.
- Reduce the cost of their college education.

Reservations about grade-skipping may be based on some faulty assumptions and interpretations, for example:

**1.** Persons who have been accelerated may incorrectly blame adolescent adjustment problems on their acceleration. Persons who were not accelerated might blame their problems on other factors.

**2.** Gifted children, on average, are better adjusted socially and emotionally than typical students. However, children with very high intelligence have special problems relating to others because of their differentness (e.g., Delisle, 1992; Gross, 1993a; Hollingworth, 1942; see Chapter 17). Because these children are the ones most likely to be skipping grades, their social problems, actually related to their extremely high intelligence, mistakenly may be blamed on acceleration.

**3.** When outsiders observe a school child who is noticeably smaller or younger than average, they may infer that the child certainly must be having social problems, even though testimony from the child him- or herself does not indicate any special problems.

To reduce the risk of problems related to grade-skipping we recommend the following guidelines, some of which duplicate the above recommendations for early admission to kindergarten or first grade:

**1.** A child should have an IQ score of 130 or higher. Feldhusen (1992; Feldhusen, Proctor, & Black, 1986) recommended that a level of mental development one standard deviation above the

mean *for the grade to be entered* also would indicate the intellectual readiness to skip a grade.[1]

**2.** Regardless of ability, for elementary students only one grade should be skipped at a time. After the child has had several years for adjustment, there may be reason to consider skipping another grade. Older students, say age 14 or upward, who are socially and emotionally mature have successfully moved directly from *junior* high school to college (Gregory & March, 1985; Stanley & McGill, 1986).

**3.** Skill gaps should be diagnosed so that the child can be assisted in acquiring any missing basic skills.

**4.** A supportive teacher, counselor, and/or group of gifted peers should be available to help the child with social problems related to grade-skipping.

**5.** Parent value systems need to be considered. Especially, if families place more emphasis on athletics than academics, grade-skipping may put considerable pressure on the student who may not be big enough to compete in some sports.

**6.** An appraisal of the child's present intellectual and social adjustment should be considered in the decision making. If the child is not showing good social adjustment in the present grade, grade-skipping cannot be assumed to improve that adjustment. Also, continued poor adjustment in the higher grade should not necessarily be attributed to the grade-skipping. Grade-skipping is not a cure-all, and a given child may require further guidance regardless of the grade-skipping decision.

**7.** Every grade-skipping decision needs to be made separately. Physical maturity, height, emotional stability, motivation, and ability to handle challenge all should be part of the decision making. Centrally important is the gifted child's need for intellectual stimulation.

**8.** Feldhusen (1992; Feldhusen, Proctor, and Black, 1986) recommended that, as with early

---

[1]One standard deviation above the mean would put the child at the 84th percentile; that is, the child would score higher in intelligence than 84 percent of the children in the grade in which the child is to be placed.

admission to kindergarten or first grade, all cases of grade-skipping be arranged on a trial basis of about six weeks. Rimm (1992b) recommended that a semester be allowed for adjustment. Although some children adjust within a few weeks, others take longer. The child should be made aware that if the advancement does not go well, he or she may request to be returned to the original grade. Counseling services should be available. Further, the child should not be made to feel he or she is a "failure" if the grade-skipping does not succeed.

Teachers and parents too often conclude that it is simply easier to avoid grade-skipping. Administratively, they are of course correct. However, teachers and parents should recognize that keeping a highly precocious child in an unstimulating environment is also making a decision—one that communicates to the gifted child that he or she is not expected to perform up to his or her capability and that social life is more important than academic challenge. That decision can be more intellectually and even socially harmful to the gifted child than the decision to skip grades. Boredom, restlessness, frustration, underachievement, and disruptiveness can be replaced by enhanced motivation, improved self-concepts, and improved study habits and productivity.

As examples of the effectiveness of elementary school acceleration, Gross (1992b, 1993, 1999) described five extremely precocious students (IQs = 160 to 200) who, because of carefully planned and monitored grade-skipping and radical subject-matter skipping, "are more stimulated intellectually, enjoy closer and more productive social relationships, and display healthier levels of social self-esteem than do equally gifted children who have been retained with age peers of average ability" (Gross, 1992b, p. 91). Rimm and Lovance (1992a, 1992b) used grade-skipping and subject-skipping to prevent or reverse underachievement in 14 high-IQ children, all of whom had been brought by parents to Rimm's Underachievement Clinic. Note the irony: The children were doing poor work—and therefore would

hardly be teachers' choices for acceleration—yet the grade- and subject-skipping provided the academic challenge needed to stimulate interest and achievement consistent with their high ability. Later, all parents and (initially reluctant) administrators agreed that acceleration was the right move.

## SUBJECT-SKIPPING

Grade-skipping sometimes is called *full acceleration* and subject-skipping therefore is *partial acceleration*. Subject-skipping involves taking classes or studying particular subjects with students in higher grades. It is especially appropriate in sequential types of subject matters, particularly reading, math, and languages, but possible in other subjects as well. Subject-skipping is therefore suitable for the student with special skills and talents primarily in a single area. The acceleration may begin in elementary school and continue through high school.

Subject-skipping has important advantages and only one major disadvantage. On the positive side, it permits the child to be intellectually challenged in a specific area of strength while he or she continues to develop appropriate grade-level skills in other areas. It also permits the child to remain with peers. Subject-skipping may be used experimentally to determine if grade-skipping later would be appropriate; the teacher can observe the academic and social adjustment of the child in the new setting and make a more confident decision about full acceleration.

Rimm and Lovance (1992a, 1992b) found that students who were first subject-skipped and later grade-skipped felt relief at no longer having to explain their participation in two different grade levels.

The disadvantage of subject-skipping is the problem of continuity. Too often a particular school or teacher may be willing to accelerate a student in a single subject, such as math, but makes no overall organizational plan for continuous progress. Therefore, the child who masters three years of math in just one may suddenly discover that he or she must repeat two of them.

However, if continuous accelerated coursework can be planned for the child, subject acceleration is an ideal approach for children with high abilities in specific areas.

## EARLY ADMISSION TO JUNIOR OR SENIOR HIGH SCHOOL

This particular acceleration alternative seems not to be popular. However, for some students the best grade to be skipped is the one just before junior or senior high school, that is, grade five or six or grade eight or nine (Brody & Stanley, 1991). From an academic perspective, the student may be ready and anxious for advanced work in the more specialized junior or senior high school. Socially, it may be an opportune time to accelerate, since new friendships develop when students from several elementary or junior high schools meet for the first time in the new school setting.

## CREDIT BY EXAMINATION

In the junior or senior high school, one cost-free mechanism for justifiable subject-skipping is credit by examination. For example, if a talented mathematics or language student feels he or she already has acquired the content of a semester course, perhaps through home study or foreign travel, the student should be allowed to "test out" of the course and, if mastery is demonstrated, receive academic credit. In addition to preventing repetition and boredom, allowing credit by examination will encourage gifted students to accept challenges, set goals, and work toward them.

As a precaution, the student should be provided with an outline of the material to be included in the test. This gives the student a fair opportunity to appraise his or her own skills and to concentrate study on those not yet mastered. Failure experienced on tests due to lack of adequate preparation or to miscommunication about test content will be an unpleasant experience for both the student and the school staff.

College credit, which permits advanced placement when the student enters college, also may be earned through examination, as in the *Advanced Placement* (AP) program described in the next section or the *College Level Examination Program* (CLEP; see, e.g., Karnes & Chauvin, 1982; Zimmerman & Brody, 1986). Unlike the AP program, CLEP does not offer courses, just examinations. CLEP examinations for college credit are available in 30 subject areas, including math, English (composition and literature), business, computer science, nursing, education, psychology, and foreign languages. The exams are 90-minute multiple-choice tests, although optional essay exams are available if colleges require them. Students taking only language exams can earn 6 or 12 college credits; students taking other CLEP exams can earn 3 or 6 college credits. The exams may be taken by anyone (e.g., juniors or seniors in high school). Before registering, one should check to determine if the college of one's choice will accept CLEP credits because not all do.[2]

## COLLEGE COURSES IN HIGH SCHOOL

Robinson and Noble (1992) observed that "for the young person whose intellectual development is markedly above average, the pace of ordinary secondary school classes is . . . like going through every day in a slow motion movie" (pp. 20–21). A solution available to many bright and motivated secondary students is taking college-level courses while in high school.

For example, with a *dual enrollment* program a student may be excused from high school for part of the day to take one or more courses on the college campus. The earned college credits may be used at the particular college when he or she is admitted, or the credits normally can be transferred to another college. Importantly, the courses also should be credited toward high school graduation requirements so that the student is not

[2]For additional information on CLEP, write to College Board, Box 1842, Princeton, NJ 08541, or phone (609) 951-1026. Schools may use 1-800-257-9558 to request information.

burdened—punished—with double the amount of coursework.

One problem is that a dual enrollment program could easily discriminate against gifted and talented poor students—suddenly a free public education is partly replaced by expensive tuition, books, and other costs. In Wisconsin, and presumably in other states, a Youth Option plan permits "public high school juniors and seniors in good academic standing to have their school districts pay for tuition, fees and books for courses at Wisconsin colleges, as long as their high schools do not offer comparable classes" (Associated Press, 2002). In Madison, in 2000–2001, 46 students took "everything from advanced calculus and chemistry to Italian and introduction to theater" (p. 2A). Statewide, 4000 high school students attended technical colleges, schools in the University of Wisconsin system, or private colleges for courses in Web design, metallurgy and welding, history, and advanced business statistics. Political eyebrows raised, however, at rumors of courses in manicuring and piano lessons.

Another desirable option, the *Advanced Placement* (AP) program, like CLEP, is sponsored by College Board. The AP program consists of college-level courses and examinations for high school students (see, e.g., Zimmerman & Brody, 1986). The courses may take the form of an honors class or a strong regular class, either of which would be taught by an instructor who follows an AP course description. Most medium-to-large high schools offer AP classes. Further, students in middle school, high school, or college or anyone else may prepare individually, perhaps with a tutor, and then take the tests. The tests are given only at high schools.

The AP program offers courses and exams in several dozen areas, such as English literature and composition, foreign languages (including Latin), chemistry, economics, music theory, calculus, psychology, history (U.S., European, art), computer science, government and politics, and biology. The exams are given over a two-week period in May of each year. The examination for each course includes a 90-minute multiple-choice test plus a 90-minute essay. Courses normally require a full year to complete. Over 1300 colleges accept AP credits, but the colleges differ in the maximum number of credits that can be used.

Generally, the factor most critical to the success of permitting—indeed, encouraging—high school students to accept the challenge of earning college credits in high school is administrative flexibility. (For additional information, contact College Board, Princeton, NJ 08541, (609) 771-7300. Regional College Board offices are listed at the end of this chapter.)

## CORRESPONDENCE COURSES

Every major university offers correspondence courses at least at the college freshman and sophomore levels. Correspondence courses thus present valuable opportunities for the talented student who lives in a rural area or a small city or town. Correspondence courses carry full college credit. They are written by professors and are supervised by college professors, instructors, or qualified graduate students. Courses are available in a variety of areas, such as college math, algebra, or statistics, or introductory psychology, educational psychology, sociology, economics, anthropology, astronomy, history, foreign languages, and others. The University of Wisconsin-Madison, offers a correspondence course in gifted education, using this text. Correspondence courses may be taken in summer, as a form of independent study, or as a form of enrichment in conjunction with a regular high school program. Typically, courses requiring student-teacher interaction or laboratories are not taught by mail—for example, biology, physics, or speech.

Considerable self-motivation and independence are needed to complete a correspondence course successfully. Students are more likely to be successful if several of them take the same course, thus permitting mutual support, stimulation, and assistance. It also is helpful if a high school faculty member can serve as advisor in case students need help.

## TELESCOPED PROGRAMS

*Telescoping* means, for example, collapsing three academic years' work into two or four years of high school into three. In the junior high school, if enough talented young mathematicians are available, a normal three-year math and algebra sequence might be taught at an accelerated pace in two years. It is less common, but the same telescoping can be used with other subjects, for example, by condensing three years of junior high school science into two years.

In high school, telescoping four years' work into three is almost entirely a counseling problem, assuming that district policies will permit such acceleration. The energetic and capable student, with the assistance of his or her counselor, simply cuts down on the "study hall" classes and schedules four years of high school requirements into a more compact and busier three. If three years is unrealistic, a three-and-a-half year program still would permit a capable student to begin college a semester early.

Planning telescoped programs can be complicated. Schools generally prefer that students design their plan before beginning even their freshman year. However, not many 13-year-olds can predict whether telescoping their high school education—trading more work for early graduation—is a good idea. A counselor who specializes in giftedness should be able to help a student make a decision and plan future coursework after the student acquires some experience in high school.

## EARLY ADMISSION TO COLLEGE

Many gifted and talented high school and even some junior high school students are permitted to enter college early on a full-time basis (Brody & Stanley, 1991; Gregory & March, 1985; Karnes & Chauvin, 1982; Olszewski-Kubilius, 1995). In some cases high school requirements are met early, as in telescoping plans. In other cases high school requirements are flexibly waived and a qualified student simply enters college full-time

without meeting all of the usual graduation requirements. With the latter plan, one must be sure that the particular college admissions office is agreeable to such short-cutting before plans reach an advanced stage.

As an example, after a successful pilot study the California State University at Los Angeles (CSULA) in 1983 installed a permanent Early Entrance Program—a full-time college program for qualified junior and senior high school-aged students (Gregory, 1984; Gregory & March, 1985). Students must be at least 14 years old. They also must produce scores on the Washington Pre-College Test or the Scholastic Aptitude Test (SAT) above the 80th percentile on either the verbal or math section and above the 50th percentile on the other. Students initially attend CSULA part-time, while continuing their junior or senior high school classes. Thus if the program is unsuitable, little is lost and usually some college credits are banked for future use. Students who eventually do register full-time appear to realize social and emotional benefits as well as intellectual ones (Gregory and March, 1985). The program works well.

Early admission to college, with or without graduation from high school, is an excellent way for a mature gifted student to accelerate his or her education. Unfortunately, many high school teachers and administrators discourage early graduation and early college admission. Also, high school students who consider this approach probably will miss opportunities for scholarships and honors and, of course, social and extracurricular activities. The early college entrant should be prepared to trade these opportunities for the challenge of college work. If the student or his or her parents have doubts about early full-time college work, the CSULA strategy of first enrolling part-time while still in secondary school will make the decision easier.

Caution is indeed required in selecting students for early college admission. Cornell, Callahan, and Lloyd (1991) emphasized that large individual differences exist in the ability of young people to adjust to college life and that early admission is inappropriate for some. In their study of 44 female students age 13 to 17 who participated in a residential (live-in) college program, over half suffered from periods of depression; a few showed suicidal tendencies; and 13 left the program due to stress. Cornell, Callahan, and Lloyd emphasized the importance of socioemotional maturity, good self-concepts, and the ability to relate well to adults, which can lead to *excellent* adjustment and healthy personality growth in early college admissions programs. They suggested also that programs in which students *commute* to college may be less stressful than residential, live-in programs.

In an unpublished report, Stanley emphasized these advantages of entering college at a younger-than-average age. Highly able youths can get more academic stimulation and breadth at a good college than during their last year or two in high school. Remaining in high school can have detrimental social and emotional consequences if such students are eager to move ahead. There is greater opportunity to interact with expert professionals. There is more time and flexibility for planning educational and other aspects of life. One also is able to enter a profession at an earlier age, allowing extra years of youthful vigorous work. Graduate and professional schools are impressed by students who graduate from college, especially an outstanding one, at a younger-than-average age. Finally, moving ahead according to one's best ability is exhilarating, motivating, and builds realistic self-confidence.

After reviewing successes and some failures of mathematically precocious college entrants, Stanley and McGill (1986) recommended that early entrants should score higher on the SAT than usual college freshman—at least 625 on the SAT-V and 675 on the SAT-M.

## RESIDENTIAL HIGH SCHOOLS

A relatively new opportunity for gifted students is special residential (live-in) high schools, such as the North Carolina School of Science and Mathematics; the Louisiana School for Math, Science, and the Arts; the Indiana Academy for Science, Mathematics, and the Humanities; the Illinois Mathematics and Science Academy; the Texas Academy of Mathematics and Science; the Mississippi School for Math and Science; the Missouri Academy of Science, Mathematics, and Computing; the Massachusetts Academy of Mathematics and Science; and the South Carolina Governor's School for Science and Mathematics (Kolloff, 2003; Stanley, 1987). These schools are based on the assumption that regular high schools simply cannot offer the number of advanced courses or a sufficiently diverse curriculum to provide for gifted students who, for example, master all the math courses the school has to offer within one or two years. Special residential programs thus are appropriate for students who are capable of mastering content much more rapidly than others and are able to engage in complex processes at high levels of abstraction (Kolloff, 2003). Stanley (1987) recommended that any state with 300 National Merit semifinalists each year should consider creating a special residential high school.

Most residential high schools admit students beginning at grade 11. However, Illinois and Alabama admit students beginning at grade 10, and North Carolina is considering 10th-grade admission. School size ranges from under 100 to over 600. Residential high schools were created through legislative action and are supported by state funds. Therefore, they are committed to ensuring a racial and ethnic composition that represents the demographics of the state (Kolloff, 2003).

Residential high schools typically are located on college campuses, which provide the needed dormitories, cafeterias, and recreational facilities, to say nothing of cultural opportunities and academic resources. However, the Illinois Math and Science Academy moved into a high school building that had been vacated. The North Carolina School of Science and Mathematics converted a former hospital into dormitories, classrooms, laboratories, a library, and recreational areas. An Arkansas residential high school in Hot Springs also is housed in a former hospital.

As indicated by their names, current residential high schools highlight math and science. For some,

AP courses in calculus, physics, chemistry, computer science, and biology form the foundation of the curriculum, enabling students to enter college with one or more years of credit in several areas.

The academic and social benefits of residential high schools seem self-evident. Nonetheless, as with any acceleration plan, criticisms have been quick. Some persons complain of a "brain drain"—the best students leave the regular high school. Others worry about the young scholars leaving home two or three years before they normally would leave for college; that contact with college students might be problematic; or that such schools will foster attitudes of superiority and arrogance.

To counter some of these issues, residential school calendars include long weekends at home as well as opportunities for outside activities. Staff are alert to signs of stress, depression, or homesickness; they watch for symptoms of adjustment problems such as missing classes, not completing assignments, excessive socializing, or social withdrawal. Residential high schools limit interaction between high school and college students by housing them separately and segregating the two groups for social and, usually, academic activities (Kolloff, 2003). Problems of arrogance are countered by requiring community service and some responsibilities for maintaining their school—a broom and mop can be humbling.

For comparison, see the description of a Russian residential school in Inset 5-2.

---

**INSET 5.2** _____

### A Russian Residential School

One remarkable example of a residential high school, or "boarding school," is the Novosibirsk Internat in Siberia (Evered & Nayer, 2000). Yes, Siberia. Novosibirsk, Siberia, was known in the former Soviet Union as "Science City." The Novosibirsk Internat opened in 1963, partly as a curious response to a Soviet requirement that high school students spend part of their day working in factories or on farms. At the Novosibirsk Internat—whose up-front goal is excellence in science and math—students "work" by participating in research at the Novosibirsk Science Center. They also take classes at the Novosibirsk State University. The science-minded boarding school includes mathematics clubs, problem-solving competitions, and participation in national mathematics and physics Olympiads.

In fact, admission criteria begin with performance in the Olympiad. The 500 most successful students spend a summer at the Novosibirsk Internat. Of these, half will qualify for admission to the Novosibirsk Internat. Once there, an awesome schedule includes a first class at 8:30 A.M. With a lunch break and an afternoon break, the last class ends at 9:25 P.M.—essentially a 13-hour day of Russian language and literature, physical education, biology, math, physics, and computer classes, which usually are taught by university faculty and include experimental work in the Science Center.

The school is alive and mostly well. However, and regrettably—from the point of view of science-minded students—the breakup of the Soviet Union has led to reduced funding, fewer programs, and fewer scientific activities. Staff also is diminished because of more attractive opportunities elsewhere, such as in other countries. To some degree, student interest in math and science also is replaced by more profitable career goals, particularly in the prestigious banking and managerial areas. Unfortunately, tuition is now charged, which puts the Novosibirsk Internat out of reach for poor but brilliant students.

## INTERNATIONAL BACCALAUREATE PROGRAMS

The International Baccalaureate (IB) programs provide excellent advanced coursework, including foreign languages, and expose students to worldwide, international concerns. At this writing, 1310 "authorized" IB programs have been installed in schools in 110 countries. Of these, exactly 1000 are the highly selective two-year high school Diploma Programmes (DP) for students age 16 to 19. There also is a Middle Years Program (MYP) and a Primary Years Program (PYP). The MYP and PYP are not prerequisites for the Diploma Programme.

With the Diploma Programme, students typically are selected by a committee of teachers, counselors, and administrators who evaluate "academic performance, attendance, conduct, extracurricular activities, motivation, and a written statement from the applicant" (Cox & Daniel, 1991, p. 158). Academically, the program draws students from above the 90th percentile. Students select one course from each of six subject groups. Either three or four courses must be two-year Higher Level (HL; 240 teaching hours) courses, the rest must be one-year Standard Level (SL; 150 hours) courses. Group 1—*Language A1* is a student's first language (e.g., English for American students), with emphasis on written and oral skills plus a study of world literature; Group 2— *Second Language* focuses on written and oral communication in a foreign language; Group 3— *Individuals and Societies* includes choices from business, economics, geography, history, Islamic history, worldwide information technology, philosophy, psychology, and social anthropology; Group 4—*Experimental Sciences* includes biology, chemistry, physics, environmental systems, and design technology, all of which cover worldwide moral and ethical matters; Group 5—*Mathematics* includes selection from four math courses or a computer course; and Group 6—*Arts and Electives* covers visual arts, music, theater, or else a second selection from Groups 1–5. Course grades reflect attainment of knowledge and skills

relative to achievement standards of IB schools worldwide.

Just 24 percent of International Baccalaureate schools offer middle and elementary school programs (MYP and PYP). Their curriculums are instructive. The five-year MYP program, which requires community service and health and social education, includes "a thorough study of various disciplines . . . [and] their interrelatedness" (International Baccalaureate Organization, n.d.). Eight areas are the students' best language; a modern foreign language; humanities (history, geography); sciences (biology, chemistry, physics); math (algebra, geometry, trigonometry, probability and statistics); arts (visual and performing); physical education (including health and team sports); and technology (computers and design technology).

The PYP (for ages 3–12) emphasizes the interrelatedness of concepts, skills, attitudes, and actions—including sensitivity to the experiences of others and social responsibility. Six areas are languages, social studies (who we are), mathematics, science and technology (how the world works), the arts (how we express ourselves), and personal, social, and physical education (how we organize ourselves).

At present, there appears to be a snag regarding college credit for high school IB students. As we noted, IB schools offer one-year Standard Level courses and two-year Higher Level courses, both of which are challenging. Writing in the *Washington Post*, Mathews (2001) noted that most American colleges will not give college credit for the one-year IB courses, although "they award credit for one-year AP courses that are no harder, and sometimes easier, than their IB equivalents." As a result, to earn college credit many IB students not only take the SL IB tests, they also must spend time and money on AP tests. One IB school administrator described each May as a "testing zoo"—in 2001 his school gave 532 IB exams and 961 AP exams. The problem is unfair and needs correcting, wrote Mathews. Poelzer and Feldhusen (1997) confirmed that 60 U.S. universities accepted only Higher Level courses for credit or advanced placement, just one accepted Standard Level courses.

For further information on the Switzerland-based International Baccalaureate Programs, see www.ibo.org.

## STUDY OF MATHEMATICALLY PRECOCIOUS YOUTH (SMPY), TALENT SEARCH, AND ELEMENTARY TALENT SEARCH

The best-known example of accelerating bright secondary students into college-level work is the highly successful *Talent Search* programs, which began at Johns Hopkins University in 1971 as Julian Stanley's *Study of Mathematically Precocious Youth* (SMPY; Stanley, 1979, 1991a; Benbow & Lubinski, 1997).

The purpose of SMPY has been to locate primarily seventh-grade students with extraordinarily high mathematics talent "and help them find the special, supplemental, accelerative opportunities they sorely need in order to move ahead faster and better in mathematics and related subjects such as physics and computer science" (Stanley, 1991a, p. 36). In an annual mathematics talent search, seventh- and some eighth-grade students are selected on the basis of Scholastic Aptitude Test-Mathematics (SAT-M) scores. Students who score at or above the 51st percentile for male college-bound high school seniors are considered mathematically precocious—they reason better mathematically than nearly all of their age mates (IQ = 135–200; Benbow & Lubinski, 1997). Students take summer mathematics classes, usually taught by a college professor. According to Stanley (1982), by working 5 to 6 hours per day these students in three weeks can master one to two years of high school algebra and geometry—they are working, not sleeping, and by eighth grade are ready for calculus.

High school SMPY participants are encouraged to pursue any of a "smorgasbord" of acceleration options. They may: (1) attend college part-time, (2) earn college credit by examination (e.g., in the CLEP or AP program), (3) skip a grade, particularly the one at the end of junior high

school, (4) complete two or more years of math in one year, (5) receive individual tutoring in advanced areas, (6) participate in an International Baccalaureate program, or (7) enter college early, either by early high school graduation or "simply by leaving high school before completing the last grade(s)" (Stanley, 1979). In every case, these students receive counseling regarding the educational alternatives that might be appropriate for them.

A few unbiased testimonials by Stanley (1979) may be of interest: "The boredom and frustration of even the average-scoring (SMPY) contestants when incarcerated in a year-long algebra class is difficult to appreciate. Often, highly able youths themselves are not aware of the extent of their slowdown, because it has been their lot from kindergarten onward. . . . Often, they take off like rockets intellectually when allowed to do so. . . . It is clear that a large reservoir of virtually untapped mathematical reasoning ability exists all around the region."

SMPY expanded in many ways. In 1979 Stanley created the Johns Hopkins Center for Academically Talented Youth (CTY), which conducted talent searches using not only the SAT-M, but SAT-Verbal and SAT-Total scores as well.

As with the Johns Hopkins SMPY and CTY, the primary activity of university Talent Search programs is accelerated summer course work, supplemented with counseling regarding educational opportunities (Lupkowski-Shoplik, Benbow, Assouline, & Brody, 2003). Many Talent Search summer programs offer AP courses that carry college credit. One Talent Search program, for example, offered 14 academically oriented classes, including computer science courses (AP), calculus (AP), geology (AP), advanced language and composition (AP), speech and debate, Latin, Greek, survey of social sciences, laboratory science, economics, and mythology. Admission to each class was based on SAT scores (e.g., one computer science course required an SAT math score of at least 450) plus registration fees and books.

Duke University offers an apparently well-funded (and nontypical) summer Talent Search program that began in 1981 with 151 students. In year 2000 the Duke Talent Identification Program (TIP) offered 99 science, math, engineering, and humanities courses on six university campuses, plus learning excursions to five international and three domestic sites. Enrollment was roughly 2300 students, apparently in junior and senior high school. The nonclassroom sites seem to be the most exciting. As director Steven Pfeiffer (2000, p. 3) asked, "Why would young people want to spend their summers in school?" For example, many students went to Costa Rica to study animal and plant life in the disappearing tropical forests. They attended lectures to learn the methodology of scientific research, then in their "jungle laboratory" they conducted mostly inde-

pendent studies alongside professional biologists. Other learning excursions were to England, Italy, Greece, and Germany.

In addition to middle school Talent Search programs, in recent years an Elementary Talent Search has emerged for grades three through six, although the grades vary with the university offering the program. The students become involved in enriching learning opportunities (e.g., independent projects, weekend enrichment classes), contests and competitions (e.g., mathematical olympiads for elementary students), mentorships, grade skipping, and other opportunities.

Table 5.2 lists universities in North America and Great Britain, and their website addresses,

**TABLE 5.2**   Talent Search and Elementary Talent Search Programs

| University and Website Address | Grade Level(s) |
| --- | --- |
| California State University, Sacramento, CA 95819<br>http://edweb.csus.edu/projects/ATS/ | Elementary and middle school<br>(northern California) |
| Carnegie Mellon University, Pittsburgh, PA 15213<br>www.cmu.edu/outreach/c-mites/ | Elementary, grades 3 through 6<br>(Pennsylvania) |
| Dublin City University, Dublin 9, Ireland<br>www.dcu.ie/ctyi/ | Middle, age 12 through 16 |
| Duke University, Durham, NC 27708<br>www.tip.duke.edu/ | Upper elementary and middle<br>(many states) |
| Iowa State University, Ames, IA 50011<br>www.public.iastate.edu/~opptag_info/mainpage.htm | Elementary and middle-school, grades<br>2 through 9 (many states) |
| Johns Hopkins University (CTY), Baltimore, MD 21218<br>www.jhu.edu/~gifted/index.html | Elementary and middle school grades<br>2 through 8 (many states) |
| Northwestern University, Evanston, IL 60208<br>http://ctdnet.acns.nwu.edu/ | Elementary and middle school, grades<br>3 through 8 (many states) |
| University of Calgary, Calgary, Alberta, Canada T2N 1N4<br>www.acs.ucalgary.ca/~gifteduc | Elementary |
| University of Denver, Denver, CO 80208<br>www.du.edu/education/ces/rmts.html | Elementary and middle, grades 5<br>through 9 (many states) |
| University of Iowa (Belin-Blank Center) Iowa City, IA 52242<br>www.uiowa.edu/~belinctr/ | Elementary and middle school, grades<br>3 through 9 (many states) |
| University of New South Wales, Sydney 2052, Australia<br>www.arts.unsw.edu.au/gerric | Elementary |
| University of Washington, Seattle, WA 98195<br>http://depts.washington.edu/cscy/ | Elementary and middle, grades 5<br>through 9 (Washington State) |

that offer a Middle-School Talent Search program, an Elementary Talent Search program, or both.

There are other SMPY-related developments. Since 1980, a continuing activity at SMPY at Johns Hopkins has been a national search for math whizzes who score above 700 on the SAT-M, which is about one in 10,000 (Stanley, 1988). These students, labeled the "700–800 on SAT-M Before Age 13 Group," are both studied and helped educationally. For example, "SMPY sends members of the group materials, especially including a long quarterly newsletter, suggesting how they can proceed faster and better in mathematics and related subjects. Also, from time to time SMPY obtains scholarships for pre-college summer experiences" (Stanley, 1988, p. 208). Since 1991 CTY assumed responsibility for locating seventh graders with SAT-M scores over 700 and began looking also for youngsters in a "630–800 on SAT-V Before Age 13 Group," also a 1 in 10,000 occurrence.

In 1986 SMPY itself had split into two branches, with the second branch established at Iowa State University by Stanley's former colleague Camilla Benbow (Benbow & Lubinski, 1997; Camilla Benbow and husband David Lubinski are both currently at Vanderbilt University). Benbow directed a summer residential Talent Search program. She also initiated a long-range Terman-like study of over 3000 intellectually talented students, largely to evaluate the impact of educational facilitation on their development. For example, Swiatek and Benbow (1992) found that after a 10-year period SMPY participants attended more prestigious colleges, and female participants were more likely to attend graduate school. Benbow and Arjmand (1990) reported that acceleration of SMPY students, male and female, produced no detrimental social or emotional effects and may have improved social and emotional adjustment.

Finally, Stanley and Benbow (1983) itemized a few benefits of SMPY participation, which presumably would apply to Talent Search as well as other forms of academic acceleration:

1. Increased zest for learning and life, reduced boredom in school, and better school attitudes.
2. Enhanced feelings of self-worth and accomplishment.
3. Reduced egotism and arrogance, due to the humbling effects of working for the first time with intellectual peers.
4. Far better educational preparation and thus improved qualifications for the most selective colleges.
5. Early college and graduate school admission.
6. Better graduate school and fellowship opportunities, due to better preparation, acquaintance with professors, and research skills.

Benbow and Lubinski (1997) added:

7. "Intellectually gifted students . . . do not achieve as highly if deprived of an education that corresponds to their level of competence" (p. 164).
8. "When differences are found, they favor the accelerates over the non-accelerates irrespective of the mode of acceleration. In addition, students are satisfied with their acceleration" (p. 164).

**SUMMARY**

Table 5.1 is a guide for planning G/T program content, summarized in the categories of basic skills, content beyond the prescribed curriculum, exposure to a variety of fields, student-selected content, high content complexity, creative thinking and problem solving, thinking skills, computer skills, affective development, and motivation.

G/T programs vary in students served, program model and goals, acceleration, enrichment, and grouping plans, instructional strategy, resources, and other dimensions.

*Acceleration* is defined as programming that results in advanced placement or credit; enrichment essentially is anything else. Both accommodate the high abilities and needs of gifted students. Both are required in any well-rounded program.

With early admission to kindergarten or first

grade, students are most likely to succeed if they are carefully screened. They should be intellectually precocious (recommended IQ = 130+), at least average in motor coordination, and possess adequate reading readiness, social/emotional maturity, and good health. Girls often are more mature. If a particular school already caters to very bright students, early admission may be unnecessary. The receiving teacher should have positive attitudes regarding early admission. Family values should emphasize academic achievement. Early admission can be on a trial basis.

Grade-skipping can improve motivation and scholarship, social relations, and self-esteem. Grade-skipping and subject-skipping also have successfully reversed some students' patterns of underachievement. The problem of missing some essential basic skills can be solved via diagnostic tests and remedial work. Research shows that social adjustment usually is not a problem. Acceleration is sometimes blamed for adolescent personal or social problems. Maladjustment due to extremely high IQ also is sometimes blamed on grade-skipping. Grade-skipping may be most successful if the student shows an IQ score of 130+, if one grade is skipped at a time, if support from a teacher, counselor, or gifted peer is available, and if intellectual and social adjustment is considered in the decision.

Subject-skipping permits the child to remain with age-mates while being challenged in a particular area of strength. Continuity with later grades probably is the only potential shortcoming.

Early admission to junior or senior high school is a socially opportune time to skip a grade.

Credit by examination encourages G/T students to accept challenges and saves repetition and boredom. College credit by examination may be earned in the CLEP and AP programs, which are highly cost effective.

In a dual enrollment program, students take college courses while still in high school. Credits from college courses taken in high school should count toward high school graduation. In the AP programs, students take college courses in an honors class, a fast regular class, or as independent study.

Correspondence courses require self-direction. It therefore is desirable for a group of students to take the same course and for a high school teacher or counselor to monitor progress.

Telescoping involves condensing a two- or three-year course, or high school program, into fewer years.

Early college admission is recommended, despite the problem of forfeiting high school honors or scholarships. Many good students are socially and academically ready, although some have experienced depression and stress. Maturity, good self-concepts, and ability to relate with adults are critical. Stanley noted that early college admission can improve social and emotional well-being, promotes interaction with professionals, impresses graduate schools, and permits one to enter a profession earlier.

Residential high schools cater mostly to high math and science talent; AP courses with college credit sometimes are offered. Critics express concern about a "brain drain," as well as the adverse effects of leaving home early and negative influences of college students. Student body composition is an issue.

The International Baccalaureate program focuses mainly on languages and international concerns. At this writing, many colleges give credit for Higher Level courses but not Lower Level courses, which may be equivalent to AP classes.

Stanley's SMPY program at Johns Hopkins University uses the SAT to identify high-level math talent among primarily seventh grade students. Students take summer math classes and are encouraged to pursue other acceleration options. CTY, an expansion of SMPY, includes verbally talented students as well as mathematically gifted ones.

Following SMPY, seventh-grade Talent Search programs currently cover the 48 contiguous states. They offer challenging courses, some of which carry AP credit, and usually educational/career counseling.

A relatively new Elementary Talent Search is available for grades 3–6.

SMPY, and now CTY, search for students who before age 13 score above 700 on the SAT-M or above 630 on the SAT-V to study and assist them. Benbow at Vanderbilt University is conducting a longitudinal study of 3000 SMPY participants.

Benefits of SMPY and Talent Search participation include improved zest for learning, better feelings of self-worth, better educational preparation, early entrance into college and a profession, and better graduate and professional school opportunities.

### APPENDIX 5.1: COLLEGE BOARD OFFICES

New York Office:
888 Seventh Ave.
New York, NY 10019
(212) 582-6210

Middle States Regional Office:
Suite 1418
1700 Market St.
Philadelphia, PA 19103
(215) 567-6555

Midwestern Regional Office:
1 American Plaza
Evanston, IL 60201
(312) 866-1700

New England Regional Office:
470 Totten Pond Rd.
Waltham, MA 02154
(617) 890-9150

Southern Regional Office:
Suite 200
17 Executive Park Dr., NE
Atlanta, GA 30329
(404) 636-9465

Southwestern Regional Office:
Suite 922
211 E. Seventh St.
Austin, TX 78701
(512) 472-0231

Denver Office:
Suite 23
2142 South High St.
Denver, CO 80210
(303) 777-4434

Western Regional Office:
800 Welch Rd.
Palo Alto, CA 94304
(415) 321-5211

# ENRICHMENT AND GROUPING

*Providing special services for the gifted and talented almost inevitably requires some special grouping. Grouping the gifted for all or part of the school day accommodates achievement and readiness levels and can serve other purposes as well.*

John Feldhusen (1989a, p. 9)

We noted at the outset of Chapter 5 that both acceleration and enrichment activities usually require grouping gifted children. This chapter will review enrichment activities and grouping plans at elementary and secondary levels.

Two preliminary thoughts are these. First, a common criticism of enrichment activities in G/T programs appears in the question "Wouldn't that be good for all children?" Of course, the answer often must be yes. Keep your antennae up for enrichment that is good for *all* students (e.g., creativity and thinking skills training, values training, college and career information, and field trips to art galleries or scientific laboratories) versus experiences that seem strictly appropriate for bright and talented students (e.g., independent work on complex projects, Talent Search, summer College for Kids, or other accelerated learning opportunities).

Second, based on interviews at 86 gifted programs in metropolitan New York, Campbell and Verna (n.d.) concluded that despite the specific type of program (grouping arrangements, curriculum organization), "Good [qualified and enthusiastic] teachers make or break programs" (p. 11). Gifted teachers agreed that you must "know your stuff" regarding student characteristics, subject matter, and teaching strategies. You must expect more, demand more, probe more, and deliver more—more material and more challenges.

## ENRICHMENT

All enrichment activities for gifted youth should be planned with "higher order" objectives in mind. One list of objectives, collated from many thoughtful sources, was presented in Table 5.1. As a reminder, the objectives were listed in the categories of:

- Maximum achievement in basic skills, based on needs, not age
- Content and resources beyond the prescribed curriculum
- Exposure to a variety of fields of study
- Student-selected content, including in-depth studies
- High content complexity—theories, generalizations, applications
- Creative thinking and problem solving
- Higher-level thinking skills, critical thinking, library and research skills
- Affective development, including self-understanding and ethical development
- Development of academic motivation, self-direction, and high career aspirations
- Development of computer skills

Enrichment strategies essentially are delivery methods for achieving *process* and *content* goals. Process goals include developing such skills— or processes—as creative thinking and problem solving, critical thinking, scientific thinking, and others (see Chapter 11). The content is the subject matter, projects, and activities within which the processes are developed.

Enrichment strategies we will review briefly include (1) independent study and independent projects, (2) learning centers, (3) field trips, (4) Saturday programs, (5) summer programs, (6) mentors and mentorships, (7) Future Problem Solving, (8) Odyssey of the Mind, (9) Junior Great Books, (10) academic competitions, and (11) using technology.

## INDEPENDENT STUDY, RESEARCH, AND ART PROJECTS

Independent study and research projects take place within many of the enrichment and grouping strategies described in this chapter and in many of the acceleration options and program models described in Chapters 5 and 7. For bright and energetic students, the possibilities for independent study and independent projects are without limit.

### Library and Internet and Research Projects

A library or Internet research project must be based on strong student interest and should be student-selected. If students have difficulty selecting a topic, a brainstorming approach is one way to identify interesting possibilities. It may be best to pose a specific problem, although the nature of the initial problem may change as the project develops. For example, some questions might be "Why and how were pyramids built?," "What are the relationships between Greek and Roman gods?," "What is the evidence for Native American migration from Asia?," or "Who the heck is Bonny Prince Charlie?" This type of research might also involve trips to a natural history museum, art gallery, or research laboratory, or visits with or phone calls or emails to relevant university faculty or other community (or national) experts.

With any independent project, it is important that a *product* be produced and that the product or performance be presented to an appropriate *audience,* either students in the class or outside groups (Renzulli and Reis, 1994, 1997). A library or Internet research project can be more than a neatly typed report. It might include a student-made video or narrated slide show; a demonstration of some activity or skill (for example, sand painting, musket loading); a tabletop demonstration (rolling 30-ton stone blocks, dinosaur models); a TV news report on the progress of the battle at Bunker Hill; a newspaper column describing recent activities in the Spanish Inquisition; an ESP test for the class; and so on.

### Scientific Research Projects

Many elementary and junior high schools organize science fairs in which each student in the science classes creates a small scientific demonstration. Ribbons are awarded to the most elaborate, well-done, or technically competent projects, usually a "first," "second," or "third" type of rating so that all participants earn a ribbon for their efforts. Projects by G/T students typically are outstanding, and their effort and ingenuity are reinforced with "first" ribbons and usually peer admiration.

With any type of research project, the teacher's main role is "the guide on the side." With elementary or secondary students, the teacher-coordinator directs the budding scientist to appropriate library, computer, or human resources for background information, helps the student clarify the problem and plan the research, aids in locating equipment and other resources and tools, and gives advice and assistance when needed.

Many children's museums will exhibit a suitable and high-quality science-related project. Outstanding high school science projects should be entered in the National Westinghouse competition, which awards $40,000 scholarships to each of 40 winners, honorable mention to 300 students, and prestige to everyone who enters. (For information on the Westinghouse Talent Search, contact Science Talent Search, 1719 N Street, NW, Washington, DC 20036; 202-785-2255.)

## Art, Drama, Creative Writing, and Other Independent Projects

Art or handicraft projects may include drawing, painting, sculpture, silk-screen, lettering, printing, batik, pottery, ceramics, photography, weaving, or other media. Students interested in theater and drama can research how plays are written and then write, direct, produce, and perform in their own. Students talented in creative writing—and perhaps others—can be coached in writing for publication. Magazines that publish student writing appear at the end of this chapter (Appendix 6.1).

Invent America is a program that provides an outlet for (what else?) inventions (www .inventamerica.com). One elementary student entered a toilet seat sprayed with luminous paint—his "Glow in the Dark Toilet Seat" now resides in the Smithsonian Institution.

A student newspaper is an especially good independent project for a small group of students. Creating a newspaper involves interviewing people, writing stories, taking photographs, and planning, designing, and printing the paper on a school computer. Students in one elementary school interviewed and photographed elderly people in a retirement home. They learned first-hand about local and state history and about such hobbies and skills as quilting, candlemaking, tatting, and blacksmithing. Their appreciation and respect for the elderly increased dramatically.

See Inset 6.1 for recommendations for organizing independent information search, research, or art projects.

### LEARNING CENTERS

Commercial learning centers can be purchased; teachers also construct learning centers. These are tabletop workstations usually for individual work. Hazel Feldhusen (1981, 1986) described using learning centers with mainstreamed gifted students. For example, she stocked a *library center* with commercial reading-skill materials and educational games; it contained a typewriter for creative writing. A *math center* included math kits,

---

**INSET 6.1**

### Recommendations for Supervising Independent Projects

Students' independent research projects should result in the personal construction of new knowledge, along with new skills in, for example, information retrieval, research and technical areas, and problem solving and creativity. Kuhlthau (1994) described six steps in independent research projects, along with feelings and emotions likely to accompany each stage:

1. Receive the assignment (uncertainty).
2. Select a problem to solve (optimism).
3. Examine for focus (confusion, frustration, doubt).
4. Form focus (clarity).
5. Collect information (confidence, having a sense of direction).
6. Prepare to present (relief, sense of satisfaction or dissatisfaction).

Kuhlthau suggested that teachers discuss the stages with students and the usual thoughts, feelings, and frustrations that accompany each stage.

---

math games, and a calculator (and calculator activities). A computer in the math center presented logic games, math challenges, spelling lessons, and "fun" computer games. Her *art center* presented a new art project each week. She supplied her *science center* with two to five science activities, and included a tape player and filmstrip viewer.

Learning centers also can teach foreign languages; geography, history, and other social sciences; handicrafts; and music appreciation. Students—gifted and others—may self-select centers and activities, or teachers and students together may plan engaging and valuable learning center goals. Learning centers may be located in the regular classroom or the building instructional materials center.

The teacher should be certain that learning center time is well spent. Learning center activities should meet some of the goals and purposes of enrichment itemized in Table 5.1. Learning centers can offer time for unsupervised fooling around.

## FIELD TRIPS

Field trips can be used as an exploratory activity, aimed at acquainting students with cultural or scientific areas or with career possibilities. Field trips also can be a source of information for students' independent projects. Either an entire class or a small group of interested students might visit a natural history museum, manufacturing plant, art gallery, planetarium, local Greek restaurant, and so on. Some carefully written requests might earn a tour of a major newspaper company, a research laboratory, or seats at a symphony rehearsal.

Field trips are most beneficial if students have specific problems to solve, questions to answer, or post-tour projects or presentations to prepare. Streaking to the gift shop and cafeteria to buy postcards and potato chips is not the main intent.

Friedman and Master (1980) emphasized that an outline of the program/tour should be planned in advance by the teacher and guide/educator. During the tour, students should be allowed to touch, respond, and question. The teacher and guide should work together to stimulate learning, with both partners commenting, contributing, and remaining open to spontaneous twists in the children's interests. Students should be encouraged to discuss and evaluate during the program.

The reader might correctly conclude that field trips are no different for gifted students than for typical students. However, if the gifted child's field trip is part of a differentiated curriculum, the preparation for the trip, the tasks of the visit, and the resulting reports or projects should be tied to advanced knowledge goals and thinking skill development.

## SATURDAY PROGRAMS

Saturday programs present a delightful benefit: They permit gifted students to meet and work with each other away from the stresses and problems of daily school requirements. Saturday programs virtually always take the form of non-credit miniclasses taught by volunteer teachers, college faculty, graduate students, or community experts—often parents of the gifted children.

Feldhusen (1991; Feldhusen, Enersen, & Sayler, 1992) noted that Saturday (and summer) programs for the gifted present opportunities for students to:

- Interact with supportive yet challenging peers.
- Learn new material at a faster pace.
- Receive instruction at more complex skill and conceptual levels.
- Work with instructors who model high level professional behavior and aspirations.
- Be exposed to topics and disciplines not ordinarily taught in regular school programs.
- Become involved in in-depth creative investigations, with opportunities to explore, inquire, investigate, and identify problems.
- Clarify and confirm their special talents and abilities.

One model Saturday program is John Feldhusen's (1991; Feldhusen & Ruckman, 1988; Wood & Feldhusen, 1996) Super Saturday plan sponsored by Purdue University. Super Saturday serves children "from age $2\frac{1}{2}$ through high school" (Feldhusen, 1991, p. 198). Each semester about 40 classes lasting nine Saturdays are offered in science, math, computers, literature, composition, foreign languages, and, for preschoolers, special enrichment areas (see examples in Table 6.1).

Parents provide transportation and pay minimal registration fees and materials charges. Teachers are university faculty and students, public school teachers, and others in the community. They must be good teachers and show energy, enthusiasm, and an interest in teaching gifted kids.

As a different model, the Gifted Child Society (1990) of Glen Rock, New Jersey, offers about 50 *one-hour* Saturday morning workshops for children from age 2 (movement, music, songs, rhythm instruments, imagination) through seventh grade. Their goal is to "challenge the learning needs and

**TABLE 6.1**   Examples of Courses Offered in the Purdue University Super Saturday Program

For Kindergarten and Lower Elementary Students
    Creative Thinking
    Mime
    Exploring Space
    Chinese
For Intermediate Elementary Students
    Art
    French
    Probability and Statistics
    Insects
For Upper Elementary Students
    TV Production
    Computers
    Native American Culture
    Chemistry
For Junior and Senior High School Students
    Economics
    Electrical Engineering
    Computers
    Horses
For College Credit
    Psychology
    French
    English Composition
    Political Science

styles of gifted children . . . [and stimulate] . . . higher levels of thinking, creativity, problem solving, and leadership. An interdisciplinary approach is used, and, where practical, courses are future oriented" (p. 2). Offerings include computer LOGO, oceanography, cartooning, metal and clay design, magic, rocketry, astronomy, drama, and "Blood and Guts Biology"—for first and second graders.

## SUMMER PROGRAMS

Most cities offer summer programs that are open to all students. Obviously, these may be capitalized upon by the teacher, parent, or counselor seeking enrichment opportunities for energetic, capable children. The National Association for

Gifted Children (NAGC) lists many summer programs on its website (www.nagc.org/summer/intro/html). The programs are listed separately for the northeastern, mid-Atlantic, midwestern, western, and southern areas of the United States plus "International," along with email and Internet addresses where available.

### Governor's School Programs

The Governor's School concept is a state-supported summer residential school for gifted teenagers. The content usually focuses on (1) math, science, and technology, (2) arts and entertainment, and (3) humanities and social studies. Currently, at least 32 states support about 43 Governor's Schools, almost exclusively serving high school students (Iowa accommodates 12- to 14-year-olds as well, and Maryland dips down to the fourth grade; Hallowell, 1991). Importantly, according to Hallowell, 24 of the 43 schools do not charge students for tuition, room, or board; of the 19 programs requiring students to pay some costs, 14 provided financial aid. Students must transport themselves to the school and arrive with some spending money.

Enthusiasm of educators and students runs high. For example, after a Governor's School experience students' likelihood of attending college increased (Cross, Hernandez, & Coleman, 1991). Said one student, "For the first time in my life, I can really be me. I can talk about opera or heavy metal music, and no one will think I'm weird."

The University of Iowa's middle school Governor's Institute accommodates about 90 seventh- and eighth-grade students, each of whom receives a $700 scholarship to cover costs. The focus each year is on leadership, a broad and critical topic. The curriculum includes five central themes: (1) understanding yourself and others, (2) developing your leadership potential, (3) developing skills of public speaking, communicating effectively, conflict resolution, and ethical leadership, (4) learning to work in groups, and (5) exploring leadership theories and models—which uses a college text. The courses emphasize analysis and critical thinking, often through debate and role-playing.

Some course highlights include a "ropes challenge course," which promotes teamwork and group problem solving, and service projects, such as visiting nursing home residents and helping disabled children at neighborhood centers. One key event in 2001 was a trip to the state capitol in Des Moines, where students chatted with two leaders, Iowa's Lt. Governor Sally Pederson and the director of a program concerned with African Americans in Iowa. Said one student of the program, "Awsome, that's all I can say. . . . This has been one of the best experiences of my life" (Warren, 2002, p. 3).

### Study Abroad Programs

A presumably expensive summer (or school year) option for gifted high school students is study abroad. Summer programs will include travel plus study of at least one country's language and culture. With school-year programs, a student lives with foreign family, attends a local school, and takes special foreign language classes (Limburg-Weber, 1999/2000; Olszewski-Kubilius & Limburg-Weber, 1999).

### Other High School Programs

A 1999 spring issue of the *National Research Center on the Gifted and Talented Newsletter* listed 22 "free summer programs for talented teens" (McCoach, 1999), which probably continue. All were for high school students. Nearly all focused on engineering and science, except for a few programs in medicine/health sciences, humanities/social sciences, and art. Over half were for minority and underrepresented students or Native American students, and some specified females or minority females. Five were residential programs with lodging paid; the rest apparently were commuter programs. One six-week program paid each high school female student $1,250. (Space will not permit details of program descriptions, locations, contacts, criteria, and so on. See

D. Betsy McCoach, 1999, or contact the NRC/GT, University of Connecticut, Storrs, CT 06269.)

### College Programs

Many colleges and universities offer summer programs (mini-courses) for gifted, talented, and creative elementary and secondary students. We described the Talent Search and Elementary Talent Search programs in Chapter 5.

As examples, Purdue University offers summer programs at four age levels. The *Pulsar* program is a two-week residential session for high school students. In 2002, a class entitled American Civil War in the West included visits to battle sites in Tennessee. Other classes were Entrepreneurship, Veterinary Medicine, Pop Art, Pharmacy, Electrical Engineering, and Movies and Mental Illness.

For students completing grades seven and eight, the *Star* program includes two one-week residential sessions. Some offerings were Aeronautical Physics, Pre-Med, Advertising, Forestry, Science Fiction, Machines and Bridges, Sculptures, Prehistoric Biology, Security and Liberty, and Suspenseful Spanish (a "haunting adventure").

At grades five and six, the *Comet* program offers three one-week residential sessions. Sample courses were Paint Without Brushes, Aquatic Underworld, Plant Biology, Writing, Civil War Adventure (students drill with a Civil War cannon), Contemporary Art, Architectural Geometry, Chemistry, and Web Page Design.

Finally, the *Meteor* day-program for grades three and four includes three one-week sessions. The first week (for all students) was Artistic Math, the second Animation Studio, and the third Phenomenal Physics.

The University of Iowa (UI) offers four summer programs. For high school students, the *Summer Institute for Creative Engineering* (SICE) is a two-week residential program offered collaboratively by the UI School of Engineering and the Belin-Blank Center (whose full name is the Connie Belin and Jacqueline N. Blank International Center for Gifted Education and Talent Development). The 2002 focus was Biomedical Engineering. Students worked with engineering faculty and practicing engineers to solve engineering problems, learning technical skills and engineering knowledge. SICE includes lectures, field trips, visits to research labs, and career counseling.

The high school *National Scholars Academy* (NSA) at UI includes two one-week residential sessions. Students study a single college-level course (e.g., Trial Style and Litigation Research, Modern Approaches to Biomedical Research) that requires "intensive exploration and application of content and skills not taught in high school. . . . The academy is designed to give you a taste of the college experience" (Belin-Blank Center, n.d.).

For students in grades six to eight, the residential *Junior Scholars Academy* (JSA) includes 14 different classes (e.g., Dropping the Bombs: Right or Wrong?, Human Genome Project, and Play/Write) that are spread over three one-week sessions. Students may attend one, two, or all three weeks.

For grades one to six, *Challenges for Elementary School Students* (CHESS) is a day program comprised of three one-week sessions. Some course offerings are Mummies and Tombs—Ancient Rome and Egypt; Detective Science; Challenge Math; Creative Approaches to Writing; and Light, Sound and Optical Illusions. The fast-paced half-day classes emphasize thinking skills. (For further information see www.uiowa.edu/~belinctr/programs/summer/index.html.)

The *College for Kids* (CfK) program at the University of Wisconsin-Madison (UW) is a three-week half-day program for 250 fifth graders. Mini-courses are just part of the plan. Following their early morning G/T seminar, each of the 27–28 teachers meets with his or her "family" of 10–12 children to practice brainstorming, problem solving, evaluation, and other thinking skills. They discuss that week's workshop, which they attend together, and the pros and cons of being gifted.

The program includes two one-week workshops in about 40 areas (e.g., chemistry, limnology, TV production, photography, dance, university history) taught by university faculty and graduate students. After their daily workshop, a family group might visit an engineering robot demonstration, the space science building, the geology museum, cows in the agricultural campus, or the UW art museum. The week between the two workshops focuses on large-group daily "extravaganzas," for example, exploding physics and chemistry demonstrations and slide lectures on astronomy and archeology. The first-hand acquaintance with UW facilities helps students value higher education.

The *Academic Talent Development Program* (ATDP) is a six-week summer program at Berkeley that serves about 1,000 students between ages 11 and 17 (Sosniak 2001). The program squares well with Sosniak's (2003) three principles for the development of talent: a lot of time and practice, a strong focus, and supportive *communities of practice* (described in Chapter 2).

Students take only one course in the ATDP program. They spend three to five hours per week in class, plus time studying at home or with classmates. They write short stories, poetry, or computer programs; put on plays; learn to translate Latin or speak Russian or Japanese; and learn the language and "stories" of archaeology, biology, or chemistry. Regarding communities of practice, students work together in and out of class; students and teachers telephone each other about classwork; students meet with professionals who share their interests; and Berkeley scientists visit the ATDP classes. Students work with archeologists at digs and marine biologists collecting samples. Accomplished poets or dance choreographers visit the classes. Noted Sosniak (2001), students learn that acquiring extremely high-level academic knowledge and skill requires a long-term and focused engagement far beyond the general education supplied by schools.

## Music, Art, Language, and Computer Camps

Many colleges and universities offer summer clinics, institutes, retreats, or camps in music, art, drama, and computers. Some sponsor foreign language camps where students eat, sleep, swim, canoe, and communicate in Spanish, French, German, or Russian. An especially good example is the *International Language Village* sponsored by Concordia College in Moorhead, Minnesota.

Although virtually none of these camps and institutes identify themselves as "programs for the gifted," students are attracted to the camp because of their talent and high interest in an area. The camps are a refreshing way to meet like-minded and like-talented friends.

## Summer Program Benefits and Problems

Olszewski-Kubilius (1997, 2003) noted that reported benefits of summer programs, which complement those for Saturday programs, include:

- Social support for learning and achievement, due to grouping with intellectual peers and support from teachers and counselors
- More suitable levels of difficulty and pace, thus combatting poor study habits and underachievement from too-easy and boring classes
- Increased understanding of university programs and college life
- Raised educational aspirations
- In residential programs, development of independence and living skills
- Increased individual risk-taking, both academically and socially
- Improved self-concept and self-esteem
- Increased acceptance of others, knowledge of different cultures, and a better worldview

Olszewski-Kubilius (2003) noted two problems that would apply to both Saturday and summer programs. First is the *continuity* issue: Will the Saturday or summer program accelerate students through material they would soon learn anyway? Must a good student repeat a course despite being well prepared for more a advanced course? Often, yes, and it's demoralizing. Second is the *access* problem: Since most Saturday and summer problems charge fees, often hundreds of dollars, do the programs exclude economically disadvantaged gifted students—students who most need the experiences? Without aid some programs may be too expensive for even moderate-income families.

## MENTORS AND MENTORSHIPS

The concept of mentoring is hardly new. In ancient Greece Mentor tutored Telemachus. Socrates was mentor to Plato, Plato to Aristotle, and Aristotle to Alexander the Great (Cox & Daniel, 1983).

Traditionally, mentorships include a community professional working with a single high school student, usually once per week, on the job, usually for a year. In gifted education the concept extends to high-ability students in both elementary and secondary school for various durations. Always, the adult mentor serves as a role model, guide, teacher, and friend. Mentoring has proven valuable for underachieving, economically disadvantaged, minority, and female students and students with disabilities (e.g., Casey & Shore, 2000; Clasen & Clasen, 2003; Duff, 2000; Goff & Torrance, 1999; Hébert & Olenchak, 2000). Indeed, Arnold and Subotnik (1995) noted that the attraction between a mentor and protégé—and the very success of the mentorship—are maximal if the mentor and mentee are closely matched in ethnicity, gender, social class, background, and values.

Some general goals of mentoring elementary students are to recognize individual students' characteristics, needs, and problems; serve as a positive role model; tutor or advise as necessary; and perhaps guide the child through home or school difficulties (C. A. Kass, personal communication, 1990). As director of teacher education and coordinator of teacher experiences in gifted education, Kass used future teachers—college students—as mentors. She noted that mentors can guide elementary students with these specific activities:

- Developing study skills
- Tutoring in difficult areas
- Composition skills and writing essays

- Developing special projects and research skills
- Learning to use the library
- Improving social relationships
- Understanding personal problems
- Exploring new interest areas

Using professionals instead of university students, Ellingson, Haeger, and Feldhusen (1986) summarized a successful mentor program for stu-

## INSET 6.2

### Mentoring a Minority, At-Risk, Underachieving 12-Year-Old

Jackson was a 12-year-old, at-risk, and economically impoverished African American fifth-grade boy with behavior problems. He was the oldest of five children, retained in first grade, and lived with his 80-year-old grandmother because his mother was in prison for burglary. Jackson also scored far into the superior range on a nonverbal intelligence test, and was keenly interested in science and math. In addition to weekly 45-minute support group sessions, his school paired him with a mentor. Together they visited a university science laboratory and a NASA museum, and Jackson had a hands-on session at a commercial design business. Further, the mentor arranged a meeting with a high school teacher who was a former space camp instructor. Meanwhile, Jackson's teacher used de Bono's CoRT (1986; see Chapter 11) problem-solving and decision-making techniques, learning contracts, and curriculum compacting to better individualize Jackson's school program, and to free up time for Jackson to study space—partly with a telescope constructed from a kit by Jackson and his former space camp instructor, and partly with the school space club that Jackson founded. Despite his virtually handicapping situation, Jackson experienced an improved self-concept, feelings of self-efficacy, academic success, and raised aspirations.

His teacher entered in her journal, "I am stunned!"

Adapted from Hébert & Olenchak, 2000.

dents as young as fourth grade. Instead of a one-on-one strategy, groups of six students met with, for example, an engineer, doctor, judge, history professor, or radio broadcaster.

In a high school program, Prillaman and Richardson (1989) used college students to mentor gifted students in grades 8 through 11, after school and on weekends for 12 weeks. The students selected an area of interest to explore, such as marine science, geology, photography, French culture, or archaeology. The college student mentors were recruited based on their expertise in an area.

In the typical high school mentorship program, the student is called a *protégé, intern, apprentice, mentee,* or *assistant.* The student visits the mentor at the job site on a scheduled basis to learn first-hand the activities, responsibilities, problems, and lifestyle associated with the particular business, art, or profession. Students normally receive high school credit for the mentorship experience. In some cases a formal work-study plan is developed in which the student is paid for working while learning.

### Online Mentoring

The Internet and email offer superb mentoring: online tutoring, ask-an-expert coaching, and linking of students with successful professionals anywhere (Duff, 2000). As an example, the telementoring program at Ursuline Academy connects females in grades 9 to 12 directly with professional women around the world. The mentor pool consists of Ursuline alumnae themselves, who in turn circulated (via email) the recruiting message to other professional females. Professionals who otherwise might be too busy are willing to share their knowledge and experience via email.

The weekly emails inform students about careers and requisite coursework and, importantly, increase career motivation—with strong incentive to take advanced classes. The telementoring includes counseling. Said one student, the program gives her "a person to talk to who went through the same experiences I am going through now" (Duff, 2000, p. 51).

An email program that helps students get in touch with experts is http://mentor.external.hp.com. A site that helps set up international telementoring is www.telementor.org.

### Good Mentors

There are many characteristics of effective mentors—persons who typically model the values, attitudes, and behaviors that the protégé will strive to emulate (Clasen & Clasen, 1997, 2003). We already noted that a good match in regard to ethnicity, gender, social class, background, and values can be crucial to the mentorship. Three assumed characteristics are high competence in an area, a strong interest in teaching young people, and a willingness to devote time to the mentorship. Especially important is the ability to provide learning experiences that are enjoyable and challenging, that enable students to use their gifts, abilities, and imagination, that bring the protégé to higher levels of thinking and problem solving, and that enable students to see their own possibilities.

### FUTURE PROBLEM SOLVING

The popular *Future Problem Solving* (FPS) program is an enrichment activity that can take place in a pullout, resource center, special class, or Saturday program, or with gifted students who are mainstreamed or clustered in the regular classroom. If your FPS team is good, it will travel to a state Future Problem Solving bowl or even to the International FPS Conference. FPS was begun in 1975 by E. Paul Torrance at the University of Georgia. It grew into a statewide Georgia plan, then a national and even international program.

The objectives of FPS are to help gifted children (1) become more aware of the future in order to deal with it actively and optimistically; (2) become more creative and learn to go beyond the obvious; (3) improve communication skills, especially speaking and writing clearly, accurately, and persuasively; (4) develop teamwork skills, such as listening, respecting, understanding, and compromising; (5) learn to use a problem-solving model and integrate it into their daily lives; and (6) develop research skills, including how and where to gather information (Crabbe, 1982).

The year-long program begins with the registration of each five-student team in one of three grade divisions, Juniors (grades 4–6), Intermediates (7–9), and Seniors (10–12). The teams are sent five problems, which they solve using the following seven-step model, based on the Creative Problem Solving (CPS) model (see Chapter 9). The teams:

1. Research the general topic.
2. Brainstorm problems related to a specific ("fuzzy") situation.
3. Select an important underlying problem from the brainstormed problems.
4. Brainstorm solutions to the underlying problem.
5. Develop five criteria by which to judge the ideas.
6. Use the criteria to evaluate the ten most promising solutions, then select the "best" solution.
7. Describe the best solution.

A typical problem in FPS begins with a one-page scenario that is read by the five-person team. The scenario is accompanied by about 20 recent magazine and newspaper articles pertaining to the issues presented. With these and other resources, the team proceeds through the above seven steps. Their single best solution is explained in essay form, with outcomes and consequences elaborated and explained.

Past problems have dealt with poverty, terrorism, garbage disposal, school dropouts, crime, drug abuse, child abuse, ozone depletion, water shortages, acid rain, medical advances, space exploration, ethics in sports, use of land, and many others. The five 2001–2002 topics dealt with alternative energy sources for the 21st century (Which will emerge? Will they be ready?); new educational options in the next 100 years (What will education be like? What options will be available?); organ donation (Will the shortage problem be alleviated? What about ethical issues?); the evolution of environmental law pertaining to habitat destruction (What issues will emerge? How will laws be changed?); and the "dot com" corporations (Will they survive? How will they impact traditional companies and consumers?).

As each problem is completed, it is sent for scoring to the state FPS organization. The first two problems are practice problems. Based on the quality of the third problem, top teams are invited to participate in the state FPS competition. For the state competition, the teams are given a topic in advance which they research. At the competition site, each team is given the problem scenario—then sequestered in a room for two hours to prepare problem statements and solutions according to the above steps. The three winning teams in the state competition, one per division, are sent to the International FPS Conference.

Another component is the Primary Division for grades K–3. These children are introduced to the problem-solving process in a noncompetitive atmosphere. There are no rules regarding team size—a teacher or coach can engage an entire class. They solve three practice problems, which are evaluated and feedback provided.

Torrance and Torrance (1978) reported student testimonials on the benefits of FPS. For example, a fifth-grade girl reported, "I learned to cooperate, to share ideas, to produce creative and clever ideas, to be excited, to learn, and to work." Rimm and Olenchak (1991) successfully used FPS to motivate underachievers. (Information is available from FPS Program, 2028 Regency Road, Lexington, KY 40503, 800-256-1499; www.fpsp.org.)

## ODYSSEY OF THE MIND

Like Future Problem Solving, *Odyssey of the Mind* (OM; formerly Olympics of the Mind) is a national and international program. Also like FPS, it is an excellent vehicle for teaching creative thinking and problem solving, along with self-confidence, interpersonal skills, and more.

The key assumption of its founders, Ted Gourley and Sam Micklus, is that the mind can be trained and strengthened through exercise with mental games just as the body is trained with physical exercise (Gourley, 1981).

The first step is to get information from http://odysseyofthemind.com, including downloading and printing a 32-page booklet that explains coaching, selecting the team, team training, brainstorming, parental involvement, age divisions, long-term problems (and scoring), style points (for creative presentation), spontaneous problems, competitions, awards, program rules, and disciplinary action for violating the rules.

There are four age divisions, all based on age on May 1. In Division I, team members must be less than 12 or in the fifth grade; Division II is less than 15 or in the eighth grade; Division III is 15 or older and attending high school; and Division IV is college students. Teams include seven members, but only five can be "on the playing field." Children in a primary (K–2) division participate in a noncompetitive creative skit. Typically, each team also registers with their state OM office.

OM provides each team with detailed directions for preparing long-term problems that will require months to plan and implement prior to the regional competitions in April or May. Performance time is eight minutes. Costs are limited, which supports buying at Goodwill. Briefly, for 2001–2002, the five long-term problems were:

1. *The Chameleon.* The team creates and drives a vehicle that changes appearance. The performance includes three different environments/settings. The vehicle is driven to each environment, where it changes appearance to blend in. The driver will also blend in.

2. *OMER's Earthly Adventures.* The OM mascot, OMER, uses creative problem solving to fix "malfunctions" that prevent three environmental preservation tasks from being completed. The team must create the illusion of OMER traveling.

3. *Center Stage.* The team creates a humorous performance based on a selection from a list of classical literature. A host sets the tone and, eventually, explains the essence of the story. The team creates a stage set and choreographs a dance. A

concluding epilogue includes a character from a different selection on the list.

**4.** *It's a Snap.* With balsa wood and glue, the team builds components of a structure that are assembled into a complete structure. Components interlock without fasteners. The structure must stay together when lifted from any piece of wood. It must support as much weight as possible.

**5.** *The Ostrich Factor.* A humorous performance includes a character who possesses the Ostrich Factor—when it hides its head it becomes invisible. A second character can see the ostrich even when its head is hidden. The ostrich hides its head five times. Once it misses a fun event; another time it reappears in a different place or time (Divisions I and II).

In the primary (K–2) division, in *Me and My Shadow* the team creates an original performance about a person's shadow. When its person is in the dark, the shadow can leave and interact with other shadows in a fantasy shadowland. At least three times, the person will go from dark to light. A signaling system advises the audience when the person is in the light.

In addition to the long-term problems, students also solve *spontaneous* (short-term) problems both in practice and on the day of competition. For example, students might be asked to improvise with a ping-pong ball ("It's a clown's nose!" "It's an egg from a plastic bird!"). Teams are awarded one point for each common idea and three points for each creative idea. They learn to give creative ideas. For further information, contact Odyssey of the Mind Programs, c/o Creative Competitions, 1325 Route 130 South, Suite F, Gloucester City, NJ 08030.

## JUNIOR GREAT BOOKS

*Junior Great Books* (JGB), a program of the *Great Books Foundation,* is a another popular enrichment program that currently is used in gifted programs in all 50 states and many foreign countries. Two goals of JGB are implementing JGB programs in grades K–12 and training teachers to be-

come JGB leaders. In one- or two-day workshops at several levels, the JGB Foundation trains teachers to ask probing questions that require students to think and interpret the literature.

The carefully selected books consist of modern and traditional literature for each grade level from kindergarten through high school. Children in kindergarten through grade four read (or hear) fairy tales and folk tales. Grades four through nine cover children's classics and modern short stories. High school students read short selections from great works of philosophy, political science, economics, and fiction. All readings have proved to be comprehensible, rich in ideas for sustained discussion of the interpretive questions, and enjoyable to read and discuss. Teachers engage students in in-depth discussions of their reading in three to five class periods per week, with homework only for high school students.

Strengthening reading skills (e.g., vocabulary), listening skills, and interpretation and inquiry are some of the benefits (Nichols, 1992), along with greater self-awareness and insights into psychological and social problems. (For further information, contact Junior Great Books, 35 East Wacker Drive, Suite 2300, Chicago, IL 60601-2298, 800-222-5870; www.greatbooks.org/progs/junior.)

## ACADEMIC COMPETITIONS

The *United States Academic Decathlon* is a challenging high school program that includes regional, state, and national competitions. Each team is composed of two "A," two "B," and two "C" students in grades 11 or 12. Each school competes in one of three categories based on school size. They compete in conversation skills, essay writing, formal speech, economics, language and literature, fine arts, mathematics, physical science, social studies, and a Super Quiz. The Super Quiz topic is provided in advance, for example, "The History of Flight from Daedalus to Kitty Hawk to Voyager." (For further information, contact United States Academic Decathlon, 10882 Kyle Street, Los Alamitos, CA 90720-2463; www.usad.org.)

The single best source of national competitions, many of which are open to students of all ages, is the book *Competitions: Maximizing Your Abilities* (Karnes & Riley, 1996a). It lists over 275 competitions in the categories of academics, fine and performing arts, leadership, and service learning. Each competition is summarized in about one page, listing the competition name, sponsor, purpose, description, eligibility requirements, dates (for applications and awards), how to enter, judging criteria, and awards. The awards include medals, ribbons, certificates, "prizes," scholarships, and in a few cases cash.

As examples, the category of academics includes subcategories of general academics (including an AP competition), business, foreign languages, language arts (10 subcategories), math, science (7 subcategories), social studies (6 subcategories), and technology. As a (cash) example of general academics, the All-USA High School Academic Team Competition is sponsored by *USA Today* to "recognize academic excellence and leadership" (Karnes & Riley, 1996a, p. 29) in students grade 9–12. Nomination forms are sent to principals and guidance counselors. Twenty "First Team" students each receive $2,500 cash plus recognition in *USA Today*. In social studies, another example from the academics category is the National Geography Olympiad. This competition involves a 50-question test given to students in grades 2 to 12 before April 10. Winners receive medals and certificates.

Fine and performing arts competitions include subcategories of drawing and poster design, music, performing arts, photography and videotaping, and visual arts. For example, under drawing and poster design, the Federal Junior Duck Stamp (JDS) Conservation and Design Program is open to grades K–12. Students' designs of ducks, geese, or swans in their natural habitat are first entered in a state JDS competition. Every student gets a certificate of participation; 100 ribbons are awarded; and a State Best of Show ribbon goes to the best designer. The National first place winner receives $2,500.

In the leadership category, the Freedoms Foundation National Awards Program is open to grades K–12 "to honor individuals and schools who promote an understanding of responsible citizenship" (Karnes & Riley, 1996a, p. 303). Students submit typed essays or speeches, or submit a ring binder substantiating the students' projects. The winner receives a $100 Savings Bond. Many others receive a George Washington Honor Medal.

With service learning, Pizza Hut sponsors the Kids' Hall of Fame open to students 14 and under "who are making a positive difference." By March 15 someone submits a 25- to 100-word description of the applicant's service. It is evaluated according to uniqueness, impact, exhibited level of commitment and responsibility, and degree of success. National winners receive a $10,000 post–high school scholarship and a trip to Washington, DC; 25 first-prize winners receive a $100 savings bond. Oh yes, contestants must not have a criminal record.

## TECHNOLOGY AND THE GIFTED

Computer and Internet technology presents endless enrichment opportunities. Computers increase students' control over learning and improve their productivity (Berger & McIntyre, 1998; Pyryt, 2003; Pyryt is pronounced "pirate").

An Internet site for anyone interested in gifted education is www.hoagiesgifted.com. It includes links to other relevant websites. Creativity is explained at the Creativity Web, http://members .ozemail.com.au/~caveman/Creative/index2.html.

Apart from computer games, an early exposure is keyboarding skills and word processing. Young writers type, save, and print their masterpieces. They learn to select fonts and type sizes, cut and paste, and use the spell check, grammar check, and thesaurus. They improve quickly in writing ability (including grammar), typing, and general computer literacy. After the basics are dozens of intricacies of word processing—setting margins, tabs, page numbers, and justification; using indents and hanging indents; creating columns, tables, and bulleted lists; inserting headnotes, footnotes, graphics, bookmarks, and the date; working with data bases; creating power-point presentations; and more.

## "Library" Research

For all students, the Internet supplies obvious "library" research possibilities. A few clicks will produce information related to virtually any subject, problem, or career field. Students invest their efforts in working with information, not finding it. Gifted students can explore topics and biographies in any depth. Biographies, for example, are at www.biography.com and http://myhero.com/home.asp.

## Important Websites

The National Association for Gifted Children (2000) published a list of websites for gifted students and their teachers. The sites present lesson plans for teachers, learning activities, problems to solve, research problems, encyclopedia-type information, access to experts, links to relevant web sites, and even cyber-visits to a shark research station and NASA's Jet Propulsion Laboratory, with pictures and sound. NRC/GT published a similar list of websites for gifted students (Vahidi, 1998).

The following is an abbreviated combined list. Note that Internet (website, URL) addresses generally begin with "http://" and most (not all) with "http://www." Be exact–if a dot, letter, or capitalization is incorrect, the website will not appear. Many websites include links to subtopics or other websites. Also note that websites come and go. All listed in this chapter were operational at the time of this writing.

*Lesson plans, project ideas, Internet resources.* For teacher lesson plans, see http://ericir.syr.edu (contains the AskERIC Lesson Plan Collection) and www.col-ed.org/cur. For research project assistance (e.g., locating experts), www.tapr.org/emissary. For locating and using Internet resources, http://execpc.com/~dboals/boals.html.

*Curriculum resource centers.* Resources for teachers, librarians, kids, and parents for differ-

ent curriculum areas and grade levels are at www.awesomelibrary.org and www.educationworld.com.

*Language arts and literature.* For reading selections, books, and/or guides to the writing process visit www.planet.eon.net/~bplaroch/index.html (grades 4–7), www.sdcoe.k12.ca.us/score/cyberguide.html, and www.ucalgary.ca/~dkbrown.

*Arts.* Art educators, museum educators, and classroom teachers find lesson plans (and an art exhibit) at www.artsednet.getty.edu.

*Music.* Music education is at www.childrensmusicworkshop.com.

*Geography and weather.* The National Geographic expeditions website is www.nationalgeographic.com/xpeditions and the U.S. Geologic Division site is http://quake.wr.usgs.gov.

*Mathematics.* Teacher resources are at http://mathforum.org, with a link to Ask Dr. Math. Two sites that present lively explorations and math challenges are www.c3.lanl.gov/mega-math and www.figurethis.org. Statistics and probability teaching resources are at www.execpc.com/~helberg/statistics.html.

*Science.* The site http://powayusd.sdcoe.k12.ca.us/dolly ("Hello Dolly") describes cloning. Astrophysics and astronomy explorations, experiments, and discussion topics are at http://hea-www.harvard.edu. NASA space activities are at www.jpl.nasa.gov. Chemistry and biochemistry are at http://chem4kids.com. Environmental education is at http://envirolink.org/envrioed. Astronomy is www.astro.washington.edu. And you can "ask the scientist" with a one-hour per week videoconference at http://space.rice.edu/hmns/dlt/video.html; the site also includes "late-breaking science news" and information about NASA and women in NASA. A telementoring site, sponsored by the National Science Foundation for high school females interested in science, engineering, and computing, is at www.edc.org/CCT/telementoring.

*Social studies.* World history and a daily quiz are at www.thehistorynet.com. Projects and activities are at http://socialstudies.com/online.html. For teachers and students, U.S. and world history, geography, cultural diversity, and more are available at http://education.indiana.edu/~socialst.

*Other online projects and ideas.* For international and cross-cultural email and pen pal exchanges, visit www.iecc.org. Ideas for world health and welfare projects are at www.iearn.org. UNICEF presents activities and quizzes and permits young adults to share ideas about world issues at www.unicef.org/voy. Connections with 90,000 kids in 103 countries plus classroom project ideas appear at www.kidlink.org. Ideas for teachers for websites, lessons, tutorials, telecollaborative activities, Spanish resources, online scavenger hunts, and more are at www.4teachers .org. Information on how to use the Internet to pursue an incredible variety of learning experiences in many areas is at http://edweb.sdsu.edu/ webquest/webquest.html.

Finally, one can tap into major newspapers (*Washington Post, New York Times, Los Angeles Times,* and others) and visit hundreds of museums such as the Field Museum of Natural History (Chicago), the Louvre (Paris), the Smithsonian Institution (Washington, DC), the Frank Lloyd Wright museum, and others.

## GROUPING OPTIONS: BRINGING GIFTED STUDENTS TOGETHER

We have noted the benefits of grouping gifted students, part-time if not full-time, many times in this text. Learning activities can be enriched and accelerated—to fit student capabilities and learning needs, develop creativity and thinking skills, reduce boredom and frustration, and combat underachievement habits by inviting students to work and think for a change. Equally important is the opportunity to interact with others like themselves for social and academic support.

In this section we will briefly summarize grouping options in three categories:

1. Full-time homogeneous classes
   Magnet schools
   Special schools for the gifted
   Private schools

School-within-a-school plans
   Special classes in the elementary school
2. Full-time heterogeneous classes
   Cluster groups of gifted students placed
     with regular students
   Individualizing in heterogeneous classes
3. Part-time or temporary groups
   Pullout programs
   Resource programs
   Part-time special classes
   Enrichment clusters
   Temporary grouping for reading and math
   Special interest groups and clubs

### Full-Time Homogeneous Grouping

The main benefit of full-time grouping of gifted students is illustrated in this anecdote recounted by Elizabeth Connor (1991) in her description of EAGLE School, Connor's private school for the gifted:

*Six-year-old Maurit announced to her family at the dinner table that she had just been selected to participate in "Wonderful Wednesdays," her public school's pullout enrichment program. Once a week she could participate in special activities in the gifted/ talented resource room instead of doing her regular classwork. Maurit's older sister, Orelia, a student at EAGLE School . . . greeted the news with delight:*

*"Oh, Maurit, that means you're gifted. Now you can come to EAGLE School!"*
*Maurit pondered this idea for a moment, then replied, "No, I don't think so. If you go to EAGLE, you have to be gifted all the time. I'm just gifted on Wednesdays."*

***Magnet Schools.*** Many large cities have adopted magnet high school plans to accommodate the needs not only of gifted and talented students, but also of regular students seeking special training for a trade or career. A clear purpose is to make high school relevant to realistic student goals, particularly for potential dropouts who view school as prison rather than a path to economic and social success. Note that gifted students, as well as low-ability students, too often become frustrated and drop out. All magnet schools offer specialized training in, say, the arts, math, science, business, or trade skills. A school also may be designated as a "superior abilities school." Students are bused in from all corners of the city or district to attend the high school that suits their educational and career interests. In some cases, they are placed in career-related part-time jobs so they may earn money and gain valuable experience while attending school. Such programs are indeed relevant, and they do meet students' needs. They also are known to reduce the dropout rate.

***Special Schools for the Gifted.***   Special schools for the gifted, either elementary or secondary, typically are a medium- to big-city alternative. The curriculum will include both traditional academic content—based upon district guidelines and requirements—plus special enriched and accelerated training in whatever academic, artistic, scientific, or personal development areas the school chooses to emphasize.

One example of a special elementary school is the Golda Meir School in Milwaukee. Students in grades three to five are selected from the entire district based upon the federal definition (general ability, specific academic aptitude, creativity, leadership, or visual or performing art talent), as reflected in test scores, grades, and teacher, parent, and peer nominations (Pfeil, 1978). A quota system is used to balance the school composition for sex, race, and representation from all districts in the Milwaukee system. Subject matter acceleration is limited in particular subjects so that students will not be advanced beyond grade level when they enter the regular junior high school.

Enrichment opportunities, however, are diverse and exciting. They include foreign language training; piano, violin, viola, and general music lessons; drama lessons from members of the Milwaukee Repertory Company; the creation of a school newspaper, aided by Milwaukee Journal reporters; field trips to Milwaukee's civic, financial, and cultural centers (between 12 and 30 trips per student per year); "MACS Packs" (math-arts-crafts-science) which offer daily student projects; and "Lunch Bunch" involvement in games, films, reading, or just visiting. There is a Classics Club which reads above-grade level books, an Advanced Science Club, a school chorus, a Student Senate, and sometimes an infant-care class featuring a real infant—a student's younger brother or sister. Enthusiasm runs high. This model school hosts many visitors.

***Private Schools.***   Achievement tends to run higher in private schools than in public schools. Therefore, private schools can be a good alternative for an accelerated education.

Some private schools cater especially to gifted and talented students (see e.g., Connor, 1991; Hollingsworth, 1991; Kelble, 1991). In Hillsborough, California, for example, the Nueva Learning Center offers training in six *R*s (reading, writing, arithmetic, rights, respect, and responsibility), piano, ballet, math, science, and more unusual topics such as organic gardening, aviation, karate, and cross-country skiing.

In Madison, Wisconsin, the EAGLE School fills a strong demand for private schooling for gifted children. Serving grades K–8, small classes of about 11 children "allow students to be explorers, scientists, mathematical puzzlers, or people in history who have solved problems" (Connor, 1991, p. 16). The curriculum—presented by 10 or 11 different specialists per week—includes art, drama, music, gym, word processing, computers, French, Spanish, science, math, language arts, social studies, and electives such as fencing, chorus, math games, robotics, or the popular art studio. See Juntune (1981) for descriptions of goals and curricula of private schools that serve gifted students.

Chapter 5 discussed state-supported residential high schools for gifted students. A related opportunity is private residential high schools for gifted students. A new and remarkable example is the Conserve School in northern Wisconsin, for grades 9–12, which opened in the fall of 2002. (The school is well funded by the late James R. Lowenstine, former president of Central Steel and Wire Company of Chicago.) The campus includes

1200 acres of woodlands, seven lakes, and 22 miles of hiking and biking trails. With 15 students per class, the school offers English, history, languages, science (with well-outfitted physics and chemistry laboratories, plus lakes and woods for biology studies), mathematics, visual arts (including studio space, pottery kiln, and photo darkroom), performing arts (including a 500-seat theater, a large music room, private practice rooms, and optional private music and voice lessons), and technology at the school's cutting-edge Technology Complex.

Conserve School emphasizes environmental conservation, leadership, ethics, creativity, and personal growth. For example, the campus "Green Machine" uses plants, bacteria, snails, and fish to process its waste water. Students learn biology and chemistry while helping maintain the Green Machine. Teamwork, health, and interpersonal skills are promoted with interscholastic, intramural, and recreational sports, including volleyball, basketball, baseball, softball, soccer, track, wrestling, golf, racquetball, running, skiing, canoeing, kayaking, sailing, weight training, fishing, ice skating, and rock wall climbing on the school's own climbing wall. Other activities include movies, dances, clubs, and private projects and hobbies at the technology and arts centers.

Tuition is $25,000 per year, but nobody pays it. Financial assistance extends as high as $24,000 per year. Busloads of inner-city students and parents visited the nonsectarian, gender-equal Conserve School during its initial recruitment period. Frankly, you have to visit Conserve School to believe it, as did your author (Davis). For information, see www.ConserveSchool.org.

**School-within-a-School.**   Similar to special classes for G/T students (next section), an entire school may be organized around a school-within-a-school concept (e.g., Witham, 1991). Here, gifted and talented students from around the district attend a particular school that also accommodates regular students. For part of the day, gifted students attend special advanced and enriched classes. They mix with other students for nonacademic subjects, such as physical education, study

hall, manual arts, and home economics and for sports and social events.

**Special Classes.**   There is a continuing interest in full-time classes for gifted and talented children—because part-time programs provide only a part-time solution. Special classes for gifted and talented students may take several forms. At the elementary level all gifted students within a particular grade level, age, or age range may be assigned to a special class. In addition to covering prescribed grade-level objectives—and usually extending beyond them—a variety of enrichment, personal development, and skill development experiences are planned. In a survey of teachers, administrators, and G/T program coordinators, 98 percent felt that special classes were "academically advantageous" to gifted students, 84 percent agreed that motivation ran higher, and 85 percent rated the special classes as good for the social-emotional development of gifted students (Feldhusen & Sayler, 1990).

In the negative column, the existence of special classes for bright students flies smack in the face of the educational reform movement, which opposes exactly this form of separation by ability. Further, some students may resist being separated physically and psychologically from regular students. It also is not unusual for other students to resent their special status and to make them feel socially uncomfortable, for example, by calling them names or by silent ostracism.

Another danger, especially at the secondary level, is that teachers of special—and more difficult—classes may grade on a normal curve, thus giving Bs and Cs to students who could easily earn As in regular courses. Grade-conscious students may avoid such "special classes."

In high school there already is a variety of college preparatory classes to challenge the abilities of gifted and talented students, for example, in chemistry, physics, calculus, art, journalism, and drama. Special classes beyond these also may be created, for example, courses in college algebra, organic chemistry, advanced physics, advanced botany, creative writing, photography, or whatever else students' needs and the school budget will allow. If some of these can be taught in accord with Advanced Placement program guidelines they may lead to college credit, as described in Chapter 5.

As an example of a special high school class, Mackin, Macaroglu, and Russell (1996) summarized their successful science seminar that extends beyond the traditional biology, botany, chemistry, and physics offerings. The course was elective and required each student to prepare a research paper, an oral presentation of the research to another class, an original research design involving the problem of interest, a poster showing the results of the investigation, and an abstract about the area of interest. Of necessity, the teacher's role changed to facilitator, mentor, or guide—most students knew more about their topics than did their boss. Among many benefits, the seminar gave students "invaluable preparation for college" (p. 49) and a continued interest in science. Uniquely, the oral presentations and posters motivated nonseminar students to become enthusiastic about science.

## Full-time Heterogeneous Grouping

*Cluster Groups.*   The phrase "cluster grouping" sometimes refers to "clustering" gifted students in special or accelerated classes. However, the proper use of *cluster grouping* means placing 5 to 10 high-ability students in one regular class per grade, along with 15 or 20 regular students. The class is taught by a teacher who has received in-service training or coursework in gifted education and wishes to differentiate the curriculum for gifted students.

The cluster group of G/T students engages in a variety of enrichment activities either individually or in small groups. To "buy time" the teacher can compact the curriculum by not requiring students to study material they already know, and by accelerating them through material they do not know. The enrichment activities should focus on advanced, in-depth content and building creativity, problem solving, research skills, or other high-level thinking skills. (Categories and specific thinking skills are described in Chapter 11.)

For example, individual students might "contract" for independent learning activities such as a library/Internet research report, an independent research project, or the mastery of an advanced math, science, computer, or language-learning assignment. Alternatively, groups of students with similar interests and abilities might work on a particular problem or project for a mutually agreed-upon period of time.

Kaplan (1974) itemized five "necessities" and "checkpoints" in planning a cluster group program: (1) develop criteria for selecting students; (2) define the qualifications and selection process for teachers; (3) clarify the teachers' responsibilities and activities; (4) plan the differentiated experiences for the cluster of gifted students; and (5) plan the support services and special resources, such as counselors and computers.

Gentry (1999) described a "well developed . . . total school cluster grouping program" (p. 52–53) in a rural—but hardly small—Midwestern elementary school with five classrooms per grade level. Some main features were that one classroom at each grade level accommodated a cluster of about eight high-achieving (G/T) students (but deliberately no "above average" students), which was taught by a trained and enthusiastic teacher. The other four classes all included clusters of above-average, average, and below-average students, and one class at each grade included a cluster of special education students, also taught by a trained and interested teacher. Teachers used between-class grouping in math and reading to challenge students at appropriate levels, along with temporary and flexible grouping.

Importantly, all teachers in the school received in-service training in gifted education pedagogy. They all held high achievement expectations. They all tried to provide challenging instruction. They experienced the common discovery that removing the highest achievers from classrooms made teaching easier—they no longer worried about accommodating the highest-ability students. The remarkable outcome was improved achievement not only for the gifted students, but for *all* students.

Winebrenner (2001) itemized these overlapping advantages of cluster grouping:

- The cluster group teacher is trained in teaching gifted students.
- Teaching five or ten gifted students, instead of one or two, is a better use of teachers' time.
- Students associate with intellectual peers, which is both rewarding (having someone to share with) and humbling (they learn that others are also smart).
- When gifted students are clustered in one classroom, new academic leaders emerge in the other classroom(s).
- With gifted students elsewhere, nonclustered classrooms have more homogeneous students. Teaching is easier and achievement can improve for all students.
- In contrast with a once-a-week pullout program, cluster teachers compact the curriculum and provide challenging learning experiences every day.
- There are no disadvantages.

***Heterogeneous Classes.*** With or without influence from the reform movement toward heterogeneous classes, some schools simply do not have special classes or programs for gifted students. Many gifted-conscious teachers in regular classrooms must use their ingenuity to provide differentiated and enriched learning experiences to their eager, fast-learning, and creative students.

One option described earlier in this chapter is learning centers, which permit worthwhile explorations into math, art, any science area, music appreciation, handicrafts, foreign languages (H. Feldhusen, 1981, 1986), thinking skills (Winebrenner, 2001), or other areas for all students, especially those who finish early or already know today's material. We also recommend using cluster groups of gifted students in the regular classroom.

Winebrenner (2001) recommended curriculum compacting—specifically, pretesting for mastery of the material to be presented—which provides time for individualized *learning contracts* and her similar *Study Guide Method* and *Resident Expert Planner.* All three strategies promote greater learning depth and complexity, higher levels of abstraction, and the avoidance of poor study habits that develop when bright students must wait for the rest of the class.

With Winebrenner's detailed learning contracts, a written agreement is prepared that lists page numbers to be read and concepts to be mastered, possible "Extension Options" (e.g., making up math story problems), as well as "Working Conditions," which include: Stay on task, don't interrupt the teacher, use soft voices, never brag about working on different activities, don't bother anyone else, and don't call attention to yourself. Teacher and student sign the contract. Children work on their contract assignment in an "Extensions Center," away from the teacher-led class. Contracts are used for individual work in math, reading (including grammar), and writing. Some contracts concern problems to be solved, such as school or personal problems.

Winebrenner's (2001) *Study Guide Method* outlines in detail, also in writing, what the student should look for in the self-directed study of "another example of what the whole class is learning" (p. 68). For example, an *American Wars Study Guide* asked students to be prepared to discuss social, political, and economic causes of the war; to describe typical battle conditions; to write a newspaper account of a related event; to summarize the war's implications for the present; and to give meanings of designated vocabulary words. "Learning Conditions" included "I will keep a Daily Log" and "I will share what I have learned . . . with the class in an interesting way . . . including a visual aid" (p. 75). "Working Conditions" were similar to those for learning contracts. Both sign. If students fail to meet the learning and working conditions, they return to the teacher-directed group for the remainder of the unit.

Winebrenner's *Resident Expert Planner,* which both also sign, is a third form used for independent study. It lists six topics, with three questions for each, plus needed materials/supplies, the format of the report, the portion to be completed at home, potential problems, and possible solutions.

Kaplan (2001) recognized the problem of teaching a prescribed curriculum in the heterogeneous classroom while differentiating the curriculum for gifted students. One solution was "paralleling," which simply means covering both the prescribed and a differentiated curriculum "in tandem." A second solution, which she called "clustering," was to use the core concepts and skills of the prescribed curriculum as "the centerpiece," while differentiated concepts and skills "reinforce the core." Both curriculums can be taught, said Kaplan, without sacrificing either.

Some teachers—in concert with counselors, parents, and students themselves—use Individualized Education Programs (IEPs) to structure the independent work of gifted students in heterogeneous classrooms, just as IEPs are used to plan education for students with learning or physical disabilities (see Inset 6.3).

Clasen (1982) itemized several alternatives available to the individual teacher in schools "where there is minimum involvement in programs for the gifted." Specifically:

- A student may be individually accelerated, perhaps by reading or working ahead or through the use of advanced or supplementary texts and workbooks.
- The curriculum may otherwise be modified to permit greater depth, more complexity, or higher levels of abstraction.
- Enrichment activities may be planned that build on or challenge the student's special abilities, for example, in creative writing, photography, or with computers.
- Academic and perhaps career advising help students understand their special capabilities and the training necessary for them to realize their potential.

---

INSET 6.3

### Using Individualized Education Programs (IEPS) with Gifted and Talented Students

Public Law 94-142, the "mainstreaming law," mandated the use of an *Individualized Education Program* (IEP) for each student classified as handicapped. IEPs also serve that other variety of exceptional student, the gifted and talented, particularly when they too are mainstreamed in the regular classroom.

For gifted students, the IEP will include:

**1.** Present levels of performance, as determined by intelligence tests, achievement tests, rating scales, and informal observations and reports by teachers, parents, school psychologists, and others.
**2.** Annual goals, which include short-term instructional goals. These goals will dictate most of the instructional methods, learning activities, and individual projects for each student required under item 3.
**3.** Specific educational services to be provided, based on the needs of the individual student. These will include special teaching strategies, special equipment, individual projects and assignments, field trips, and others.
**4.** The extent to which the student will participate in the regular program versus special G/T classes and activities.
**5.** A projected date for initiation and the anticipated duration of the services.
**6.** Evaluation procedures and appropriate objective criteria, which may result in a review and revision of the IEP.
**7.** A schedule for determining whether the objectives are being achieved.

Treffinger (1982) itemized 60 suggestions for teaching gifted students in the regular classroom. Some examples are:

- Use pretests or mastery tests to permit students to test out of material they already know (compacting).
- Use individualized learning packets, learning centers, and mini-courses, particularly in the basics.
- Allow time every day for individual or small-group projects.
- Incorporate creative thinking into subject areas.
- Help students to learn the meaning of higher-level thinking processes, such as *analysis, synthesis,* and *evaluation,* and to plan independent projects around these processes.
- Bring guest speakers to describe their careers or unusual hobbies.
- Use cross-age and peer tutoring.
- Help students to understand their own strengths, interests, learning strategies, and preferences, and to become sensitive to those of others.
- Explore many points of view about contemporary topics, and allow students the opportunity to analyze and evaluate evidence and conflicting ideas and opinions.
- Help gifted students set personal and academic goals.

Finally, note that if gifted and talented children in heterogeneous classrooms are not truly involved in differentiated curriculum and learning activities, one cannot say that the school is providing for their needs.

## Part-Time and Temporary Grouping

*Pullout Programs.* The old standby in programming for gifted and talented students is the *pullout* program. With minor variations, elementary students are pulled out of their regular classes once or twice per week for two to three hours per session to participate in special enrichment activities, guided usually by a district G/T teacher/coordinator. Often, one coordinator serves an entire district by conducting a pullout class in a different school each afternoon. The meeting place usually is called a *resource room* because it provides special reading material and equipment resources. As with other special classes and cluster grouping, pullout activities focus on acquiring knowledge and skills and strengthening creativity and thinking skills, communication skills, and self-concept development.

It is ironic that this most popular programming design also is the more severely criticized. A common statement is that pullout programs are a poor solution to the full-time problem of being gifted. Also, it is relatively expensive, largely because of the G/T coordinator's salary. Further, friction develops when teachers are saddled with the dilemma of permitting students to miss regular classwork or requiring them to make it up—thus punishing them for their G/T participation. Most pullout programs assume that G/T kids can afford to miss some regular content, and students are not held responsible for missed work.

Another problem is that students may not be comfortable being visibly separated from classmates and classified as "gifted." Still another classic criticism is that pullout curricula frequently include too much "fun and games" and too little theory-based training (Renzulli and Reis, 1985, 1991).

More positively, the pullout program is a popular and often successful means of bringing G/T students together for social and intellectual support, and for the special differentiated and enriched training they deserve. When it has a well-planned, challenging, and integrated curriculum, this program can offer gifted children good opportunities for developing high-level skills.

As one example, Cohen, Duncan, and Cohen (1994) studied peer relations in the Memphis CLUE pullout program. Fifty-three students in grades four to six met in a separate room with their CLUE teacher twice per week, $2\frac{1}{2}$ hours per session, to work on problem solving, generating alternatives, and individual and group projects.

Children were encouraged to self-monitor and self-evaluate. Social relationships also were discussed. CLUE children showed superior social relationships—earning high sociometric and popularity scores.

***Resource Programs and Resource Rooms.***   The phrases *resource program* and *resource room* are used rather freely. Because pullout students are sent to a resource room, pullout programs are sometimes called *resource programs* or *resource-room programs.*

The present meaning of *resource program* is a district-wide pullout plan in which gifted students are transported to specially equipped and taught resource rooms or enrichment centers for one or two sessions per week.

In Ankeny, Iowa, the *Ankeny Gifted and Talented Education* (AGATE) program uses city buses to transport K–9 students to a junior high school equipped with AV equipment, books, magazines, a science lab, a language corner, games, plants, a piano, and miscellaneous materials for independent projects. The enrichment curriculum has included such activities as astronomy, including building a telescope; rocketry, with student-made—and launched—rockets; film animation; journalism, resulting in a newspaper; foreign languages; American Sign Language; art; literature; theater; photography; oceanography; and more (Juntune, 1981). Students alternate mornings and afternoons and days of the week to avoid missing the same activities in their home classes.

***Part-time Special Classes.***   Special classes (discussed under Full-Time Homogeneous Grouping) also may be offered as part-time or temporary options. For example, in *Project Horizon* (Seattle, Washington) elementary school G/T students are placed in self-contained classes for 50–70 percent of the school day. Their differentiated experiences include independent projects, accelerated subjects, and small-group enrichment activities, all of which aim at developing creative and other high-level thinking skills.

***Enrichment Clusters.***   As we saw earlier, a "cluster group" was 5 to 10 gifted students "clustered" full-time in one classroom per grade level, where they receive the attention of a teacher trained in gifted education. *Enrichment clusters* are different. An enrichment cluster is a group of students—not necessarily identified as gifted (Reis, Gentry, & Maxfield, 1998; Renzulli, 1994)—from several grades who share a common interest, for example, in engineering, writing, drawing, archeology, snakes, paleontology, sign language, dairy farming, or creating a school newspaper (Reis, Westberg, Kulikovich, & Purcell, 1998). The group of students meet with an adult who is an expert in the area (e.g., a teacher, parent, or other community member) at designated times during the week for about 10–12 weeks. Enrichment clusters go into considerable depth. For example, students interested in snakes or paleontology learn also scientific methods of inquiry and assume the role of biologist or paleontologist. Students interested in learning to speak French also learn about French and other cultures.

No lesson plans are prepared in advance. Rather, three questions provide direction: (1) What do people with an interest in this area do? (2) What knowledge, materials, and other resources do they need? (3) How can the product or service have an impact on an intended audience. As we will see in Chapter 7, Renzulli's Enrichment Triad and newer models include creating products that impact an audience. The principle is that real-world innovators produce for an audience, not just for themselves.

Students are exposed to advanced content, resources, and methodologies, and they acquire new concepts, new vocabulary, and new tools. They learn about an area, then develop authentic products, services, performances, or presentations.

Reis et al. (1998) emphasized these four principles of enrichment teaching and learning:

- Each student is different.
- Learning is more effective when students enjoy what they do.

- Learning is more meaningful when content and process are learned while solving a real problem.
- While some formal instruction is necessary, a major goal is promoting knowledge and thinking skills via the application of what students have learned; they construct their own meaningfulness.

***Temporary Grouping for Reading and Math.*** In Chapter 1 we reviewed the advantages of within-class grouping and cross-grade grouping, both of which adjust teaching to match student achievement or ability (Kulik, 2003). Such grouping normally is restricted to student differences in reading and math ability or achievement. A study with 645 fourth- and fifth-grade students from all socioeconomic levels in four school districts confirmed that students who (1) received math instruction in different achievement groups in the same class (within-class grouping) or (2) went to a different class for suitable instruction (Joplin plan, cross-grade grouping) achieved at higher levels than control students who received traditional whole-class instruction (Teiso, 2002). Further, teachers preferred and enjoyed having students change classrooms for math, which reduced heterogeneity among students. The students enjoyed both grouping plans, especially cross-grade (Joplin plan) grouping. There was no damage to students' self-esteem. On the downside, while teachers appreciated the need for ability/achievement grouping, they had concerns about logistics and classroom management aspects of such arrangements.

***Special Interest Groups and Clubs.***   Most secondary schools have these, although they are rare in the elementary school. G/T-conscious teachers at any level can assume the leadership necessary for organizing these enriching activities for interested students. There are drama clubs, German clubs, French clubs, computer clubs, chess clubs, math clubs, and others.

The teacher-leader can organize meetings, competitions, research projects, field trips, and meetings with community experts and can provide career information and guidance. One also can organize mini-courses, taught either by teachers or community experts, dealing with special interest areas such as music writing, computer programming, jewelry making, aviation, or other academic, career, or hobby topics. Clubs and courses may meet before or after school or on Saturdays.

## COMMENTS ON ENRICHMENT AND GROUPING

When we modify or "differentiate the curriculum" for gifted students, as per all of the enrichment and grouping strategies in this chapter, and as noted by Westberg and Archambault (1995), it means that we:

- Use advanced content.
- Provide depth, for example, by teaching interrelationships among bodies of knowledge.
- Accelerate the pace of instruction.
- Group students according to skill level or interest area.
- Allow independent, self-directed learning.
- Strengthen higher-level thinking skills, such as via questioning (Chapter 11) and projects that demand analysis, planning, creativity, interpretation, and evaluation.
- Allow independent, advanced-level projects.
- Use outside mentors, at elementary as well as secondary level.
- Compact already learned or quickly learned curriculum to provide time for independent learning or projects.
- Use learning or interest centers.

Westberg and Archambault (1995) and their colleagues visited ten elementary schools that had been identified as successfully teaching gifted students. Despite program differences, six repetitive themes emerged.

First, effective teachers had advanced training in gifted education, stemming from graduate degrees and inservice training that presented new teaching techniques.

Second, teachers were motivated. They were willing to make changes, spend extra time, and sometimes fail in trying to differentiate learning for gifted students.

Third, teachers collaborated with each other, with curriculum specialists, and with gifted education specialists to plan instruction for high-ability students.

Fourth, teachers used a variety of approaches to differentiating curriculum and instruction—all aimed at determining *what* students will learn, *how* they learn, and how they will *demonstrate* their learning. They modified the curriculum, set high standards, located mentors, encouraged independent projects, and created flexible instructional groups.

Fifth, teachers received clear support from their principals and superintendents.

The sixth recurrent theme was a "supportive atmosphere" or "collaborative culture" that encouraged teachers to experiment with and adopt new practices, such as flexible staffing patterns and new curricula.

## SUMMARY

Many enrichment activities are good for all students, not just the gifted. Qualified and enthusiastic teachers are critical. Worthwhile enrichment should be guided by the types of objectives in Table 5.1, Chapter 5.

Enrichment strategies are delivery methods for achieving process and content goals.

Independent projects can involve library/Internet research, scientific research, art, drama, creative writing, or others.

Commercial or teacher-made learning centers can teach languages, science, math, computers, social studies, creative writing, music appreciation, and others.

Field trips are good experiences for regular and gifted students. The teacher and the guide/educator should preplan any tour. Students should have problems to solve or questions to answer.

Feldhusen's Super Saturday is a model Saturday enrichment program.

Many cities offer summer programs. Governor's Schools are summer programs for gifted secondary students. At the Iowa Governor's Institute, seventh- and eighth-grade students learn ethical leadership. Study abroad programs can take place during the summer or academic year. Some free high school summer programs offer valuable learning experiences for minorities and females.

Many universities, such as Purdue University, the University of Iowa, the University of Wisconsin-Madison, and UC Berkeley, offer "college for kids" types of summer programs, largely mini-courses. The Berkeley Academic Talent Development Program supports Sosniak's concept of *communities of practice*.

Music, art, language, and computer camps are valuable summer programs. Bright and motivated students self-select. Summer programs can aid independence, understanding of college life, educational aspirations, goal-setting, self-esteem, risk-taking, acceptance of others, and more.

Mentor programs traditionally involved on-the-job, one-to-one interaction of a high school student with a community professional. In some programs, university students or professionals mentor elementary students, sometimes mentoring small groups of students. At Ursuline Academy, female high school students were mentored via email by professional women around the world. One trait of good mentors is providing enjoyable and challenging learning experiences that stimulate thinking and help students see their possibilities.

Future Problem Solving helps children become future-oriented and strengthens creativity, problem solving, communication and teamwork skills.

Odyssey of the Mind includes long-term problems, worked on over the school year, and short-term problems.

Junior Great Books acquaints students with classic literature and strengthens reading, interpretation, and discussion skills.

The United States Academic Decathlon is a national high school program involving competitions in a variety of academic areas.

The book *Competitions: Maximizing Your Abil-*

*ities* lists 275 national competitions for students of all ages in the areas of academics, fine and performing arts, leadership, and service.

Computer technology—the Internet—presents endless opportunities for "library" research of any topic or career. Keyboarding and word processing comprise an early exposure. NAGC and NRC/GT list important Internet sites in many areas for teachers and gifted students.

In the category of full-time homogeneous grouping, magnet high schools draw students to the particular school that accommodates their needs and educational/career interests. Special schools, elementary or secondary, enrich and accelerate the education of gifted students.

Private schools usually produce higher average achievement than public schools; some private schools are designed for gifted and talented students.

With the school-within-a-school plan gifted students attend special classes for part of the day and mix with regular students for other, usually less academic classes.

Special classes for gifted students may be created in the elementary or secondary school. Some problems are that the concept is contrary to the reform movement toward heterogeneous classes; some students may resist being separated; other students may resent the special status; and teachers may grade the more difficult class on a curve. High schools already provide differentiated opportunities for bright and motivated students.

Under full-time heterogeneous grouping, cluster grouping involves placing a group of five to ten gifted students in the same regular class for special assignments. Curriculum may be compacted to allow time for enrichment activities. The cluster grouping program described by Gentry, in which all teachers received training in G/T strategies, raised achievement for gifted and all other students.

In heterogeneous classes, gifted-conscious teachers can use learning centers or compact the curriculum, perhaps with pretesting. Winebrenner used compacting to provide time for three similar independent learning activities, all requiring a written agreement: learning contracts, Study Guide Method, and Resident Expert. Kaplan described two methods for covering the prescribed curriculum while differentiating for the gifted: "paralleling" (covering both the prescribed and a differentiated curriculum) and "clustering" (elaborating on core concepts of the prescribed curriculum).

IEPs may be used to individualize instruction for mainstreamed gifted students.

Some other suggestions for teaching the gifted in a regular classroom include individual acceleration, enrichment activities in a student's interest area, academic and career advising, compacting learning centers and individualized learning packets, incorporating creativity into regular subject areas, helping students plan projects that develop thinking skills, guest speakers, cross-age and peer tutoring, and helping gifted students to set goals.

In the category of part-time and temporary grouping, pullout programs, the most common elementary level G/T plan, involve sending gifted students to a resource room for one or two afternoons per week. It is criticized for being a part-time solution. Other problems include, for example, dealing with missed work.

A resource program is a district-wide pullout plan in which students travel to a resource room once or twice per week.

Special classes may be used on a part-time as well as full-time basis. For example, elementary students may attend special classes for part of the day; secondary students may be bused to a district-wide special class in, say, accelerated math or humanities. Honors programs use part-time special classes.

An enrichment cluster is a temporary group of students from several grades who have a common interest. They are taught by an adult expert in the area.

Special interest groups and clubs are a good outlet for students whose enthusiasm and ability exceed the regularly offered coursework.

Final comments on enrichment repeated recommendations to use advanced content, provide depth, accelerate instruction, group according to skill or interest, allow independent learning, focus on developing thinking skills, use outside mentors, compact the curriculum, and use learning centers. Westberg and Archambault reported six main themes of schools that successfully teach the gifted: teachers had advanced training, they were motivated, they collaborated with each other, they used a variety of ways to differentiate the curriculum and teach, administrators were supportive, and the atmosphere supported new practices.

## APPENDIX 6.1   MAGAZINES THAT PUBLISH STUDENT WORK

*Child Life*
Box 567
1100 Waterway Blvd.
Indianapolis, IN 46206

*Children's Album*
Box 6086
Concord, CA 94524

*Children's Digest*
Box 567
1100 Waterway Blvd.
Indianapolis, IN 46206

*Creative Kids*
GCT Inc.
Box 6448
Mobile, AL 36660

*Flip Magazine*
Art Center
265 Emmett Street
Battle Creek, MI 49017

*Highlights for Children*
803 Church Street
Honesdale, PA 18431

*Kid City*
1 Lincoln Plaza
New York, NY 10023

*Listen*
"Graffity"
6830 Laurel Street, NW
Washington, DC 20012

*McGuffy Writer*
400-A McGuffy Hall
Miami University
Oxford, OH 45056

*Odyssey*
Kalmback Publishing Company
1027 North 7th Street
Milwaukee, WI 53223

*Prism*
1040 Bayview Drive
Suite 223
Fort Lauderdale, FL 33304

*Scholastic Scope*
Student Writing
730 Broadway
New York, NY 10003

*Spinoff: Gifted Children Monthly*
Box 115
Sewell, NJ 08080

*Stone Soup*
Box 83
Santa Cruz, CA 95063

*Wombat*
365 Ashton Drive
Athens, GA 30606

*Young Authors' Magazine*
Theraplan, Inc.
3015 Woodsdale Blvd.
Lincoln, NE 68502

# CHAPTER 7

# CURRICULUM MODELS

*Research tells us that gifted behaviors can be developed in a far broader spectrum of the school population than the small percentage of students who are usually identified by high scores on intelligence or achievement tests.*

Joseph Renzulli and Sally Reis (1985, p. 3)

Curriculum models provide a theoretical framework within which specific enrichment activities may be planned. This chapter will briefly summarize ten curriculum models. In most cases—but not all—the models and their prescriptions are consistent and complementary, permitting a teacher-coordinator to draw ideas from two or more curriculum models simultaneously. Also, the Schoolwide Enrichment Model (Renzulli, 1994; Renzulli & Reis, 1997), the Pyramid Model (Cox, Daniel, & Boston, 1985), and the Autonomous Learner Model (Betts, 1985, 1991; Betts & Kercher, 1999) supply extensive details regarding program philosophy, recommended selection procedures, curriculum content, and specifics of carrying out the entire plan. For example, details of the Schoolwide Enrichment Model fill a 500-page book (Renzulli & Reis, 1997). Other models make general and specific recommendations, then leave it to the teacher-coordinator to fill in the particulars. These are the 11 models:

1. Enrichment Triad Model (Renzulli, 1977; Renzulli & Reis, 1997, 2003)
2. Schoolwide Enrichment Model (Renzulli, 1994; Renzulli & Reis, 1997, 2003)
3. Multiple Menu Model (Renzulli, 1988)
4. Pyramid Model (Cox, Daniel, & Boston, 1985)
5. Purdue Three-Stage Enrichment Model (Feldhusen & Kolloff, 1986; Moon, 1995, 1996)
6. Guilford/Meeker Structure of Intellect Model (Guilford, 1967, 1977, 1988; Meeker, 1969; Meeker and Meeker, 1986)
7. Autonomous Learner Model (Betts, 1985, 1991, Betts & Kercher, 1999)
8. Multiple-Talent Totem Pole Model (Schlichter, 1997; Schlichter & Palmer, 1993; Taylor, 1986, 1988)
9. Programming at four ability levels (Treffinger & Sortore, 1992a).
10. Multidimensional Curriculum Model (Morelock & Morrison, 1999)
11. Constructing Differentiated Curriculum for the Gifted (Kaplan, 1986)

## ENRICHMENT TRIAD MODEL: RENZULLI

The Enrichment Triad Model (Renzulli, 1977; see also Renzulli & Reis, 1985, 1997, 2003) is the best known and most widely used model for guiding "what to do" for gifted students. The plan has been implemented almost entirely with elementary students but can be used effectively with secondary students as well.

### The Triad Model in the Elementary School

As an overview, the three more-or-less sequential but qualitatively different steps in the *Enrichment Triad Model* appear in Figure 7.1.

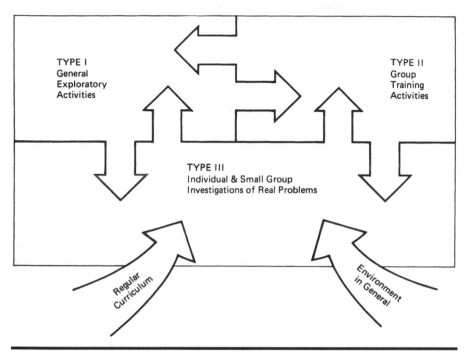

**FIGURE 7.1**    Renzulli's Enrichment Triad Model.

From J. S. Renzulli, *The Enrichment Triad Model: A Guide for Developing Defensible Programs for the Gifted and Talented.* Mansfield Center, CT: Creative Learning Press, 1977. Reprinted by permission.

***Type I enrichment.***    The main purpose of Type I enrichment, General Exploratory Activities, is to expose students to a variety of topics, disciplines, events, hobbies, persons, places, interest areas, and occupations that are not a normal part of the curriculum (Renzulli & Reis, 2003). Type I experiences may include, for example, demonstrations, guest speakers, performances, films, videotapes, and slide presentations. Students with gifted potential might find ideas for a later Type III research project. Appendix 7.1 at the end of this chapter, based on ideas from Renzulli (1977) and Reis and Burns (1987), lists over 200 possible Type I topics, some of which are categories (e.g., languages, history).

***Type II enrichment.***    The purpose of Type II enrichment—group training activities—is to promote

the development of a broad range of thinking and feeling processes (Renzulli & Reis, 1997). While these skills, abilities, attitudes, and strategies should be developed in *all* students, "an escalation of process development should be a primary goal of programs that serve gifted and talented students" (Renzulli & Reis, 1985). Renzulli (1994) especially recommended developing general and specific skills in the five categories of Table 7.1. Some Type II enrichment activities will relate specifically to gifted students' independent projects, for example, techniques for writing a play script, silk screening, or using scientific equipment.

Additional affective concerns, which will be elaborated in Chapter 8, include helping students form good self-concepts and feelings of high self-worth; helping them develop constructive social and interpersonal values; increasing their awareness

**TABLE 7.1**   Type II Skill Categories

*Cognitive Training*

1. Analysis skills
2. Organizational skills
3. Critical thinking skills
4. Creativity skills

*Affective Training*

5. Intrapersonal skills
6. Interpersonal skills
7. Dealing with critical life incidents

*Learning-How-to-Learn Training*

8. Listening, observing, perceiving
9. Note taking and outlining
10. Interviewing and surveying
11. Analyzing and organizing data

*Developing Advanced Research and Reference Procedures*

12. Preparing for Type III investigations
13. Library skills
14. Using community resources

*Developing Written, Oral, and Visual Communication*

15. Written communication skills
16. Oral communication skills
17. Visual communication skills

From Renzulli (1994), by permission of Creative Learning Press.

of others' perceptions, points of view, problems, and handicaps; and increasing their educational and career motivation, in part by helping them understand that they can control their destinies (Davis, 2003a, 2003c).

Incidentally, many programs for the gifted focus exclusively on Type II process activities—creativity, thinking skills, affective development, and others. In their article entitled "Developing Defensible Programs for the Gifted and Talented," Renzulli and Smith (1978a) warned that too strong an emphasis on process activities defi-

nitely is not defensible, which brings us to Type III enrichment.

***Type III enrichment.***   With Type III enrichment the student pursues a self-selected problem—in original research, art, writing, theater, designing a home page, and so on—that leads to an original product. Students should act as *producers* of knowledge and art, not just consumers.

The purposes of Type III enrichment are to help students (1) apply knowledge, motivation, and creativity to a self-selected problem or area of study; (2) acquire advanced understanding of the content and methodology in a particular area; (3) develop skills of self-directed learning (planning, organizing, using resources, managing time, making decisions, and evaluating one's performance); and (4) develop self-confidence, task commitment, and feelings of accomplishment (Renzulli & Reis, 2003).

The teacher, as "guide on the side," helps with clarifying the problem, designing the project, locating materials and equipment, and recommending information sources or community experts. Ten steps for helping teachers guide students through Type III projects are summarized in Table 7.2 (Renzulli, 1994).

**TABLE 7.2**   Steps for Guiding Students through Type III Projects

1. Assess, find, or create student interests.
2. Conduct an interview to determine the strength of the interest.
3. Help find a question to research.
4. Develop a written plan.
5. Help locate multiple resources.
6. Provide methodological assistance.
7. Provide managerial assistance.
8. Help identify the final product and outlets.
9. Provide feedback and escalate the process.
10. Evaluate, with the student, the process and product according to appropriate criteria.

From Renzulli (1994), by permission of Creative Learning Press.

## Outlets for Creations

It is important for students to have audiences for their Type III products, as with adult artists, scientists, and other professionals. Gifted students too are product-oriented, and they also wish to hold up their accomplishments and perhaps inform or influence a particular audience.

Local organizations such as historical societies or science or dramatic groups can be suitable audiences. Displays of work also can be set up in children's museums, shopping malls, hospital foyers, the district school office building, or the state capitol—or at least the school hallway. Children's magazines and sometimes local newspapers publish children's writing and research reports. (See the list of magazines that publish students' work in Appendix 6.1, Chapter 6.) If children's art shows and science fairs are not available, an energetic G/T teacher-coordinator can think about creating some. Local newspapers like a human-interest story, and good publicity will not hurt any teacher or G/T program. Appreciative audiences for dramatic productions and puppet plays, and perhaps other kinds of products, can be found in children's hospitals and retirement homes. You can invite the press to these also. Of course, the student's own class is a ready audience, for example, for a video production, a weaving or pyramid-building demonstration, or a report on school and community attitudes about year-round schooling.

## Secondary Triad Model

The *Secondary Triad Model* (Reis & Renzulli, 1986) includes the same three types of enrichment as the original model. However, it requires a high school reorganization in the form of creating *talent pool* classes within each discipline. The *talent pool* concept has appeared several times in this text. In Reis and Renzulli's (1986, p. 274) summary definition, "it is easiest to think of them as the top 15 to 20 percent of the general population in either general ability or in one or more specific areas of ability in the major categories of school achievement (i.e., math, science, language arts, etc.)."

The recommended selection of students for these classes follows the *Talent Pool Identification Plan* presented in Chapter 4, which is based on ability, achievement, and creativity test scores, as well as peer, parent, teacher, and self-nominations—or, in the high school model, simply a strong interest in conducting a Type III project in a subject area such as English, math, or art. Talent pool members receive a thorough orientation to the Triad model and descriptions of talent pool classes, either in an assembly program for talent pool students or individually.

The self-contained special classes in each discipline teach a regular curriculum that is compacted to permit time for Types I and II enrichment activities and Type III independent projects. Type I enrichment includes exposing students to a broadened range of knowledge in the particular subject area, which helps them select Type III projects. Type II enrichment, as in the elementary school Triad model, includes creativity, problem solving, study skills, research and reference skills, and other thinking and affective skills, as well as skills related to the specific subject area.

Type III projects will be of high quality, perhaps requiring the consulting services of outside professionals. Regarding audiences, projects might be, for example, published in professional journals or presented to appropriate local groups. Such audiences motivate high quality work because they "add a dimension of reality and relevance" (Reis and Renzulli, 1986, p. 283).

## SCHOOLWIDE ENRICHMENT MODEL

We hope the reader appreciates the challenge of summarizing two thoughtfully written fat books containing four billion details (Renzulli, 1994; Renzulli & Reis, 1997), or even the 15-page summary in Renzulli and Reis (2003), in the next few pages. As an example of the complexity, see the summary 63-cell cube in Figure 7.2, briefly explained later. First, some SEM highlights.

The *Schoolwide Enrichment Model* (SEM) is

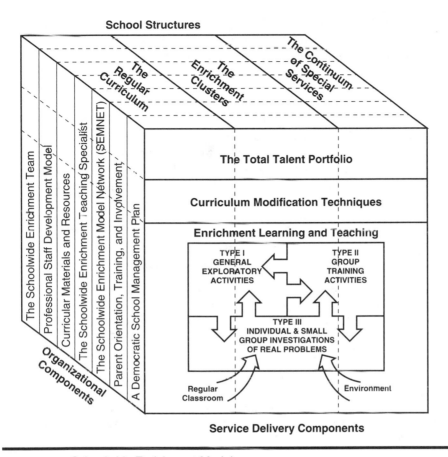

School Structures

The Continuum of Special Services

The Enrichment Clusters

The Regular Curriculum

The Schoolwide Enrichment Team

Professional Staff Development Model

Curricular Materials and Resources

The Schoolwide Enrichment Teaching Specialist

The Schoolwide Enrichment Model Network (SEMNET)

Parent Orientation, Training, and Involvement

A Democratic School Management Plan

Organizational Components

**The Total Talent Portfolio**

**Curriculum Modification Techniques**

**Enrichment Learning and Teaching**

TYPE I
GENERAL
EXPLORATORY
ACTIVITIES

TYPE II
GROUP
TRAINING
ACTIVITIES

TYPE III
INDIVIDUAL & SMALL
GROUP INVESTIGATIONS
OF REAL PROBLEMS

Regular
Classroom

Environment

**Service Delivery Components**

**FIGURE 7.2**  Schoolwide Enrichment Model.

Renzulli, J. S., & Reis, S. M. (1997). *The schoolwide enrichment model: A how-to-guide for educational excellence*. Mansfield Center, CT: Creative Learning Press. Reprinted with permission. Available from www.creativelearningpress.com.

an adaptation of the earlier *Revolving Door Identification Model* (RDIM; Renzulli, Reis, & Smith, 1981), with the new name emphasizing the literally schoolwide focus of the program. Like the RDIM, the SEM is based on the Enrichment Triad Model. One reviewer, displaying uncanny perceptiveness and foresight, said this of the Revolving Door IdentificationModel, "The RDIM [now SEM] probably will be recognized as one of the most significant and revolutionary contributions to gifted education to date" (Davis, 1981b).

The first high-appeal feature is Renzulli's *talent pool* approach to identification and selection.

As we noted in Chapter 4, the usual strategy is to identify about 5 percent of the school's population in the fall, after which teachers stop worrying about who is "gifted" until fall of the next year. The students who are "in" begin participating in wonderful learning activities, most often in a pullout format; and parents of excluded students, and sometimes the excluded students themselves, complain of unfairness and elitism.

With the SEM, about 15 to 20 percent of the students are selected for the talent pool. Although schools may select students however they wish, Renzulli (1994) and Renzulli and Reis (1997) recommend the procedure described in Chapter 4.

The selection process is intended to *include* students, not *exclude* them; when in doubt, admit. Further, students not initially selected who strongly wish to conduct an independent project probably will be allowed to do so and become part of the talent pool. Identification thus continues year round, the program serves more students, and the SEM generally avoids charges of unfairness and elitism.

The second high-appeal feature is the *school-wide* one. We noted that Enrichment Types I and II are good for all students. In the SEM concrete plans are made to incorporate Types I and II enrichment in every class.

An abbreviated orientation for all students (from Renzulli & Reis, 1985), appears in Inset 7.1. This orientation contains an explanation of the Three-Ring Model, the Enrichment Triad Model, and their participation in Types I and II enrichment. Note the invitation to all students to develop an interest in pursuing a Type III project. The orientation would be presented by the SEM resource teacher.

---

**INSET 7.1** _____

### Schoolwide Enrichment Model: Orientation for All Students

Good morning, my name is _____, and I'm here to explain our enrichment program to you today. Have any of you seen this poster on my door (show poster or slide of Enrichment Triad Model)? Well, this is a picture of the model that we use for our enrichment program. Do any of you know what *enrichment* means? . . . Good, now let's talk about the Enrichment Triad Model.

Three different types of activities are a part of this model. Type I activities bring all of you in touch with topics, ideas, and areas of study you may never have heard about before. . . . You might learn about architecture, anthropology, art history, or other topics. Type I's are for *all* of you. . . . It may be a film or a speech, slide show, a display in your classroom, or even a beautiful poster . . . Now, if any of you get very excited about a Type I, you should tell you classroom teacher. Remember that and we'll talk about why later.

The second part of the Triad Model is Type II activities. Type II involves skills that will help you become better at research, problem solving, writing, and even thinking. For example, you may learn how to complete an independent project, how to work on your own, or how to have lots of ideas. (If available, show slides or posters about creativity or critical thinking.) All of you will have some classroom involvement in Type II, but some of you will be involved in extra Type II training.

Let's talk abut why! How many of you have ever seen this before? (Show poster or slide of three-ring model). This is our definition of what we call *gifted behavior*. Every single one of us is capable or able to show gifted behaviors in some areas in our lives. Some people do but some people do not! One of the things we hope our enrichment program will do is show and teach young people how to develop or learn to display gifted behaviors. How many of you are good at running? How many of you can draw well? How many of you can sing well? How many of you are good at daydreaming? Well, all of us have different talents. One part of this program will be to help you find your talent area! But some people in this room already have shown what they are good at doing. Some people in this room finish their school work early and are very good at subjects like reading, science, or math. Do you know who they might be? . . . These students will be coming to work on Type II in a resource room (with me or with _____) once or twice a week. . . . We call those students members of the Talent Pool. (Mention separate art or music Talent Pools, if they are to be established).

**INSET 7.1 Continued**

Being in the Talent Pool means that students will do some other Type II work at a time that your teacher believes they can leave your class. . . . Any of you may be able to become involved in the Talent Pool by doing excellent work, but remember—you are all going to be involved in Type I and Type II activities in your classroom anyway!

Now, being in the Talent Pool doesn't mean that someone is gifted! (point to three-ring sign). We believe that gifted behavior happens when someone has above average ability and *also works very hard.* That is what task commitment is all about! We also believe that gifted behavior happens when someone takes his or her creativity and works hard to be creative in the area where he or she has an above average ability. How many of you know what creativity is? (Show three-ring sign again). This is where gifted behavior occurs and this is what the third part of the Enrichment Triad Model is all about. (Show Triad Model again). Type III Enrichment is only for students who are willing to work very hard in an area in which they are interested. (Show examples of Type III enrichment products.) Type IIIs involve a lot of work. Some people work for many months and sometimes even a year or more to finish their Type IIIs.

Any of you can decide to try to do a Type III investigation. You should have some kind of question that you want to answer, some type of problem that you want to solve, or a very strong interest in some area like local history or creative writing or architecture. If you want to try a Type III, either your classroom teacher or I can help you. The first thing you should do is tell your teacher you have an idea and complete this Light Bulb (show slide or poster of an Action Information Message). Remember, a Type III starts to happen when you get your three rings together (hold up three-ring sign)! Now are there any questions?

Remember, *any* of you can fill out a light bulb to become involved in a Type III. . . . Any questions? (Review Types I, II, and III Enrichment.)

---

Abbreviated from Renzulli and Reis (1985), by permission of Creative Learning Press.

Talent pool and other students request permission to pursue a Type III investigation by filling out a "Light Bulb"—an Action Information Message—that the regular teacher forwards to the resource teacher (Figure 7.3). If the project is approved, the student works with the resource teacher to plan and carry out the project, which may require a few days, weeks, or months. About 50 to 60 percent of talent pool students muster the creativity and motivation to pursue at least one Type III project each year.

Talent pool students receive several types of enrichment and related services. They receive the same *general enrichment* experienced by other students, but they also receive Type II enrichment related to skills needed for their particular project.

In addition, Talent Pool students are helped to identify interests that might lead to a Type III project. For example, Renzulli's *Interest-a-Lyzer* helps students identify interests in arts and crafts, science, creative writing, the legal/political area, mathematics, computers, management, history, athletic and outdoor activities, performing arts, business, consumer action, ecology, and so on.

Another important component is *curriculum compacting,* noted several times in earlier chapters. Curriculum typically is compacted in basic skill areas, particularly math but also language arts, science, and social studies. We mentioned earlier that pretests (e.g., end-of-unit tests) can assess mastery. An accelerated instructional pace also produces extra time. Students' grades and

TO: _____ Talent Pool Class Teacher

_____ Program Coordinator

_____ Other

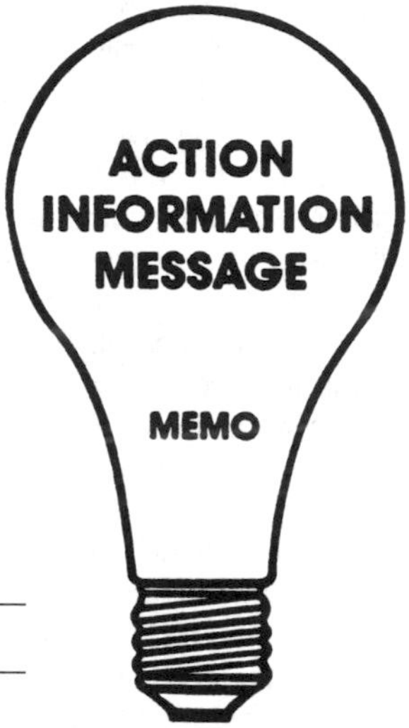

**ACTION
INFORMATION
MESSAGE**

FROM: _____ Student (print name)

_____ Teacher (print name)

_____ Other

**MEMO**

General Curriculum Area: _____

_____

Idea for Investigation or Study: _____

_____

_____

In the space below, provide a brief description of evidence of high levels of task commitment or creativity on the part of a student or small group of students. Indicate any ideas you may have for advanced level follow-up activities, suggested resources or ways to focus the interest into a first-hand investigative experience.

Date Received_____

Date of Interview_____

Mentor Located _____ Yes _____ No

Name of person who will be responsible for facilitating this Type III

**FIGURE 7.3**   Action Information Message.

classwork, standardized achievement test results, portfolios, counselor recommendations, or interviews with the student, the parents, or the teacher also can indicate content mastery before instruction (Renzulli, 1994; Renzulli & Reis, 1997).

In today's atmosphere in which competency testing evaluates student achievement—and supposedly teacher and administrator competence—one concern is whether compacting lowers student achievement. Reis, Westberg, Kulikovich, and Purcell (1998) examined the preinstruction and postinstruction *Iowa Test of Basic Skills* (ITBS) achievement scores of 335 elementary students (grades two to six) throughout America who "demonstrated superior ability and advanced content knowledge before instruction." Despite eliminating 36 percent to 54 percent of the mathematics or language arts content, the results showed no ITBS differences between gifted students whose curriculum had been compacted versus gifted students who received the regular instruction—which included material they already knew. Further, median scores were over the 90th percentile on all subscales for the compacted students. Renzulli and Reis (1994) also reported no lowering whatever of elementary students' achievement with compacting; science achievement actually increased; school attitudes improved; and both students and teachers liked compacting. See the Compactor (Renzulli, 1994) in Figure 7.4.

The books *Schools for Talent Development* (Renzulli, 1994) and *Schoolwide Enrichment Model* (Renzulli and Reis, 1997) present plenty of step-by-step explanations, examples, plans for organizing Type II activities in the regular classroom, Type I and Type II activity forms, materials specification forms, checklists for preparing Type III fairs, lists of outlets for Type III projects, descriptions and responsibilities of the Schoolwide Enrichment Team, teacher training activities (for example, a simulation of dealing with questions that newspaper reporters typically ask about programs for the gifted and talented), and more. There are forms for nearly everything—nomination forms, management plans, Light Bulbs, class-survey sheets, parent questionnaires, student

questionnaires, teacher questionnaires, letters to inform parents of their child's participation, student (and parent) product evaluation forms, and so on. Some of the forms serve as staff accountability checks, motivating everyone to do his or her job.

Let's return to Figure 7.2. Three central aspects of the SEM do not appear in this illustration of the SEM. First, Renzulli and Reis (2003) note two forms of giftedness. *Schoolhouse giftedness* is test-taking or lesson-learning giftedness, measured by IQ tests, and often used to select students for gifted programs. *Creative-productive giftedness,* partly self-defining, is developing original material and products that are designed to have an impact on one or more audiences. History does not remember high-IQ giftedness; it remembers "the creative and productive people of the world" (p. 186). Two other critical components not in Figure 7.2 are the talent pool concept and curriculum compacting.

Briefly, the top plane of the SEM in Figure 7.2 is *school structures,* which includes the regular curriculum, enrichment clusters (as described in Chapter 6), and the continuum of special services (such as counseling, acceleration, mentorships, and other connections with out-of-school persons and resources). The front plane is *service delivery components.* The total talent portfolio is a management form that summarizes three types of information about each student: abilities (test scores, product evaluations), interest areas, and style preferences (e.g., lecture, learning centers; analytic or synthetic thinking; written, oral, or artistic expression). Curriculum modification techniques refers to ways to increase enrichment and in-depth experiences "so that all students are challenged" (Renzulli & Reis, 2003, p. 190). The third component is enrichment learning and teaching via the enrichment triad model. The left-side plane of Figure 7.2 includes seven *organizational components,* which are partly self-explanatory (see Renzulli & Reis, 1997, for details).

There are four pivotal points: (1) each learner is unique in ability, interests, and learning styles; (2) learning is most effective when students enjoy

Name ________ Age ________ Teacher(s) ________ Individual Conference Dates and Persons
School ________ Grade ________ Parent(s) ________ Participating in Planning of IEP ________

________ ________ ________ ________

| Curriculum Areas to be Considered for Compacting | Procedures for Compacting Basic Material | Acceleration and/or Enrichment Activities |
|---|---|---|
| Language Arts: Holt 14:<br>Units 2–6, Pretest Units 2–6<br>Decoding/encoding skills<br>Language skills | Unit and level tests in Holt Language Arts. (Student) will participate in all language activities except those involving decoding and encoding skills, language skills already mastered, and any kind of repetitious "seatwork." | *Advanced Exposure in Language Arts:* To read biographies for the purpose of enriching her background in literature and to see how the following human value applies to her selections: "Determination and courage are often necessary to achieve one's goals." |
| CTBS scores:<br>Vocabulary 6.5<br>Comprehension 9.5<br>Total Reading 7.9<br>Language Mechanics 9.9<br>Language Expression 9.9<br>Total Language 9.8 | Time gained from this will go toward (Student's) advance exposure in Language Arts. | Amelia Earhart, Anne Bradstreet<br>Phillis Wheatley, Mahalia Jackson<br>Abigail Adams, Dolly Madison<br>Harriet Beecher Stowe<br>Also, (student) will choose novels from the Newbery Award Series to increase her vocabulary and understanding. |
| | | *Advanced Exposure in Science:*<br>8 trips to regional science center for ________<br><br>*Resource Room:* 5 hours per week. Types I, II, and III activities to develop creative thinking and problem solving. |
| | | Resource Room: 5 hours per week. Type I, II, and III activities developing creativity thinking, critical thinking, and critical problem solving. |

From Renzulli, J. S. (1994). *Schools for talent development: A practical school plan for total school improvement.* Mansfield Center, CT: Creative Learning Press. Copyright © by Creative Learning Press, P.O. Box 320, Mansfield Center, CT 06250. Modified and reproduced by permission.

**FIGURE 7.4** Individual Educational Programming Guide: The Compactor.

the learning task; (3) learning is both enjoyable and meaningful when knowledge and thinking skills are acquired while working on a real problem; and (4) a major goal is to impart knowledge and thinking skills via students' own construction of meaning.

Finally, to reduce worries about not getting the SEM exactly right, Renzulli and Reis concede that there is no such thing as a "pure" Triad/SEM program. Each school district will examine its own philosophy and resources and adopt those parts of SEM that fit well in the existing school district structure.

## MULTIPLE MENU MODEL

Renzulli's (1988) *Multiple Menu Model* focuses on teaching content and thinking processes in efficient and interesting ways. Five planning "menus" provide guidance for designing curriculum.

*Knowledge Menu.* This menu recommends a desirable sequence for teaching knowledge in a particular area. It includes four subcategories or steps. First, *location, definition, and organization* helps the learner see the "big picture" of a field. A branching diagram may be used to illustrate the organization and subdivisions of a field, along with the characteristics and mission of each subdivision. The curriculum designer (teacher) presents the purposes of a field; subareas of concentration; kinds of questions asked in subareas;

sources of data; basic reference books and professional journals; major data bases; major events, persons, places, and beliefs; and insiders' humor, trivia, scandals, and so on.

Second are *basic principles and functional concepts.* Basic principles are generally agreed-upon truths in an area. The concepts are largely the vocabulary of a field, as found in a glossary.

Third, *knowledge about specifics* refers to important facts, conventions, trends, classifications, criteria, principles and generalizations, and theories and structures that comprise a field. About 95 percent of the information in a field will be in this "warehouse of information," according to Renzulli.

Fourth, *knowledge about methodology* refers to standard investigative procedures in an area, namely, how to identify problems, state hypotheses, identify data sources, locate or construct data-gathering instruments, summarize and analyze data, draw conclusions, and report findings.

*Instructional Objectives/Student Activities Menu.* The first of four subsections of the instructional

**TABLE 7.3**  Multiple Menu Model

| | |
|---|---|
| Knowledge Menu | Location, definition, and organization (general organization of a field) |
| | Basic principles and functional concepts |
| | Knowledge about specifics |
| | Knowledge about methodology |
| Instructional Objectives/ Student Activities Menu | Assimilation and retention (listening, reading, etc.) |
| | Information analysis (e.g., classifying, interpreting) |
| | Information synthesis and application (output, e.g., writing) |
| | Evaluation |
| Instructional Sequence Menu | Gaining attention, presenting objectives, relating to previous material, presenting material, evaluating performance, transfer and application |
| Instructional Strategies Menu | Drill and recitation, lecture, discussion, peer tutoring, learning center activities, simulation and role playing, learning games, independent study, others |
| Artistic Modification Menu | Teachers' creative contributions (e.g., personal knowledge and experiences, beliefs, insider information, interpretations, controversies, biases, etc.) |

From Renzulli, 1988.

objectives/student activities menu, *assimilation and retention,* refers to information *input* processes: listening, observing, touching, reading, manipulating, note taking, and so on. The second section of this menu, information analysis, suggests ways to achieve greater understanding, for example, by classifying, ordering, gathering data, interpreting, thinking of alternatives, and concluding and explaining. The third section, *information synthesis and application,* deals with the *output* or products of the thinking processes, for example, writing, speaking, constructing, or performing. Finally, the fourth subsection, *evaluation,* concerns review and judgment of information according to personal values or conventional standards.

***Instructional Strategies Menu.*** The instructional strategies menu itemizes teaching and learning options familiar to most teachers, for example, drill and recitation, lecture, discussion, peer tutoring, learning center activities, simulation and role playing, learning games, and independent study.

***Instructional Sequence Menu.*** The instructional sequence menu describes an accepted way to sequence events to help students learn: gain attention, inform students of objectives, relate the topic to previous learning, present the material (with active or passive student roles), assess performance, provide feedback, and provide opportunities for transfer and application.

***Artistic Modification Menu.*** Finally, Renzulli recommends that teachers "make their own creative contribution" to the lesson to increase interest and excitement. The artistic modification menu suggests sharing personal knowledge and experiences, beliefs, insider information, interpretations, controversies, biases, or "additional ways teachers might personalize the material."

Many components of the Multiple Menu Model are standard good teaching practices. However, as Renzulli states, it does "direct us to consider a broad range of options, and to interre-

late the many factors that must be considered." For teachers of the gifted, the Multiple Menu Model provides an organizational framework for developing special curriculum in areas not typically covered in ordinary school programming. Table 7.3 outlines the Multiple Menu Model.

## PYRAMID PROJECT: COX

The *Pyramid Project* is widely known and contains many excellent pro-gifted features. On the downside, first, this early 1980s model barely preceded the most vocal criticisms (e.g., Oakes, 1985) of educational plans that group gifted students and active reform toward heterogeneous classes. Second, the pyramid model requires a not-easy large-scale revision of a district's schools and school goals.

The Pyramid Project grew from many of the conclusions and recommendations of the Richardson Study, a survey of existing G/T programs (Cox, 1986; Cox, Daniel, & Boston, 1985; Cox & Daniel, 1988). Some pertinent conclusions were: many current programs for the gifted make no provision for the brightest and most creative youngsters; rigid cutoff scores unreasonably exclude many able learners; many programs are fragmented and discontinuous; and the popular pullout plan is (you guessed it) a part-time solution to a full-time problem that is problematic and divisive, for example, causing students to miss work they need or to make up work they do not need.

Said Cox, the goal of the Pyramid Project is to provide appropriate instruction for all capable students of all ages, from above-average to the highly gifted, in all subjects every day. About one-fourth of all students in Cox's pioneering greater Forth Worth, Texas, Pyramid Project are defined as "able learners."

As represented in the broad base of the Pyramid Model (Figure 7.5), the largest number of able learners receive advanced material in the regular classroom, for example, using learning centers, flexible grouping (e.g., for math and

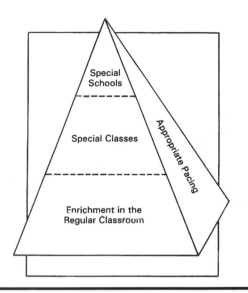

**FIGURE 7.5**  The Pyramid Concept.

Reprinted from *Educating Able Learners: Programs and Promising Practices* by June Cox, Neil Daniel, and Bruce O. Boston, copyright © 1985. Reprinted by permission of J. Cox, Gifted Students Institute, and the University of Texas Press.

language arts), cluster grouping, individualized instructional methods, cross-grade grouping, curriculum compacting, and resource room enrichment and projects. Cox argued that classroom teachers can do the job of enrichment if they get training, support, and guidance. She recommended Renzulli's Enrichment Triad Model as a good curriculum guide.

Moving to the midsection of the pyramid, a smaller group of more superior students are placed in full-time special classes. Also, students can participate in dual enrollment—elementary students can enroll concurrently in middle school for their strongest subjects, middle school students can enroll in high school, and high school students may take college courses.

At the top of the pyramid, the smallest number of students—the most capable and with the most specialized needs—are served by special (magnet) schools. At the high school level, these schools usually stress math, science, language, the arts, or an International Baccalaureate program.

However, concede Cox, Daniel, and Boston (1985), special schools for students at the top of the pyramid are a big-city option (e.g., the Bronx High School of Science). At the elementary level, smaller school districts accommodate able students in the regular classroom, using options noted above. If possible, special elementary classes are created for students at the top two pyramid levels. Secondary schools in these smaller districts use special (advanced) classes, for example, in math, science, English/language arts, history/social studies, and fine arts; honors courses; AP courses; and concurrent enrollment arranged with a local junior college.

The concept of *flexible pacing* runs from the base to the peak of the pyramid—the plan requires teachers to recognize that all students do not learn at the same rate. Noted Ondo and Session (1989, p. 47), "Basic to the pyramid concept . . . is the conviction that students should move ahead as they master content, concepts, and skills. Schools accelerate the educational process for bright students either by moving students to higher grade levels in their areas of accomplishment or by bringing the advanced material down to students." Ondo and Session noted that flexible pacing primarily takes these forms in the Pyramid model: early entrance policies, advanced level courses, dual enrollment, compacted courses, grade skipping, and credit by examination.

The Pyramid plan requires longitudinal and interdisciplinary planning by committees of teachers and administrators; continuous staff development; support services, such as special clerical help and a resource teacher; a manageable record-keeping system that allows teachers to monitor individual student progress; and cooperation among parents, administrators, and teachers.

A summary of thoughtful Richardson Study recommendations—as valid today as then—appears in Table 7.4.

**TABLE 7.4** Summary Recommendations from Richardson Study

| | |
|---|---|
| Administration | Develop a written philosophy consistent with the goals and values of the district. |
| | Select a coordinator early to participate in the planning. |
| | Assess the current program(s) for able learners. |
| | Adopt flexible pacing at all levels. |
| Discovering Talent | Include a larger group of "able learners" than is usually identified as "gifted." |
| | "Cast a wide net"; keep entrance requirements modest; avoid arbitrary cut-offs. |
| | Assess abilities; use these results to guide programming decisions. |
| | Recognize multiple measures of multiple types of intelligences. |
| | Encourage parents and primary teachers to note children's abilities. Discovering and nurturing talent are interdependent. |
| | Observe creativity and problem solving, which indicate ability and interest. |
| | Use puzzles and games to discover talents; note symbol systems other than verbal. |
| | Be thoughtful of minority groups; supplement testing with characteristics checklists. |
| | Use out-of-level testing. |
| | Avoid labeling selected children as "the gifted," which implies others have no gifts. |
| | Maintain a psychologically safe environment. |
| Program | Use counselors for assessment, students' affective needs, program selection, and career/college counseling. |
| | Do not try to create a comprehensive program at once; piece together a mosaic. |
| | Be sure programs are sequential and integrated throughout the system. |
| | Offer program options across disciplines, grade levels, and levels of intelligence. |
| | Encourage projects that use authentic inquiry methods and yield real products. |
| | Use concurrent enrollment at all levels—elementary/middle school, middle/high school, high school/college. |
| | Recognize that some students benefit from early college admission. |
| | Use mentorships and (in high school) internships. |
| | Use area museums and arts organizations. |
| | Encourage students to use after-school, Saturday, and summer programs. |
| | Consider specialized schools and residential schools. |
| | Balance acceleration with enrichment activities for diverse intelligences. |
| Staff Development and Teacher Support | Assume staff development to be a continuous process. |
| | Coordinate teaching strategies with learning styles of able students. |
| | Encourage thinking and questioning skills. |
| | Arrange joint planning among K–12 teachers, with attention to content sequence. |
| | Help teachers develop an efficient record-keeping system to monitor student progress. |
| | Use nearby colleges as resources for staff development and curriculum innovations. |
| Evaluation | Plan program evaluation in early program development stages (e.g., to establish baseline data). |
| | Conduct comprehensive and regular program evaluations to assess accountability, program success, and impact on students. |
| | Employ external and internal evaluators to assure objectivity and add credibility. |

From Cox, Daniel, & Boston, 1985.

## PURDUE THREE-STAGE ENRICHMENT MODEL: FELDHUSEN AND KOLLOFF

The *Purdue Three-Stage Enrichment Model* (Feldhusen & Kolloff, 1986; Moon, 1995, 1996) centers upon three levels of skill development. While fostering creativity clearly is central, the training also aims at strengthening many types of thinking skills, convergent problem solving, research skills, and independent learning.

Stage 1 focuses upon the development of basic *Divergent and Convergent Thinking Abilities.* Instructional activities include relatively short-term, teacher-led exercises and workbook activities mainly in creative thinking but also other thinking skills in verbal and nonverbal areas. Content and basic skills in science, math, and language arts also can be included in Stage I. Creativity workbooks by Stanish (e.g., 1977), and thinking skills workbooks by Harnadek (e.g., 1976) and Black and Black (e.g., 1987, 1988) may be used in Stage 1.2.

Some creativity exercises are, for example, listing unusual uses for trash bags, thinking of improvements for a bicycle, predicting outcomes of unlikely events (What would happen if there were no television or no McDonald's?), or "designing a vehicle of the future using anything you might find in a junkyard" (Feldhusen & Kolloff, 1981). These kinds of exercises are assumed to develop such creative abilities as ideational fluency, originality, flexibility, and elaboration. Thinking skills exercises might stretch logic, critical thinking, analysis, synthesis, evaluation, decision-making, classification, comparison, or analogical thinking abilities. (Creativity workbooks and exercises are described in Chapter 10; thinking skills programs and workbooks appear in Chapter 11.)

Stage 2, called *Development of Creative Problem Solving Abilities,* focuses on more complex and practical strategies and systems. Included are creative thinking techniques (e.g., brainstorming and the *synectics* methods; see Chapter 10); the Creative Problem Solving (CPS) model; Future Problem Solving, which uses the CPS model; Odyssey of the Mind; and other problem-solving applications and experiences.

Stage 3 activities aim at the *Development of Independent Study Skills.* Said Feldhusen and Kolloff (1981), "Stage 3 projects should involve gifted youngsters in challenging efforts to define and clarify a problem, ambitious data gathering from books and other resources, interpretation of findings, and the development of creative ways of communicating results." Some examples of Stage 3 projects are writing haiku, short stories, or plays (which are produced); investigating alternate waste disposal systems (which one group presented to the Lafayette City Council); and researching backgrounds of community leaders (which one group presented on local radio).

The Purdue Three-Stage Model might be implemented in a pullout plan, using the first few weeks for Stage 1, followed by Stage 2 activities through weeks 12 or 16, and Stage 3 independent study and projects thereafter.

## STRUCTURE OF INTELLECT MODEL: GUILFORD AND MEEKER AND MEEKER

Many people are acquainted with Guilford's original 1967 *Structure of Intellect* (SOI) model of intelligence, which included 120 cells created from the combinations of four *contents, six products,* and five *operations* (see Figure 7.6). The cells represent specific mental abilities. The SOI cube represents Guilford's theory of intelligence—one that contrasts sharply with a single IQ view of intelligence. For the record, the cube was extended to 150 cells in 1977 and to 180 cells in 1988. Joy Paul Guilford, who never used his first name, invested over three decades creating tests to measure those 180 abilities.

As an example, the darkened slab of the model in Figure 7.6 includes the operations of *divergent production.* Somewhere in that slab is a cell identified as the "divergent production (operation) of symbolic (content) units (product)," or just *DSU.* Two tests of DSU—or word fluency—ask the examinee to list words that include one, two, or

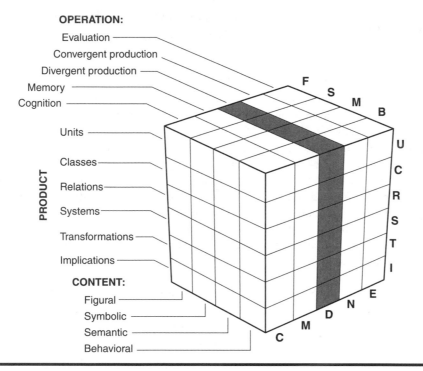

**FIGURE 7.6**    The Guilford (1967) Structure of Intellect Model.

From J. P. Guilford, *The Nature of Human Intelligence* (New York: McGraw-Hill, 1967). Reprinted with permission.

three specified letters; or list words that rhyme with a specified word (for example, *roam*).

Meeker and Meeker's (1986) 90 SOI abilities—or 90 kinds of intelligence—are comprised of all combinations of Guilford's original five *operations* and six *products,* but just three *contents* (figural, symbolic, semantic). As of 2002, the Meekers' SOI Systems offered services in general education, reading, remedial education, training/retraining, career counseling, math—and gifted education. Their services ranged from assessing reading readiness in kindergarten to rehabilitation in corrections institutions. The basic approach is diagnosis by SOI tests, then remediation of the learning problem by SOI training modules. SOI Systems offers over 100 training modules, each of which "is focused on one learning ability . . . [and] which are based on the Structure of Intellect theory" (SOI Systems, n.d.).

There are two gifted education contributions. The first is identification. Early on, Mary Meeker (1978) observed that many children from non-English-speaking, low-education, low-income families had not developed the cognitive abilities necessary for school success. And IQ-based selection criteria did not pick them for gifted programs. In response, the Meekers used the SOI tests to evaluate *many* cognitive abilities—and the tests proved successful in identifying giftedness in diverse populations as well as regular student populations. For example, the group-administered SOI Test of Learning Abilities—Form CR (SOI-LA) measures 24 SOI abilities. For each student, a bar-graph profile displays each of the 24 scores falling into the "disabling," "functioning," or "gifted" category. Patterns of strength and weakness are apparent.

One interesting feature is the ability of Meekers' SOI-LA to identify students with learning disabilities who are also gifted. A profile might show severe weakness in semantic abilities, but strong giftedness in figural and/or symbolic abilities.

The Meekers' second contribution is training modules to strengthen each student's already-gifted abilities as well as the student's weaker abilities, both determined by the student's profile of SOI test scores. A unique feature is Meekers' attention to "near-gifted" students. The SOI approach helps the near-gifted become gifted, if they wish to develop their abilities. Using the Meekers' training modules, the near-gifted can score higher on the SOI tests and qualify for G/T selection. (For information, see www.soisystems.com on the Internet, or email them at info@soisystems.com.)

## AUTONOMOUS LEARNER MODEL: BETTS

As with the Renzulli and Reis (1997) *Schoolwide Enrichment Model* (SEM), George Betts's (Betts & Kercher, 1999) *Autonomous Learner Model* (ALM) is a comprehensive programming guide (Figure 7.7). As its name suggests, a core goal is to help students become independent and responsible learners by giving them increased responsibility for their own learning. Other central goals are to help students develop more positive self-concepts; comprehend their own giftedness; develop social skills; increase their knowledge in a variety of subject areas; develop their thinking, decision-making and problem-solving skills; and ultimately become responsible, creative, independent learners. Such goals square well with the purposes of G/T programs.

Also resembling the SEM, Betts's ALM may be incorporated into the regular classroom for all learners. At the same time, an "advanced" ALM may be used with gifted students in a pullout/resource room program that meets, preferably, for about $2\frac{1}{2}$ hours twice per week. In junior or senior high school the ALM would be installed as an elective course.

Space will not permit an adequate explanation of the many details of Betts's model; the interested reader should see Betts and Kercher (1999).

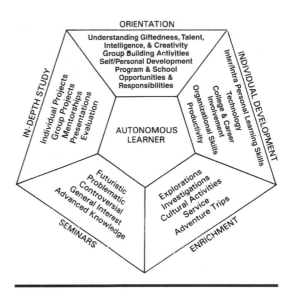

**FIGURE 7.7**   The Autonomous Learner Model. From George Betts and J. K. Kercher (1999). Reprinted with permission of ALPS Publishing.

Information on publications and conferences is available at www.alpspublishing.com.

As an overview, the *Autonomous Learner Model* divides into the five major dimensions summarized in Figure 7.7: orientation, individual development, enrichment activities, seminars, and in-depth study.

***Orientation.*** The *orientation* dimension acquaints students, teachers, administrators, and parents with central concepts in gifted education (e.g., the nature of giftedness and creativity) and the specifics of the *Autonomous Learner Model* (e.g., program goals, opportunities, expectations). Students learn about themselves and what the program has to offer.

In the regular classroom for all students, the emphasis is not on understanding giftedness but on multiple intelligences, creativity, and talents of all children and youth.

In the resource room with gifted students (and perhaps the regular class) group building and self-understanding exercises help students learn more about one another and themselves and about group processes. A sample exercise is "Find Someone

Who. . . ." Students each have a 32-cell matrix with one characteristic (e.g., plays chess, loves math, goes to concerts) in each cell. They move about asking each other to sign any square that fits them. After names are gathered and the students seated, they volunteer what they learned and what the experience was like for them. "I Am" poems include 18 sentence stems that students complete. The poem lines begin with, for example, I am _____, I pretend _____, I feel _____, I touch _____, I worry _____, I cry _____, I am [again] _____.

***Individual Development.*** The *individual development* dimension of the ALM focuses more clearly on developing skills, concepts, and attitudes that promote lifelong independent, self-directed learning. As shown in Figure 7.7, five basic dimensions are inter- and intrapersonal learning skills (e.g., social skills, self-understanding, thinking skills, research skills), technology, college and career involvement, organizational skills, and productivity (for efficiently managing information).

In the regular classroom, and for all children, the teacher would develop skills that are seen as essential for all students—particularly self-understanding, thinking and feeling, productivity (e.g., study, goal-setting) skills, and even career exposure. For most of the school year, the ALM in the regular classroom includes the two dimensions of orientation and individual development, although Betts considers explorations and investigations—enrichment activities—a "must" for students to become lifelong learners.

***Enrichment Activities.*** As we know, enrichment is content beyond the regular curriculum. In the ALM, one type of enrichment is differentiation of curriculum by the teacher. The other is differentiation by the student. For example, students already may have preferred topics or "passion areas," that they wish to pursue. They also study "related passion areas" plus unrelated areas. Students may explore an area and make a presentation about it to the group; they may conduct a research-type investigation; they may participate in cultural activities, such as visiting a museum, play, concert, speech, or art display; they may perform a service, such as working with the elderly or collecting food or money for shut-ins; or they may plan an "adventure trip," such as studying the geology and archaeology of the Grand Canyon or the cultural aspects of San Francisco.

***Seminars.*** The *seminar* dimension is designed to give each person in a small group of three to five students the opportunity to research a topic and present it in a seminar format to the rest of the group. Students learn to proceed through three steps of presenting general information to promote understanding of the topic; facilitating discussion of the topic to involve the audience in thinking; and bringing the discussion and activities to a close.

Like enrichment activities, seminars are valuable experiences and can be arranged for all students.

***In-depth Study.*** Finally, in the dimension of *in-depth study* students pursue areas of interest in long-term individual or small-group studies. These activities resemble Renzulli Type III projects, and students decide what will be learned, what help will be necessary, what the final product will be, how it will be presented, and how the entire learning process will be evaluated. Completion of an in-depth study, whether by gifted students in the resource room or students in the regular classroom, is considered the highest level of autonomous learning.

Overall, the Autonomous Learner Model is a thoughtful and excellent programming guide that has been installed in many schools and districts in the United States and Canada. The Betts and Kercher (1999) book includes self-rating and teacher rating forms for assessing students' social and emotional attitudes (e.g., "needs to be more accepting of others"), abilities (e.g., "communicates ideas," "solves problems effectively"), behavior (e.g., "works independently"), and other areas. An action plan, essentially an IEP, summarizes pretests and compacting plans, acceleration plans, and interest/passion areas. There also is a teacher nomination form, a parent referral form, and a student application form, and many specific exercises and activities aimed at promoting self-understanding, educational goals, service activities, and more.

## TALENTS UNLIMITED MODEL: SCHLICHTER

In Chapter 1 we reviewed Taylor's (1978, 1986) *Multiple-Talent Totem Poles* (Figure 1.3) as an approach to defining giftedness, one that argues that if you look at enough talents, almost everyone will be at least above average (if not outstanding) in something.

Schlichter's (1986, 1997; Schlichter & Palmer, 1993) *Talents Unlimited* is a staff development model for training teachers to recognize and nurture student potential in the six talents described by Taylor (1978). The training involves four major categories of activities:

1. Introductory sessions on multiple talent theory and 22 specific thinking skill components
2. Modeling and demonstration of talents instruction
3. Classroom practice teaching sessions
4. One-to-one and small-group planning sessions

As examples of how teachers are coached in concepts and strategies for teaching the talents: *productive thinking* is strengthened by having students generate many, different, and unusual ideas and add details. *Decision making* involves having students outline, weigh, make final judgments, and defend a decision on the alternatives to a problem. *Planning* involves designing the means to implement an idea—identifying needed resources, planning the steps, pinpointing possible problems, and making improvements to the plan. *Forecasting* requires students to make predictions about possible causes and/or effects of various phenomena. Teaching *communication* focuses on using and interpreting verbal and nonverbal forms of communication to express ideas, feelings, and needs. *Academic* talent is strengthened via acquiring information and concepts to form a good knowledge base in a given topic.

Said Schlichter, students themselves should be taught Taylor's totem pole model so they can become actively involved in improving their thinking skills. The *Talent Train* (Figure 7.8) is used —by adding car after car to the academics engine—to help explain the Talents Unlimited model to elementary children. The *McTalent Burger* (Figure 7.9) introduces secondary students to the model; the basic academics bun represents the knowledge base that is enhanced with the other tasty ingredients represented by the five creative and critical thinking talents.

**FIGURE 7.8** The Talent Train, for Introducing Elementary Students to the Talents Unlimited Model.

Reprinted by permission of Carol Schlichter. Original concept by artist Donna H. Goodman.

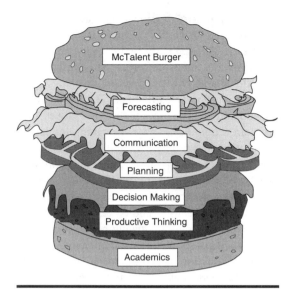

**FIGURE 7.9**   The McTalent Burger, for Explaining the Talents Unlimited Model to Students in Grades 7–12.

Reprinted by permission of Carol Schlichter. Original concept by artist Donna H. Goodman.

## PROGRAMMING AT FOUR ABILITY LEVELS: TREFFINGER AND SORTORE*

Treffinger and Sortore (1992a) do not call their four-level suggestions a *model*. However, it clearly helps guide the planning of enrichment and acceleration options. First, they emphasize developing the capabilities of *all* students. Second, as in the pyramid model described earlier, their plan stresses that different talents and interests among students demand different program activities.

At Level 1, *Services for All Students,* the authors suggested:

- Creative and critical thinking
- The higher levels of Blooms's taxonomy (application, analysis, synthesis, evaluation; see Chapter 11)

*©1992 Center for Creative Learning. From *Programming for Giftedness Series, Volume I: Programming for Giftedness—A Contemporary View,* by D. J. Treffinger and M. R. Sortore.

- Independent projects, both individual and in small groups
- Accommodation of student learning styles
- General exploratory activities (e.g., speakers, field trips, assembly programs, interest development centers)
- Individualized progress in basic skill areas
- Exposure to new topics and areas, such as foreign languages or fine arts
- Activities based on student interests

Level II, *Services for Many Students,* includes:

- Involvement in Great Books
- Odyssey of the Mind
- Future Problem Solving
- Solving real problems (e.g., problems students care about and feel strongly about, rather than artificial workbook problems)
- Young authors—creative writing activities and conferences
- Readers' theater—in which amateur actors read lines while acting the parts
- Young inventors—activities and competitions
- Computer explorations
- Science fairs, math competitions
- Performing and visual arts, band, chorus, theater, debate
- Clubs and academic interest groups
- Personal and career counseling services
- Curriculum compacting
- After school and/or summer enrichment courses or programs

At Level III, *Services for Some Students,* directed toward an even smaller number, we find:

- Available newspapers, literary magazines, and the like
- Guest speakers and in-depth follow-up seminars
- Individual music, drama, or art lessons
- Advanced classes in academic areas
- Solving community problems
- Internship (or shadow-a-professional) experiences

- Complex or extended projects, individual or small group
- Summer talent search programs
- "Testing out" of courses; credit by examination
- Peer teaching opportunities
- Participation in special programs sponsored by colleges and universities for talented students

At the most select Level IV, *Services for a Few Students,* the authors proposed:

- Enrollment in higher level (high school or college) courses
- Grade acceleration or even multiple-grade advancement
- Mentors
- The presentation of student work to outside groups (e.g., to historical societies or governmental agencies)
- Publication of student work in outside sources
- The development and conduct of research or service projects

## MULTIDIMENSIONAL CURRICULUM MODEL: MORELOCK AND MORRISON

As an important preliminary in their *Multidimensional Curriculum Model* for young gifted children, Morelock and Morrison (1999) remind us of Vygotsky's influential *zone of proximal development* concept. The principle notes (logically) that learning takes place when challenging material or skills can be mastered with sensitive adult guidance. The learning task cannot be too difficult nor already mastered. The teacher's job is to keep learning tasks in each child's "zone"—on the edge of their learning, and with success likely.

While the Treffinger and Sortore (1992a) model presents a four-level hierarchy of activities, the *Multidimensional Curriculum Model* emphasizes five levels of increasing complexity and abstractness within an area. It can be used in mixed ability (heterogeneous) classes or with homogeneous groups of gifted children. As shown in Figure 7.10, the child—and his or her existing knowledge and interests—are the starting point. "From there, learning flows outward—always growing and increasing in depth of content, complexity, and abstractness" (Morelock & Morrison, 1999, p. 197).

Using math as an example, in Level 1, *direct experiences,* the children classify, tally, and draw graphs based on their own experiences. Level 1 activities are identical for gifted and regular young children. In Level 2, *extension into proximal experiences,* the teacher builds on existing knowledge and introduces more varied and sophisticated "in-the-zone" learning experiences. For example, children might compare the amounts of fuel needed to fill the tanks of one anothers' family cars. Then they figure out how much fuel might be needed to fill the fuel tanks of motorcycles, limousines, buses, trucks, and tractors, which can be ranked according to likely tank size. Level 3, *addition of contextual dimensions,* includes the introduction of still more abstract and complex concepts and materials. For example, children can explore why different vehicles travel different distances on the same amount of fuel. Level 4, *further extension into multiple contexts,* involves greater depth and more contexts, with extra activities for children with extraordinary potential or talent. For example, children might contrast the unique design and requirements of race cars with family cars, and compare sizes of tires and engines. Finally, Level 5, *further extension crossing disciplines,* includes still higher complexity and abstractness and becomes interdisciplinary. For example, children can compare the dimensions and weight of their paper airplanes, estimate their speed, and time the actual speed. Then "They develop hypotheses about how design characteristics affect travel speed" (Morelock & Morrison, 1999, p. 199).

The Morelock and Morrison model draws attention to how—keeping Vygotsky's *zones of proximal development* in mind—increasingly abstract and complex experiences can be effectively taught to young gifted children.

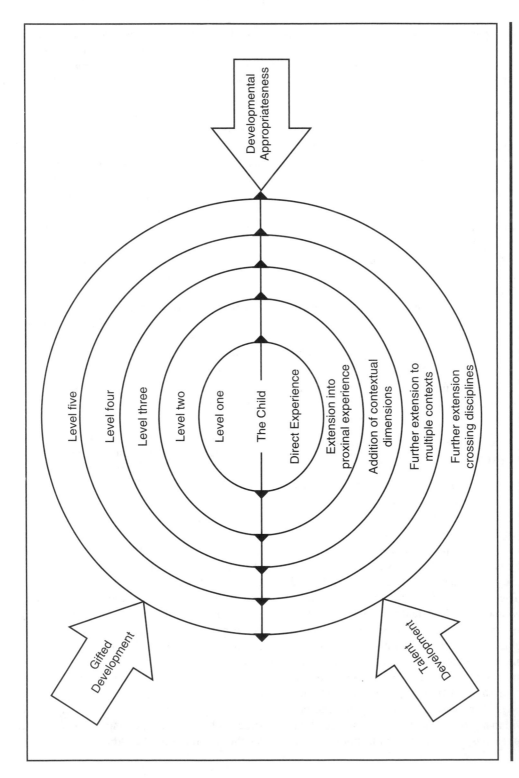

**FIGURE 7.10** Morelock and Morrison's (1999) Multidimensional Curriculum Model.
Reprinted with permission of *Roeper Review.*

## CONSTRUCTING DIFFERENTIATED CURRICULUM FOR THE GIFTED: KAPLAN

As we know, *differentiated curriculum* refers to learning experiences built around the needs, abilities, and interests of gifted students. Kaplan's (1986) model for constructing differentiated curriculum mainly looks at the integration of three qualitatively different components: *content, process,* and *products.* Kaplan helps us take a closer and deeper look at each component.

*Content* refers to knowledge and information defined as useful, important, and interesting to gifted students. In includes facts, ideas, concepts, generalizations, principles, theories, and systems, all of which may be related to historical, contemporary, and even futuristic considerations. Multidisciplinarity—extensions to other subject areas—is recommended. A core question is: What should a gifted student know as a result of studying a subject area or discipline?

*Process* refers primarily to complex thinking skills such as critical and creative thinking, but includes research skills (such as using information retrieval systems), learning-to-learn skills, technological skills, basic academic skills, and even life skills. Such skills are integrated in the sense that, for example, the skill of *verification* involves gathering information (a research skill) and sequencing that information (a basic skill).

Selecting a student *product* is important. It requires the integration of content knowledge with the mastery of many skills. The product serves both as a vehicle for learning as well as verification that learning took place. As a curricular opportunity, the product should allow exposure to several types of communication (e.g., written, oral, illustrative, and physical models), including variety within each category (e.g., written stories, editorials, abstracts, slogans, and proposals). Researching and creating a product also should exercise several production skills, which Kaplan (1986) named as (1) applying technology, (2) organizing time and resources, (3) establishing a bond with the product and valuing its worth to an audience, (4) appreciating significant contributors, and (5) identifying outlets for sharing products.

Finally, in addition to content, process, and product, Kaplan draws attention to the important *affective* component of curriculum for the gifted, which includes improved self-understanding as an individual and a contributor, valuing learning and productivity, and an awareness of the roles and responsibilities of leaders (see Chapter 8).

## COMMENT

The thoughtful program planner should consider all of the models in this chapter and what each has to offer. At mentioned earlier, most (not all) models are consistent with one another, which allows the planner to draw ideas and strategies from many models, even if a single model (e.g., Renzulli's Enrichment Triad) is adopted officially. Select what seems to best meet the needs of your students, which might require plucking elements from several models.

## SUMMARY

Some of the eleven curriculum models make highly specific procedural recommendations, others make more general suggestions.

In Renzulli's Enrichment Triad model, Type I Enrichment (general exploratory activities) exposes students to a variety of topics; Type II (group-training activities) focuses on creativity and other thinking skills, learning-to-learn skills, communication skills, and information retrieval skills; Type III is investigations of real problems. Types I and II are appropriate for all students. Outlets and audiences for Type III projects are important.

The Secondary Triad Model requires Talent Pool classes, similar to honors classes, in each discipline. Compacting "buys time" for Type III projects in the particular area.

The Schoolwide Enrichment Model is a complete programming guide that includes Types I and II enrichment in the regular classroom for all students. Talent pool students—and other students—can volunteer for Type III projects.

Curriculum compacting and identifying student interests are central. Two thick books present many details. Renzulli and Reis distinguish between schoolhouse and creative-productive giftedness. A summary cube model presents the three dimensions of school structures (e.g., enrichment clusters), service delivery components (e.g., curriculum modification techniques), and organizational components (e.g., the schoolwide enrichment teaching specialist).

Renzulli's Multiple Menu Model is a series of five planning guides or menus that suggest sequences and alternatives for teaching content efficiently: a knowledge menu, instructional objectives/student activities menu, instructional strategies menu, instructional sequence menu, and an artistic modification menu.

Based on the Richardson study, the Pyramid Project is a pre-detracking three-level schooling plan intended to overcome many problems and criticisms of G/T programs. Above-average students are mainstreamed in the regular classroom, more able students are placed in full-time special classes, and the most able students attend magnet or residential schools.

Feldhusen's Three-Stage Enrichment Model focuses mainly on fostering creative thinking but also on research and independent-learning skills and positive self-concepts. Stage 1 develops basic divergent and convergent thinking abilities, as well as basic skills, largely with short-term exercises. Stage 2 involves more complex creative problem solving, partly by teaching creativity techniques and using Future Problem Solving and Odyssey of the Mind. Stage 3 develops independent study and research skills via independent projects.

The Meekers use 90 of Guilford's (1967) 120 SOI abilities for (1) identifying giftedness and (2) diagnosing specific ability weaknesses, then strengthening them using SOI Training Modules. The SOI approach identifies gifted minority students and gifted students with learning disabilities. "Near-gifted" students can qualify for gifted programs also with SOI Training Modules.

Betts's Autonomous Learner Model, a rela-

tively complete programming guide, includes the five main dimensions of orienting students and others to giftedness and to the content and purposes of the ALM program; individual development in areas of self and interpersonal understanding, learning and thinking skills, technology, and career development; student-selected enrichment; small seminars; and individual or small-group in-depth studies.

An early Taylor Multiple-Talent Totem Pole Model suggests that learning activities focus upon developing academic ability, creativity, planning/organizing, communicating, forecasting/predicting, and decision making/evaluating. Schlichter's Talents Unlimited program trains teachers to teach totem pole talents.

Treffinger and Sortore suggested activities intended to develop talents at four levels of student ability. Services for *all* students included creative and higher-level thinking skills and exposure to new topic areas; services for *many* students included Future Problem Solving, compacting, and computer labs; services for *some* students included advanced classes and complex projects; and services for a *few* students included grade acceleration, concurrent enrollment, and mentors.

The Morelock and Morrison Multidimensional Curriculum Model uses Vygotsky's *zone of proximal development* to describe five levels of increasing complexity and abstractness. Level 1, the only level for all young children, emphasizes learning tasks based on children's own experiences. Level 2 builds on existing knowledge with more varied and complex learning experiences. Level 3 adds other contexts to supply additional abstract and complex concepts. Level 4 extends learning into new contexts. Level 5 adds still higher complexity and abstractness with interdisciplinary activities.

Kaplan's model takes a close look at three pivotal G/T considerations: content (e.g., facts, ideas, principles, theories), process (e.g., thinking, research, computer, and learning-to-learn skills), and product, which integrates content knowledge with many process skills. Kaplan also notes such affective matters as self-understanding and leadership.

## APPENDIX 7.1 TOPICS FOR ENRICHMENT ACTIVITIES

### Visual Arts, Performing Arts

Acting
Antiques
Architecture
Art appreciation
Art history
Art in various cultures
Artists
Ballet
Batik
Calligraphy
Candle making
Cartooning
Costume design
Dance, choreography
Dance history
Designing (clothes, toys, machines, etc.)
Drawing

Film making (animation, drama)
Folk art
Folk music
Graphics
Jewelry making
Leather craft
Macrame
Mime, pantomime
Movie making
Music composition
Music history
Musical instruments
Musicians
Opera
Painting
Photography, cameras
Plays
Political satire

Pottery, ceramics
Print making
Puppet making
Radio shows
Rug hooking
Sculpture (clay, metal, wood, etc.)
Shakespeare
Silk screening
Slide show making
Soft sculpture
Television
Theater—dramatic production, acting techniques, dramatic literature, set design, lighting, creative dramatics, improvisational theater, history of theater, makeup
Weaving

### Math and Science

Aeronautics
Agriculture
Anatomy
Animals, animal behavior
Aquarium planning
Archaeology
Astronomy
Biology
Botany
Brain science
Chemistry
Computer repair
Conservation
Diseases
Ecology
Electricity, electronics
Energy—solar, geothermal, tidal, wind, etc.

Engineering
Evolution
Forestry
Fossils
Genetics
Geology
Horticulture
Ichthyology
Marine biology
Math—algebra, geometry, measurement, math puzzles, statistics, probability
Medicine, health
Metals
Meteorology
Microbiology
Microscopes
Minerology, rocks

Money management
Natural resources
Nuclear energy
Nutrition
Optics, optometry
Ornithology
Physics
Physiology
Pollution
Prehistoric animals
Reptiles
Robots
Rocketry
Scientists
Solar power
Space, space travel
Veterinary science

*continued*

Based largely on Renzulli, 1977, and Reis and Burns, 1987.

## Computers, Internet

Computer resources for gifted students (e.g., help with math; learning about giftedness at www.gtkids.org; creativity and thinking skills; summer programs at universities; Future Problem Solving, Odyssey of the Mind; Junior Great Books; International Baccalaureate program)

Computer search and resources (e.g., city maps, weather, history, biographies, travel, geography, finding persons)
Stock market information and operation, stock quotes, stock trading

Word processing (introductory, sophisticated)
Writing music on the computer
Computer repair
Any other topic

## Literature, Writing, Communication

Broadcasting
Journalism
Literature appreciation
Mysteries

Mythology
Play writing
Poetry writing
Public speaking

Short story writing
Speed reading
Sports writing

## Social Sciences, Culture, Language

African American history
Alcohol, drug abuse
Ancient Egypt, Greece, Rome, China
Anthropology
Archaeology
Aztecs, Mayas, Incas
Careers
Children, child development
Civil rights
Contemporary cultures
Crime, criminology, prisons
Current events
Death, dying
Debate
Divorce
Editorial writing
Elections, voting
Etymology

Famous people
Festivals, holidays
Folklore
Foreign languages
Future thinking
Geography, mapping
Geology
Government (U.S., foreign)
Handicapped people
History (local, state, U.S., Russian, military, etc.)
Humor
Law, courts
Legends, myths
Linguistics
Minority groups
Newspapers

Parapsychology, occult
Philosophy
Poetry
Political cartoons
Political science
Population problems
Prehistoric life
Presidents
Problems of the elderly
Psychology, mental illness
Public opinion surveys
Religion
Sign language
Social problems
Sociology
Travel
Women's rights

## Business, Economics

Accounting
Advertising
Banking
Careers

Economics (models, theories)
Finance
Insurance
Law, lawyers

Operating a small business
Stock market
Transportation, trucking

## Miscellaneous

Bicycles, bicycling
Bridge
Careers
Chess
Coins, stamps
College preparation

Creativity
Gardening
History of football
Horses
Interior decorating
Karate

Law enforcement
Magic
Running
Sailing
Test taking

# CHAPTER 8

# LEADERSHIP, AFFECTIVE LEARNING, AND CHARACTER EDUCATION

*Education should . . . be focused on the emotional, moral, and ethical development of the student rather than on preparation for success in the work world.*
Annemarie Roeper (1995, p. 142)

*If we want leaders who will promote . . . the components we have identified in Operation Houndstooth [e.g., optimism, moral courage, sensitivity to human concerns, sense of destiny], then giftedness in the new century will have to be redefined.*
Joseph S. Renzulli (2003, p. 84)

This chapter looks at two important goals of programs for gifted students: *leadership* and *affective learning*. Leadership is one of the five U.S. Department of Education categories of giftedness. Gifted and talented students often are labeled *tomorrow's leaders*. As emphasized by Sisk (1993, p. 493), "Society cannot nor will not survive without intelligent, imaginative leadership. Leadership training for gifted students can provide leaders who have both the intellectual and creative potential to lead." In recent years, several writers have clarified characteristics of leaders, the nature of leadership, and how leadership traits and skills can be taught to gifted and other students. We will explore some of these.

The topic of affective learning runs through many chapters in this book. We have repeatedly stressed the importance, for example, of building good self-concepts, healthy social adjustment, high academic and career aspirations, constructive attitudes and values, and self-motivated learning. These topics are important for all gifted students, but take special significance in relation to at-risk gifted—students who are culturally different or economically disadvantaged (Chapter 12) or underachieving (Chapter 13); students with disabilities (Chapter 15); and sometimes female gifted students (Chapter 14). Chapter 17 on counseling, especially, will focus on understanding and aiding the self-understanding and social and emotional development of gifted students.

## LEADERSHIP

As mentioned in Chapter 3, Renzulli (2003) tied leadership to affective learning (which includes character education) quite clearly: Instead of just helping bright students to become educated, affluent, and high-consumption professionals, gifted education should promote a strong concern for less fortunate individuals plus a leadership capability—which includes a predisposition to take action and correct problems. Many enrichment programs involve students in community service with these two goals in mind: concern for others and a willingness to help. Renzulli used the term *social capital,* which refers to valuing freedom, justice, civic participation, and a diverse population.

At the National Research Center on the Gifted and Talented (NRC/GT), the relatively new

Operation Houndstooth focuses on promoting six core and interacting topic areas (instead of self-interest and consumerism): *optimism* (hope, sense of competence stemming from hard work), *courage* (moral conviction, psychological and intellectual independence, freedom from fear of group rejection), *romance with a topic or discipline* (absorption, passion, self-actualization), *sensitivity to human concerns* (empathy, altruism, insight), *physical and mental energy* (charisma, curiosity, vitality, excitability), and *vision and a sense of destiny* (sense of direction, sense of power to change things, achievement motivation). The term *Houndstooth* refers to the hounds tooth background [pattern] underlying the three-ring conception of giftedness (Renzulli & Reis, 2003, p. 76). NRC/GT Information on Operation Houndstooth is available at www.gifted.uconn.edu.

The following sections review further definitions and conceptions of leadership, then turn to other ideas about what is taught when you "teach leadership."

## LEADERSHIP DEFINITIONS: TRAITS, CHARACTERISTICS, AND SKILLS

Different leadership traits and skills naturally are required for different leadership situations—consider leading the Boston Pops Orchestra, the Lewis and Clark expedition, or the U.A.W. Or consider Renzulli's (2003) remarkable example of leadership, a fifth-grade girl who instigated a plan to reduce harassment of a badly nearsighted boy and supervised the creation of large-print illustrated books that he could see. At the same time, there are traits and skills that seem to characterize all leaders.

One definition of leadership is found in the Renzulli and colleagues (2001) leadership rating scale, reproduced in Appendix 4.5, on which teachers evaluate student leadership according to the following criteria:

1. Carries responsibility well and can be counted on to do what has been promised
2. Is self-confident with both age-mates and adults; seems comfortable when showing personal work to the class

3. Is well liked
4. Is cooperative, avoids bickering, and is generally easy to get along with
5. Can express him- or herself clearly
6. Adapts to new situations; is flexible in thought and action and is not disturbed when the normal routine is changed
7. Enjoys being around other people
8. Tends to dominate; usually directs activities
9. Participates in most school social activities; can be counted on to be there
10. Excels in sports

Plowman (1981) itemized six aspects of leadership in the form of adjectives. *Charismatic* refers to an almost mystical ability to instill others (partly by example) with a sense of mission and to energize them to think and act to achieve objectives. *Intuitive* includes the ability to sense what is about to happen via an extrapolation of current events or a keen sensitivity to subtle cues. It includes the ability to sense the needs of individuals and groups and to respond to those needs even before they are expressed. *Generative* refers to creativeness: defining problems in new ways and creating unusual ideas, processes, and courses of action. *Analytic* includes seeing component parts of systems and analyzing their individual contributions. *Evaluative* involves judging the effectiveness or efficiency of activities or programs. *Synergistic* aspects "are those which make the unbelievable happen"—goals are reached in half the expected time, or production is five or ten times what was expected.

Plowman (1981) also reported the results of a 1980 California Association for the Gifted Annual Conference in Los Angeles in which 16 traits of leadership were identified.

1. Assertive decision making
2. Altruistic
3. Persuasive/innovator
4. Sensitive to the needs of others
5. Ability to be a facilitator
6. Goal-oriented
7. Strong communication skills
8. Integrity

9. Organizational ability
10. Resourceful
11. Risk-taker
12. Charismatic
13. Competent (knowledgeable)
14. Persistent (hangs in there)
15. Accepts responsibility
16. Creative

Tannenbaum (2000) looked at *social leadership* as the ability to help a group reach its goals while bettering human relationships with a group. Specifically in regard to building G/T programs, Moon and Rosselli (2000) distinguished between individual and committee leadership. *Champions* are individuals committed to making changes, and given leeway by institutional structures will do so. *Broad-based advisory groups,* which include stakeholders, guide program development efforts through district policies.

Sisk (1993) observed that "one finds about as many definitions of leadership as there are persons writing about the concept of leadership" (p. 491). She noted that the Great Man Theory defines a leader as one who possesses vision, power, authority, and dynamic personal attraction. However, she preferred to define a leader as one who "helps others lead themselves" (p. 492). They encourage initiative, autonomy, and inventiveness; they bring out the best in others. Sisk's *Interactive Creative Leadership Model,* described later, evolves around the traits of *vision* to see things as they can be, *courage* to take risks, *absorption* in the creative act, and *talent recognition,* which includes the realization and appreciation of one's ability to become a creative leader. Note that Sisk's first three points—vision, courage to take risks, and absorption in the creative act— are three basic traits in Renzulli's Houndstooth project.

The traits or "aspects" of leadership in the above lists can be viewed as objectives or competencies for a leadership curriculum. That is, G/T students can be helped to understand these traits and skills, and to acquire them through practice.

## LEADERSHIP TRAINING

Recommendations and strategies for leadership training invariably include some combination of (1) teaching students about leadership styles and traits, along with principles of group dynamics; (2) putting students into leadership roles; and (3) teaching them component skills of leadership.

Magoon (1980), for example, recommended:

**1.** *Classroom monitorships,* in which students assume responsibility for regulating the behavior of peers (for example, in lineups) or other jobs (blackboard or A-V duties). Such activities teach leadership and followership, including the notion that there are menial tasks that must be carried out for the system to function.

**2.** *Mentorships,* in which gifted and talented students tutor peers or younger students. The mentors learn to communicate in an acceptable and challenging manner.

**3.** *In-school leadership projects,* identified via brainstorming, such as improving student behavior (for example, in the halls or cafeteria), improving the physical plant (e.g., in classrooms or restrooms, or temperature or noise levels), or solving problems related to, for example, curriculum selection, classroom rules, safety, or sanitation.

**4.** *Community projects,* in which students tackle neighborhood problems or undesirable conditions. This activity requires the development of communication skills, tact, diplomacy, and patience.

**5.** *Simulations,* which can involve, for example, establishing "banks" and "stores," making rules, and establishing a legal system for maintaining the rules.

Magoon (1981) proposed that students be exposed to the "topic and content" of leadership itself. For example, training can include teaching students about leadership and followership, principles of participatory democracy, group processes, and characteristics of leaders, along with developing communication skills. Magoon's strategy is "based, in part, on a leadership program that has been classroom tested with talented and gifted students for over three years with exciting results."

Plowman (1981) recommended strengthening leadership with exercises aimed at developing the component skills of critical thinking, decision making, persuading, planning, and evaluating. More complex objectives included helping students understand others' needs, and showing them ways that changes are made in political, social, economic, and other spheres.

Parker (1983) suggested that leadership could be trained by strengthening the four component skills of *cognition* (especially research and investigative skills), *problem solving* (including creative thinking), *interpersonal communication* (including self-awareness, concern for others, cooperation, and conflict resolution), and *decision making*.

Maker's (1982) suggestions for leadership training include providing practice in leading, helping students understand leadership, and teaching them component skills. She recommended that during the school year the G/T teacher should allow gifted students to assume progressively more leadership responsibilities. For example, they can teach small groups of students, a task that intrinsically requires leadership, and they can take responsibility for various projects. She noted that a teacher can raise understanding and awareness of leadership via discussions of leadership qualities, focusing partly on which traits help make leaders successful and why. Also, the teacher can foster discussion skills, public speaking, and group control and group dynamics skills.

Thomson (1989) described a unique approach to leadership training that was part of a summer sixth-grade *College Days for Kids* program. One of 25 mini-courses, entitled *Operation Adventure* and taught by ROTC staff, focused on two characteristics of leadership: problem solving and courage. On the first Friday, students took a brisk walk through a nature preserve. Student teams solved imaginary challenges, such as: How can we create a moving "human trolley" to cross a swamp filled with alligators? The importance of good communication skills quickly became evident.

The second Friday presented a true hair-raiser. After proper coaching and safety training, they rappeled from a 20-foot tower—each student eagerly making his or her "jumps." Thomson noted that the activity "gives the students opportunity to practice initiative and determination in the face of somewhat frightening circumstances" (p. 59). They also learned followership in the sense that they must trust their ROTC leaders. The ROTC staff were good models of leadership in showing qualities of professionalism, enthusiasm, and sensitivity to the children's needs. One student said of the experience, "It made you believe in yourself."

## Leadership Skills Development Program: Karnes and Chauvin

Karnes and Chauvin (2000) developed a two-part Leadership Skills Development Program aimed at upper elementary and secondary students. The first part of the program centers on their *Leadership Skills Inventory* (LSI). The LSI evaluates these kinds of leadership traits and skills:

*Fundamentals of leadership,* including understanding leadership styles and terms

*Written communication,* including outlining, speech writing, and report writing

*Speech communication,* including defining one's view on an issue, delivering speeches, and giving constructive criticism

*Values clarification,* including identifying things that one values, understanding the importance of free choice, and affirming one's choices

*Decision making,* including gathering facts, analyzing the consequences of decisions, and reaching logical conclusions

*Group dynamics,* including serving as group facilitator, achieving consensus, and achieving compromise

*Problem solving,* including identifying problems, revising problem-solving strategies, and accepting unpopular decisions

*Personal development,* including self-confidence, sensitivity, and personal grooming

*Planning,* including goal setting, developing timelines, and creating evaluation strategies

The LSI provides a profile of leadership abilities and skills for each student and for the group as a whole. It thus serves as a needs assessment instrument and guides the planning of a leadership development program based upon individual and group weaknesses. Because the results are shared with students, they learn about the nature of leadership and leadership skills, and they receive an objective assessment of their own present leadership skills. This record is used as a basis for later evaluation of progress.

The second part of the training stems from the *Leadership Skills Activities Handbook*. The handbook contains activities designed to strengthen each skill or trait described on the LSI. For example, one LSI item reads "I am ambitious and desire success." The coordinated activity in the handbook is leading a discussion on "how the self-confident person views success." The student-leader would pose such (supplied) questions as "Are all leaders success-oriented? How important is this quality to a leader?"

The culminating activity for the Leadership Development Program is a student's written "plan for leadership." Each student is asked to think about everything he or she learned about leadership, then formulate a plan to put these skills into action. The student formulates objects, a timeline, and a list of resources. Field tests of the Leadership Skills Development Program have shown positive results.

## Leadership Education: Richardson and Feldhusen

Richardson and Feldhusen's (1986) book *Leadership Education* was written primarily for secondary students participating in leadership education programs. The book presents a balanced mix of theory and principles, characteristics of leadership, guides for becoming an effective leader, plus activities and problems designed to exercise and strengthen leadership traits and skills.

To explain leadership, Richardson and Feldhusen reviewed four types of leaders. The *personality* approach defines a leader as one who possesses a constellation of personality traits that are attractive to others, for example, confidence, humor, and popularity. Students with these traits often are elected to school leadership positions. Leadership as a form of *persuasion* is based on the ability to "convince or inspire others to follow their directions, orders, or commands . . . to inspire people to action." Leadership as a *power relation* goes to the person with the highest rank, as in democratic government or clan leadership. Finally, a leader can be a self-directed and motivated person who *initiates action and maintains structure* when working toward group goals, as when a private citizen organizes a group to combat drug use or automobile deaths among young people.

To help students understand leadership, Richardson and Feldhusen explain that good leaders are confident and have good self-esteem. They take risks and admit mistakes. They tend to be responsible, empathic, and more assertive and extroverted than average. Good leaders also are good speakers, good listeners, and can give directions, lead discussions, and write well. They have good interpersonal skills, delegate authority, and are prepared to help others. They have good organization and planning skills; they can involve group members in a task and clarify the goals and issues. They develop group cohesiveness and an atmosphere of respect, cooperation, and teamwork; avoid harsh criticism; are fair; make decisions based on majority views; protect rights of individual members; help all members to achieve their personal goals; are good at public relations—keeping the community informed and supportive; and understand parliamentary procedures.

Students learn steps to use in leading discussions, and steps to use in brainstorming and problem solving. The authors also suggest tips for reading body language and nonverbal communication; communicating effectively; making introductions; writing letters; preparing a speech; setting and clarifying individual and group goals; planning meetings; planning work activities for the group; serving as a committee chairperson; and serving as a committee member.

Overall, the book not only provides convincing evidence that leadership can be taught, it carefully explains and provides exercises in the skills and traits needed to improve one's leadership ability.

## Interactive Creative Leadership Model: Sisk

Sisk (1993) described a leadership training program that emphasizes six "productive thinking and feeling behavioral strategies of leadership" (p. 498). The first is *setting goals,* which gives students practice in creating objectives, plans, priorities, and hopes. The second strategy is *responding to the future,* which includes helping students develop a future-focused perspective, for example, with simulations such as planning a City of Tomorrow. *Developing a success syntax,* the third strategy, means teaching the order of activities that leads to creative production—knowing when to do what and in what order. The fourth leadership strategy is *gaining self knowledge,* which involves, for example, journal writing, independent study, or imagining yourself 30 years in the future. *Becoming interpersonally competent,* the fifth strategy, involves becoming more aware of oneself during the leadership functions of planning, initiating, controlling, supporting, informing, and evaluating group behavior. Finally, the sixth strategy is helping students in *coping with value differences and conflict,* for example, by learning conflict resolution and negotiating strategies. Sisk also noted that value differences can aid motivation (to solve the problem), help reasoning (to rise above emotional responses), present different perspectives, and even aid group cohesion.

The plan has been used in the secondary level Texas Governor's Honors Program, a three-week summer residential program. According to program staff and alumni, students acquired a "more positive attitude toward learning and . . . enhanced leadership skills that impact their school and community" (p. 504).

## Leadership Education by Telecommunications

Telephone and television were used to teach leadership traits and skills to gifted middle school students in four rural school districts (University of Wisconsin-Eau Claire, 1992).[1] Table 8.1 presents the discussion guide that all students reviewed and discussed via telephone. Before the telecommunications session began, the students had read several selections pertaining to popularity, giftedness, and leadership. The main objectives of the session were to help the seventh and eighth graders become sensitive to the differences between *leadership* and *popularity,* and to better understand the variety of leadership roles within schools and communities.

**TABLE 8.1**    Leadership—Distance Learning

1.  What different kinds of student leadership exist in your school and community? Let's all list these.
2.  What are the characteristics leaders need in any two of these?
3.  Are these characteristics the same in both or are there differences?
4.  What do all leadership roles seem to have in common?
5.  What is the importance of talk in leadership? What is the place of listening?
6.  What are some types of leadership in adult communities?
7.  What kinds of school leadership are likely to lead toward adult leadership roles?
8.  What kinds of school leadership will not be likely to lead to adult leadership?
9.  What does the story *Gifted Kids Have Feelings Too* have to do with school leadership and lifetime leadership?
10. How do the articles on popularity relate to school leadership and lifetime leadership?

Prepared by Sylvia Rimm for the University of Wisconsin-Eau Claire (1992).

[1]Written and conducted by Sylvia Rimm.

## AFFECTIVE LEARNING

In our early discussion of characteristics of gifted and talented children we noted that, compared with the average, G/T students are better able to understand moral issues and to be honest, truthful, and ethical (e.g., Howard-Hamilton and Franks, 1995). If they are moderate-to-high achievers, they also are likely to have good self-concepts, high self-esteem, and reasonably high levels of achievement motivation. However, just as we try to strengthen the cognitive skills of students who already are cognitively superior, we also can help affectively superior students to better understand themselves and their values, to be more empathic toward others, and generally to acquire high-level values, ethics, achievement needs, and humanistic attitudes (e.g., Davis, 2003a, 2003c).

It also is true that some gifted students do go astray morally and legally, and many drop out of high school and college. They forfeit both their full development and self-actualization and their potential contributions to society.

The following five sections will examine, first, the nature of the self-concept—how it is formed and how its protection can lead to subtle defensive behaviors. We next look briefly at how the classic Kohlberg (1974) stages in moral development can serve as a guide for teaching moral and ethical thinking. The remaining sections review curriculum content and strategies for imparting constructive attitudes, awarenesses, values, and humanistic thinking, as well as the qualities of a humanistic teacher.

## SELF-CONCEPT

Feelings of personal competence and self-esteem are tied closely to experiences of success. For adults, there are many types of success experiences that can strengthen feelings of adequacy and self-esteem—for example, job or career success or success as a parent, church member, home decorator, bowler, union member, and so on. For children, however, feedback from schoolwork and the teacher is extremely important in telling each child whether he or she is a capable and worthwhile person. The following are some dynamics of self-concept development:

**1.** Developing healthy self-concepts in students is an educational goal in itself. In addition, because a student who feels capable and confident will be more motivated and have higher academic and career aspirations, promoting good self-concepts also is a means of stimulating higher school achievement.

**2.** There are many facets of the self. A person may perceive, for example, an academic self, a social self, an emotional self, and a physical self. Gifted students sometimes have better academic selves than social selves.

**3.** The self-concept is organized, relatively stable, and evaluative. The evaluative component (self-esteem) relates to mental health—a person may or may not like his or her self-concept. Rimm (2003) noted that underachieving gifted students have lower self-esteem than high-achieving students (see Chapter 14). Also, according to Carl Rogers (1949) mentally healthy people see their *actual* selves as similar to their *ideal* selves.

**4.** The *mirror theory* of self-concept development assumes that the self-concept is created via assessments (reflections) from others.

**5.** The *self-accepting* student understands him- or herself and therefore is aware of strengths and weaknesses. This student values himself despite weaknesses. The *self-rejecting* student considers him- or herself of little worth and may have other symptoms of maladjustment.

**6.** Academic failure implies low worth as a person and prevents students from maintaining feelings of competence. Failure after great effort is especially devastating to feelings of competence (Covington and Omelich, 1979).

**7.** Excuses and rationalizations, constructed to explain why the effort did not succeed, will protect the self-concept.

**8.** Self-esteem and pride are greatest when the student succeeds at a difficult task; the success is attributed to both high ability and high effort (Covington and Omelich, 1979).

**9.** Most critically, feelings of self-esteem and self-worth are a highly treasured commodity. *All students are strongly motivated to protect their feelings of self-esteem.* Roeper (1995) confirmed that "it is this inner self, the unique self of each human being, that is the central point of their lives" (p. 142).

The Piers-Harris Children's Self-Concept Scale (Piers, 1984) is the industry standard for assessing self-concept in school-age students. Subscales evaluate self-perceptions of being well-behaved, intellectual and school status, physical appearance, absence of anxiety, popularity, happiness, and an overall global self-concept score. Lewis and Knight's (2000) study of 368 gifted students across grades 4–12 showed that males saw themselves as less anxious and more popular than did females, but females saw themselves as better-behaved than did males. Lewis and Knight also reported that middle school students saw themselves as significantly worse behaved than did elementary or high school students.

### Attributions and Defense Mechanisms

Most often, the gifted student succeeds. The person's history of success inspires confidence in his or her abilities, a sense of responsibility for his or her actions, and feelings of control over his or her environment. When failure occurs, it typically is attributed to lack of effort, not lack of ability. Failures therefore may be used constructively to evaluate shortcomings and prepare for next time. The person has temporarily fallen short of a goal, not fallen short as a person (Covington and Beery, 1976).

Many students, however, are motivated not by strong needs to succeed but by strong needs to avoid failure. And when failure threatens, any of several defense mechanisms may be used to ward off threats to the self-esteem.

One is *deliberate underachieving:* There will be no humiliation or destroyed self-esteem due to poor performance if the student does not really try. If the fear-of-failure student *accidentally* scores high on a test or paper there is a bonus. Doing well without trying is clear evidence of extra-high ability, thus reinforcing the underachievement pattern. In college, an effortless "gentleman's C" maintains the illusion of intellectual superiority without testing the scholar's actual abilities.

If one's need to avoid failure becomes combined with a strong need to achieve, the result may be *compulsive high achievement.* Again, with feelings of self-worth tied closely to classroom success, this individual makes more and more self-demands in order to sustain a high level of achievement.

Also, excuses can protect the fragile ego of a fear-of-failure student. Failure is simply attributed to external causes, not internal ones. Such students blame anything and everything: "The test was unfair," "My friends wouldn't let me study," "My computer wasn't working right," or just "I wasn't feeling good." Ironically, these students may not accept credit for successes either, because success implies the ability and obligation for continued good work.

The case history of Dan, a real-life underachiever unable to take credit for success, is instructive. Dan had been a consistent C student when he came to Rimm for underachievement counseling. After one quarter his achievement had improved sufficiently to earn him a place on the honor roll. When the counselor asked Dan how he felt about his achievement, he replied, "I like it, but I guess I was just lucky." He even had thanked his English teacher for "giving" him an A. The counselor pointed out to Dan that he had both improved his study habits and increased the time he spent learning. He finally acknowledged, hesitantly, that there probably was some relationship between his new efforts and the improved grades.

One recommended solution to self-defeating, self-perpetuating defense mechanisms is individualized instruction. By engaging fear-of-failure students in independent-learning assignments, success is redefined in terms of meeting or exceeding one's own standards, not publicly competing with others for classroom rewards and recognition. According to Covington and Beery (1976), when students are not forced to compete they will set reachable, realistic goals, and these provide both the best challenge and the best conditions for a satisfying success.

## MORAL DEVELOPMENT: THE KOHLBERG MODEL

Based on research with the same group of 75 boys over a period of twelve years, Lawrence Kohlberg (1976; Power, Higgins, & Kohlberg, 1989) developed a model of moral thinking that is valuable for understanding sequential stages in moral development and teaching moral thinking.

Kohlberg's six stages of moral development are divided into three main levels, each containing two stages. In both stages of the *preconventional* level (ages 0–9) the orientation is toward the physical consequences of an action, regardless of any higher level notions of right or wrong. Thus in Stage 1 obedience and good behavior are valued because they avoid punishments. This "might makes right" stage is characteristic of preschool children. In Stage 2 "right" action is that which produces rewards and satisfies one's needs or the needs of others—who will reciprocate ("You scratch my back, I'll scratch yours").

In the *conventional* level (ages 9–15), behavior is heavily influenced by conformity pressures, strict stereotypes, social conventions and expectations, and rules and laws. Thus in Stage 3 good behavior is that which pleases others or avoids disapproval, producing the "good boy–good girl" orientation. There is much conformity here. In Stage 4 right action is based upon rules and authority, "doing one's duty," and respecting the system. Laws are to be obeyed, not revised, leading to the "law and order" syndrome. Many adults do not rise above conventional moral thinking.

The highly desirable *postconventional* level includes the acceptance of universal and personal moral principles (for example, "Do unto

others . . .") that are valid apart from authority. In Stage 5 right action is defined by general rights and standards that have been examined and agreed upon. Personal values and opinions present the possibility of rationally changing these rights and standards. For the chosen few, Stage 6 includes self-chosen principles and ethics based upon such universal principles and rights as justice, equality, and respect for individual differences.

Kohlberg found that children and adolescents comprehend all stages up to their own and understand only one additional stage. Importantly, *they preferred this next stage.* Children move to the next stage when they are confronted with the appealing views of peers who are in this higher stage.

In one study of gifted students ages 9 to 15, Karnes and Brown (1981) found that the tendency to make Postconventional responses was positively correlated with age and verbal intelligence scores. The authors concluded that gifted students may reach Level III (postconventional) moral reasoning during their secondary school years, a level attained by only 10 to 15 percent of adults. Using Rest's (1988) Kohlberg-based Defining Issues Test, Howard-Hamilton (1994; Howard-Hamilton and Franks, 1995) in two studies also found that gifted adolescents scored at higher levels of moral reasoning than other students. That is, they possessed a stronger justice-orientation with greater emphasis on moral principles and individual rights.

As for teaching for moral development, Kohlberg (1976) suggested that teachers expose children to concepts just *one step higher* than their current stage and encourage them to think at this more mature stage. Children also may be given opportunities to think about moral matters by role-playing someone who has been treated rudely or cheated. A related strategy is to discuss moral dilemmas and let children practice making moral decisions that require high-level moral thinking.

High school English teacher Joan Weber (1981) used moral dilemmas from literature to encourage higher-level moral thinking. For example, *Old Man Warner* by Dorothy Canfield describes a 93-year-old obstinate man who, despite family pressure, refuses to move in with relatives or even move closer to town. Weber asks her class, "What should the man do? Why? Would it make a difference if he lived in a big city? If he were physically ill? If he were a woman and not a man?" Literature is a rich source of personal problems and conflicts centering on moral issues and values.

Especially for students who are gifted, Kohlberg's six stages themselves can help them understand moral thinking. What is "good" and what is "bad" about preconventional, conventional, and postconventional thinking? Should we get stuck at the conventional level? Discussions of universal values, based upon the impact of our behavior upon others (e.g., honesty, fairness, pleasantness, helpfulness, empathy, dependability, and respect for others' rights), along with valuing safety, a good education, and staying out of prison, also would be valuable in developing good moral thinking.

## AN AFFECTIVE, HUMANISTIC CURRICULUM

Character and values are in a crisis. Daily headlines describe record numbers of robberies, shootings, rapes, drug deals, and gang violence, to say nothing of dropping out, racism, rudeness, an absence of empathy, and indifference to others' rights. Teenagers go to prison, babies get tossed into dumpsters, and families are emotionally shattered—all because some young people do not think about the consequences of their actions, consequences for themselves, for others, for everyone's families, and for their own future lives. At least 12 states currently receive government grants to develop citizenship and character education programs (O'Brien, n.d.).

It is true that bright students, on average, better understand moral issues and productive values, and are less likely to behave as per the preceding paragraph. Nonetheless, we must help *all* children—from gifted and privileged to at-risk and gang-prone—to understand values and to decide consciously that constructive values will help them live happier and more successful lives, and that poor values will hurt them personally and may destroy their lives.

The Character Education Partnership is a relatively new national nonprofit organization devoted to improving education for moral and ethical growth. One conference description (Character Education Partnership, 2002) mentioned these central topics:

- Student intellectual, ethical, moral, and emotional growth
- Helping students grapple with domestic and worldwide issues from a moral and ethical foundation
- Involving young people in character-based citizenship projects
- Involving parents
- Integrating character education with academic subjects in support of academic standards
- Using civics and social studies to explore democratic values and ethics
- Ways teachers, counselors, and administrators can become better prepared to be educators of character
- Developing new in-service character education curricula and programs
- Implementing models that build caring environments

We will look now at some programs and strategies for developing these critical components of affective learning and student self-concepts.

### Ideas for Promoting Positive Values: Fantini

Over two decades ago, Fantini (1981) itemized a number of suggestions for creating an affective, humanistic curriculum for children. For example:

**1.** Emphasize the desirability of "caring" values and behaviors as they relate to the self, to others, and to nature and the environment. Specifics might relate to clarifying values and ethics and understanding ecology, principles of health and hygiene, and related topics.

**2.** Students can learn and discuss the difficulties of persons with disabilities and the elderly.

**3.** Students can learn about people, both common and famous, whose behavior demonstrates humanistic, caring values.

**4.** High school students can become involved in community service programs, working in day-care centers, hospitals, or nursing homes or other centers for the elderly. These assignments may be voluntary or mandated as a graduation requirement. Students may receive course credit or recognition on their school records.

Elementary school children can make gifts or perform plays for the elderly or hospitalized; take leadership in recycling efforts; participate in drives to collect food, coats, hats, and gloves for poor families; and help in highway cleanup projects. (For example, in Lucerne, Switzerland, your author (Davis) noticed recycling bins on an elementary school grounds—a super way to raise recycling awareness.)

**5.** Students can participate in walk-a-thons or similar activities aimed at raising research funds for persons with cancer, multiple sclerosis, AIDS, heart disease, and other charitable causes.

**6.** Students can review social issues, for example, relating to refugees seeking asylum in America, political prisoners, military actions, migrant workers, and so on, from the perspective of humaneness.

**7.** Importantly, while the above are good for all children, gifted children can initiate, plan, implement, and evaluate such social action projects, perhaps as Renzulli Type III enrichment.

## MATERIALS AND STRATEGIES FOR ENCOURAGING AFFECTIVE GROWTH

### Values Clarification

*Value clarification* strategies are a long-standing way to help gifted and other students explore their beliefs and feelings. Affective education leader Sidney Simon (Simon, Howe, & Kirschenbaum, 1978) described 79 values clarification strategies. One of the authors' favorites, which can be modified and revised for any student population, cen-

ters on a list of attitudes and behaviors (see Table 8.2). The question is asked, "Are you someone who . . . ?" and the student checks yes (A), maybe (B), or no (C)—requiring the student to decide on the spot that he or she *strongly favors,* is *neutral toward,* or is *opposed to.* Discussion follows, of course.

The traits in Table 8.2 list only a few of the hundreds of possibilities. Simon and Massey (1973) suggested that students will have a rousing time brainstorming lists of behaviors that could include such items as "Blushes at a compliment?" "Talks loudly when nervous?" "Cheats on unfair tests?" "Gambles on parking tickets?" and so on.

In today's world, Table 8.2 could be extended by adding: Are you someone who . . . Would carry a gun? Would shoot another young person? Would sell drugs? Would like to go to prison? Would join a gang? Will destroy your health? Will be rude and nasty? Will think about other people's rights? Will ruin your future by dropping out of school? Will become an educated and successful adult?

Adolescents will be intrigued by listing personal traits and then responding "yes," "maybe," or "no" to the question, "I am looking for someone who is . . ." Other values clarification strategies include writing letters to newspapers expressing views on issues, or classifying yourself as a Cadillac person or a Ford Escort person and then discussing reasons why.

One unfortunately out-of-print book, *Affective Education Guidebook* (Eberle & Hall, 1975), is jammed with exercises for clarifying feelings and teaching values. For example, in their *Mini-Speech* strategy, students draw a topic from a sack and prepare a two- to four-minute speech that expresses feelings about the matter. Some topics are:

- I think I'm pretty good at . . .
- Compared to most people, I'm different because . . .
- I like people who . . .
- Getting along with another person is easy if . . .
- My feelings are hurt when . . .

Class discussion follows each mini-speech.

**TABLE 8.2**    Are You Someone Who . . . ?

(A = yes, B = maybe, C = no)

| A | B | C | Are you someone who: |
|---|---|---|---|
| | | | 1. Likes to break the curve on an exam? |
| | | | 2. Likes to stay up all night when friends visit? |
| | | | 3. Will stop the car to look at a sunset? |
| | | | 4. Puts things off? |
| | | | 5. Will publicly show affection for another person? |
| | | | 6. Will do it yourself when you feel something needs doing? |
| | | | 7. Will order a new dish in a restaurant? |
| | | | 8. Could accept your own sexual impotence? |
| | | | 9. Could be satisfied without a college degree? |
| | | | 10. Could be part of a mercy killing? |
| | | | 11. Is afraid alone in the dark in a strange place? |
| | | | 12. Is willing to participate in fund raising? |
| | | | 13. Eats when you are worried? |
| | | | 14. Can receive a gift easily? |
| | | | 15. Would steal apples from an orchard? |
| | | | 16. Is apt to judge someone by his or her appearance? |
| | | | 17. Would let your child drink or smoke pot? |
| | | | 18. Watches television soap operas? |
| | | | 19. Could kill in self-defense? |
| | | | 20. Needs to be alone? |

From Sidney Simon* and Sara Massey, "Values clarification," *Educational Leadership,* May, 1973. Reprinted with permission of the Association for Supervision and Curriculum Development. Copyright © 1973 by the Association for Supervision and Curriculum Development. All rights reserved.

*For information about current Values Realization materials and a schedule of nationwide training workshops, contact Sidney Simon, Old Mountain Rd., Hadley, MA 01035.

With the *What's It Like?* exercise, students clarify and identify their own feelings and learn that their behavior can make other people feel good or uncomfortable. Students discuss "What's it like" when:

- People yell at you.
- Someone tells you that you have done something very well.
- Somebody doesn't do what they said they would.
- You get a gift you didn't expect.

Students and teachers can brainstorm more "What's it like" questions. The class also can reverse the roles, for example:

- "What's it like to yell at people?"
- "What's it like to tell someone they have done something very well?"
- "What's it like to give someone a gift they don't expect?

*In What Ways?* asks students to answer the questions "In what ways might I . . ."

- Show my appreciation to those who are helpful to me?
- Give pleasure to others?
- Show a person that I value her or his friendship?
- Gain the respect and love of all human beings?

The *What Kind of Person Are You* exercise likely was inspired by the "Are you someone who?" strategy of Simon, Howe, and Kirschenbaum (1978). Students mark the "Hardly Ever," "Sometimes," or "Always" column in response to the statements "I am the kind of person who . . ."

- Tells people when they do good
- Puts out a foot to bother or trip someone
- Cuts in line at the drinking fountain
- Listens and tries to understand what others are saying
- Makes smart-aleck remarks to others
- Says "please" and "thank you"
- Finds fault with others

Eberle and Hall's (1975) had this advice to teachers about clarifying feelings and values: "Be happy, feel good, and work proudly—you are doing something for the infinite good of your pupils, yourself, and the larger community" (p. 13).

## Magic Circle

The *Magic Circle* technique helps children learn "why people are sometimes happy or unhappy, how to feel good about themselves, and how to get along with others" (Lefkowitz, 1975). Seven to twelve children in a circle—few enough to maintain everyone's attention—voluntarily respond to "Today's Topic," such as "I felt good when . . . ," "I felt bad when . . . ," "I made someone else feel good when . . . ," or "Something I can do (or wish I could do) is . . ." The teacher encourages learning and understanding with follow-up questions such as "Who can tell me why Dizzy Jones felt good on the roller coaster?" or "Why was he proud of himself?"

## Teaching Values: Two Books

Two books for teaching character and values education are *Character Education* (Davis, 2003a) and *Values Are Forever* (Davis, 2003c). Both books aim at grades four to eight. Both books help students understand and make commitments to these types of universal values: honesty,

responsibility, empathy, compassion, education, health, good school and work habits, respect, self-respect, regard for others' rights, caring for our environment, and positive life goals.

Some information, exercises, and activities relate to teenage problems. Younger children must be prepared in advance for the values questions and difficulties (e.g., theft, drugs, gangs, smoking, dropping out) they will face in middle and high school. *When they become teenagers, for many it is too late.*

Activities include, for example, "What would happen if . . . ?," brainstorming, reverse brainstorming, visualization (empathy), problem solving, crossword puzzles, word-search puzzles, and discussion-prodding real-world examples of self-destructive values. Two quizzes are a *Rights Quiz* and a *Quiz About Your Values,* both intended to help students make conscious decisions about values matters. Similarly, the *Final Examination: Values and Your Dreams* asks students whether each of 22 statements "Will Help My Life" or "Will Hurt My Life." For example, "Friends and people who love you are valuable. You should treat them with honesty, fairness, and friendliness," "It's a good idea to be a nasty, grouchy, sarcastic person—and maybe a bully too," and "It's good to have empathy, to try to understand other people's feelings."

The exercises try to help young people understand and make commitments to constructive values and behavior; understand that our values determine who we are; respect others' rights; empathize with persons (victims) whose rights are violated; value education, achievement, and career preparation; and become inoculated against media content and peer pressures that promote rudeness, underachievement, crime, drugs, and lack of concern for others' rights.

Children are helped to think about what their adult lives will be like if they adopt self-destructive values, such as dropping out, ignoring their health, joining a gang, or becoming an under-educated and under-trained person. This is compared with what life can be like if they adopt caring and constructive values, including valuing education and training. Students basically are asked: Do you want the American Dream? Then go for it!

With *brainstorming,* students are asked, for example, "Why should we be honest?" "What rights do students (parents, teachers, siblings, store clerks) have?" "How many reasons can you think of to get as much education as you can?"

With *reverse brainstorming* we find "How many ways can you destroy your health?" "How can we be VERY rude and discourteous at school?" "How many ways can you prove beyond any doubt that you are an irresponsible, undependable, and untrustworthy slob?"

In *"What would happen if . . . ?"* exercises students imagine and think about the outcomes of hurtful behavior. For example, what would happen if everyone were a thief? If the school were vandalized every night? If nobody was friendly to anybody else? If we all ignored all safety rules? If everyone in the school wasted as many school supplies as they possibly could?

With *analogical thinking* students make imaginative comparisons. For example: How is a good person like a good pizza? How is trustworthiness like a good movie? How are bad friends like Monopoly money? How is sharing like Saturday?

*Empathy* and *visualization* exercises are similar. In both, the teacher leads students through an episode that elicits empathy, compassion, and positive values. For example:

> Imagine that Dayvene's mother gave her a new digital watch for her birthday. She loved her new watch and did not want to scratch it. So she put it in her locker—and somebody stole it!

A variety of follow-up questions ask: How does Dayvene feel? What does she think about after this happens? What will Dayvene's mother think? How will she feel? Was the thief thinking of Dayvene's feelings? Why not? Was the thief thinking only of himself or herself? What kind of people steal from lockers? Are they considerate? Thoughtful? Intelligent? Do they think about other people's rights and feelings? Are you the kind of person who would do this?

Using a *questioning and discussion* approach, *Character Education* describes how everyday events can be used to teach character education and values. For example: "I saw a couple of fifth-graders smoking this morning. Is smoking good for you? Is smoking smelly and expensive? Is our health important? What happens if we do not take care of our health?" "Someone in this room was being rude to another person. Do we like people to be rude to us? Should we be nasty and unpleasant and rude to other people?" (Davis, 2003a).

Davis's *problem-solving* approach follows just two steps. The first is *clarifying* an affective problem. The teacher can ask: Why is the situation bad? Why is it wrong? When does this happen? Who is hurt? How do we hurt ourselves? How are others affected? What would happen if everyone did this? The second step is *finding solutions* for what can or should be done. The teacher might probe for ideas with: What are some examples of correct behavior? What would a helpful, thoughtful person do? What would earn us respect from others? How might we help the victims?

Finally, both books warn students that "people are playing with your head." That is, peer influence (including gang influence), television (especially the violent Saturday and evening cartoons, MTV, and "professional wrestling"), and movies present lots of poor values, particularly violence, overdone sexiness (e.g., on MTV), coarse vocabulary for children (e.g., on the early-evening *Sopranos*), and sometimes anti-everything stupidity, as with the now-defunct *Beavis and Butt Head*. "These shows are fun to watch, but they can teach values that might hurt you!" (Davis, 2003b).

## THE HUMANISTIC TEACHER

A teacher who has internalized humanistic and character-education values will be better able to communicate these values to students, both in direct teaching and by serving as a good role model. Pine and Boy (1977) listed the characteristics of such a humanistic teacher. We can view the traits as ideals toward which we all should work. The self-actualized, humanistic teacher:

1. Thinks well of himself or herself; he or she has a good self-concept
2. Is honest and genuine; there is no conflict between the real inner person and the role-playing outer person
3. Likes and accepts others
4. Lives by humanistic values; is honestly concerned with the welfare of fellow humans and the improvement of human society
5. Is sensitive and responsive to the needs and feelings of others
6. Is open to the viewpoints of others, to new information and experiences, and to his or her own inner feelings
7. Exercises control over his or her life and environment
8. Initiates needed changes
9. Is responsive, vibrant, and spontaneous, and tries to live optimistically and energetically

If there is one enrichment topic in this text that is "good for all children," it is teaching positive attitudes and values.

## SUMMARY

Two goals of gifted education are promoting leadership and aiding students' affective development. Leadership is one category of giftedness in the federal definition; our gifted and talented students are tomorrow's leaders. Affective learning and character education concern self-concept, personal and social adjustment, career aspirations, moral thinking, and related topics.

Renzulli's Operation Houndstooth ties leadership to affective learning by promoting optimism, moral courage, strong absorption with a topic, sensitivity to human concerns, physical and mental energy, and vision and a sense of destiny, instead of consumerism.

We reviewed several lists of characteristics of leadership. Renzulli's 10-item leadership rating scale emphasized, for example, responsibility,

self-confidence, likableness, flexibility, enjoyment of people, and a tendency to dominate.

Plowman noted charisma, intuitiveness, creativeness, and the ability to analyze and evaluate situations. A California gifted conference listed, for example, good decision making, altruism, persuasiveness, sensitivity to others' needs, communication skills, integrity, organizational ability, competence, and risk taking.

As part of a leadership training program, leadership traits may be used as objectives and competencies.

In developing G/T programs, according to Moon and Rosseli, leadership is by individual "champions" or advisory groups.

In contrast with the "Great Man Theory," Sisk defined a leader as one who helps others lead themselves.

Leadership training includes some combination of teaching students about leadership styles, traits, and group dynamics; placing students in leadership roles; and teaching students component skills of leadership, such as communication, creative problem solving, planning, decision making, and others.

Magoon described five leadership training activities: classroom monitorships, mentorships, in-school leadership projects, community projects, and simulations.

Plowman emphasized teaching critical thinking, decision making, persuading, planning, evaluating, understanding others' needs, and how decisions are made.

Parker recommended teaching problem solving and research skills, interpersonal communication skills (including conflict resolution), and decision making.

Maker recommended allowing G/T students progressively more leadership responsibilities as the year progresses.

Operation Adventure focused on two characteristics of leadership. Problem solving was exercised in solving imaginary team challenges; courage was strengthened by rappelling from a tower.

Karnes and Chauvin's Leadership Skills Development Program included (1) using their

*Leadership Skills Inventory* to assess leadership traits and skills, and then (2) prescribing leadership activities from their *Leadership Skills Activities Handbook* to strengthen each weak skill. Each student also prepares a written plan for leadership.

Richardson and Feldhusen's high school book *Leadership Education* teaches types and characteristics of leaders; steps to use in leading discussions, brainstorming, and problem solving; and other specific leadership skills, including goal-setting, communication, and planning.

Sisk emphasized six "thinking and feeling" leadership strategies of setting goals, developing a future focus, developing a success syntax (learning what to do in what order), gaining self-knowledge, becoming interpersonally competent, and coping with conflict.

One effort used telephone and television to teach leadership to gifted students in rural school districts. The focus was a discussion of leadership as it relates to popularity and giftedness.

Gifted students usually attain higher levels of moral thinking. High-achieving students usually have good self-concepts. The self-concept is tied closely to success experiences, which makes feedback from schoolwork and the teacher extremely important for children. Academic failure implies low self-worth.

Developing good self-concepts is a goal in itself. We have many "selves" (academic, social, emotional, physical). The self-concept is organized, stable, and evaluative. Underachieving G/T students have poor self-concepts. The self-concept may be formed by mirrored reflections from others. Self-accepting students are aware of strengths and weaknesses. Self-rejecting students feel of little worth. Academic failure implies low worth, especially after great effort. Excuses protect the self-concept. Self-esteem is greatest with success at a difficult task. All students try to protect their treasured self-esteem.

The Piers-Harris Scale assesses students self-concept. Subscales evaluate self-concepts of being well-behaved, intellectual and school status, physical appearance, anxiety, and popularity.

Male gifted students saw themselves as less anxious, females as better behaved.

Students may be achievement and success oriented, or motivated by fear of failure. Deliberate underachieving helps avoid feelings of failure, as does compulsive high achievement or attributing failures to external causes. Individualized learning is one solution to self-defeating defensive behaviors.

Kohlberg's six stages of moral development are in three levels. In the two stages of the preconventional level, right action avoids punishment and satisfies one's needs or the needs of others (who will reciprocate). In the two stages of the conventional level, correct behavior is defined by strict social conventions. In the two stages of postconventional thinking, right action is defined by universal and self-determined principles. Children understand all previous stages and one more, and prefer this next one. Research indicates that gifted adolescents tend to think at the postconventional level.

Children should be exposed to moral thinking at the next higher level. They should have opportunities to think about moral problems, for example, using moral dilemmas. Kohlberg's stages themselves can be taught.

The Character Education Partnership organization seeks to promote moral and ethical growth. Some suggestions are helping students grapple with ethical aspects of world problems, involving students in citizenship projects, integrating character education with academic subjects (especially civics and social studies), helping teachers and administrators become better educators of character, and developing character education curricula.

Fantini emphasized teaching "caring" values, discussing problems of the elderly and disabled, teaching about people who demonstrate humanistic values, involving students in community service (e.g., recycling, food drives) programs, and reviewing social issues. Gifted students can design and carry out social action projects.

Values clarification strategies (Simon and colleagues; Eberle and Hall) help students explore their beliefs and feelings. One activity is "Are you someone who . . . ?" Another is "What's it like when . . . ?"

In a Magic Circle, children learn how to get along with others and feel good about themselves.

*Character Education* and *Values Are Forever* try to help students in grades four to eight understand and make commitments to values relating to, for example, honesty, responsibility, empathy, others' rights, and education. The books use, for example, "What would happen if . . . ?", brainstorming, visualization (empathy), problem solving, crossword and word search puzzles, and quizzes, as well as real-world examples.

The humanistic teacher has a good self-concept, likes others, initiates change, and is honest and genuine, forward-growing, sensitive, creative and adventurous, confident, and open to other viewpoints.

# CHAPTER 9

# CREATIVITY I
## THE CREATIVE PERSON, CREATIVE PROCESS, AND CREATIVE DRAMATICS

*When I examined myself, and my methods of thought, I came to the conclusion that the gift of fantasy has meant more to me than my talent for absorbing positive knowledge.*
Albert Einstein

*There must be motivation and . . . persistence, courage, and love of one's work. There has to be "the blazing drive."*
E. Paul Torrance (1995, p. 267)

There can be no more important topic in the education of gifted and talented children than *creativity*. Indeed, the two interrelated purposes of gifted education are (1) to help these children and adolescents become more self-actualized, creative individuals; and (2) to better enable them to make creative contributions to society. As stated by Cropley and Urban (2000), "modern research on creativity, intelligence, and achievement showed that although students with high IQs obtained good grades both at school and university, they were consistently outstripped by those with not only a high IQ but also high creativity" (p. 485).

This chapter and Chapter 10 are designed to help the reader better understand creativity and creative students, and to suggest ideas for stimulating creative growth. This chapter will review some basic features of creativity: (1) traits and characteristics of creative people and some important creative abilities; (2) the nature of the creative process; and (3) creative dramatics. The important topic of testing for creative potential was discussed in Chapter 4 in conjunction with identification. Chapter 10 will focus more specifically on teaching for creative development.

## CHARACTERISTICS OF CREATIVE PERSONS

Chapter 2 summarized recurrent personality, motivational, and biographical characteristics of creative children and adults. To review briefly, creative people frequently are high in self-confidence, independence, risk-taking, energy, enthusiasm, adventurousness, curiosity, playfulness, humor, idealism, and reflectiveness. They tend to have artistic and aesthetic interests, to be attracted to the complex and mysterious, and to need privacy and alone time. They tend to be more perceptive and intuitive. Importantly, they are willing to tolerate the ambiguity that accompanies engaging in creative problem solving. The majority of these traits originally were uncovered by Frank Barron (1969, 1988) and Donald MacKinnon (1978) in their classic Berkeley studies of creative architects, writers, and mathematicians.

Further, as we also noted earlier, some traits will be troublesome to teachers. Especially, the admirable characteristics of independence and high energy, combined with nonconformity and unconventionality, may lead to stubbornness, resistance to teacher (or parent) domination, uncooperativeness, indifference to accepted con-

ventions, cynicism, too much assertiveness, slop-
piness, low interest in details, a tendency to
question rules and authority, forgetfulness, overactivity, uncommunicativeness, and the feeling
that the rest of the parade is out of step. Because
of their high energy, eagerness, inquisitiveness,
rapid talking, and overactivity, some creative students have been diagnosed as having attention
deficit hyperactivity disorder (ADHD). They are
medicated to calm them down (Cramond, 1994).
The nasty problem is: Some gifted students *do*
have ADHD (Kaufman, Kalbfleish, & Castellanos, 2000). (The ADHD problem is elaborated
in Chapter 15.)

While we are on the topic of mental problems,
one-fourth to one-third of historically eminent persons (Walberg, 1988) and the majority of eminent
artists and writers (Richards, 1990, 1999) were or
are manic-depressive or otherwise mentally disturbed. Noted Simonton (2003), "genius-level talents probably reside at the delicate boundary
between a healthy and an unhealthy personality" (p.
362). Such unconventional persons may entertain
bizarre thoughts and analogies and, in manic periods, produce many outstanding works. But those
who "go too far . . . into never-never land may never
develop their gifts" (p. 362). Noted Richards, if Vincent van Gogh had been given antidepressants, he
might have delightedly exclaimed, "I feel like painting happy . . . clowns on black velvet!" (p. 300).
Your authors know of no contemporary research
relating creative giftedness or productivity to psychoses in school-age populations.

The biographical traits listed earlier included
some unsurprising ones, namely, a background
filled with creative activities and hobbies. Frequent performances in dramatic productions is a
very strong indicator of creativeness, since such
performances necessarily require important creative traits (humor, energy, aesthetic interests,
confidence, and risk-taking, for example). More
subtle biographical characteristics of creativity
include preferring friends who are younger and
older, having had an imaginary playmate as a
child, and a tendency to believe in psychic phenomena (and a higher than average likelihood of

having psychic experiences). Naturally, not all
characteristics apply to all creative students.

Many of these (positive) traits probably can be
enhanced by a creativity-conscious teacher.
Indeed, as we will see in the next chapter, there is
every reason to believe that attitudes and personality traits can be changed to produce a more flexible, creative, and self-actualized person.

Torrance (1979, 1981b) itemized other nontest
indicators of creativeness in the kinesthetic and
auditory areas:

Shows skillful, manipulative movement in
crayon work, typing, piano playing, cooking, dressmaking, and so on
Shows quick, precise movements in mime,
creative dramatics, and role playing
Works at creative movement activities for
extended periods of time
Displays total bodily involvement in interpreting a poem, story, or song
Becomes intensely absorbed in creative movement or dance
Interprets songs, poems, or stories through
creative movement or dance
Writes, draws, walks, and moves with rhythm
and is generally highly responsive to sound
stimuli
Creates music, songs, and so on
Works perseveringly at music and rhythmic
activities

The characteristics listed here and in Chapter 2
should help the reader recognize creative children
and adolescents in the classroom. The lists also
might improve one's patience with the obnoxious
student who shows too many of the negative traits.
Perhaps the energy, unconventionality, stubbornness, inquisitiveness, and so forth require constructive redirection.

Note also that many academically average and
below average students will demonstrate marvelous creative talent, for example, in art, dance,
or any other area in which the student possesses
special knowledge and skills.

Is it easy to recognize creative talent? See
Inset 9.1.

INSET 9.1

## Is It Easy to Recognize Creative Talent?

While an awareness of traits of creative people will help us recognize creative students, we are not likely to reach perfection in our identification of creative talent. Consider these creative persons who were *not* recognized by their teachers, professors, or supervisors:

- *Albert Einstein* was four years old before he could speak and seven before he could read; he performed badly in almost all high school courses.
- *Thomas Edison* was told by his teachers that he was too stupid to learn.
- *Werner von Braun* failed ninth-grade algebra.
- *Winston Churchill* was at the bottom of his class in one school and twice failed the entrance exams to another.
- *Pablo Picasso* could barely read and write by age 10. His father hired a tutor—who gave up and quit.
- *Louis Pasteur* was rated mediocre in chemistry at the Royal College.
- *Charles Darwin* did poorly in the early grades and failed a university medical course.
- *F. W. Woolworth* worked in a dry goods store when he was 21, but his employers would not let him wait on customers because he "didn't have enough sense."

- *Walt Disney* was fired by a newspaper editor because he had no good ideas.
- *Caruso's* music teacher told him, "You can't sing, you have no voice at all!"
- *Louisa May Alcott* was told by an editor that she could never write anything popular.
- *Charles Dickens*, *Claude Monet*, *Isadora Duncan*, and *Mark Twain* never finished grade school.
- *George Gershwin*, *Will Rogers*, both *Wright brothers*, and newscaster *Peter Jennings* dropped out of high school; *Harrison Ford* (Indiana Jones) and *Leo Tolstoy* flunked out of college.
- *David Suchet*, who portrays Hercule Poirot in the British Agatha Christie TV series and stars in many British and American movies, laughingly described how several acting schools would not admit him because he was too short, could not sing, and showed no promise as an actor.
- A 1938 letter found in 1991 said that western movie star *Gene Autry* "needed to improve his acting," that an acting course was "evidently wasted," and that "he needed darker make-up to give him the appearance of virility." Replied the 83-year old Autry, "A lot of that is true."

While amusing, such historical facts raise our awareness of the complexity and subtlety of creative talent.

## CREATIVE ABILITIES

There are a great many intellectual abilities that contribute in one way or another to creative potential. Indeed, it would be difficult to isolate mental abilities that have nothing to do with creativeness. The list below includes seemingly important creative abilities. Most have appeared elsewhere in the creativity literature, especially in Torrance's work (Torrance, 1962, 1965, 1979, 1980, 1987, 1995). The first four are the classic Guilford/Torrance *fluency, flexibility, originality,* and *elaboration* abilities, which are measured by the Guilford (1967) tests and the *Torrance Tests of Creative Thinking* (Torrance, 1966). Some people have mistakenly assumed that these four are a definitive and exhaustive list of creative abilities, which is not true at all.

*Fluency.* The ability to produce many ideas in response to an open-ended problem or question. The ideas may be verbal or nonverbal (e.g., mathematical or musical). Other names are "associational fluency" or "ideational fluency."

*Flexibility.* The ability to take different approaches to a problem, think of ideas in different categories, or view a situation from several perspectives.

*Originality.* Uniqueness, nonconformity.

*Elaboration.* The important ability to add details, develop, embellish, and implement a given idea.

*Problem finding, problem sensitivity, problem defining.* An important and complex syndrome that includes abilities to (1) detect difficulties, (2) detect missing information, (3) ask good questions, (4) identify the "real" problem, (5) isolate important aspects of a problem, (6) clarify and simplify a problem, (7) identify subproblems, (8) construct a problem on which to work, (9) propose alternative problem definitions, and (10) define a problem more broadly. Abilities 9 and 10 open the problem to a wider variety of solutions.

*Visualization.* The ability to fantasize and imagine, "see" things in the "mind's eye," and mentally manipulate images and ideas (Daniels-McGhee and Davis, 1994).

*Ability to regress.* The ability to think like a child, whose mind is less cluttered by habits, traditions, rules, regulations, and a firm knowledge of "how it ought to be done."

*Analogical thinking.* The ability to borrow ideas from one context and adapt them to another context; or the ability to borrow a solution to one problem and transfer it to another problem.

*Evaluation.* The important ability to separate relevant from irrelevant considerations; to think critically; to evaluate the "goodness" or appropriateness of an idea, product, or problem solution.

*Analysis.* The ability to analyze details, separate a whole into its parts.

*Synthesis.* The ability to see relationships, to combine parts into a workable, perhaps creative whole.

*Transformation.* This includes the ability to adopt something to a new use; see new meanings, implications, and applications; or creatively change one object or idea into another. Transformation is an extremely important creative ability.

*Extend boundaries.* The ability to go beyond what is usual, to use objects in new ways.

*Intuition.* The ability to make "mental (intuitive) leaps," make inferences, or see relationships based on little information; the ability to "read between the lines."

*Predict outcomes.* The ability to foresee the results of different solution actions and alternatives.

*Resist premature closure.* The ability to defer judgment and not jump on the first idea that comes along. Many students are deficient in this ability.

*Concentration.* The ability to focus on a problem for long periods of time, free from distractions.

*Logical thinking.* The ability to deduce reasonable conclusions, and to separate relevant from irrelevant.

*Aesthetic thinking.* Sensitivity to and appreciation of beauty in art, design, and nature.

Some other creative abilities are the ability to see structure in chaos; avoid mental sets and perceptual sets; think critically; anticipate consequences; make good decisions; understand complex issues; and adapt present knowledge to new problems (Davis, 2003b; Tardif & Sternberg, 1988).

If we take a broad view of "creative abilities," many other thinking skills to be described in Chapter 11 also could be seen as abilities important to creative thinking and problem solving, for example, planning, reasoning, considering all factors, prioritizing, discovering relationships, and making inferences. Some creative personality traits also could be viewed as "abilities," for example, independence, risk taking, humor (which is always built of surprising idea combinations), curiosity, reflectiveness, perceptiveness, tolerance for ambiguity and disorder, spontaneity, artisticness, open-mindedness, adventurousness, and probably others (Davis, 2003b). Of course, in any scientific, business, artistic, or social field there are innumerable learned skills and abilities that are essential for creative thinking within the particular knowledge area.

## THE CREATIVE PROCESS

There are several ways to view the creative process (Davis, 1998). First, the traditional approach is to describe a sequence of *stages* through which one might proceed in solving a problem creatively. Second, the creative process can be viewed as a *change in perception*—literally "seeing" new idea combinations, new relationships, new meanings, or new applications that simply were not perceived a moment before.

A third approach to understanding the creative process is to examine creative thinking *techniques*—strategies used by creative individuals to produce the new idea combinations and relationships that comprise creative ideas and products. Creativity techniques appear in Chapter 10.

## STEPS AND STAGES IN THE CREATIVE PROCESS

### The Wallas Model

The best-known set of stages in the creative process is the *preparation, incubation, illumination,* and *verification* stages suggested in 1926 by Graham Wallas. The *preparation* stage includes clarifying and defining the problem, gathering relevant information, reviewing available materials, examining solution requirements, and becoming acquainted with other innuendos or implications, including previous unsuccessful solutions. This stage basically involves clarifying "the mess."

The *incubation* stage may best be viewed as a period of "preconscious," "fringe conscious," "off-conscious," or even "unconscious" activity that takes place while the thinker, perhaps deliberately, is jogging, watching TV, playing golf, eating pizza, or snoozing. Guilford (1979) suggested that incubation takes place during reflection, a pause in action, and that some people simply are more reflective than others. Many creative people keep a pad and pencil on their bedstand or a small notebook (idea trap) in their pocket in order to jot down ideas for incubated problems.

The third, *illumination* stage is the sudden "Eureka" or "Aha!" experience. A solution appears, usually suddenly—although it may follow weeks of work and incubation—that seems to match the requirements of the problem.

The final *verification* stage, as the name suggests, involves checking the workability, feasibility, and/or acceptability of the illumination.

Wallas's four stages resemble steps in the classic scientific method: State the problem and propose hypotheses (*preparation*), plan and conduct research (during which *incubation* seems unavoidable), then evaluate the results (*verification,* which had better include one or more *illuminations*). Note also that the stages are not an invariant sequence. Stages may be skipped or the thinker may backtrack to an earlier stage. For example, preparation often leads directly to a good, illuminating idea. Or if the verification confirms that an idea will not work or will not be acceptable, the thinker may skip back to the preparation or the incubation stage.

One often-noted oversight was ignoring a step of *implementation:* The solution must be elaborated and carried out. Cropley's (1997; Cropley & Urban, 2000) extension of the Wallas model solves this oversight and others. His seven steps are *preparation, information* (learning or remembering special knowledge), *incubation, illumination, verification, communication* (achieving closure, gaining feedback, showing the product to others), and *validation* (evaluating relevance and effectiveness by judges, e.g., a teacher).

### A Two-Stage Model

The creative process often, if not always, involves two fairly clear steps: A *big idea* stage and an *elaboration* stage (Davis, 1998). The big idea stage is a period of fantasy in which the creative person is looking for a new, exciting idea or problem solution. After the idea is found, perhaps using a personal creative thinking technique, the elaboration stage includes idea development, elaboration, and implementation. For example, the artist must do preliminary sketches and create the final work; the novelist must put words on the page—and then revise and re-revise; and the research scientist or business entrepreneur must organize the details and sequentially carry out the work necessary to implement the big idea.

## Creative Problem Solving Model

The Creative Problem Solving (CPS) model is an extremely useful set of five stages originated by Alex Osborn (1963) and more recently articulated by Sidney Parnes (1981) and by Donald Treffinger and his colleagues (Treffinger, Isaksen, & Dorval, 1994a, 1994b). In addition to the five steps represented in Figure 9.1, Parnes and Treffinger and colleagues described a sixth step, the preliminary one—called *mess finding*—of locating a challenge, opportunity, need, or problem to which to apply the model. To be accurate, Osborn (1963) described his original model in just three stages, which subsume the others: (1) *Fact finding* included identifying a problem *and* gathering facts; (2) *idea-finding* is unchanged; (3) *solution-finding* included evaluating *and* implementing ideas.

We will look briefly at the five core steps of *fact finding, problem finding, idea finding, solution finding* (idea evaluation), and *acceptance finding* (idea implementation). The five steps are useful because they guide the creative process— they tell you what to do at each step to eventually produce one or more creative, workable solutions. One noteworthy feature, represented by the diverging and converging lines at each step in Figure 9.1, is that each of the five steps first involves a divergent-thinking phase, in which lots of ideas (facts, problem definitions, potential solutions, evaluation criteria, implementation ideas) are generated, and then a second convergent phase in which only the most promising ideas are selected for further exploration.

*Fact finding.* The first stage, *fact finding,* involves "listing all you know about the problem or challenge" (Parnes, 1981). For example, let's say the problem is thinking of ways to stimulate creativity in an elementary classroom. An individual or group first would list all of the facts they could think of relating to training creative thinking and perhaps to the nature of creativity and creative abilities. Parnes recommends the use of *who, what, when, where, why,* and *how* questions. That is:

Who is or should be involved?
What is or is not happening?
When does this or should this happen?
Where does or doesn't this occur?
Why does it or doesn't it happen?
How does it or doesn't it occur?

The list of ideas is then convergently narrowed to a smaller number of facts that might be especially productive.

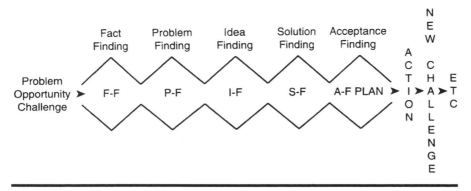

**FIGURE 9.1**   The Creative Problem Solving (CPS) Model.

***Problem finding.***    The second stage, *problem finding,* involves listing alternative problem definitions. One principle of creative problem solving is that the definition of a problem will determine the nature of the solutions. It helps to begin each statement with, "In what ways might I (we) . . ." (e.g., find lists of strategies, locate someone who knows about training creativity, locate books on the topic, have the kids themselves solve the problem, and so on).

One or more of the most fruitful definitions is selected for the next stage.

***Idea finding.***    *Idea finding* is the brainstorming stage in which ideas are freely listed for each problem statement accepted in the second stage.

***Solution finding.***    In the fourth stage of *solution finding,* criteria for idea evaluation are listed, for example: Will the strategy strengthen important creative abilities? Will it strengthen good creative attitudes? Will it teach usable creative thinking techniques? Will it cost too much? Will it take too much time? Are the materials available? Will the principal, other teachers accept it? Will the children enjoy it? And so on. The list may be reduced to the most relevant criteria.

Sometimes, an *evaluation matrix* is prepared, with possible solutions listed on the vertical axis and criteria across the top (see Figure 9.2). Each idea is rated according to each criteria (perhaps on a 1 to 5 scale), the ratings are entered in the cells, and then totaled to find the "best" idea(s).

***Acceptance finding.***    Finally, *acceptance finding* (or implementation) amounts to thinking of "ways to get the best ideas into action" (Parnes, 1981). It may involve creating an *action plan* (Treffinger, Isaksen, and Dorval, 1994a, 1994b). Treffinger (1995a) and colleagues noted that acceptance finding involves searching for *assisters* and *resisters*. Assisters are people ("key players"), essential resources, and the best times, places, and methods that will support the plan and contribute to successful implementation. One also must identify *resisters*—obstacles such as con-

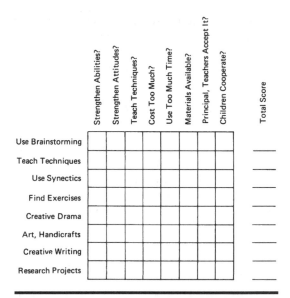

**FIGURE 9.2**   Example of an Evaluation Matrix. Each idea is rated on a 1 (low) to 5 (high) scale according to each criterion. Total scores are then tallied.

trary people, missing materials, bad timing, ineffective methods, or other matters that can interfere with acceptance. Said Treffinger, one makes the best possible use of assisters, and avoids or overcomes sources of resistance.

In his inspiring book *The Magic of Your Mind,* Parnes leads the reader through problem after problem with the goal of making the five steps habitual and automatic. That is, when encountering a problem, challenge, or opportunity, one quickly would review relevant facts, identify various interpretations of the problem, generate solutions, think of criteria and evaluate the ideas, and speculate on how the solution(s) might be implemented and accepted.

After Parnes's 30 years as president of the Creative Education Foundation and lots of experience teaching creative problem solving, learning these steps—supplemented with creative attitudes and some idea-finding strategies—is his best recommendation for becoming a more creative problem solver and a more effective, self-actualized human being.

In the classroom, the CPS model would be used to guide a creative-thinking session that (1) improves students' understanding of the creative process, (2) exposes them to a rousing creative-thinking experience, and (3) solves a problem. With much practice with the steps, students might become habitual creative thinkers, as Parnes intended.

Parnes (1981) noted that "the five steps are a guide rather than a strict formula. Frequently, a change of sequence may be introduced into the process; and it is always advisable to provide plenty of opportunity for incubation." Over one and one-half chocolate sundaes, which Parnes ordered, he explained to one author (Davis) that people tend to use the five stages too rigidly. On a napkin he scribbled a star-shaped model enclosed in a circle (Figure 9.3), emphasizing that—if it helps the creative process—one may flexibly move directly from any one step to any other.

Treffinger, Isaksen, and Dorval (1994a; see also 1994b) described how *hits* and *hot spots* can be used in the five CPS steps. *Hits* are ideas that strike the problem solver as important break-throughs—directions to be pursued further because they could

form the basis for a good solution. Groups of related hits are called *hot spots*. Hot spots thus are "groups of several (two or more) hits that all deal with a common theme, issue, or important dimension of the mess" (p. 45). In the convergent part of each CPS step, hits and hot spots are excellent leads for further exploration.

The CPS model may be taught to secondary students and even elementary children, as in the book *CPS for Kids* (Eberle and Stanish, 1985). The *Future Problem Solving* program, summarized in Chapter 6, is based on the CPS model.

Finally, an important message in the CPS model is that enrichment programs for teaching creative thinking should not focus totally on the brainstorming and divergent thinking that comprise stage 3, *idea finding*. Realistic creative thinking includes at least the other CPS stages of clarifying the mess, gathering facts and data, generating or selecting a problem definition, evaluating the ideas, and implementing the chosen solution(s).

## THE CREATIVE PROCESS AS A CHANGE IN PERCEPTION

Many creative ideas and problem solutions result from a change in perception—the usually abrupt experience of "seeing" a new idea combination, new relationship, new meaning, new application, or new perspective on a problem. This phenomenon occurs whether the transformation is a simple modification of a cookie recipe (e.g., substituting mint candies for chocolate chips) or a complex discovery in engineering, medicine, or astronomy.

One simple way to illustrate the sudden perceptual change is with visual puzzles. For example, look at Figure 9.4. There is one main, meaningful figure, created in fact from a photograph. After you find this figure, try to locate (1) a flying pig, (2) an Al Capp *Li'l Abner* character with a snaggle lower tooth, (3) a woman with her hair in a bun reclining on a sofa (she is in white). If you can find these easy (?) ones, you may proceed to (4) the Road Runner (heading left), (5) Harry Belafonte, (6) Popeye, (7) Blackbeard the Pirate, (8) a side profile of Jesus, (9) right next to

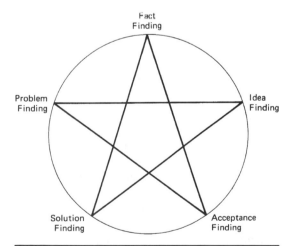

**FIGURE 9.3** An Alternative Conception of the Creative Education Foundation Stages Emphasizing That One May Flexibly Move from Any Stage to Any Other.

**FIGURE 9.4** Visual Puzzle.

Reprinted with permission of Charles Scribners Sons, an imprint of Macmillan Publishing Company, from *Creative Actionbook* by Sidney J. Parnes, Ruth Noller, and Angelo M. Biondi. Copyright 1976 by Charles Scribners Sons.

Jesus a lady in a bouffant hairdo, and (10) E.T. You will find yourself exclaiming, "Oh! There it is!" or "Now I see it!" The solutions are outlined at the very end of this chapter.

We do not understand this sudden perceptual change or mental transformation particularly well. It some simple cases the "Eureka!" seems due simply to viewing (or visualizing) one or two objects or ideas, and then mentally modifying them, combining them, or otherwise creating a new meaning or relationship; or to suddenly seeing a relationship between your problem and a more familiar one. For example, a candy bar mogul, always alert for new products, may receive a sample package of macadamia nuts on an airline flight and instantly "see" a chocolate/macadamia treat.

The discussion of creative thinking techniques in the next chapter will outline some unconscious creative processes that have been made conscious, knowable, and teachable. Most of these techniques force the thinker to "see" new relationships and transformations of ideas.

## CREATIVE DRAMATICS

Creative dramatics definitely is a unique classroom activity. As with other creativity exercises, creative dramatics stimulates divergent thinking, imagination, and problem solving. It also may strengthen sensory awareness, concentration, control of the physical self, discovery and control of emotions, humor, self-confidence in speaking and performing, empathic and humanistic understanding of others, and even critical thinking (e.g., Carelli, 1981; Cresci, 1989; Davis, Helfert, & Shapiro, 1992; McCaslin, 1974; Way, 1967). It also is as fun as it is beneficial. Sessions are not difficult to lead: The two main requirements are a good sense of humor and enough energy to crank up a people machine or wade through a peanut butter swamp.

A sample of creative dramatics activities are described in the categories of *warm-ups, movement exercises, sensory and body awareness exercises, pantomime, and playmaking.*

### Warmup Exercises

Any creative dramatics session must begin with some simple loosening up exercises. These movements stretch a few muscles but require little or no thinking. The leader narrates and illustrates. Some suggestions are:

*Holding Up the Ceiling.*   Students strain to hold up the ceiling, slowly letting it down (to one knee), then pushing it back up into place.

*Biggest Thing, Smallest Thing.*   Everyone stretches his or her body into the "biggest thing" he or she possibly can. No one has any trouble guessing what the second part of the exercise is.

*Stretching.*   There are many ways to stretch. One strategy is to have students begin with their heads and work down, stretching then relaxing every part of the body. Vice versa, begin with the toes. Either may be done lying down.

*Warmup at Different Speeds.*   Children run in place in slow motion, then speed up until they are moving very fast. Variations include jumping, skipping, or hopping.

### Movement Exercises

*Circles.*   The group stands in a large circle. Each participant, in turn, thinks of a way to make a circle by using his or her body. It may be a fixed or moving circle, using part or all of the body. All others must make the same circle. Names add to the fun—"This is a halo circle," "This is a shoulder circle," "This is a chicken circle," "This is a Groucho Marx circle." Circles will be more original if originality is clearly encouraged.

*Mirrors.*   Everyone needs a partner. One person becomes a mirror who mimics the movements of the partner. Roles are reversed in about three minutes.

*Circus.*   Each child becomes a different circus performer or animal. Variations include the leader directing what every one should be, for example, tightrope walkers, trained elephants, lion tamers, jugglers, and so forth.

*People Machines.*   This is a favorite (at least with college students). There are two main strategies. Students can form groups of six to twelve persons and take 10 or 15 minutes to design and practice their machine. They are performed one at a time for the others, who try to guess what the machine is. (Warning: Don't allow the machine to dismantle prematurely just because someone guesses what it is.) Alternatively, with the *add-on* method an idea for a machine is agreed upon and then one person starts the action. Others add themselves. Sounds—beeps, dings, buzzes, pops, and so on—are recommended. One of the best is an old-fashioned pinball game, which can absorb fifty volunteers, including a pinball player and several preferably crazy balls.

*Obstacles.*   With chalk, the leader draws a "start" and "finish" line on the floor, about eight feet apart. One at a time, each student makes up an imaginary obstacle that he or she must climb over (past, through, under, around) to get from start to finish. Since only one person participates at a time, it works best with small groups.

*Robot Walk.*   Each person is a robot with a unique sound and walk. Whenever one robot touches another robot, both stop, sit down, and begin again to rise with a new sound and a new walk.

*Balloon Burst.*   There are two main versions. First, each person is a balloon who is blown up, and up, and up. The balloon can be released and zip around the room, or else blown up until it pops. In the second version the entire group is one balloon that is blown up to the limit, then bursts.

***Creative Locomotion.***    Have children walk like a Crooked Man, the Jolly Green Giant, Raggedy Ann, a robot, and so forth; run like a squirrel, mouse, Miss Muffett frightened by a spider, or the slowest person in the world running for a bus; jump like a kangaroo, popcorn, a jack-in-the-box; or walk through a peanut butter swamp, flypaper, a jungle, tacks, deep sand, or deep Jell-O. The leader and students call out new characters, animals, substances, surfaces, and so on.

***Making Letters.***    Have individuals or two people shape their bodies to become alphabet letters. Others guess the letter. A small group can spell a word.

***Imaginary Tug-of-War.***    Ask for ten volunteers (or pick them, if reluctance prevails). They are divided into two five-person teams. The leader narrates: "This side is struggling hard and seems to be winning. Now the other side is recovering. Look out! The rope broke!" Warn them to listen to the narrator and be sure they hear the last instruction.

## Sensory and Body Awareness

***Trust Walk (or Blind Walk).***    This is a must. Each person has a partner. The member with eyes shut, or blindfolded, is led around the room, under tables and chairs, and allowed to identify objects by touch, smell, or sound. Students walk down the hall, get a drink of water, try to read names or numbers on doors (such as "Boys"), go outside and explore trees, the sun, shade, a flower, and so on. Partners trade roles after about 10 minutes. Ask about experiences and discoveries in a follow-up discussion.

***Exploring an Orange.***    Give everyone an orange to examine closely. How does it look, feel, smell, taste? What is unique about your orange?

Take the orange apart and examine and discuss the colors, patterns, and textures. Eat the orange.

***Listening.***    Have students sit (or lie) silently, listening first for sounds that are close, then for sounds that are far. "What do the sounds remind you of?" As an option, students can describe the sounds with their hands.

***Smelling.***    Small bottles are prepared in advance, with familiar scents such as vanilla extract, Vicks Vaporub, peanut butter, used coffee grounds, cinnamon, cloves, rubbing alcohol, lipstick, and so on. In small groups the scents are passed around and students discuss the memories that are stimulated by each smell. The smells also can be imagined, for example, how does the smell of warm apple sauce and cinnamon make you feel?

***Touching.***    Have students touch many surfaces, concentrating fully on the feel. Use strange objects (e.g., a piece of coral) and familiar ones (e.g., a piece of tree bark). Paper sacks keep the objects hidden from view.

## Pantomime

Many of the movement and sensory exercises cited thus far include an element of pantomime (e.g., circus, people machines, tug-of-war, creative locomotion). With more "serious" pantomime, students create situations with physical movements, facial expressions, and even eye movements as they perform in an imaginary environment. With encouragement, students can use their faces, hands, and bodies to express sadness, glee, love, fear, surprise, and so on. Pantomime activities can be relatively short-term, or lengthier mini-plays without lines.

Some pantomime activities include:

***Invisible Trunk.***    Six to ten students form a circle. In turn, each person lifts the lid on an invisible trunk, removes something, does something with it, then puts it back in the trunk and closes the lid. Others spontaneously guess the object and activity. The action may go around the circle two or three times.

***Invisible Balls.***   An invisible ball is passed from person to person several times around a small circle (or up and down each row in a class). As each person receives the ball, it changes size, shape, weight, smell, and so forth.

***Magic Stick.***   Taking turns, students improvise with a wooden dowel or other stick—or any other object, for that matter. They can "pass" if temporarily stumped.

***Inside-Out.***   Children become fish in a tank or zoo animals in cages. Others look in.

***Animal Pantomimes.***   Each child moves to the center of the circle to pantomime his or her animal. Others guess the animal. For variety, two or three animals can act out a simple plot, for example, a cat sneaking up on a mouse; a bear looking for honey but finding bees; a bull spotting some picnickers; a squirrel and a bluejay both trying to get the same piece of bread; a rabbit and a turtle preparing for a short race. Students can think of more.

***Creating an Environment.***   This exercise is much like an add-on people machine. Students think of and create an environment, such as a bowling alley, people in a boat fishing, a playground, ballet class, fish and seaweed in an aquarium, gym class, football team warming up, farm animals, a car wash, a dentist's office with waiting room, and so on. The class can think of more.

***Miscellaneous Pantomime.***   Many brief sketches can teach students to pay high attention to movements and expressions. As some examples: a jolly McDonald's counterperson waiting on two or three impatient customers, a fussy person trying on hats or shoes, scared mountain climbers unable to go up or down, three stooges hanging wallpaper or performing heart surgery, a grouchy cab driver in 5 o'clock traffic getting a worried

person to the airport, the president of the United States being locked out of the official airplane, and others.

### Playmaking

Playmaking involves acting out stories and scenes without a script. To improve the expressiveness of movements and gestures, a sketch may be practiced without lines, that is, in pantomime. With one straightforward strategy, students are given a simple scene (plot), characters are explained, and then students improvise the action.

Way (1967) suggested that mini-plays need not be silly. They can involve, for example, miners working against time to reinforce a mine about to cave in; slow-moving astronauts assembling something in space; toy shop toys or museum displays coming alive at the stroke of midnight; Californians experiencing an earthquake; or witches and goblins cooking up a magic brew with improvised important ingredients. Historical episodes, folklore, mythology, fairy tales, nursery rhymes, and animal stories also present possibilities: the Boston Tea Party, Columbus discovering America, Goldilocks and the Three Bears, Cinderella, and others.

A more structured playmaking strategy might run as follows. After a few warmup exercises, the leader tells a story. Then leader and students review the sequence of events—what happened first? Second? Third? The group then discusses characterization, considering physical, emotional, and intellectual qualities (limping, slow, quick-stepping, nervous, angry, happy, excited, calm, conceited, dull-witted, scientific-minded). The play typically is broken down and worked out scene by scene. The group may first act out a scene without dialogue to explore movements and expressions. After improvements, it is replayed with improvised dialogue. A given scene may be replayed many times, with different students trying different roles. As above, ideas may be found in historical or mythological material, or in children's books, nursery rhymes, or other stories. Also, students can brainstorm plots and ideas.

For playmaking with gifted students, Carelli (1981) noted that the students may select the theme, assign responsibilities, plan and implement the activities, including researching the particular historical or mythological event, and evaluate both the process and the final product.

Creative dramatics virtually always elicits excited feelings of creativeness—it's not every day that students experience being blind or pretend to be a robot, a bird in a cuckoo clock, or a squeaking gear in a people machine that does nothing. They are given a perfectly logical reason to stretch their imaginations and humor. The activities may be used with any age group from an elementary school pullout program to a high school drama class to a college creativity class.

In Davis's former college creativity class—with chairs out of the way in a classroom or sometimes in a lecture hall with 80 students—a progressively more creative and rousing session typically included holding up the ceiling and biggest thing, smallest thing (warmups), imaginary tug-of-war, and some combination of circles, mirrors, trust walk, invisible box, invisible balls, and always people machines (group strategy *and* add-on strategy, usually a pinball machine). A creative experience for all.

## SUMMARY

Creative development is a central G/T topic. In lifetime achievement, high-IQ students are outperformed by bright students who also are creative.

Creative students tend to be independent, risk-taking, energetic, curious, witty, idealistic, artistic, attracted to the mysterious and complex, and to need alone time.

Negative traits include stubbornness, resistance to domination, uncooperativeness, cynicism, tendencies to question rules, uncommunicativeness, and others.

Some high-energy bright and creative students are incorrectly classified as having ADHD, although some gifted students do have ADHD.

Many eminent persons—especially in the arts—are manic-depressive or show other symptoms of psychoses. Such problems apparently aid imagination and unconventionality.

Biographical characteristics include a background of creative activities and having had an imaginary playmate, psychical experiences, and theater experience.

Torrance suggested a number of characteristics of creativeness in the kinesthetic and auditory areas, for example, skillful movement and talent in dance and music.

In addition to the popular fluency, flexibility, originality, and elaboration, important creative abilities include, for example, a syndrome that encompasses problem finding, problem sensitivity, and problem defining, along with abilities pertaining to visualization, analogical thinking, evaluation, intuition, resisting premature closure, logical thinking, seeing structure in chaos, avoiding mental sets, and making good decisions.

Many thinking skills (e.g., planning, prioritizing, discovering relationships, making inferences) and creative personality traits (e.g., humor, curiosity, independence, risk taking) may be considered creative abilities.

The creative process may be viewed, first, as stages in creative problem solving. Wallas's four stages are preparation, incubation, illumination, and verification. Cropley added three more stages of information, communication, and validation. A two-stage model includes a big idea stage followed by elaboration and development.

The Creative Problem Solving model includes fact finding, problem finding, idea finding, solution finding (idea evaluation), and acceptance finding (idea implementation), and sometimes a preliminary stage of "mess finding" (identifying a problem). Solution finding may involve an evaluation matrix. In acceptance finding Treffinger noted "assisters" and "resisters"—people, methods, or resources that affect progress. He also described "hits" and "hot spots," groups of good ideas. Parnes advised that, if helpful, the five steps may be used in any order.

The creative process also may be viewed as a change in perception—seeing new idea combinations, new relationships, new meanings, new implications, and new applications. This sudden change in perception is not well understood.

Creative dramatics seeks to strengthen divergent thinking, imagination, problem solving, sensory awareness, discovery and control of emotions and the physical self, humor, self-confidence, and empathic understanding. Five categories of activities include warmups, movement exercises, sensory and body awareness, pantomime, and playmaking.

Solutions to Visual Puzzle

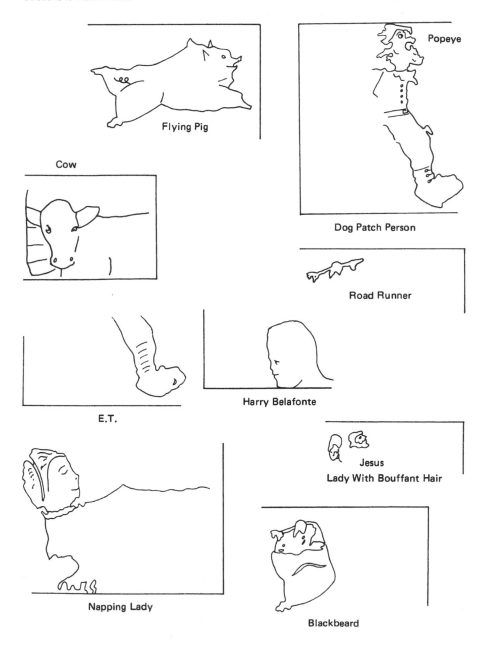

Flying Pig

Popeye

Dog Patch Person

Cow

Road Runner

E.T.

Harry Belafonte

Jesus
Lady With Bouffant Hair

Napping Lady

Blackbeard

# CHAPTER 10

# CREATIVITY II
## TEACHING FOR CREATIVE GROWTH

*I know that it is possible to teach children to think creatively. . . . I have done it; I have seen my wife do it; I have seen other excellent teachers do it. I have seen children who had seemed previously to be "non-thinkers" learn to think creatively, and I have seen them continue for years thereafter to think creatively.*

E. Paul Torrance (1995, p. 269)

## CAN CREATIVITY BE TAUGHT?

Can creativity be taught or are you born with it? The answer is *yes* and *yes*. Some people are born with a special combination of creative genius and intelligence that, activated by high motivation and a sense of destiny, leads them to dream their dreams and implement their creations that make the world a better place. The names of Leonardo da Vinci, Wolfgang Mozart, Marie Curie, Thomas Edison, Albert Einstein, George Washington Carver, and Georgia O'Keeffe come to mind. No amount of creativity training can elevate an average person to such lofty creativeness.

*At the same time, it is absolutely true that everyone's personal creativity can be improved.* In the case of gifted and talented children, efforts to strengthen their creative abilities—and get them to use the abilities they were born with— can have visibly dramatic effects, for example, as evidenced in the marvelous products and performances in the Future Problem Solving and Odyssey of the Mind programs.

Many teachers already are creativity conscious and integrate creativity exercises into class work perhaps daily. For example, some teachers arrange independent projects in language arts, science, or art areas. Such projects help students develop such creative problem-solving attitudes and skills as independence, problem defining, information gathering, idea generating, evaluat-

ing, decision-making, and communication, along with valuable technical skills.

Some teachers give divergent thinking exercises, either as a classroom brainstorming activity or in asking students individually to write their ideas. Divergent thinking problems may or may not be tied to the subject matter at hand. For example, teachers might ask students to think of unusual uses for ping pong balls or for the math balance scales; improvements for bicycles or better ways to evacuate the building in case of fire; or clever ways to make the school burglar proof or keep the hallways clean. Some ask "What would happen if . . . ?" questions: What would have happened if gasoline engines were never invented? If nobody went to school? If Jefferson had not arranged the Louisiana purchase? If we didn't have any fingers? If nobody could spell or write a correct sentence? Many workbooks are filled with divergent thinking and other creativity exercises and activities. Some favorites are *Hearthstone Traveler* (Stanish, 1988), *Mindglow* (Stanish, 1986), *Hippogriff Feathers* (Stanish, 1981), *I Believe in Unicorns* (Stanish, 1979), *Sunflowering* (Stanish, 1977), *Teaching Is Listening* (Gordon & Poze, 1972a), *Strange and Familiar* (Gordon & Poze, 1972b), *Making It Strange* (Gordon, 1974), and *New Directions in Creativity* (Renzulli, Callahan, Smith, Renzulli, & Ford, 2000).

Further, as we saw in Chapter 8, teachers interested in character and values education can use "What would happen if . . . ?", brainstorming, and other creativity thinking techniques taught in this chapter to help students understand character and values and make commitments to productive, not self-destructive, ones. "What would happen if everyone were always rude to everybody else?" "How many ways can we think of to make a new student feel welcome?" (Davis, 2003a, 2003c).

Some teachers review biographical information about creative people, such as the training, lifestyles, attitudes, and thinking habits of Edison, Einstein, Curie, or Picasso. They might ask students to research the life of a creative person, and even design and create a learning center that explains the person's thinking style, personality, struggles, and accomplishments. On parents' night, students can even dress as famous creative characters and explain "what it's like being me" (Betts & Kercher, 1999). The goal of the biographical approach is to help students better understand creativity and creative people, and possibly motivate them to acquire some of the attitudes and technical talents they have learned about.

## GOALS OF CREATIVITY TRAINING

The above strategies are logical efforts to "teach creativity." However, creativity training might be better structured if we itemize the main goals and objectives of such training and then review ways to achieve each objective (see, e.g., Davis, 1987, 1989a, 1998, 2003b). The list is brief and uncomplicated. We will look at:

- Raising creativity consciousness, teaching creative attitudes, and strengthening creative personality traits
- Improving students' understanding of creativity
- Strengthening creative abilities through exercise
- Teaching creative thinking techniques
- Involving students in creative activities

Our recommendation is that a sensible creativity training effort should include *all* of these objectives and their corresponding activities. By a remarkable coincidence, a sensible order of objectives and their related learning activities exactly matches the order in which these topics are presented.

## CREATIVITY CONSCIOUSNESS, CREATIVE ATTITUDES, AND CREATIVE PERSONALITY TRAITS

*Increasing creativity consciousness and creative attitudes is the single most important component of teaching for creative growth.* Creative attitudes are taught in every creative thinking course and program, and for good reason. To think creatively a person must be consciously aware of creativity. He or she must value creative thinking, appreciate novel and farfetched ideas, be open-minded and receptive to the zany ideas of others, be mentally set to produce creative ideas, and be willing to take creative risks, make mistakes, and even fail. Sternberg (2000a), in fact, argued that high creativity stems from conscious decisions, for example, to redefine problems, overcome obstacles, do what you love to do, and believe in yourself.

In Torrance's (1995) list of 20 suggestions for fostering creativity in school experiences, about half dealt with raising creativity consciousness and altering attitudes, such as "Teach children to value their creative thinking," "Develop tolerance of new ideas," and "Develop constructive criticism, not just criticism" (p. 44).

Many students are capable of creative achievements. However, they do not think about creativity or appreciate the importance of creativity for their personal growth—for developing their talents and potential, for coping successfully with their world, and for simply getting more out of life. Students also should become more aware of the importance of creative innovation in the history of civilization and for solving society's present and future problems. Indeed, without creative innovation and creative people we still would be living in caves during our short and sick lives, and digging roots and clubbing rodents for lunch.

## Strengthening Creative Personality Traits

Creative personality traits are tied closely to creative attitudes and awarenesses. We normally do not speak of "teaching personality traits." However, teachers can reward and encourage the (positive) kinds of traits and behaviors that relate to creative thinking—confidence, independence, enthusiasm, adventurousness, a willingness to take risks, curiosity, playfulness, humor, time alone for thinking, interest in complexity, perceptiveness, and artistic and other aesthetic interests. Cropley and Urban (2000) suggested these important attitudes and personality traits that may be strengthened in the classroom: autonomy, ego strength, positive self-concepts, preference for complexity, tolerance for ambiguity, and acceptance of all (even contradictory) aspects of one's own self.

Regarding "contradictory" aspects of the self, Barron (1969) and others noted long ago that creative persons accept traits traditionally associated with the opposite sex. More recently, Cropley and Urban (2000) reported this "integration of opposites": stereotypically masculine traits of autonomy, self-confidence, and toughness with stereotypically feminine traits of sensitivity, intuition, and responsibility. Even with brilliant natural potential, would a Hell's Angel pursue a career in ballet?

Teachers can also foster creativity by encouraging students to learn independently, not harshly judging student ideas, tolerating "sensible" errors, encouraging flexible thinking, promoting self-evaluation, encouraging fantasy and imagination, helping students cope with frustration and failure, accepting students as they are, helping students resist peer pressure to conform, rewarding courage as much as being right, and being aware that a child's "difficult" behavior could be a manifestation of creativity (Cropley & Urban, 2000; Fleith, 2000; Rejskind, 2000).

Teachers also may take a direct approach: Help students understand each creative attitude and trait and why it is essential for creativeness.

## Creative Atmosphere

Creative attitudes and awareness relate closely to the notion of a creative atmosphere, an environment where creativity is encouraged and rewarded. Carl Rogers (1962) called it *psychological safety,* a prerequisite for creative thinking. In brain-storming it is called *deferred judgment*—the noncritical, nonevaluative, and receptive atmosphere where fresh and even wild ideas may be safely proposed.

It is an ancient and honored principle of psychology that rewarded behavior will persist and become stronger, while punished or ignored behavior will disappear. A creative atmosphere rewards creative thinking and helps it become habitual.

## Blocks to Creativity

Creative attitudes and predispositions may be aided by raising students awareness of blocks and barriers to creative thinking, which may be categorized as *perceptual, cultural,* and *emotional* (Davis, 1998, 1999; Simberg, 1964). With *perceptual blocks* we become accustomed to perceiving things in familiar ways, and it simply is difficult to view them in a new and creative way. As an illustration of a perceptual block, given BSAINXLEAT-NTEARS, cross out six letters to find a meaningful word. (See footnote when you give up.*)

*Cultural blocks,* as with perceptual blocks, result from learning and habit. With cultural blocks we have the creativity-squelching effects of traditions, conformity pressures, and social expectations, which along with "fear of being different" will nip creativeness in its proverbial bud.

Conformity pressures and social expectations can take the form of idea squelchers. The following are some favorites, condensed from a longer list by Warren (1974; Davis, 1998). Think about installing an innovative G/T program as you read these:

It won't work. . . .
It's not in the budget. . . .
We've never done it before. . . .

---

*The solution is BANANA. What did you cross out?

We're not ready for it yet. . . .
What will parents think? . . .
We're too small for that. . . .
We have too many projects now. . . .
Somebody would have suggested it before if it
    were any good. . . .
You'll never sell it to the union. . . .
We can't do it under the regulations. . . .
It's not in the curriculum. . . .
It'll mean more work. . . .
I'll bet some professor suggested that. . . .

Such idea squelchers are the products of unreceptive, inflexible, and uncreative attitudes.

It is true, of course, that the human processes of socialization, education, and even healthy peer relations necessarily require a good measure of conformity. *However, children and adults should realize that there is a time for conformity and a time for creativity.*

*Emotional blocks* are the insecurities and anxieties that interfere with creative thinking. Here we find temporary states, such as job anxieties, school pressures, emotional problems, or health concerns. We also have more permanent emotional blocks, such as a chronic fear of making mistakes or failing, fear of being different, fear of rejection, fear of supervisors, timidity, a poor self-concept, or other persistent anxieties.

Some of us need a whack on the side of the head to jostle us out of our uncreative attitudes (see Inset 10.1).

---

## INSET 10.1

### A Whack on the Side of the Head

One popular book on stimulating creativity, written for corporate readers, was entitled *A Whack on the Side of the Head* (von Oech, 1983). The entire book focused on removing 10 mental blocks. As his book title suggests, it can take a whack on the side of the head to jolt us out of our anti-creative attitudes.

The first mental block, *The Right Answer*, is the well-learned assumption that there is one right answer. Not so. We should look for the second right answer, the third right answer, and more. A later "right answer" probably will be more creative.

Von Oech's second block, *That's Not Logical*, is based on the common assumption that logical thinking is better than illogical thinking. However, illogical thinking stimulates the imaginative play and new perspectives that can generate creative ideas.

A third block to creative thinking is *Follow the Rules*. Instead of following the rules, said von Oech, we should play the revolutionary and challenge rules. He recommended holding "rule-inspecting and rule-discarding" sessions.

Pressure to *Be Practical* is his fourth block. Instead, we should ask creativity stimulating "what if" questions, and encourage "what-iffing" in others.

*Avoid Ambiguity* is the fifth block. In fact, a period of ambiguity is an integral part of creative problem solving. Such ambiguity inspires imaginative solutions.

Von Oech's sixth block is *To Err Is Wrong*. While a fear of making mistakes inhibits trying new things, creative innovation necessarily requires making errors and even failing. Thomas Watson, founder of IBM, claimed, "The way to succeed is to double your failure rate" (von Oech, 1983, p. 93).

The seventh block is the notion that *Play is Frivolous*. Countless creative innovations and scientific discoveries have been born by playing with ideas; and childlike thinking, humor, and playing with ideas are common traits of creative people.

Block number eight is *That's Not My Area*. This block is an excuse for not even trying to solve a problem. Further, many innovations are born by adapting ideas from outside a field.

*Don't Be Foolish*, block nine, is another cultural barrier. Said von Oech, you occasionally should play the fool, and you certainly should be aware of when you or others are putting down a creative "fool."

Finally, the tenth block is the self-squelcher: *I'm Not Creative*. If you seriously believe this, you will be correct.

Do you need an occasional whack on the side of the head?

INSET **10.2** _____

## Tips for Strengthening Creativity

- *Know when to be creative and when to conform.* For example, be creative in artistic and research projects; do not be creative on multiple-choice exams or by violating normal school requirements.
- *Find out what you are best at.* Experiment and explore; take risks and challenge yourself. You might discover new talents.
- *Be motivated from inside yourself, not from the outside.* Work to please yourself; do things that interest you. Seek satisfaction in a job well done.
- *Do not let personal problems stop your thinking and work.* Accept that everyone sometimes has problems and try to take them in stride. Work can take your mind off problems.
- *Do not take on more—or less—than you can handle.* Find the balance that allows you to do a thorough job but without accomplishing less than you could.
- *Be persistent.* Do not let frustration, boredom, or fear of failure stop your creative work. Finish what you start—but also know when to quit if you hit a dead end.
- *Make your environment more creative.* Do your parents, teachers, and friends support your creative efforts? Does your room inspire creative thinking? Can you change your environment to make it more creative?

Based on Sternberg (1990), by permission of Free Spirit Publishing.

Fortunately, a heightened creativity consciousness and creative attitudes are a natural outgrowth of most types of classroom creativity exercises and activities. As we noted in Chapter 2, the main difference between people who *have* creative abilities and those who *use* their creative potential lies in attitudes, awareness, and related creative personality traits that predispose people to think and behave in creative ways. Sternberg (1990) itemized tips that encourage students to develop creative habits and traits—and to use them (see Inset 10.2).

## UNDERSTANDING THE TOPIC OF CREATIVITY

Any creativity training will have more impact and make a more lasting impression if students are helped to understand the topic of creativity. There is a large body of information that contributes to this understanding (see Cropley & Urban, 2000, Davis, 1998, or Treffinger, Sortore, & Cross, 1993, for an overview). Some main topics that could comprise lessons "about creativity" are:

The importance of creativity to self and society
Characteristics of creative people
The nature of creative ideas as modifications, combinations, and analogical relationships
The nature of the creative process: stages, changed perceptions, modifying, combining, analogical thinking
Creative abilities
Theories and definitions of creativity
Tests of creativity and the rationale underlying them
Creative thinking techniques
Barriers to creative thinking, including Von Oech's ten blocks

As we noted above, biographies of well-known creative people provide a useful way to teach students about desirable creative characteristics, attitudes, habits, and lifestyles. The *Torrance Tests of Creative Thinking* may be used as the basis for a lesson in the meaning of *fluency, flexibility, originality,* and *elaboration* and their importance in creative thinking.

Students also can learn principles of creative thinking such as:

- Creativity will help you live a more interesting, successful, and enjoyable life.
- Creative people are not rigid; they look at things from different points of view.
- Creative people are aware of pressures to conform—to be like everybody else.
- Creative thinking includes taking risks and making mistakes—and the more creative the idea, the greater the risk of mistakes and failure.
- Creative people play with ideas, consider lots of possibilities, use techniques, think analogically, evaluate their ideas, and get their ideas into action.
- Creative people use their talents, not waste them.

## STRENGTHENING CREATIVE ABILITIES

In Chapter 9 we itemized abilities that logically underlie creativity. It is a common and reasonable strategy to try to strengthen creative abilities through practice and exercise, the same way we strengthen skills of reading, math, typing, solving chemistry problems, and shooting baskets.

We will look again at some of those abilities, noting strategies, exercises, or materials that aim at strengthening each ability. Note that most activities not only exercise creative abilities but also implicitly raise creativity consciousness and bend attitudes in a creative direction.

Note also that there is a thin to nonexistent line between creative abilities and many thinking skills. Bloom's (1974) classic higher-order thinking skills of *analysis, synthesis,* and *evaluation* were listed in Chapter 9 as creative abilities. Other "thinking skills" such as *critical thinking, reasoning, planning,* and *organizing* are obviously essential to creative problem solving. Thinking skills are discussed in Chapter 11.

*Fluency, Flexibility, Originality, Elaboration.* Many types of questions and problems will exer-

cise these traditional creative abilities. As we noted earlier, students can do the exercises as a class, perhaps following brain-storming rules, or else individually. One of the most involving methods is to divide students into problem-solving teams. All teams work on the same problem and then report all or their best ideas to the entire class. Students often are surprised at the different problem interpretations, approaches, and ideas from the other groups.

Some useful types of exercises for stimulating fluency, flexibility, originality, and elaboration are as follows.

**1.** With "What would happen if . . . ?" exercises students list consequences for unlikely events. The events may be imaginary or potentially real. What would happen:

If each person had an eye in the back of his or her head?
If we did not have books?
If the British had won the Revolutionary War?
If the only musical instruments were drums?
If there were no gravity in this room?
If people with blond hair were not allowed in hotels or restaurants and could not vote?
If the earth shifted and your town became the north pole?
If Edison had become a plumber and we had no light bulbs?
If no one ever smiled?
If everyone were a litterbug?
If we had no bricks or wood to build homes?
If we had no automobiles, TV, video games, peanut butter, bicycles, football?

**2.** Thinking of *product improvements* is another type of open-ended question. Students may be asked to think of improvements for any product or process—pencils, desks, jogging shoes, classrooms, skateboards, pianos, school lunches, soda pop, kitchen sinks, the school (or city) bus system, Cracker Jacks, bathtubs, computers, bicycles, jogging shoes, and so on.

**3.** Thinking of *unusual uses* for common objects is probably the single oldest creativity test item; it also makes a good exercise. How might we use discarded rubber tires? A coat hanger? Empty plastic gallon milk containers? A wooden stick? A sheet of paper? Leftover and wasted cafeteria food?

**4.** Posing *problems and paradoxes* is intrinsically interesting and challenging. A problem may require a solution, or a puzzling situation may require a logical explanation. The problem may be realistic or fanciful. For example: How can bicycle thefts be eliminated? How can the lunch menu be improved? What can we buy for parents for Christmas or Hanukah for twenty dollars? How can the school (family) light bill be reduced? How can our health be improved? What can be done for Mr. Smith, a former night watchman who is 55 years old, out of work, with no special skills? How could we remove a stubborn elephant from the living room? How can the three bears prevent burglaries?

Here are some examples of problems requiring explanations: The principal suddenly cancels recess. Why? The grass behind billboards in pastures is often lush. Why? Ten paintings were discovered missing from the art gallery, but there was no sign of a break-in. How could they have disappeared?

**5.** With *design problems,* students can design an ideal school, an airplane for hauling nervous kangaroos, a better lawnmower, more functional clothes, safer ways to travel, a more efficient way to serve lunch in the cafeteria, new sandwiches or other treats for McDonald's, a better mousetrap, and so on.

Looking more specifically at each ability, *fluency* can be exercised by having students list things, for example, that are round, square, sweet, sour, blue, white, made of metal, made of wood, long and slender, short and stubby, smell good, taste bad, or have sharp edges. Some *flexibility* exercises ask students to look at things from different perspectives: How does this room look to a tidy housekeeper? a hungry mouse? an alien from outer space? How does a highway look to a tire? a

crow? a lost pilot? *Elaboration* exercises require the learner to build upon a basic idea, for example, developing the dog walking or cat petting machine in detail—measurements, materials, costs—or elaborating and embellishing a short story, drawing, invention, class outing or field trip, or creative dramatics people machine.

***Sensitivity to Problems.*** Exercises aimed at strengthening problem sensitivity should have the learners find problems, detect difficulties, or detect missing information. Therefore, one type of exercise is having students *ask questions* about an ambiguous situation or even a common object. For example, what questions could you ask about clouds, Mexico, Mickey Mouse, a typewriter, the moon, or the school lunch program? Another type of problem sensitivity exercise would begin with "What don't we know about . . . ?" Or "What is wrong with . . . ?"

***Problem Defining.*** *Problem defining* is a complex ability. Relevant exercises would evolve around:

Identifying the "real" problem. What really needs attention (fixing)? What are we really trying to do?

Detecting missing information. What's missing here? What else do we need to know?

Identifying important aspects of a problem. What's relevant? Essential? What should we focus on? What can we ignore?

Clarifying and simplifying the problem. Checkout service at a discount store is very slow. What needs to be done?

Identifying subproblems. What problems are related to the main problem? What problems will follow from each solution?

Proposing alternative problem definitions, as in the "In what ways might we . . . ?" tactic of the CPS model (Chapter 9).

Defining the problem more broadly to open up new solution possibilities. What is it, generally, that we wish to accomplish? What is a broader view of this problem?

***Visualization and Imagination.*** *Visualization* and *imagination* are obviously central creative abilities (e.g., Daniels-McGhee and Davis, 1994). Three books filled with imagination stimulation exercises are *Put Your Mother on the Ceiling* (DeMille, 1973), *Scamper* (Eberle, 1995), and *200 Ways of Using Imagery in the Classroom* (Bagley and Hess, 1984). All ask students to relax, shut their eyes, and visualize some colorful narration, for example: "Now put a light bulb in each hand. . . . Hold your hands straight out to the side. . . . Pretend that your light bulbs are jet engines. . . . Run down the street for a take off. . . ." (Eberle, 1995).

Another exercise guaranteed to elicit visualization is a creative writing activity suggested by Helman and Larson (1980): "Cut out headlines from a newspaper dealing with unusual stories and have the kids make up the stories." The familiar grocery store rags provide an endless supply of candidate headlines. Some winners include: "Angry Dad Sells Bratty Kids," "Baby Born Talking Gives Dad Winning Lottery Numbers," "Lightning Bolt Zaps Coffin—And Corpse Comes Back To Life!" "Titanic Survivor Afloat for 65 Years," "Teacher Picks Up Hitchhiking Ghost," and "Woman Weds Two-Headed Man— And Gets Sued for Bigamy!"

***Analogical Thinking.***    As we will see in the next section, analogical thinking is not just a cognitive ability, it also is the single most common and important creative thinking technique used— consciously or unconsciously—by creatively productive people (Davis, 1998; Gordon, 1961). Many activities for exercising analogical thinking appear in workbooks by Gordon (1974), Gordon and Poze (1972a, 1972b), and Stanish (1977, 1986, 1988). A teacher or G/T coordinator also can make up his or her own with the format "How is a hamburger like a good day at school?" "What animal is like a bass fiddle? Why?" "What kind of weather (animal, fish, vegetable, car, book, fish, sport, magazine, etc.) is like you?" And perhaps "What color is sadness?" or "How can noise be seen?" In the next section we will see the *direct*

*analogy method,* which involves finding ideas by asking how nature has solved similar problems, for example, "How do animals, birds, and plants keep warm in winter?" "What could have given a cave dweller the idea for a spear? What do you think was the connection?"

***Resisting Premature Closure.***    Most children and adults are guilty of grabbing the first idea that presents itself. However, considering lots of ideas and deferring judgment are two of the most basic principles of creative problem solving, principles that students should thoroughly understand. Brainstorming, with heavy emphasis on the rationale behind deferring judgment, should help with this pivotal ability (or attitude).

## Other Creativity Exercises

There are many types of creativity and problem-solving exercises that may be used to strengthen creative abilities. Some are relatively simple divergent thinking exercises; others ask for more complex aesthetic products or solutions to difficult invention or design problems.

Shallcross (1981) created exercises that could be integrated into specific subject matter. As some examples:

1. Sculpt something using leaves, rocks, paste, and a paper bag (art).
2. List ways to get children to enjoy brushing their teeth (health).
3. Invent a one-step "meal-in-one" (home arts).
4. Plan a mystery or soap opera series using the morphological synthesis approach (language arts; described in next section).
5. Think of new ways to measure time, water, air, or height (math).
6. Have someone strike three notes on a piano. Use them as the basis for a melody (music).
7. Invent stretching exercises for joggers (physical education).
8. Brainstorm ways endangered species might be preserved (science).
9. Brainstorm ways different cultures could learn to understand each other better (social studies).

A workbook by Stanish (1988), *Hearthstone Traveler,* includes instruction and exercises in these areas: poetry writing (cinquains, diamanté), creative writing, humor, analogical thinking, values, recognizing patterns in nature, idea-finding techniques, the CPS model, idea evaluation, and more. Consider the cinquain writing strategy:

Select a title word (for example, merry-go-round).

Brainstorm words (or phrases) associated with the title (for example, wild horses, beasts, children, music, mirrors, ticket to ride).

Brainstorm a second list of "-ing" words descriptive of the title (for example, smiling, laughing, playing, circling, spinning, galloping, running).

Brainstorm a third list of feeling words also ending in "-ing" (for example, exciting, wondering, thrilling, mastering, owning the world, riding high).

Write the title on one line, two associated words on the second line, three "-ing" words on the third line, four feeling "-ing" words on the fourth line, and another word associated with the title on the fifth line.

One result:

Merry-go-round
Music, wild horses
Galloping, playing, laughing
Thrilling, wondering, mastering, owning the world
Ticket to ride.

Said Stanish, such cinquain may be used to write about oneself, to capture the essence of a reading assignment or an important person one has studied, or as the conclusion to a unit of study. Try it. Some of Stanish's (1988) other exercises include:

In what ways is our circulatory system like a tree?

Investigate the use of spirals in computer art, Van Gogh paintings, the human face, the horns of animals, floral patterns, religious temples.

If I were a hawk, in what ways might I assert an opinion?

Something that few people know about me is . . .

Create a humorous drawing that merges two meanings of a word (for example, horn, school, bark, sock, punch).

What kind of sound would an exclamation point (question mark, dollar sign) make?

Invent a Rube Goldberg machine, with at least five steps, to time your suntan (walk your dog, tickle an armadillo's stomach).

## PERSONAL CREATIVE THINKING TECHNIQUES

Personal creative thinking techniques are methods that are developed and used, consciously and unconsciously, by every creative person regardless of the subject or content of his or her creations. This topic lies at the core of central questions such as "Where do ideas come from?" and "What is the nature of the internal creative process?" (Davis, 1981a).

Most personal techniques are *analogical* in nature. That is, the innovator based the idea for the creation on a news event, an historical event, or an earlier book, movie, melody, art or architecture style, invention, scientific discovery, business idea, some other previous innovation, or some phenomenon in nature. Indeed, whenever we hear the phrase "was inspired by . . ." or "was based upon . . . ," we can be sure that a deliberate or accidental analogical technique was used by the innovator.

An important point is that every single one of the standard techniques described in the next section originated as a personal creative thinking technique—a method that some creative person used in his or her day-to-day high-level creative thinking. The standard techniques are unconscious methods made conscious, knowable, and teachable.

To present the flavor of personal creative-thinking techniques, let's look at a few examples. In science, Einstein used what he called "mental experiments." In his most noted example, he once imagined himself to be a tiny being riding through space on a ray of light, which helped him develop his general theory of relativity.

In art we find recurrent subjects and styles with every famous painter, reflecting their personal creative thinking techniques. Picasso, for example, is known for his African, harlequin, blue, and pink (rose) periods, during which his paintings were inspired by particular themes. He also deliberately disassembled faces and other elements and put them back together in more original arrangements. Paul Gauguin painted South Pacific natives in his unique style, time and again. Edgar Degas is noted for his graceful ballerinas. Renoir's trademark is his soft pastel, female subjects and still lifes. Georges Seurat used a "dot" style (pointillism), often with water and sailboats as subjects.

Seurat's most famous painting, *Sunday Afternoon on the Isle of La Grande Jatte,* inspired the Broadway musical *Sunday Afternoon in the Park with George.* Andrew Lloyd Weber's *Cats* was based on T. S. Eliot's *Old Possum's Book of Practical Cats.*

Even Leonardo da Vinci reportedly wandered Italian streets, sketchbook in hand, looking for interesting faces for his painting *The Last Supper.* Throughout art history, ideas for paintings have been taken from mythology, the Bible, or historical events.

All of Franz Liszt's *Hungarian Rhapsodies* were drawn from the folk tunes of Hungarian gypsies. Tchaikovsky, too, developed folk tunes into symphonies. Aaron Copland's marvelous *Appalachian Spring* was based on the folk tune *Simple Gifts.* Even the ever-popular *Star Spangled Banner* came from an English drinking song.

Cartoonists continually use deliberate analogical thinking to find ideas. For example, after the Gulf War, Saddam Hussein was portrayed as the powerless Wizard of Oz behind the curtain—"I am Saddam the great and powerful!" See also the *Far Side* cartoon.

Former columnist-humorist Art Buchwald also used deliberate analogical thinking—borrowing

**THE FAR SIDE**                    **By Gary Larson**

**Moses as a kid**

The Far Side.

ideas and concepts from one area and using them to make a humorous political comment in another. In one column he borrowed ideas from TV soap operas and used them to discuss a new "Seamy, Steamy Tale of Power and Greed—The Budget of the United States Government":

> I couldn't put it down. I kept turning the pages to see what government programs would be cut next. It's more frightening than *Rosemary's Baby.*
>
> You mean it's a thriller?
>
> It's more of a whodunit. Or, specifically, who's doing it to whom. It's about money and power, the struggle for survival, death and taxes and man's fate in a world he never made.
>
> Any sex?

The military chapters are very sexy, particularly the love scenes between the President of the United States and the new weapons that the Pentagon has seduced him into buying.

You mean the President is in bed with the military-industrial complex?

All through the book! Some of the scenes are so hot that Tip O'Neill has threatened to ban the book in Boston . . .*

Toward the end of the sixteenth century, Holinshed's *Chronicles,* a history book, was published. William Shakespeare used it extensively as a source of ideas for *Macbeth, Henry IV, Henry V, Henry VI, Richard II,* and other plays. He drew from Plutarch's *Lives* to write *Antony and Cleopatra* and *Coriolanus. Troilus and Cressida* came from various accounts of the story of Troy.

Contemporary novelists and screenwriters continue to draw ideas analogically from identifiable sources. As just one example, Pearl Harbor inspired *From Here to Eternity, Tora, Tora Tora!,* and *Pearl Harbor.* In an interview, the screenwriter of *High Noon* confessed that the inspiration for his award-winning suspense western came from the intimidation of writers and actors in Hollywood by organized crime in the 1950s.

The *Star Wars* series was based partly on an effective personal creative thinking technique used by George Lucas. While writing the script for *Star Wars,* Lucas read books on mythology. Said Lucas in a *Time* magazine interview, "I wanted *Star Wars* to have an epic quality, and so I went back to the epics." Thus we find a young man who must prove his manhood to himself and to his father; who rescues a princess in distress; who has an older and wiser mentor (actually two, Ben Kenobi and Yoda); and who battles with a villain, Darth Vader. Some western movies have been built deliberately around the same principles.

Professional comedians also use personal creative-thinking techniques, both for their unique type of humor and for their original delivery.

*Reprinted by permission of Art Buchwald.

Comedian Don Rickles insults people, using the same insults again and again ("Shut up dummy, you're makin' a fool of yourself!"). Rodney Dangerfield's "I don't get no respect" theme makes him one of America's most successful comedians. He continually puts himself down: "When I was born the doctor told my mother, 'I did everything I could, but he's gonna be okay.'" "I couldn't play hide-and-seek 'cause nobody wanted to find me!" "I remember when I called this girl for a date. She said, 'Sure, come on over, nobody's home.' So I went over an' nobody was home!" "Last week I went to a psychiatrist. He said 'I think you're crazy.' I said I wanted another opinion, so he said 'Okay, I think you're ugly too!'" The list of creations and innovations produced via personal creative thinking techniques, usually analogical in nature, could be endless. At the same time, we should not lose sight of unexplainable creative genius and inspiration. Consider the marvelous *Harry Potter* books and movies. Although Ernest Hemingway drew ideas from his travels and World War II, he also said, "the stuff comes alive and turns crazy on ya'."

## Developing Personal Creative Thinking Techniques

There are several ways students may be encouraged to develop personal creative thinking techniques. First, students should understand how even extraordinarily creative people have "found" ideas. This demystifies creativity and helps convince students that they also can legitimately build upon existing ideas without feeling "uncreative." After all, if William Shakespeare, Franz Liszt, George Lucas, and Art Buchwald can borrow plots, tunes, and ideas, so can they.

Second, some recurrent personal creative thinking techniques may be teachable. For example, some techniques include:

**1.** Deliberately using analogical and metaphorical thinking. For example, in aesthetic creations students can find ideas by looking at what others have done and where their ideas came from.

Students can learn to ask: What else is like this? What has worked for others? What could I adapt from similar problems or situations? Does history, the Bible, or other literature suggest ideas? What would professionals do (Davis, 1998)?

**2.** Modifying, combining, and improving present ideas.

**3.** Starting with the goal—perhaps an ideal or perfect solution such as having the problem solve itself—and working backward to deduce what is required to reach that goal.

**4.** Asking yourself how the problem might be solved 50, 100, or 200 years in the future.

Because personal creative thinking techniques develop (1) in the course of doing creative things or (2) from instruction by people who use and understand such techniques, G/T students should become involved in such inherently creative activities as art, photography, creative writing, acting, journalism, independent research, or other activities requiring creative thinking and problem solving.

Mentorships may be especially good, since they involve many hours of direct, personal work with a creative professional. Field trips lead to exposure to experts, to creative ideas, and to sophisticated elaborations and embellishments of ideas.

Visitors also can teach personal creative thinking techniques. For example, school districts in some states contract with a different visiting artist or writer each school year. In this way children have a close view of the creative processes of a variety of artists during their school years. University and industry researchers and other creative professionals also may be invited to share their experiences related to creative discoveries and creative thinking.

## STANDARD CREATIVE THINKING TECHNIQUES

There are several well-known methods for producing new ideas and new idea combinations that are taught in most university and professional creativity training courses. The strategies also may be taught to middle and high school students, and to gifted and talented elementary students. One lively workbook, *Imagination Express* (Davis & DiPego, 1973), incorporates standard creative thinking techniques into a fantasy story about a Saturday subway ride from Kansas City to Pittsburgh to Dublin to Tokyo to Santa Monica and back. It also teaches good creative attitudes and awarenesses.

The techniques of brainstorming, attribute listing, the CPS model, and others are taught, for example, in the workbooks by Stanish (1977, 1979, 1981, 1988) in a form comprehendible to young learners.

It is worth repeating that every standard creative thinking technique began as a personal technique that some creative person explained and thus made conscious and teachable.

### Brainstorming

In the case of brainstorming, it was Alex Osborn, cofounder of the New York advertising agency Batten, Barton, Dursten, and Osborn and founder in 1954 of the Creative Education Foundation, who identified the conditions and listed the rules for brainstorming. The main principle is *deferred judgment:* Idea evaluation is postponed until later. Deferred judgment implicitly creates a receptive, creative atmosphere—an appreciation for novel ideas and a predisposition to find them. Osborn (1963) noted, simply enough, that any type of criticism or evaluation interferes with thinking of imaginative ideas: You cannot do both at once. And the purpose of any brainstorming session is to generate a long list of possible problem solutions.

Brainstorming may be used in the classroom for (1) teaching brainstorming as an effective creative thinking technique, (2) practicing creative thinking (thus strengthening attitudes and abilities), and perhaps (3) solving some pressing school problem, such as high absenteeism, messy school grounds, drug problems, traffic problems, bicycle thefts, raising money, selling play tickets, and so on.

Osborn's four ground rules are simple:

**1.** *Criticism is ruled out.* This is deferred judgment, which contributes to the creative atmosphere essential for uninhibited imaginations.

**2.** *Freewheeling is welcomed.* The wilder the idea the better. Seemingly preposterous ideas can lead to imaginative yet workable solutions.

**3.** *Quantity is wanted.* This principle reflects the purpose of the session: to produce a long list of ideas, thus increasing the likelihood of finding good problem solutions.

**4.** *Combination and improvement are sought.* This lengthens the idea list. Actually, during the session students will spontaneously "hitchhike" on each other's ideas, with one idea inspiring the next.

Variations on brainstorming include *reverse brainstorming,* in which new viewpoints are found by turning the problem around. For example: How can we *increase* vandalism? How can we *increase* the electric bill? How can we *stifle* creativity? How can we *decrease* morale? Reverse brainstorming quickly points out what currently is being done incorrectly and implicitly suggests solutions. With *stop-and-go* brainstorming, short (about 10-minute) periods of brainstorming are interspersed with short periods of evaluation. This helps keep the group on target by selecting the apparently most profitable directions. In the *Phillips 66* technique small groups of six brainstorm for six minutes, after which a member of each group reports either the best ideas or all ideas to the larger group.

It is easy to run a classroom brainstorming session. The teacher begins by discussing creativity and creative ideas, which leads to brainstorming as one method that stimulates creative thinking. The four brainstorming rules are discussed and a problem selected, such as "How can we raise money for new playground equipment?" or "How can we turn the classroom into a foreign planet?" A volunteer scribe lists ideas on the blackboard. The teacher-leader's role is to ask, "Anyone else have an idea?" or the leader might specifically ask quieter students if they have ideas they wish to contribute. If a serious problem (for example, messy hallways) is the focus, the leader can give the group 48 hours advance notice of the problem. Gifted and talented students can learn to organize and lead brainstorming sessions.

*Idea Evaluation.* Listing wild ideas does not represent the complete problem-solving process. Therefore, a brainstorming session can be followed by an idea evaluation session. Idea evaluation would be most important if the class intended to present the school principal (or the mayor) with some blue-ribbon solutions to a real current problem. The group can brainstorm evaluation criteria such as: Will it work? Can the school afford it? Will the community (parents, principal, mayor) go for it? Is adequate time available? Are materials available? As we saw in the previous chapter, the most relevant criteria would be listed across the top of an *evaluation matrix,* the specific ideas in rows down the left side. Table 10.1 shows one evaluation matrix that was constructed to evaluate ideas brainstormed for the problem "How can we build school spirit?" The total scores are a guide to ideas that students may wish to pursue.

The use of objective criteria:

**1.** Helps evaluate the ideas in a mostly unbiased manner.

**2.** Helps students learn to evaluate as part of the overall creative problem-solving process.

**3.** Teaches an effective evaluation technique, one that is used in both the CPS model and Future Problem Solving.

**4.** Requires students to consider many components and views of the problem.

**5.** Often helps the group explore its values relative to the problem at hand. What criteria are truly relevant?

**6.** Prevents idea evaluation from becoming a personal attack on specific children.

**7.** Helps children understand that thinking of "silly" and "far-fetched" ideas truly can lead to good, practical solutions to problems.

**TABLE 10.1**    Example of Evaluation Matrix

| IDEAS | | CRITERIA | | | | | | |
|---|---|---|---|---|---|---|---|---|
| | Cost | Effect on Teachers | Educational Effects | School Spirit Effect | Effect on Students | Effect on Community | Totals |
| Buy class sweatshirts | +3 | +2 | +1 | +3 | +3 | +3 | 15 |
| Establish school baseball team | −2 | +2 | 0 | +2 | +2 | +2 | 6 |
| Start interclass competition | 0 | 0 | +1 | +3 | +2 | 0 | 6 |
| Get new school building | −3 | +3 | +2 | +3 | +3 | −2 | 6 |
| Get rid of "hoods" | −3 | 0 | −3 | +1 | −3 | −3 | −11 |

| POSITIVE EFFECTS | NEGATIVE EFFECTS |
|---|---|
| +3 = Excellent | −1 = Slightly Negative |
| +2 = Good | −2 = Somewhat Negative |
| +1 = Fair | −3 = Very Negative |
| 0 = Not Applicable | |

Evaluation sessions may follow the use of any of the creative thinking techniques in this section.

### Attribute Listing

Robert Crawford (1978), designer of *attribute listing,* argued, "Each time we take a step we do it by changing an attribute or a quality of something, or else by applying that same quality or attribute to some other thing." Attribute listing thus is both a *theory* of the creative process and a practical creative thinking *technique.* Following Crawford's definition, there are two forms of attribute listing: (1) *attribute modifying* and (2) *attribute transferring.* Either strategy may be used individually or in a group.

*Attribute Modifying.*    The problem solver lists main attributes (characteristics, dimensions, parts) of a problem object, then thinks of ways to improve each attribute. For example, a group of students might invent new types of candy bars or breakfast cereals by first writing important attributes (size, shape, flavor, ingredients, color, texture, packaging, nutritional value, name, intended market, and so on) on the blackboard, and then listing specific ideas under each main attribute. Particularly good combinations are picked out of the lists of ideas. Not-so-good ideas—the two-pound "Popeye's Delight" candy bar containing spinach and steroids and created for muscle-builders—will keep enthusiasm high. In university design engineering courses the attribute modifying strategy is called the *substitution method* of design.

Fran Striker (n.d.; see also Shallcross, 1981) used attribute listing to generate radio and TV episodes for his *Lone Ranger* series. Striker used the attributes of *characters, goals, obstacles,* and *outcomes.* In the first column he listed specific ideas for *characters,* broadly defined to include objects and animals. *Goals* included things the character(s) wanted to become, to achieve, or to happen. *Obstacles* could be the law, stupidity, soft-heartedness, or a desert. *Outcomes* could include bargaining, sacrificing one's pride or position, or using one's wits. With this technique, augmented by stacks of western novels, Striker produced plenty of ideas.

The attribute listing technique is simple and it works—whether used for inventing breakfast cereals, writing short story plots, or solving any other problem in which attributes can be identified. For example, "dirty hallways" might be attacked by listing such attributes as student habits, student awareness, available trash containers, disciplinary consequences, and or other aspects of the problem. Students would "list" specific ideas for improving each "attribute."

*Attribute Transferring.*   This is a pure case of analogical thinking—transferring ideas from one context to another. We noted above how deliberate analogical thinking is used by creative persons in many aesthetic and scientific areas. As one classroom application, ideas for a creative and memorable parents' night or open house might be found by borrowing ideas from a carnival or circus, Disneyland, *E.T.,* the "Wild West," a funeral parlor, McDonald's, or a *Star Wars* or *Harry Potter* movie.

## Morphological Synthesis

The *morphological synthesis* technique is a simple extension of the attribute listing procedure (Allen, 1962; Davis, 1998). Specific ideas for one attribute or dimension of a problem are listed along one axis of a matrix, ideas for a second attribute are listed along the other axis. Plenty of idea combinations are found in the cells of the matrix. One sixth-grade class invented new sandwich ideas with the morphological synthesis technique (Figure 10.1). With a third dimension (type of bread) you would have a cube with three-way combinations in each cell. Davis (2003a, 2003c) used morphological synthesis to generate hundreds of exercises for teaching values and moral thinking.

The method may be used with a half-dozen dimensions by listing ideas in columns. The columns may be cut into strips that can slide up or down to create hundreds (thousands) of combinations found by reading horizontally.

## Idea Checklists

Sometimes, one can find a *checklist* that suggests solutions for your problem. For example, the *Yellow Pages* are often used as a checklist for problems like "Who can fix my TV?" or "Where can I get a haircut?" High school counselors have used the *Yellow Pages* for career counseling ideas. A gift store catalogue—or browsing through a gift store, clothing store, book store, cheese-and-sausage store, or gourmet kitchen/food shop, which often can be done on the Internet—is also using an idea checklist.

Some idea checklists have been designed especially for creative problem solving. The most popular of these is Alex Osborn's (1963) *73 Idea-Spurring Questions* (Table 10.2). Take a few extra seconds as you read through this list and think of how a mousetrap, a backpack, a can of soda pop, or a poster advertising a school play might be improved by the suggestions on the list. Ideas will be elicited virtually involuntarily.

The checklist technique sometimes is called the *SCAMPER* method: *S*ubstitute, *C*ombine, *A*dopt, *M*odify-Magnify-Minify, *P*ut to other uses, *E*liminate, *R*everse-Rearrange.

## Synectics Methods

*Synectics,* from the Greek word *synecticos,* means the joining together of apparently unrelated elements. It was his work with creative-thinking groups that led William J. J. Gordon, originator of the synectics methods, to identify strategies that creative people use unconsciously. He made these strategies conscious and teachable in a form for adults (Gordon, 1961; Gordon and Poze, 1980) and for children (Gordon, 1974; Gordon and Poze, 1972a, 1972b; see also Stanish, 1977, 1986, 1988).

*Direct Analogy.*   With this method the person is asked to think of ways that similar problems are

A sixth grade Milwaukee class used the morphological synthesis method to generate 121 zany ideas for creative sandwiches. Can you find a tasty combination? A revolting one? If you add a third dimension, with five types of bread, how many total ideas would you have?

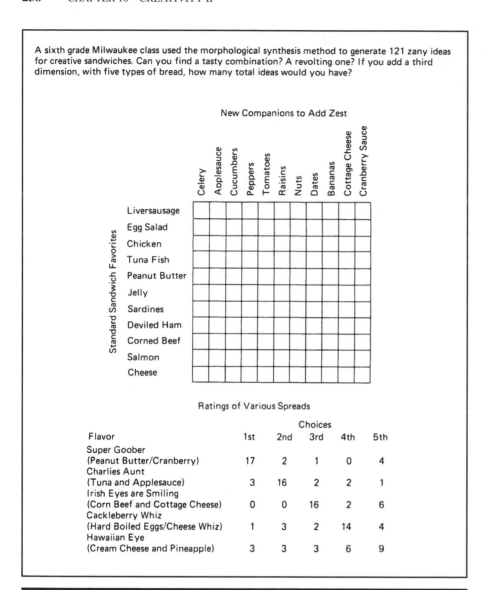

New Companions to Add Zest

Standard Sandwich Favorites:

| | Celery | Applesauce | Cucumbers | Peppers | Tomatoes | Raisins | Nuts | Dates | Bananas | Cottage Cheese | Cranberry Sauce |
|---|---|---|---|---|---|---|---|---|---|---|---|
| Liversausage | | | | | | | | | | | |
| Egg Salad | | | | | | | | | | | |
| Chicken | | | | | | | | | | | |
| Tuna Fish | | | | | | | | | | | |
| Peanut Butter | | | | | | | | | | | |
| Jelly | | | | | | | | | | | |
| Sardines | | | | | | | | | | | |
| Deviled Ham | | | | | | | | | | | |
| Corned Beef | | | | | | | | | | | |
| Salmon | | | | | | | | | | | |
| Cheese | | | | | | | | | | | |

Ratings of Various Spreads

| Flavor | Choices | | | | |
|---|---|---|---|---|---|
| | 1st | 2nd | 3rd | 4th | 5th |
| Super Goober (Peanut Butter/Cranberry) | 17 | 2 | 1 | 0 | 4 |
| Charlies Aunt (Tuna and Applesauce) | 3 | 16 | 2 | 2 | 1 |
| Irish Eyes are Smiling (Corn Beef and Cottage Cheese) | 0 | 0 | 16 | 2 | 6 |
| Cackleberry Whiz (Hard Boiled Eggs/Cheese Whiz) | 1 | 3 | 2 | 14 | 4 |
| Hawaiian Eye (Cream Cheese and Pineapple) | 3 | 3 | 3 | 6 | 9 |

**FIGURE 10.1**    A Morphological Sandwich.

From *Creativity Is Forever,* 4th ed., by G. A. Davis (Dubuque, IA: Kendall/Hunt). Used with permission.

solved in nature by animals, birds, flowers, weeds, bugs, worms, lizards, and so on. For example, ideas for conserving energy could be found by asking how animals keep warm in winter.

In a creativity workshop for the elderly, many expressed concern for their personal safety. With a synectics approach the problem became, "How do animals, plants, and birds protect themselves, and how can these ideas help the elderly?" The list included spray cans of skunk scent, slip-on fangs and claws (mildly poisonous), a compressed air can that screams, an electronic transmitter that

**TABLE 10.2**   Osborn's "73 Idea-Spurring Questions"

Put to other uses? New ways to use as is? Other uses if modified?

Adopt? What else is like this? What other idea does this suggest? Does the past offer a parallel? What could I copy? Whom could I emulate?

Modify? New twist? Change meaning, color, motion, sound, odor, form, shape? Other changes?

Magnify? What to add? More time? Greater frequency? Stronger? Higher? Longer? Thicker? Extra value? Plus ingredient? Duplicate? Multiply? Exaggerate?

Minify? What to subtract? Smaller? Condensed? Miniature? Lower? Omit? Streamline? Split up? Understate?

Substitute? Who else instead? What else instead? Other ingredient? Other material? Other process? Other power? Other place? Other approach? Other tone of voice?

Rearrange? Interchange components? Other pattern? Other layout? Other sequence? Transpose cause and effect? Change pace? Change schedule?

Reverse? Transpose positive and negative? How about opposites? Turn it backward? Turn it upside down? Reverse roles? Change shoes? Turn tables? Turn other cheek?

Combine? How about a blend, an alloy, an assortment, an ensemble? Combine units? Combine purposes? Combine appeals? Combine ideas?

secretly "yells" for police assistance, traveling only in groups, camouflage, or disguises (for example, wearing a police uniform), and others.

***Personal Analogy.***   Imagine you are a piece of candy sitting quietly with your candy friends on the shelf of the local drugstore. A little boy walks in, places a nickel on the counter and points at you. How do you feel? What are your thoughts? Describe your experiences for the next fifteen minutes. The purpose of such exercises is to give elementary students practice with the *personal analogy* creative thinking technique. With this strategy, new perspectives are found by becoming part of the problem, usually a problem object. What would you be like if you were a highly efficient can opener? A captivating short story? A truly exciting and valuable educational learning experience for children?

***Fantasy Analogy.***   Problem solvers think of fantastic, farfetched, perhaps ideal solutions that can lead to creative yet practical ideas. Gordon sees *fantasy analogy* as a type of Freudian wish fulfillment. For example, one can ask how to make the problem solve itself: How can we make the hallways keep themselves clean? How can we get parents to want to attend open house? How can we get the School Board to want to give us a new instructional materials center? Some years ago, design engineers probably asked: How can we make refrigerators defrost themselves? Ovens clean themselves? Automobile brakes adjust themselves? This was employing fantasy analogy.

***Symbolic Analogy.***   A fourth synectics technique is called *symbolic analogy*; other names are *compressed conflict* or *book titles*. Your dictionary will call it *oxymoron*. The strategy is to think of a two word phrase or "book title" that seems self-contradictory, such as "careful haste" or "gentle toughness." The compressed conflict would be related to a particular problem and would stimulate ideas. For example, the phrase "careful haste" might be used by educators or firefighters to stimulate ideas for quickly and safely evacuating a large school building. "Gentle toughness" might stimulate ideas for designing automobile tires, durable fabrics, or long-distance bicycles.

An exercise from a synectics workbook, *Teaching Is Listening,* by Gordon and Poze (1972a), includes a direct analogy, personal analogy, and symbolic analogy:

1. What animal typifies your concept of freedom? (Direct analogy)
2. Put yourself in the place of the animal you have chosen. Be the thing! Describe what makes you feel and act with so much freedom. (Personal analogy)
3. Sum up your description of the animal you chose by listing the "free" and "unfree" parts of your animal life.

   Free: _____

   _____

   Unfree: _____

   _____

4. Express each of these parts of your life in a single word. Put together these two words and refine them into a poetic, compressed conflict phrase.

   _____        _____

   _____        _____

   _____        _____

5. Circle the phrase you like best. Write a new essay about freedom. Use any material you may have developed in this exercise.

Synectics methods can be used in the classroom either as creativity exercises or as material for lessons in techniques of creative thinking.

As a final note on creativity techniques, a five-volume series of activity books for students at different grade levels (K–8) uses brainstorming and other "forced relationship" techniques to improve students' "ideational fluency and originality . . . [and] the ability to speculate and imagine" (Renzulli et al., 2000, p. 2). As with virtually all creativity training efforts, the activities will also strengthen creativity consciousness and other creative attitudes. As a sample activity, students are given an improbable situation and asked for consequences: "What would happen if there were no such thing as darkness or night?" (p. 2). Follow-up activities include asking students for improbable situations for which classmates can think of consequences. The activities are intended to elicit humor and playfulness—legitimate parts of creativity. (For further information, visit www.creativelearningpress.com.)

### Implementation Charting

*Implementation charting* helps gifted children see implementation as a realistic next step in creative thinking, following the generation of ideas and the selection of one or more workable solutions. With implementation charting, students prepare a chart specifying both the *persons responsible* for implementing components of the idea(s) and a *completion deadline.* For example, if the best idea for increasing school spirit were to sell school sweatshirts, then an implementation chart such as the one in Table 10.3 might be suitable.

Note that there is more than one role of *evaluation* in creative problem solving. In the present example, the initial ideas were evaluated in an evaluation matrix (Table 10.1). After the idea(s) are selected and the project implemented, a later evaluation can determine if the project was successful and if it should be continued.

### INVOLVING STUDENTS IN CREATIVE ACTIVITIES

The most logically sound answer to the question "How can we teach creativity?" is this: Involve students in activities that intrinsically require creative thinking and problem solving. It is virtually assured that creative attitudes, abilities, and skills will be strengthened in the course of this creative involvement. It is no accident that Renzulli's Type III Enrichment (Renzulli and Reis, 1997; see Chapter 7) focuses on developing creativity via individual or small group projects and investigations of real problems. Appendix 7.1 lists topics

**TABLE 10.3**   Implementation Chart for Selling School Sweatshirts

| ACTIVITY | PERSON RESPONSIBLE | TIME FOR IMPLEMENTATION |
|---|---|---|
| 1. Ask permission for project | Ron | March 10 |
| 2. Design sweatshirt | Mary, Ruth | March 15–20 |
| 3. Approve design | Student Council | March 22 |
| 4. Review possible sweatshirt sellers | Barb, John | March 15–20 |
| 5. Make recommendation to Student Council | Student Council | March 22 |
| 6. Order sweatshirts | Barb, John | March 24 |
| 7. Organize student sales campaign | Tom, Mary & Allan | March 22–31 |
|    a. Posters | Bob, Andy | March 25 |
|    b. Article in school newspaper | Alice | March 25–31 |
|    c. Article in community newspaper | Allan | March 28 |
| 8. Actual beginning of sales | Tom, Mary & Allan | April 10 |
| 9. Student Sweatshirt Day | Ron, Mary & Ruth | April 12 |
| 10. Evaluation of success of project | Original Brainstorming Group | April 20 |

in art, science, literature, and so on, that will stimulate creative thinking and problem solving. We particularly recommend the Future Problem Solving and Odyssey of the Mind programs, which were designed to teach creativity through involvement with real problems and projects.

The G/T teacher-coordinator should be continually alert for opportunities to exercise creative thinking and problem solving in content areas. Available opportunities also might be expanded. Are music, science, and art programs adequate? Are students encouraged to become involved in scientific and aesthetic activities? Are community resources and mentors being used to good advantage?

*A knowledge base.*   As a consideration, on one hand—and contrary to some strong opinions—it

*is* possible to think creatively "in the abstract." One does not need a great fund of specialized knowledge to brainstorm ideas for improving local traffic conditions, making parents' night more exciting, or making Wanda the guinea pig a little happier. Many such problems were suggested earlier. On the other hand, one does need a good knowledge base for making creative contributions in a specialized area, which happens with independent research projects and with real-world creative innovations whose inspiration grows out of education and experience.

**CREATIVE TEACHING AND LEARNING**

Torrance (1977) stated that "people fundamentally prefer to learn in creative ways." These ways include exploring, manipulating, questioning, experimenting, risking, testing, and modifying ideas. Said Torrance, learning creatively takes place during the processes of sensing problems, deficiencies, or gaps in information; formulating hypotheses or guesses about a problem; testing the hypotheses, revising and retesting the hypotheses; and then communicating the results. He explained that problems arouse tension, thus motivating the learner to ask questions, make guesses, and test the adequacy of the guesses, correcting errors and modifying conclusions if necessary.

Some recommendations for creative teaching, partly from Torrance (1995), include the following:

Maintain high teacher enthusiasm.

Accept individual differences, for example, in preferred ways of learning, learning rates, faults, and so forth.

Permit the curriculum to be different for different students.

Communicate that the teacher is "for" rather than "against" the child.

Encourage and permit self-initiated projects.

Support students against peer conformity pressures.

Allow or encourage a child to achieve success in an area and in a way possible for him or her.

Respect the potential of low achievers.

Do not be blinded by intelligence test scores; they do not tell the whole story.

Do not let pressure for evaluation get the upper hand.

Encourage divergent ideas; too many "right" ideas are stifling.

Teach how to test each idea systematically.

Create necessities for creative thinking.

Create "thorns in the flesh."

Make resources available for working out ideas.

Encourage the habit of working out the full implication of ideas.

Provide for active and quiet periods.

Try to be "adventurous of spirit."

Do not be afraid to wander off the teaching schedule and try something different.

Torrance (1981a, 1981c, 1995; see also Millar, 1995; Hébert et al., 2002) summarized some signs that creative learning is taking place, which partly represent benefits of creative teaching and learning. These include improved motivation, alertness, curiosity, concentration, and achievement; a charged atmosphere "tingling with excitement"; the combining of activities that cut across curriculum areas; improved communication of ideas and feelings; a boldness in ideas, drawings, stories, and so on; improved self-confidence; improved creative growth and creative expression; a reduction of unproductive behavior, behavior problems, hostility, vandalism, and apathy; and an increase in enthusiasm about school and learning and improved career aspirations.

Creativity training and creative teaching can indeed make a difference for gifted, normal, and even troubled students.

## SUMMARY

Creativity can be increased. Many teachers incorporate creativity training activities into their classrooms.

Goals of creativity training include increasing creativity consciousness and creative attitudes and personality traits, helping students understand creativity, strengthening creative abilities, teaching creativity techniques, and involving students in creative activities.

Creativity consciousness and creative attitudes include an awareness of creativity, valuing creativity, a predisposition to think creatively, a willingness to make mistakes, and others. A teacher can reinforce creative personality traits (e.g., confidence, curiosity, risk taking, playfulness, artistic interests); promote independent learning, self-evaluation, and fantasy and imagination; help students cope with failure and peer pressure to conform; establish a creative atmosphere, and raise awareness of blocks to creative thinking.

Creative persons accept personality traits stereotypically associated with the opposite sex, such as autonomy, confidence, and toughness (masculine) along with sensitivity, intuition, and responsibility (feminine).

Helping students understand creativity can involve lessons on the importance of creativity, characteristics of creative people, creative abilities, theories of creativity, creativity tests, creativity techniques, blocks and barriers to creativity, and important principles of creativity.

Many types of exercises exist for strengthening creative abilities such as fluency, flexibility, originality, sensitivity to problems, problem defining, visualization, analogical thinking, and others. Shallcross suggested exercises that are tied to specific subject areas. Stanish's workbooks include simple and complex (e.g., poetry writing, inventing) exercises.

Personal creativity techniques, usually analogical, are used by every creatively productive person. Examples were cited from science, art, music, political cartooning, political satire, theater, moviemaking, and comedy.

Students may be helped to develop personal creativity techniques by explaining the techniques used by others; teaching such problem-solving strategies as looking for analogically related solutions; working backward from an ideal goal; involvement in creative activities; and instruction from creative professionals who use such techniques.

Standard creative thinking techniques are commonly taught in creativity courses and workshops.

Brainstorming is based on deferred judgment. Variations include reverse brainstorming, stop-and-go brainstorming, and the Phillips 66 procedure.

Students may be taught idea evaluation with an evaluation matrix.

The attribute listing technique takes two forms, modifying important problem attributes and transferring attributes from one situation to another, which is analogical thinking.

Morphological synthesis, an extension of attribute listing, is a matrix approach to generating ideas.

Osborn's "73 Idea-Spurring Questions" is an idea checklist designed for creative problem solving.

Four synectics methods include direct analogy, looking for ways that similar problems have been solved in nature; personal analogy, in which ideas are found by becoming a problem object or process; fantasy analogy, in which the thinker looks for farfetched, perhaps ideal problem solutions; and symbolic analogy, using two-word conflicts to stimulate new perspectives.

Implementation charting includes assigning responsibilities and deadlines. Project success can be evaluated.

Involving students in creative activities—such as independent research projects, Future Problem Solving, and Odyssey of the Mind—is a sound way to develop creative skills, abilities, attitudes, and awarenesses.

A deep knowledge base is important for creative contributions in a specialized area, but not for classroom creativity exercises.

According to Torrance, creative teaching and learning includes exploring, questioning, experimenting, testing ideas, and other activities. Creative learning includes sensing a problem; formulating hypotheses or guesses; testing, revising and retesting the hypotheses; and communicating the results.

Some recommendations for creative teaching included maintaining high enthusiasm, accepting individual differences, encouraging self-initiated projects, looking beyond IQ scores, encouraging divergent thinking, creating necessities for creative thinking, providing resources for working out ideas, and others.

Creative learning can result in improved motivation, achievement, creativity, self-confidence, school attitudes, and others.

# CHAPTER 11

# TEACHING THINKING SKILLS

*Intelligence can be learned, nurtured, and grown. Ability is a repertoire of skills and habits that continuously and incrementally expands.*
Arthur Costa (2003, p. 325)

The topic of *thinking skills* is sufficiently important that expert Arthur Costa (2003) uses the phrase interchangeably with "intelligent behavior" itself. While basic *g* is considered largely fixed (e.g., Gottfredson, 2003), according to Costa developing students' thinking skills is equivalent to helping them become more intelligent, or at least behave more intelligently. He has a good argument.

In today's schools teachers want to strengthen the ability of all students to analyze, compare, classify, synthesize, generalize, discriminate, infer, plan, predict, see cause-effect relations, make good decisions, and more. We want children to think critically, logically, and evaluatively, for example, about the credibility of messages from salespersons, politicians, and others with strong biases and personal interests (e.g., Lipman, 1991). Noted Costa (2003), "while these capacities are innate, their refinement, procedures, and applications may need to be brought to the conscious level through direct instruction" (p. 327).

Because of gifted students' higher potential and likely professional future, there is a special place in their education for teaching skills for effective thinking.

Three basic approaches to "teaching thinking" run throughout this chapter:

- Strengthening thinking abilities and skills through practice and exercise (*indirect approach*).
- Helping students learn conscious and deliberate strategies for reasoning, problem solving, and critical thinking (*direct approach*).

- Increasing students' understanding of their own and others' thinking (*metacognition*—thinking about thinking).

We will look at several lists and taxonomies of thinking skills that can help create a thinking skills curriculum. We also will review Bloom's higher taxonomic levels of educational objectives (application, analysis, synthesis, and evaluation), which has been a standard guide for teaching thinking. A key part of the chapter is teaching *critical thinking*—a skill that is weak in too many children and adults. Also, we review some good-quality published thinking skills programs and exercise books. Finally, we look at criteria for selecting materials and activities for thinking skills training.

## ISSUES

By way of introduction, the following issues pertain to teaching thinking skills:

*Should thinking skills instruction be infused into existing subjects, taught as a separate subject or course, or both?* Integrating thinking skills into the existing curriculum seems most appealing to teachers and administrators. Finding space for yet another subject is indeed troublesome. Language arts and science, for example, are logical places to impart thinking skills because of the natural role of analysis, reasoning, critical thinking, analogical thinking, evaluation, and others (de Bono, 1983). If possible, we recommend both integrating (infusing) thinking skills into existing subjects as well as teaching thinking as a separate topic or even course.

*What should be the content—the skills—for students of different ages?* We know that young children think concretely, older students more abstractly. Based on a six-year research project, Reis (1990b) recommended introducing specific thinking skills approximately in the sequence shown in Table 11.1. The skills introduced at each level would continue to be practiced and reinforced at higher grade levels.

*How does one best teach thinking?* Alvino (1990) noted that, for some, teaching thinking means only a minor modification of their usual teaching patterns, for example, asking more questions that stimulate students to apply, synthesize, analyze, evaluate, or think critically or creatively, along with modeling "good thinking" habits. For other teachers, creating a "thinking classroom" involves radical changes in teaching and expectations of students. Reis (1990a) said not to tackle too much: "Students who are taught fewer thinking skills, but in greater depth, learn them better" (p. 46). She recommended that teachers introduce

just a few skills, teach them step by step, demonstrate how to use them in a content area or project, and make certain students practice each skill several times during the year.

Beyer (1988) essentially elaborated on Reis's (1990a) logical steps, although he stretched the teaching procedure to six partly redundant steps: The teacher (1) introduces the skill by presenting the name, synonyms, a definition, and steps in using the skill, and then asks where students may have used the skill in or out of school; (2) guides practice with the skill, allowing students to apply the skill and reflect on what they did; (3) allows self-directed practice in additional situations that require the use of the skill, for example, in response to teacher questions; (4) shows students how to transfer the skill to other subjects and contexts; (5) guides practice in the new contexts; and (6) allows students to use the thinking skill independently, for example, in response to teacher questions, end-of-chapter questions, essay assignments, and with new subjects and contexts.

Costa's (2003) four components of a thoughtful thinking skills program appear in Inset 11.1,

**TABLE 11.1** Introducing Thinking Skills at Different Grade Levels

| | |
|---|---|
| Early Elementary Grades (K–2) | *Creative thinking*—brainstorming plus other fluency, flexibility, originality, and elaboration exercises; guided imagery |
| | *Critical and logical thinking*—comparing, contrasting, classifying; patterns and figural relationships |
| Middle Elementary Grades (3–4) | *Creative problem solving and decision making*—creative problem solving (CPS model), future problem solving |
| | *Critical and logical thinking*—deductive and syllogistic reasoning; analogical reasoning; also learning-to-learn skills |
| Upper Elementary and Middle School Grades (5–8) | *Critical and logical thinking*—interpreting, inferring, hypothesizing; analyzing propaganda and bias |
| | *Metacognitive skills*—planning, monitoring, evaluating |

Based on Reis (1990b).

along with a list of 16 important "habits of mind."

Thinking skills may be taught *directively*, as above, by explaining the thinking skill first, then presenting examples for practice. Or a teacher may prefer an *inductive* approach, allowing students to practice the thinking skill first, then letting them reflect on the steps and explain (induce) the rule (Beyer, 1988).

*How does one evaluate the mastery of thinking skills?* Usual achievement tests do not evaluate the mastery of such skills. Some published thinking skills materials include their own tests. Three standardized tests for measuring thinking skills are the *Cornell Critical Thinking Tests,* the *Ross Test of Higher Cognitive Processes,* and the *New Jersey Test of Reasoning Skills.* (The *Cornell Critical Thinking Tests* are available from Critical Thinking Books and Software, P.O. Box 448, Pacific Grove, CA 93950. See http://criticalthinking.com/index .html.) The problem is that such tests may not measure what you have taught—and if the tests show "no improvement" in thinking skills (which you did not teach), your teaching and your gifted program both become suspect.

A teacher likely can design suitable tests to evaluate students' mastery of *classifying, inferring, predicting, planning, recognizing relationships,* and *detecting causes and effects,* and even more complex thinking skills such as *evaluating*

---

**INSET 11.1** _____

### Components of a Thinking Skills Program (From Costa, 2003)

Arthur Costa (2003) described four components of a well-developed program for teaching "habits of skillful thinking" or "habits of mind."

Imagine four concentric circles—like a dart board. In the center, *judiciously selected content* refers to the subject within which the thinking skills will be taught and applied. Content influences the selection of thinking skills in the sense that, for example, a scientific problem will require skills related to logic and scientific control, while social and aesthetic content requires skills related to ethics and artistic judgment. An attractive content also motivates students: "Content activates and engages the enquiring mind" (p. 326).

The second circle is *instruction in the thinking skills* themselves: "the basic tools of effective thinking . . . [which] need to be brought to the conscious level through direct instruction" (p. 327).

The third circle is named *solving problems that require the application of skillful thinking.* Students are exposed to ambiguities, anomalies, conflicts, dilemmas, enigmas, obstacles, or paradoxes that require resolution. Thinking skills are organized into strategies, said Costa, that we call *creativity, problem solving,* and *decision making.*

Finally, Costa's outside circle is *habits of mind;* dispositions or inclinations to use the thinking skills in suitable circumstances. Students must come to value the thinking skill, be alert to opportunities to use it, be capable of using it, and make a commitment to improve the particular thinking skills.

While there is an infinite number of habits of mind, Costa listed these sixteen comparatively complex thinking skills as especially important:

- Persisting when a solution is not readily apparent
- Managing impulsivity
- Listening to others with understanding and empathy
- Thinking flexibly
- Thinking about our own thinking (metacognition)
- Striving for accuracy and precision
- Asking questions and posing problems
- Applying past knowledge to new situations
- Thinking and communicating with clarity and precision
- Gathering data through all senses
- Creating, imagining, innovating
- Responding with wonderment and awe
- Taking responsible risks
- Finding humor
- Thinking independently
- Remaining open to continuous learning

*bias and credibility* and *explaining an author's intentions.*

*How much of teaching thinking skills actually is teaching "attitudes" or "traits"?* A lot. Some important thinking skills are inseparable from personality dispositions, for example, respect for evidence, a willingness to search for reasons and alternatives, a willingness to withhold or even reverse judgments based on facts, open-mindedness, tolerance for ambiguity, sensitivity to others' views (Alvino, 1990; Lipman, 1991), and of course a creativity consciousness (Davis, 1998).

## INDIRECT TEACHING, DIRECT TEACHING, AND METACOGNITION

### Indirect Teaching of Thinking Skills: Strengthening Abilities Through Exercise

Thinking skills may be taught in a comparatively subtle, *indirect* fashion through practice and exercise—the same way we strengthen arithmetic and typing skills. For example, a teacher can strengthen classification skills through instruction and practice with classification problems, including multiple classifications and subclassifications. Similarly, to teach analogical thinking a teacher can use simple exercises of the *dog*: *cat*:: *canine*: _____? variety.

In addition to workbook exercises, Costa (1986; Costa and Lowery, 1989) and Swartz and Perkins (1990) recommended that teachers pose problems and ask questions. For example, teachers can ask "Why," "What if," and "How" questions, not just "What" questions. They can have students explore paradoxes, dilemmas, and discrepancies. Teachers also can ask students to compare, classify, evaluate, find similarities and differences, find analogical relationships, induce principles, extrapolate, and so forth. For seatwork, teachers can create their own exercises or use published ones. A Problem Box permits students to suggest problems for the class to work on. A classroom Think Tank provides a place where students can spend time working on a favorite interest or project.

Teachers can model pertinent thinking skills by "thinking out loud" while analyzing, evaluating, reasoning, or creating.

## Direct Teaching: Knowing Why, When, and How

Many complex thinking skills can be taught *directly* as conscious techniques for reasoning and dealing with problems (e.g., Beyer, 1988; Costa, 2003; Costa & Lowery, 1989; Reis, 1990a). For example, as we will see, critical thinking may be taught by helping students evaluate biases, qualifications, and ability to observe; to examine whether a statement is an assumption or an opinion; and to evaluate whether particular conclusions necessarily follow. Creative thinking may be taught directly, for example, by helping students learn when and how to use the CPS model, brainstorming, and other creative thinking techniques (Davis, 1998). *If thinking skills are to be taught, direct instruction is essential.*

One particularly noteworthy program for the direct teaching of complex thinking skills is the *CoRT* (Cognitive Research Trust) *Thinking Program* created by Edward de Bono (1973, 1983, 1985). de Bono's lessons and exercises teach such skills as evaluating, taking other perspectives, planning, prioritizing, and many others as conscious and deliberate thinking strategies. Students are helped to understand each skill and *why, when,* and *how* it should be applied. We will look at de Bono's strategies in a later section.

While analogical thinking can be indirectly taught using simple analogy problems, it also may be taught as a conscious and deliberate skill. For example, students can be asked to use the language of a rocket launch or a football game to write an essay on "What I did last summer"; borrow ideas from the Cinderella story to create a cartoon about some current news event, as a political cartoonist might; or apply ideas from nature's animal defense systems to design a burglary-prevention system for the school.

Later in this chapter we will review several programs for exercising thinking skills and abilities (indirect approach) and for directly teaching more complex thinking strategies.

### Metacognition

*Metacognition* is thinking about our own thinking. Self-monitoring and self-reflecting lie at the core of metacognitive activity. It is a key characteristic not only of experts, but of gifted persons as well (e.g., Hong, 1999). Certainly, students should be aware of their own thinking and differences between their thinking and that of others (Sheppard & Kanevsky, 1999). Hong noted that some high-level thinking activities relate closely to metacognition, for example, planning, predicting, setting goals, questioning, evaluating, rehearsing, selecting actions, selecting strategies, using existing knowledge to create ideas, and selectively connecting new information to existing knowledge.

Leader (1995) recommended the use of written daily journals, summaries, expectations, and self-evaluations, along with debriefing and closure sessions, to promote self-reflection and therefore metacognition. For example, her students address: What did I learn? How did I learn? What do I still want to find out? Which way of learning is easiest for me? Why? What are my strengths? Leader's strategy also included direct instruction in the vocabulary of critical and creative thinking (e.g., "This is creative and here's why.").

Sheppard and Kanevsky (1999) helped fifth-grade students think about their own thinking with a "mind-machine" analogy. While solving problems, students were asked to draw and describe a machine that represented how their mind worked. For example, one student said her mind was like a steam iron—it takes a wrinkled piece of information and straightens it out. Another student used a video camera analogy—"When I know how to use it, it works. But when I don't it's hard to work out" (p. 269). Students agreed that after the training, they better understood how their mind worked.

As we will see later, the de Bono CoRT strategies are good examples of a metacognitive approach to teaching thinking skills. Students come to understand the advantages of using a particular technique, when the technique may be profitably used, and the steps involved in using it.

Metacognition includes helping students to understand the sources of their own ideas, view-points, attitudes, and values, and also where others' ideas and values come from. For example, Barell (1984, 1991) recommended that instead of just arguing their own viewpoint, students try defending others' positions: What do students think of the proposal for a new swimming pool? What do taxpayers think? Custodians? Teachers? Also, a teacher can ask—or students can ask themselves—why they thought of a particular question and what the question means to them.

Costa (1986) described three components of thinking about thinking that he called *metacognition, epistemic cognition,* and *brain functioning,* all three of which suggest worthwhile enrichment content. His metacognition referred to students' conscious understanding of problem solving. That is, when solving a problem, students should consciously identify what is known and what needs to be known; plan a course of action before they begin; monitor themselves while executing the plan (and consciously back up to adjust the plan as needed); and evaluate their success upon completion. Other aspects of metacognition included classroom discussions of what is going on inside their heads while thinking, and comparing different students' approaches to problems and decision making.

Costa's epistemic cognition is the study of how knowledge is produced. Here, students might learn about the lives, works, and thinking processes of famous composers, artists, philosophers, and scientists. Discussion would focus on, for example, differences and similarities between artists and scientists, creative processes used by artists, poets, and scientists, and the possible use of scientific inquiry for solving social problems.

Finally, students can learn about brain functions, for example, related to learning and memory, emotions, dreaming, and mental disorders. To these we suggest discussion of thinking styles and personality dimensions such as right-brain versus left-brain thinking processes; reflectiveness versus impulsiveness; global versus analytic (forest versus trees) thinking; being a morning (lark) or a night (owl) person; sensation-seeking (thrill-seeking; Farley, 1986); and internal versus external locus of control—which is an especially important thinking style related to achievement and career success. An internal locus of control person feels responsible for successes, failures, and his or her destiny; an external locus of control person blames others for failures, attributes success to luck, and generally feels like a sock in the laundromat of life.

Metacognition also can include teaching about individual differences in preferred ways of studying and learning. Some students will prefer visual modes, others auditory, and others tactile. Some prefer lectures, independent study, group work, learning games, high activity, and so forth. Take a vote on preferences and discuss differences in selections. Ask students to share impressions of ways of teaching that make them think.

Shore and Kanevsky (1993) noted, "Capable students and experts know more . . . they better know what they know . . . their existing knowledge is highly interconnected and new knowledge is immediately linked in many ways to prior knowledge" (p. 137). Metacognitive abilities and operations direct, control, and drive the use of thinking skills. Metacognition is important indeed.

## TYPES OF THINKING SKILLS

According to Reis (1990b, p. 44), "Teachers need a plan. This plan should consist of a well-thought-out list (taxonomy) of skills, a timetable for teaching them, and effective teaching techniques." As one possible list, the thinking skills in Table 11.2 were assembled from various sources. Most of the skills are relatively complex; they also are interrelated. For example, *evaluation* and *deductive reasoning* both involve abilities to compare, interpret, consider relevance, consider implications, predict outcomes, and so on. Complex processes such as creative thinking, critical thinking, problem solving, and decision making involve

**TABLE 11.2**   Thinking Skills

**Creativity and Creative Problem Solving** (Chapters 10 and 11)

| | |
|---|---|
| **Critical Thinking:** | Evaluating bias, credibility, consistency, qualifications, recency of information |
| | Evaluating primary vs. secondary sources, inferences, validity of reasons |
| | Identifying assumptions, opinions, claims, ambiguities, missing parts of an argument, adequacy of definitions, appropriateness of conclusions |
| **Problem Solving:** | Problem clarifying and defining |
| | Selecting relevant information |
| | Identifying and evaluating alternatives |
| | Drawing conclusions and making inferences |
| **Reading:** | Finding main ideas |
| | Justifying interpretations |
| | Explaining authors' intentions |
| | Drawing logical inferences, implications, conclusions |
| | Relating feelings to specific content |
| **Writing:** | Stating and defending an idea |
| | Sequencing appropriate information |
| | Elaborating |

(*continued*)

**TABLE 11.2 Continued**

| | | |
|---|---|---|
| **Writing: (cont.)** | Communicating clear relationships | |
| | Expressing feelings, values | |
| | Arguing persuasively, logically | |
| | Developing story plots | |
| | Creating mood | |
| **Science and Research:** | Identifying needed processes and information | |
| | Questioning, formulating hypotheses | |
| | Estimating, guessing | |
| | Observing, measuring | |
| | Applying principles | |
| | Extrapolating, interpolating | |
| | Discovering trends, patterns, cause-effect relationships | |
| | Reading charts, graphs, tables | |
| | Generating graphs from data | |
| | Recognizing mathematical relationships (weight, distance, time) | |
| **Reasoning Skills:** | Deductive reasoning | Inductive reasoning |
| | Analogical reasoning | Verbal reasoning |
| | Figural/spatial reasoning | Justifying |
| | Synthesizing, combining | Analyzing assumptions |
| | Recognizing logical relationships | Elaborating |
| **Classifying Skills:** | Comparing, contrasting | Sequencing, ordering |
| | Part-whole relationships | Overlapping classes |
| **Planning Skills:** | Following directions | Planning steps |
| | Following rules | Prioritizing |
| | Setting goals and objectives | Considering implications |
| **Evaluating Skills:** | Identifying errors | Making decisions |
| | Asking questions | Making inferences |
| | Evaluating generalizations | Interpreting |
| | Recognizing assumptions, beliefs, opinions | Setting criteria |
| | Recognizing essential and nonessential | Determining relevance and irrelevance |
| | Making applications to real life situations | Summarizing |
| | Predicting consequences | Verifying |

a great many subskills and abilities. Table 11.3 presents a related list created by the Association for Supervision and Curriculum Development. Still a third list appears later in this chapter. These lists, along with previously mentioned strategies and perhaps published programs described later, can help a teacher plan a defensible thinking skills curriculum.

**TABLE 11.3**   Core Thinking Skills

*Focusing Skills*
(directing attention to selected information)

  1. *Defining problems*—clarifying problem situations.
  2. *Setting goals*—establishing direction and purpose.

*Information gathering skills*
(acquiring relevant data)

  3. *Observing*—using one or more senses to acquire information.
  4. *Questioning*—seeking new information by formulating questions.

*Remembering Skills*
(storing and retrieving information)

  5. *Encoding*—storing information in long-term memory.
  6. *Recalling*—retrieving information from long-term memory.

*Organizing Skills*
(arranging information so it can be used more effectively)

  7. *Comparing*—noting similarities and differences between two or more entities.
  8. *Classifying*—grouping according to common attributes.
  9. *Ordering*—sequencing according to a given criterion.

*Analyzing skills*
(clarifying by identifying and distinguishing among components and attributes)

  10. *Identifying attributes and components*—determining characteristics and parts.
  11. *Identifying relationships and patterns*—recognizing ways elements are related.

*Generating skills*
(using prior knowledge to add new information)

  12. *Inferring*—reasoning beyond available information to fill in gaps.
  13. *Predicting*—anticipating or forecasting future events.
  14. *Elaborating*—using prior knowledge to add meaning to new information and to link it to existing structures.
  15. *Representing*—adding new meaning by changing the form of information.

*Integrating skills*
(connecting and combining information)

  16. *Summarizing*—abstracting information efficiently and parsimoniously.
  17. *Restructuring*—changing existing knowledge structures to include new information.

*Evaluating skills*
(assessing the reasonableness and quality of ideas)

  18. *Establishing criteria*—setting standards for making judgments.
  19. *Verifying*—confirming the accuracy of claims.
  20. *Identifying errors*—recognizing logical fallacies.

Adapted from Association for Supervision and Curriculum Development, 1988, by permission.

Nobody ever said the topic of *thinking skills* was uncomplicated.

## HIGHER ORDER THINKING SKILLS: BLOOM

### Bloom's Taxonomy of Educational Objectives

When educators speak of *thinking skills,* their first association is the top portion of Bloom's taxonomy of educational objectives (Bloom, 1974; Bloom, Engelhart, Furst, Hill, & Krathwohl, 1956). "Bloom's taxonomy" made an international impact on education by drawing attention to the difference between "low-level" academic knowledge, which is commonly taught, and "higher-level" thinking skills, which everyone suddenly seemed to realize were rarely taught. The taxonomy was designed as a guide for writing instructional objectives. It therefore helps one plan a thinking skills curriculum, teaching strategies, and learning experiences. Table 11.4 lists the six levels of the taxonomy, along with examples of

**TABLE 11.4**  Taxonomy of Educational Objectives: Cognitive Domain

| Category | Examples |
|---|---|
| **Knowledge** | Defining terminology, symbols<br>Recalling facts, names, examples, rules, categories<br>Recognizing trends, causes, relationships<br>Acquiring principles, procedures, implications, theories |
| **Compre-hension** | Rephrasing definitions<br>Illustrating meanings<br>Interpreting relationships<br>Drawing conclusions<br>Demonstrating methods<br>Inferring implications<br>Predicting consequences |
| **Application** | Applying principles, rules, theories<br>Organizing procedures, conclusions, effects<br>Choosing situations, methods<br>Restructuring processes, generalizations, phenomena |
| **Analysis** | Recognizing assumptions, patterns<br>Deducing conclusions, hypotheses, points of view<br>Analyzing relationships, themes, evidence, causes and effects<br>Contrasting ideas, parts, arguments |
| **Synthesis** | Producing products, compositions<br>Proposing objectives, means, solutions<br>Designing plans, operations<br>Organizing taxonomies, concepts, schemes, theories<br>Deriving relationships, abstractions, generalizations |
| **Evaluation** | Judging accuracy, consistency, reliability<br>Assessing errors, fallacies, predictions, means and ends<br>Considering efficiency, utility, standards<br>Contrasting alternatives, courses of action |

From Metfessel, Michael, and Kirsner. Instrumentation of Bloom's and Krathwohl's taxonomies for the writing of educational objectives. *Psychology in the Schools* (1969), *6*, 227–310. Reprinted by permission.

learning activities at each level. Many of the thinking skills from Tables 11.2 and 11.3 have found their way into one category or another.

The six levels of the taxonomy describe progressively higher levels of cognitive activity. While the *knowledge* and *comprehension* levels naturally are necessary for all students, teachers of gifted students, especially, will want them to *apply* rules, principles, or theories; *analyze* components, relationships, hypotheses, patterns, and causes and effects; *synthesize* parts into creative solutions, plans, theories, generalizations, designs, and compositions; and *evaluate* the accuracy, value, efficiency, or utility of alternative ideas or courses of action. As a general rule, students progress from learning activities at the knowledge and comprehension levels to the four higher-level thinking skills. Activities at the four highest levels do not necessarily occur in a specified order, although a final evaluation usually manages to be last.

Some gifted-oriented educators use the two pyramids in Figure 11.1 to illustrate the different emphases that can be placed upon different taxonomic levels for regular students and for gifted students. The instructional focus for regular students is greatest at the knowledge and comprehension levels. Gifted students, who should grasp information and relationships more rapidly, can invest more time at the higher levels. The inverted pyramid is misleading in suggesting that evaluation should receive the absolutely largest proportion of emphasis, but you get the idea.

An important and common use of Bloom's taxonomy is to guide classroom questions at the different levels. Hunkins's (1976) key verbs for posing knowledge, comprehension, application, analysis, synthesis, and evaluation questions appear in Table 11.5. Take a minute or two and make up a few questions at each level using her key words.

Finally, many teachers teach the taxonomy itself to students, acquainting them with different

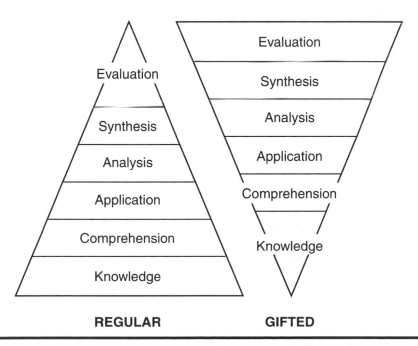

**FIGURE 11.1** Based on Bloom's taxonomy, these pyramids illustrate the notion that with gifted students, more time should be invested on higher-level activities and objectives, compared with the reverse for regular students.

**TABLE 11.5** Key Words for Questioning at Bloom's Six Taxonomic Levels

| Level | Key Words | | | |
|---|---|---|---|---|
| **Knowledge** | What | Distinguish | Recall | Write |
| | When | Identify | Reorganize | Which |
| | Who | List | Show | Indicate |
| | Define | Name | State | Tell How |
| **Comprehension** | Compare | Distinguish | What | |
| | Conclude | Estimate | Fill in | |
| | Contrast | Explain | Give an example of | |
| | Demonstrate | Extend | Hypothesize | |
| | Differentiate | Extrapolate | Illustrate | |
| | Predict | Rearrange | Infer | |
| | Reorder | Rephrase | Relate | |
| | Which | Inform | Tell in Your Own Words | |
| **Application** | Apply | Build | Construct | Demonstrate |
| | Develop | Plan | Solve | Indicate |
| | Test | Choose | Show Your Work | Check Out |
| | Consider | How Would | Tell Us | |
| **Analysis** | Analyze | Discriminate | Relate | |
| | Categorize | Distinguish | Explain | |
| | Describe | Recognize | What Assumption | |
| | Classify | Support Your | What Do You | |
| | Compare | Indicate The | | |
| **Synthesis** | Write | Suggest | Plan | |
| | Think of a Way | How | Formulate a Solution | |
| | Create | Develop | Synthesize | |
| | Purpose a Plan | Make Up | Derive | |
| | Put Together | What Conclusion | | |
| | What Would Be | What Major Hypothesis | | |
| **Evaluation** | What Is | Select | | |
| | Choose | Which Would You Consider | | |
| | Evaluate | Defend | | |
| | Decide | Check | | |
| | Judge | What is Most Appropriate | | |
| | Check The | Indicate | | |

From Hunkins, 1976. Reprinted by permission of the author and Allyn & Bacon, Inc.

levels of learning, thinking, and skill development. As shown in Inset 11.2, fifth-grader Monica Blanton (1982) understood the taxonomy very well.

### Thinking Skills: How Would Socrates Teach Them?

Teaching and stimulating thinking by asking questions sometimes is called the *Socratic method.* Paul et al. (1989) organized "Socratic questions" that elicit *clarifying, analyzing assumptions, probing reasons and evidence, analyzing viewpoints or perspectives, analyzing*

*implications and consequences,* and *questioning* (see Table 11.6). Many of the questions focus on critical thinking as evaluating, which will be clarified in a following section.

### CRITICAL THINKING

The phrase *critical thinking* is used rather loosely. It has been taken to mean carping criticism, wholesale skepticism, thoughtful contemplation, analytic thinking (including the analysis of propaganda), reflective (not compulsive) thinking, problem solving, Bloom's evaluation level of thinking, all of Bloom's higher-level thinking

---

**INSET 11.2** _____

### Bloom's Taxonomy Revisited

I like your magazine very much. I read about "Bloom's Taxonomy on Bloom's Taxonomy." I am one of Alice Krueger's fifth grade students at Offerle Middle School.

I'm sending in questions on *Mrs. Frisby and the Rats of NIMH* to put in *G/C/T*. I would appreciate it if you did.

Yours truly,
Monica Blanton

Mrs. Frisby and the Rats of NIMH

Knowledge—Name Mrs. Frisby's four children in order of age.

Comprehension—Restate Mrs. Frisby's first talk with Brutus the time in the rosebush.

Application—Illustrate Mrs. Frisby flying on Jeremy's back going over the river.

Analysis—Break down Mrs. Frisby's big problem and see how many little problems you can find.

Synthesis—Write a new ending to the story pretending Timothy had died.

Evaluation—Pick three animals of those six that were mentioned in the story. Try to find a new name you think would be better than the one in the book. Tell why you think your names would be better.

---

Source: *G/C/T* (Sept.–Oct. 1982), 22. Reprinted by permission.

**TABLE 11.6** A Taxonomy of Socratic Questions

### Questions of Clarification

- What do you mean by _____?
- What is your main point?
- Could you give me an example?
- Could you explain that further?
- How does _____ relate to _____?
- Could you put that another way?
- What do you think is the main issue here?
- How does this relate to our discussion (problem, issue)?
- Jane, would you summarize what Richard said? . . . Richard, is that what you meant?

### Questions that Probe Assumptions

- What are you (they) assuming?
- What could we assume instead?
- All of your reasoning depends on the idea that _____. Why have you based your reasoning on _____ rather than _____?
- You seem to be assuming _____. How would you justify taking this for granted?
- Is it always the case? Why do you think the assumption holds here?

### Questions that Probe Reasons and Evidence

- How do you know?
- Are those reasons adequate?
- Do you have any (good) evidence for that?
- Is there reason to doubt that evidence?
- How could we go about finding out whether that is true?
- What other information do we need to know?

### Questions about Viewpoints or Perspectives

- Why have you chosen this perspective rather than that perspective?
- Could anyone else see this another way? Why?
- What would someone who disagrees say?
- How could you answer the objection that _____ would make?
- What is an alternative?
- How are Roxanne's and Ken's ideas alike?

### Questions that Probe Implications and Consequences

- What are you implying by that?
- When you say _____, are you implying _____?
- If that happened, what else also would happen as a result? Why?
- Would that necessarily happen or only probably happen?
- If this and this are the case, then what else also must be true?

### Questions about the Question

- How can we find out?
- How could someone settle this question?
- Is this the same issue as _____?
- What does this question assume?
- Why is this question important?
- Does this question ask us to evaluate something?
- Do we all agree that this is the question?
- To answer this question, what questions would we have to answer first?

Adapted from Paul et al. (1989) by permission.

skills, all important ("critical") thinking skills, careful thinking, logical thinking (especially!), independent thinking, and the abilities to evaluate biases, assumptions, inconsistencies, opinions, and other questionable sources of information.

We will examine critical thinking as *evaluating* and as *problem solving,* which, as we will see, can be related.

## Critical Thinking as Evaluating

Swartz and Perkins (1990) defined *critical thinking* as "critical examination and evaluation . . . of beliefs and courses of action" (p. 37). As one of their examples: It is said that Columbus discovered America. How do we know? What are the grounds for believing that? If historical documents are involved, what evidence is there that they are sound?

According to Swartz and Perkins, in critical thinking we aim at critical judgment about what to accept as reasonable and/or what to do, and we seek reliable information to use as evidence in supporting our judgments.

A few decades ago Ronald R. Allen and his colleagues (Allen, Kauffeld, and O'Brien, 1968; Allen and Rott, 1969) created workbooks to teach critical thinking in relation to ideas and assumptions implicit in such everyday media as comic strips (e.g., the far right *Orphan Annie* and the sexist *Beetle Bailey*), advertising and sales pitches, political messages, movies, and television shows.

Most of Allen's specific critical thinking abilities are worth incorporating into any thinking skills curriculum, for example:

1. The ability to appraise a speaker's testimony (a statement issued by a source) in terms of the source's ability to observe accurately.
2. The ability to evaluate the particular biases of a source.
3. The ability to appraise the source's qualifications necessary for making an informed statement.
4. The ability to appraise whether the source is consistent with himself or herself and other sources.

5. The ability to appraise whether the source's information is the most recent available.
6. The ability to differentiate between primary—first-hand—and secondary sources.

Other of Allen's principles emphasizing critical thinking and reasoning involve:

> Evaluating inferences
> Evaluating reasons given for a claim
> Checking the reliability and adequacy of information
> Following logically valid lines of reasoning
> Detecting missing parts of an argument
> Discerning the relevance of objections
> Recognizing appropriate conclusions

In his Cornell Project on Critical Thinking, Robert Ennis (1962, 1964) compiled a number of aspects of critical thinking that also stress evaluation of sources or statements. Said Ennis, students should learn to judge whether:

1. There is ambiguity or contradiction in a line of reasoning.
2. Something is an assumption.
3. A statement is specific enough.
4. A conclusion necessarily follows.
5. An observation statement is reliable.
6. An inductive conclusion is warranted.
7. The real problem has been identified.
8. A definition is adequate.
9. A statement by an alleged authority is acceptable.

We will see in a later section that Lipman's (1988, 1991) *Philosophy for Children* program also includes critical thinking in the evaluation sense by teaching students to recognize inconsistent and contradictory statements, underlying assumptions, cause-effect relationships, and truth in syllogistic reasoning.

## Critical Thinking as Problem Solving

To Budmen (1967), critical thinking is problem solving or an act of inquiry. He emphasized, however, that critical thinking differs from more objective scientific problem solving in that critical thinking involves values, emotions, and judgment. Budmen's message to teachers was that students should learn that there are problems for which there is no single solution—only alternatives and judgments. Said Budmen, "What to consider in arriving at these judgments, how to identify the alternatives and make the choices, is what the process of critical thinking is all about."

Budmen stressed that problems best suited for critical thinking should be problems without a single right answer. He outlined four steps that could be taught. The first step—the heart of the issue—is to identify one's own assumptions, feelings, beliefs, and values relating to an issue. Second, one examines all sides of an issue. Third, one examines possible actions and their probable results. "More than anything else, students must understand that all behavior has consequences." Finally, the process requires a choice among alternatives—a decision.

Also viewing critical thinking as problem solving, Dressel and Mayhew (1954) reduced a long list of critical thinking abilities to five central ones.

1. The ability to define a problem, which includes the abilities to break complex elements into simpler, familiar and workable parts, identify central elements, and eliminate extraneous elements.
2. The ability to select pertinent information for the solution of a problem, including the ability to recognize unreliable and biased sources of information, as well as information that is relevant and irrelevant to the solution of the problem.
3. The ability to recognize stated and unstated assumptions, and unsupported and irrelevant assumptions.
4. The ability to formulate relevant hypotheses and check the hypotheses against the information and assumptions.
5. The ability to draw valid conclusions and inferences, detect logical inconsistencies, and judge the adequacy of a conclusion.

## MODELS, PROGRAMS, AND EXERCISES FOR TEACHING THINKING SKILLS

As we indicated earlier, thinking skills may be taught as a separate course or subject, for example, in an elementary pullout program or part of an honors course in secondary school, or they can be integrated into existing subjects. A separate course could stress creativity, problem solving, critical thinking, logical thinking, analogical thinking, character and values education (Davis, 2003a, 2003c), as well as other skills listed in Tables 11.2 and 11.3; the skills in Bloom's higher taxonomic levels (Tables 11.4 and 11.5), and the taxonomy itself; thinking skills aimed at coping with personal problems, such as making good decisions (Davis, 2003a, 2003c; Nelson-Jones, 1990); and the exercising of more specific thinking skills and abilities in Table 11.7. Commercially available

**TABLE 11.7** Some Specific Thinking Skills Taught in Critical Thinking Books and Software Workbooks

| | |
|---|---|
| **Figural Similarities** | |
| Matching Shapes | Dividing Shapes into Equal Parts |
| Combining Shapes | Finding Patterns |
| Matching Congruent Figures | Matching Similar Figures |
| Drawing Lines of Symmetry | Matching Volume |
| Matching Congruent Solids | Recognizing Views of a Solid |
| Combining Solids | Using Grids to Enlarge Figures |

*(continued)*

TABLE 11.7   **Continued**

### Figural Sequences

Figural Sequence Problems
Producing Reflections
Matching Pattern Pieces

Rotating Figures Problems
Paper Folding
Producing a Pattern

### Figural Classifications

Classifying by Shape
Describing Characteristics
Matching Classes by Shape
Finding Shape Exceptions
Multiple Classifications

Classifying by Pattern
Describing Classes
Matching Classes by Pattern
Finding Pattern Exceptions
Overlapping Classes

### Figural Analogies

Analogies—Select and Supply Problems
Describing Figural Analogies
Making up Analogies

### Verbal Similarities and Differences

Selecting Antonyms
Denotations

Selecting Synonyms
Connotations

### Verbal Sequences

Following Directions
Completing Phrases
Similarities
True-False Tables
Describing Locations
Deductive Reasoning
Discriminating Degree of Meaning

Writing Directions
Opposites
Following Yes-No Rules
Finding Locations with Maps
Describing Directions
Time Sequences

### Logical Relationships

Negation
Disjunction ("or") Rules
Cause-Effect Words
Schedules

Conjunction ("and") Rules
Implication ("if-then") rules
Intervals of a Day, Year
Time Zones

### Flowcharting

In Problem Solving
A Cycle
In Comparison Shopping

A Sequence
In Planning

### Verbal Classifications

Parts of a Whole
General to Specific
Explaining Exceptions
Overlapping Classes
Diagramming Classes
Sentences with Classes and Subclasses

Classes and Members
Distinguishing Relationships
Sorting into Word Classes
Branching Diagrams

### Verbal Analogies

Antonym/Synonym Analogies
"Kind of" Analogies
"Used to (for)"
Creating Analogies

Association Analogies
"Part of" Analogies
"Degree of" Analogies

materials and programs would be useful for such a course or subject.

The following sections summarize programs, models, strategies, and exercises for teaching thinking skills. Space will not allow full descriptions, so interested readers should see the original sources for more complete information. The first two models, the de Bono CoRT approach and Lipman's *Philosophy for Children,* take a direct approach: Students fully understand that they are learning about *thinking;* they learn the meaning and purpose of each thinking skill; and they learn why, when, and how the skill should be used.

The remaining programs, including *Project IMPACT, Instrumental Enrichment,* and Critical Thinking Press and Software workbooks, take a more indirect approach in strengthening simple and complex abilities via practice.

## CoRT STRATEGIES: DE BONO

The place is Maracaibo, second largest city in Venezuela. There is a meeting of about 20 people (doctors, parents, government officials) to discuss the setting up of a new medical clinic. For three hours the arguments flow back and forth—in the usual fashion.

Suddenly, a 10-year-old boy who has been sitting quietly at the back of the room because his mother could not leave him alone at home approaches the table.

He suggests to the group that they "do an AGO (set the objectives), followed by an APC (outline alternatives), and then an FIP (set priorities) and, of course, an OPV (analyze other people's views). In a short while there is a plan of action.

That 10-year-old had participated in the routine thinking skills program that is now mandated by law in all Venezuelan schools (de Bono, 1985).

Edward de Bono (1973, 1983) created a delightful set of materials for the direct teaching of thinking as a skill. The CoRT (Cognitive Research Trust) program requires little or no special teacher training and apparently is enjoyable for both students and teachers.

As one example, the PMI technique is a simple and effective way to teach evaluation. Students learn that ideas, suggestions, proposals, activities, or virtually anything else may be intelligently evaluated by looking at the good points or *pluses* (P), the bad points or *minuses* (M), and points that are neither good nor bad, just *interesting* (I). Students learn the reasons (principles) behind PMI, and they practice applying the technique. The principles explain that:

> By using the PMI approach one will not hastily reject an idea that initially looks bad.
> Vice versa, one will not too quickly adopt a good-looking idea that has serious but overlooked disadvantages.
> Some ideas are neither good nor bad, just interesting and relevant and may lead to other ideas.
> Without using a PMI, one's emotions may interfere with clear judgments.
> With a PMI you pass judgment on an idea after it is explored, not before.

Small groups of fifth-grade G/T students in a College for Kids program directed by one author (Davis) did PMIs on "being gifted." They discovered they were not unique in having social problems at school, and they improved their appreciation for themselves and their high potential.

There are six sets of lessons with 10 lessons in each set, for a total of 60 lessons covering about 50 thinking skills. Many lessons teach complex thinking strategies that require the use of several previously learned skills; for example, *planning* requires subskills of *considering all factors* and *itemizing goals and objectives.* Each lesson usually is organized into these six sections:

**1.** *Introduction.* An introduction defines and explains the skill. For example, with the *Consider All Factors* (CAF) skill students learn that whenever they make a decision or choose something there are always many factors to consider. If they leave out some factors, their choice may turn out to be wrong. Further, they can try to see what factors other people have left out of their thinking.

**2.** *Example.* A sample problem (or statement) is presented and the skill is applied. For instance, in London a law was passed that required all new buildings to provide parking in the basement. They neglected to consider that basement parking would encourage people to drive to work, and so traffic congestion was worse than ever.

**3.** *Practice.* Four or five practice problems give students first-hand experience using the skill. For example, what factors are involved in choosing a hair style? What factors would you consider if interviewing someone to be a teacher?

**4.** *Process.* In a class or group discussion, students consider, for example, whether it is easy to leave out important factors; when it is important to consider all factors; what the difference is between a PMI and a CAF; what happens when others leave out important factors; and whether one needs to consider all factors or just the important ones.

**5.** *Principles.* Usually five sensible principles are presented, which amount to reasons for and advantages of using the skill, as illustrated in the PMI technique above.

**6.** *Project.* These are additional practice problems.

CoRT thinking skills are not tied to any particular subject area. Thinking is taught as a subject in its own right and as a conscious and deliberate metacognitive skill. Many of the CoRT thinking skills are described briefly in Inset 11.3.

## PHILOSOPHY FOR CHILDREN: LIPMAN

Matthew Lipman's (1988, 1991; Lipman, Sharp, & Oscanyan, 1980; Sharp & Reed, 1992) *Philosophy for Children* program is unique in taking the form of stories for children and teenagers. The program has produced significant improvements in reading, interpersonal relations, ethical and moral understanding, reasoning, and critical thinking (Lipman, 1981; Weinstein & Laufman, 1981). At this writing, *Philosophy for Children* is used in 50 countries.

Six textbooks, each accompanied by a teacher's guide book, aim at ages 5–6 (*Lis*), 6–8 (*Rebecca*),

9–10, (*Thinking Stories, 1*), 11–12 (*Lisa*), 13–14 (*Suki*), and 15–17 (*Golden City*). In the stories fictional children and teens spend much of their time thinking about thinking, with clear examples of good thinking and bad thinking—including thinking about ethical, moral, aesthetic, logical, and philosophic matters ("What is reality?" "What is the mind?" "What is goodness?" "What is fairness?"; [Accorinti, 2002]), as well as more traditional thinking skills. The idea, of course, is for student-readers to identify with the characters, "think along" with them, and adopt good thinking habits and skills. Exercises follow the stories, but the main emphasis is upon story content and the teachers' follow-up discussions.

A few of the thinking skills and related attitudes taught in *Philosophy for Children* are:

*Cause-effect relationships.* Does this statement necessarily imply a cause-effect relationship: "He threw the stone and broke the window."

*Recognizing consistent and contradictory statements or ideas.* For example, can you be a true animal lover, yet still eat meat.

*Identifying underlying assumptions.* What is the assumption underlying a statement such as "I love your hair. What beauty parlor did you go to?"

*Learning part-whole and whole-part relationships.* Students might be asked to evaluate the truth of "If Mike's face has handsome features, Mike must have a handsome face."

*Making generalizations.* Students draw generalizations from sets of facts, such as "I get sick when I eat raspberries; I get sick when I eat strawberries; I get sick when I eat blackberries."

*Analogical thinking.* Students practice analogical thinking with problems like "germ is to disease as candle is to (a) wax, (b) wick, (c) white, (d) light.

*Syllogistic reasoning.* "All dogs are animals; all Lhasa Apsos are dogs." What valid inference can we draw from this?

*Reversibility and nonreversibility.* "No" statements are reversible: No submarines are kangaroos, and therefore no kangaroos are submarines. However, "all" statements are nonreversible: All

## CoRT Thinking Skills: de Bono

Edward de Bono's (1973) CoRT thinking skills are taught in a direct, metacognitive fashion. Children consciously understand the value of each skill and when, why, and how it should be applied. The following are brief descriptions of some of the 50 CoRT thinking skills.

Thinking of good points (pluses), bad points (minuses), and interesting points of ideas, suggestions, and proposals.

Considering all factors when making choices or decisions.

Thinking of consequences (short-term, medium-term, long-term) of actions.

Thinking of goals and objectives, including seeing other people's objectives.

Planning, which includes skills of considering all factors and itemizing goals and objectives.

Prioritizing, for example, relevant factors, objectives, and consequences.

Thinking of many alternatives, possibilities, and choices, for example, in interpreting causes or in considering alternative actions.

Decision making, which requires considering the factors involved, objectives, priorities, consequences, and possible alternatives.

Seeing other points of view, which exist because other people may consider different factors, see different consequences, or have different objectives or priorities.

Selecting something according to your needs and requirements, that is, according to "best fit."

Organizing by analyzing what needs to be done, what is being done, and what is to be done next. One may need to consider all factors and think of alternatives.

Focusing on different aspects of a situation, that is, knowing when you are analyzing, considering factors, thinking of consequences, etc.

Concluding a thinking project, perhaps with ideas, an answer to a question, a problem solution, an action, or conceding an inability to solve the problem.

Recognizing opinions vs. facts as two types of evidence.

Recognizing evidence that is weak, strong, or key.

Recognizing points of agreement, disagreement, and irrelevant points.

Being right by referring to facts, authority, etc.

Supporting an argument by using value-laden words, such as right, proper, fair, or sincere versus ridiculous, dishonest, devious, stupid.

Being wrong in an argument because of exaggerating, making a (e.g., factual) mistake, or by having prejudiced (fixed) ideas.

Challenging existing ways of doing things as a means of stimulating new ideas.

Improving things by identifying faults and thinking of ways to remove them.

Solving problems by thinking about problem requirements.

Recognizing information that is given vs. information that has been omitted, but is needed.

Recognizing contradictory information, which can lead to false conclusions.

Recognizing guesses based on good information ("small guesses," e.g., the sun will rise tomorrow) vs. guesses based on little information ("big guesses," e.g., the final score of a future football game).

Distinguishing between ordinary emotions (e.g., anger, love, fear, sorrow) and those concerned with one's view of oneself (ego-emotions; e.g., pride, power, insecurity).

Understanding that values determine thinking, judgments, choices, and actions.

Each of us has things we value highly, and things to which we give a low value.

And more.

model airplanes are toys, but not all toys are model airplanes.

*Independent thinking.* Should we always follow the majority?

*Taking other perspectives.* Can you see this issue from their point of view?

*Caring.* Concern for the welfare of others.

Other thinking skills in the *Philosophy for Children* materials address creativity, understanding descriptions and explanations, universal and particular statements ("All birds are blue" vs. "This bird is blue"), hypotheses, impartiality, consistency, reasons for beliefs, alternatives, and others.

Intelligence expert Robert Sternberg (1984b) said of Lipman's materials, "No program I am aware of is more likely to teach durable and transferable thinking skills than *Philosophy for Children*." However, Sternberg also warned that students in inner-city schools may have trouble identifying with the middle-class story characters and their types of problems. Further, poor readers or students of low-average ability may have trouble dealing with the program.

## PROJECT IMPACT

Another impressive thinking skills program is the middle-school level *Project IMPACT* (Improve Minimal Proficiencies by Activating Critical Thinking; Orange County Department of Education, 1981; Winocur and Maurer, 1997). In her review of Project Impact, Zinner (1985) commented:

> The projects' merits were tested and the results were remarkable. . . . Teachers noticed improvement in students' high-level questioning abilities . . . use of vocabulary, motivation in class, attendance . . . reading and math scores . . . students enjoy the lessons so much they request them . . . teachers themselves say *IMPACT* has improved their teaching style

and renewed their enthusiasm for their career as well . . . it was selected as an Exemplary/Incentive Project and a Model Staff Development Program by the California State Department of Education . . . the U.S. Department of Education ranked it first among 24 funded projects.

In a hierarchical fashion, Project *IMPACT* aims first at strengthening *enabling* skills of observing, comparing, contrasting, grouping, classifying, ordering, sequencing, patterning, and prioritizing. Next are *process* skills of analyzing facts and opinions, relevant and irrelevant information, reliable and unreliable sources, questioning, inferring meaning of statements, cause-effect relationships, generalizations, predictions, assumptions, and points of view, including prejudice. Finally, the program focuses on *operations,* including inductive and deductive reasoning and the evaluation skills of judgment and decision making.

To illustrate, one lesson entitled Can You Zooley? focuses on deductive reasoning. The learner studies the arrangement of large and small, round and rectangular, patterned drawings representing zoo animals (see Figure 11.2). A series of questions requires the learner to analyze the illustration and deduce information about the creatures. Try it. If you get stumped, answers appear at the very end of the chapter:

1. Which family is visiting the polar bears?
2. Which is the family of spiders?
3. Whose son has Mr. Crocodile just swallowed?
4. Which swimming family has only three sons?
5. Which family has just three daughters?
6. Is the polar bear's cub male or female?
7. Which is a family of snakes?
8. Which is a kangaroo?
9. What will be the surname of the elephant's baby that is soon to be born?
10. What is the zookeeper's name?

The materials are engaging.

# Can You Zooley?

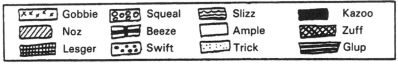

**FIGURE 11.2** "Can You Zooley?" Lesson from Project IMPACT.

Reprinted by permission of S. Lee Winocur, Ph.D., Center for the Teaching of Thinking, Project IMPACT.

## INSTRUMENTAL ENRICHMENT: FEUERSTEIN

Reuven Feuerstein spent several teenage years in Nazi concentration camps. He later helped children and adults migrate to Israel and studied at the University of Geneva and the Sorbonne. In Israel he studied the educational needs of immigrants, many of whom would be classified by intelligence tests as retarded. He designed a program to change the cognitive structure of retarded performers and to transform them into autonomous, independent

thinkers, capable of initiating and elaborating ideas (Makler, 1980).

Feuerstein's (1980a, 1980b) *Instrumental Enrichment* program was designed to address:

Impulsivity
Egocentric thinking and behavior
Recognizing, defining, and solving problems
Considering two or more sources of information at once
Analyzing, making comparisons, categorizing
Planning, testing hypotheses

Recognizing the need for logical evidence
Accurately using time and space dimensions

Instrumental Enrichment is a three-year program that can be accelerated for gifted students. It is designed for students around age 9 and above, those ready for Piagetian formal operational thinking. Teachers cannot obtain the materials unless they complete Instrumental Enrichment training. (For information regarding materials and teacher training, contact Frances Link, Curriculum Development Associates, 1211 Connecticut Ave., Washington, DC 20036.)

There are 13 types of exercises, each of which is said to strengthen a number of underlying abilities. Two examples follow.

***Organization of Dots.*** Students are presented with amorphous arrays of dots of varying complexity. Their task is to identify and outline specified geometric figures, such as squares, diamonds, and stars, by connecting dots. This exercise is said to strengthen the projection of visual relationships, discrimination of form and size, constancy of form and size across changes in orientation, use of relevant information, discovery strategies, perspective, restraint of impulsivity, labeling, precision and accuracy, planning, determination of starting point, systematic search and comparison to model, and motivation (Feuerstein, 1980a).

***Orientation in Space.*** A picture is presented containing, for example, a house, a bench, a garden, and a tree (Figure 11.3).

To the right is a boy who is facing left, right, front, or back. Imagine each picture of the boy in the center of the garden. By filling in a table, the student describes the position of each object in the picture relative to each orientation of the boy. The exercise is said to teach the ability to use concepts and stable systems of reference (concrete, abstract, and interpersonal) for orientation in space; defining the problem; simultaneous use of several sources of information; systematic work; hypothetical and inferential thought as a basis for logical conclusions; how to summarize data using a table; precise and accurate communication of information; and reduced egocentricity.

In addition, comparison exercises strengthen classification abilities and the abilities to find similarities and differences between objects, events, and ideas. Verbal and nonverbal syllogisms strengthen formal logic, including the use of sets, subsets, and intersecting sets. Students infer validity, find relationships, discover principles, and choose and process data.

The cognitive functions taught in Instrumental Enrichment fall into three categories of *input* (e.g., organizing information), *elaboration* (e.g., evaluating relevance of information), and *output* (e.g., expressing problem solutions).

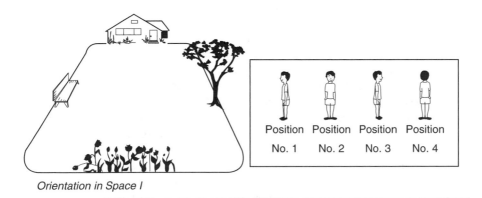

*Orientation in Space I*

**FIGURE 11.3** Illustration from Orientation in Space Problem.
Reproduced by permission of Curriculum Development Associates.

Evidence for the effectiveness of the FIE program amounts to observations by teachers' aides and project administrators in Tennessee, Toronto, New York City, and Louisville, who independently agreed that after Instrumental Enrichment training, children:

Used Instrumental Enrichment strategies in other subjects.

Read and followed directions spontaneously.

Improved their accuracy of observation and their inclusion of more relevant detail.

Improved their precision; they began spontaneously correcting their own mistakes.

Increased their social sensitivity, willingness to listen to others, tolerance of others' opinions, and willingness to help others.

Became more willing to defend their opinions on the basis of evidence.

Improved the relevance and completeness of their answers and their readiness to cope with more difficult problems.

Improved their feelings of success and their self-image.

Hobbs (1980) described Feuerstein's (1980a) book *Instrumental Enrichment* as "an intellectual achievement of formidable proportions . . . Few single works in psychology equal it in originality, ingenuity, scope, theoretical importance, and potential significance." Frances Link (personal communication), an Instrumental Enrichment workshop leader, said, "It's fantastic. It changes teachers."

## CRITICAL THINKING BOOKS AND SOFTWARE

One broad-based approach to teaching thinking skills through exercise is found in the several dozen workbooks and computer software programs produced by Critical Thinking Books and Software (formerly Midwest Publications). (For information, contact Critical Thinking Books and Software, P.O. Box 448, Pacific Grove, CA 93950; http://criticalthinking.com/index.html.) The many workbooks by Howard Black and Sandra Black (e.g., 1988), Anita Harnadek (e.g., 1979), and others include hundreds of exercises designed to strengthen dozens of simple and complex thinking skills, some of which focus on math, writing, science, and history. A sample of the thinking skills these authors try to strengthen appeared in Table 11.7 on pages 258–259.

The following are examples of exercises found in the workbooks by Black and Black and Harnadek. The reader likely can create original ones.

*Analogical Thinking.* Analogical reasoning exercises take the classic form *speedometer : velocity :: thermometer : _____ (degree, light, temperature).* Nonverbal (figural) analogical reasoning can be exercised with geometric figures, as shown in Figure 11.4. Other figural analogy problems require students to draw the one missing figure or to create a pair of figures that have the same relationship as the given pair.

*Inductive Thinking.* Inductive thinking abilities are exercised in sequence problems that require students to induce a figural relationship among three (or four) patterns in a sequence, and then draw the next pattern in the series.

Verbal sequence exercises ask students to line up a sequence of three words (e.g., *believe, deliberate, read*) in order of size, degree, or, in this case, order of occurrence.

*Deductive Reasoning.* One type of exercise sought to teach deductive reasoning with problems that require the logical elimination of alternatives. A matrix is provided that the thinker uses, in conjunction with a series of clues, to eliminate untenable possibilities and eventually find the one correct solution. For example, Angelo, Becky, Conrad, and Doreen are an actor, a bellhop, a comedian, and a trapeze artist; Doreen is not in show business, and Angelo is not the actor. Using these clues and the matrix in Figure 11.5, match each person's name and occupation. (Note that two occupations, in 1978, implied gender.)

Similar "mind-bender" exercises require the learner to figure out who is younger or taller than whom or in Black and Black (1984) the correct order of historical events.

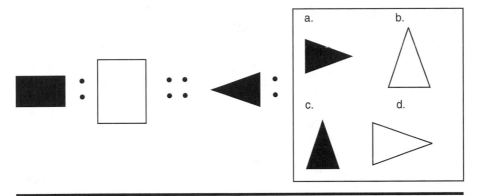

**FIGURE 11.4**  Example of Figural Analogy Problem.
From Black and Black (1984). Reprinted by permission of Critical Thinking Press and Software.

***Classifying.***   Classifying is important. If we could not classify, based on shared characteristics, we would be unable to cope with our complex world.

Classification skills are taught by presenting groups of geometric patterns and asking students to induce the commonality among members. Multiple-classification exercises teach students that objects simultaneously can be members of several classes, depending upon which characteristics one attends to. For example, a black parallelogram can belong to "Group A" because it is a parallelogram and to "Group B" because it is black.

Other exercises focus on helping students learn the meanings of such classification-related concepts as *overlaps with, is separate from,* and *is included in.*

With verbal classification exercises, students are asked to select which one of five words does not belong: *pencil, chalk, rabbit, crayon, pen.* (Nothing is more frustrating than trying to write with a dull rabbit!)

***Verbal Relationships.***   Many exercises help students learn verbal relationships by using *antonyms, synonyms, similarities,* and *opposites,* sometimes

|  | Actor | Bellhop | Comedian | Trapeze Artist |
|---|---|---|---|---|
| Angelo |  |  |  |  |
| Becky |  |  |  |  |
| Conrad |  |  |  |  |
| Doreen |  |  |  |  |

**FIGURE 11.5**  Deductive Reasoning Exercise from Harnadek (1978).
Reprinted by permission of Critical Thinking Press and Software.

in verbal analogies (e.g., *cease : stop :: proceed :* _____.

***Cause and Effect.*** Understanding cause-and-effect relationships may be considered a type of inductive thinking—given an effect, one induces cause (Harnadek, 1979). Some exercises aim at strengthening cause-and-effect thinking by giving students a short illogical scenario and asking them "Do you think this is right? How come?" or "What do you think?" For example, "Only countries with military forces have wars, therefore we should not have military forces in our country."

***Part-Whole Relationships.*** To strengthen students' understanding of part-whole relationships, one exercise is: Given four words (*acrobats, animals, clowns, circus*) students identify which word represents the whole and which words are its parts.

***Following Directions.*** One easily neglected thinking skill is the self-management behavior of following directions. In one exercise students practice attending carefully to directions:

> Use a whole sheet of paper. Draw the design exactly as directed.
> **a.** Draw a line from top to bottom that is one-fourth the page width from the left edge.
> **b.** Divide this vertical line into four equal parts.
> **c.** Divide the right edge into four equal parts.
> **d.** Connect the points one-fourth of the way from the top.
> **e.** Connect the points one-fourth of the way from the bottom.
> **f.** Write "I" in the top right rectangle.
> **g.** Write "DIRECTIONS" in the lower right rectangle.
> **h.** Write "FOLLOWED" in the square.

Any teacher who wishes to find ideas and exercises for strengthening innumerable types of thinking skills should request a Critical Thinking Books and Software catalog or visit their website.

## THINKING SKILLS AND CHARACTER EDUCATION

We mentioned earlier that many thinking skills relate closely to attitudes and personality dispositions. We mentioned also that Lipman's (1988, 1991) *Philosophy for Children* program emphasizes ethical and moral thinking along with other thinking skills. The three-part Character Education Thinking Skills model in Table 11.8 puts thinking skills into three categories: Simpler ones that are not necessarily tied to teaching character and values; intermediate thinking skills that logically would contribute to moral and ethical thinking; and thinking skills that directly emphasize ethical and moral thought, and that comprise the substance of character education books by Davis (2003a, 2003c; see Chapter 8) and the *Philosophy for Children* books by Lipman.

In today's world, thinking skills related to empathy, respecting rights, honesty and responsibility, pleasantness, and valuing education and achievement are critical thinking skills indeed.

## OBSTACLES TO EFFECTIVE THINKING

Vail (1990) described a variety of personal, home, and school factors that block students' ability to think. Some comparatively simple problems are being hungry or tired—with similarly simple solutions of switching the time for demanding classroom thinking activities, keeping snacks on hand, and talking to parents about TV watching versus sleep.

Another problem, common to gifted children, is *perfectionism,* which we will elaborate in Chapters 13 and 17. When the curriculum shifts from "How do you spell . . . ?" to "Why do you think . . . ?" the perfectionist student may attempt to parrot an answer from the book or otherwise deliver a teacher-pleasing reply instead of thinking. For students who have gotten by on memorizing and reciting, Vail recommended exercises that reward originality instead of conformity.

Many personal problems can interfere with children's ability to think clearly, for example, a

**TABLE 11.8**   Character Education Thinking Skills Model

| Examples of Simpler Thinking Skills | Examples of Thinking Skills that Contribute to Character Development | Examples of Thinking Skills That Build Good Character |
|---|---|---|
| Observing | Reasoning, thinking logically | Empathy |
| Comparing | Clarifying problems | Respecting others' rights |
| Sequencing | Drawing conclusions | Honesty and responsibility |
| Classifying | Deducing causes and effects | Valuing self-respect |
| Estimating | Analyzing relationships | Caring and compassion |
| Extrapolating | Making inferences | Accepting differences |
| Seeing part-whole relationships | Considering implications | Understanding others' problems |
| Reading charts | Determining relevance and irrelevance | Patience, pleasantness, and courtesy |
| Recalling facts | Evaluating | Valuing education and achievement |
| Reorganizing | Explaining | Accepting consequences |
| Rephrasing | Predicting outcomes | |

Based on Davis (in preparation).

death or divorce in the family (for which they may feel responsible and guilty) or family pressures for correct answers and high grades. In the classroom some obstacles to thinking are a mismatch between the student's learning style (e.g., visual) and the teacher's teaching style (e.g., verbal), or an emotional environment that is stressfully competitive or otherwise potentially humiliating. School and district expectations of high achievement test scores (does the word *accountability* ring a bell?) also can damage a teacher's plans for teaching thinking—despite the fact that teaching thinking is more valuable in the long run (Vail, 1990).

On the positive side, noted Vail, feelings of confidence, belonging, and dignity, along with courage, resilience, curiosity, diligence, and humor, will aid the freedom to think and learn.

## SELECTING THINKING SKILLS, EXERCISES, AND MATERIALS

de Bono (1983), Sternberg (1983), and Treffinger, Isaksen, and McEwen (1987) itemized criteria for assessing the value and usefulness of thinking skills strategies and programs. A composite of their lists includes:

1. The program should not require extended training. However, training should be available through workshops or printed resources.
2. A good program should be usable by teachers of varying abilities, not just gifted or highly qualified teachers.
3. The program should be robust enough to "resist damage" as it is passed from the training source to the teacher, and from the teacher to students.
4. The program should use "parallel design." If some parts are taught badly or skipped, what remains still will be usable and valuable.
5. The program should be enjoyable for teachers and children.
6. Materials should be attractive, appropriate to students' interests, and motivating.
7. Important thinking skills should be addressed; objectives should be specified.
8. The program should improve metacognitive skills—students should be helped to understand thinking and thinking skills.

9. There should be examples of practical applications of the methods and techniques.
10. Involvement should be active, not passive, with opportunities for transfer and application of the training.
11. It is desirable to have both individual and group activities.
12. It is desirable to relate the thinking skills training to other curriculum content—so students can experience the thinking skills "in action."

As with all G/T enrichment, the program must be suited to students' needs.

## SUMMARY

Teaching thinking skills may be equivalent to teaching intelligent behavior.

Issues in teaching thinking skills include whether they should be infused into existing subjects or taught as a separate course or subject, selecting which skills to teach at different ages, selecting the best way to teach thinking skills, and evaluating mastery of thinking skills. Some thinking skills include attitudes and dispositions.

Reis recommended teaching fewer skills in greater depth.

Beyer recommended six steps of introducing the thinking skill, guiding practice, allowing self-directed practice, showing students how to transfer the skill, allowing practice in new contexts, and letting students use the skill independently. Costa recommended four steps of (judiciously) selecting content, teaching the thinking skills, and exposing students to conflicts and dilemmas that require application of the skills—all leading to suitable "habits of mind."

Students may be taught directively (rule then examples) or inductively (examples then rule).

Thinking skills may be taught indirectly via practice with, for example, classification, analogy, logical reasoning, and other kinds of problems. Thinking skills also may be taught directly as conscious techniques for reasoning and solving problems.

Metacognition is thinking about thinking. It includes understanding why, when, and how problem-solving strategies should be used and thinking about one's own thinking, the thinking of others, and sources of ideas. Metacognition can encompass teaching about brain functions, personality and thinking styles, and preferred ways of learning.

Teaching thinking requires a list of skills to be taught. One list included creativity, critical thinking, and problem solving; skills in reading, writing, and science; and reasoning, classifying, and evaluating skills. Another list included the categories of focusing, information gathering, remembering, organizing, analyzing, generating, integrating, and evaluating.

The best known higher-level thinking skills are the application, analysis, synthesis, and evaluation levels of Bloom's taxonomy. The taxonomy guides teacher questioning. Gifted students should spend more time with higher level thinking skills, less at the knowledge and comprehension levels.

Paul et al. proposed a taxonomy of Socratic questions in the areas of clarification, examining assumptions, reasons and evidence, viewpoints, implications and consequences, and the question or problem itself.

"Critical thinking" is interpreted in many ways. This section explains critical thinking as evaluating the biases, qualifications, and consistency of speakers, and evaluating assumptions, opinions, beliefs, ambiguities, whether inferences and conclusions follow, and others. Critical thinking as problem solving includes teaching students to identify assumptions and values, examine different sides of an issue and possible actions, and make decisions (Budmen); or else teaching students to define a problem, select pertinent information, recognize assumptions, formulate hypotheses, and draw conclusions (Dressel and Mayhew).

de Bono's CoRT strategies directly teach thinking as conscious skills that are independent of specific subject areas. About 50 CoRT thinking skills teach evaluating, considering all factors, identifying goals and objectives, projecting consequences, planning, prioritizing, and others.

Lipman's Philosophy for Children program takes the form of children's stories that teach, for example, cause-effect relations, identifying assumptions, analogical thinking, independent thinking, taking other perspectives, and caring.

Project IMPACT was designed to strengthen enabling skills (e.g., comparing, classifying), process skills (e.g., analyzing facts, assumptions, cause-effect relationships), and operations (e.g., reasoning, evaluating).

Feuerstein's Instrumental Enrichment program was designed to strengthen a variety of thinking skills and abilities via such exercises as organization of dots and orientation in space.

The Critical Thinking Press and Software workbooks contain exercises designed to strengthen simple and complex skills such as analogical reasoning, classifying, cause-effect relations, deductive reasoning, and following directions.

Many important thinking skills relate to developing good character, such as empathy, respecting rights, honesty, responsibility, valuing education and achievement, and others.

Some obstacles to effective thinking include being hungry or tired, perfectionism, personal problems, learning style mismatches, a competitive environment, and a district emphasis on accountability. On the other hand, feelings of confidence, belonging, curiosity, diligence, and others will help students learn and think.

Criteria for selecting materials and strategies include, for example, usability by teachers of varying abilities (without extended training), attractiveness and enjoyability, effectiveness in teaching important transferable skills, a focus on students' metacognitive understanding of thinking and thinking skills, practical applications of the thinking skills, active involvement, individual and group activities, and relatability to school content.

---

### Solutions to *Can You Zooley*? Exercise

1. The **Zuff** family. They are the only family group outside of the cages. The polar bears must be **Tricks**.

2. **Lesger**. They have eight legs.

3. The **Beeze** son, and the crocodiles must be **Gobbies**. This is the only small animal "inside" a different type of large animal. We also learn that rectangles are male.

4. The **Squeal** family. They have fins and three little sons (rectangles).

5. The **Lesger** family. They have three little circles (females), no rectangles (males).

6. Male. It's a rectangle.

7. The **Slizz** family. They have no legs.

8. The **Swifts**. They seem to have two legs and a big tail, with a little one attached to the front of the mother.

9. **Ample**. This is the only family with a small animal inside an adult female.

10. **Glup**. He is the only adult by himself outside of the cages.

# CHAPTER 12

# CULTURAL DIVERSITY AND CHILDREN FROM LOW SOCIOECONOMIC BACKGROUNDS
## THE INVISIBLE GIFTED

*Simply put, the significant and constant increases in both the number and proportion of racial/ethnic minority and economically disadvantaged children in the public school population are not reflected in programs for the gifted and talented.*

Mary M. Frasier and A. Harry Passow (1994, p. viii)

The scene is the principal's office in an inner-city elementary school. The principal, an African American woman, is bright, determined, dedicated, and very professional; she has been carefully selected from among many competitors to lead a daring new approach to educating inner-city youngsters. Many of these children, with learning and social problems, had been written off as "nonlearners" by teachers in other schools. Today, several members of the school board who are interested in the goals and methods of this innovative "fundamental" school program interview the principal. Their questions begin with the *whos, whys,* and *hows* of this unique school. She answers that the school is based on certain fundamentals: carefully selected staff, parent involvement, basic skills, mastery learning, firm discipline, and homework.

Then a significant question:

"Ms. Jones, how will you teach your gifted students?" And the response:

"In this school we have no gifted children."

Culturally different and economically disadvantaged African American, Hispanic American, Native American, and White children living in large urban centers, in poor rural areas, and on Indian reservations rarely are identified or de-scribed as gifted or talented. They are grossly underrepresented in programs for the gifted. Their formal educational needs are assumed to be only in basic skills areas, and their adjustment to school and learning almost always involves strict discipline. Their cultural and language differences plus their lack of exposure to mainstream U.S. culture usually combine to obscure from society the gifted children among them. These gifted minority and disadvantaged children typically proceed invisibly through school until they drop out or, with luck, graduate.

In addition to their wholesale exclusion from G/T programs, the families and peers of minority and poor children also typically do not reinforce the development of their intellectual or creative talents. They clearly are in need of strong school support. This chapter will discuss the special needs of these children, factors that contribute to their academic success, identification methods, programming and counseling strategies, and special considerations for rural gifted children.

## LEGISLATION

In 1977 Congresswoman Shirley Chisholm introduced legislation to include funding for gifted and talented minority and culturally different children within the Elementary and Secondary Education Act. She immediately was confronted with the reality of widespread misunderstanding of these students (Chisholm, 1978). She pointed out that her Caucasian colleagues did not seem to recognize the existence of *gifted* minority children and that they assumed that all minority children were in need of academic remediation. Her African American colleagues, with little apparent support, questioned her sponsorship of programs that "did nothing but promote (discriminatory) IQ testing and money for affluent white children." In her keynote address before the National Forum on Minority and Disadvantaged Gifted and Talented, Chisholm lamented the failure of our educational institutions to nurture the talents of gifted disadvantaged students. She faulted U.S. education for (1) inadequate methods for recognizing talent among culturally different children and (2) insufficient funding to provide special programs for these children.

The late 1960s and the 1970s saw the introduction of major educational and social programs to improve opportunities for minority, culturally different, and economically disadvantaged children. The Elementary and Secondary Education Act, Head Start programs, educational TV programs for children (*Sesame Street, Electric Company*), bilingual educational funding, and court-ordered desegregation all contributed to enhancing educational preparation and opportunities. The actual educational and social impact of these investments has been both controversial and difficult to evaluate. However, some statistics were encouraging. For example, the percentage of minority students who dropped out decreased dramatically. According to a 1977 U.S. Department of Commerce report, in the mid-1950s 50 percent of African American youth and 60 percent of Hispanic American youth dropped out of school. By 1977 24 percent of African American and 42 percent of Hispanic American students dropped out. For White students over a similar period of time, dropout rates decreased from 20 percent to 13 percent.

In 1988, Congress passed the Jacob K. Javits Gifted and Talented Students Education Act (P.L. 100–297), which funded the National Research Center on the Gifted and Talented as well as a multitude of educational programs throughout the United States. The research conducted by the National Research Center and the programs are specifically dedicated to identifying and programming for gifted and talented youth with disadvantages. More new research has been conducted in this area of gifted and talented education since 1988 than in any other period. However, it is too early to assess the long-term impact of this targeted programming and research on gifted children.

## SPECIAL NEEDS

It was estimated that by the year 2000, one in three Americans would be non-Caucasian (Banks, 1991; Hyland, 1989). The Census Bureau further projected that by the same year, 18 percent of the youth population of our country would be Hispanic American. Reis, Hébert, Díaz, Maxfield, and Ratley (1995) pointed out that Hispanic Americans are the most undereducated in our country. Hispanic Americans are underrepresented in honors and college-bound tracks (Orum, 1986), and only 5 percent of the children enrolled in gifted programs are Hispanic American. As of 1997, only 55 percent of Hispanics 25 years or older had graduated from high school, and 7.4 percent had graduated from college (Ovando, 2001).

A 1992 report by the U.S. Department of Education indicated that dropout rates for African American and white students have continued to decline, but Hispanic American dropout rates have remained high. From 1972 to 1991, the report showed dropout rates for African American students went from 21.3 percent to 13.6 percent; for White students, 12.3 percent to 8.9 percent. The 1991 dropout rate for Hispanic American students was 35.3 percent (Watertown, Wisconsin Daily Times, Sept. 16, 1992). On a visit to a school in North Dakota, it was indicated to author Rimm that the dropout rate for a Native American population in that area runs as high as 50 percent. While these reports indicate some improvements for some minority groups, the statistics remain unacceptable.

A study of 28,000 students in the Public Schools of Montgomery County, Alabama, showed a higher percentage of African American and Hispanic American students working below the standard of performance for mathematics at every grade level (Norman, 1988; Figure 12.1). Pool (1990) found that on a test of high-level mathematical proficiency, 7.6 percent of the White students performed at a high enough level to be channeled toward science and engineering. Only 1.2 percent of Hispanic Americans and 0.3 percent of African Americans attained a similar level. For those who are qualified, recruitment is enthusiastic. Major universities and small colleges alike search for minority students talented in the sciences and offer

them significant scholarship help. The demand is there, but the supply is lacking.

As we look to gifted minority youth who could direct their talents toward science or mathematics, we would hope to find increasing numbers of Ph.D.'s. There are actually *fewer* African American males earning Ph.D.'s in science than earlier (Pool, 1990). Although the numbers for African American females have increased slightly, that has not compensated for the decrease in males. There has been a slight increase in the number of Hispanic American males and females receiving Ph.D.'s in the "hard sciences," but they account for only 2 percent of the natural science and engineering doctorates, which is low considering Hispanic Americans account for 7 percent of the working-age population.

In educational research the numbers of African American Ph.D.'s decreased from 9.2 percent of

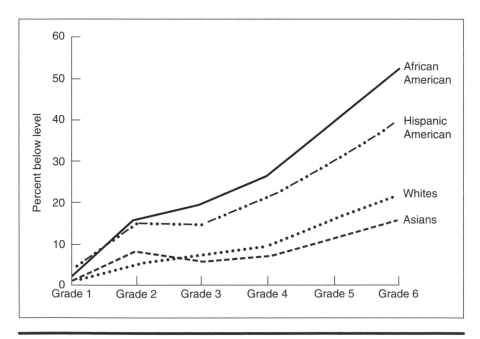

**FIGURE 12.1**  Falling Behind. Percentage of students in Montgomery County schools by racial/ethnic group and grade level who are working below the standard of performance for mathematics at each grade.

From Norman (1988). Reprinted by permission of the American Association for the Advancement of Science.

all educational research Ph.D.'s (691) in 1975 to 7.0 percent (421) in 1986 (Frierson, 1990). Furthermore, half of all African American faculty members are at predominantly African American colleges, therefore reducing their effectiveness as mentors to African American students who attend other universities.

These alarming statistics emphasize the importance of early identification of gifted disadvantaged and minority students and programming for their giftedness. The executive summary from the report *No Gift Wasted* (Alamprese & Erlanger, 1988) warns educators that disadvantaged students are not yet sufficiently served by elementary and secondary gifted programs. Its main findings follow:

• Minority students are underrepresented in programs designed to serve gifted and talented students. Although minorities make up 30 percent of public school enrollment, they represent less than 20 percent of the students selected for gifted and talented programs.

• Whereas students from low-income backgrounds comprise 20 percent of the student population, they make up only 4 percent of those students who perform at the highest levels on standardized tests (those who score at the 95th percentile or above).

• High school seniors from disadvantaged families (in which the mother did not complete high school) are less than half as likely to have participated in gifted and talented programs as more advantaged seniors.

• Disadvantaged students are far less likely to be enrolled in academic programs that can prepare them for college and are about half as likely to take coursework in advanced math and science than more advantaged students. Only 2 percent of high school seniors from poor families take calculus, whereas approximately 7 percent of those from more advantaged backgrounds do.

Estimates of the underrepresentation of minority students in gifted programs vary between 30 and 70 percent (Richert, 1987). Frasier (1990) and Baldwin (1987) noted that IQ cut-off scores

effectively preclude the identification of disadvantaged and culturally diverse gifted students, including many African American students.

A survey conducted by Patton, Prillaman, and VanTassel-Baska (1990) summarized the paucity of programs serving disadvantaged gifted learners. Surveys were returned from 52 of the 54 states or state entities surveyed. Three states had no programs that focused on disadvantaged gifted learners. Approximately 30 percent of the states reported "frequent" use of "low socioeconomic status" in identifying gifted students, while 35 percent of the states used the SES variable "a little" or "not at all." Race and ethnicity were not mentioned at all, very little, or a moderate amount in identification by 62 percent of the states. Only 29 percent indicated that a race or ethnicity variable was heavily emphasized. The results of the survey were not encouraging.

## FACTORS RELATED TO SUCCESS FOR DISADVANTAGED YOUTH

Literature that includes differentiated information on the successes of disadvantaged children can provide insights into appropriate programming to encourage success of these gifted youth.

Werner (1989) provided impressive information in a 30-year study of 201 high-risk children from the Hawaiian island of Kauai. These children had experienced multiple risks, including moderate to severe perinatal stress, chronic poverty, troubled family environments, and parents with fewer than eight grades of education. While two-thirds of these children developed serious problems, one-third grew into adults who "lived well, worked well, and played well." They were successful in accomplishing educational and career goals; 46 of them completed college. Werner termed these children *resilient* and documented the characteristics in their childhood that appeared to support their success despite their extreme disadvantages.

The critical factor for these resilient children appeared to be their informal support networks. Many mentioned a teacher who had been a role model during periods of family disorganization. Others mentioned a youth leader, a favorite minister, participation in 4H, the school band, a cheerleading team, or the "Y." These important people or activities seemed to help the children develop meaning and a sense of personal control over their lives.

The Werner study was the first of a large number of significant studies identifying resilience among disadvantaged youth. Javits legislative funding provided significant further research. The findings of the separate studies support each other.

VanTassel-Baska (1989) used a case study approach to determine the dynamics underlying the success of 15 economically disadvantaged gifted adolescents who had attended public schools in the midwest. She uncovered important home and school variables that can help parents and educators guide disadvantaged youth. Aspirations, expectations, and standards of parents and the extended family were high for these children. Mothers were extremely influential, and for some children grandmothers were critical. Fathers and grandfathers also were cited as important.

School was pleasant and productive for these children. Many were *A* students. For those who had been accelerated, it had been a positive experience. Involvement in extracurricular activities appeared extremely helpful. Also, the students had many positive relationships with teachers. While they had friends, peer influence did not play a critical role in their educational or career plans.

An important difference between the Werner (1989) and VanTassel-Baska (1989) studies lies in the role of family versus community. In Werner's research the disadvantaged children all came from dysfunctional families, and the needed support came from school and community sources. In the VanTassel-Baska study good family relationships seemed critical. One might conclude that the assistance of community members becomes crucial in the absence of role models and high expectations in the disadvantaged child's family.

There is great stress on students of diverse minority backgrounds. Not only do they encounter barriers getting accepted into gifted programs, but after they are identified as gifted their family and peers may actively or passively fail to support their talent development (Robinson, Reis, Neihart, & Moon, 2001).

Ford (1994a) summarized research on the characteristics of resilience among gifted African American youth (described later). Internal locus of control, a positive sense of self, and feelings of empowerment were characteristics cited by Hauser, Vieyra, Jacobson, and Wertlieb (1989). Taylor (1991) found resilient Black youth to be mature and academically and socially confident, and Clark (1991; also Ford, 1993) considered them to have bicultural identities and to believe in the American dream.

Taylor (1991) and McLoyd (1990) described resilient African American youth as having positive school experiences and strong family values and actively participating in religious affairs. Positive and strong peer relations were added to the characteristics of resilience by Garmezy (1991). These characteristics serve as protection for African American youth and promote social and academic success.

Developing resilience of three urban gifted Latino young men was described by Hébert (1996) as including supportive families that emphasize school success, mentors and role models, and involvement in extracurricular activities.

A qualitative study of twelve high-ability African American girls in an urban elementary school differentiated the characteristics of achievers and underachievers (Leppien, 1995). The achieving girls had a strong belief in self. They used learning strategies to maintain academic performance and deal with the negative effects of peer culture. They acknowledged the importance of teacher, school, and family support. The underachievers used negative behaviors (e.g., rebelliousness) to maintain a belief in themselves, had poor learning and behavior strategies, were unsuccessful in managing the peer culture, and acknowledged fewer support systems.

In another study characteristics of female achievers included involvement in multiple activities, independence, resilience, and dedication to

**TABLE 12.1**  Factors Influencing Achievement

- Belief in self
- Personal characteristics
- Support systems
- Participation in special programs, extracurricular activities, and summer enrichment programs
- Appropriately challenging classes
- Realistic aspirations

Adapted from S. M. Reis, T. P. Hébert, E. I. Díaz, L. R. Maxfield, & M. E. Ratley (1995).

a career (Reis et al., 1995). These high-achieving students were extremely supportive of other achieving students. Male high achievers also were involved in multiple activities, had positive personal traits, and a positive peer group. They, too, had reasonable career aspirations. Table 12.1 lists factors influencing achievement.

In reviewing a study by Arnold and Denny of 81 valedictorians, Moses (1991) itemized roadblocks to post-high school achievement of gifted minority students. The group as a whole was very successful. However, the study found that while White middle-class students had considerable family support, the eight African American and Hispanic American students struggled with financial issues, family support, and "fitting in" at predominately White colleges. The intellectual self-esteem of women students decreased after they entered college, despite their grades being higher than those of many men. They also often lowered their career expectations. The difficulties that minority gifted students will face in college should undoubtedly be part of their guidance preparation in high school if we wish to increase the likelihood that they will complete college.

Ford and Harris (1997) studied the racial identity of 152 African American male and female gifted and regular adolescents. They found that achievers and females tended to have more positive racial identities than underachievers and males. Furthermore, gifted students had more positive racial identities than regular students. Earlier, Harris and Ford (1991) noted the conflict between maintaining racial identity and striving

for academic honors—largely the "acting White" issue. Likewise, Tonemah (1991) and Duran and Weffer (1992) pointed out that the achievement ethos is in conflict with cultural values for both Native Americans and Mexican Americans. Despite conflicts, a follow-up study of a sample of minority students who scored above the 95th percentile on their ACT Assessment included 64 African Americans, 20 Native Americans, 85 Mexican Americans, and 50 Asian Americans (Kerr and Colangelo, 1994). The mean grade-point average of the students was 3.35. The most popular college major chosen by far was engineering. Natural sciences were the next most popular. These students credited their success to their personal efforts and the support of their families. Many of them stated that they had to "prove" their talents to the larger society.

## IDENTIFICATION

Minority and culturally different gifted children are not easily identified. Indeed, because of cultural bias in test instruments and other identification methods, many typical procedures actually obscure their giftedness—by "proving" these children are *not* gifted. Because actual achievement often is not outstanding, identification must be based upon superior *potential* instead of superior performance. At least 34 states now advocate the use of multiple criteria for the identification of gifted children (Gallagher & Coleman, 1992). Furthermore, the authors note, 38 states have specific instructions to school districts to include the special needs of culturally diverse and disadvantaged populations in the identification of gifted students.

Frasier (1997) reminds us that despite these instructions minority populations remain underrepresented in gifted programming. She related this identification problem to two main issues: "(1) differences in test performance among racial, cultural, or ethnic groups; and (2) the effects of cultural, economic, and language differences or deprivations on the ability of minority students to achieve at levels associated with giftedness" (p. 498).

A major problem in identifying poor and minority gifted children comes from the focus on homogeneity rather than heterogeneity. Group stereotypes are perpetuated because of the tendency to characterize all members of a minority group with the attributes of group members who perform the least well (Banks, 1993; Tonemah, 1987). This section will review typical identification methods and evaluate their usefulness for populations that are culturally different and economically disadvantaged. It will also recommend other identification procedures that in some cases will be more effective.

### Intelligence Tests

High intelligence test scores on either group or individual tests are one valid way to identify intellectually gifted minority youngsters. However, an average or even low IQ score may be a poor or misleading indicator of student ability if the child comes from a culturally deprived or culturally different environment.

This issue is exceedingly complex. There are frequent and continuing debates regarding *cultural bias* in mental testing and the dust is far from settled. For example, some argue that the lower average scores of minority groups are simply evidence of discriminatory test bias. From this perspective, intelligence tests "have devastating labeling—and pigeon-holing—effects . . . and they are nothing more than an Anglo yardstick designed to make whites look ingenious, and Blacks

and other minorities stupid" (Hoffman, 1964). For another view, Arthur Jensen (1976; see also Jensen, 1980), known for his "racial differences" hypothesis, argues that intelligence tests show practically no evidence of differential culture bias, by which he means that the tests predict school success for both minority and majority cultures.

Thorndike and Hagen (1977) argued for the usefulness (prediction ability) of intelligence tests, but further noted that (1) the tests do not determine a person's ability, they simply suggest strengths and weaknesses; (2) they describe how a person is doing at the present time; and (3) we should consider the cultural, personal, and family background in interpreting test scores.

Frasier, Garcia, and Passow (1995) agree strongly that IQ tests are racially biased. In their review of assessment issues, they claim there are three major reasons for the underrepresentation of minority groups in gifted programming:

1. *Test bias.* Standardized testing is unfair to ethnic minorities for cultural and language reasons.
2. *Selective referrals.* Teacher attitudes and knowledge about minority students and the schools they are likely to attend influence fewer referrals.
3. *Reliance on deficit-based paradigms.* The focus on deficits makes recognition of strengths of minority children difficult.

New paradigms for identification are recommended by the authors. However, the challenge of designing these paradigms still lies ahead.

Educators and psychologists—whether liberal or conservative, African American, Hispanic, Native American, or White—will agree that culturally different students are more likely than the average student to have a difficult time when taking tests of *verbal ability* (vocabulary, comprehension). These tests, of course, are based upon middle-class English. The problem is that subcultural languages such as African American English, Hawaiian pidgin, or Navajo or other Native American languages are different, and so the person's linguistic structures, categories, and associations also are different. Group intelligence tests depend heavily on language ability and therefore are more likely to be biased than individually administered tests. As we saw in Chapter 4, the Wechsler tests separate subtests and IQ scores into *verbal* and *performance* (nonverbal) components, thereby allowing a bright child with deficient English to score high. Several authors have commented on large Wechsler verbal/performance discrepancies of Native American children, due at least in part to language and cultural differences (e.g., Kryaniuk & Das, 1976; Scruggs & Cohn, 1983).

Helms (1992) pointed out that some African American cultural issues could negatively affect cognitive ability testing for these students (see Table 12.2). Among other recommendations for cultural equivalence in standardized testing, she suggested the use of separate racial group norms.

The use of IQ tests for Asian American students presents different issues. Woliver and Woliver (1991) and Plucker (1996) pointed out several important weaknesses in our understanding of gifted Asian American students. In the area of assessment, there may be some Asian American populations that will be disadvantaged if traditional assessments are *not* used. Plucker also emphasized that little is said about creative development in discussions of Asian American populations. Finally, he reminds educators that the dominant

**TABLE 12.2**   African Cultural Components in Cognitive Ability Testing: Hypothesized Effects of African-Centered Values and Beliefs

| Dimension | General Description | Influence on Test Responses |
|---|---|---|
| Spirituality | Greater validity of the power of immaterial forces in everyday life over linear, factual thinking. | It may be difficult to separate relevant aspects of the test stimuli from factors caused by luck or circumstance. |
| Harmony | The self and one's surroundings are interconnected. | The ambiance in which one takes the test may influence one's responses. |
| Movement | Personal conduct is organized through movement. | Active test-taking strategies may result in better performance than sedentary ones. |
| Affect | Integration of feelings with thoughts and actions. | Feelings may facilitate or hinder test performance; respondent may find it difficult to "understand" persons in test stimuli who act without feeling. |
| Communalism | Valuing of one's group(s) more than individuals. | Performance may be influenced when a person perceives that it represents the group. |
| Expressive | Unique personality is expressed through one's behavioral style. | Test taker may choose the more imaginative response alternative. |
| Orality | Knowledge may be gained and transmitted orally and aurally. | Test performance may differ when the person is tested orally and aurally. |
| Social time | Time is measured by socially meaningful events and customs. | The belief that obtaining a "good" answer is more important than finishing on time may lead the test taker to "waste" time. |

Adapted from Helms (1992).

role of males in most Asian cultures must influence achievement for girls (Lee & Cynn, 1991). Consideration of the heterogeneity of Asian cultures also is important for both identification and programming for gifted Asian American students.

In sum, any identification process based on intelligence/aptitude tests will surely underidentify disadvantaged gifted students, students with underdeveloped potential. A high IQ score, of course, is convincing evidence of high intellectual ability among culturally different and poor children, just as with majority children. However, many gifted minority and economically disadvantaged children will be overlooked if intelligence tests are used as the only or the most important identification instrument. Their use is recommended, but average or low scores should be interpreted with caution, and in consideration of the language, cultural and family background, and the circumstances of testing.

### Achievement Tests

Achievement tests typically are administered at regular intervals in virtually every school system, and so achievement information is readily available. However, while standardized achievement tests are highly recommended as an identification tool for most populations, with culturally different students they are plagued by exactly the same problems as intelligence tests. Therefore, while it is critical that achievement scores not be misused because of cultural bias, it certainly is reasonable to use them as one index of gifts and talents for minority children. As with IQ scores, children who produce high scores on achievement tests are showing good evidence of special kinds of giftedness. However, in culturally different populations gifted children may not score high on these tests despite their giftedness. Achievement tests alone, then, are not a sufficient measure for the identification of gifted minority and poor children.

Because achievement test scores often are used to deny entrance into gifted programming to disadvantaged students, Lynch and Mills (1990) designed a program to improve the achievement

of 45 high-potential sixth-grade students in the Pasadena Unified School District. The group included a high proportion of African Americans and Hispanic Americans as well as socioeconomically disadvantaged students. Their Skills Reinforcement Project (SRP) was sufficiently effective to allow nine of these students into gifted programming without recourse to affirmative action, proof that achievement test scores can be improved rapidly with a little hard work.

### Creativity Tests

Creativity tests, both divergent thinking tests and self-descriptive inventories (see Chapter 4), can be very helpful in selecting minority and culturally different children for participation in G/T programs. Specifically, they are useful in identifying highly creative children who are not motivated to achieve and who may not score high on ability or achievement tests. For both kinds of creativity tests, there has been research with minority children that supports their use.

The *Torrance Tests of Creative Thinking* (Figural Form, particularly) have been used in several research projects with minority children. For example, Solomon (1974) found that minority children scored *higher* than other children in some areas of creative thinking in grades 1 and 3. At the fifth-grade level there were no significant differences between scores of minority and other children. Torrance (1971; see also Torrance, 1995) summarized the results of 16 different studies designed to evaluate racial or socioeconomic differences in Torrance Test scores. The results varied, with some favoring the minority children and others favoring majority children, but overall his conclusions supported the notion that there is no racial or socioeconomic bias in open-ended tests of creative thinking.

The *Group Inventory for Finding (Creative) Talent (GIFT)* and the *Group Inventory For Finding Interests (GIFFI*; Davis & Rimm, 1980; Rimm, 1976) are self-report inventories that evaluate personality characteristics, attitudes, interests, and biographical information known to be associated with creativeness. Studies by Rimm and Davis (1976, 1980; Davis & Rimm, 1982) indicated that *GIFT* and *GIFFI* are valid for identifying creative potential in both rural and urban socioeconomically disadvantaged populations, as well as among specific ethnic groups, including African American, Hispanic American, and Native American minority students. GIFT and GIFFI also are available in Spanish.

Central to the appropriate use of divergent thinking tests such as the Torrance Tests or personality/biographical inventories is the recognition that (1) scores from a single creativity test should be combined with other information, such as teacher ratings of creativity or scores on a second creativity test, in order to reach a valid decision; and (2) low creativity test scores absolutely must never be used to eliminate children from G/T programs. Creativity tests are not perfect; there simply are too many types of creativity and creative people. However, creativity tests can identify creatively gifted children, majority and minority, who may not be identified in other ways.

## Matrix Identification Models

Matrix identification models have been developed to bring together data from a variety of sources and to specifically include variables that will help identify minority and disadvantaged gifted children. The *Baldwin Identification Matrix* (Baldwin, 1985; see Chapter 4) combines objective and subjective criteria and has been reported to be effective for increasing the number of African American students identified for gifted programs (e.g., Dabney, 1983; Long, 1981; McBeath, Blackshear, & Smart, 1981).

## Teacher Nominations

In many instances, teacher nominations of giftedness are a highly suspect and invalid identification strategy (see Chapter 4). Nonetheless, it continues to be the most popular identification method used. For minority and poor children, the teacher nomination method creates special

hazards. "Teacher pleasers," who are neat and clean, nicely dressed, who speak middle-class English, and who turn in their work neatly done and on time, are likely to be named as "gifted." Other students—poor, African American, Hispanic American, or Native American—are automatically "disadvantaged" by many teachers in the nomination process. Shade (1978) found that African American gifted achievers, despite their giftedness, receive less praise and attention and more criticism in the classroom than their nongifted African American counterparts. Clark (1983) observed that there remains the persistent attitude that gifted children are not found in certain populations.

On the other hand, a sensitive and caring teacher who is knowledgeable about characteristics of gifted children may, in fact, be the very best identifier of the culturally different gifted child. Furthermore, such a teacher may be able to guide and inspire a talented child who does not score high on any ability or achievement test.

Several studies cast serious doubt on the validity of teacher nominations for culturally different students. For example, when teachers use rating scales that include language items in rating Hispanic LEP (Limited English Proficient) students, the teachers may neglect students' verbal proficiency in Spanish and evaluate only their English proficiency (Fernandez, Gay, Lucky, & Gavilan, 1998). Peterson and Margolin (1997) found that Anglo teachers often passed over Hispanic and other minority group gifted students because of their own cultural mainstream definition of *giftedness*. Even when rating scales were used to identify 274 fifth-grade students, the extent to which Hispanic students were acculturated into the mainstream culture increased the likelihood that they would be identified by teachers as gifted (Masten, Plata, Wenglar, & Thedford, 1999). Peterson (1999) also discovered that classroom teachers' cultural perceptions of giftedness were pivotal in underidentifying African American, Hispanic, Native American, immigrant Asian, and low-income Anglo children for gifted programs.

The nomination procedure will be greatly improved by educating teachers regarding characteristics of gifted and talented minority children, some of which are different than usual characteristics of giftedness. For example, Gay (1978) researched common characteristics of gifted African American children and compared them to parallel characteristics of other gifted children. Her list of 11 characteristics stems from twenty years of teaching experience with African American children and three years of teaching in a program for the gifted and talented (see Table 12.3).

The present authors might repeat an earlier warning in relation to Gay's item 11 in Table

**TABLE 12.3** Comparative Characteristics of Giftedness

| Concepts from the Literature | Manifestations of Gifted Characteristics in Gifted African American Children |
|---|---|
| 1. Keen observation | Picks up more quickly on racist attitudes and practices; may feel alienated by school at an early age. |
| 2. Interest and ability in perceiving relationships | Seeks structure and organization in required tasks; may be slow to motivate in some abstract activities. |
| 3. Verbal proficiency, large vocabulary, facility of expression | Many African American children have large vocabularies inappropriate for the school setting; thinking in African American English may hinder the facility of expression in standard English. |
| 4. Breadth of information | Difficult to determine many areas of experiential knowledge for African American children. |
| 5. Questioning, curious, skeptical | Though some ask too many "wrong" questions, some may have been conditioned to suppress questioning behavior. |
| 6. Critical, evaluative, possessing good judgment | Explores (in perception of relationships) better or wiser choices; reads behavioral implications. |
| 7. Creative, inventive, original | Makes up games and activities; expresses original ideas in other ways. |
| 8. Power of concentration, long attention span | Some have extremely strong concentration due to persistent noise in their environment; may also express displeasure at having to stop an activity. |
| 9. Independence | Need for less supervision is especially pronounced in African American gifted. |
| 10. Diversity of interests and abilities | Frequently has artistic, musical, creative writing, psychomotor, or leadership talent in addition to global intellectual ability; may neglect school work due to other interests. |
| 11. Academic facility and strength | Good at basic school tasks; may not show expected achievement due to inferior schooling. |

From J. E. Gay, "A Proposed Plan for Identifying Black Gifted Children," *Gifted Child Quarterly, 22* (1978), 353–359. Reprinted by permission.

12.3. Gifted African American children may perform only at an average level in school because of socioeconomic, language, motivational, personal, or cultural disabilities. Therefore, students should be considered potentially gifted if they earn high ratings on many of the first ten characteristics, with or without actual "good" school achievement.

Swenson (1978) constructed a helpful list of characteristics of creativeness in a culturally different and socioeconomically deprived urban school area. Her list came from information generated by 36 teachers and was based on observed original behavior related to classwork, art, and antisocial—yes, *antisocial*—behavior (see Table 12.4). Because teachers are accustomed to disciplining children for antisocial behavior they may overlook the creativity exhibited in such behavior (see especially items 2, 9, 18, 23, and 24 in Table 12.4).

**TABLE 12.4**   Characteristics of Creativity in Culturally Different Students

1. Repeats activities so that he or she can do them differently.
2. Invents imaginative lies.
3. Shows that he or she sees hidden meanings, cause-and-effect relationships that are not obvious.
4. Writes and illustrates stories without being asked to do so as an assignment.
5. Utilizes free time by making up games or making something from paper and material scraps as opposed to more structured activities.
6. Finds many answers to a situational question.
7. Lets his or her imagination "run" when writing a story; sees more possibilities.
8. Finds activities for spare-time work with little or no additional help.
9. Decorates the border of his or her paper when doing an assignment.
10. Doesn't copy other children's ideas in art.
11. Builds and constructs things using unusual materials; uses ordinary materials in different ways.
12. Interrelates his or her experiences and draws on them with ease in discussions.
13. Doesn't let classroom events go unnoticed; questions them.
14. Accomplishes things on his or her own without help.
15. Writes poems and stories in his or her spare time.
16. Asks unusual questions during class discussions.
17. Makes up his or her own ideas when the class does a project together.
18. Suggests to the teacher alternate ways of doing an activity.
19. Is willing to risk friendship to express his or her feelings or thoughts.
20. Enthusiastic about new activities in music and art.
21. Goes beyond what is required in class assignments; makes his or her work "fancier."
22. Comes up with fresh, original comments or an unusual correct answer when there is more than one correct answer.
23. Finds new ways to get attention.
24. Tries original ways to get out of work he or she doesn't want to do.
25. Takes the initiative when he or she wants to know something; reads or asks questions without prompting.

From J. E. Swenson, "Teacher-Assessment of Creative Behavior in Disadvantaged Children," *Gifted Child Quarterly, 22* (1978), 338–43. Reprinted by permission.

## Parent Nominations

Appropriate gifted programming should encourage parent identification. However, in order for parent identification to be effective for minority children, special efforts are necessary to educate those parents about characteristics of giftedness and the advantages of gifted programming for their children.

A survey sent to White, Hispanic American, and African American parents of children in a gifted and talented program of a large urban district yielded an important clue to the underrepresentation of minority children in gifted programming (Scott, Perou, Urbano, Hogan, & Gold, 1992). Parents were asked about the characteristics that had suggested to them that their child was gifted and current characteristics of their gifted child. They also were asked if they had requested an evaluation of their child for placement in the gifted program. There were no significant differences between the groups for the first two questions, but significantly fewer minority parents than white parents had requested that their children be evaluated for programming. This finding seems to underline the importance of reaching parents of minority children and involving them in the identification of giftedness (e.g., Scott et al., 1992).

## Peer Nominations

Peers of economically deprived or culturally different gifted children usually do not place a high value on school achievement. However, they are as aware of gifts and talents among their friends and classmates as are other young people. Bernal (1979), for example, found that members of a particular ethnic group almost always can identify the "smartest" among their peers.

In order to identify unusual intellectual, creative, or leadership ability, it may be necessary to look beyond the classroom to the out-of-school cliques and crowds. One interesting approach is to meet with students named by peers as out-of-school "leaders." These leaders can explain characteristics of culturally valued giftedness within their own peer culture (Bernal, 1979; Bruch & Curry, 1978), gifts that might qualify the person for the special opportunities of a G/T program. In inner-city areas, for example, creative approaches to self-maintenance or even survival may be reasonable arenas in which to discover giftedness. Culturally valued art and music talent, which is known to peers but not expressed in the classroom, also would be important information for the identification of giftedness. Finally, the "different" or lonely child in a minority culture, even though he or she does not value intellectual pursuit, may be considered suspect for unusual talent. The child may well have special interests and talents, suppressed due to peer pressures, that should be cultivated in a G/T program.

## Additional Identification Plans

Frasier (1991a; Frasier & Passow, 1994) summed up the goal of alternative identification models by indicating that we need a paradigm that "accommodates both the children we are missing and the children we are finding." The *Frasier Talent Assessment Profile* (F-TAP) was designed to combine test and nontest criteria and is based on the following four assumptions (see Figure 12.2):

1. Methods to locate gifted children from diverse cultural backgrounds can be developed without eroding program quality and without requiring excessive data collection or excessive expenditures of time.
2. Identification methods should rely on assessing dynamic rather than static displays of gifted behaviors.
3. A profile, rather than cutoff scores or weighting systems, provides the most effective and efficient way to display data for interpretation from test and nontest sources.
4. Results from identification procedures should be used to design programs and develop curricula for gifted students.

Frasier's F-TAP will include aptitude and achievement test data as well as self-report and observational information in *data categories* such

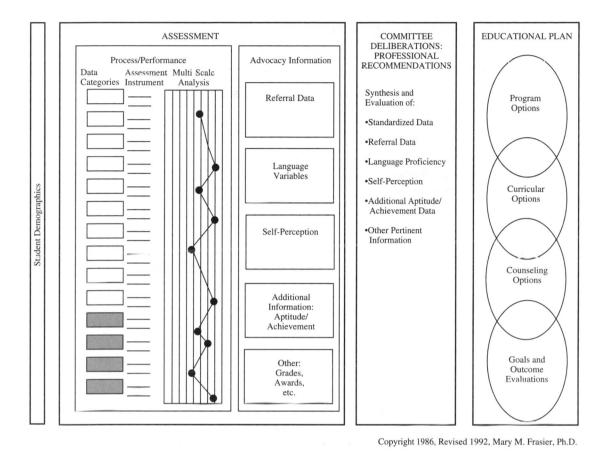

Copyright 1986, Revised 1992, Mary M. Frasier, Ph.D.

**FIGURE 12.2**  The Frasier Talent Assessment Profile (F-TAP).
Reproduced by permission of Mary M. Frasier.

as intelligence, specific academic talents, motivations, creativity, and others (see F-TAP discussion in Chapter 4).

Two programs that effectively use dynamic "activity" approaches to identifying gifted African American students, rather than "static" test scores, are the Program of Assessment, Diagnosis, and Instruction (PADI; Johnson et al., 1985) and the Potentially Gifted Minority Student Project (Alamprese & Erlanger, 1988). These approaches appear to be less culturally biased than others, and thus increase the number of minority students identified (Patton, 1992).

Woods and Achey (1990) increased the per-

centage of racial/ethnic minority students in the Academically Gifted (AG) Project by 181 percent by using a *series* of evaluations. While some students qualified at the first step, based on group aptitude and achievement testing, other students were permitted to proceed through two other steps of group and individual testing. The use of a variety of objective measures were successful in identifying additional gifted minority students for the AG Project while following the traditional definition of gifted adopted by North Carolina. Table 12.5 compares the AG and traditional methods of identification. The AG Project method differs from the traditional method in that it

**TABLE 12.5**    Differences Between Academically Gifted Project Procedures and Traditional Academically Gifted Program Procedures

| AG Project Procedures | Traditional Procedures |
| --- | --- |
| 1. Systematic review of existing test scores for all racial/ethnic group students in grades 2–5 to generate a target group (pool) of students to be tested. | 1. Parent, school, peer, and self nominations. |
| 2. Informative group meetings with parents of students eligible to participate in the Target Group held prior to initiating the evaluation sequence. | 2. Individual conferences held with parents following each group evaluation and, when administered, individual evaluations. |
| 3. Target group students progress automatically through the evaluation sequence. | 3. Students retested only at the request of parents or school-based committee personnel. |
| 4. Two full-time educational diagnosticians assigned specifically to the AG Project. | |

From Woods and Achey (1990), by permission of *Roeper Review.*

encourages additional testing for those who would not have qualified in the initial testing.

The Rural and Migrant Gifted Project provides a successful model for identifying gifted Hispanic American students (Ortiz & Gonzalez, 1991). It involves the administration of a shortened version of the *Wechsler Intelligence Scale for Children-Revised* (WISC-R) (Ortiz & Gonzalez, 1989), both in English and Spanish. The criteria used for effective selection of gifted Hispanic American students were:

1. Information provided by the teacher on the prescreening form.
2. Performance on the WISC-R screening test (students performing in the 85th to 94th percentile are considered *accelerated,* while those scoring at the 95th percentile or higher are considered *gifted*).
3. Achievement test records (same criteria are applied as in the WISC-R screening test, but in specific academic areas).
4. Motivation and behavior factors.

Promising improvement in the identification of culturally different gifted children has been found using *dynamic assessment,* which was developed in an effort to evaluate immigrant children in Israel who have learning problems (Feuerstein, Rand, & Hoffman, 1979). Dynamic assessment involves a test, then an intervention that teaches test-taking skills, followed by a retest (Kirschenbaum, 1998). Gifted children make significantly greater improvement after the intervention than do average children. G. Chaffey (personal communication, August 29–30, 2001), University of New England, Armidale, Australia, recently used dynamic assessment to identify gifted Australian Aboriginal children age 8 to 11. He found significant changes in the children's mean scores from pre- to post-test, but more important he found very large improvements for the gifted children. In the pretest, no children scored above the 90th percentile. After the intervention, 7 of the 84 participants scored above the 90th percentile. Kirschenbaum noted that the test-taking strategies can be taught by teachers. Furthermore, teachers who learned the intervention tasks viewed themselves as better able to recognize skills of children in economically disadvantaged populations.

Several promising studies have used Gardner's (1983; see Chapter 1) theory of multiple intelligences to identify giftedness among minority children. Plucker, Callahan, and Tomchin (1996) developed their assessment instruments by modifying the original Multiple Intelligence Assessment Technique (Udall & Passe, 1993; Maker, 1993). Their MI assessment involved 13 checklists, ratings, and activities to measure four intelligences: spatial, logical-mathematical, linguistic, and interpersonal intelligences. The sample included over 1800 kindergarteners and first graders from 16 schools, many of whom were of ethnically diverse and/or low socioeconomic backgrounds. More ethnically diverse students were identified as gifted, and the MI-based procedure was found reliable. However, questions about predictive validity indicated that further research was needed.

The Problem Solving Assessment (PSA), based on Multiple Intelligence Theory (Gardner, 1983) and assessment research (Maker, 1993; Sternberg, 1984b, 1988a), was used to assess 1100 students in a large school district in southeastern U.S. (Reid, Romanoff, Algozzine, & Udall, 2000). Positive correlations were found with other measures, and different and more diverse populations were identified as gifted. Sarouphim (1999) reviewed research using the DISCOVER assessment (Maker, 1996; see Chapter 4), which also is based on Gardner's theory of multiple intelligences, and reaffirmed its usefulness in identifying different kinds of giftedness among diverse populations. She cautions about the importance of a match between identified giftedness and appropriate programming. For example, programs for logical-mathematical students might be inappropriate for children with high interpersonal intelligence but average logical-mathematical intelligence. While her advice seems logical to any educator, it is not so easy to match program to type of giftedness in the real world of schools.

Creative efforts to identify gifted students with disadvantages are indeed being developed. Hopefully, future research will add to effective identification procedures, which are, of course, the first steps to cultivating giftedness in diverse populations.

## Quota Systems

One reasonable solution to minority representation in G/T programs is the quota system. A fixed percentage of culturally different children are included in a program, based upon the percentage of those students in the school or district and regardless of comparative test scores or grades. The quota system assumes that the same percentage of minority students are gifted and talented as majority students. As one might guess, this is a much debated assumption. A central issue is the fairness to majority students who are excluded and who, according to objective criteria, appear more qualified.

The effectiveness of the quota system has been born out by a longitudinal study of minority students identified by the Racine school system using a quota system (Smith, LeRose, and Clasen, 1991). Twelve years later, of the 24 students identified by the quota system for a gifted program, *not one had dropped out,* compared to 45 percent of 67 equally able minority students who were in regular school programs. Admitting minority students to gifted programs can make a dramatic difference.

## PROGRAMMING FOR GIFTED STUDENTS WHO ARE CULTURALLY DIFFERENT

Programming for culturally diverse and socioeconomically disadvantaged gifted and talented children can include any of the curriculum options for acceleration, enrichment, and grouping described in earlier chapters. However, there are important additional components that should be given special consideration: (1) maintaining ethnic identity, (2) extracurricular cultural enrichment, (3) learning style differences, (4) counseling, (5) parent support groups, (6) development of significant models, (7) accelerated and enriched curriculum, and (8) career education. While it may not be possible to include all of these components at the outset, it is desirable to include all of them eventually if minority gifted children are to have an optimal opportunity to develop and use their abilities.

The important findings by Reis, Hébert, et al. (1995) certainly should be considered in planning programs for gifted students to ensure that the special needs of minority students are included. In their study of highly able African American, Hispanic American, and White underachievers in an urban high school, school factors, family factors, personal factors, and community factors were found to adversely affect achievement. All of these factors will be considered later in this chapter.

Other factors that adversely affect successful placement of economically disadvantaged African American students in gifted programs were outlined by Ford (1994b). For example, she points out that African American students are likely to feel socially isolated in classrooms in which there is no racial and cultural diversity. Furthermore, they may feel peer pressure if they participate in a pullout program.

Ford noted that families of disadvantaged students require a better understanding of gifted programs than most typical families. Many of the parents have negative memories of their own school experiences and may be resistant to any special school experience for their children. Ford also stressed the importance of multicultural training for teachers and counselors and the recruitment of culturally diverse teachers and counselors in order to keep students in gifted programming once they are identified.

Table 12.6 shows characteristics of exemplary teachers of culturally diverse gifted students suggested by Ford and Trotman (2001). The authors make it clear that these characteristics are over and above the typical characteristics expected of exemplary teachers of the gifted.

To build resilience in African American youth, Ford (1994a) recommended the following promising strategies:

**1.** *Improving family-school community relations.* Achievement test scores of African American youth improve if parents participate in school.

**2.** *Self-concept enhancement.* Counseling, academic enrichment, and the provision of role models and mentors will improve self-concept and thus resilience.

**3.** *Improving social and emotional relations.* Group experiences, multicultural curriculum, consideration of learning style differences, and teaching of social competence within the community environment are techniques for building social and emotional resilience.

## Maintaining Ethnic Identity

The *assimilationist* position holds that upward mobility in the United States requires conformity to the language, culture, and rules of the majority Caucasian population. Assimilationists further point out that minority subcultural values prevent or at least discourage integration into the majority community, and thus limit the minority person's educational and socioeconomic opportunities (Banks, 1979). Exum (1983) noted that assimilationist attitudes of African-American families, who wish to succeed and be accepted in the White world, not only may be pro-white but even anti-African American.

On the other hand, the *cultural pluralist* position emphasizes the importance of pride in one's ethnic identity as an important part of educational and career achievement. Cultural pluralists note the close relationship of ethnic pride to the development of healthy self-concepts, and therefore consider heterogeneity and diversity to be beneficial to both individual and cultural growth.

Ogbu (1992) emphasized that cultural diversity continues to be poorly understood and that minority students, whose cultural frames of reference often are oppositional to those of American mainstream culture, face greater difficulties in learning.

Gifted programming generally gives lip service to a cultural diversity point-of-view. However, a survey by VanTassel-Baska, Patton, and Prillaman (1989) suggested that program policies typically do not include accommodations for diversity.

**TABLE 12.6**   Characteristics of Effective Teachers of Gifted Diverse Students

| Characteristics of Gifted Education Teachers | Characteristics of Multicultural Education Teachers | Characteristics of Gifted Multicultural Education Teachers |
| --- | --- | --- |
| Knowledge of the nature and needs of gifted students. | Knowledge of the nature and needs of diverse students. | Knowledge of the nature and needs of students who are gifted and diverse. |
| Ability to develop methods and materials for use with gifted students. | Ability to develop methods and materials for use with diverse students. | Ability to develop methods and materials for use with students who are gifted and diverse. |
| Skills in individualized teaching. | Skills in addressing cultural differences in students' learning styles, cognitive styles, and behavioral styles. | Skills in addressing individual and cultural differences. |
| Skills in teaching higher level thinking skills and questioning techniques. | Skills in teaching higher level thinking skills and questioning techniques using multicultural resources and materials. | Skills in teaching higher level thinking skills and questioning techniques using multicultural resources and materials. |
| Ability to identify gifted students. | Ability to recognize the strengths of diverse students. | Ability to recognize the strengths of students who are gifted and diverse. |
| Seeks to develop students' self-concept. | Seeks to develop students' concept as a person of color (i.e., racial identity). | Seeks to develop students' sense of self as a gifted individual and diverse individual. |
| Skills in counseling gifted students. | Skills in counseling diverse students (multicultural counseling skills). | Skills in counseling students who are gifted and diverse. |
| Skills in creating an environment in which gifted students feel challenged and safe to explore and express their uniqueness. | Skills in creating an environment in which diverse students feel challenged and safe to explore and express their uniqueness. | Skills in creating an environment in which diverse gifted students feel challenged and safe to explore and express their uniqueness. |

Source: Ford, D. Y., & Trotman, M. F. (2001). Teachers of gifted students: Suggested multicultural characteristics and competencies, *Roeper Review, 23*(4), 235–239.

Some practical classroom ideas for teaching students to value diversity by enhancing sensitivity are suggested by Baldwin (1991, 1993):

**1.** Help students experience what it feels like to be different. Students can use masks and become members of another ethnic group; they should stay "in character" for at least 48 hours. A journal and discussion of emotions can be used.

**2.** Have students produce resource books on different cultural groups. Include books, films, activities, field trips, and local resource people.

**3.** Use games that have been developed for the

purpose of placing persons in the roles of other ethnic groups.

**4.** Use other activities such as debates, unfinished stories, and fictional stories such as *Kindred* (Butler, 1988) to develop sensitivity toward different ethnic groups.

If a G/T program serves students in a multicultural area, explicit objectives of the program should include the provision of multiethnic experiences and, for minority persons especially, the development of positive ethnic identity.

Kitano (1991) summarized the differences between assimilationist and pluralist perspectives for gifted programs in Table 12.7.

Ford, Howard, Harris, and Tyson (2000) and Ford and Trotman (2001) characterized culturally responsive classrooms as including the following ingredients: culturally relevant instruction (see

also Patton & Townsend, 1997), equity training, a holistic teaching philosophy, a "we-us-our" or communal philosophy, respect for students' primary language, culturally congruent instructional practices, culturally sensitive assessment, student-family-teacher relationships, and a diverse teaching staff. This last component will require that schools be assertive in recruiting minority teachers to gifted education. According to a survey conducted by Ford, Grantham, and Harris (1997), minority teachers are often discouraged from working with gifted students. Perhaps minority *teachers* also suffer from underidentification of their giftedness.

### Extracurricular Cultural Enrichment

The cultural enrichment that comes from attending concerts, theater, and ballet and visiting exhi-

**TABLE 12.7**   Summary of Assimilationist and Pluralist Perspectives

|  | Assimilationist | Pluralist |
|---|---|---|
| Source of under-achievement | Within child based on culture and experience; need for intervention aimed at deficits | Within system or within interactions between system and child; need for empowerment of child |
| Purpose of Schooling | Transmission of mainstream values toward maintenance of core culture | Understanding many cultural perspectives toward creation of a society that values diversity |
| Identification | Standardized assessment | Alternative assessment, nonbiased assessment, multiple measure assessment |
| Instructional Processes | Focus on individual achievement; helping child fit the school | Focus on democratic structures; changing school to fit the child |
| Curriculum | Problem solving and critical thinking applies to mainstream culture and history | Problem solving and critical thinking applies to culture and history of many groups; building skills to transform society |

From Kitano (1991), by permission of the *Journal for the Education of the Gifted.*

bitions, art galleries, and museums usually is provided by the families of middle-class gifted children. For the socioeconomically deprived child, these experiences typically are nonexistent or limited to occasional school excursions. Exposure to the arts can be a valuable experience for deprived gifted children, as well as good reinforcement for their participation in the gifted program. Importantly, such exposure will strongly reinforce students' own artistic or scientific efforts and talents.

For maximum benefit, art or science experiences should be tied to other knowledge, skill, or creative components of the G/T program. For example, historical backgrounds of particular artists, composers, or scientists would add knowledge and depth to the experiences. Also, discussions of the antecedents and idea sources of particular products or performances, or comparative evaluations of various works, would further embellish the event. "What would happen if . . . ?" or "In what other ways might we. . . . ?" questions add creative and futuristic thinking to the experiences. Students also can do further research, prepare written or oral reports to the class, or write stories, newspaper columns with photos, or news reports about a person or event. Finally, as we noted earlier, field trips are most beneficial when students are armed with specific objectives to be met and questions to be answered before they climb onto the bus.

School funding for many enrichment experiences is certain to be limited or even absent. Ideally, travel and admissions monies would be built into the original program budget. If not, local industries, businesses, or civic groups may be encouraged to fund specific trips. For the business owner, such sponsorship has the attraction of combining a small tax-deductible investment with a superb public relations opportunity (news coverage).

### Learning Style Differences

Learning style differences should be considered in every classroom. Differences may vary within cultured groups as well as between them. One recent study was specific to cultural differences.

Learning style differences were analyzed for 54 African American, 61 third generation Mexican American, and 40 third generation Chinese American sixth-, seventh-, and eighth-grade gifted students in Chicago to determine if there were group differences in preferences for noise, light, visual modality, studying in the afternoon, or persistence (Ewing & Yong, 1992). All groups preferred bright light, studying in the afternoon, a cool and quiet environment, and less mobility. Chinese American students preferred the visual modality more than the other two groups. African Americans expressed a preference for the kinesthetic modality, and Mexican Americans indicated they did not like the auditory modality. At least among these groups of gifted minority students, learning style differences did not vary significantly (Ewing & Yong, 1992).

Adapting to such groups would seem to be accommodated easily. On the other hand, increased use of the kinesthetic and visual modalities might be effective for all three groups. A study of whether achievement actually improves if accommodation to different learning styles is changed would lend credibility to purposeful modification.

### Counseling

The support that comes from an intact and secure family structure is less available to many economically disadvantaged or culturally different students. While family problems are not unique to students in these groups, it is true that complicated and temporary marital relationships, alcohol abuse, mobility, and other forms of stress and instability are common. According to one U.S. Census, for example, 36 percent of African American families are single-parent and female-headed. Health, hygiene, and nutritional values may be minimal. Peer pressure *not* to achieve is strong. In some difficult circumstances, survival itself takes strong precedence over educational achievement and developing gifts and talents. A study by Lee and Smith (1999) found social support positively related to learning in Chicago schools, but that social support depended on schools' specific efforts to create supportive environments.

Gifted children need shelters, persons to whom they can go when intellectual, social, developmental, and even safety and survival needs are threatened. This shelter should include an adult, particularly an empathic and professional counselor, who understands the local economic and ethnic realities and who cares about the welfare of all children. Exum (1983) recommended that counselors in minority areas should, first, increase their knowledge about the community, for example, by becoming acquainted with population characteristics, availability of resources, availability of public transportation, community leadership styles, and the particular types of problems that come to the counselors' attention. Second, Exum noted that the counselor's credibility and trustworthiness will be enhanced if he or she becomes more visible in the community, perhaps by serving on multicultural committees and by patronizing minority businesses. A third recommendation was for counselors to be flexible in scheduling appointments—using evenings and weekends—because so many parents of minority children cannot attend counseling sessions during the regular work day. Generally, said Exum, counselors should seek to build personal relationships with minority families, because "parents are much more responsive to counselors whom they believe have a genuine personal interest in their children."

Counseling that takes place within school becomes especially important in economically disadvantaged schools. Referrals to outside-of-school psychologists are unlikely to be followed through by parents who don't have the means to pay for such services.

Informal counseling by concerned adults played an extremely important role for the successful disadvantaged youth in the Kauai study (Werner, 1989). Teachers, ministers, and club leaders can be encouraged to support gifted students who may not have the family support and expectations that are important for disadvantaged gifted adolescents.

Harris (1991) emphasized the importance of peer support among gifted new immigrants who came mainly from third world countries. Steinberg, Dornbusch, and Brown (1992) also underscore the critical role of peer culture in achievement. They concluded that the peer group both mediates positive or negative family effects and directly influences attitudes toward achievement. For example, with Asian American students peer support toward academic excellence can offset negative parenting effects. Unfortunately, among African American adolescents, the positive influence of parenting often is undermined by a negative peer environment.

The antilearning peer pressure terms used for African American students (acting White) and Native American students ("apples"—red on the outside, white on the inside) may be a reflection of more than peer pressure. Ogbu (1994) reminds us that education has not taken into consideration that some minority groups have cultural frames of reference that are oppositional to the frames of reference of the American mainstream. Academic success for these families may truly represent leaving the cultural community to join the White majority culture. For disadvantaged minority children, achievement could feel like betrayal to their own race. Their racial identities may well be tied to opposing mainstream educators. Even their teachers who are of similar race may not be considered a part of their cultural community. Educators thus are faced with the complex task of proving to children that school education is not "white" education, but truly has multicultural value. Counseling by minority group counselors is particularly encouraged to help minority groups internalize the importance of education.

Certainly a critical goal of counseling must be to develop a peer support group for academic excellence among gifted youth. Summer enrichment programs can be an effective means of providing peer support for students who are not supported in their intellectual pursuits in their own schools. Cooley, Cornell, and Lee (1991) found that 35 high-ability African American students were entirely accepted by white peers in a summer enrichment program and also were comparable on measures of self-concept and academic self-esteem.

Providing social support systems for disadvantaged gifted youth may be critical. Studies of gifted middle class youth have emphasized the importance of family support. If that support is not available, interventions that provide positive substitute support are promising (Olszewski-Kubilius, Grant, & Seibert, 1994).

The SMART (Science and Mathematics Advocacy and Recruitment for Teaching) program, sponsored by Northwestern's Center for Talent Development and the Chicago Urban League, is designed to provide social support for minority high school students who are economically disadvantaged (Olszewski-Kubilius et al., 1994). The program components that provide social support are listed as:

- Weekly after school clubs
- Tutoring and academic support
- Cultural enrichment activities
- An intensive summer program
- A professional person who serves as mentor

Goals of the SMART program include successful high school graduation, college enrollment, election of teacher training, and college graduation. The long-term goal is for these students to become successful, full-time science and mathematics teachers, preferably in Chicago's public schools. It is too soon to evaluate so comprehensive a program, but it seems to provide some key supports.

## Parent Support Groups

Although every gifted program should encourage parent education and involvement, parents of socioeconomically deprived and culturally different children have a special and greater need. These parents will become supportive and involved only if (1) they understand their child's gifts and talents and (2) they understand the opportunities available to the gifted in our society. Further, they are more likely to assist their children and contribute to the G/T program if they do not see the program as elitist (e.g., for WASPs only) or as threatening. For example, parents may resist a G/T program if they believe the program will psychologically separate them from their children or cause their children to respect them less. It may be frightening to parents with little education to learn that their child is very bright and on a track toward a middle-class education that, they believe, could alienate the child from them.

On the other hand, if the program emphasizes *positive cultural identity,* fears of alienation should be reduced. Parents also will have an avenue for relating to and making contributions to the program. Parent meetings in which the G/T program and activities are explained and the above problems addressed, and in which parents share problems and optimism, will benefit the program and the gifted children involved.

High expectations by parents were crucial for the successful women from diverse backgrounds in a study by Rimm, Rimm-Kaufman, and Rimm (1999; Rimm & Rimm-Kaufman, 2001). Also, a study of the relationship between parental expectations and school performance of fourth- and fifth-grade students showed significant differences among Asian American, Latino, and European American families in expectations of children's educational achievement and grades (Okagaki & Frensch, 1998). Encouraging high expectations is foundational for gifted children's achievement. Unfortunately, some parents who found their own school experience discouraging may unintentionally discourage success for their children. Teacher communication to these parents may assist them in recognizing that their gifted children can achieve well.

Enhanced parenting skills should be part of parent support group activities. Shade (1978) emphasized that African American children who do well in school and on achievement tests tend to have parents or guardians who:

1. Maintain a quality of communication that stimulates the child's problem-solving ability, independence, and productivity.

2. Express warmth, interest, affection, and encouragement.
3. Establish close family ties.
4. Maintain structure and order for the child.
5. Establish goals of performance.
6. Use control mechanisms that include moderate amounts of praise and blame, moderate amounts of punishment, and no authoritarian tactics.
7. Give assistance when requested or when the need is perceived.

Shade also concluded that the parent-child interaction is more important to achievement than either family socioeconomic status or family structure.

The *No Gift Wasted* program (Alamprese & Erlanger, 1988) heavily encourages parent participation. For example, some of its projects required parents to learn about the activity and sign an agreement for their children's participation. The Potentially Gifted Minority Student Project (Alamprese & Erlanger, 1988) took the responsibility of keeping parents informed of their children's progress through telephone calls and written reports. There always was more involvement by parents in elementary school programs; parent participation in high school programs was limited.

Harris's (1991) gifted program, which included new immigrants, stressed the importance of using the parents' own language to communicate the importance of parent involvement.

Eight keys for parents to help children find success at school are presented in Table 12.8. The basis for these keys comes from Hine's (1994) study of the family factors that supported high achievement among ten gifted high school students. Her findings were used to prepare a guide for the parents of Puerto Rican students. Hine's discoveries are, of course, cross-cultural and need to be communicated to all families. However, disadvantaged families are especially vulnerable to pressures that do not encourage their pro-school and learning support.

Middle to upper-middle income white parents have led the advocacy movement for gifted education in this country. Parent advocacy by parents of economically disadvantaged and African American children has been lacking (Baytops, 1994). The causes of lack of advocacy are many. Impor-

---

**TABLE 12.8**  Eight Keys for Helping Children Find Success at School

1. Let your child know you value achievement in school.
2. Help your child to develop strong language skills.
3. Parents must make their children understand that they believe their children *will* be successful both in school and, later, in the workplace.
4. Parents must provide a strong family support system for their children.
5. Parents who nurture a strong family bond at home help their children to develop a positive image of themselves and their culture and to gain the self-confidence necessary to meet the challenges they face at school and in the community.
6. Help your child understand that, with preparation and hard work, his or her future can be bright. Instant success stories do not usually happen in real life. The great majority of successful adults had to deal with many challenges and obstacles along the way.
7. Do not let your child use cultural biases or prejudices held by people at school or in the community as an excuse for failure.
8. Parents should become involved in their child's school and extracurricular activities. By encouraging a social bond with the school and the community, they will help him or her to grow in confidence and self-esteem.

Adapted from C. Y. Hine (1994).

tant among them are the historically bad relationships between these groups and schools (e.g., Comer, 1988). Education may not be a high priority of those who are struggling to meet more basic needs. However, it is in everyone's interests to convince all parents that schools and gifted programs can make a difference for their children.

## Development of Significant Models

*Significant others* are persons who exercise a major influence on the attitudes of individuals. Chapter 13 on underachievement will emphasize the critical role of parents, as significant others, in the modeling of achievement values. Shade (1983) pointed out that for African American youth, significant others extend beyond the immediate family to include the extended family, the media, and White society. Mother, concluded Shade, is the strongest family influence upon African American students' school performance. Studies of occupational choice (Pallone, et al., 1973) indicated that African American high school girls were most influenced by their mothers, while boys were most influenced by persons holding the job to which they aspired. A study of African American college freshmen by Shade (1978) found that parents ranked last in influence, while peers, teachers, counselors, friends, and siblings ranked at the top. In contrast, earlier studies of African American college students showed mothers (Gurin & Epps, 1966) or parents (Olsen, 1970) to have the greatest influence. In the Rimm research (Rimm et al., 1999; Rimm & Rimm-Kaufman, 2001) parents, other relatives, and teachers were all found to be extremely important mentors.

A unique mentoring program that pairs middle school gifted students with extremely disadvantaged kindergarten children who show indicators of giftedness is part of Project Synergy (Wright & Borland, 1992; Inset 12.1). The adolescents receive guidance for their mentoring. The project staff also attempts to involve the family for more complete support. One has to believe that significant life experiences are taking place for these children.

These studies again emphasize the importance of parent achievement models for academic success. They also point to an important gap: The disadvantaged African American matriarchal family rarely provides a male achievement model for its adolescent boys.

Disadvantaged gifted boys are in almost desperate need of achievement-oriented males to serve as role models for achievement. In the absence of appropriate models, television media (Fedler, 1973; Leifer, et al., 1974) and peer and street culture (Perkins, 1975) strongly influence African American adolescent male youth. In one study (Bridgemen & Burbach, 1976), a videotape of African American male youth being rewarded for excellence in school resulted in a significant increase in academic expectations by the African American male viewers.

The concept of an all African American male academy has become a resounding answer to the recognized need for positive role models for primary-grade African American inner city males (Holland, 1991). In addition to providing appropriate role models in teachers and administrators, adult male volunteers from business and industry participate and involve boys in tutoring or learning projects. The first such program was known as Project 2000 because the kindergarteners with whom the program began in the 1988–1989 school year would graduate in the year 2000. The project was adopted by an all-male community service organization, the Washington, DC, chapter of Concerned Black Men, Inc.

The model of the all African American male academy has since been adopted in many urban areas and has been expanded to include all African American female academies as well. These experimental models are based on the following objectives and principles

1. Examining the effectiveness of gender specific instructional strategies.
2. Obtaining release-time for employees in the public and private sectors to serve as volunteers in classrooms.
3. Investigating ungraded primary grade models.

## Adolescent Mentors

Six-year-old **Jenny** lives in central Harlem with eight siblings and her pregnant, crack-addicted mother. Her father, an alcoholic, does not live with the family. He is not missed. Home is chaotic, cacophonous, and squalid to a degree that defies belief. Garbage rots in paper bags scattered throughout the apartment, providing a home for vermin and play objects for Jenny's siblings. Because of her mother's incapacity, the care that Jenny receives borders on neglect. She frequently comes to school in filthy, disheveled clothes that reek of urine.

Jenny's elementary school offers little in the way of respite from the adversities that have defined much of her existence. Classes are crowded, and a significant proportion of the children in each classroom have severe educational and behavioral difficulties. The physical plant might have been described as spartan before it fell on hard times. Today, other adjectives spring to mind. Classroom supplies are virtually nonexistent; teachers make do with next to nothing or buy materials with their own money. Art projects are of necessity monochromatic; there are only enough crayons for each child to have one. Unsurprisingly, the school is facing the threat of decertification by the state due to a persistent record of low student achievement.

Outside Jenny's school and apartment building, the environment is harsh and unforgiving. Crime is a constant presence. Street arguments frequently erupt into violent confrontations. The sidewalk is littered with crack vials and the inert bodies of men and women who have found surcease of their pain in the oblivion of alcohol and drugs.

The daily challenges that Jenny faces seem insurmountable. Yet, she is a survivor. Her inquisitive nature, her tenacious spirit, and the support and encouragement of her kindergarten teacher have enabled her to learn in spite of circumstances that would crush many adults.

Jenny has an intuitive facility with numbers. Although she has received virtually no formal instruction in the subject, she has somehow learned enough arithmetic to score at the 83rd percentile for children of her age on a test of early mathematical ability. Jenny is also quite adept verbally. She is teaching herself to read, and she writes imaginative stories using inventive spellings. By any reasonable metric, especially in light of her circumstances, Jenny is a gifted child.

**Narissa** is an eighth-grader who lives in Brooklyn with her single mother and other members of her extended family. Economic deprivation and crime stalk Narissa's life as persistently as they do Jenny's. Last summer, she and her family were evicted from their apartment for nonpayment of rent. That same week, Narissa spent three days on the witness stand in a murder trial giving testimony about a cross-fire shooting involving warring drug dealers, a shooting to which she was the only witness.

Nevertheless, Narissa is an unusually intelligent and sensitive adolescent. It is her good fortune to attend the De La Salle Academy, a middle school for bright urban, minority students in New York City, for which her family pays token tuition, and where she is considered to be an exemplary student. She considers the two-hour commute from Brooklyn to the Upper West Side of Manhattan to be a small price to pay for the education she is receiving.

Jenny and Narissa were brought together by Project Synergy at Teachers College, Columbia University, Jenny as a potentially gifted student receiving educational services, Narissa as a mentor.

From L. Wright and J. H. Borland (1992). By permission of *Roeper Review.*

4. Emphasizing team teaching.
5. Establishing secondary homerooms led by teacher-advisors who will keep the same group of children throughout their junior or senior high school careers, thereby providing them with an adult within the school who can serve as a mentor.

At this time the results appear promising. Providing achievement role models is critical to en-

**INSET 12.2** _____

## CURRICULUM IDEAS FOR ESTABLISHING MALE ACHIEVEMENT MODELS

1. Videotapes of achievement-oriented males in various careers (e.g., doctor, lawyer, professor, businessman). Men should tell about childhood experiences that fostered achievement.

2. Videotapes of a panel of minority gifted children (males and females) discussing their problems and successes in achievement. Emphasis may be placed on cultural pride and achievement.

3. Cultural intermediary—a young man who is achievement oriented and "streetwise" to meet with and counsel adolescent boys.

4. Speaker series—weekly talks by successful minority community persons (male and female) about their careers and their lifestyles.

5. Lunch seminars for small groups of students with minority community persons to talk about achievement.

6. Parenting classes for fathers only, led by a male counselor or teacher who also is a parent.

7. Parenting classes for single mothers with the specific goal of assisting them in establishing appropriate minority role models.

8. General parenting classes with emphasis on the importance of appropriate role models.

9. Video- and audiotapes of the parenting classes for fathers only, single parents, and general parenting available for loan to parents unable to attend classes.

10. Student interview assignments with achieving adults. Collection of interviews may be assembled into a book for discussion and review.

11. Bibliography of books emphasizing the childhoods of successful minority persons.

12. Visits to college campuses, including meeting with minority college students.

13. Involvement in summer and Saturday college campus enrichment programs.

14. Funding for minority teachers to spend extra personal time with minority adolescents in and out of school enrichment activities (one to one or small groups).

15. Funding for special interest mentor activities with successful adults.

---

hancing giftedness in populations of disadvantaged students and should be a requirement of every gifted program for disadvantaged students. Some recommendations are included in Inset 12.2. While this Inset addresses mainly male models, the suggestions also are applicable to providing appropriate female role models.

### Accelerated and Enriched Curriculum

Research by Ford (1993) seems to document a need for more challenging curriculum for disadvantaged gifted children more than it points to individual motivation problems. In her study of average, above average, and gifted African American students, Ford found gifted students to be most supportive of an achievement ideology and average students least supportive. Paradoxically,

the very same fifth and sixth grade students who believed in the relationship of schooling, hard work, and effort to success in life did not exert the effort they espoused. Although 88 percent of the gifted males considered school very important, 94 percent reported low levels of effort. Among the gifted girls, 94 percent considered school to be very important, yet 87 percent reported low levels of effort. Despite low effort, these students earned relatively good grades. Low effort should be considered an indicator of underachievement (Rimm, 1995d). If children are not making an effort, regardless of their grades they are underachieving. If the children in the Ford study continue to get good grades without effort, one might ask if teachers' expectations were low because the children were African American or disadvantaged.

Runco (1993) emphasized creativity as an important objective for disadvantaged students. Although he indicates that most recommendations for creativity would be similar to those recommended for all gifted students (Chapters 9 and 10 on creativity), there are three areas of emphasis for disadvantaged students:

1. *Provide a stimulus-rich environment.* Disadvantaged children may have less exposure to stimulating materials at home.
2. *Use nonverbal materials.* Verbal materials may be biased against disadvantaged students.
3. *Focus on independent and small group assignments.* These provide opportunities for disadvantaged children to follow their own interests.

## Career Education

Career education is an important priority for all students. One problem for disadvantaged gifted students, however, is that "career education" traditionally focuses on occupations and careers that seem suitable or available only to the majority children in a particular school. Thus a curriculum program in a middle-class high school will feature college preparatory coursework and a professional career orientation. A high school in a minority or economically depressed area might focus on blue-collar occupations. There is a noticeably reduced awareness and valuing of college training and professional careers and, thus, a reduced opportunity for the necessary preparation.

Career education for the gifted child in a lower-SES environment, of course, should stress the professional opportunities available and the necessary educational preparation. However, a realistic career education program also must emphasize the lifestyles, values, ethics, and goals that accompany particular professional careers (Moore, 1979; Perrone, 1997). To compete successfully, the disadvantaged gifted child must acquire the many subtle attitudes and skills that accompany a given profession—attitudes and skills learned at home by children of educated professional parents.

An important—indeed, crucial—component of career education is the involvement of suitable mentors. These are professional persons of similar ethnic backgrounds who have, in fact, emerged from difficult socioeconomic circumstances. They need to share their experiences, their problems, and their strategies for success with gifted young disadvantaged people. Presentations, mentorships, and on-the-job visits are good ways to provide gifted youth with a taste of career and life goals worth working for. The mentors also can help students understand that within the professional areas there *will* be support; and further, that once high-level positions are attained, both intrinsic and extrinsic rewards will make the educational and economic struggle worthwhile. Professional persons from disadvantaged backgrounds typically are very sensitive to the problems of culturally different and poor gifted youth and are motivated to help.

As an example, the Texas Governor's Honors Program, which follows the theme of Leadership in a Multi-Cultural Society, provides not only in-depth leadership instruction but also instructors and seminar speakers who serve as models and mentors to inspire these gifted students of diverse cultures to look toward college (Sisk, Gilbert, & Gosch, 1991).

An important component of career education should be visits to college campuses and, if possible, participation in gifted programs on these campuses. Tennessee State University is one of many universities that is making an effort to attract ethnically diverse students to summer programs to inspire young scientists to consider a biomedical education beyond high school (Adams, 1989). Participation in such programs provides appropriate role models and peer support, an enriched educational opportunity, as well as an opportunity to live and feel more comfortable on a college campus.

Insights from a career counseling program in a major urban center in the midwest provides some additional goals for college counseling programs. Fifty-five disadvantaged gifted students were enrolled in the program to prepare them for college (Olszweski-Kubilius & Laubscher, 1996). As a result of the program, enrolled students changed some of their plans for financing their college education and recognized that college would be lonelier than they had anticipated. Compared to a group of economically advantaged students in a summer preparation program, a three-year follow-up study found the students to experience college as significantly more boring, dull, and snobbish. They had more difficulty adjusting socially and forming attachments to their university.

Clearly, career education should include preparation for the social and cultural integration that will help disadvantaged students feel more socially comfortable in college environments.

Disadvantaged students require assistance in financial planning and will require direction in finding scholarships or other funding assistance. The second author of this book is especially conscious of this issue because the guidance counselors at her high school in Perth Amboy, New Jersey, Edward and Henrietta Herbert, made the difference in her attending college by providing her with this important information.

The extraordinary value of a well-designed career education program for gifted disadvantaged youth is that it may guide very talented persons to become fulfilled and productive individuals, individuals who will make those "valuable contributions to self and society." However, if these gifted youth meet only dead ends and frustration and have no outlet for the development and expression of their talents, society not only will lose their positive professional contributions but also may be taxed (literally) by their negative contributions. Farley (1986) argued that high energy levels can be channeled either into creative and productive outlets or, in the case of many low-SES adolescents, into delinquency and self-destructiveness.

### Effectiveness of Programming for Gifted Students Who Have Disadvantages

The new emphasis on programming for gifted and talented students with economic and cultural disadvantages is effective in many school districts.

Yong (1994) administered tests for self-concept, locus of control, and "Machiavellianism" (deceitfulness) to 169 ethnically diverse middle school gifted students in Chicago schools. Self-concepts for the African American group were slightly better than those for the Mexican American and Asian American groups. No significant differences were found between groups for locus of control or Machiavellianism. Self-concept was significantly correlated with internal locus of control and low Machiavellianism. Mean scores for this group indicated they had high self-concepts, internal locus of control, and low Machiavellianism. These three characteristics have been correlated with high achievement in other studies, thus supporting the important impact of gifted programming on ethnically diverse populations.

In a study including 147 gifted seventh and eighth graders, of which 97 were considered middle SES and 50 lower SES, and 56 were African American and 91 Caucasian, VanTassel-Baska, Olszewski-Kubilius, and Kulieke (1994) drew the following important conclusions:

• Self-esteem tends to be high among gifted students regardless of ethnicity, gender, or socioeconomic class.
• The greatest differences were found between advantaged and disadvantaged, supporting the concept that class may be more important than ethnicity in impeding achievement. Disadvantaged students believed they had less support from classmates. They also felt less academically and socially competent.
• Gender differences also were found, with females feeling less academically and socially competent. They also felt they received less social support from classmates than did their male counterparts.

A dramatically successful program, A Better Chance (ABC), has for the past 30 years identified more than 8000 talented minority children and fostered and supported their education (Griffin, 1992). Recognizing the difficulty in using test scores for identification, they used the following additional measures: A strong sense of self, an independent mind, a questioning attitude, and a willingness to take risks and persevere. The effectiveness of selecting these children and matching them to appropriate high-level educational settings is best born out by the extraordinary results. Consider this sample of postsecondary education by ABC graduates:

**Degrees completed or in progress**

| | |
|---|---|
| Bachelor's | 96% |
| Master's | 38% |
| Doctor's | 7% |

There is much that educators of the gifted can learn from ABC.

## GIFTED PROGRAMMING IN RURAL AREAS

The word *rural* typically elicits images of farms and farming communities located far from urban centers. In fact, there are four categories of *rural communities,* defined as communities with fewer than 2500 people (Colangelo, 1999). In addition to (1) farm areas, there also are (2) rural fishing villages, as in New England and Alaska, (3) isolated logging towns, as in America's Northwest, and (4) reservations and small towns in the West and Southwest, home to many Native American and Mexican-American people.

Gifted students who live in rural areas may be greatly disadvantaged. Sparse populations, poverty, traditional rural values, small school size, and inadequate school finances all contribute to the paucity of gifted programming. Spicker, Southern, and Davis (1987), Colangelo (1999), Colangelo, Assouline, Baldus, and New (2003), and Davalos and Griffin (1999), noted the following problems in providing gifted education for rural students:

- Resistance to change makes it difficult to initiate new offerings for gifted students.
- There is less parental pressure for gifted programs.
- A smaller budget prevents expensive educational programs (e.g., a district G/T coordinator), particularly if the program is perceived as benefitting only a small number of select students.
- Rural isolation prevents access to universities, libraries, other schools, teacher training, and cultural opportunities, as well as exposure to professional careers.
- Teachers in rural secondary schools have more preparations across several different subjects, making it difficult for them to keep up with newer, specialized information.
- There typically are fewer counselors, school psychologists, and curriculum specialists to assist the faculty in building programs for the gifted.
- In accord with the national movement, there is a trend toward heterogeneous grouping and "teaching all students as if they are the same" (Davalos & Griffin, 1999, p. 308).
- The needs of gifted students are not understood. There also may be confusion about acceleration.
- With small enrollments, there will be few gifted peers.
- A belief in self-sufficiency and local control make it less likely that rural districts will seek outside assistance from state agencies or universities to develop gifted programs.
- Some adults may feel threatened by a "brain drain."

At the same time, many features of rural schools and communities promote social and emotional support that encourages school achievement and could aid innovation (Colangelo, 1999; Davalos & Griffin, 1999). For example:

- Smaller class size allows greater student-teacher contact, and promotes a warm, interactive, and family-like atmosphere; greater social and emotional support; and a sense of belonging.
- Everyone is acquainted, which promotes respect among students, respect for the teacher, and hard work.

- There is good rapport between teachers and administrators, and close interaction between school and community.
- With less bureaucracy, administrators can more easily mobilize the smaller teaching staff to implement instructional improvements and schoolwide changes.
- There are strong family ties and family support of educational activities.
- There is greater community stability, compared with the mobility often found in urban settings (Spicker, Southern, & Davis, 1987).

Attempts to identify giftedness in a rural Mexican population in the southwest United States were successful in terms of increasing community involvement and enhancing a culturally relevant understanding of giftedness (Reyes, Fletcher, & Paez, 1996). Table 12.9 includes a list of char-

acteristics of giftedness arrived at by community parents and teachers. Although most of these characteristics would seem to be relevant in any community, a few surely are culture specific (e.g., ability to learn a new language, knowledge of nature and farming).

As one solution, innovative educators can encourage cooperation among small school districts. For example, a consortium of school districts brought Purdue University and seven rural public schools together to provide comprehensive in-service training for their teachers, a resource center, and a broad range of effective programming for gifted and talented students (Ruckman & Feldhusen, 1988).

Witters and Vasa (1981) found the itinerant (traveling) consultant model to be effective in providing services to rural gifted children. Still another solution is for volunteer community persons to take an active role in gifted programs, if

**TABLE 12.9** Characteristics of Giftedness Identified by Community, Teachers, and Parents

- Is curious about knowing the how and why.
- Thinks of unusual ways to solve problems.
- Is able to influence or persuade others.
- Is clever at making things out or ordinary materials.
- Understands the importance of culture and family.
- Has the ability to learn a new language.
- Knows how to interact and to get along with people.
- Is a decision maker.
- Has abilities in the arts (music, drawing, dancing, etc.).
- Has a good sense of humor.
- Has above-average physical coordination.
- Has a good memory.
- Has good skills in organizing and planning.
- Likes to make up stories or poems.
- Is able to express his or her feelings.
- Understands the importance of nature in relation to farming (the weather, the moon, the soil, the stars, etc.).
- Is able to adapt to a variety of situations or to new surroundings.
- Helps others solve problems.
- Thinks about what he or she wants and sets goals to accomplish it.
- Is aware of and sensitive to the feelings of others; is liked by a lot of people.
- Is a self-starter; initiates and does things without being told.

school staff are unable to provide suitable programming (Yoder, 1985).

Telecommunications, including electronic bulletin boards (Southern & Spicker, 1989), televised in-services for teachers (Clasen & Clasen, 1989; Lewis, 1989), and "distance learning" using television and telephones (University of Wisconsin-Eau Claire, 1992) are being incorporated effectively to heighten awareness of faculty and provide peer group interaction to overcome the spatial separation of gifted students in rural areas. Technology holds great hope for expansion of opportunities for rural gifted students.

Rural adolescent girls have few female role models in science. Jacobs, Finken, Griffin, and Wright (1998) examined the influences on 220 high school girls for staying in science. Variables that were important for keeping rural girls in science, in addition to their intrinsic interest, included their science GPA, their friends' support of science, extracurricular science activities, and their mothers' support of their interest in science. The research emphasizes the importance of building supportive environments to encourage rural girls toward science.

A key focus is teacher education—raising awareness of gifted students' academic, social, and emotional needs, as well as educational strategies that accommodate their learning rates and interests. Many of the same (low-cost) strategies that are effective in larger communities are—or would be—effective in rural schools (Colangelo, 1999; Colangelo, Assouline, Baldus, & New, 2003; Davalos & Griffin, 1999). For example, distance learning with computers provides opportunities to explore any topic—art, math, geology, history, space science, and so on—in any depth (see Chapter 6), as well as to provide email contact with gifted peers. Other strategies include grade acceleration; tutoring across grade levels (Colangelo, 1999); using learning contracts (and individualizing learning generally); cluster grouping to solve problems or produce creative products (Davalos & Griffin, 1999); mentoring, perhaps using secondary students, available local professionals, or email contacts (e.g., Duff, 2000, see

Chapter 6); allowing gifted students to work at their own pace with topics of personal interest, which may be at a higher grade level; and allowing cross-grade movement that matches student capability with suitable curriculum, for example, a gifted fourth-grade student may require middle-school math and sciences classes.

As resources, the Rural Council on Rural Special Education at Kansas State University can be reached at www.ksu.edu/acres/; the National Rural Education Association at Colorado State University can be reached at www.colostate.edu/orgs/NREA/; the Rural Challenge organization in Granby, CO, can be reached at www.ruralchallenge.org/; and the ERIC Clearinghouse on Rural Education and Small Schools (Appalachia Educational Laboratory) can be reached at www.ael.org/eric/.

Despite some progress, education for the gifted in small rural schools is in its infancy, and most gifted children in rural schools are not served by appropriate programming (Spicker, Southern, & Davis, 1987).

## SUMMARY

Minority students are underrepresented in gifted programs. Current legislation allows funding for research, programming, and identification of gifted and talented youth who are disadvantaged.

Dropout rates for minority students have improved in recent years but remain unacceptably high. Hispanic Americans are the most undereducated in our country, and both Hispanic American and African Americans are underrepresented in gifted programming.

Few Hispanic American or African American students show high-level mathematical proficiency; few earn Ph.D. degrees.

Studies have shown that support from either the family or others in the community can help gifted disadvantaged students develop their potential.

Characteristics of resilience, such as internal locus of control, positive self-worth, maturity, academic and social confidence, belief in the

American Dream, positive school experiences, strong family values, and positive peer relations, serve as protection and promote social and academic success for African American youth.

There is a conflict between maintaining cultural identity and striving for academic honors for minority students. Successful minority students credit their success to their personal efforts and the support of their families. Gifted, achieving, and female students were found to have more positive racial identities than average, underachieving, and male students.

Low IQ or achievement tests scores may be misused to "prove" the absence of giftedness. Because average or below-average achievement can be common among gifted disadvantaged, identification must be based on potential rather than actual academic performance.

While a high IQ score is valid evidence of giftedness, an average or low score may be misleading and IQ tests may be racially biased.

Family, cultural, and language differences and testing circumstances must be considered. African-centered values and beliefs can affect ability testing. An understanding of Asian cultures is an important factor in both identification and programming for gifted Asian American students.

While high achievement is good evidence of talent in particular areas, achievement tests scores suffer from the same problems as intelligence test scores.

Research indicates that creativity tests such as the Torrance Tests of Creative Thinking and the GIFT and GIFFI inventories are good instruments for identifying creative disadvantaged and minority students.

The Baldwin Identification Matrix is helpful in identifying gifted minority students.

Teacher nominations may favor members of the majority culture and were found to underidentify African American and Hispanic students in several studies. Gay compiled a list of characteristics of gifted African American children; Swenson itemized characteristics of creativity in culturally different students.

Parent nominations are important in the identification of gifted students, especially if parents are made aware of the characteristics of giftedness and the advantages of gifted programming for their children. Peer nominations also are a good identification strategy.

The Frasier Talent Assessment Profile combines test and nontest criteria to identify gifted disadvantaged students.

Identification methods based on activity rather than static test scores, using a series of evaluations instead of just one, and using a shortened WISC-R administered in Spanish and English have increased minority participation in gifted programs.

Other promising identification methods include the use of dynamic assessment in a pretest, teaching test-taking intervention, followed by a post-test, and identification tasks based on Gardner's (1983) theory of multiple intelligences.

Quota systems assume that gifts and talents exist in equal proportions in all cultural groups and assure their proportional representation in G/T programs.

Programming options described in earlier chapters may be used with disadvantaged and minority students. However, additional components should be included: (1) maintaining ethnic identity, (2) extracurricular cultural enrichment, (3) learning style differences, (4) counseling, (5) parent support groups (6) using significant models, (7) greater emphasis on enrichment, and (8) career education. School, family, personal issues, and community all must be considered.

Ford and Trotman suggested characteristics of exemplary teachers of culturally diverse gifted students.

Cultural pluralism includes maintaining ethnic identity; cultural pride is central to self-esteem and educational and career success. Assimilationism refers to conforming to the majority (Caucasian) system. Differences between the two positions influence many aspects of programming for gifted students.

Culturally responsive classrooms should include culturally relevant instructional training, equity instructional training, a "we-us-our" or communal philosophy, respect for students' primary language, culturally congruent instructional practices, culturally sensitive assessment, student-family-teacher relationships, and a diverse teaching staff.

Extracurricular enrichment can include knowledge, skill, and creative objectives. Accommodation to different learning styles should be considered in every classroom.

Counseling is important. Exum recommended that counselors learn about the local community, become visible, and be flexible in scheduling appointments. Informal counseling by concerned adults in the community is valuable.

A support group of gifted peers is beneficial to lessen antilearning peer pressure and feelings of culture disloyalty; summer enrichment programs create such peer groups. The SMART program is designed to provide social support for minority economically disadvantaged high school students.

Parents are more likely to support G/T programs and to become involved if they understand the importance of the program for their child's future, and if they are not threatened by the program or its possible effects on their child. Parent meetings aid in educating parents regarding G/T programs, and allow parents to share problems and optimism. Helping parents set high expectations for their children is crucial.

Disadvantaged gifted children—especially males—need achievement models, as provided in all African American male and all African American female academies.

Accelerated and enriched curriculums emphasizing creativity are important for challenging gifted disadvantaged students and should focus on providing a stimulus-rich environment, using nonverbal materials, and providing independent and small group assignments.

Career education must include not only career options and the preparation needed to attain them, but the lifestyles, ethics, and goals that accompany various professions. Mentors—professional persons from similar disadvantaged backgrounds—are a vital component of career education programs. College visits and college counseling are valuable.

In studies of the effectiveness of gifted programming for disadvantaged students, the characteristics of high self-concept, internal locus of control, and low Machiavellianism were correlated with high achievement and support the important impact of gifted programming on ethnically diverse populations.

Many problems impede the development of gifted programs in rural areas, for example, sparse populations, smaller budgets, and fewer support personnel. Some solutions are increased community involvement, an understanding of giftedness, cooperation among several small districts, itinerant consultants, volunteer community members, the use of telecommunications, and such low-cost G/T strategies as computer information searches, grade acceleration, learning contracts, cluster grouping, mentoring, and allowing cross-grade matching of ability with curriculum.

# CHAPTER 13

# UNDERACHIEVEMENT
## DIAGNOSIS AND TREATMENT

*Student performance that falls noticeably short of potential, especially
for young people with high ability, is bewildering and perhaps the most
frustrating of all challenges both teachers and parents face.*
Sally Reis (1998a, p.12)

The underachieving gifted child represents both
society's greatest loss and its greatest potential
resource. The child has the potential for high
achievement and significant contributions, but is
not using that talent in productive ways. Statistics
tell us that as many as half of our gifted children
do not perform up to their abilities in school (National
Commission on Excellence in Education,
1983). Studies of high school dropouts estimate
that between 18 percent and 25 percent of the students
who do not graduate are in the gifted range
of abilities (Solorzano, 1983; Renzulli & Park,
2000). The Carnegie Corporation's (1996) report,
*Years of Promise,* further certifies the seriousness
of the underachievement problem in the United
States. The report states:

Make no mistake about it, underachievement is
not a crisis of certain groups: it is not limited to
the poor; it is not a problem afflicting other people's
children. Many middle- and upper-income
children are also falling behind intellectually.
Indeed, by the fourth grade, the performance
of most children in the United States is below
what it should be for the nation and is certainly
below the achievement levels of children in
competing countries (p. 2).

Richert (1991a) is convinced that even these
large figures are underestimates of the amount
and degree of underachievement because the figures do not include underachievers who were not
identified because IQ scores were the criterion.
IQ scores, even of individually tested students,
are frequently lowered by the underachieving
pattern (see Harry's scores on next page). It is
difficult to measure the exact magnitude of the
problem, but it is large.

Furthermore, although some underachievers
may reverse their underachievement in college
and in life, most continue their pattern of underachievement. Comparisons of 73 gifted achievers
and gifted underachievers four years after high
school graduation (Peterson, 2000) showed that
achievers continued achieving, had more years of
college, higher college GPAs, greater campus involvement, and had earlier and greater certainty
about their career directions. To shed some hope
in the direction of maturity's effect on achievement, 26 percent of the high school underachievers did become achievers in college and had
GPAs of at least 3.0.

Because the child's special abilities are recognized, the nonproductiveness often leads to frustration for parents, teachers, and even the child.
However, if the underachieving pattern can be reversed, the child can make unusual progress in
skill acquisition and in positive, productive work.
In view of the child's history of underachievement,
the extent of positive change after appropriate intervention usually is quite surprising. Extraordinary motivation to achieve or superachievement

may indeed be the flip side of the underachievement coin (Rimm, 1991b).

This chapter will review the characteristics, causes, and dynamics of underachievement, along with a strategy for reversing this costly syndrome.

## DEFINITION AND IDENTIFICATION OF UNDERACHIEVEMENT

*Underachievement* is defined as a discrepancy between the child's school performance and some index of his or her actual ability, such as intelligence, achievement, or creativity scores or observational data. Although many studies use more technical definitions, the discrepancy between potential and actual productivity seems to be part of all definitions (Richert, 1991a).

### Test Scores

The chief index of actual ability is test scores. Despite all the faults and problems related to testing, despite test unreliability and measurement error, and despite all the biases that need to be considered related to low test scores, it seems apparent that children cannot score extraordinarily high on tests purely by accident. Test-taking skill alone cannot account for test scores that consistently fall two or more standard deviations above the mean, that is, above the ninety-seventh percentile. Unusually high scores then, whether on intelligence, achievement, or creativity tests, indicate special abilities or skills not apparent in the underachieving child's usual schoolwork.

The unusual story of Harry's reversal of underachievement (Rimm, 1995d) provides evidence of how underachievement may lower test scores and how the reversal of underachievement may cause those test scores to increase again. Harry's parents were uncertain whether their son was an underachiever or if he simply had average ability, so they sought help at Rimm's Family Achievement Clinic. Harry's primary-grade teachers had described him as gifted, but by sixth grade his teachers considered him an average student with average grades and test scores. After regular col-

lateral therapy with Harry's parents and only a few sessions with Harry, he gradually reversed his underachievement. Figures 13.1 and 13.2 show the improvement in Harry's IQ and achievement test scores from sixth through eighth grade. His Wechsler IQ score went from 110 to 125 by eighth grade. Harry showed further improvement in high school. His 650 SAT score and his 3.6 grade point average, which included honors and AP courses, reflected the giftedness his earlier teachers had described. Harry's college 3.5 grade point average, his admission into medical school, and his success as a medical student further confirmed his early childhood gifted diagnosis.

### Intelligence Test Scores

If a child is identified as gifted, even based on intelligence test scores alone, it is important to compare the child's *actual* school performance to the performance that would be *expected* based on those IQ scores. There are several statistical concepts that may be used in this kind of comparison, especially *grade equivalent scores, mental age* (MA) *equivalents, stanines,* and *percentiles.* For example, a third-grade child of 8 years 6 months may produce intelligence test scores in the ninth stanine (top 4 percent) or a mental age equivalent score of 10 years 2 months, but his or her usual classroom performance might range between the fourth, fifth, and sixth stanines—strictly at grade level. Any of these statistical yardsticks are satisfactory for helping to define underachievement operationally in order to identify children who need help.

However, using *current* test scores alone may underidentify underachievement because scores may be artificially lowered by lack of motivation, tension, negative attitudes toward testing, or many years of not learning in school. Earlier test scores can be important for alerting educators to a child's real potential.

A frequent error in the identification of underachievers is to use a *fixed* number of months or years below grade level as a criterion of underachievement. For example, first-grade children

**IOWA TESTS OF BASIC SKILLS**

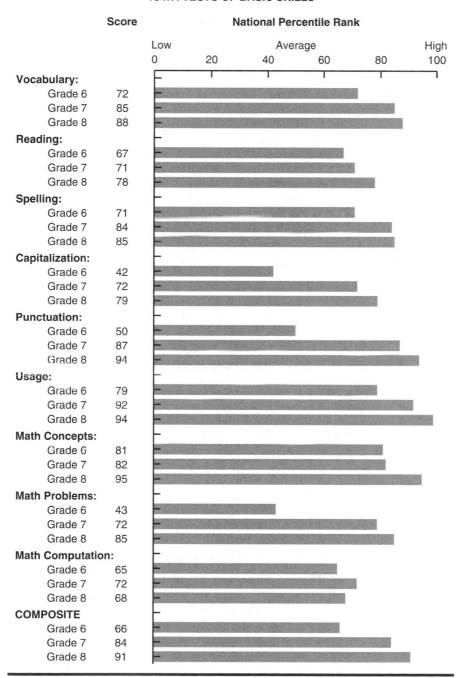

**FIGURE 13.1**   Cognitive Abilities Test (Harry).

Source: *Why Bright Kids Get Poor Grades,* by S. B. Rimm, Crown Publishers, New York, 1995.
Reprinted by permission.

**FIGURE 13.2**    Iowa Tests of Basic Skills (Harry).

Source: *Why Bright Kids Get Poor Grades,* by S. B. Rimm, Crown Publishers, New York, 1995. Reprinted by permission.

who are six months below their expected achievement level will have far more serious underachievement problems than eighth graders performing one full year below the expected level. For the younger children six months may represent being 50 percent behind where they should be; for the eighth-grade children one year represents only 12.5 percent behind expected performance. The main problem related to using a constant number of months is that younger children with underachievement problems are likely to be overlooked because the discrepancy between actual and expected achievement does not appear to be large enough in terms of actual months, even though the problem is quite serious. Because underachievement can be treated more easily when diagnosed early, it is critical to recognize this common identification error (Rimm, 1995d; Whitmore; 1986).

## Achievement Test Scores

Many schools do not routinely administer group intelligence tests, but virtually all schools regularly use published (standardized) and/or teacher-made achievement tests. These provide an objective basis for determining the levels of information and skills

that a child has mastered. To evaluate underachievement, the teacher can compare actual school performance (for example, the quality of reports, projects, homework, math or reading proficiency, or class participation) with the achievement test scores. A pattern of continuous decline in group achievement test scores also is a sure sign of underachievement (Rimm, 1995d).

## Creativity Test Scores

High scores on divergent-thinking tests such as the *Torrance Tests of Creative Thinking* (Torrance, 1966) or on creative personality inventories such as GIFT and GIFFI (Rimm, 1976; Rimm & Davis, 1980, 1983) strongly suggest that the child has talent in the area of creative and productive thinking. However, high creativity scores do not assure high achievement. On the contrary, some fairly common characteristics of creative students—such as nonconformity, resistance to teacher domination, impulsiveness, and indifference to rules—may cause the creative child serious difficulties in achieving within the classroom structure (Davis, 2003). Some highly creative students are dramatic underachievers, since their personalities and thinking styles are quite at odds with that required for classroom success. Rimm (1987b, 1995d) found that creative underachieving students often defined their identity in terms of nonconformity. Their concern for thinking and acting differently than others actually prevented them from achieving and making classroom efforts. Typical patterns Rimm finds among underachieving students who come to her clinic are scores of 98 or 99 percentile for the GIFT or GIFFI inventories and below 10 percentile for the Achievement Identification Measure (AIM; Rimm, 1986). AIM is an inventory completed by parents that describes achievement patterns, with low scores representing underachievement (Rimm, 1995d). Other creative students, however, apply their unique talents to classroom assignments and requirements and achieve at the level of students with much higher tested intelligence (Getzels & Jackson, 1962).

Children with high creativity scores but only somewhat above average IQ scores (110–130) have very high potential for making creative contributions (Rimm, 1987c; Renzulli, 1986; Renzulli and Reis, 1985, 2003). If students in this category are not being productive in school, they should be identified as gifted underachievers, even though their intelligence and achievement test scores may not be in the "gifted" range.

## Observation

Some underachieving gifted children do not perform well on any test due to poor test-taking habits. For example, they may not be motivated to do well. On a group test some students may answer questions randomly. On an individually administered test they may fear making mistakes, so they "play dumb" or avoid answering questions unless they are certain of the correct answer. Teacher and parent observations provide the only basis for identifying these gifted children; there will be little or no objective evidence.

Teachers may note class behaviors, comments, or vocabulary that suggest that the child has much more intellectual, creative, or artistic potential than he or she is exhibiting in school work.

Teachers, however, can recognize these behaviors only if they are aware of the characteristics of gifted children. Teachers must remain open to the possibility of discovering giftedness in children already labeled as "average" or even "below average" (remember Harry!). *Many such gifted underachievers are never discovered.*

Commonly used checklists and rating scales for gifted programs do not include traits of gifted underachievers. Hall's (1983) study of teacher identification procedures found that four gifted children described by the following statements had been considered "below average" students, although their IQ scores were above 130.

Student A. Makes excuses for not doing assignments, doesn't take an interest in things, passive, dependent.

Student B. Doesn't get along with others, doesn't do his work, likes to tell jokes.

Student C. Talks too much, doesn't listen, wastes time.

Student D. Immature, quiet, withdrawn, short interest span.

Teachers who are aware of characteristics of both underachieving and achieving gifted students can make important observations that will help identify gifted underachievers.

Parents also are in a unique position to observe the talents and capabilities of their own gifted children, even if the children are not high achievers. Note that teachers and principals typically feel uncomfortable and threatened by "pushy" parents who insist their child is gifted. Educators should assure these parents that their perceptions will be given full consideration if they can provide specific evidence of their child's giftedness. If the anecdotal material appears reasonably convincing, further testing may indeed support the parents' observations. If the anecdotal material does not suggest giftedness, the teacher or principal can explain why such behavior does not represent special talent by comparing it to behavior of typical children and highly talented children.

Parent observations that indicate the child makes little effort on assigned homework or study can certainly verify underachieving behavior even when school grades are reasonably good. If gifted students earn good grades effortlessly, the curriculum is not sufficiently challenging and they are underachieving. Further, they may not be prepared to cope with challenging curriculum and competition when it occurs (Rimm, 1995d).

### Underachievement Test Scores

Three tests have been expressly developed for the identification of underachievement syndrome. *Achievement Identification Measure* (*AIM*; Rimm, 1986) is a parent report inventory used with children in grades 1–12. *Group Achievement Identification Measure* (*GAIM*; Rimm, 1987a) is a self-report inventory for students in grades 5–12. *Achievement Identification Measure-Teacher Observation* (AIM-TO, Rimm, 1988a) is a teacher observation instrument to be used for students in

Grades 1–12. These inventories were normed with general student populations and are highly reliable ($r = 0.89$, $0.90$, and $0.97$ for AIM, GAIM, and AIM-TO, respectively). All instruments provide a test score that allows one to compare each student to the norm based on characteristics related to high achievement. Subscale scores, described in Table 13.1, provide information on the types of problems the children are exhibiting. The manuals that accompany the tests provide a guide to the interpretation and use of the scores.

AIM, GAIM, and AIM-TO are most useful in identifying children suspected by teachers and parents of being gifted underachievers. The tests also can be used to identify underachieving gifted children already in programs. That is, they can uncover high-risk children with characteristics of underachievement whose superior abilities mask the problems that are likely to appear later if not prevented.

**TABLE 13.1**  Subscale Scores for AIM, GAIM, and AIM-TO

COMPETITION

High scorers enjoy competition, whether they win or lose. They are good sports and handle victories graciously. They do not give up easily.

RESPONSIBILITY

High scorers are responsible in their home and schoolwork. They tend to be well organized and bring activities to closure. They have good study habits and understand that their efforts are related to their grades.

ACHIEVEMENT COMMUNICATION

Children who score high are receiving clear and consistent messages from parents about the importance of learning and good grades. Their parents have communicated positive feelings about their own school experiences and there is consistency between mother and father messages of achievement.

INDEPENDENCE/DEPENDENCE

High scorers are independent and understand the relationship between effort and outcomes. They are able to share attention at home and in the classroom.

RESPECT/DOMINANCE

High scorers are respectful toward their parents and teachers. They are reasonably well behaved at home and school. They value education. They are not deliberately manipulative.

## CHARACTERISTICS OF UNDERACHIEVING GIFTED CHILDREN

Studies of gifted underachievers have identified characteristics that are typical of these children. Joanne Whitmore (1980) summarized some of the most important traits in an identification checklist (Table 13.2). If ten or more of these characteris-

tics are checked, she suggests this would indicate that the child should be further evaluated to determine if the child is indeed a gifted underachiever.

The characteristic found most frequently and consistently among underachieving children is *low self-esteem* (Fine & Pitts, 1980; Rimm, 1995d; Whitmore, 1980). These students do not believe they are capable of accomplishing what their fam-

**TABLE 13.2**   A Checklist to Identify Gifted Underachievers

Observe and interact with the child over a period of at least two weeks to determine if he or she possesses the following characteristics. If the student exhibits ten or more of the listed traits, including all that are asterisked, individual intelligence testing (Stanford-Binet or WISC-R) is recommended to establish whether he or she is a gifted underachiever.

_____*poor test performance

_____*achieving at or below grade-level expectations in one or all of the basic skill areas: reading, language arts, mathematics

_____*daily work frequently incomplete or poorly done

_____*superior comprehension and retention of concepts when interested

_____*vast gap between qualitative level of oral and written work

_____exceptionally large repertoire of factual knowledge

_____vitality of imagination, creative

_____persistent dissatisfaction with work accomplished, even in art

_____seems to avoid trying new activities to prevent imperfect performance; evidences perfectionism, self-criticism

_____shows initiative in pursuing self-selected projects at home

_____*has a wide range of interests and possibly special expertise in an area of investigation and research

_____*evidences low self-esteem in tendencies to withdraw or be aggressive in the classroom

_____does not function comfortably or constructively in a group of any size

_____shows acute sensitivity and perceptions related to self, others, and life in general

_____tends to set unrealistic self-expectations; goals too high or too low

_____dislikes practice work or drill for memorization and mastery

_____easily distracted, unable to focus attention and concentrate efforts on tasks

_____has an indifferent or negative attitude toward school

_____resists teacher efforts to motivate or discipline behavior in class

_____has difficulty in peer relationships; maintains few friendships

From Joanne Whitmore, *Giftedness, Conflict, and Underachievement* (Boston, MA: Allyn & Bacon, 1980). Copyright © 1980 by Allyn & Bacon, Inc. Reprinted by permission.

ily or teachers expect of them or what they should expect of themselves. The low self-esteem they feel may, in fact, be directly related to these pressures to "be gifted" (Rimm, 1987c; Adderholdt-Elliott, 1989).

Low self-esteem is not always internally consistent nor observable to the outsider. Plucker and Stocking (2001) discovered that among 131 gifted adolescents studied, academic self-concept was not always generalizable. Thus a student who has excellent mathematics skills is likely to have a positive self-concept in the area of mathematics, but that self-concept may have a negative effect on self-concept in the verbal area. When your author (Rimm) asks young clients about how smart they are compared to their classmates, they often describe themselves in segmented ways, some of which are realistic and some more negative in their areas of weakness because of their strengths in other areas. Here's a case study example:

Sixteen-year-old Craig is gifted and achieving in art. His art teacher describes his work as phenomenal, specifically referring to Craig's speed, creativity, and the excellence of his products. Craig explains that he shuts down and feels anxiety in math and English because he could never reach the high standards set by his art teacher. His thoughtful but rationalized defense is that it makes no sense to put effort into areas in which he cannot be as successful as he can be in his talent area. "Fast," "brilliant," "extraordinary," and "creative" are his only acceptable standards. His self-concept is excellent as it relates to art but is seriously damaged for math and English.

Related to their low self-esteem is their sense of low personal control over their own lives (Rimm, 1995d). If they fail at a task, they blame their lack of ability; if they succeed, they may attribute their success to luck. Thus they may accept responsibility for failure but not for success.

This attribution process in educational achievement has been related to Seligman's (1975) concept of *learned helplessness*. If a child does not see a relationship between efforts and outcomes, he is not likely to make an effort to achieve. This pattern is characteristic of many gifted underachievers. Weiner (1985) also emphasized that a child's performance will be strongly influenced by whether he or she attributes successes and failures to ability, effort, task difficulty, or luck. Especially, attributing success to *effort* leads to further effort while attributing success to *task ease* or *luck* does not.

Low self-esteem leads the underachiever to nonproductive *avoidance behaviors* both at school and at home, secondary characteristics of under-achievement (Whitmore, 1980). For example, underachievers may avoid making a productive effort by asserting that school is irrelevant and that they see no reason to study material for which there is no use or, as Craig mentioned above, at which they aren't very good compared to their real talent areas. Students may further assert that when they are really interested in learning, they can do very well and then cite the examples of a favorite course or project. These kinds of avoidance behaviors protect underachievers from admitting their lack of self-confidence, or worse, their feared lack of ability. If they studied, they would risk *confirming* the possible shortcomings to themselves and to important others. If they do not study, they can use the nonstudying as a rationale for the failure, thus protecting their valuable feelings of self-worth (Covington & Beery, 1976; Fine & Pitts, 1980; Rimm, 1995d). Some familiar examples of defensive excuses appear in Figure 13.3.

Extreme rebellion against authority, particularly school authority, provides another route to protect the underachiever. The student seems eager to tell teachers, the principal, the superintendent, and even the board of education exactly how they ought to run the school. An indignant Craig, who was described earlier, came to your author (Rimm) with a petition signed by most members of his freshman class stating that the teachers at his school were not teaching useful information. Faulting the school helps the underachiever avoid the responsibility of achieving by blaming the system.

**HIDDEN MEANINGS:**
On Not Getting Down to Work

*Whatever subject I pick, it won't be as good as Mary's topic.*

*My video production is going to look ridiculous. I'm afraid they'll laugh at me.*

*What if lasers are too complicated to study?*

**FIGURE 13.3**   Avoidance Behaviors Often Take the Form of Defensive Excuses.

From Hershey & Crowe, 1989. Reprinted by permission of *Gifted Child Today*.

Expectations of low grades and perfectionism—though apparent opposites—also serve as defense mechanisms for the underachieving child. If the underachiever expects low grades, he or she lowers the risk of "failure." Note that low goals are consistent with a poor self-image and low self-confidence.

By contrast, achieving children set realistic goals that are reachable, and failures are constructively used to indicate weaknesses needing attention.

Perfectionism provides a different protection. (Perfectionism is elaborated in Chapter 17.) Since perfection is unachievable, it provides the child with ready excuses for poor performance. For example, students can boast that they set their goals higher than most people, so of course they cannot always succeed. The students thus provide a rationale for failure and do not need to label themselves as incompetent (although they may indeed feel incompetent).

Adderholdt-Elliot (1989) named five characteristics of perfectionistic students that contribute to underachievement: *procrastination, fear of failure,* an *all-or-nothing mindset* (even one *B* means failure), *paralyzed perfectionism* (if there is a risk of failure, do nothing), and *workaholism* (which leads to burnout, depression, and a lost balance among school, family, and friends).

Hostettler (1989) described the relationship between perfectionistic habits acquired in elementary school and high school underachievement. He taught a class of tenth-grade *gifted* underachievers whose standardized achievement test scores were above the 85th percentile, yet their mean grade-point average (GPA) was 1.85. Most of them were failing English, French, and/or algebra. However, high school records showed that in sixth grade the usual GPA of these bright students was 4.0— straight *A*—and typical teacher comments were "perfect student," "marvelous," "wonderful," "doing beautiful work," "impossible to improve," and "set for big things." Two conclusions seemed in order: First, the students' own high grades coupled with superlative feedback led to perfectionistic self-expectations. Second, these students showed a common late onset of underachieving because perfectionistic students do well when the curriculum is easy enough to permit "perfect" achievement but become underachievers when work becomes difficult, that is, in secondary school.

Closely related to the issue of perfectionism is the gifted underachiever's inability to function in competition unless they view themselves as winners (Rimm, 1995d). Students in a clinic setting rarely admit this problem when asked; however, when the *Achievement Identification Measure* (Rimm, 1986) was factor analyzed to create achievement subscale scores, the main factor included items related to competition, for example, "My child loses his or her temper if he or she fails at something," "My child brags a lot when he or she wins at something" (negatively scored), "My child enjoys competition, win or lose," and "My child is a good sport whether he or she wins or loses."

Parent observations of underachievers confirm that these children avoid competitive activities in and out of the classroom, *unless they perceive themselves as highly likely to win.* Instead of viewing losing as temporary, they see themselves as losers, quit, and do not seem to have the resilience to recover from failure experiences. Many young adults who were underachievers as children concede that their early inability to cope with competition was a critical component of their avoidance patterns, although they also acknowledge they would never have admitted their feelings about competition at the time. Donna Draves (a pseudonym), television news anchor (Rimm, Rimm-Kaufman, & Rimm, 1999), confessed to feelings of competition she had during childhood that she would never have admitted to if she had been required to use her real name for the study. For example, she admitted that she wanted to quit ballet lessons because she was no longer the best dancer in class, not because the lessons were boring as she had told her parents. Donna avoided math and sports because she feared she could never do as well in those areas as her brother. She also gradually left her peer group because she won a speech competition (encour-

aged by her teacher), and her peers did not value winners, but a new group of peers did.

EPA Director Christie Whitman's description of her underachievement in some subjects follows (Rimm & Rimm-Kaufman, 2001):

> My father set very high standards, perhaps too high. He insisted, "Anything worth doing is worth doing well," so when I wasn't good at things, I would retreat. I did well with the subjects that interested me, like English, history, and creative writing, but in Latin, math, and grammar, I did miserably. I think part of it was being spoiled. I developed a defense mechanism, which was "If I don't try, it's not that I'm dumb, it's that I didn't try." I didn't give myself a chance to prove myself. It's not something I'm dearly proud of and I certainly never mentioned it to my children when they were growing up.

Underachievement of gifted students may appear even at the college level if students have not learned to function in competition. The U.S. Department of Education reported that of the top 5 percent of high school graduates, 40 percent do not graduate from college (DeLeon, 1989). While the reasons for noncompletion of college may be more than an inability to function in competition, the second author's clinical experience with gifted students who lose confidence in competitive college environments provides evidence for this serious underachievement problem. Here is an example:

> *Bruce was a National Merit Scholar and valedictorian of his very academic high school. He had received few Bs during his entire educational experience. He was well liked and well adjusted. He loved computers and became engaged in almost every kind of learning.*
>
> *Bruce attended the University of Wisconsin-Madison. His freshman year went reasonably well, but in his sophomore year, his grades declined. After the first semester of his junior year, his grades were too low for him to be permitted to continue.*
>
> *Bruce worked at a fast-food restaurant while planning his future. He said he completed a report in his*

*senior year of high school about how he thought the school could improve. It never occurred to him then to ask for more challenge. He had been happy and interested. Bruce said he never realized then how many highly intelligent students there were in the world, nor had he ever had an assignment in high school that he could not easily do. He "hit his first wall" in college and backed away in defeat.*

*When the counselor asked Bruce about returning to school, he said that, of course, he planned to graduate eventually. When he was further asked if he believed he would be able to graduate, his immediate response was "no" (Rimm, 1995d).*

Achieving students recognize a competitive environment as one in which they may experience success or failure, yet they take the risks in full awareness that they may not be the top (most perfect) scholars.

Two directions of avoidance behaviors have been described by Kaufmann (1986) as *withdrawal* responses or *aggressive, hostile* responses. In a related fashion, Rimm (1995d) found underachievers to exhibit their defenses by *dependency* or *dominance*. Figure 13.4 shows these two directions. Conforming underachievers differ from those in the nonconforming category in their visibility. That is, conforming dependent and dominant students have the characteristics that may lead to greater underachievement problems, but their underachievement is not obvious. Nonconforming dependent and dominant underachievers already are exhibiting serious problems. The prototypical names used in Figure 13.2, Passive Paul, Rebellious Rebecca, and so on, are used to emphasize the main characteristics of these underachievers, but any one child typically exhibits a group of these symptoms. Rimm also points out that some underachievers exhibit both dependent and dominant qualities.

Richert (1991a) summarized how others' expectations can influence gifted children not only in the area of achievement (or underachievement) but in values, creativity, self-esteem, social relations, and "emotional impact" (Table 13.3). Richert's ideal pattern, and one to be encouraged, is to neither fully accept nor reject others' expec-

tations, but *transcend* them with *healthy self-expectations,* which will optimize achievement, independence, creativity, self-acceptance, and so on. Note that Kaufmann, Rimm, and Richert show considerable agreement in their descriptions and interpretations of behavior of underachieving gifted children.

## Other Characteristics of Underachievers

Because underachieving children avoid effort and achievement to protect their precarious self-esteem, other characteristics arise that support the pattern of underachievement. These include deficient academic skills (Fine & Pitts, 1980), poor study habits, peer acceptance problems, poor school concentration, and home and school discipline problems. These indicators of underachievement seem to be the visible "tip of the iceberg" characteristics that result mainly from the avoidance behaviors that protect underachievers from the primary problem, low self-esteem and the related feelings of low personal control.

Skill deficiencies may cause several kinds of problems. Redding (1990) found that gifted underachievers did as well as gifted achievers on tasks that required holistic information processing, but could not perform as well with detailed or computational tasks requiring precision. Rimm (1991b) similarly found that gifted underachieving elementary children performed well in tasks requiring information, abstract reasoning, and vocabulary, but poorly on tasks that required rapid copying of codes. If writing is difficult, some gifted children will avoid writing assignments in favor of verbal tasks. Rimm (1995d) facetiously labeled this characteristic "pencil anxiety." Their poor coordination has little to do with coordination with Legos or screwdrivers—only pencils.

Further, because many elementary-age children equate "fast" with "smart," poor writers may worry that their slow writing confirms they are not as "smart" as they or their parents and teachers believe them to be (Rimm, 1991b).

Hayes, Norris, and Flaitz (1998) compared narrative language skills of 20 eighth-grade gifted

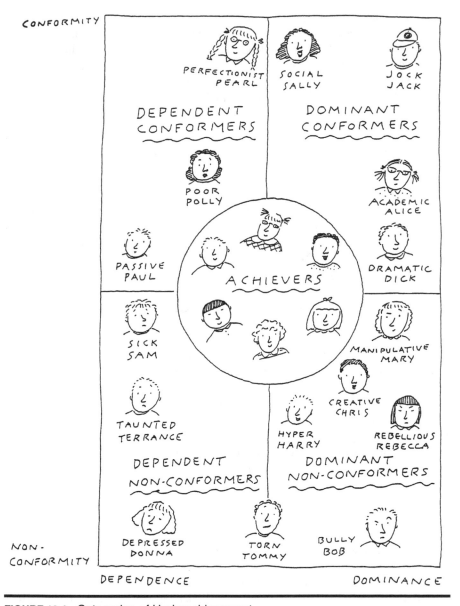

**FIGURE 13.4** Categories of Underachievement.

Source: *Why Bright Kids Get Poor Grades,* by S. B. Rimm, Crown Publishers, New York, 1995. Reprinted by permission.

achievers and underachievers and found significant problems in the language skills of the underachieving gifted. Perhaps the roots began with early "pencil anxiety" (Rimm, 1995d), or perhaps their language problems were simply unidentified early, and the feelings of inadequacy in one language subject initiated defensive patterns in related subjects.

**TABLE 13.3**   Patterns of Response to Expectations

| Aspects of Potential | Accept | | Reject | Transcend |
| --- | --- | --- | --- | --- |
| | Conformity | Withdrawal | Rebellion | Maximizing |
| Ability Achievement Productivity | Successes satisfy others Extrinsically motivated | Safe mediocrity Evades pressure to perform | Failure/Rejects external expectations | Satisfies own values Intrinsically motivated |
| Values | Based on norms Externally dependent | Evades external judgment | Reacts against | Independent |
| Creativity | Repressed Fear of failure | Repressed/Refuses to take risks | Divergent Negative | Creative Risk taker |
| Self-Esteem | Insecure/Dependent on others' perceptions External locus of control | Follower/Avoids competition External locus of control | Dependent Internalizes negative external judgment External locus of control | Independent Self-accepting Internal locus of control |
| Social Relations | Roles that lead to rewards/Pleases others | Follower/Avoids competition | Loner or gang leader isolated or domineering | Withdraws or takes leadership May have few friends |
| Emotional Impact of Experiences Vulnerability | Reinforces dependence on external rewards and approval for self-esteem | Reinforces feeling of self-dissatisfaction and fear of judgment | Punishment Betrayal Rejection | Potency: Asserts control over own life Compassion |

© 1990 E. Susanne Richert

## ETIOLOGIES OF UNDERACHIEVEMENT

Children are not born underachievers. Under-achievement is *learned* behavior, and therefore it can be unlearned. Underachievement can be taught by families, by schools, or by cultures. The last, cultural underachievement, its etiology and treatment, is discussed in Chapters 12 and 14, focusing on culturally different students and females. The following sections will describe rituals and reinforcements that maintain patterns of underachieving in the home and school. Recognizing factors that cause, support, and reward underachievers should help the reader understand the dynamics of underachievement and therefore should assist in preventing and reversing the problem.

## FAMILY ETIOLOGY

When families of underachieving children are compared to families of achievers (Zilli, 1971; Rimm & Lowe, 1988), certain characteristics become apparent. Some of these characteristics are difficult to alter, but some can be changed easily by concerned parents once they are aware of the dynamics. Among the characteristics resistant to change are general poor family morale and family disruption (French, 1959) caused by death or divorce. Among those that can be changed relatively easily are parent overprotection, authoritarianism, excessive permissiveness, and inconsistencies between parents. These frequently result in manipulative rituals and parent identification problems that almost always can be recognized.

These family problems appear across socio-economic strata. For example, the family etiology model was noted by Baker, Bridger, and Evans (1998) in their study of preadolescent under-achievers. Further, the authors found a combined, more complex etiology model that included individual, family, and school etiology. In Hébert's (2001) qualitative analysis of young men in urban classrooms, he, too, found a complex etiology that included individual, family, and classroom. An analysis of college-age achievement by King (1998) found family etiology so important that he recommended using the Family Environment Scale for identifying college students at high risk for underachievement.

As part of the family pattern, sibling issues were included by Hébert (2001). Competition between siblings, which identifies one child as a hard-working achiever and the other as a gifted but unwilling-to-work underachiever, is found frequently as part of the family etiology (Rimm, 1995d).

It is helpful for teachers to be familiar with "problem family" patterns, because an understanding of these patterns will help the teacher communicate with parents more effectively. Also, family patterns that include manipulations by a child can be extended into the classroom. Thus a sensitivity to underachieving patterns can help the teacher avoid being manipulated.

### Identification and Modeling

Terman and Oden's (1947) study of lower-achieving gifted men showed that their most significant characteristic was *non*identification with their father. Rimm (1984; Rimm & Lowe, 1988) similarly found that underachievers frequently did not identify with the same-gender parent. Interestingly, however, some identified very strongly with a same-gender parent—if that parent appeared from the child's perspective also to be an underachiever or to be giving the child messages that "avoiding schoolwork is acceptable."

Freud (1949) explained identification with the same-gender parent as a product of the resolution of the Oedipal or Electra complexes. During the phallic stage of development (ages 3 to 5), said Freud, the child finds himself or herself romantically attached to the opposite-gender parent. Recognizing that the parent already has a partner, the child sees the impossibility of the affair and resolves the issue by unconsciously identifying with the same-gender parent. This identification purportedly causes the child to adopt the behaviors, conscience, and appropriate gender role of that parent. The three-year-old boy walking in Daddy's shoes or the girl imitating Mommy's telephone conversation is said to be evidence of this early identification.

While conceding that it is nice for children to love their parents, contemporary social learning theorists question whether identification truly stems from the unconscious resolution of a sexual conflict. Rather, they describe identification and imitative behavior in terms of *modeling* (Bandura, 1986; Meichenbaum, 1977). Research by Mussen and Rutherford (1963) and Hetherington and Frankie (1967) indicated that the parent model chosen for identification and imitation depends largely on a combination of three variables, *as perceived by the child:* (1) nurturance, (2) power, and (3) similarities between the parent and child.

The *nurturance* variable is very straightforward. The child tends to identify with, and model the behavior of, the parent who is highly nurturant. There may be an especially warm, loving relationship between the parent and a particular child or children in the family. If that parent is an underachiever, or does not stress achievement, the child may adopt similar attitudes.

The way that *power* influences identification, imitation, and underachievement is sometimes direct and at other times more complicated. In the most direct way, if one parent is definitely more powerful from the child's perspective, but does not value education or school achievement, the identifying child is not likely to perform well in school. Teachers need to be aware of this pattern because they may see only the concerned mother of an underachieving boy at parent conferences.

However, it may be the *father* with whom the conference should be taking place. It is difficult to motivate a boy who identifies with his father, if the father and the boy view education as "women's work."

Some typical, more complicated power patterns that foster underachievement in children are described by Rimm (1995d, 1996a) as "Father is an Ogre," "Daddy is a Dummy," "Mother is an Ogre," and "Mother is the Mouse of the House." These power patterns tend to arise because parents unintentionally compete with each other to establish their own childrearing approach as best or to feel like the "good parent." The impact of the rivalry to establish oneself as the better parent is that the other person is given the role of "bad" or "dumb" parent. Rimm indicated that awareness by parents of these rituals frequently is sufficient to encourage a change in parenting approaches. This awareness may make a major difference for underachieving gifted students.

In the first pattern, "Father is an Ogre," the father is viewed as successful and powerful, the mother as kind and caring. Often, a closer view of the home life shows a father who wears a big "No!" on his forehead. That is, he firmly prohibits many of the activities the children wish to pursue. However, the children learn to bypass his authority by appealing to their kind, sweet mother. Mother either manages to convince Dad to change his initial decision or surreptitiously permits the children to carry out their desired activities anyway. Children quickly learn the necessary manipulative maneuvers.

The ritual worsens because as the children grow older the father begins to recognize his lack of power over his family, and he becomes more and more authoritarian as he tries to cope with his powerlessness. In response to his increasing authoritarianism, the mother feels an increasing need to protect and defend her children. In desperation she invents new approaches to sabotaging her husband's power in the belief that she is doing the best thing for her children. Although girls in this family are likely to be achievement-oriented because they see their mother as power-

ful and positive, boys will tend to underachieve. They see no effective model in their father, who appears both hostile and powerless. They may fear and resent him but are not likely to want to emulate him.

"Daddy is a Dummy" is a slightly different but equally disruptive ritual. This syndrome is often discovered in homes where Mother has a college education that includes courses in education and psychology. Dad has no college education or one that did not include psychology. Mother is certain that she knows the "correct" way to bring up the children, which, according to her training, should include an important father role. However, whenever Dad attempts to play his parent role, Mother corrects him and explains a better way in which he can play his part. Dad feels uncomfortable and powerless in handling the children and makes every effort to withdraw, sometimes to 70 hours a week at the office. If Mother insists that he come home, the television screen becomes his escape. Sons again tend to be the underachievers in this family since they see their father as either powerless, absent, or as expressing passive-aggressive behavior. These underachieving boys often assume the same passive-aggressive posture in front of the television screen.

In the third parenting pattern, "Mother is an Ogre," we find a disciplinarian mother and a kind, sweet, but undisciplined father. This results in at least two more poor patterns for identification. (1) If the disciplinarian mother is viewed by the children as fair and strong and supported by "kind father," this provides a weak male image for the sons but a strong mother figure for female identification. (2) However, if the mother's discipline is overruled by the father, we have potential models for underachievement for both male and female children. The boys may identify with Father because he is viewed as powerful, but he models some characteristics and habits that make for underachievement—ignoring or violating (Mom's) rules, procrastination, and lack of discipline and perseverance. To the girls, Mother may be viewed as insignificant sound and fury and therefore cannot become the model for an achieving daughter because of the children's perceptions of both her powerlessness and her continuous anger.

"Mother is the Mouse of the House" is the "dummy" ritual that results in rebellious adolescent daughters. It begins with a conspirational alliance between father and daughter—"daddy's little girl." Mother is not included in the special relationship and is treated as if she were not as intelligent as Dad. The daughter is typically a very good student in elementary school and pleases father, mother, and her teachers. By fourth or fifth grade, although good achievement continues at school, an unexplainable conflict between mother and daughter begins at home. Father takes the role of mediator, or worse yet, rescuer for his daughter who has learned to convince her daddy that she is right and that mother is too controlling and overreacting. This manipulative ritual continues until adolescence when father begins to worry about teenage dangers from which he must protect his daughter. He then takes a firmer discipline position and will no longer give in to his daughter's persuasion. In frustration and surprise at her new ineffectiveness, the daughter may attempt manipulating her mother for support. Mother, impressed by the improved mother-daughter relationship, may then ally herself with her daughter. The manipulations increase and vary between mother-daughter opposed to father and father-daughter opposed to mother. Eventually and usually by high school, the parents identify the manipulations and unite in desperation to control their adolescent who seems to be pushing all limits. The adolescent, who has earlier managed to do exactly what she chose, now feels overcontrolled by her parents and rebels. Her rebellion sparks a series of punishments increasing in severity, which in turn causes more rebellion. The adolescent underachievement becomes only one of the symptoms. more severe behaviors, including alcohol and drug abuse, depression, and/or sexual promiscuity, become the acting-out behaviors that capture adult attention. Underachievement is viewed as a minor offense in comparison.

Although these four parenting rituals may appear separately in some families, they sometimes appear simultaneously in the same family. Parents actually may take "good" or "mean" roles differently for each child in the family. They also may change roles between early childhood, later childhood, and adolescence. The crucial issue for underachievement is that if children are exposed to one parent who challenges them and another parent who shelters them, they learn to "take the path of least resistance" and automatically back away from challenge, with the protection and support of the sheltering parent.

In order to prevent a child from developing an underachieving pattern, parents must compromise their points of view to avoid either overpressuring or overprotecting their children so that an appropriate and positive challenge message is issued by both parents. This permits children to accept challenge and please both parents, who have set reasonable expectations for them.

In addition to nurturance and power, the third variable that affects identification is the *similarity* the child sees between himself or herself and a parent. This similarity provides a good basis for gender-role identification. High similarity between mother and daughter or between father and son strongly supports same-gender identification when nurturance and power of the parents are equal. However, unusual similarities in appearance, abilities, interests, or personality between boys and mothers or between girls and fathers may lead to cross-gender parent identification. Cross-gender parent identification can contribute strongly to either achievement or underachievement. Achievement motivation may be strengthened by female identification with a powerful and effective father if he is intellectually oriented, but weakened if he is not intellectually oriented. However, only underachievement appears to be fostered by the cross-gender identification of sons with their mothers.

In the relationships that develop after a divorce or in single-parent households, ogre and dummy rituals become more complex and further increase the likelihood of underachievement. It has been predicted that by the year 2000, 61 percent of the children born in 1987 will spend at least part of their childhood in a single-parent home (Kutner, 1991). Although the prognosis for family etiology of underachievement is not optimistic, hopefully further research in new family styles will provide a blueprint for avoiding underachievement in the non-traditional family.

Other research has produced findings that relate child-parent identification to achievement and underachievement. For example, Lamb (1976) and Zilli (1971) found that if father is absent from the home, boys are more likely to be underachievers. Parish and Nunn (1983) discovered that boys and girls whose fathers left home (or died) before the children were 13 tended to be low in internal locus of control, a trait strongly related to achievement. In relation specifically to quantitative abilities, if Father is absent, both boys' and girls' math aptitudes and achievement are more likely to be weak (Carlsmith, 1964). However, girls and boys who identify strongly with father are more likely to have good problem solving, math, and science skills (Helson, 1971).

As we will see in Chapter 14, Rodenstein and Glickauf-Hughes (1979) found that a girl's attitude toward a career will be strongly and positively influenced by a successful working mother. However, this holds true only if there is a good family attitude toward Mother's employment and Mother's role conflict is minimal. Almquist and Angrist (1971) similarly emphasized that in order to aspire to a career, young women need good role models who can demonstrate that marriage and a career can be combined successfully.

In summary, the identification literature clearly supports the significance of identification with good parent models as an important family factor in high achievement. The lack of that identification, or the identification with a poor parent model, seems to be related to underachievement. Parents who view their own lives as interesting and successful and who model an equitable and respectful husband-wife relationship provide ideal role models for both male and female children.

## Gender Issues in Underachievement

Although gender issues will be described in Chapter 14, it is worthwhile to look at gender differences as they relate specifically to underachievement in this chapter. The patterns found by Kerr (1995, 1997), Shaw and McCuen (1960), Richert (1991a), and Rimm (1995d; Rimm, Rimm-Kaufman, & Rimm, 1999) appear to be consistent. Gifted boys start their academic underachievement earlier than gifted girls. Rimm finds that 90 percent of the elementary children who come to her clinic are males. Underachievement in her clinic population increases for girls by the middle and high school years. Among students who begin their underachievement at the college level, more are females.

One reason for gender differences in the onset of underachievement may lie in educational, family, and peer traditions. Most elementary teachers are female, and mothers have taken primary responsibility for home-school communications. Girls thus receive strong encouragement to achieve from female models. Many successful women in the Rimm and colleagues (1999) report idolized their elementary school teachers. Further, by middle school, peer pressure plays an important part in female underachievement, with peers tying brains and achievement to being a "nerd" (Brown & Steinberg, 1990; Rimm, 1990a; Rimm, Rimm-Kaufman, & Rimm, 1999; Rimm & Rimm-Kaufman, 2001). Finally, Table 13.4 sketches some striking differences in the videotaped behavior of second-grade boys and girls and equally striking differences in reactions to that behavior by men and women.

## Manipulative Rituals and Counteridentification

The situation in which a parent identifies with his or her child is called *counteridentification*. The parent who counteridentifies with the child invests himself or herself in the child's activities and empathically shares efforts, successes, and failures. A familiar example of counteridentification is the

**TABLE 13.4** Men's and Women's Reactions to Videotapes of Behavior of Second-Grade Boys and Girls

Videotape 1: The Boys

The second-grade boys are physically restless; their idea of what to do involves physical activities. They are continually aware of the hierarchical framework they are in, and they do what they can to mock and resist it; and they show their affection for each other in an oppositional format. They directly disagree with each other, but their disagreement is a natural response to the putdowns and mock assaults that are initiated.

Videotape 2: The Girls

The second-grade girls' conversation in the same situation includes nothing that resembles the ways of talking for the boys. The girls, too, are aware of the authoritarian framework they are in, but they are complying with it rather than defying or mocking it. Far from playfully attacking each other, they support each other by agreeing with and adding to what the other says. Rather than colluding to defy authority, they reassure each other that they are successfully complying. In contrast to the teasing by which each boy implies that the other is doing things wrong, the girls offer assurance they are doing things right.

Typical Female Response to the Videotapes

Women subjects thought Jane and Ellen were sweet little girls. They were touched by the girls' eagerness to fulfill the experimenter's request. The little boys made them nervous. They wished they'd *sit still!* They thought their joking silly and didn't like their teasing and mock attacks. They felt sorry for poor Kevin, who kept trying to smooth down his hair and was told that another little boy didn't like him.

Typical Male Response to the Videotapes

Men subjects reacted very differently. They thought the boys cute, and they found their energy and glee touching. They were sympathetic to the boys' impulse to poke fun at the situation and defy the experimenter's authority. The girls seemed to them like a pair of "Miss Goody Two-Shoes." Some commented that they didn't trust the girls' behavior; they felt that little children couldn't really enjoy sitting still or trying to be on their best behavior to please the experimenter.

Adapted from Tannen (1990).

vociferous father who argues desperately with the referee at the Little League baseball game as if it were he who had been unfairly called "out." Counteridentification is not always bad. Many parents vicariously enjoy seeing their children excel in sports or other talent areas, attend prestigious colleges, or travel—activities that the parents missed in their own youth.

Counteridentification has not been thoroughly explored in research, but it appears to have the potential to influence either high achievement or underachievement. The potential for positive contributions to achievement comes mainly from the parents' sharing of skills and their investment of time and resources. As mentioned in Chapter 2, Bloom (1985; Sosniak, 2003) found that the early training of extremely talented youth included coaching by one or both parents who had a strong personal interest in the particular talent field. Bloom emphasized that the parent provided an early and influential model for the child. Based on Bloom's descriptions, it is likely that most of the parents counteridentified with their talented child.

On the negative side, several forms of counteridentification can lead to manipulative rituals by children, supporting underachievement. Two such rituals begin with kind, empathic parents who try to be helpful to their children and try to understand their points of view. In one negative ritual rooted in counteridentification the child manipulates parents into completing his or her homework. This extremely common problem begins innocently enough. The child does not understand an assignment and goes to the parent for an explanation. The counteridentifying parent not only explains the assignment but in order to prevent the child's "suffering" continues to work with the child. The parent explains the assignment step by step, over and over. The child soon learns that he or she needs only to briefly express confusion and the parent is brought quickly to his or her side for the evening. Together they complete the daily assignments. When father or mother does not cooperate, the child may punish the parent by failing the assignment, thus encouraging the parent to be more helpful with the next homework.

It is not surprising that as time progresses the child finds the assignments more difficult and takes longer and longer to complete the work. Not only has the child found comfortable reinforcement in the form of attention from mother or father, the child loses confidence in his or her ability to achieve independently. Since mother or father is now carrying the responsibility for much of the work, the child may no longer believe it is possible to learn the required skills.

An early manifestation of this dependent pattern in the classroom is a child seeking continuous aid from unsuspecting teachers. For example, this is the child who typically waits until instructions have been given twice and then raises his hand and innocently announces, "Ms. Jones, I just don't understand what I'm supposed to do."

This dependent pattern sometimes has its origins in an early teacher recommendation to a parent. For example, in a primary grade a teacher may have suggested that a parent regularly help the child with homework. Teachers should be cautious in making such recommendations and should be explicit in the kinds of help that they suggest so that this help does not lead to overdependence.

This dependent ritual is relatively easy to change if identified early but very resistant to change in the high school years. By then, there is a sizable gap between the student's developed skills and those necessary to succeed. Furthermore, by this time the youth has little remaining confidence in his or her school-related competence. The sad example from this author's (Rimm) clinic of a twelfth-grade young man with an IQ of 160 who believed he could not accomplish his homework without his mother's help reminds us of how maladaptive dependence can be.

The second maladaptive ritual that stems from counteridentification is one in which parents convey *too much power* to their gifted children and the children become dominant or aggressively manipulative. Because the children appear so bright and because they use adult vocabulary and adult reasoning, parents find themselves interacting with them almost as adult peers long before the children have attained the wisdom to match their verbalizations (Fine & Pitts, 1980). Parents and sometimes teachers may be awed by the child's adultlike rationalizations for why they need not perform routine school tasks. To their own detriment, these children learn to manipulate their parents and teachers, frequently bypassing skill development because the work is "boring" or "irrelevant." Further, they may claim there is no reason to write material that they can answer orally, and they may depend on their verbal precociousness until writing skills actually become deficient.

Dominant children also may manipulate their parents and teachers into permitting them to avoid assignments in which they are less confident by using their talent area as an excuse. More than one musically or artistically gifted student has managed to avoid "irrelevant" math or science assignments by claiming to need time for his or her special talent (Rimm, 1990b). Furthermore,

## CALVIN AND HOBBES

CALVIN AND HOBBES ©1992 Watterson. Dist. by Universal Press Syndicate.

creatively gifted underachievers often have a history of avoiding tasks they describe as "boring" because they believe they must function creatively all the time. While talented students must have extra time to devote to their special interests, these kinds of avoidance habits can become manipulative rituals that deprive them of taking responsibility for learning (Rimm, 1987b).

The teacher who works with dominant students must recognize that the verbally powerful child needs to be carefully led to the conclusion that he or she must learn and study. Opposing this child will lead to a no-win battle, and antagonism is the likely result. Recognizing the power pattern that exists at home can help the teacher guide this child in the classroom. Whitmore (1986) described the necessary relationship as a problem-solving partnership. This alliance minimizes the potential for conflict and an adversarial relationship.

We have seen that *intuitive responses* by parents and teachers can reinforce underachievement—make matters worse. For example, with dependent students an intuitive reaction is to do too much (e.g., homework) for them; with abrasive dominant students a natural reaction is to "put them in their place" by overreacting and overpunishing. Less natural, *counterintuitive* measures are more effective. For example, with dependent children adults should insist that the children take small steps forward *independently,* even when they show signs of pressure. For dominant students, attitudes of respect, compromise, working together to solve problems, along with a negotiated and fair agreement regarding school work is a successful strategy for reversing underachievement. Parents and teachers should put such agreements in writing and hold to them firmly to avoid again becoming victims of manipulation.

In a comparison of families of gifted underachievers and families of gifted achievers, Rimm and Lowe (1988) found considerably more dysfunction among families of underachievers. Also noticeably absent from the families of underachievers were the modeling of intrinsic and independent learning, a positive commitment to their careers, and respect for schools and teachers.

That last component of family etiology is worth emphasizing. Erickson and Ellett (1990) point out that American educators, during the last three decades, have been more concerned with students' rights than responsibilities. Perhaps more emphasis at home and in the media on students' personal responsibilities, coupled with a clear message of respect for educators, would be an effective means of encouraging student achievement.

## SCHOOL ETIOLOGY

The gifted child often is exposed to the "good year, bad year" syndrome. Archambault and Hallmark (1992; Renzulli, 1992) found that 42 to 62 percent of the 7000 teachers in their study had absolutely no exposure to methods for teaching the gifted. Teachers without training supply most of the "bad years." However, other teachers—even without training in gifted education—do detect and provide for the special needs of gifted children, creating the "good years." Fortunately, not all "bad years" are devastating. Most gifted children are resilient enough to function well even in a less-than-responsive environment. However, certain personal and classroom conditions seem to create problems for the gifted child and seem to initiate or accelerate underachieving behavior patterns.

### School Climate

Whitmore (1980) described classroom environments that appear to cause and support underachievement. The main characteristics were a lack of respect for the individual child, a strongly competitive climate, emphasis on outside evaluation, inflexibility and rigidity, exaggerated attention to errors and failures, an "all controlling teacher," and an unrewarding curriculum. We will look more closely at the effects of inflexible and competitive classrooms.

*Inflexible Classrooms.* The inflexibility and rigidity that demonstrate lack of respect for the individual child provides a strong reinforcement for gifted underachievers. The intellectually gifted child learns faster and integrates information more easily. The creatively gifted child thinks differently and asks frequent questions. The rigid teacher, however, adheres to an organized schedule that allows little flexibility for those who differ in speed or learning style. The gifted child quickly discovers that rapid completion of assignments usually leads to more assignments. These typically are not more challenging or more exciting but "busy work" to keep the active child occupied.

Initially, the gifted child may be pleased and motivated by the special treatment by the teacher. Eventually, as the child finds the busy work unchallenging and boring, he or she concludes that these additional assignments are punishment for rapid work. To avoid the punishment, the child slows his or her pace and no longer completes assignments before the rest of the class. However, since the student's mind remains active and alert, he or she usually must find other diversions such as daydreaming, troublemaking, or surreptitiously reading an exciting book. In some cases the diversions become powerful reinforcers that distract the child from completing even the regular assignments, which appear dull by comparison. Consider this actual case:

> *Robbie, eight years old, was a highly verbal child with an IQ in the very superior range. However, he was two years behind in mathematics and never completed his math assignments. His problem became clear after he was observed in class by the psychologist. On his lap, hidden from the teacher's view, was a book he was reading while the teacher explained the math assignment. The book was shifted to underneath the math book while students were to be doing math written work. Robbie moved further and further behind in mathematics, which was taught too slowly for his quick mind, but he read many exciting books. He was referred to the psychologist as having a "learning problem."*

At the 1992 Annual National Rimm Underachievement Institute in Pewaukee, Wisconsin, John Feldhusen, a long-time leader in gifted education, shared his own story of surreptitious reading to avoid his childhood school boredom. Perhaps many adults committed to gifted education recall their own techniques for coping with inflexible and dull classrooms. Can you, the reader, recall your own novel adjustments?

Reis (1998a) described the dilemma of her stepson, Mark, as "dropping out with dignity" and explained that his school performance was directly related to a combination of curriculum content and his liking of his teachers. His complaints of too-easy work were valid in totally inappropriate lower-track courses, where his earlier underachievement had led him. His experience is an example of how underachievement can leave gifted students helplessly placed in inflexible environments.

In addition to busy work, other ritual punishments tend to discourage the gifted child from achieving in the rigid, inflexible classroom. For example, if the gifted child responds too frequently in class or asks too many questions, he or she is not called on to speak. However, if the ignored child waves his or her hand too enthusiastically, calls out answers, or talks excitedly to a neighbor, he or she is rewarded with a scolding. The scoldings may serve either to reinforce or punish the child. If the child views them as punishment, he or she stops responding, deciding that such enthusiasm is somehow inappropriate to the school setting. If the child views the scoldings as reinforcing, he or she increases the talking out of turn and the hand waving, which become nuisances to both teachers and peers. Either way, enthusiasm for learning and thinking is diminished.

***Competitive Classrooms.*** The classroom where competition and comparative evaluation are heavily stressed is a serious problem for underachievers. The announcement of grades to the class, the comparisons of students' test scores, the surprise expressed by a teacher when a student scores higher or lower than expected, and the continuous ranking of students all foster extreme competition within the classroom. That competition is attached to extrinsic evaluations of performance based on objective criteria that, from the perspective of the child, are viewed as the true measure of his or her competence and worth. Children who are already strong achievers and continue to find themselves at the top of the class may become even more motivated to achieve in very competitive environments. However, even for highly motivated children too much emphasis on extrinsic rewards may detract from the intrinsic rewards of learning and creativity.

It is underachievers, of course, who are most dramatically affected by the severe competition (Covington & Beery, 1976). Underachievers, who do not have a clear sense of their own competence, are informed on a daily basis that they are not measuring up to the standards of excellence of the classroom. These children are given objective evidence of average or below-average abilities. Since competitive achievement is the only source of teacher recognition and rewards in the classroom, and since these children do not believe they are capable of attaining that recognition, they search for other classroom rewards or other evidence of personal worth, or adopt the defensive measures noted earlier in this chapter and in Chapter 8.

A highly competitive environment may be a "good year" or a "bad year" for the achieving gifted child. For the underachieving gifted child it is always a "bad year," because it provides convincing evidence of his or her incompetence. While an *overly* competitive environment causes problems for many students, learning to function in a gradually more competitive environment is appropriate for students who must adjust to real-world competition (Rimm, 1992a, 2003).

## Negative Expectations

Rosenthal and Jacobson's (1968) book *Pygmalion in the Classroom* inspired a landslide of research, most of which strongly supports the notion that a teacher's expectations can have a dramatic impact on children's self-concepts and school achievement (Good & Weinstein, 1986; Keneal, 1991). The problem is that for children, teachers and school success are the major—if not the only—source of feedback concerning one's ability, competence, and worth (Covington & Beery, 1976). The teacher who sends messages of negative expectations usually will find exactly what he or she expects: Both regular and gifted students will underachieve. As a perhaps surprising source of negative expectations, Felton and Biggs (1977) concluded that "remediation, as it is sometimes practiced, may help the student to label herself as *stupid,* and this, in turn, may affect the teacher's attitudinal responses to that individual. This means that underachievement may be caused directly in the classroom and in the 'helping' provided there."

Not all gifted children will respond to the negative attitudes and expectations of a teacher by poor achievement. Some few may see this attitude as a special challenge and make additional efforts to meet that challenge. However, the underachieving gifted child, whose self-concept already is poor, normally will perceive the teacher's expectations of failure as a confirmation of his or her own poor self-evaluation. Another true story:

*It was fall conference time for fifth-grade parents. Any teacher can relate to the early confusion of matching the correct parents with students. There were two Amys in Mrs. James' class. One Amy was an excellent and positive student, but the other Amy was quite the opposite.*

*The second Amy's parents entered the classroom and introduced themselves. Mrs. James, assuming these to be parents of the first Amy, immediately exclaimed glowing praise for their delightful daughter. Amy's parents' faces reflected shock. Their response was, of course, enthusiastic. Mrs. James, immediately realizing that these parents belonged to the other Amy, regrouped quickly. Still on a positive note, she explained that Amy did have a few problems.*

*The description of Amy's problems never dampened the parents' enthusiasm. They returned home after the conference to tell Amy that this would surely be her best year in school. Amy, too, was delightfully surprised. She agreed that this would surely be a wonderful year.*

*Amy ended fifth grade with a B average, in startling contrast to her D average of the year before, a very dramatic impact of teacher expectation.*

Kolb and Jussim (1994) found that teachers' low expectations for a child help create a climate that encourages underachievement. They found that teachers may assign lower grades to gifted children who do not follow classroom behavioral norms. Furthermore, they concluded that teacher expectations of improved performance may lead to the reversal of underachievement for some students.

## Peer Pressure and Underachievement

Attitudes of peers toward achievement has a dramatic impact on achievement. By fifth grade, many children begin to believe it is "not cool" to achieve. Terms such as "brain," "geek," "dork," or "dweeb" bring tears to the eyes of many reasonably mature middle school students. The peer pressures continue in many communities through high school (Brown & Steinberg, 1990; Kinney, 1993). Clasen and Clasen (1995) interviewed forty middle and high school students participating in a Jacob Javits program for minority gifted students. Sixty-six percent of the students considered peer pressure to be the primary force against their getting good grades. Some students identified good friends as buffers from that peer pressure; their friends encouraged their achievement.

### An Unrewarding Curriculum

Although complaints from the underachieving gifted child that the school curriculum is irrelevant, dull, or unchallenging may only be a defensive avoidance ritual, it is often a real difficulty. Gifted children are particularly vulnerable to the "unrewarding curriculum" problem because of their intellectual and creative needs. Gifted children are often anxious to question, criticize, discuss, and learn beyond the levels that are appropriate for most students in the class. If the students are not challenged by the curriculum, they will find stimulation outside of the curriculum, and school will indeed be viewed as dull and boring. It is not uncommon for gifted underachievers who perform poorly in school to achieve excellence in nonschool-related activities in which they create their own rewarding "curriculum." Consider this case:

*Ron was described as a poor reader and disinterested in school. In fourth grade he rarely completed assignments, daydreamed, performed his class work sloppily, and in general was considered a below-average student. At home he was immersed in comic books or baseball. He read and enjoyed literally thousands of comic books. As for baseball, he had easily committed to memory baseball statistics of the previous 20 years and talked knowledgeably about batting averages and pitching records that involved mathematics well beyond what he had learned in school. The same skills he seemed unable to apply in the classroom setting were readily exhibited in his areas of true interest—comic books and*

*baseball. A more rewarding curriculum could have brought together Ron's interests and abilities and expanded both.*

### Matching Efforts with Outcomes

Whitmore (1986) emphasized that gifted underachievers are not "lazy" or "unmotivated," merely unmotivated for schoolwork. Underachievement syndrome among gifted children may have been caused by complex family and school situations, but it nonetheless is critical that children understand the relationship between effort and outcomes.

The educational needs of gifted children are best served by classrooms that provide intrinsically motivating curriculum (Goldberg & Cornell, 1998; Rea, 2000). Rea described *optimal motivation* as an experience in which students became absorbed in a task. They are most likely to experience motivation when challenge, interest, and arousal are present. That intrinsic motivation builds the relationship between effort and outcome.

Figure 13.5 (from Rimm, 1987b) illustrates how the appropriate relationship can lead either to achievement or underachievement. Quadrant 1 represents achievement. Children demonstrate appropriate effort. They have learned to work hard. They understand perseverance and have ap-

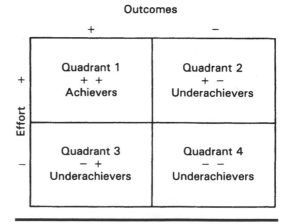

**FIGURE 13.5** Relationship between Effort and Outcomes.

propriate skills. Intrinsic enjoyment of challenge is part of the process and easy tasks are accomplished quickly in order that they may pursue more challenging activities. Their goals are set appropriately high but not beyond their abilities. They continue to achieve as long as they see the relationship between effort and outcome.

Quadrant 2 leads to underachievement when efforts are appropriate but goals or outcomes are set either too low or too high. In the cases of goals set too low, these children may have internalized a message from parents, society, or their peers that being "smart" is not as important as being well-adjusted or popular. Intellectual accomplishment is less valued than beauty or athletic prowess, and they do not wish to be "geeks" or "nerds."

Examples of goals that are set too low by teachers come from unchallenging cooperative learning environments in which gifted children too frequently play the role of teacher (Rimm, 1992b; Robinson, 1997, 2003) or when gifted children must conform to a heterogeneous group. Here's a sample case:

> Alex, an extremely gifted young man with somewhat poor social skills, was involved in a cooperative learning group where part of the assigned task was to draw a college campus. Alex could not convince his fellow students to design the campus to show more academics than athletics. Figure 13.6 (top) reflects Alex's description to the therapist of his reasons for frustration. The bottom figure is the drawing he made when he was given the opportunity to work independently.

The Quadrant 2 problem of goals set too high may appear in a highly competitive school environment in which, despite the child's excellent intelligence and study skills, good grades are not attainable. If parents set expectations beyond children's abilities (and some do), this too will have the impact of establishing "too high" goals.

Generally, if goals are set too low, children will stop making an appropriate effort; they have learned that it is easy to achieve those lower outcomes. If goals are set too high, they give up in desperation because they do not believe that any amount of sustained effort will make a difference in accomplishing these difficult outcomes.

Quadrant 3 leads to underachievement syndrome when achievement outcomes are set at a reasonable level, but the process of making an effort has not been learned appropriately. That is, parents and children value good grades and school performance. Report card grades initially reflect the excellent performance, and children feel positive about school. However, activities are not sufficiently challenging and the children learn that achievement is easy, that success is readily attainable, and that learning and study should be effortless. Occasionally they may comment on boredom or lack of challenge, but as long as grades continue to be high they exhibit no problem behaviors. Unfortunately, they do not develop the good habits of perseverance, dealing with challenge, or intense study. At some point in their academic development the curriculum material becomes more complex, the student population becomes more competitive, or both. Their goals continue to be appropriately high but they have not learned the processes or efforts required to produce the desired outcomes. Some students adjust to the additional needed effort. Others hide behind their threatening feelings. They worry that they are not as smart as they would like to be and they invent or discover a whole herd of rituals and excuses that prevent them from making a good effort.

Quadrant 4 represents the most advanced stage of underachievement syndrome. It appears after children described by Quadrants 2 or 3 have not functioned as achievers for a period of time. Quadrant 4 underachievement takes place when children's efforts and skills both show deficiencies for such a long period of time that the children give up on reasonable goal setting. Teachers rarely identify these children as gifted because their intelligence or creativity are no longer exhibited in the classroom. Even parents begin to doubt their children's abilities. In conversation they may refer to the past when, they recall, their children were smart, but at this point they have given up on high-level goals and are willing to

**FIGURE 13.6** Alex's representation of the cooperative learning group's drawing of a college campus (top), and his own version of a campus (bottom).

INSET 13.1

## Are Schools Teaching Gifted Children to Underachieve?

Two major changes are taking place in many schools today that are likely to contribute to underachievement by gifted children.

**1.** By uncritically hopping on the detracking bandwagon many schools have abolished *homogenous ability grouping*—and gifted programs along with it. As we saw in Chapter 1, research (e.g., Kulik, 2003) shows clearly that gifted children who are grouped for acceleration and enrichment, compared to gifted students in nonaccelerated and nonenriched classes, outperform the latter substantially—academically, nearly one year on a grade-equivalent scale. Further, if curriculum is too easy, gifted students are not likely to learn perseverance and develop an internal locus of control—the idea that personal effort leads to success (Laffoon, Jenkins-Friedman, & Tollefson, 1989).

**2.** Some schools emphasize *cooperative learning* in forms that minimize competition. To the extent that gifted students do not learn to compete, they will be ill-prepared for the competition they will face in college. They also may suffer decreased self-confidence that comes from a balance of successes and failures. An even greater danger of cooperative learning is that, as in heterogenous grouping, bright students simply are not challenged by assignments geared to the "group."

Because lack of an internal locus of control, poor functioning in competition, and not making a good effort are typical characteristics of underachievers, *schools adopting heterogeneous grouping and cooperative learning may now be teaching underachievement*. Gifted students may interpret the two trends to mean "don't bother to work hard."

The famous quote by Plato says it well: "What is valued in one's country is what will be cultivated." High individual achievement and creativity appear to be less valued in today's quest for equity.

---

settle for their children earning a high school diploma.

Inset 13.1 suggests that school curriculum that adopts heterogeneous grouping and cooperative learning may, in a *de facto* way, be teaching underachievement.

### THE TREATMENT OF UNDERACHIEVEMENT

As we have seen, the underachieving gifted child continues to underachieve because the home, school, and/or peer group support that underachievement. The student is not motivated to achieve, and there probably are deficiencies in skills necessary for achievement. Working below one's ability affects both immediate educational success and eventual career achievement; it is an important problem requiring attention.

While it may seem like a tall order to reverse a long-standing pattern of underachieving, Rimm's strategies have proven successful in case after case (Rimm, 1995d). She has found that the treatment of underachievement involves the collaboration of school and family in the implementation of six steps of her TRIFOCAL Model (see Figure 13.7):

1. Assessment
2. Communication
3. Changing Expectations
4. Role Model Identification
5. Correction of Deficiencies
6. Modifications of Reinforcements

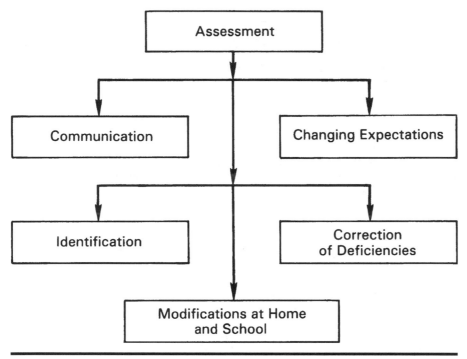

**FIGURE 13.7** TRIFOCAL Model for Reversing Underachievement.

Most of these concepts have been described in this chapter. It is important to note that to reverse underachieving patterns, all six steps must be implemented approximately *simultaneously*.

Biographical studies of achievers who indicate they previously had been underachievers show that all six steps usually are included in the change process. These "spontaneous changers" typically initiated their turnabout with Steps 3 or 4, the discovery of a positive model for identification or a change in expectations of important others, for example, a teacher, boyfriend, girlfriend, or spouse. These relationships, which are common in spontaneous underachievement conversion, need to be recognized as important elements in the deliberate treatment of underachievers. Parents and teachers must remain aware of the central role they play in the implementation of the critical six steps, particularly in the areas of setting expectations and finding or becoming a good model. In addition to using the TRIFOCAL

Model, parents and teachers should be equipped with "patience, dedication, and support" (Hoffman, Wasson, & Christianson, 1985).

### Step 1: Assessment of Skills, Abilities, Reinforcement Contingencies, and Types of Underachievement

The first step in underachievement reversal is an assessment that involves the cooperation of the school psychologist, teachers, and parents. The school psychologist should have primary involvement in this process. However, since few school districts allocate time for gifted children within the psychologist's role, it may be necessary for the guidance counselor, G/T coordinator, or classroom teacher to assume some of the responsibility. Ideally, the person should (1) have some background in measurement, (2) be sensitive to various learning and motivational styles and problems, (3) be knowledgeable in behavioral learning theory, and (4) be aware of the special characteristics of gifted and creative children.

The *individual* intelligence test is a highly recommended first assessment instrument. That venerable IQ number has the potential to communicate important expectations related to the child's true abilities. Since the child has not been motivated, it is likely that *group* intelligence test scores have underestimated his or her intellectual potential. Also, it is characteristically difficult to score above 125 on some group intelligence tests, a serious problem for intellectually gifted students. Therefore, the WISC-III or the *Stanford-Binet* (Form LM) should be individually administered by a psychologist.

Even with these individually administered tests there are problems. As we noted in Chapter 4, the highest possible score on the Wechsler tests is 155 and on the Stanford-Binet, fourth edition, 164. Also, IQ scores run lower on the new Stanford-Binet and WISC-III tests. The Stanford-Binet (Form LM) remains the best intelligence test for evaluating gifted children, despite being outdated and not measuring spatial skills. Further, underachieving gifted children often have uneven skills; thus, several tests may need to be administered in combination to identify strengths and problem areas.

During testing, the examiner should be especially aware of particular task-relevant characteristics of the child: symptoms of tension, attention to the task, perseverance at the task, responses to frustration, problem-solving approaches, defensiveness, and responses to personal encouragement by the examiner. These reflect, in miniature, approaches to educational tasks that the child very likely uses in the classroom and at home.

Intelligence testing should be followed by individual achievement tests to assess strengths and deficits in basic skills, particularly reading and math.

A creativity test or inventory, which can be administered by the teacher or psychologist, also should be part of the assessment. These produce not only a norm-referenced creativity score but also descriptions of abilities, characteristics, and interests that are relevant to understanding the child's personality, creative potential, and learning style. The GIFT and GIFFI tests include subscale scores such as *Independence, Self-confidence,* and *Risk-taking* that provide important insights for understanding underachievement.

GAIM can be used for children from Grades 5 through 12, while AIM and AIM-TO can be completed by parents or teachers of all children. The scores provide a description of the extent and type of the child's underachievement. Subscale scores reveal whether the child is mainly dependent or dominant or a mixture of both. Scores also permit insights regarding parent consistency in messages about achievement.

Finally, parent and student interviews also can be very helpful in identifying underachieving patterns unintentionally maintained at home and school. Examples of parent and student interviews, which can be adapted, are available in the *Guidebook for Implementing the Trifocal Underachievement Program in Schools* (Rimm et al., 1989). Ideally both parents should be at the interview. If only one appears, it is important to ask about the other parent's relationship to the child. Overall, the analysis of student abilities and home and school reinforcement contingencies is critical to the second step of the underachievement modification program.

### Step 2: Communication

Communication between parents and teachers is an important component of the cure for underachievers. Either a parent or the teacher may initiate the first conference, but the initiator must assure the other person of support, rather than placing blame. If it appears to a teacher that the parents are not interested in or capable of working with him or her, the teacher should select another child advocate in the school, for example, a counselor, gifted coordinator, or resource teacher. Reversing an underachievement pattern without parental assistance is not as efficient, but it is possible.

The content of the communication between parents and teachers should include a discussion of assessed abilities and achievements as well as formal and informal evaluations of the child's expressions of dependence or dominance. These are especially important in order that adults at home and at school do not fall into the trap of continuing to reinforce these problem patterns (Rimm, 1991a).

### Step 3: Changing the Expectations of Important Others

Parent, teacher, peer, sibling, and self expectations can be difficult to change. As noted above, IQ scores, if higher than anticipated, are very effective in modifying expectations. Anecdotal information also can provide convincing evidence of the child's abilities. For example, a teacher convincing an adolescent or his or her parents of the child's mathematical talent can explain that the child solves problems in an unusually clever way or seems to learn math concepts more quickly than anyone else in the class. A psychologist trying to convince a teacher that a child has unusual talent can describe the unusual vocabulary or problem-solving skills that the child revealed during testing. *Specific* descriptions of unusual strengths are good evidence of giftedness.

Changing self and peer expectations can be done in individual therapy, in group counseling sessions, and in classroom settings. Even a teacher of the gifted, who is not trained as a counselor, can be effective in helping gifted students, underachieving or otherwise, to better understand realistic goal-setting, perfectionism, competition, and peer pressure better. A book designed specifically to help gifted students learn about these topics is *Gifted Kids Have Feelings Too* (Rimm, 1990a), which includes stories and poems for and about preadolescents and adolescents. An accompanying discussion and activity book, *Exploring Feelings* (Rimm & Priest, 1990), is for teachers and counselors to use in classrooms or counseling sessions.

It is important to underachieving children that parents and teachers be able to say to them honestly that they believe in their ability to achieve. The expectations of these important others are basic to the personal change in self-expectations

that is necessary to reverse from underachievement to high achievement. In their longitudinal research with bright fourth-, fifth-, and sixth-grade underachievers, Jackson, Cleveland, and Mirenda (1975) showed that positive expectations by parents and teachers had a significant long-range effect on achievement in high school. Bloom's (1985; Sosniak, 2003) studies of talent development found that parents of research neurologists and mathematicians always expected their children to be very good students.

Since sibling competition frequently is a causal component of underachievement syndrome, changing the expectations of siblings also is important. In the sibling rivalry that often exists, an achieving child may have assigned to a brother or sister the role of "loser" and changing that role may be threatening to the "winner." An individual and personal communication to the "winner" about the expected change is helpful. Parents should provide the assurance that the sibling's status change will not displace the achiever's role. Genetically and environmentally a "whole smart family" is not only possible, but likely. This explanation may deter the achiever from subtly trying to keep the underachiever in his or her underachieving status.

Because it is difficult to change the expectations of persons who know the child, changing the child's school environment sometimes is an effective measure. Changing schools is a drastic step to take unless one is reasonably certain that the change will make a worthwhile difference. If extraordinarily gifted children are stifled by school environments that set only average goals and expectations, the children sometimes will change their entire achievement pattern when put in an environment that expects and values high achievement. However, for most children it is more realistic to try to change relevant expectations within the school.

### Step 4: Model Identification

A critical turning point for the underachieving child is the discovery of a *model* for identification. All other treatments for underachievement dim in importance compared with strong identification with an achieving model. As noted above, Bloom's (1985; Sosniak, 2003) biographical research with highly talented students showed that parents modeled the values and the lifestyles of successful achievers in the child's talent area. Radin (1976) argued that the best family environment for a gifted boy is provided "when a father is perceived as competent and strong, is pleased with his job, and permits his son to master tasks independently." Since this ideal situation is rarely provided for the gifted underachiever, parents and teachers need to help the student find a good model for identification.

Research on parent identification (e.g., Mussen & Rutherford, 1963) indicates that the selected parent identification figure is nurturant, powerful, and shares common characteristics with the child. These same characteristics can be used to locate an appropriate achieving model for the underachieving gifted child. As a warning, however, an underachieving adolescent sometimes selects a powerful, nurturant model who shares the *underachieving* characteristics of the adolescent. This person then becomes a strong model for underachievement.

Underachieving children should be matched with an *achieving* person to serve as a model for them. The person selected can serve in a model capacity for more than one child. His or her actual role may be tutor, mentor, companion, teacher, parent, sibling, counselor, psychologist, minister, scout leader, doctor, and so on. However, the model should have as many of the following characteristics as possible:

**1.** *Nurturance.* The model must care about the child assigned. Many adults are pleased to encourage youth with whom they can counteridentify.

**2.** *Same gender.* Although identification with an opposite-gender model is possible, the similarity in gender facilitates identification.

**3.** *Similarities to child.* These may include religion, race, interests, talents, physical disabilities, physical characteristics, socioeconomic backgrounds, specific problem experiences, or any other characteristics that will create the necessary easy rapport. When the child realizes that the model can be truly understanding, empathic, and sympathetic—because the model has experienced similar problems—rapport is more easily established and the process of identification is facilitated.

**4.** *Openness.* A model's willingness to share his or her own real problems in establishing him- or herself as an achiever is important for encouraging communication and identification and for motivating the underachieving child.

**5.** *Willingness to give time.* Achieving adults frequently have shortages of this most precious commodity. However, it is not possible to be an effective, positive model without providing time. It can be work time, play time, or talk time. Models who work on tasks with their child or play with their child can be most effective. It becomes possible for the child to see first hand such important achievement characteristics as responding to challenge, winning and losing in competition, reasoning styles, leading, communicating and relating to others, and experiencing successes and failures.

**6.** *Sense of positive accomplishment.* Although the model's life need not be perfect, the model must exhibit to the child the sense that his or her achievements have been personally fulfilling. Achievement involves sacrifice and postponed gratifications. The underachiever must recognize that these costs and postponements are worthwhile.

Research by Emerick (1992) on students who reversed their underachievement found that they often attributed their reversal to a teacher who was an important inspiration in their lives. A longitudinal study of disadvantaged children in Hawaii (Werner, 1989) showed that teachers, ministers, and other important adults were important as role models for achievement.

The concept of important role models is now being used in hundreds of school programs where community members volunteer to participate in mentorship programs. The concept of all-male and all-female academies for African American students (Holland, 1991) is intended to provide appropriate role models for underachievers in disadvantaged populations.

Richert (1991a) summarizes role model importance well by the following statement: "The single most awesome influence educators and parents have are as role models."

## Step 5: Correcting Skill Deficiencies

The underachieving gifted child almost always has skill deficiencies as a result of inattention in class and poor work and study habits. However, because he or she is gifted, the skill deficiencies can be overcome reasonably rapidly. This is less of a problem for a young child because the deficiencies are less likely to be extensive.

Tutoring should be goal-directed with movement to a higher reading or math group or acceptance into an accelerated class the anticipated aim. It should be of specified duration, for example, weekly for two months until the child takes a proficiency test, rather than ongoing. Ideally, the tutor should be an experienced and objective adult who recognizes the child's underachievement *and* giftedness. Parents or siblings are not appropriate since the personal relationships are likely to cause the child additional pressure and dependency. The correction of skill deficiencies must be conducted carefully so that (1) the independent work of the underachieving child is reinforced by the tutor, (2) manipulation of the tutor by the child is avoided, and (3) the child senses the relationship between effort and the achievement outcomes. Charting progress during tutoring helps visually confirm the rapid progress to both child and tutor.

## Step 6: Modification of Reinforcements at Home and School

The analyses in Step 1 will certainly identify some of the manipulative rituals discussed earlier in the home and school etiology sections. These behaviors need to be modified by setting important long-term goals and some short-term objectives that can ensure immediate small successes for the child both at home and at school. These successful experiences can be reinforced by rewards—anything from gold stars or extra art time to special outings with parents or money.

There are several considerations in determining the rewards to be used. First, they must be meaningful to the child. Money may seem unimportant to a six-year-old, while stars are not particularly motivating to the adolescent. They also must be within the value system and range of possibility for the givers of the rewards. Schools usually do not use money as a reward, and parents may not want to pay (bribe) their children to learn. There are, however, effective rewards within the value system of parents and within the capabilities of teachers to administer—for example, free time. The rewards should not be too large. In fact, they should be as small as possible yet effective enough to motivate behavior. They can be increased in value as necessary; but if one already has used large rewards, small rewards will no longer be effective. It is important always to supply the rewards agreed upon, and to pay them on a regular basis immediately after the activity is successfully completed. Rewards may be based on activities completed, or based on the quality of the activity. Rewards should never be paid for incomplete work or when the work is not attempted.

Modification of reinforcements at school includes much more than reward schedules. For example, acceleration by subject or grade skipping are appropriate reinforcements for some underachievers (Rimm & Lovance, 1992a, 1992b). Participation in Future Problem Solving was found to be effective in reversing underachievement (Rimm & Olenchak, 1991). Encouraging a student's strong interests in the classroom also may facilitate the reversal of underachievement (Emerick, 1989). Independent studies and curriculum compacting were used effectively by a sixth-grade teacher as part of the reversal of underachievement for her students (Lemley, 1994).

Modifying reinforcements for homework and study are an important component of reversing underachievement. However, this modification by itself will not be sufficient. Dozens of other recommendations for home and school changes are described by Rimm (1995d) in her book on underachievement syndrome.

### Treatment beyond Home and School

The preceding recommendations for the treatment of underachievement at home and school are effective with many children and adolescents if the underachievement is not complicated by heavy involvement in drugs, alcohol, crime, or serious depression. However, even the adolescent who shows a long history of "complicated" underachievement also may be able to reverse the underachieving pattern, as well as drug, crime, or other problems. In addition to the parent and educator working together, this youth is likely to need attention by a psychologist specializing in such problems.

### SUMMARY

Underachievement by gifted students is a great loss for them and for society. It is defined as a discrepancy between students' high ability and mediocre or poor school productivity. The Carnegie Corporation's *Years of Promise* (1996) documents it as a continuing problem in the United States.

Intelligence, achievement, and creativity scores can be used to help diagnose underachievement. If the gifted student is a poor test-taker, observation by teachers or parents is necessary for determining giftedness. Prolonged underachievement may cause test scores to underestimate a child's abilities, as in Harry's case. Rimm researched parent and student inventories that identify underachievers and describe patterns of their problem behaviors.

Whitmore prepared a checklist of characteristics of gifted underachievers. The authors describe characteristics that include low self-esteem; defensive avoidance of threatening academic tasks;

and deficiencies in skills, study habits, peer acceptance, school concentration, and discipline.

Perfectionistic tendencies may cause underachievement, especially in high school when work gets difficult due to procrastination, fear of failure, and related avoidance behaviors. Many underachieving gifted students have difficulty functioning in competitive situations, unless they believe they can win.

Avoidance behavior can take the form of aggression or withdrawal (Kaufmann, 1986), which is similar to Rimm's identified patterns of dominance or dependence.

Richert noted that others' expectations influence achievement, values, creativity, self-esteem, social relations, and "emotional impact." She recommended transcending others' expectations with healthy self-expectations.

Underachievement is learned and can be unlearned.

Gifted underachievers are less likely to identify with their same-gender parents, unless the parent also is an underachiever or does not value achievement. Freud explained identification as an unconscious product of resolving Oedipal or Electra complexes. Social learning theorists emphasize the importance of a nurturing relationship, perceived power in the parent, and similarities in child-parent characteristics.

Several parent-power patterns foster inappropriate identification and underachievement. Research shows worse achievement for males in father-absent homes, and worse math and problem-solving skills for both males and females in father-absent homes. Successful career mothers serve as effective models for achieving girls.

In elementary school more boys than girls are underachievers; but due apparently to peer pressure and different behavior patterns (aggressiveness versus conformity), increasing numbers of girls become underachievers in middle and high school and college.

Counteridentification can lead parents to spend time with their children and reinforce the development of academic, artistic, or athletic skills. It also can lead to manipulation by children and to underachievement. If parents complete the child's homework it will encourage excessive dependence. If parents give their highly verbal children too much power, the children may manipulate their environments to avoid effort.

Creative students may dodge academic work by claiming they must spend time on, for example, their art or music interests.

Counterintuitive responses by parents and teachers can help reverse underachievement. Dependent children must take small steps independently; dominant children require respect, support, and fair agreements on school work.

Underachievers tend to come from dysfunctional families without good achievement models. Dysfunctional family patterns are discovered across socioeconomic strata. An emphasis on responsibility plus respect for teachers and education is recommended.

Teachers who recognize and provide for gifted students create their "good years"; other teachers who cannot, their "bad years." Inflexible teachers, who may pile on extra busywork, encourage underachievement.

Teachers may ignore or scold the hand-waving, question-asking gifted student, who then stops responding in class.

Too much competition in the classroom is devastating to underachievers, whose self-concept is damaged by repeated evidence of incompetence.

Low expectations of teachers become self-fulfilling prophecies and help create a climate that encourages underachievement. Remedial work may label a student as inept. Attitudes of peers toward achievement also have a dramatic impact on achievement.

An unrewarding curriculum prevents the gifted child from fulfilling needs to question, discuss, criticize, and so forth. A history of underachievement in combination with inflexibility may lock gifted underachievers out of challenging classes.

Underachievers must come to understand the relationship between effort and outcomes (goals). Cooperative learning groups can lead to low goal-setting and lack of challenge for gifted students.

The **TRIFOCAL** model for reversing underachievement requires six steps: (1) assessment of skills, abilities, reinforcement contingencies, and types of underachievement; (2) communication between parents and teachers; (3) changing the expectations of parents, teachers, peers, and siblings; (4) locating an achieving identification model; (5) correcting skill deficiencies; and (6) modifying home and school reinforcements that support underachievement.

Involvement in challenging opportunities such as acceleration or participation in Future Problem Solving can stimulate achievement.

Professional psychological help is needed if underachievement is complicated by drugs, crime, or other serious problems.

# CHAPTER 14

# THE CULTURAL UNDERACHIEVEMENT OF FEMALES

*Learning about the obstacles faced by many talented women will help us to enable gifted girls to learn how to plan and overcome difficulties which have hindered their mothers' and grandmothers' journeys toward their dreams and aspirations.*
Sally Reis (1998b, p. 4)

The education of gifted women has been a low priority throughout history, a matter that has led to wholesale female underachievement. Many gifted girls have been, and continue to be, systematically discouraged by peers, family, and sometimes teachers and counselors from using their talent in productive ways. Reis (1987) pointed out that the underachievement of adult women is indeed a different concept than that which is measured by grades in school and might be better defined as "what a person believes can be attained or accomplished in life." The discrepancy between the giftedness observed in girls' school achievement and their talent development in adulthood has been aptly labeled by Olshen (1987) as the "disappearance of giftedness in girls."

History shows that leading educators and psychologists had played a deliberate role in limiting educational opportunities for females. While many early educators simply ignored the education of females, some were explicit in designing education to maintain women's subservience to men. Smith (1981) quoted one of the most influential educators of the eighteenth century, Jean-Jacques Rousseau, regarding his theory for the education of "Sophie," the ideal girl.

Women's entire education should be planned in relation to men. To please men, to be useful to them, to win their love and respect, to raise them as children, care for them as adults, counsel and console them, make their lives sweet and pleasant. These are women's duties in all ages and these are what they should be taught from childhood on.

Smith also reminds us that Sigmund Freud and Carl Gustav Jung, two illustrious leaders of early psychoanalytic psychology, described what they perceived as inferior female characteristics. Freud noted the main traits of femininity as narcissism, masochism, and passivity. Jung described the mentally healthy female as being more emotional and less rational and logical than an equally mentally healthy male.

G. Stanley Hall (1844–1924), another leading psychologist and educator, reflected Freud's views in recommending that education for women "should aim at nothing but motherhood." Edward L. Thorndike, early in this century, progressed only slightly beyond Hall, suggesting that education is not likely to "harm women's health" and that some women could even be educated toward careers, provided those careers involved nurturing roles (Smith, 1981). All of these quaint views both reflected and reinforced prevailing social attitudes.

A survey of 544 graduates of a highly selective school for gifted females found that among those who graduated between 1910 and 1979 who had careers, almost half (46 percent) became teachers, 28 percent went into social work, and only 10 percent were physicians or engineers. Seventy-three percent of the respondents described themselves as homemakers (Walker, Reis, & Leonard, 1992).

A book by Margaret Rossiter (1995), *Women Scientists in America: Before Affirmative Action, 1940–1972,* dramatically recalls how different the world of science was. Although World War II mobilized women scientists into the laboratory, women were forced to leave their occupations after the war. Not only did they lose their jobs, but they no longer were recruited into universities or colleges because they were supposed to be mothers, not scientists.

David Noble (1992) begins his book, *A World Without Women,* with "the absence of women from the world of science has been so pervasive historically that it has been taken as a given, something to be overcome, perhaps, and never really explained." Green (1992), a reviewer of the above-mentioned book, questions further: "Why is it that the greater the percentage of women's participation in a given intellectual sphere, the more the general prestige of the sphere declines?" She ponders the reasons for the historical ignoring and underdevelopment of women's intellectual capabilities.

A unique exception to the shutting out of women from science took place in eighteenth-century Bologna, Italy (Cielak-Golonka & Morten, 2000). The University of Bologna encouraged women scientists to compete on an equal footing with men, and there were indeed distinguished women scientists who flourished in that environment. Laura Bassi (1711–1778) was the university's first female professor. She occupied a chair in physics while managing a complex family life. She and her husband, a physician, parented twelve children. It was rumored that her family interfered with her publication productivity.

With "only" six children, Anna Marnadi Manzolini (1716–1774) managed to publish a great deal in the area of anatomical studies and achieved fame for her anatomical models. Her fear of corpses, combined with her artistic talent, motivated her to produce exact anatomical models of organs. This served Anna two purposes: she could teach well from the models, and she could avoid constant use of the corpses, which she dreaded.

Apparently, even in the eighteenth century dads were influential in encouraging women scientists. Maria Gaetana Agnesi (1718–1799) was a brilliant professor of mathematics and wrote a celebrated book in her field, but acknowledged she had become an accomplished professor of mathematics only to please her father.

For the most part, only women from wealthy families were permitted to study science, but an exception was Maria Dalle Donne (1778–1842), who was a peasant girl from very modest surroundings. Her cousin, who was a priest, recognized her intelligence and encouraged her to study medicine. She became the director of the Department of Midwifery at that same University of Bologna.

Except for the Italian oasis of science and, of course, Marie Curie's scientific contributions, it was assumed by most men and women alike that women couldn't be scientists. A sad example was Mileva Maric, Albert Einstein's first wife (Gabor, 1996), whom he initially wrote about as "an equal." He indicated in his letters to her that he looked forward to their working together on relative motion and credited her, at least initially, for stimulating his thinking. Einstein soon tired of being married to a scientist and rejected being a family man as well. He divorced Maric, leaving her to do all the parenting, and he married a woman "who placed no intellectual demands" on him. We shall never know Maric's contributions to Einstein's early work or about her pioneering role in physics.

In this country, there were very few women in medicine, law, business, government, art, serious media, or music until the 1960s (Rimm & Rimm-Kaufman, 2001). Consider how strange the perceptions about women were just a generation ago. Women who played in symphony orchestras were instructed to wear their hair back, dress in pants, and sit toward the center of the orchestra to keep their gender hidden. Even stranger assumptions were made about men. For example, men could design, manufacture, sell, and be executives of huge companies that produced washing machines; yet they didn't seem to know how to run them to help with the home laundry.

Considering women's history, the status of women has changed dramatically. Although we are far from equity, this chapter will help to identify how far gifted girls have come and how far we need to go before equity is achieved. This chapter will review and update some statistics and opinions regarding the present status of women in the work world and life satisfactions of working versus nonworking women. It also will review arguments and data regarding biological gender differences, along with information regarding the other viewpoint—that observed differences are sociocultural in origin and are maintained by mechanisms that support female underachievement. Suggestions for teaching and counseling gifted females and for reducing gender-role stereotyping, bias, and discrimination also will be itemized. Finally, we will extend the school-home model for modifying general underachievement, described in Chapter 13, to reversing underachievement patterns in gifted girls.

## PRESENT STATUS OF WOMEN: WOMEN IN THE WORK FORCE

An analysis of the present status of women in the work force continues to provide the best documentation for the argument that many gifted women are indeed functioning as underachieving adults.

Reis and Callahan (1989) appropriately entitled one paper *Gifted Females: They've Come a Long Way—or Have They?* Recent statistics document women's slow progress toward equality in many areas. Salary differentials continue and have actually become greater (National Committee on Pay Equity, 2000). According to 2001 statistics released by the Census Bureau, full-time working women earned only 73 percent as much as full-time working men, down from 1998 when they earned 74 percent and 1996 when they

earned 75 percent (Reis, 1998b). The Census Bureau attributed this differential to men's larger growth in earnings.

Even in specific careers there is a pay differential (Lipson, 2001). Figure 14.1 shows the pay differentials for some careers that are typical for men and women. In all cases the salary is higher for men. In all professional specialties, women earn 76 percent of men's earnings, but Figure 14.2 shows that in some professional specialties, women earn as much as 87 percent of what men earn. Women hold 53 percent of the 21 million

| Pediatrician | |
|---|---|
| Men | $138,174 |
| Women | $116,331 |
| Gap | 16% |
| **Secretary** | |
| Men | $32,400 |
| Women | $22,500 |
| Gap | 31% |
| **Teacher** | |
| Men | $43,000 |
| Women | $35,050 |
| Gap | 18% |
| **Software Engineer** | |
| Men | $57,799 |
| Women | $47,143 |
| Gap | 18% |
| **Nurse** | |
| Men | $44,500 |
| Women | $39,100 |
| Gap | 12% |
| **Lawyer** | |
| Men | $125,000 |
| Women | $ 99,400 |
| Gap | 20% |

**FIGURE 14.1**   Fair Pay at Work.

Sources: National Committee on Pay Equity and Working Woman (July/August 2001).

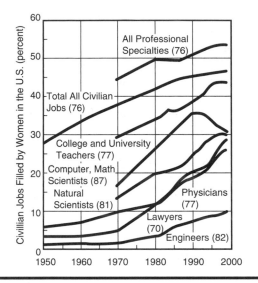

**FIGURE 14.2**    Civilian Jobs Filled by Women in the U.S. (percent).

Source: U.S. Bureau of the Census and Bureau of Labor Statistics.

Figures in parentheses indicate women's earnings as a percent of men's earnings in 1998. The trend lines show decennial census data for 1950–1980 and five-year moving averages thereafter.

professional jobs in the United States, but only 28 percent of professions with yearly compensations above $40,000. Doyle (2000) pointed out that the salary differential within the higher-paid professions is directly attributed to either the fewer hours women work or their selection of the lower-paying specialty areas within these professions, for example, pediatrics rather than orthopedic surgery.

Rubenstein (1997) supports this finding by noting that women's earnings approach 98 percent of men's among young people who have not yet had children, and salaries are very close to parity with men for older women who never married but focused mainly on their careers.

An analysis by Kaplan and colleagues (1996) reflects poorly on equality in academia. Even after adjusting for differences in academic productivity, work time, institutional support of research, and family responsibilities, salaries of women in academic pediatrics were lower than men's. After citing other similar findings in academic institutions, Kaplan and colleagues concluded, "These findings suggest a pervasive prejudice against women manifested throughout academia as well as in medicine" (p. 1288), thus explaining why the proportion of women in senior ranks has not changed since 1986.

The 1999 Department of Labor statistics data underscore the cumulative effect of lower salaries (Glasneen & Crowley, 1999). Average lifetime earnings of women aged 50 are $496,000 compared to the average lifetime earnings of $1.1 million for men of the same age.

Areas of great progress for women appear to be biology and business. By 1986, the numbers of men and women earning bachelor degrees in the biological sciences showed almost no gender difference, and there was an extraordinary relative increase in the numbers of women majoring in business. The business share of all degrees earned by women changed from 2.8 percent in 1970 to 21.7 percent in 1986 (Turner & Bowen, 1990).

In an earlier edition of this book, we asserted that even this apparent progress was balanced by a downside because women with MBAs earned so much less than men. In 1990 Stacey showed that in the first year after receiving an MBA, men earn a salary that is 12 percent higher on the average than that of women.

The good news is that there have been dramatic changes in women's success in business since then. Over seven million companies are now owned by women, a 78 percent increase since 1987 (Belton, 1996). Even more impressive, women MBA graduates now outpace men in starting salaries by $5000. Furthermore, these women had better GMAT scores, more prior work experience, and greater participation in honorary societies than men (Kunde, 1995). A *New York Times* story claims that Wellesley graduates now scoff at glass ceilings (Dobrzynski, 1995b). This school's graduates include the most women directors of Fortune 500 companies and only slightly fewer than the University of California at Berke-

By Mike Keefe for USA TODAY, Reprinted by Permission

ley (top ranking) who are senior executives in business.

A Catalyst (2001) census shows that as of 2000, women comprised 12.5 percent of all corporate officers in the Fortune 500 companies, up from 8.7 percent in 1996. They also reported only four female CEOs of Fortune 500 companies, and although four is insufficient to encourage optimism, that is twice the number in 1996. These figures, which are far from equitable, represent improvements over times when the boards of Fortune 500 companies were entirely male and there were no female CEOs.

In medicine, too, there is improvement but also a downside. Despite the 45 percent of U.S. medical school entrants today who are women (Association of American Medical Colleges, 2000), there is a "glass ceiling" effect in both medical practice and at medical colleges. In medical practice, the smallest percentage of women is found in the higher-paying residency programs, while in less lucrative specialties there are higher percentages of women. For example, 65 percent of pediatric residents are women, while only 7.8 percent and 6.9 percent of the orthopedic surgery and tho-

racic surgery residents, respectively, are women (Association of American Medical Colleges, 2000). Although that may be related to women's choices, the environment of some academic specialties is clearly not hospitable to women, as illustrated by a comment by one orthopedic surgeon (Rimm, Rimm-Kaufman, & Rimm, 1999):

> A comment in medical school made my drive to be a surgeon stronger. On my third year surgery rotation, the attending doctor (a Navy captain) said, "Back when I was a resident, ships were made of wood, men were men, giants roamed the halls, and (looking directly at me) women went into nursing. That was 1987. (p. 302)

According to other female orthopedic surgeons who participated in the Rimm study, surgery specialties continue to discourage women.

Medical colleges don't seem to be faring much better. Tesch, Wood, Helwig, and Nattinger (1995) found that 11 years after graduating from medical school, only 59 percent of the female graduates were associate or full professors compared to 83 percent of the male graduates. In the

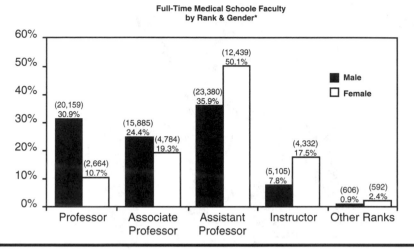

**FIGURE 14.3**   Full-Time Medical School Faculty by Rank & Gender*.

Source: *Women in U.S. Medicine, Statistics 1999–2000,* Association of American Medical Colleges. Retrieved June 18, 2001, from the World Wide Web: http://www.aamc.org/about/progemph/wommed/stats00/summary.html. Reprinted with permission of the Association of American Medical Colleges.

full professor rank, there were 23 percent males compared to only 5 percent females. The authors described this not as a glass ceiling effect but as a "sticky floor." Medical schools do seem to continue to have a very sticky floor.

Figure 14.3 compares more recent statistics for males and females at the various ranks of medical colleges. With three times the percentage of males as females at the highest rank of professor and more than twice the percentage of females as males at the lowest instructor level, it seems obvious that women are not being promoted at the same pace as men. As to chairs of departments, only $7\frac{1}{2}$ percent are women and 20 percent of medical schools have no women chairs at all (Association of American Medical Colleges, 2000).

Furthermore, in medical school administration for the 1986–87 academic year, only 1.6 percent of all medical school deans, 9.6 percent of associate deans, and 20 percent of all assistant deans were women (Martin, Parker, & Arnold, 1988). Twelve years later, there are only 4 women deans among the leadership of 125 medical schools, only a $1\frac{1}{2}$ percent increase. There are higher per-

centages of women associate and assistant deans, 30.6 percent and 37.6 percent, respectively (Association of American Medical Colleges, 2000).

As documented by the accompanying cartoon, even Blondie has learned about the glass ceiling effect.

The increase in percent of women in science and engineering is dramatic and hopeful (Farnham, 1988; National Science Foundation, 2000). However, the continued underrepresentation of women in most fields of science provides graphic proof of the underachievement of gifted women (see Figure 14.4 and Table 14.1).

The glass ceiling persists. There continue to be major differences in promotion to higher academic ranks in the areas of the physical sciences, mathematics, and engineering even when the number of published papers is adjusted for age (Sonnert & Holton, 1996). The National Academy of Science (NAS) is very concerned because its minute female membership (only 5.9 percent) proves that there is a serious problem (Fox, 1999). The first ever NAS symposium was organized to examine the barriers facing women,

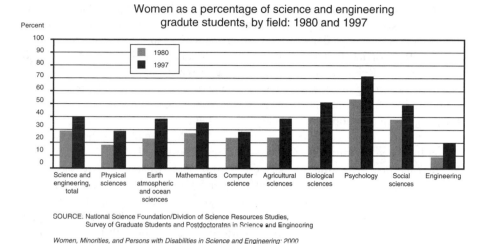

**FIGURE 14.4**   Women as a Percentage of Science and Engineering Graduate Students, by Field: 1980 and 1997.

Source: National Science Foundation/Division of Science Resources Studies, Survey of Graduate Students and Postdoctorates in Science and Engineering.

*Women, Minorities, and Persons with Disabilities in Science and Engineering: 2000*

**TABLE 14.1**   Percentage of Scientists and Engineers in the Labor Force Who Are Women: 1993, 1995, and 1997

| Occupation | 1993 | 1995 | 1997 |
|---|---|---|---|
| **Total scientists and engineers** | 22.8 | 22.4 | 22.8 |
| Computer/mathematical scientists | 30.7 | 28.9 | 27.3 |
| Life and related scientists | 34.3 | 34.9 | 36.2 |
| Physical and related scientists | 21.5 | 21.6 | 21.9 |
| Social and related scientists | 50.5 | 49.9 | 52.1 |
| Engineers | 8.6 | 8.6 | 9.1 |

Source: National Science Foundation/Division of Science Resources Studies, 1997 SESTAT (Scientists and Engineers Statistical Data System).

*Women, Minorities and Persons with Disabilities in Science and Engineering: 2000*

minorities, and the disabled. A major concern is the declining proportion of women in science as they move through their education and into the academic workforce. Although more girls are taking early math and science courses in middle school, by college and graduate school the number declines. Questions about "unconscious discrimination" against women and women's "lack of aggressiveness in asking for equality" were posed. It was concluded that "chilly" environments toward women in science continue to exist in both academia and industry.

The status of women in education further documents female underachievement. Elementary and, to a lesser degree, secondary teaching have long been known as female stereotyped professions. In 1980 approximately two-thirds of all K–12 educators were female (Smith, 1981). However, not only is the upper echelon of power in elementary and secondary education predominantly male, but the average salary of female teachers is 18 percent below that of males (Lipson, 2001), and again reflects dramatic achievement inequities for females: Only 13 percent of school superintendents are women (Educational Research Service, 2000). Leadership in teachers' organizations shows similar inequities, with most local, state, and national positions held by men (Reis & Callahan, 1989). As a positive note, according to a 1988 government study, beginning in 1983 the number of women earning Ph.D. degrees in education has exceeded the number of men.

College administration had been a virtual *no-woman's land*. In 1972 a *Time* magazine article recommended, "If a woman wishes to become a college president, she is advised to become a nun." At the time, just 1 percent of college presidents were women, and virtually all were nuns.

On the positive side, as in other traditionally male professions, the number of women entering college administration is increasing (e.g., Reis & Callahan, 1989). The percentage of college presidents who are women has risen to 12 percent (Hartman, 1994). Although opportunities may not abound, one no longer needs to be a nun to qualify. Even Princeton University now has its first woman president, Shirley Tilghman (Marshall, 2001).

Opportunities have gradually expanded for women in law and government (Hartman, 1994). Twenty-five percent of lawyers are women, but only six percent have achieved partnership status. At this writing, women hold 14 percent of the seats in the Senate and 13.6 percent of the seats in the House of Representatives (Learning Network, 2001). From an international leadership perspective, although women make up close to 14 percent of the 40,000 publicly elected offices, they lead only 9 of the 190 nations around the world (American Association of University Women, 2001). That's less than one half of one percent.

Overall, while the trends are in a positive direction, they still document the underachievement of gifted women in most of the prestigious careers in our society.

## LIFE SATISFACTIONS OF WOMEN

In the post–World War II years, even a woman who attended college was expected to achieve life satisfaction vicariously through her husband's career. Her success was tied to his success, along with success in the wife, mother, and home manager role she would play. Qualities of being "good-looking" and "sexy" were part of her definition as a woman (and probably still are). Her primary allegiance was toward her family, while the primary allegiance of her husband was toward his career.

Eminent developmental psychologist Erik Erikson (1959) described the *identity crisis*—deciding who and what you are—as being resolved later for a woman than for a man and as tied directly to marriage, her husband's career, and the birth of their first child. Identity was wrapped in the nurturing role. Adams (1981) suggested that women were caught in a "compassion trap," based on the belief that their most important function was to provide tenderness and compassion.

Note, too, that sociocultural stereotypes allowed a man to receive encouragement and support for his demanding career and professional accomplishments. However, a talented woman did not have a nurturing and supporting "wife" available, nor was anyone particularly anxious to take over home and child-rearing responsibilities for her. That has changed considerably for both men and women. A recent University of Maryland survey found that, compared to a generation ago when men rarely did housework, men do approximately 10 hours of housework a week (Kleiman, 2000). Women's hours of housework have decreased from an average of 30 to 17.5 hours a week, still almost twice as many as men and about two-thirds of the total. This is progress.

This dramatic waste of the talents and contributions of women might be justified if women perceived themselves as fulfilled and happy in their housewife role. Surely, the nurturing of future generations is a critically important contribution to society, as is the support of men who make professional contributions. Research indicates that while some women do find high life satisfaction as homemakers, on the average life satisfaction—including self-esteem and feelings of competence—is greater for working and career women (Birnbaum, 1975). Bernard (1972), for example, found that housewives who derived their identity solely from their role as wife and mother were most likely to suffer the effects of *housewife syndrome*—a sense of helplessness and hopelessness, depression, and a loss of self-esteem. The years devoted to caring for one's family seem to deprive many women of their sense of autonomy, leaving them with feelings of complete dependence. Even their teenagers turn to them and suggest that they "get a life." Furthermore, 93 percent of teenagers surveyed indicated they planned to work outside the home (Roper Starch Worldwide, 1998).

Career women usually derive much satisfaction from their work and the recognition they receive (Rodenstein & Glickauff-Hughes, 1979). Nadelson and Eisenberg (1977) reported that husbands of professional women found them to be "more stimulating" people. A recent survey found that 97 percent of working women feel successful in their work (Oxygen/Markle Pulse, 2000).

A study by Holahan (1981) of life satisfactions of gifted females from Terman's research found that at a mean age of 66, career women expressed greater overall satisfaction with their lives than did homemakers and job holders. There were no significant differences between the latter two groups.

Life satisfaction was a qualifier for a study of over 1000 successful women (Rimm et al., 1999; Rimm & Rimm-Kaufman, 2001). When the participating women were asked what they found most satisfying about their careers, "challenge," "creativity," "making a contribution," and "fulfillment" were selected most frequently for the overall group. Only a third of the women selected either "financially satisfying" or "prestigious" as a reason for recommending their careers to other women.

There were differences in the reasons for the women's career satisfaction among career groups. Fewer of the business executives, artists, and musicians felt they were making contributions compared to the women who were in government and medicine. Also, more of the women in the traditional fields of teaching, nursing, homemaking, and mental health believed they were making contributions.

The women who described their careers as fulfilling did not necessarily perceive they were financially satisfied. The women in business indicated most financial satisfaction, but they less frequently selected "making a contribution" and "fulfilling" for career satisfaction. The legendary "starving artists" indicated least financial satisfaction.

## THE HOME–CAREER CONFLICT

Although working outside the home usually provides more self-satisfaction and life satisfaction, gifted women are caught in a very common conflict. The alternative to the *housewife syndrome* is the *working wife* or "Queen Bee" syndrome, a demanding superwoman role that requires

**MARVIN**                                                    **by Tom Armstrong**

women to meet the obligations of a challenging and worrisome job plus fulfill the traditional responsibilities of cleaning, shopping, cooking, laundry, and child care—and be a loving and supportive wife as well.

Poloma (1972) interviewed 53 couples in which the wives were involved in the male-dominated professions of law, medicine, and college teaching. These woman used one or more of the following four techniques for managing the home-career conflict.

**1.** *They looked at the **benefits** of combining a career and a family, rather than the costs.* As one woman explained, "I am a better mother because I work and can expend my energies on something other than over-mothering my children."

**2.** *They decided in advance which role came **first** in the event of conflicting demands.* In virtually every case, family crises took precedence over career crises. If the baby sitter did not show up or a child got sick, the wife, not the husband, missed work that day.

**3.** *They **compartmentalized** the two roles as much as possible, keeping work and family distinct.* Few of the women brought work home with them, for example, although their husbands often did.

**4.** *They **compromised**.* The wives controlled the extent of their career commitment to fit the circumstances of their family lives—how the husband's work was going, his income, the ages and number of children, the husband's support (or lack of it), and so on. "When one or more of these factors is out of kilter, the wife makes the necessary adjustment to manage role strain," Poloma found.

For the professional woman with a family, there is no easy solution to the continuous conflict of her roles. If she is committed to her career, she feels guilty for not fulfilling her nurturing commitment to her family. If she considers family first, she is criticized and feels guilty for not being sufficiently dedicated to her career.

Yet the women in the Rimm study (Rimm et al., 1999; Rimm & Rimm-Kaufman, 2001) found creative approaches to managing complex careers. "Gathering" food at the supermarket was sometimes substituted for cooking. A variety of child-care approaches included relatives and day care. In many families husbands shared child-care responsibilities, and in a few families husbands took on parenting and home responsibilities as full-time jobs. The husband of Katherine Hudson, CEO of the Brady Corporation, liked to call himself the CEO of 10357, their home address.

As Reis (1998b) pointed out, not all women are successful in meshing their needs with husbands and families. Some of the women she studied had to cope with divorce before they could be allowed to fulfill their own identity goals. She cautions young women to ask questions of their partners before developing lifelong relationships.

Not all of the successful women selected a linear path in pursuing their careers. Instead, there were a variety of sequences that were followed. Table 14.2 shows the optional sequences selected by the married women in the study. In actuality, there were permutations and combinations of these sequences. Teenage girls planning careers should be encouraged to discuss these potential sequences and understand that each sequence has both rewards and penalties, some of which are shown in Table 14.3. Some careers cannot be achieved in some sequences. That is, if a girl prioritizes a family choice above a career choice, certain careers will not be possible because there may not be sufficient time for specialized training.

Consider a further analogy proposed by Mary Catherine Bateson at the second annual Matanus-ka-Susitna Women's Conference in Wasilla, Alaska, in 1997. She compared women's lives to putting an addition on a home. She pointed out that when families add to their homes, they not only add a room or two, but they typically change the uses of other rooms and reorganize the entire house. Bateson thus maintains that with the longer life spans and healthier active lifestyles of women today, not only can their lives expand and

**TABLE 14.2**   Optional Sequence Patterns for the Married Women in the Study

| Pattern 1: Traditional | Pattern 2: Delayed Career | Pattern 3: Linear Career | Pattern 4: Late Bloomer |
|---|---|---|---|
| College | College | College | High School Graduation |
| Marriage | Brief Career | Graduate or Professional School (Optional, depending on career) | Marriage (or parenting before marriage) |
| Wife/Parent/ Volunteer | Marriage | Early Career and Marriage | Preschool Parenting |
| Wife/Volunteer or Brief Career | Preschool Parenting | Early Career and Preschool Parenting | School-Age Parenting and College Attendance |
| | School-Age Parenting and Return to School or Career | Middle Career and School-Age Parenting | Early Career |
| | Early Career Middle Career Peak Career | Peak Career | Middle Career |

From: *See Jane Win,* S. Rimm, S. Rimm-Kaufman, and I. Rimm, copyright © 1999 by Sylvia Rimm. Used by permission of Crown Publishers, a division of Random House, Inc.

be redesigned in a fashion to provide more time for relationships, parenting, careers, explorations, and so on, but they can also change the sequences and directions of those activities. Although women may not be able to achieve everything all at once, their remodeled lives may permit them to attain much of what they wish to accomplish in alternating sequences.

For women today, 35 or 40 is not too old for beginning a career, starting a family, reappraising one's lifestyle, or initiating a new phase of life. Some active and healthy women in the Rimm research began new careers and reeducated themselves even into their 60s and 70s. For example, wildlife photographer Frances Bayless, who had been a teacher, began her study of photography at the Cleveland Institute of Art when she was 62. Now in her 70s, she photographs penguin families in Antarctica in −70°F temperatures. Special Leica cameras have been designed for her that don't use batteries, but Frances's own batteries keep running despite her age, and she has newfound energy for her life and her creative photography.

In the area of science, although women are generally published less than men are, there is some documentation that marriage has an enhancing effect on scientific productivity, and parenthood does not adversely affect that productivity (Cole & Zuckerman, 1987). Among eminent female scientists, married women published more than single women and this did not change if married women had children. The most significant factor that increased the rate of publication was marriage to another scientist. Maria Goeppert Mayer, renowned physicist and the second woman to ever receive a Nobel Prize, recommended that

**TABLE 14.3**    Rewards and Penalties of Career Sequences for Women with Families

|  | *Rewards* | *Penalties* |
|---|---|---|
| **I. Traditional Sequence** | Time to focus on raising children | Dependency on husband |
|  | Psychological and energy support for breadwinner | Identity tied to husband and children |
|  | Cadre of volunteers in community | Frequent lack of confidence and life satisfaction |
|  |  | Often remained at lower status in later career |
| **II. Delayed Sequence** | More time for children than linears | Frustration at delay of career |
|  | Head start on careers compared to traditionals | Loss of confidence during early parenting years |
|  | Potential for some high status careers | Some careers not open because of age |
|  |  | Change in family dynamics sometimes cause problems |
| **III. Linear Sequence** | High status, interesting career availability | Pioneered dealing with gender bias |
|  | Rapid upward mobility in career | Difficulties with finding marriage partner |
|  | More immediate develop-ment of confidence | Less focused caring for children |
|  |  | Problems balancing family life |
|  |  | Increased fertility problems |
| **IV. Late Bloomers Sequence** | Time to spend with children | Frequent economic difficulties |
|  |  | Loss of confidence during early parenting years |
|  |  | Difficulties returning to education |
|  |  | Late start in career |
|  |  | Many career fields closed |
|  |  | Problems with changing family dynamics |

her female students marry scientists who share their research interests so they might at least be able to continue their research. Mayer herself was offered a faculty position shortly before she received the Nobel Prize (Gabor, 1996).

The timing of when the "mommy track" begins apparently has a negative effect on women's scientific careers (Healy, 1992). A study of 460 former National Science Foundation postdoctoral fellows found that women who began their families during their postdoctoral years did not achieve academic and leadership positions that were as high as those of other women or men.

The constraints on married women's careers in medicine are quite dramatic (Martin, Parker, & Arnold, 1988). The divorce rate of women physicians is twice that of males. Among married male physicians, 90 percent had children, in contrast with 60 percent to 70 percent of married female physicians. The women physicians had fewer children and were older when they had them. Child-care arrangements of male and female physicians are dramatically different, with half of the wives of male physicians providing full-time child care and another 33 percent providing a major part of child care. Among women physicians, 75 percent stated they had major responsibility for household and family care, and husbands were responsible for between 0 percent and 5 percent of the child care. Women physicians depended on full-time household help, day care, and relatives for child care.

Perhaps the most telling statistical comparison between male and female physicians was the response to a question that asked if they had changed their career plans or behaviors because of family responsibilities. None of the men had, while 44 percent of the women had made such changes.

Griffith (1999) reported that more doctors are marrying doctors; however, opportunities are not quite equal. Of 1208 physicians that responded to a survey, 22 percent of the male physicians and 40 percent of the female physicians were married to doctors. Twenty-four percent of those women reported rearranging their schedules to fit their children, while very few male physicians reported changes in schedules for care giving.

Another study (Potee, Gerber, & Ickovics, 1999) found that of 566 women physicians who had graduated from Yale medical school, 82 percent of those over 40 were mothers. Women physicians who had no children were more likely to be in time-consuming surgical specialties, less likely to be in primary care, and more likely to work full time than the women physicians with

children. The research underscores further need for maternity leaves and child care for physicians.

Women continue to struggle with the home-career conflict, and there are surely many successful women balancing that dual responsibility. One survey (Roper Starch Worldwide, 1998) found that both working moms and stay-at-home moms spend about the same amount of time with their children. No wonder, then, that some feel impossibly stretched. A *New York Times* poll found women's perceptions to be pessimistic (Dobrzynski, 1995a). They believe they are given lower-level assignments with little chance for advancement, discriminated against in the workforce, and are missing the skills to be business executives. They claim they are being more careful of where they choose to work. Furthermore, they perceive that successful women (those paid more than the bottom 25 percent of men of the same age) were more often divorced and childless compared with women who are not as successful (Wallich, 1996).

The lesser success may indeed be attributable to women professionals putting their career goals on hold when they have their children (McEvoy, 1993). This has led to their settling for lower pay and less prestigious occupations. McEvoy adds, "Who could possibly predict what effect a little face with drool and dimples and sometimes a smile will have on one's future?" (p. 91)

Reis's (1995) study of 67 gifted women in graduate programs in education found the persisting conflict between family and career seems to have become a permanent thread in the stories of women's attempts at achievement. For most, their personal and family lives were barriers to their talent development.

Note also that a woman without a career may not have the resources to cope with unpredictable life circumstances such as illness, the death of her spouse, or divorce. All young women, and especially high-potential ones, should have both the encouragement and the opportunity to receive training, develop their talents, and become professionals. The door must remain open, and gifted females must have the support of parents, teachers, school counselors, future partners, and society.

## SEX DIFFERENCES OR GENDER DIFFERENCES

Reis and Callahan (1989) emphasize the importance of distinguishing between *sex* and *gender* differences; the first relating to the biological and the latter to the sociocultural. Separating the two provides a basis for determining the extent to which the underachievement of women can be modified. Sex differences are biologically determined and could be viewed as potentially limiting the achievements of gifted women. However, gender differences related to sociocultural norms —stereotypes, bias, and discrimination—can be changed, and the correction of these problems may be seen as freeing women to achieve equally with men.

Sonnert and Holton (1996) describe two different models for looking at career differences between males and females in the sciences. The *deficit model,* they explain, is based on the existence of exclusion, both formal and informal. That is, women receive fewer opportunities for successful careers. The second model, called the *difference model,* assumes that there are deeply ingrained differences in behavior, outlook, and goals between men and women. These may be innate or the result of different socialization.

Here's an example of how these models could be used in interpreting male-female differences: Sonnert and Holton found that 70 percent of the men compared to 52 percent of the women in their study considered their scientific ability to be above average. Twenty-five percent of the women and only 5 percent of the men thought they should have had the confidence to be more assertive. If these self-assessments are viewed according to the difference model, one would assume that women cannot be as successful in science because they do not possess sufficient confidence. However, the deficit model, which this author (Rimm) sees as a better fit, explains that structural obstacles cause women to lose con-

fidence and adjust their ambitions and self-expectations downward.

## Biological Differences

Velle (1982) reviewed research on biologically-based behavioral differences between the sexes, differences that conceivably could limit achievements of women. Although some of the research was based on animal behavior, some also involved human subjects.

*Levels of Physical Activity.*   Velle attributes high levels of male physical activity to hormonal influences in the brain during fetal development. He cited research with horses and monkeys. He also reminds us that castration of male domestic animals invariably produces quieter animals. His only example of actual human gender differences in activity came from research reported by Restak (1979), which showed that hyperkinesis (abnormally high levels of physical activity) is found in boys much more frequently than in girls. The hyperactivity that accompanies about 50 percent of all learning disabilities in school children is known to be largely a boys' problem (e.g., Heward & Orlansky, 1992).

*Aggression.*   Velle cited animal studies linking the male hormone testosterone with aggression. He also documented human studies that indicated that boys display more aggressive behavior than girls and suggested that this is related to adolescent competitive behavior.

*Tomboyism.*   *Adrenogenital syndrome* is an abnormal condition in girls characterized by masculinization of external genital organs. It apparently is caused by excessive androgen hormones during fetal development (Money, 1987). Girls with this syndrome always have corrective surgery and are raised as girls. However, despite their female socialization, most of them show characteristics usually considered masculine, such as interest in sports and athletics, preference for boys' clothes and toys, preference for a professional career to marriage, higher physical activity levels, and a lack of interest in caring for small children, hence the nickname *tomboyism.* These findings support the reality of biologically determined gender differences that, in tomboyism cases, can override environmental and sociocultural influences.

***Cerebral Dominance Differences.*** In the past three decades, specialization of the left brain hemisphere for speech and verbal abilities and logical and sequential thinking, and the right hemisphere for spatial and other nonverbal abilities, has been continuously researched (e.g., Springer & Deutsch, 1985). Assumptions about abilities related to sex differences based on the more specialized use of one side of the brain or the other are highly controversial and not well supported by any documented research. However, Levy-Agresti and Sperry (1968) reported finding stronger right-hemisphere dominance for males, resulting in higher spatial abilities. Buffery and Gray (1972), in clear contradiction, argued that better male bilateral development—equal development of both sides of the brain—is responsible for the apparently superior spatial skills of males.

Levy (Kimura, 1985) theorized that differential brain pattern organizations for the sexes may be due to differences in rates of development both before and after birth, with the left hemisphere developing more quickly in girls and the right hemisphere in boys. The impact of this difference in rate would favor verbal skills in females and spatial skills in males.

PET (positron emission tomography) scanning continues to find differences between the male and female brains (Begley, 1995). Women have more neurons in their temporal lobes and have a larger corpus callosum and anterior commissure than men, thus leading to more communication between the two hemispheres of the brain, enabling women to be more proficient in language and intuition, as well as in recognizing melodies and tones of the voice.

If there are hemispheric differences between the sexes, no research makes it clear whether the hemisphere differences cause the differential spatial ability or whether cultural conditions cause the differential hemispheric development.

## Sociocultural Differences

Although gender differences can be described and to some degree even quantified, research cannot delineate the exact extent to which specific differences are cultural versus biological in origin. However, studies of the changing role of women in society provide good documentation that many differences are indeed *not* biologically based.

The pink or blue blanket that identifies gender differences almost at birth is the first step in giving differential direction to the sexes. Next comes the infant's nursery, with pastel colors, lace, frills, and dolls for girls and bright colors, heroes, spaceships, and dump trucks for boys. The expectations of *docility* and *conformity* for girls throughout early childhood initiate the gifted girl to her eventual underachieving role in society.

In the process of developing her *Bem Sex-Role Inventory,* Bem (1974) itemized stereotyped characteristics associated with men and women. Interestingly, characteristics considered "masculine" also are typical of successful people, for example: *aggressiveness, ambitiousness, analytical ability, assertiveness, competitiveness, leadership ability, independence,* and *self-reliance.* Characteristics in the "feminine" column included those that might be associated with mothering or, at best, a narrow range of nurturant, female-dominated occupations, for example: *affection, cheerfulness, compassion, gentleness, love of children, shyness, understanding,* and *warmth.*

Bem's stereotyped traits continued to be reinforced by textbooks, literature, and the media. For example, there are "girls' books," such as *Little Women* and *Little House in the Big Woods,* and "boys' books," which include tales of mystery, adventure, risk-taking, and accomplishment (Sadker, Sadker, & Hicks, 1980). Even in more recent history textbooks only 2 percent of space is devoted to women (Sadker & Sadker, 1994). Sternglanz and Serbin (1974) analyzed gender-role stereotypes of ten of the then most popular children's TV shows. They found half to have no female characters at all, while the others had twice as many males as females. Furthermore, females were portrayed as not making or carrying out plans; they were punished if they were too active or aggressive; and they continuously deferred to males. Male characters were highly active, aggressive, and socially dominant, and they made plans and carried them out. The TV picture has not changed much.

Can gifted girls overcome the impact of families, schools, and sex-role stereotyped literature and media on their own self-perceptions? If we are to help girls, we will have to start early. Eccles, Wigfield, Harold, and Blumenfeld (1993) found that by first grade girls believed they were less competent in athletics and mathematics. On the other hand, they had higher beliefs in their competence in reading and music. In contrast, boys had higher competence beliefs in their athletic and mathematical abilities, and fewer indicated that they felt competent in reading and music. Only with high levels of awareness and some deliberate "counterconditioning" will we be able to overcome these gender stereotypes.

## MATHEMATICS ABILITY

The most prominent and heated argument related to differential abilities regards whether males have superior mathematical abilities (Armstrong, 1980; Benbow, 1986, 1992a, 1992b; Benbow & Stanley, 1980, 1981, 1982, 1983; Fennema & Carpenter, 1998; Fennema, Carpenter, Jacobs, Franke, & Levi, 1998a; Kerr, 1997; Pallas and Alexander, 1983; Wiley & Goldstein 1991; see also Benbow & Lubinski, 1997; Stanley, 1994; Stanley & Benbow, 1983).

Until recently considerable research pointed to differences in math achievement beginning at adolescence. Cramer and Oshima (1992) blame girls' lesser achievement on girls seeing success in math as contradictory to peers' expectations of their roles. They also point out the importance of "attribution training" so girls can succeed in junior high math. This would include awareness of gender-role stereotyping and its negative effects and also the termination of self-defeating beliefs.

Almost all studies have found that the math difference seems to widen over the school years, becoming quite prominent by junior high school (Maccoby & Jacklin, 1974). Giele (1978) and Fennema (1980), in fact, concluded that male and female math abilities are about equal in childhood, but at about age 12 or 13 boys begin to show superiority. Even computer use declines for girls as they approach adolescence (Enrico, 1995). At a fast-paced computer summer program that was made up of 75 percent girls, despite their quick acquisition of skills, the girls assumed that boys were better at computers than they were. Girls tend to use computers differently than boys do. They are more likely to use them for word processing or education, while boys are more likely to use them for games, most of which are related to typical male interests.

A longitudinal study by Hall (1980) of 59 gifted students (29 boys and 30 girls) from preschool through grade 12 found no significant gender differences in arithmetic or spatial abilities or SAT-Math scores. She attributed her unique findings to an environmentally specific sample. The students were mainly from a university environment where many of the females' fathers were Ph.D.'s and cross-gender support for education was evident.

A male/female math comparison study in Hawaii of students in grades 4, 6, 8, and 10 found superior achievement for *females* over males (Brandon, Newton, & Hammond, 1987). An analysis by ethnic background of these students further indicated that gender differences favoring girls were smaller for Caucasian students than for Japanese American, Filipino American, and Hawaiian children.

Camilla Benbow and Julian Stanley (1980, 1981, 1982, 1983)—basing their work on years of SAT-M scores collected for thousands of students in Stanley's *Study of Mathematically Precocious Youth* (SMPY)—concluded that their data support a biological superiority of male math ability, which could be related to male superiority in spatial tasks. They indicated that environmental influences are not likely to so dramatically affect the "extreme absence of extraordinary female talent" among students involved in the SMPY talent search. A November 1983 Associated Press news release, based upon an article in *Science* magazine (Benbow & Stanley, 1983), noted that in the years 1980, 1981, and 1982 Benbow and Stanley found that the average SAT-Math score for 19,883 gifted seventh-grade boys was 416. For 19,937 gifted girls the average score was a noticeably lower 386. Average SAT-Verbal scores were almost identical, 367 for boys and 365 for girls. Further, boys outnumbered girls by better than 2 to 1 among those scoring above 500; by better than 4 to 1 among those who scored over 600; and by almost 13 to 1 in the group scoring 700 or higher (113 boys, 9 girls). Benbow and Stanley "could not find substantial differences in attitude, background, or previous mathematical training between boys and girls." See Inset 14.1 for one

possible physiological explanation of gender differences in mathematical talent.

Benbow and Arjmand (1990) further reported in the longitudinal Study of Mathematically Precocious Youth (SMPY) that males achieved better in sciences in college and that the aspirations of females declined significantly during their college years. Rimm found in her clinical work that a fear of low grades often prevents girls from risking the competitive and difficult science courses and may be in part responsible for preventing women from taking these more challenging courses.

Among the successful women who participated in the Rimm research (Rimm et al., 1999; Rimm & Rimm-Kaufman, 2001), women in the areas of science, medicine, and business tended not to experience grade decline in mathematics in middle school and were more likely to take advanced math courses in high school. They attributed their taking advanced courses to simply liking math or to the influence of parents and

---

**INSET 14.1**

### Does Math Genius Have a Hormonal Basis?

Harvard Medical School neurologist Norman Geshwind proposed that excess testosterone or unusual sensitivity to testosterone during fetal life can alter brain development (Kolata, 1983). Specifically, the right hemisphere of the brain (instead of the usual left) becomes dominant for language abilities, and the person is likely to be left-handed. Further, such individuals—mainly boys, of course—are predisposed to (1) such speech abnormalities as autism, dyslexia, or stuttering, (2) certain kinds of giftedness, particularly artistic, musical, or mathematical, and (3) disorders in the body's immune system. Said Geshwind, "If you get the mechanism adjusted just right you get superior right hemisphere talents, such as artistic, musical, or mathematical talent. But the mechanism is a bit treacherous. If you overdo it, you're going to get into trouble."

According to *Science* magazine writer Gina Kolata, Benbow and Stanley were intrigued by this

possible explanation of male superiority in math talent, and promptly contacted their very best students (those who scored above 700 on the SAT-M) to see if they were left-handed or had immune system disorders. "To their surprise and delight, they find that Geshwind's predictions hold up beautifully in their group" (Kolata, 1983). Twenty percent of the mathematically talented students are left-handed, which is more than double the proportion of left-handedness in the general population. A full 60 percent have immune system disorders (allergies, asthma)—which is five times the expected rate.

When Benbow and Stanley contacted students in their list who were less mathematically talented, the students also were less likely to be left-handed or to have immune disorders.

While Geshwind agrees that the data for the precocious students "fit in perfectly, to put it bluntly," he also concedes, "There's been—understandably—an enormous degree of skepticism."

teachers. Women in the more verbal professions were less likely to take advanced math courses and indicated in their research questionnaires that they were disinterested or they feared the difficulty of mathematics. An important main difference between the women in medicine and nursing was that those in nursing preferred not taking math courses or found them difficult.

Analyses of male/female differences in math test scores continue to be reported, and results are mixed. Feingold (1988) reported that there had been a significant decrease in male-female gender differences in arithmetic and figural reasoning in the previous 33 years, and Linn and Hyde (1989) also found decreases in gender differences for both mathematics and science. Hyde and Fennema (1990) did a meta-analysis of gender differences in math achievement and aptitude and found that differences that favored males increased with the selectivity of the sample, highly selective samples showing greater differences favoring males. Becker and Forsythe (1990) examined 10 years (Grades 3–12) of Iowa Test of Basic Skills and Iowa Test of Educational Development data and found that at the upper percentiles, males scored significantly better in mathematics.

Stanley (1992) stunned an audience of educators with his report of higher average scores for males on the majority of 86 subtests of aptitude and achievement tests, including the Graduate Record Examination (GRE), Scholastic Aptitude Tests (SAT), the American College Testing Program (ACT), and Advanced Placement (AP) tests. For example, males scored higher than females on all 17 of the subject area tests of the GRE, with political science, math, chemistry, engineering, and history showing the largest gender differences. There were no differences in Verbal GRE scores but large differences favoring males in Quantitative GRE scores. On the Law SAT (LSAT), females scored the same as males. Females scored higher than males on the English portion of the ACT but generally lower on the other tests (Social Studies, Math, Natural Sci-

ence). Females also scored higher on the French AP test, but lower on computer science, physics, chemistry, and calculus. There were no differences on the Spanish and English literature AP subtests.

Stanley found the matter perplexing and unexplainable, particularly since females generally are better students.

Despite the large numbers of analyses of ability test differences, the test score differences apparently do not reflect high school grade differences. Among the 1989 SAT examinees, for example, 54 percent of the females and 46 percent of the males reported an *A+* grade-point average, and 58 percent of the females and 42 percent of the males reported an *A* grade-point average (Educational Testing Service, 1989a). Furthermore, Kelly-Benjamin (1990) reported that when females are allowed additional time in the SAT they outperform males, indicating they are quite capable of the work but at a slightly slower average pace.

Three new studies suggest that gender differences in math and computers develop earlier than adolescence, thus supporting the theories that either very early school environments differentiate gender math skills, or there is a biological basis for math differences. A study by Nancy M. Robinson and colleagues of the University of Washington, Seattle (as cited in Holden, 1998), provided a mathematics-enriched environment for one-half of a group of 276 children between the ages of $5\frac{1}{2}$ and 8 who were identified as mathematically gifted. The boys in the control group (not given math enrichment) gained more than the control girls in math skills; and the boys in the enrichment group, which gained significantly more than the control group, also maintained their lead in math achievement.

A study of 82 first- through third-grade children's mathematical strategies did not actually show better overall math performance for either gender, but showed differences in gender strategies in solving math problems, which may explain later gender differences in mathematics (Fennema

& Carpenter, 1998; Fennema et al., 1998a; Fennema et al., 1998b). The researchers found that girls tended to use concrete strategies like counting or modeling, while the boys tended to use more abstract strategies. The researchers point out that their research may indeed call into question earlier studies that identified gender differences in mathematics beginning only in adolescence.

Beisser (2000) observed differences in style of computer use as early as kindergarten. While boys had their hands on the mouse, girls tended to verbalize instructions, watch, and talk. Beisser considered that the girls were "marginalized" by the boys' active hands-on approach even at that young age.

*An absolutely crucial consideration is that no ability is totally and exclusively related to gender.* Research reports are based on average test scores involving large numbers of students. There is always near-total overlap in the distributions of male and female ability and achievement test scores.

## Culture-Based Explanations of Gender Differences in Math

The counterarguments to a biological explanation of male math superiority assert mainly that any gender differences in mathematics ability are cultural in origin. Some specific arguments are these:

*Cultural Stereotypes.* During adolescence, society encourages boys more often than girls to show superior intellectual ability to attract members of the opposite sex. However, girls, in accord with cultural stereotypes, may believe that boys do not like girls who excel in math and therefore do not seek to develop mathematical abilities (Fox, 1977). When in 1992 a talking Barbie Doll included in her mechanical conversation the statement "Math is really hard," women protested loudly and Mattel withdrew the stereotyped message ("Barbie's Remarks," 1992).

A longitudinal study of high school valedictorians in Illinois found that two-thirds of the females settled for careers significantly lower than their educational attainment would justify, compared to only 10 percent of the males (Arnold & Denny, 1985). Benbow (1992a) reported that of the top 1 percent of women in math ability, only 3 percent stayed in the math/science pipeline compared to 32 percent of the males in the study. Alper (as cited in Adams, 1996) found that among 730,000 sophomore girls who expressed interest in science and engineering in 1977, less than 1 percent had achieved a doctorate degree in either field by 1992. Sue V. Rosser is quoted as saying "The [science] pipeline is leaking women," a leak that begins in middle school (American Association of University Women, 1991).

Parent expectations make a difference in perpetuating these cultural stereotypes (Dickens & Cornell, 1993). In a study of 165 high-ability adolescent girls, mother and father expectations rather than role model identification made the difference in the adolescent mathematical concept. Thus parents either carry on the cultural stereotype or change it, and that makes the main difference for girls. Jacobs and Weisz (1994) also found parents' stereotypic beliefs to affect both girls' attitudes and their actual math performance, and Callahan et al. (1996) discovered that even girls with high abilities in math or science perceived that their parents discouraged their attendance at specialty schools for math, science, or technology.

In a study of 117 African American middle school gifted students, it was found that gifted girls had a positive attitude about math and science and considered these subjects to be important. They also believed in their abilities to be successful in these domains. However, males in the study continued to think of math and science as male domains (Yong, 1992). Some things are changing and some simply are not.

Kolata (1980) emphasized the impact of cultural influences on attitudes toward math in a summary statement about the Johns Hopkins SMPY research. "Although fewer girls than boys qualify for the accelerated math courses . . . , even fewer girls enroll in them." While females who select math study achieve as well as males, few females choose to study math (Fennema & Sherman, 1978).

The cultural stereotype that females are not as capable in mathematics and science adversely affects their estimates of their own talents (Heller & Ziegler, 1996). However, improvements can be made with retraining and positive environments. In research studies involving attributional retraining conducted in a German high school and with university students in physics and mathematics (Ziegler & Heller, 2000), female students showed significant improvements in their science and math performance. In another study (Zeldin & Pajares, 2000), where self-efficacy was found to be critical for women in mathematical and scientific careers, the women's positive belief in themselves was fostered by relationships with others within their academic and career settings. Although intentional training as well as supportive environments can remove cultural stereotypes, major societal commitments must be made to affect the long-held stereotypes that women are less capable in mathematics and mathematical sciences.

***Unequal Math Training.***   Based upon her review of research on mathematics learning, Fennema (1980) argued that conclusions about male superiority often have been based on studies in which the number of previous math courses has not been controlled; that is, males with more math background have been compared to females with less background. However, Fox (1981; also Benbow & Stanley, 1980, 1981, 1983) noted that the mathematics talent searches conducted at Johns Hopkins University for the SMPY program were at grades 7 and 8, when males and females had equal math training.

Table 14.4 compares high school advanced math and science courses taken by males and females between 1982 and 1987. While there are increases for both males and females, the rates of increase for females unfortunately are not as high as for males (Educational Testing Service, 1989b).

***Father Identification.***   As we saw in Chapter 13, several studies (e.g., Sutten-Smith, Rosenberg, & Landy, 1968) reported that early father absence, before age 8 or 9, has a depressing effect on later math scores of both males and females. They hypothesized that children learn a mathe-

**TABLE 14.4**  Percentage of High School Graduates Who Took Selected Mathematics and Science Courses by Sex, 1982 and 1987

| Courses | Males | Females | Difference |
| --- | --- | --- | --- |
| Trigonometry 1982 | 12.9 | 11.3 | 1.6 |
| Trigonometry 1987 | 21.9 | 19.0 | 1.9 |
| Pre-calculus 1982 | 6.0 | 5.5 | .5 |
| Pre-calculus 1987 | 13.6 | 11.3 | 1.2 |
| Calculus 1982 | 5.3 | 4.2 | 1.1 |
| Calculus 1987 | 7.6 | 4.7 | 2.9 |
| Chemistry 1982 | 31.7 | 30.0 | 1.7 |
| Chemistry 1987 | 46.3 | 44.5 | 1.8 |
| Physics 1982 | 18.2 | 10.0 | 8.2 |
| Physics 1987 | 25.3 | 15.0 | 15.0 |

Source: "Nation at Risk Study as Part of the 1987 High School Transcript Study," Tabulations, May 19, 1988, Westat, Inc. for the U.S. Department of Education, National Center for Educational Statistics, Tables 33 and 41.

matical problem-solving thinking style from their fathers. Helson (1971) similarly reported that creative women mathematicians and scientists tended to identify with their fathers. As noted previously, Hall (1980) attributed the strong math achievement of the gifted girls in her longitudinal study to support by fathers. It therefore is possible that learning mathematical thinking and problem solving may take place informally in the family through the process of identification with the father. Since boys are more likely to identify with their fathers than girls, boys logically would acquire superior mathematics abilities.

***Different Toys.***    Another hypothesis is that gender-role stereotyped toys improve visual-spatial abilities for boys more than for girls. Trains, model airplanes, race cars, trucks, electrical sets, Legos, Tinker Toys, and other construction toys all are more likely to be played with by boys. These toys may enhance spatial skills more than the typical dolls, tea sets, coloring books, jump ropes, and needlecraft supplied to girls. A visit to a typical preschool or kindergarten class reminds one of how infrequently girls will be found in the block corner or boys in the doll house.

***Teacher and Parent Expectations.***    Mathematics has been considered a male domain by both students and teachers. Ernest (1976) found in interviewing teachers that 41 percent thought boys were better at math than girls, while none thought girls were better. Since teacher expectations may affect achievement by as much as 20 percent (Brophy, 1982; Good & Weinstein, 1986), a *self-fulfilling prophecy* can help perpetuate mathematics as a male domain.

Also rooted in cultural stereotypes and expectations, Brody and Fox (1980) found that parents of gifted boys were more likely to see a career in mathematics for their son than were parents of gifted girls.

Parsons, Adler, and Kaczala (1982) and Dickens (1990) came to similar conclusions. Parent and teacher expectations about children's math

abilities had a significant impact on their mathematics achievement. However, Raymond and Benbow (1989) did not find parent encouragement of math different for gifted girls than for gifted boys. They did indicate that the typical gender role stereotyped parent behaviors, with fathers more involved with their gifted children in quantitative areas and mothers more concerned with verbal areas, provide stereotyped role models affecting math preferences.

Further insight into female mathematics and teacher expectations comes from a study by Hallinan and Sorensen (1987), which found that "girls with high aptitude in mathematics are less likely to be assigned to the high-ability group than boys" (p. 71). Such inappropriate grouping is likely to impact on girls taking advanced math and science classes despite their aptitude for these courses.

Male and female self-perceptions about their math abilities may be reinforced by teachers who see girls as working harder and producing better work in math and science (Siegle & Reis, 1994). Although the work is perceived as better, however, the girls do not receive higher grades that reflect the better quality. Teachers indicated that they did not believe girls had lesser abilities than boys, but perhaps the grades told the real story and therefore affected the girls' lesser self-perceptions.

***School Support.***    In an analysis of schools that successfully teach math and science to girls, Casserly (1979) found that teachers in those schools were not threatened by mathematically gifted girls, that they used older females to tutor younger girls, and that they began good programs before the sixth grade—before girls come to view math as a male subject. Fox (1974) similarly found that girls were successful in a math program for the gifted when school personnel were enthusiastic and supportive of the girls. When Gavin (1996) surveyed 16 female mathematics majors in a highly selective liberal arts college, the women revealed that parental and teacher encouragement was critical for them. Most of these math majors recall being recognized by peers and teachers alike as top math students during their precollege school years.

## Importance of the Math Differences Hypothesis

Differential skill in mathematics is a critical issue in relation to the professional development of gifted females. Male-dominated fields that convey high status and good financial rewards (for example, medicine, engineering, architecture, pharmacy, computer sciences, and all physical sciences) *require skill in mathematics*. A lack of preparation clearly prevents most females from ever entering many challenging and rewarding professions. Said then-president Reagan in his 1983 State of the Union address to Congress, "If a child has not acquired good mathematical training by age 16, he or she will never be able to enter the fields of engineering or science."

## DIFFERENCES IN EXPECTATIONS, ACHIEVEMENT ORIENTATION, AND ASPIRATIONS

Differences in mathematical preparation create real barriers to the entrance of females into many male-dominated professions. In addition, family, school, and peer expectations discourage a strong achievement orientation, risk-taking, independence, and self-confidence in girls. These pressures can lead to low aspirations that, in turn, result in underachievement.

### Family Expectations and Identification

High educational achievement and high career aspirations begin at home. Both mother role-modeling and father expectations have a compelling influence on the achievement orientation of gifted girls.

In regard to career aspirations, many researchers (e.g., Marini, 1978; Radin, 1974; Rimm et al., 1999; Rimm & Rimm-Kaufman, 2001; Sutherland, 1978) concluded that career modeling by mothers motivates females to have higher educational and career aspirations.

Fathers' direct expectations of their daughters also may influence female achievement. Radin and Epstein (1975) found that fathers' short- and long-term academic expectations of their daughters were positively correlated with measures of the girls' intellectual functioning. Many of the successful women in nontraditional careers in the Rimm research (Rimm et al., 1999; Rimm & Rimm-Kaufman, 2001) credited their fathers' high expectations for their career success.

Gender-stereotyped expectations of girls—and all women—by their fathers (Lynn, 1974) and dominating fathers (e.g., Heilbrun, 1973) appear to have a negative effect on girls' achievement.

Research on the comparative importance of the mother versus the father role-model for female achievement is not always consistent, nor are the dynamics uncomplicated. Helson (1971), noted earlier, found that creative women mathematicians tended to be oldest daughters who identified with their fathers. Bardwick (1971) also emphasized the importance of girls' identification with their fathers in order to learn important achievement traits such as independence and self-esteem. Drews and Teahan (1957) and Pierce and Bowman (1960), however, concluded that mother dominance was critical in encouraging girls to become career-oriented achievers. Although more of the successful women in the Rimm research (Rimm et al., 1999; Rimm & Rimm-Kaufman, 2001) in both traditional and nontraditional careers identified with their mothers than with their fathers, the highest percentage of women who identified with their fathers were those in science and medicine. On the other hand, some of the successful women were cautioned by their full-time homemaker mothers to find their own identities and not be dependent on men. Their mothers served as models of what *not* to do, with advice of what to do.

A study of 60 high-ability females, 42 of whom had left home to participate in an early college entrance program, found a consistent association between self-perceived competence and the quality of communication with parents (Callahan, Cornell, & Loyd, 1990). Better communication with mothers was associated with favorable self-perceptions of both job competence and "romantic appeal." Callahan, Cunningham, and Plucker (1994) also found family influence to be important in helping gifted girls cope with barriers to their achievement. Some family encouragements that seemed particularly important were mothers as role models and the observation of discussion, debate, and decision making in their homes.

Incidentally, the influence of the media on parents may also impact on their children. Reports of the Benbow and Stanley (e.g., 1980) research on gender differences in math reasoning appeared in many popular magazines and newspapers. Jacobs and Eccles (1985) discovered that parents exposed to these research findings changed their math expectations of their daughters. Compared to other mothers, mothers who read about the research appeared to expect *less* of their girls in terms of math success. The effect of the exposure on fathers was to increase the importance of their daughters' taking calculus and higher math. Apparently, although the media coverage seemed to encourage mothers to provide an easy way out for their daughters, it inspired fathers to come to their defense.

In conclusion, despite some special circumstances and exceptions, career-oriented mothers do indeed provide strong role models that, along with positive and supportive father expectations, influence educational and career achievement of gifted girls.

## Peer Expectations

From early adolescence, and sometimes before, peer expectations play a strong part in directing achievement. Because high intelligence and an achievement orientation sometimes are considered masculine characteristics, girls risk being considered "unfeminine" if they become too involved in school achievement.

Brown and Steinberg (1989) reported peer pressure to get good, but not outstanding, grades. Kramer (as cited in Reis & Callahan, 1996) found that gifted girls deliberately underestimated their abilities for fear that high abilities would cause peers to view them as socially less competent or unattractive. The Rimm research (Rimm et al., 1999; Rimm & Rimm-Kaufman, 2001) found that 40 percent of the successful women described themselves as less social than typical, and many reported paying a social price for their good grades. The successful women managed their peer pressure by finding peer groups that shared their interests and respected their intelligence. For example, Cleveland Orchestra flutist Martha Aarons recalled coming home in tears daily from middle school after being taunted and teased as "hairy legs" and "brainiac." At summer music camp, however, she felt accepted among her orchestra friends, and by high school her youth orchestra pals provided her with a good social life. As an adult, Martha finds her social skills to be a strength. African American neurosurgeon Alexa Canady, known as a "math nerd," didn't fit in with the high school mainstream but was comfortable with her intellectual crowd and not lonely. Teenage girls should be made aware that they are not alone, and peer pressure need not cause them to underachieve to be popular.

Perhaps the tides are turning, at least in some schools. In some recent studies of girls in gifted programs, African American and Puerto Rican girls indicated positive and supportive peer relationships and pride in their high achievement (Yong, Spielhagen, & Reis, et al., as cited in Reis & Callahan, 1996).

As to peer pressure on girls who participate in gifted programming, Read (as cited in Reis & Callahan, 1996) found that girls tended to drop out of gifted programming more than boys. In early grades there were more girls participating than boys, but by tenth grade there were more boys than girls in gifted programming.

By college age, parent attitudes toward gifted women's career choices appear less important than peer attitudes, especially those of male peers. For example, Trigg and Perlman (1976) found that females were more likely to apply to graduate school in less traditional areas if their male friends encouraged them to do so. According to Horner's (1972) classic "fear of success" syndrome, girls suppress high achievement and success because of their fear of "failing as a female." As one immediately pertinent finding, Horner found that females who received career encouragement from their male friends were less likely to experience fear of success.

Grant, Battle, and Heggoy (2000), using a multiple-case-study design, tracked seven gifted females after high school graduation. The women had all been raised in rural settings. All proceeded through college in expectation of combining a career and marriage in a dual-career family, and they remained committed to that career search. They believed their parents continued to be strong influences while they were in college. All the women changed their initial majors by the end of their freshman year. When they changed from mathematics and sciences to more traditional verbal majors, they blamed it on their dislike of the college course work. The women's experiences included transfers between institutions, multiple changes in majors, taking more than the typical amount of time to finish college, and career indecision. All the women persisted in completing college. The authors recommended that career guidance for college women would be a major help to them because these women's search, although continuous, seemed haphazard, unplanned, and in need of guidance.

## School Expectations

From nursery school onward we find continuous documentation of school biases that deter an achievement orientation for females. Serbin and O'Leary (1975) compared differential treatment of boys and girls in 15 nursery school classes and recorded the following behaviors that they felt would reinforce aggressiveness, confidence, and independence in boys but not in girls. Boys were encouraged to work on their own much more often than girls. Teachers rewarded girls for being

dependent by responding more when they were near but gave similar attention to boys regardless of physical distance. All 15 teachers gave more attention to boys than girls, including more individualized instruction and more tangible and verbal rewards.

Rimm-Kaufman (1996) compared the adjustment to kindergarten of inhibited (fearful) children to that of uninhibited (outgoing) children. There was no gender difference in the adjustment for the inhibited children. However, for uninhibited children there were surprisingly rapid gender changes. Observations of "circle time" over a four-month period in 31 classes showed an increase in volunteering by uninhibited boys but a dramatic decrease in talking and volunteering by uninhibited girls. Rimm-Kaufman also noted a difference in teachers' attitudes when children "acted out." For example, the teachers' typical response to boys' behavior was "boys will be boys," but for girls it was, "there must be something wrong with her" or "she's immature" (and this was only kindergarten).

Siegle and Reis (1998) found that teachers concluded that female students worked harder and produced better-quality work; however, girls did not receive higher grades than boys. The teachers also concluded that their male and female students had similarly high abilities except in language arts, where they rated the females higher. This represents progress in teacher expectations because earlier research found that teachers believe males had higher abilities in math and science. Despite the equal expectations of teachers, the gifted girls in the study did not rate themselves as high as did the boys in social studies, science, or math, although the girls did rate themselves higher than the boys did in language arts. The researchers suggested that the teacher perceptions of greater effort by the girls caused the girls to assume they had lesser abilities.

The AAUW report, *How Schools Shortchange Girls* (American Association of University Women, 1992; McKay, 1994), focused on some critical disadvantages with which girls cope in public schools:

- Girls receive less attention than boys in the classroom.
- African American girls get even less attention than other girls.
- Sexual harassment of girls by boys is increasing.
- Girls are included less in textbooks.
- Girls are advancing in math but declining in science.
- Boys get more scholarships than girls, based on SATs, even if grades are the same.
- The decrease in girls' self-esteem is three times greater than boys.
- Only half of girls take pride in their schoolwork.
- Teachers allow boys to try again but tend to take over for girls.

Despite the multitude of disadvantages that affect girls in schools, the same report finds that girls achieve better in college than boys. However, as we know from the first part of this chapter, the accumulation of small disadvantages adversely affects career achievement for women.

When teacher feedback is given to children, Dweck and Bush (1976; Nichols, 1979) found that poor performance often is described as "lack of ability" in girls, while similar poor performance is noted as "not working hard enough" with boys. This difference is important. If poor performance is seen by students (girls) as lack of *ability,* then increased effort will not solve the problem. However, if poor performance is interpreted as lack of *effort,* then the students (boys) will be motivated to work harder to achieve (Weiner, 1985).

Casserly (1979) reported gender differences in willingness to take Advanced Placement courses. Although girls outnumber boys in traditionally "female" Advanced Placement courses (for example, English, Spanish, and French), girls usually take fewer Advanced Placement courses than boys in math, history, classics, German, and all sciences. In analyzing differences between schools that produce high-achieving girls and those that do not, Casserly identified two disarm-

ingly simple factors: (1) The schools producing high-achieving girls used a tracking program that made Advanced Placement classes a natural sequence, and (2) teachers both actively recruited girls for the Advanced Placement classes and expected them to be high achievers.

From preschool to college, then, and despite improvements in recent years, many teachers and counselors by innuendo and by action unconsciously discourage females from developing their talents equally with males.

## Self-Expectations

Female aspirations and achievement orientations surely are changing. This change includes altered self-perceptions and self-expectations. If gifted females are to develop their talents and make their contributions to society they must acquire confidence and strong achievement needs, and they must make plans for a sound education.

Noble (1989), who focuses on problems of gifted females in her clinical practice, reported that gifted females often are unaware of and/or frightened by their own potential. She believes these inappropriate self-expectations are related to concerns about rejection by families, teachers, and peers; growing up in impaired families; and families that underestimate their abilities.

Self-expectations of females also are changing. Karnes and D'Ilio (1989) questioned 49 gifted boys and 48 gifted girls (Grades 4–6) about their gender-related impressions for a list of 34 leadership positions. Although boys continued to have more traditional gender-role stereotyped biases, females did not. Girls believed that most leadership roles are suitable for either gender.

Research suggests four important factors that seem to be linked to lower self-expectations and aspirations of females: (1) a lower sense of competence, (2) a tendency to attribute failures to oneself and successes to external factors, (3) lower achievement motivation, and (4) the "fear of success" syndrome mentioned earlier. These undoubtedly are interrelated and together decrease the likelihood of gifted women aspiring to challenging professions.

***Low Sense of Competence.*** First, studies of the sense of competence among women repeatedly show that, on average, women exhibit lower feelings of competence than do men. For example, Stake (1981) found that females tended to score lower than males in predicting their future ability to perform well in high-level careers. Addison (1981) similarly found that in evaluating their own performance, females tended to underestimate their degree of success while males tended to overestimate it.

Gifted girls seem to be extremely susceptible to the loss of confidence at adolescence (Klein & Zehms, 1996). Although overall self-concept scores declined for both gifted and nongifted girls between grades three and five, and again between grades five and eight, eighth-grade gifted girls scored lower in the areas of intellectual and school status and popularity than the nongifted eighth-grade girls.

Fox, Sadker and Engle (1999) suggest that the lowering of girls' sense of intellectual competence may be part of the reason that girls lag behind boys in critical college, graduate school, and professional tests. Girls start to lose ground to boys on standardized tests around the middle school years, the same time they seem to begin to lose self-esteem. Perhaps their lack of confidence causes them to avoid risk taking, such as intelligent guessing of answers where they have only partial knowledge (Ben-Shakhar & Sinai and Gallagher & DeLisi, as cited in Fox, Sadker, & Engle 1999). In reviewing the research literature, Reis (1998b) found that gifted girls were less likely to lose confidence in their abilities if they were involved in gifted programs and numerous extracurricular activities compared to gifted girls not in such programs.

In a program in which gifted seventh- and eighth-grade students were given an opportunity for grade acceleration, only 54 percent of the girls chose acceleration, compared to 73 percent of the boys (Fox, 1977). Said Fox, girls were less confident in trying something new and were more fearful of failure. They also experienced more problems of self-esteem—which were unrelated to actual ability—and were more fearful of peer rejection. Hall (1982) similarly reported that girls were less likely than boys to enter college early.

Denny (cited in Callahan, 1991) studied self-perceptions of competence of a group of high school valedictorians. At graduation, 23 percent of the males and 21 percent of the females rated themselves "far above average." By the end of their sophomore year of college, that percentage decreased one point for males and 17 points for females—only 4 percent of the females continued to perceive themselves as highly competent.

Arnold (as cited in Fox et al., 1999), in a 15-year study of high school valedictorians, found that although there were more female than male valedictorians, and those females surpassed the males on all measures of college achievement, the female valedictorians lost confidence in their intelligence in college, and many of them lowered their career aspirations to traditional female career paths, voicing early concerns about the difficulties of combining career and family.

***Attributional Differences.*** The lower confidence that females exhibit is reflected in studies of the causal attributions they make. Studies of both children and adults report a similar gender-related tendency (Deaux, 1976; Frieze, 1975; Post, 1981). Females tend to attribute their successes to hard work or to luck but their failures to lack of ability. Males tend to follow the reverse attribution process, blaming others, bad luck, or their lack of effort for failures but crediting their own high abilities for successes.

In a study of sixth-, seventh-, and eighth-grade girls, the attribution of success to hard work or luck persisted. None of the gifted females acknowledged their excellent abilities (Callahan, Cunningham, & Plucker, 1994). However, as mentioned earlier in this chapter (Heller & Ziegler, 1996; Ziegler & Heller, 2000), attribution may be taught.

*Low Achievement Motivation.*   Our third factor in female underachievement is low achievement motivation. The need to achieve is a highly consistent personality trait that begins developing as early as the second grade (Atkinson, 1974; McClelland, 1976).

Efforts to teach achievement motivation basically encourage the learner to think as achievement-oriented individuals do; that is, to (1) value success and achievement, (2) accept moderate risks, (3) set realistic and achievable goals, and (4) feel confident that he or she can achieve these goals.

We have seen throughout this chapter that cultural stereotypes, biases, and home and school expectations work to reduce female independence and aggressiveness and, consequently, their needs for high-level academic and career achievement. Achievement motivation leaders McClelland (1976) and Atkinson (1974) attribute needs for achievement to learning, rather than heredity, and point to parental influence in childhood as the crucial factor.

As an interesting historical fact, in an 873-page compilation of research into achievement motivation, a single footnote commented on achievement motivation research with women (Atkinson, 1958).

## EDUCATING GIFTED FEMALES

Society no doubt will continue to improve in providing a support system in which gifted women may develop their potential equally with men. Schools, however, must take a leadership role in fostering this equal development. In this section the model explored in Chapter 13, dealing with underachievement, will be used to provide some realistic guidelines that can help teachers, counselors, and parents reverse underachievement in females. That model includes the following steps:

1. Assessing skills, abilities, and home and school reinforcement contingencies.
2. Improving communication between home and school.
3. Changing the expectations of important others.
4. Improving model identification.

5. Correcting skill deficiencies.
6. Modifying reinforcements at home and school.

Since cultural underachievement is a more extensive problem than individual underachievement, there will be some additional special problems that educators must consider in programming for underachieving girls.

## Assessing Skills, Abilities, and Reinforcement Contingencies

School district administrators, principals, teachers, counselors, and others need, at the minimum, to ask the following questions:

1. Are gender-role stereotyped books, films, and other media avoided in the classroom and library?
2. Are spatially oriented activities, such as mathematics and computer work, introduced early so that both girls and boys begin learning these skills before peer pressures intervene?
3. Are females equally encouraged to participate in competitive activities?
4. Are counselors and teachers being educated in the opportunities for and abilities of females?
5. Are students and their parents being educated regarding the broad range of opportunities for females?
6. Are girls encouraged to take leadership roles in the school?
7. Are gifted girls encouraged to take advanced courses in all curricular areas?
8. Are students exposed to a variety of successful, professional female models?
9. Are opportunities available for assertiveness training for females?
10. Are some all-female group guidance experiences being provided, so that girls may deal with problems related to femininity, self-confidence, and an achievement orientation?
11. Are efforts being made to erase the stigma of a high achievement orientation for females?
12. Are girls from lower SES families being informed about careers they have had little exposure to (McCormick, 1997)?

13. Are gifted girls being counseled to expect to take financial responsibility for themselves and their families, and are they learning about careers that provide financial security (McCormick, 1997)?

14. Are the rewards for career achievements for females being stressed equally with those for males?

To the extent that answers to these questions reflect nonencouragement of high-level educational and career aspirations for gifted girls, changes should be made.

## Communication between Home and School

Gifted coordinators, guidance counselors, and classroom teachers may all become involved in coordinated efforts to communicate with parents about the achievement, course selection, and career expectations for gifted girls. A series of short letters to the parents of gifted students, including some specific suggestions of ways in which parents can help encourage gender equity and female talent development, may help. One example of such a letter appears in Inset 14.2. Notice that only one topic is addressed in this letter, encouraging girls to take higher-level mathematics and science courses. Other topics for brief letters could include strengthening the girl's career orientation, building confidence, the value of higher education, the role of risk-taking in success, and perhaps even the eventual division of household chores. In each case, it is important to emphasize the rewards available to females who develop their abilities and to encourage parents to reward girls for accepting special challenges. This is a difficult message to give many parents; they have been socialized in a culture that has fostered underachievement in women, and therefore they themselves usually are guilty of reinforcing gender-role stereotypes.

## Changing the Expectations of Important Others

Teachers, parents, and girls themselves must acquire the expectation that females can achieve. Providing teachers, parents, and gifted students with evidence of female achievement in traditionally male-dominated fields is a most effective method of changing expectations. Internship programs (in which girls work with women executives and other women professionals), career women guest speakers, and field trips to see the accomplishments of talented women all provide living evidence of female accomplishment. Local professional women's organizations, such as American Association of University Women or the local chapter of the National Organization for Women, may be pleased to cooperate with such projects.

Opportunities to hear, see, and work with high-achieving women can be supplemented by reading and research projects that provide students with the opportunity to learn about achieving women and to understand the training and personality characteristics needed for high career achievement. The study of women's achievements in the arts, sciences, and in literature will help gifted girls, their teachers, and their families to recognize the reality of female talent and accomplishment.

Reis and Dobyns (1991) prepared an annotated bibliography of nonfictional books and curricular materials for gifted females that are intended to help girls change their self-expectations. See Appendix 14.1 at the end of this chapter.

Father expectations are important for the success of their daughters (Rimm et al., 1999; Rimm & Rimm-Kaufman, 2001). Fathers who act as coaches and believe in their daughters' abilities to achieve and accomplish are instrumental in encouraging their daughters to succeed in nontraditional careers for women. On the other hand, fathers who act the role of handsome knight and emphasize appearance, popularity, and encourage

INSET 14.2

### Challenge Senior High School

Dear Mr. and Mrs. Kirkpatrick:

We would like to recommend that your daughter Sara select Calculus, Advanced Biology, and Advanced Chemistry among her courses in grade 12. Her past performances in mathematics and science suggest that she would benefit from these challenging courses. These courses are complex and do involve more homework than some other selections that she might make. As a result, some high school students, particularly females, are hesitant in selecting them for fear that they may not perform as well as they typically have performed. Mainly, these students worry about a negative effect on their grade-point average or about peer pressure that may make high-level science or math courses appear to be more male-related.

We hope that Sara will be encouraged to select these courses because advanced courses in science and math can provide many more career options for her. Challenge Senior High School has taken the following steps to encourage capable girls to select these difficult courses:

1. Course grades are weighted so that a "B" grade in these courses is the equivalent of 4 points or an "A" in easier courses.
2. Courses are taught by both male and female teachers who were selected based on their willingness to provide extra support and help in these challenging courses.
3. Guest lecturers from professional science and mathematics areas will provide information to students on career areas in science and mathematics.
4. Women guest lecturers will share with girls their experiences on how to combine careers and homemaking roles.
5. Students who select these courses will be eligible for Advanced Placement testing and may therefore be able to earn college credits during their senior year in high school.

You or Sara may want to chat with me further about our special program to encourage bright female students to fulfill their intellectual potential. Please don't hesitate to call me to discuss Sara's special concerns. We will also be holding a special meeting for gifted girls and their parents in early March and I hope to meet you at that time.

Sincerely yours,

*Margaret Nellon*

Margaret Nellon
Guidance Counselor

a flirtatious relationship with their daughters may trap their daughters into assuming that happiness will always depend on men's approval. These girls may miss the opportunity to establish their own identities. Reis (1998b) emphasized how important it is for gifted girls to establish their personal identities if they are to realize their potential.

Surprisingly, dads who may be either emotionally or physically distant by reason of their work or divorce may not have any effect on their daughters' achievement (Rimm et al., 1999; Rimm & Rimm-Kaufman, 2001). Women in the Rimm study who were raised in environments where fathers did not dominate but had strong mothers learned great independence and often took strong leadership roles, particularly related to leading other women. Some of the women married later in life and some chose not to marry at all, perhaps because they were less comfortable in their relationships with men.

School contacts with fathers can help them to set high expectations for their daughters and to be effective coaches.

Peer expectations are perhaps the most difficult area in which to effect change. One way to encourage peer reinforcement is to provide coeducational group meetings for gifted students, both educational and semisocial. The kind of rapport and mutual support that usually develops in such meetings encourages all gifted students to challenge themselves. Discussion in which students air their concerns (for example, regarding risk taking or the career-homemaker conflict) helps give females the support they will need. Discussions of careers that are appropriate for all gifted students will emphasize the acceptability and desirability of female talent development. The rapport established among gifted peers also can create a more supportive and rewarding social life for gifted girls, which is an important variety of peer reinforcement.

Another important approach to building support for girls' achievement is to encourage an all-girls support group. Successful women in the Rimm research (Rimm et al., 1999; Rimm & Rimm-Kaufman, 2001) frequently acknowledged that a girls group (Girl Scouts, girls schools, and girlfriends) provided the source of their self-esteem, leadership, and goal direction. Unexpectedly, Rimm et al. found that more than half of the successful women in their study were Girl Scouts, and many described the goal direction and independence they learned from Girl Scouts. Furthermore, in a cross section of 473 women listed in *Who's Who in America,* 64 percent indicated they once belonged to Girl Scouts (Girl Scouts of the U.S.A., 1991). Rimm's book for middle schoolers, *See Jane Win*, was written to help girls raise their personal expectations for success (Rimm, 2003a).

## Model Identification

Although there are fewer female models with whom gifted girls may identify—for example, women doctors, lawyers, researchers, astronauts, or executives—there are many more than there were when this textbook was first published in 1985. Successful women are often eager to provide the aspiring gifted girl with the assurance that it is possible for a woman to achieve a career goal and at the same time enjoy a satisfying marriage if she so chooses.

Research by Arnold and Denny (1985) found that female high school valedictorians who continued to achieve interacted closely with college faculty and professionals. Kaufmann and colleagues (1986) also verified the importance of mentors for successful females in their study of Presidential Scholars. Having a mentor appeared to equalize the income of women and men.

Educators need to help girls locate appropriate role models. The models can share with gifted girls the experiences, rewards, frustrations, and decision-making processes that accompanied their accomplishments. In view of their own difficult experiences, they often enthusiastically share insights with gifted young women. Silverman (1991) recommends that teachers or counselors arrange opportunities for girls to shadow women professionals to observe them at work. McCormick (1997; see also Duff, 2000) suggested email mentors as a source of inspiration and information.

A surprising finding emphasized the importance of the appropriateness of mentors. Both female and male college students whose mentors were women left their scientific fields in greater proportion than those whose mentors were men (Sonnert & Holton, 1996). One participant in the study remarked that she was "deterred, rather than attracted" by her female advisor in college about whom she said, "The more you got to know her, the more you realized she'd given up all personal life to be a scientist. She had a very lonely and isolated life" (p. 67). Fortunately, the same study also reports that positive experiences with female role models were more common.

### Correcting Skill Deficiencies

The skill deficiencies of gifted girls usually are found in math and science, although the gap between male and female math achievement is diminishing (e.g., Gutbezahl, 1995). Such deficiencies can be prevented by encouraging high school girls to take the necessary advanced courses, which will permit their eventual entry into desirable college majors and prestigious careers. Girls continue to be underrepresented in advanced high school math classes (Kerr, 1997).

One good approach to attracting girls to advanced math classes is to encourage women teachers to teach them. Also, reasonable grading criteria, good teaching, and smaller classes that allow individual attention can make these classes more attractive to all students and less threatening to gifted girls. Many students, male and female, avoid math classes in fear of lowering their grade-point averages, which reduces their chances for high school awards and college admission and scholarships. If advanced math course grades are weighted such that an *A* earns 5 points instead of the usual 4, and so on, gifted males and females both will be less intimidated by the courses. Some secondary schools have implemented such a grading plan.

Cooperative learning groups have been recommended for teaching math to girls (American Association of University Women, 1992). However, in a high school study gifted girls preferred traditional grouping to cooperative groups (Drzewiecki & Westberg, 1997).

Females can be encouraged to receive tutoring in high school mathematics if they find it difficult. Tutoring can facilitate the acquisition of math concepts, increase scores on the SAT-M, and may be important in increasing the academic confidence of females (Olszewski-Kubilius et al., 1990).

We should note that not all areas in which some females are deficient are academic. Teachers and counselors must ensure that gifted girls are helped in developing autonomy, self-esteem, self-confidence, a willingness to compete, leadership, and assertiveness.

### Changing Reinforcements at Home and School

This last step is probably the most critical one. Gifted girls frequently are reinforced for being good, perfect, pretty, and well-adjusted. None of these reinforcements helps prepare them for careers ahead. Here are some recommendations for change.

*Perfectionism.* Take the word *perfect* out of your vocabulary at home and at school. Each time parents and teachers tell girls that they have completed a task "perfectly" or that they are "perfect," they reinforce pressure toward perfectionism. Fathers must be especially careful not to describe their little girls in those extreme terms. Fathers usually believe it to be a compliment that builds confidence, but girls internalize it as an expectation and impossible pressure.

*Social Life.* Although making friends can be positive, aloneness and independence are equally valuable. Do not make a child feel uncomfortable in independent activities. Encourage alone time. In her study of the childhoods of eminent women, Kerr (1985, 1997) found that they spent an unusual amount of time alone. She cited Gertrude Stein and Eleanor Roosevelt as examples. Most eminent women had a sense of being "different." The importance of spending time alone as well as the sense of being different were also characteristic of the successful women in the Rimm study (Rimm et al., 1999; Rimm & Rimm-Kaufman, 2001). Overemphasizing the importance of being "well adjusted" has the impact of internalizing a pressure to be popular and to make excessive compromises to please others.

*Challenge.* The girl who gets all As and pleases everyone is not anxious to take the risk of acceleration or other extra challenge. Explain that you would rather she take the risk of doing harder work even if she is not as successful. Expect her to do more than is required and encourage her to take accelerated courses even if they are difficult. It is better to experience difficulty early and to learn to persevere and struggle than to have eight or ten years of perfect work that is easily accomplished. Pressure for perfection prevents risk taking.

*Appearance.* Refuse to emphasize appearance. Whether she is pretty or not, from early on do not make a fuss about attractiveness. Reasonable neatness and cleanliness are acceptable values. Early emphasis on beauty and Barbie dolls becomes an internalized pressure to be thin, to wear excessive makeup, and to concentrate on fashion instead of intellectual accomplishment, kindness, creativity, and other important values. This is contrary to the advice given by Marone (1988) in her popular book, *How to Father a Successful Daughter.* She recommends that fathers praise their daughter's appearance. Since praise conveys the praiser's value system, paying too much attention to appearance, and not enough to intellect and creativity, will surely bias the daughter's perception of what's important. If fathers hope that their daughters will become models, fashion queens, or fashion designers, emphasis on appearance probably is appropriate. The Rimm study (Rimm et al., 1999; Rimm & Rimm-Kaufman, 2001) found that very few successful women considered themselves fashion leaders when younger.

*Competition.* Teach little girls about realistic competition. Do not protect them from failure

experiences. Do not just "let them win" at games. Teach them either to laugh at their losses or to analyze them for future learning. Even friendly insults help them to build some resilience to criticism. Do not let them use tears to attract unnecessary protection or shelter.

Sports provide excellent opportunities for teaching girls how to function in competition (Rimm, 1995a, 1995b; Wildenhaus, 1995; Rimm, Rimm-Kaufman, & Rimm, 1999; Rimm & Rimm-Kaufman, 2001). More female coaches might encourage girls to participate.

*Careers.* As a mother, if you are a career woman do not apologize for your work. Let your daughter know that you and she are better off because you have a career, not only for the money but for the way you feel about yourself and for the independence you can permit her. Space shuttle commander Eileen Collins truly began to admire her mother when her mother began her secretarial job with the local prison parole board (Rimm & Rimm-Kaufman, 2001). Eileen's mother seemed happier and more confident, which helped Eileen to understand the importance of a woman's having a career. If you are an educator, let girls know you are proud of your career so they will not assume that you work only because you must have a salary. Pride in your career will inspire your daughter toward pride in establishing her own career. Meckstroth (1989) recommended that parents encourage their daughters to develop a close relationship with a woman who likes her and is in love with her own life and work.

*Male Attitudes.* Perhaps the most difficult reinforcer to change is male attitudes toward females. Convincing gifted boys to appreciate intelligent and assertive females will help prevent the pressures that girls feel about appearing too intelligent. Explaining to males that the best kind of relationships come from mutual respect rather than a perceived need to feel more intelligent than females is a critical key to supporting intelligent thinking and acting in girls. Gifted girls tend to like gifted boys, but the latter often feel threatened in the company of very bright girls. Also, the deemphasis on appearance or the "pretty girl" message to sons and male students will make for better self-actualization of both females and males.

***All-Girl Classes or Schools.*** Some evidence suggests that all-girl classes and all-girl schools help some females to take leadership positions and courses they otherwise would avoid (e.g., Riordan, 1990). All-female classes for math and science can make a difference (Lee, 1995; Math Theory Gains Ground, 1994). Pollina (1995) found that girls in all-female math and science classes perform better and have more self-confidence than other girls. Although the research findings on girls' schools are not absolutely clear, girls' schools are thriving (Lewin, 1999). Applications at Manhattan's independent girls' schools increased 69 percent between 1991 and 1999.

Taking a lead from successful achievement in math and science established by all-girl schools, public schools have attempted to permit girls to take math in girls-only classes. Results indicate that girls are more willing to participate in class and are learning more in the female environment. However, there's a hitch! All-girl classes may be counter to the 1954 court ruling against segregation by sex. Some school districts seem to be managing to stay within the law by inviting anyone to join these classes specifically geared to girls' interests. So far, teenage boys have opted not to enroll. However, some boy sooner or later will see all-girl classes as a special challenge and that may end public school attempts to provide single-sex education.

Jefferson Leadership Academies in Long Beach, California, became the first public schools to segregate their entire 1100 students by gender (Haynes, 1999). The students seem to like it. Research will follow, but other schools are already following suit.

Tidball (1986) reported that women's colleges produce the largest proportion of women who go on for Ph.D. degrees. Sebrechts (1992) pointed

out that more women in women's colleges select math and science majors, compared with those in other colleges (Table 14.5). She maintains that women who are intellectually talented in science and math continue to select women's colleges, possibly to avoid sociocultural pressures about women's inability to succeed in these disciplines. Subotnik and Strauss (1990) found that girls in an all-female school performed better in Advanced Placement calculus classes than girls in all-female classes in a mixed-gender school.

Compared to women students from coed universities, twice as many students from women's colleges become engineers, scientists, and mathematicians. Furthermore, graduates from women's colleges continue their education in graduate and professional school more often than other college women (Dunn, 1995). Former Wellesley President Nannerl Keohane stated: "It's the difference between breathing fresh air and smog. The sexism—smog—isn't there at a women's school." In 1990 women graduating from women's colleges earned $5000 more than men and twice as much as women with traditional college degrees. Obtaining a master's degree increases a woman's income by 50 percent. It increases a male's by only 16 percent (Mann, 1994).

In the American Association of University Women's latest report, *Growing Smart: What's Working For Girls* (Hansen, Walker, & Flom, 1995), the authors came to conclusions that seem to fit well with the steps of the TRIFOCAL Model described in Chapter 13:

- Girls need to be included in the academic and social life of schools.
- Girls need women mentors.
- Encourage hands-on participation, especially in math and science.
- Consider single-sex classes, especially in math and science.
- Involve families in girls' education.
- Provide decision-making opportunities for girls.
- Create community youth programs for girls.

**TABLE 14.5** Percentages of Students Enrolled in Selected Majors, by Year at Women's and Coeducational Colleges.

| | Women in Women's Colleges | Women in Other Colleges | Men |
|---|---|---|---|
| **1971** | | | |
| Economics | 1.2 | .5 | 2.9 |
| Life Sciences | 3.8 | 2.8 | 5.3 |
| Physical Sciences | 1.4 | .8 | 3.9 |
| Mathematics | 3.6 | 2.5 | 3.2 |
| **1976** | | | |
| Economics | 2.1 | .6 | 2.3 |
| Life Sciences | 6.4 | 4.4 | 7.0 |
| Physical Sciences | 1.8 | .9 | 3.4 |
| Mathematics | 2.1 | 1.5 | 1.9 |
| **1981** | | | |
| Economics | 3.2 | 1.2 | 2.4 |
| Life Sciences | 6.1 | 4.0 | 5.1 |
| Physical Sciences | 1.9 | 1.2 | 3.8 |
| Mathematics | 1.6 | 1.0 | 1.3 |
| **1986** | | | |
| Economics | 4.0 | 1.4 | 2.9 |
| Life Sciences | 5.4 | 3.6 | 4.1 |
| Physical Sciences | 1.7 | 1.2 | 3.2 |
| Mathematics | 2.3 | 1.5 | 1.8 |

Source: National Center for Education Statistics, U.S. Department of Education. From Sebrechts (1992).

## SUMMARY

The education of gifted women historically has been largely ignored. Some early influential educators publicly specified a nurturing domestic role for women. The mobilization of women scientists during World War II and the flourishing women scientists at the University of Bologna during the eighteenth century provide early proof of how important opportunity is for gifted women. The concept of a "disappearance of giftedness in girls" implies that they excel in childhood but frequently underachieve as adults. Until recently, women have been drawn to female-dominated careers—teaching, social work, and homemaking.

In the work force, women continue to be dramatically underrepresented in most traditionally male professions. Salaries also are comparatively poor, although women seem to have found success in some areas of business and science.

Women are underrepresented in educational administration in elementary and secondary schools, in college teaching, and in college administration. While women's entry into "male careers" is improving, the percentage of women at higher salaries and upper ranks in these fields still is low, especially in medicine. This is has been called the "sticky floor" effect. Even the National Academy of Sciences is concerned about the pipeline that seems to be "leaking" women scientists as they continue into the workforce.

Women's life satisfactions stereotypically had been tied to their husbands' career success plus success as a wife and mother. On average, working and professional women show higher life satisfaction—greater self-esteem and greater feelings of competence—than full-time housewives.

A study of over 1000 successful women reported that they found their careers satisfying because they provided challenge, creativity, opportunities to make a contribution, and fulfillment.

The main problem is the home-career conflict. While there is no easy solution, some women decide in advance which role comes first (the family), compartmentalize the two roles, and often compromise to fit husband and family needs. In the area of science some documentation indicates that marriage may have an enhancing effect on scientific productivity, particularly if the woman is married to another scientist. Generally, women continue to try to balance the dual responsibilities, and lower success may be due to female professionals putting their careers on hold to have children. Men now do approximately one-third of home and family chores.

Not all successful women choose linear careers. Some choose delayed or traditional sequences, and some successful women are late bloomers.

Career differences between successful males and females can be analyzed with two models: The *deficit model,* based on exclusion, and the *differences model,* based on deeply ingrained differences in behavior, outlook, and goals.

Research suggests biological gender differences in levels of physical activity and aggression. Some scholars claim stronger right-hemisphere spatial abilities for males. Tomboyism produces girls with many masculine interests and traits.

Sociocultural differences in the treatment of the sexes begin almost at birth. Differences exist in room decorations and toys and stereotyped characteristics, for example, as reflected in Bem's *Sex-Role Inventory.* Textbooks, literature, and the media, especially television, reinforce gender-role stereotypes.

The most heated debate centers on math ability. Studies find that math achievement differences between males and females become evident in adolescence and are most evident in gifted students. New studies show differences in math strategies used by girls and boys as early as first grade.

Counterarguments propose that the math differences may be due to (1) cultural stereotypes, (2) unequal math training, (3) boys' identification with father, (4) different types of toys, (5) teacher and parent expectations, and (6) lack of school support. The issue is important because a lack of mathematical training will close—and is closing—permanently the doors to high-status and well-paying male-dominated careers.

High educational and career achievements are related to family expectations. Identification with mother, especially a career mother, appears important. Fathers' expectations of their daughters also influence achievement. Gender-role stereotyped family expectations work against girls' achievement. Research shows that creative women mathematicians tend to identify with their fathers. Traits of independence and self-esteem also may be learned from fathers. Career modeling by mothers is an important motivation for girls. High expectations by both parents appear to have the greatest positive effect on successful women.

Peer attitudes and expectations often depress female achievement. School expectations reward male independence, confidence, and aggressiveness, but reward female conformity. These stereotypical expectations begin as early as nursery school. Female poor performance sometimes is attributed to lack of ability; male poor performance to lack of effort, leading boys to work harder.

Schools that successfully produce high-achieving girls make Advanced Placement classes a natural part of the sequence and actively recruit girls for Advanced Placement classes. School counselors sometimes perpetuate cultural stereotypes and often counsel girls to avoid math and science. Regarding self-expectations, women tend to have a lower sense of competence and self-esteem, attribute failure to lack of ability, and have lower achievement motivation. Attribution training can improve achievement.

Rimm's six-step model is a guide for dealing with female underachievement. Appropriate mentors are important for fostering the success of women, and e-mail extends the availability of mentors. Sports provide opportunities for girls to learn how to function in competition.

All-girl classes, Girl Scouts, girl friendship groups, and all-girl schools seem to foster leadership and the acceptance of academically challenging coursework.

**APPENDIX 14.1**

## Selected Bibliography of Nonfiction Books and Curricular Materials to Encourage Gifted Females

*Sally M. Reis and Sally McClure Dobyns*

| Publisher | Year | Title | Author | Brief Description |
|---|---|---|---|---|
| **ART** | | | | |
| VSE Publisher<br>212 South Dexter<br>Denver, CO 80222 | 1987 | History of Women Artists for Children | Epstein, Vivian Sheldon | History of women in art told through brief biographies of 29 women artists of distinction. Includes example of each artist's work. (grades PS–6) |
| **AWARENESS** | | | | |
| Advocacy Press<br>P.O. Box 236<br>Santa Barbara, CA 93120 | 1984 | Choices: A Teen Woman's Journal for Self-awareness and Personal Planning | Bingham, Mindy; Edmondson, Judy; and Stryker, Sandy | A journal for adolescent girls. Includes chapters about attitudes of society toward women, economics, values and decision-making, assertiveness, future planning for education, family and work, financial aid for education. Beautifully illustrated, open-ended exercises, readable format, cartoons, appropriate quotations. Highly recommended! |
| Avon Books<br>P.O. Box 767<br>Dresden, TX 38225 | 1978 | Pulling Your Own Strings | Dyer, W. W. | A "how-to" book which focuses on being a decision-maker and action-oriented person. Sample dialogues, strategies, checklists. Great for planning activities for bright females. |
| Bantam Press<br>666 5th Avenue<br>New York, NY 10103 | 1987 | Free to Be . . . You and Me | Thomas, Marlo; Steinem, Gloria; and Pogrebin, Letty Cottin | Collection of stories and songs designed to expand children's horizons. Includes: "The Story of X" about stereotypes, and "Atlanta," a fairy tale about a princess who is a winner and decides her own future. |
| National Black Child Development Institute Washington, DC | 1987 | Beyond the Stereotypes: A Guide to Resources for Black Girls and Young Girls | Moore, E. K.; Vassall, M. A.; and Wilson, J. | This reference book provides lists of books, sound recordings and videos, annotated and classified by age group. (3–7, 8–11, 12–15, 16 and up) |
| Stein and Day Publishers<br>Scarborough House<br>Briarcliff Manor, NY 10510 | 1983 | Beyond Bartlett | Cooper, Jilly, and Hartman, Tom | Quotations by and about women. |
| The Time Inc.<br>Magazine Co.<br>Rockefeller Center<br>New York, NY 10020 | 1990<br>(fall) | Women: The Road Ahead<br>*Time:* Special Issue | | This special issue of *Time* includes women in politics, inequality around the globe, profiles of 10 extraordinary women, women in the 21st century and the changing family. |
| **BIOGRAPHY** | | | | |
| Aristoplay<br>P.O. Box 7028<br>Ann Arbor, MI 48107 | | Great Women | | Three terrific biographical card games to introduce players to outstanding American women. Each game played like rummy. Ages 10 to adult. |
| Little, Brown & Co.<br>(Joy St. Books) | 1989 | Ragtime Tumpie | Schroeder, Alan | Tumpie, a young black girl who later becomes famous as dancer Josephine Baker, longs to find the opportunity to dance amid the poverty of St. Louis in the early 1900s. (grades K–4) |

| Publisher | Year | Title | Author | Brief Description |
|---|---|---|---|---|
| **BIOGRAPHY** (Continued) National Women's Hall of Fame 76 Fall Street, P.O. Box 335 Seneca Falls, NY 13168 | 1989 | Phases and Phrases | | Includes biographical information and charcoal illustration of all 42 women in the National Women's Hall of Fame, including Susan B. Anthony, Mary Cassatt, Margaret Mead, Eleanor Roosevelt, Elizabeth Cady Stanton, Harriet Tubman. |
| Penguin USA 120 Woodbine Street Bergenfield, NJ 07621 | 1973 | They Led the Way: Fourteen American Women. (Original title: Women Themselves) | Johnston, Johanna | Brief biographies of American women instrumental in American history. (grades 2–6) |
| **CAREERS** The Equity Institute: Maryland Box 30245 Bethesda, MD 20814 | | From Here to There: Exploring the Apprentice-to-Journey-Worker Career Ladder with Girls and Boys in Grades 1–9. A Multimedia Approach | | Of interest to young gifted girls, not because they will grow up to work in the trades, but because children are fascinated with details about nontraditional work. Stories, worksheets, filmstrips, plays, math, games, history, and problem solving. |
| VSE Publisher 212 South Dexter Denver, CO 80222 | 1980 | The ABC's of What A Girl Can Be | Epstein, Vivian Sheldon | From Architect to Zookeeper—illustrated non-traditional career possibilities for young girls to consider. (grades PS–3) |
| **CURRICULAR MATERIALS** Feminist Press 311 W. 94th Street New York, NY 10128 | 1981 | Books for Today's Young Readers | Bracken, Jeanne; and Wigutoff, Sharon | An annotated bibliography of recommended fiction for ages 10–14. |
| Feminist Press 311 W. 94th Street New York, NY 10128 | 1986 | Feminist Resources for Schools and Colleges: A Guide to Curricular Materials | Chapman, Anne (Ed.) | An essential resource for school and college teachers. Entries include books, articles, pamphlets, films, and cassettes. Subject areas covered include American and European history, literature, the social sciences, mathematics, and art. |
| Learning Publications, Inc. P.O. Box 1326 Holmes Beach, FL 33509 | 1980 | Boys and Girls Together: Non-sexist Activities for Elementary Schools | Cain, Mary Alexander | Activities for establishing sex equity in the classroom using materials already found in the classroom. |
| National Women's Hall of Fame 76 Fall Street P.O. Box 335 Seneca Falls, NY 13168 | 1986 | The Times and Triumphs of American Women | Scott, Elaine (Ed.) | An educational kit featuring women from past and present who have contributed to the development of our country. Arts, athletics, education, government, humanitarianism, and science. Exercises. (grades 4–9) |
| **HISTORY** Aristoplay P.O. Box 7529 Ann Arbor, MI 48107 | | Noted Women | | A graceful time-line poster highlighting distinguished women from the mid-18th century to the present. 24" x 24". |
| Feminist Press 311 W. 94th Street New York, NY 10128 | 1981 | Women Have Always Worked: An Historical Overview | Kessler-Harris, A. | Overview of women's work experiences in the United States. Focuses on tension between women's work inside and outside the home; weaves together material about immigrant and black women; wealthy, poor, and middle-class women. |

## APPENDIX 14.1 (Continued)

| Publisher | Year | Title | Author | Brief Description |
|---|---|---|---|---|
| **HISTORY** (Continued)<br>Houghton Mifflin<br>One Beacon Street<br>Boston, MA 02108 | 1979 | Women of America:<br>A History | Berkin, C., and<br>Norton, M. | Traces circumstances of women in America from 1600 and looks at the future of women. Protestant and Quaker views of women, Irish working women, Chinese immigrant women, the feminization of academe, the role of women in World War II. Suggestions for further reading. |
| National Women's History Project<br>7738 Bell Road<br>Windsor, CA 95492-8515 | | National Women's History Month | | Excellent resources for infusing women into the study of history. Books, films, posters. |
| VSE Publisher<br>212 South Dexter<br>Denver, CO 80222 | 1984 | History of Women for Children | Epstein, Vivian Sheldon | For children from preschool age through 4th grade, this book balances its message of women's plight through the ages by listing achievements of women of all races. |
| **INVENTION**<br>William Morrow & Co. Publishers<br>39 Plymouth Street<br>Fairfield, NJ 07007 | 1988 | Mothers of Invention: From the Bra to the Bomb, Forgotten Women and Their Unforgettable Ideas | Vare, Ethlie Ann, and Ptacek, Greg | Women were the co-inventors of everything from penicillin to the bomb. This excellent resource celebrates female inventors. |
| **LITERATURE**<br>Houghton-Mifflin<br>One Beacon Street<br>Boston, MA 02108 | 1976 | By Women: An Anthology of Literature | Kirschner, L., and Folsom, M. | Eighty-eight selections, classical to contemporary. Works of more than seventy writers, including Willa Cather, Emily Dickinson, Katherine Mansfield, Edna St. Vincent Millay, Anais Nin, Flannery O'Connor, Katherine Anne Porter, Jessamyn West, Virginia Woolf. Biographical sketch of each writer. |
| W. W. Norton<br>500 Fifth Avenue<br>New York, NY 10036 | 1985 | The Norton Anthology of Literature by Women: The Tradition in English | Gilbert, S. M., and Gubar, S. | Landmark collection by over 150 women authors, including Jane Austen, Ann Bradstreet, Phyllis Wheatley, Sojourner Truth, Grace Paley, Maya Angelou, Margaret Atwood, Alice Walker. |
| **MATH**<br>Eureka Catalog<br>Lawrence Hall of Science<br>University of California<br>Berkeley, CA 94702 | 1985 | Math for Girls and Other Problem Solvers | Downie, Diane; Slesnik, Twila; and Slenmark, Jean Kerr | Curricular ideas and game sheets, including problem solving and other activities geared to make mathematics more interesting and enjoyable for upper elementary and secondary grade students. |
| Gallopade Publishing Group<br>235 East Ponce de Leon<br>Suite 100<br>Decatur, GA 30030 | 1989 | Math for Girls: The Book with the Number to Get Girls to Love and Excel in Math! | Marsh, Carole | Stories, puzzles, games, and problems to make math enjoyable. Topics designed to appeal to girls include parties, music, tennis, pizza, and friends. (grades 3–9) |

| Publisher | Year | Title | Author | Brief Description |
|---|---|---|---|---|
| **OUT-OF-PRINT-BUT-WORTH-A-TRIP-TO-YOUR-LIBRARY** | | | | |
| Addison-Wesley Publishers South Street Reading, MA 01867 (800) 447-2226 | 1978 | Math Equals: Biographies of Women Mathematicians and Related Activities (out-of-print 1989) | Perl, Teri | Biographies of female mathematicians are presented as are their major contributions. |
| Atheneum | 1973 | Girls Are Equal Too: The Women's Movement for Teens | Carlson, Dale | Grades 6–7 |
| Feminist Press | 1982 | Everywoman's Guide Colleges and Universities | Howe, Florence, et. al (Eds.) | For young women interested in attending a college or university that has services, options, and female role models. It can be used as a check against colleges of interest to see how they rate in opportunities for young women. |
| Garrard | 1971 | Susan B. Anthony: Pioneer in Women's Rights | Peterson, Helen S. | Grades 3–6 |
| Lothrop | 1967 | Petticoat Politics: How American Women Won the Right to Vote | Faber, Doris | Grades 7 and up |
| McGraw | 1971 | Single Standard | Harris, Janet | Grades 7 and up |
| Prentice-Hall, Inc. | 1981 | Equal Their Chances: Children's Activities for Nonsexist Learning | Shapiro, Kramer, and Hunerberg | |
| Putnam | 1975 | Women in Sports Series | Haney, Lynn | Titles include Chris Evert, I Am A Dancer, Perfect Balance, Show Writer, Skater's Profile, Ride 'em Cowgirl. |
| Random House | 1972 | Young and Female: Turning Points in the Lives of Eight American Women | Ross, Pat | Grades 6 and up |
| T. Y. Crowell | 1959 | Women Who Led the Way: Eight Pioneers for Equal Rights | Boynick, David | Grades 7 and up |
| Warne | 1963 | Women Who Made History | Boter, Mary C. | Grades 7–9 |
| Watts | 1972 | Women's Rights | Stevenson, Janet | Grades 5–7 |
| | 1980 | Women of Crisis II—Lives of Work and Dreams | Coles, R., and Dell, J. H. | |
| | | What Can She Be? | Lothrop, Lee, and Shephard | Grades 2–5 A series of books each featuring women in a non-traditional career. Careers include Architect, 1974; Computer Scientist, 1979; Framer, 1976; Film Producer, 1977; Geologist, 1976; Lawyer, 1973; Legislator, 1978; Musician, 1975; Music Librarian, 1975; Newscaster, 1973; Police Officer; Veterinarian, 1972. |

# CHAPTER 15

# GIFTED CHILDREN WITH DISABILITIES

*Many individuals who possess exceptional intellectual qualities are overlooked due to masks that hide their abilities.*
Alexinia Baldwin and Wilma Vialle (1999, p. xi)

Typically and unfortunately, gifted children with disabilities are recognized only for their disability, not for their gifts and talents. Their special needs stemming from the disability are provided for by mandated programs in special classes and special schools funded by state and federal government. Since most disabling conditions do not preclude or prevent giftedness, it is logical to expect the same percentage of gifted and talented students among students with disabilities as in the general population. However, labeling the child as having a disability plus attending to the priority needs of the disabling condition usually obscures the creative, artistic, intellectual, or scientific talents of the child. They are thus much less likely than nondisabled gifted children to be identified as gifted and included in school programs that help develop their special talents.

This chapter will explore the needs and problems of children with disabilities, their identification, and some programming ideas directed toward accommodating those needs.

## NEEDS OF GIFTED STUDENTS WITH DISABILITIES

The Office of Special Education Programs (OSEP; 1994, 1995) reports that 5.3 million children were served by special education programs during the 1993–1994 school year. The number of children served annually has increased by 1.6 million since 1976–77, the first year such data was reported by OSEP. The area of largest increase was in children classified as having spe-

cific learning disabilities (SLDs; see Figure 15.1). The number of children in most other categories actually declined. Students classified with SLDs make up more than 5 percent of all students aged 6–17 enrolled in school.

The gifted disabled are individuals with exceptional ability or potential and who are capable of high performance despite such disabilities as hearing, speech, vision, orthopedic, or emotional impairments, learning disabilities, or other health problems, either singly or in combination (U.S. Congress, 1975; Yewchuk & Lupart, 1993). Other federal definitions include retardation, which may be the only disability that precludes most forms of giftedness. Nonetheless, programs for gifted students with disabilities are rare, even though state and federal funding agencies typically specify that such students must be included in any funded G/T program. At the time Eisenberg and Epstein (1981) initiated their program, they discovered that there were *no* special programs designated for gifted students with disabilities in all of New York City.

Until the 1970s it was assumed that *giftedness* and *disability* were mutually exclusive categories (Grimm, 1998). A 1989 study in Texas found 91 percent of the school districts had not identified learning disability students for gifted programming. In 1995 Grimm conducted a similar study in Minnesota and found 81 percent of the programs to be serving disabilities within their gifted programs. There has been progress.

Legislation clearly states that children with disabilities must be served. However, Schnur and

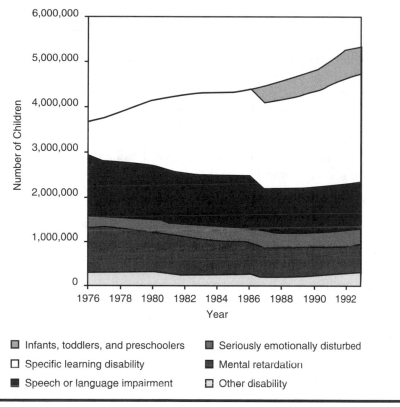

Infants, toddlers, and preschoolers    Seriously emotionally disturbed

Specific learning disability    Mental retardation

Speech or language impairment    Other disability

**FIGURE 15.1**   Number of Children up to Age 21 in Special Education Programs by Disability Category, 1976 to 1993.

Data on this graph come from the Office of Special Education Programs and show both the increase in the number of children receiving special education services and the change in their classification over time. The decrease between 1986 and 1987 in all of the categories except preschool occurs because, prior to 1987, preschool and younger children receiving special education services were counted in the individual categories, but in 1987 they were assigned a separate category.

- Since 1976–77, the number of children served annually has increased by 1.6 million, almost 45%.
- The increase in the number of children served is almost completely attributable to the growth in the number of children classified as having specific learning disabilities.

Sources: **1976 to 1989:** National Center for Education Statistics. *120 years of American education: A statistical portrait.* T. D. Snyder, ed. Washington, DC: NCES, January 1993, p. 44, Table 12; **1990 and 1991:** National Center for Education Statistics. *The condition of education.* Washington, DC: NCES, 1994, p. 301, Table 45-1 (includes children ages 0 to 5); **1992:** Office of Special Education Programs. *Implementation of the Individuals with Disabilities Education Act: Sixteenth annual report to Congress.* Washington, DC: U.S. Department of Education, 1994, p. 9, Table 1.4; p. 41, Table 2.5; and p. 52, Figure 2.1; **1993:** Office of Special Education Programs. *Implementation of the Individuals with Disabilities Education Act: Seventeenth annual report to Congress.* Washington, DC: U.S. Department of Education, November 1995, Table AA14, Table AA1 (0 to 5).

Stefanich (1979) pointed out that the disabled gifted child may be omitted from special services (the special education class, a reading teacher, psychological services, Individualized Education Programs) if he or she is functioning reasonably well within the regular classroom. This means that an intellectually gifted child who performs at grade level, but whose achievement nonetheless is depressed by his or her disability, would not necessarily be provided with any special services because his or her performance is equivalent to that of average classmates. To the extent that the special services would individualize evaluation and instruction, help the gifted child remediate academic weaknesses, help the child compensate for the disabling condition, and/or develop individual talents, such special attention is lost.

Bireley (1991) noted that children with low-incidence disabilities such as hearing or visual impairment usually are taught by trained specialists. Their inexperience with gifted children may cause them to focus more on the impairment, thus making it less likely that they will identify the giftedness. Furthermore, Peterson (1993) found that gifted people who are deaf don't seem to be comfortable with the "gifted" label.

Several studies have shown that mainstreamed children with disabilities, particularly emotional disturbances, frequently are not accepted by peers in the regular classroom (e.g., Heward & Orlansky, 1992; Yewchuk & Lupart, 1993). Generally, the greater the severity of the problem, the greater the degree of social rejection.

An example of a low-incidence disability is autism (Cash, 1999). The unique overlap between giftedness and autism shows itself in unusual talents among some autistic persons. For example, Temple Grandin, who is autistic, was diagnosed as deaf and brain-damaged at age two but tested with an IQ of 137 at age eight. As an adult who earned her Ph.D. at age 42, she continues to struggle with social behaviors. She has made unique contributions, including dozens of papers and books on both autism and animal science, and has designed equipment including the human squeeze machine to relieve tension. In an interview

Grandin commented, based on autistic characteristics that Einstein showed, "You wonder why there are no Einsteins today? It's probably because they flunked their GREs" (Baldwin & Vialle, 1999, p. 222).

Researchers are discovering more and more autistic persons (Rimland, 1995; Donnelly & Altman, 1994) who are indeed gifted and talented, and also have noted eminent individuals who have autistic traits (Grandin, 1995; Donnelly & Altman, 1994). In addition to Albert Einstein, included in the celebrated list of eminence with autistic characteristics are Bill Gates, Bobby Fischer, Howard Hughes, Sir Isaac Newton, and Vincent Van Gogh. Their extreme ability to concentrate, their poor social skills, and their extraordinary visual talents are characteristic of autism. Nevertheless, they are known for their gifted contributions, not their autism.

Baum and Owen (1988) found gifted students with learning disabilities (LD) to be the most disruptive in class. These students felt less effective in school compared with other gifted students and even with average LD students. A study by Vespi and Yewchuk (1992) found that gifted LD children had good self-esteem despite their learning difficulties. The children were eager to talk about their *strengths,* and their parents and teachers confirmed their healthy self-concepts. However, the children assumed that learning tasks would be easy for them and were not prepared for the difficulty of learning activities in an area of disability (e.g., language). Their frustration, tension, and fear of failure led to defensiveness.

Swesson (1994) pointed out that the identification of a disability immediately leads teachers to the lowering of expectations for the student almost regardless of the student's giftedness. The students tend to react to these lowered expectations with genuine feelings of inadequacy. Making things worse, Birely (1991) reminds us that the higher goals of gifted students may be especially frustrating to achieve when the student has a disability.

Neihart (1999b) reviewed the research literature on emotional disturbance in regard to anxiety problems, depression, self-concept, and social adjustment and found no increased emotional problems associated with giftedness. Gallucci, Middleton, and Kline (1999a, 1999b) and Garland and Zigler (1999) compared the behaviors of gifted and nongifted children and did not find any more behavioral problems among gifted children. In the Gallucci et al. research, creativity scores from the Torrance tests were compared to scores on the Child Behavior Checklist (CBCL), and there was no statistical relationship between the two. Furthermore, suicidal behaviors of gifted children do not seem to be more frequent than those for average children (Gust-Brey & Cross, 1999). These research conclusions bring parents of emotionally disturbed gifted children little comfort or support for their children's needs.

There is an important shortcoming in these research conclusions. Many gifted children with emotional disturbances are simply not identified as *gifted,* and do not participate in gifted programming. They are thus eliminated from the kinds of comparisons that have been made by these researchers.

Neihart (1999b; see also Richards, 1999; Simonton, 2003) summarized a large number of studies that found mood disorders with artistic adults, specifically, and a significantly greater rate of depressive illnesses among creative artists and writers. There is no evidence that these adults were identified for either gifted programs or special education programs during their childhoods.

The 1986 Amendments to the Education for all Handicapped Children Act, P.L. 99–457 (Renamed in 1990 *Individuals with Disabilities Education Act*), not only extended special educational services to 3- to 5-year-olds but assisted states in implementing intervention services for handicapped infants and toddlers (Krauss, 1990). For the first time, the service recipient was defined as the *family* in addition to the child, and an *Individualized Family Service Plan* (IFSP) was required. Furthermore, Yell and Espin (1990) believe that the U.S. Congress passed The Handicapped Children's Protection Act of 1986 (HCPA), P.L. 99–372, in response to court rulings that seemed to undercut

parents' opportunities to dispute school decisions. This law allows parents to take legal action when they feel their children are not receiving an appropriate education.

Clearly, we are dramatically underserving a segment of the population that has high potential for personal development and achievement and for making high-quality contributions to society. Among outstanding creative individuals who have disabilities, Karnes, Shwedel, and Lewis (1983) listed Ludwig van Beethoven, Thomas Edison, Helen Keller, and Franklin D. Roosevelt. We might add the names of musicians George Shearing, José Feliciano, Stevie Wonder, and Ray Charles, all of whom are blind; violinist Itzhak Perlman, crippled by polio; and Hollywood personality Jack Paar, former Tonight Show host, who stutters. Unlike most gifted persons with disabilities these people are noted for their gifts and talents, not their disabilities.

In sum, gifted children with disabilities continue to be ignored, programs for them are lacking, and their problems are compounded by sometimes severe social problems and rock-bottom feelings of self-worth and personal integrity. As Baldwin and Vialle (1999) point out, it is indeed time to lift the mask.

## IDENTIFICATION

Identifying gifted children with disabilities usually is difficult. A major problem is that their gifts usually remain invisible to teachers and sometimes even parents. Eisenberg and Epstein (1981) described their G/T program for students with disabilities in which forms for nominating gifted and talented students with disabilities were sent to designated New York City schools serving a full 60,000 disabled students. *Not one student was nominated.*

Another problem is that the disability itself may obscure the *expression* of the special gifts and talents. For example, blindness, deafness, and some learning disabilities have the effect of slowing development and may result in deceptively lower IQ scores. Children who are blind and deaf, because of their sensory deficits, tend to be more concrete in their thinking, which will hardly help the abstract reasoning necessary for a high IQ score. Children with dyslexia will certainly suffer on verbal components of an intelligence test, although Marx (1982) suggested that these children may have much higher than normal spatial-oriented giftedness. Other disabilities (for example, emotional disturbance or social maladjustments, orthopedic or health impairments, speech or language impairments) also can interfere with obtaining an accurate high score on an intelligence test.

In some cases then, the intelligence test—the most commonly used instrument for identifying gifted children—may add a handicap to the discovery of giftedness among already disabled children.

The combination of giftedness and disability thus can deliver a double disadvantage. The disabilities of such students may hide their giftedness, causing them not to be identified for gifted programs. Further, their high intellectual abilities may mask their disabilities, causing them to be overlooked for learning disability programs (Olenchak & Reis, 2001).

A dramatic example of overlooking gifted students who are learning disabled comes to us from two surveys in Texas (Boodoo et al., 1989). Of the 180 responses by special education centers, 91 percent reported *no* gifted LD children. There were 143 responses from gifted and talented programs, and 77 percent of these reported no gifted LD children in their programs. A later survey of 388 gifted coordinators in Texas found that only 75 school districts reported the selection of gifted children with learning disabilities for gifted programming (Tallent-Runnels & Sigler, 1995). The modifications made by those districts to identify learning disabled gifted children are included in Table 15.1.

Minner (1990) discovered that when teachers studied near-identical vignettes of children, they were less likely to identify for gifted programming those students who also were described as having a learning disability.

An example of a case in which a disability resulted in dependency and underachievement with the effect of obscuring giftedness is Kevin:

*Kevin, a nine-year-old fourth grader, was totally blind. He was a very good looking child and was small for his age. His disability and his young appearance invited adults to "take care of him" and do much more for him than was appropriate.*

**TABLE 15.1** Modification in the Gifted Program Selection Process

| Modification | Number of Districts |
| --- | --- |
| Alternate forms of tests or alternate tests | 13 |
| Open screening | 8 |
| Waiving of some criteria | 6 |
| Several criteria | 6 |
| Product portfolios | 5 |
| Nonverbal tests | 4 |
| Teacher recommendation | 4 |
| Interviews | 2 |
| Case studies | 2 |
| Probationary status in the program | 2 |
| Modified administration of tests | 2 |
| Search for strengths | 1 |
| No grades | 1 |

Source: The Status of the Selection of Gifted Students with Learning Disabilities for Gifted Programs by M. K. Tallent-Runnels and E. A. Sigler, *Roeper Review, 17*(4), May/June, 1995.

*Kevin's initial evaluation indicated his WISC-R verbal IQ score to be 109. It had been recommended that he repeat fourth grade. One year after the initial evaluation and after the dependency patterns were changed and the skills gaps were closed by tutoring, Kevin's IQ score as tested by the same unbiased tester, who had no knowledge of the treatment program, was 141. Kevin appeared to everyone to be a very bright child, but his dependent underachieving behavior related to his blindness had a major impact on lowering his ability scores and the initial nonidentification of his giftedness.*

The Wechsler Intelligence Scales are the most frequently used intelligence tests and are often used in modified form with children with disabilities. Brown (1984) suggested that other tests, which are specifically designed and normed for children with disabilities, may be more appropriate. Examples of such instruments are the Nebraska Test of Learning Aptitude (Hiskey, 1966), used with children who are deaf and hearing impaired; the Arthur Adaptation of the Leiter International Performance Scale (Arthur, 1950) for children who are deaf, hearing impaired, and who have speech or language difficulties; the Blind Learning Aptitude Test (Newland, 1969); and The Pictorial Test of Intelligence (French, 1964), for children with motor disabilities. Other tests for children with handicapping conditions are described by Bauman and Kropf (1979), Salter and Tozier (1971), and Sullivan and Vernon (1979). Notice that the tests for students who are handicapped date back to the 1960s and 1970s. Revisions seem rare.

Karnes (1979) reported that identifying gifted children with disabilities through observation was more difficult than with "normal" children and requires a prolonged observation. Providing inservice workshops for teachers of the disabled, which focus on characteristics of giftedness and the identification of gifted and talented children, should help the teacher identification and nomination process. Eisenberg and Epstein (1981) noted that in their search for gifted children with disabilities, teachers would select conforming students, not the highly active, energetic ones. Concluded Eisenberg and Epstein, teachers definitely needed direction.

In observing possibly gifted children with disabilities, one would, of course, watch for the types of characteristics and behaviors described in Chapter 2, along with an additional interesting one. As Eisenberg and Epstein described their gifted children with disabilities, they "understand faster, ask questions, zip through math—and they are terribly disruptive." With "normal" gifted students, disruptiveness is a trait that sometimes appears because the child is bored or frustrated in school. Because frustration and stress can be everyday matters for gifted students with disabilities it is not surprising that *disruptiveness* can be a good indicator of giftedness with these children.

The identification procedure used successfully by Eisenberg and Epstein (1981) included IQ and achievement scores, which conveniently were already on file. They also used the Renzulli et al. (2001) rating scales, not only the frequently used Learning, Motivation, Creativity, and Leadership scales (see Chapter 4), but also the less well-known Art, Music, Drama, and Communications scales. As noted above, when first approached via a mailing of nomination forms, not one teacher of students with disabilities spontaneously nominated a single child for participation in the Eisenberg and Epstein program. However, after looking over the Renzulli rating scales, many began *calling* (not writing) the program coordinator with the same urgent message: "Hey, I think I've got a kid for you!" The rating scales themselves served as quick in-service training for identifying gifted children with disabilities.

Especially good indicators of giftedness from the Renzulli Learning scale were:

Possesses a large storehouse of information about a variety of topics.

Has rapid insight into cause-effect relationships; tries to discover the how and why of things; asks provocative questions; wants to know what makes things (or people) "tick."

Is a keen and alert observer; usually "sees more" or "gets more" out of a story, film, etc., than others.

Especially good items from the Motivation scale were:

Becomes absorbed and truly involved in certain topics or problems; is persistent in seeking task completion.

Prefers to work independently; requires little direction from teachers.

Eisenberg and Epstein also found peer nominations and self-nominations to be valuable; more valuable, in fact, than teacher nominations. The peers knew who were bright, creative, and fast-learning. Many students with disabilities *nominated themselves* as gifted or talented, and "nine out of ten were right!"

Johnson, Karnes, and Carr (1997) described a Parent Checklist and a Teacher Checklist designed especially for identifying gifted youngsters with disabilities. Both instruments focus on the six areas of the 1972 federal definition: intellectual ability, specific academic talent (with scales for reading, math, and science), creativity, leadership, visual and performing arts (with scales for art and music), and psychomotor abilities. Scores on the two checklists are combined and tabulated on a Talent Identification Summary. Decisions regarding talent are made by teams comprised of parents, teachers, and ancillary staff. Following Renzulli, the authors assume that 10 to 20 percent of a class is potentially gifted. In their words, "A 'wide net' approach is used to make sure that potentially gifted disabled children are not overlooked" (p. 522).

To help in the identification of gifted children with disabilities, Maker (1977) recommended that (1) disabled students should be compared with others who have the same disability, and (2) characteristics that enable the child to effectively compensate for his or her disability should be weighted more heavily. For example, if an orthopedically impaired student cannot write, his compensating verbal and cognitive abilities should receive more weight; if a student cannot speak, his written, artistic, and creative talents should be examined. In addition to these two points, Silverman (1989; see also Silverman, 2003) added these recommendations: (1) Allow these children into the gifted program at least on a probationary or "guest" basis to see if they are capable of achieving higher level work. (2) Place extra weight on the child's performance in areas unaffected by the disability. (3) Cutoff scores should be dropped 10 points to take into account a depression of scores due to the disability.

As for creativity, the Renzulli Creativity Scale mentioned above apparently is useful. The *PRIDE* (Rimm, 1982), *GIFT* (Rimm, 1976) and *GIFFI* (Davis and Rimm, 1980, 1982) creativity inventories have been specifically validated for use with children with learning disabilities and also should be usable with students with other disabilities.

LaFrance (1995) recommended the use of the Torrance Tests of Creative Thinking, Figural Form B, for identifying gifted children with learning disabilities based on her identification research with 90 students. In comparing gifted, gifted with learning disabilities, and regular groups with learning disabilities (30 students in each group), she found that the gifted students with learning disabilities exhibited humor, emotion, richness of imagery, and cognition that separated them from the less talented group of students.

Children with cerebral palsy who are not able to communicate with speech are not likely to be identified for gifted programming. However, the dramatic work of Willard-Holt (1994) should remind teachers that even children with such extreme disabilities can thrive in gifted programs. Jan was identified for gifted programming at age 6, and Brad elected to participate in the research study at age 14. Data was collected over a three-year period. The researcher concluded that these students exhibited the following characteristics of giftedness: advanced academic abilities, a broad base of knowledge, quickness of learning and recall, sophisticated sense of humor, curiosity, insight, maturity, desire for independence, and the use of intellectual skills to cope with their disabilities. Perhaps this brief poem by Jan summarizes most effectively how critical it is not to overlook talents in children who are severely disabled:

### Lost seeds

*Poems are meant to be pomegranates*
*Like my poems for no one*
*Days go by because I just forget how I felt*
*Poems can steal no one's imagination*
*When they rot on the tree*
*Like unpicked fruit*

## Identification of Gifted Children with Learning Disabilities

As with other disabilities, gifted children with learning disabilities also are often overlooked by typical G/T program selection procedures (e.g., Brody & Mills, 1997; Reis, McGuire, & Neu, 2000; Tallent-Runnels & Sigler, 1995). They may function at or below grade level and may exhibit deficits in cognitive ability, including long- or short-term memory problems, visual or auditory processing weaknesses, and/or visual-motor integration problems (Suter & Wolf, 1987). Spatial disabilities, which lead to problems with math, also are common. Cognitive areas of giftedness found among many learning disabled children are good problem-solving skills, abstract thinking abilities, and excellent oral communication skills (Daniels, 1983; Hadary, Cohen, & Haushalter, 1979; Whitmore, 1980). Behavior problems, poor self-concepts, and dependent behaviors complicate the identification of both the giftedness and the learning disability.

Rimm (1995d) pointed out that sometimes children who are labeled as "learning disabled" in school actually are dependent underachievers. Table 15.2 includes characteristics that may help separate children with learning disabilities from those who are underachieving. Separating the two categories for the purpose of differential treatment is important.

Dole (2000) noted that although more boys are identified as learning disabled, there is a greater risk factor for girls. Recent research (Lyon, Alexander, & Yaffe, 1997; Shaywitz et al., 1997) shows that girls have as many learning disabilities as boys, but are identified later because they show fewer behavioral problems. Later identification of learning disabilities decreases the opportunity for improvement in those difficulties (Lyon et al., 1997).

The WISC-R or WISC-III frequently is used for the identification of children with learning disabilities. The "scatter" or differences between subtest scores (Lutey, 1977) and significant discrepancies between Verbal and Performance scores (Kaufman, 1976a, 1976b, 1979a, 1979b; Wees, 1993) often are used to identify a learning disability. While the average Verbal-Performance discrepancy is 9.7 IQ points, Schiff, Kaufman, and Kaufman (1981) found an average Verbal-Performance discrepancy of 18.6 points for a gifted learning disabled group. A full 87 percent showed a higher Verbal than Performance score, although in Wees's Canadian program, all but two students had higher Performance scores, several as much as 20 points higher.

An examination of the case histories of 17,000 children referred to the Temple University Reading Clinic between 1952 and 1979 produced 322 (246 boys, 76 girls) who were both gifted and learning disabled. Large Verbal-Performance discrepancies of 15 points or more were found for half of the gifted sample. *Similarities* (abstract verbal reasoning) and *comprehension* (common-sense thinking) subtests were highest for these students, while *digit span* and *arithmetic* were lowest. Note that the latter two subtests require considerable concentration and attention, which are often poor in children with learning disabilities (Satler, 1982).

Fox and Brody (1983), Maker and Udall (1983), and Rosner and Seymour (1983) all have suggested a multidimensional approach to identifying gifted students with learning disabilities. Such an approach might include the WISC-III, achievement tests, teacher and parent reports, creativity tests, and interviews with the child.

Finally, as with the similarly difficult challenge of identifying gifted disadvantaged and minority children, using a *quota system* will ensure that children with disabilities are examined closely for gifts and talents and that many will be placed in programs for the gifted. The identification of gifted students with disabilities will continue to be difficult. However, a sensitivity to characteristics of

**TABLE 15.2** Ways to Discriminate between Dependence and Disability

| Dependence | Disability |
|---|---|
| 1. Child asks for explanations regularly despite differences in subject matter. | Child asks for explanations in particular subjects that are difficult. |
| 2. Child asks for explanation of instructions regardless of style used, either auditory or visual. | Child asks for explanations of instructions only when given in one instruction style, either auditory or visual, but not both. |
| 3. Child's questions are not specific to material but appear to be mainly to gain adult attention. | Child's questions are specific to material and once process is explained, child works efficiently. |
| 4. Child is disorganized or slow in assignments but becomes much more efficient when a meaningful reward is presented as motivation. | Child's disorganization or slow pace continues despite motivating rewards. |
| 5. Child works only when an adult is nearby at school and/or at home. | Child works independently once process is clearly explained. |
| 6. Individually administered measures of ability indicate that the child is capable of learning the material. Individual tests improve with tester encouragement and support. Group measures may not indicate good abilities or skills. | Both individual and group measures indicate lack of specific abilities or skills. Tester encouragement has no significant effect on scores. |
| 7. Child exhibits "poor me" body language (tears, helplessness, pouting, copying) regularly when new work is presented. Teacher or adult attention serves to ease the symptoms. | Child exhibits "poor me" body language only with instructions or assignments in specific disability areas and accepts challenges in areas of strength. |
| 8. Parents report whining, complaining, attention getting, temper tantrums, and poor sportsmanship at home. | Although parents may find similar symptoms at home, they tend to be more sporadic than regular, particularly the whining and complaining. |
| 9. Child's "poor me" behavior appears only with one parent and not with the other; only with some teachers and not with others. With some teachers or with the other parent the child functions fairly well independently. | Although the child's "poor me" behaviors may appear only with one parent or with solicitous teachers, performance is not adequate even when behavior is acceptable. |
| 10. Child learns only when given one-to-one instruction but will not learn in groups even when instructional mode is varied. | Although child may learn more quickly in a one-to-one setting, he/she will also learn efficiently in a group setting provided the child's disability is taken into consideration when instructions are given. |

Some children who are truly disabled have also become dependent. The key to distinguishing between disability and dependence is the child's response to adult support. If the children perform only with adult support when new material is presented, they are too dependent whether or not there is also a disability.

Source: *Why Bright Kids Get Poor Grades* by S. B. Rimm, Crown Publishers, New York, 1995. Reprinted with permission.

giftedness and a willingness to look beyond the too-visible disability will aid in the discovery of talent.

The National Association for Gifted Children established a policy statement for gifted children with learning disabilities, excerpts from which are shown in Inset 15.1.

**Identifying Gifted Children with Attention Disorders**

*Attention Deficit-Hyperactivity Disorder* (ADHD), *Impulsive-Hyperactive* and *Inattentive* types, are the new, catch-all diagnoses for children, gifted or otherwise (Rimm, 1995c). These disorders are

## Students with Concomitant Giftedness and Learning Disabilities
## (Excerpts from NAGC Position Paper)

Due to a specific learning disability, an increasing number of students are not achieving up to their potential despite the fact that they demonstrate high ability or gifted behavior. These students exhibit characteristics of both exceptionalities: giftedness and learning disabilities. Their gifted behaviors often include keen interests, high levels of creativity, superior abilities in abstract thinking and problem-solving prowess. Similar to their peers with learning disabilities, they frequently display problems in one or more of the following: reading, writing, mathematics, memory, organization, or sustaining attention.

NAGC recognizes three types of students who could be identified as gifted learning disabled: (1) identified gifted students who have subtle learning disabilities, (2) students with a learning disability but whose gift has not been identified, and (3) unidentified students whose gifts and disabilities may be masked by average school achievement. School policies concerning identification and entitlement to specialized educational services can contribute to the under-identification and inappropriate programming for these youngsters. Given that gifted students with learning disabilities do not necessarily perform below grade level, discrepancy analysis should be based on their potential compared to their classroom performance.

Identifying students' abilities and gifts should be based neither on classroom performance nor on total test scores in achievement or intelligence. Rather, to identify students' gifts, schools should analyze individual subtest scores and patterns on tests of intelligence as well as emphasize authentic assessment of talent within specific domains using student products, audition, and interviews.

Students who have both gifts and learning disabilities require a dually differentiated program: One that nurtures their gifts and talents while accommodating for learning weaknesses. Without appropriate identification and services, the gifts of these students will likely be lost.

characterized by difficulty with concentration, distractibility, impulsivity, disorganization, and hyperactivity for the first diagnosis, and all characteristics but the last for the second diagnosis. Table 15.3 lists characteristics for diagnosing ADHD in children.

While it is tempting to latch on to a "sure cure," and while statistical data reassures parents that stimulant medication is appropriate for some children, it is critical that parents and teachers understand that all tests for attention disorders are observational.* There are absolutely *no* definitive biological tests for attention deficit disorders at this time. Doctors, teachers, and parents deduce a biological cause from observations of children's behavior without any biological evidence whatever.

A great deal of research has been conducted to understand attention disorders. While findings are suggestive of possible neurochemical imbalances, even the best-known specialists admit that "definitive empirical support has been lacking" (Anastopoulos & Barkley, 1991, p. 16). Zametkin (1991) explains that after two decades of an extensive search for biochemical markers for ADHD, findings have been disappointing. He further indicates that it may be a long time before an underlying cause of the disorder is found and recognizes that interacting biological and psychosocial variables may cause ADHD. Breggin (1991) asserts that "the idea that Ritalin or other stimulants correct biochemical imbalances in the brain of hyperactive children . . . is false on two counts."

*Yes, *stimulant* drugs, Ritalin or Adderall, are used to calm hyperactive children. One theory (Farley, 1986) is that such drugs raise the child's internal level of mental arousal (stimulation) to a more comfortable level, thus reducing the need for additional external stimulation.

**TABLE 15.3**   Characteristics of Attention Deficit-Hyperactivity Disorder

*Attention Deficit-Hyperactivity Disorder, Predominantly Inattentive Type*

A.   Often fails to give close attention to details or makes careless mistakes in schoolwork, work, or other activities.
B.   Often has difficulty sustaining attention in tasks or play activities.
C.   Often does not seem to listen when spoken to directly.
D.   Often does not follow through on instructions and fails to finish schoolwork, chores, or duties in the workplace (not due to oppositional behavior or failure to understand instructions).
E.   Often has difficulty organizing tasks and activities
F.   Often avoids, dislikes, or is reluctant to engage in tasks that require sustained mental effort (such as schoolwork or homework).
G.   Often loses things necessary for tasks or activities (e.g., toys, school assignments, pencils, books, or tools).
H.   Is often easily distracted by extraneous stimuli.
I.   Is often forgetful in daily activities.

*Attention Deficit-Hyperactivity Disorder, Predominantly Hyperactive-Impulsive Type*

**Hyperactivity**
A.   Often fidgets with hands or feet or squirms in seat.
B.   Often leaves seat in classroom or in other situations in which remaining seated is expected.
C.   Often runs about or climbs excessively in situations in which it is inappropriate (in adolescents or adults, may be limited to subjective feelings of restlessness).
D.   Is often "on the go" or often acts as if "driven by a motor."
E.   Often talks excessively.

**Impulsivity**
F.   Often blurts out answers before questions have been completed.
G.   Often has difficulty awaiting turn.
H.   Often interrupts or intrudes on others (e.g., butts into conversations or games).

Source: *Diagnostic and Statistical Manual of Mental Disorders,* 4th ed. Washington, DC: American Psychiatric Association, 1994.

First, there is no known biochemical imbalance in these children, and second, it generally is accepted that Ritalin has the same calming effect on normal children regardless of diagnosis or behavior (Anastopoulos & Barkley, 1991, p. 16).

Ritalin is overused and misused (e.g., Safer & Krager, 1988). Incredibly, a teacher of gifted children in Florida reported that *half* of her students were taking Ritalin for ADHD (Rimm, 1991a). One teacher of an enthusiastic 10-year old boy (IQ = 180), known to the first author (Davis), recommended that the active child be put on Ritalin. This boy's problem was solved by finding a new teacher and, later, a special school that valued his energetic giftedness.

Ritalin produces side effects for some children, including loss of appetite (and some growth), tics, insomnia, nausea, stomachaches, headaches, depression or sadness, social withdrawal, flattened emotions, and loss of energy (Breggin, 1991). Ritalin does calm a great many children and even helps them focus attention; it also makes them more compliant in the classroom.

Needless to say it would be better if ADHD children could learn to function well without medication. Many of the symptoms of attention disorders can be controlled behaviorally, but some children do require both medication and behavioral help in order to work to their abilities in school.

The growing interest in attention deficit disorders has caused a serious problem (Baum, Olenchak, & Owen, 1998). There has been an overdiagnosing of the disorder by parents, teachers, and professionals. Ritalin, Adderall, and other stimulant medications are being hailed as a magical cure by many. The problem is especially severe for gifted children. For example, Webb (1993) reminds us that some of the characteristics used to identify ADHD (Table 15.3) resemble those of high-intensity, high-energy gifted children. Also, characteristics that identify high creativity are similar to some of those listed as indicative of children with ADHD (Cramond, 1994; Leroux & Levitt-Perlman, 2000). Reif (1993) reminds us that an unchallenging curriculum for gifted children can also cause children to show ADHD-like symptoms. Here's a dramatic story:

*Anna had a school history of diagnosed learning disabilities and underachievement. She also had solid symptoms of Attention Deficit Hyperactivity Disorder (Inattentive Type). By her junior year in high school, she had almost reversed her underachieving habits and was coping well with her reading disability. Her important strengths were math, spatial abilities, and creative problem solving. She was determined to major in engineering in college but was concerned with her difficulty in attending to lectures and concentrating on her reading. Her father had found his use of Ritalin very effective for his own inattention problems, and there is ample research that suggests ADHD may be genetic.*

*At the suggestion of Rimm, Anna was put on Ritalin for a trial period. She was a freshman in college in a difficult engineering program, and at age nineteen was capable of carefully monitoring the effects of the medication. Her observations should give all adults who suggest medication some important thoughts to consider.*

*Anna found that the Ritalin was extremely helpful to her concentration during lectures. However, during her engineering problem-solving classes, if she had taken Ritalin, she was so focused she couldn't seem to produce any creative ideas. In her words, "Ideas just wouldn't come." Anna needed to carefully monitor the amount of medication she took and*

*actually used much less than the doctor initially had suggested. The doctor's first recommended dosage caused Anna to feel like she was on a "high" very similar to the feelings she would get if she drank too much coffee. Anna continues to use Ritalin for lectures but refrains from using it when creativity is called for.*

In considering a request for medication for a student, parents and teachers may wish to remember that although focus and attention are extremely important for some kinds of learning, it can be dysfunctional for idea production. Children may not be mature enough to report these dysfunctional effects, and they may not be readily observable by teachers.

Although it's important to emphasize the problems of overmedication, it's also critical to consider that giftedness may mask ADHD, and ADHD may mask giftedness (Leroux & Levitt-Perlman, 2000; Kaufmann, Kalbfleisch, & Castellanos, 2000; Zentall, Moon, Hall, & Grskovic, 2001). Flint (2001) emphasized that the double exceptionality of (1) giftedness and ADHD is common, and (2) giftedness does not provide protection from the difficult symptoms of ADHD.

Consistency, appropriate limit-setting, curriculum changes, and emphasis on positive interests and accomplishment are some of the many alternative approaches that can be used for gifted children who are presently being diagnosed with ADHD (Rimm, 1995c, 1995d). Some will require medication. While some gifted children are easy to raise, many of them frustrate their parents and teachers to tears and guilt. There is no easy way out of so great a challenge.

## CRITICAL INGREDIENTS OF PROGRAMS FOR GIFTED CHILDREN WITH DISABILITIES

Programming for gifted children with disabilities may vary in type and content to the same extent as for other gifted children. It can include the same acceleration, enrichment, grouping, and counseling tactics, and with the same view toward developing the child's strengths, promoting high achievement, and enhancing creative and other high-level thinking skills. However, the program also must include some special components based on additional needs related to the handicapping condition.

Instead of categorizing the student first as having a disability and second as gifted, the G/T program should view the child primarily as a gifted child, but one who may need some special assistance because of his or her disability. The primary emphasis thus should be on the recognition and facilitation of the child's strengths. A secondary focus is to prevent the disability from becoming a deterrent to the development and expression of the child's talent.

Although different disabilities create different obstacles, there are a core of obstacles that appear to be critical for almost all children with disabilities. It is these that we address as priorities for gifted programs that include children with disabilities.

## REDUCING COMMUNICATION LIMITATIONS

Countless high-achieving college students with disabilities have learned effective and socially acceptable ways to compensate for their disabling conditions. Blind students use tape recorders, study with sighted friends, and make easy arrangements to take exams orally. Students with severe visual impairment will obtain (usually at government expense) head-mounted devices or other machines that magnify the pages of standard college texts. Students who are deaf will bring a sign language interpreter to class, parking the smiling interpreter squarely next to the on-stage lecturer. Orthopedically impaired students scoot from building to building in electric wheelchairs; if they cannot write they also will use tape recorders and take exams orally. Dyslexic students pay maximum attention to lectures and illustrations, with little time devoted to frustrating printed words. On one hand, these students are admired for their courage and ingenuity. On the other, as energetic and talented individuals they simply are doing what they must do.

Regardless of the compensatory device used, students with disabilities are usually required to invest more time than normal students. Successful attorney Martha Lindner, who is dyslexic (Rimm & Rimm-Kaufman, 2001), discovered that she needed to invest three times more time than average students in her homework and study in order to feel adequately intelligent.

All persons with disabilities must compensate as best they can for their limitations. In school, they must be able to perceive, respond, and express themselves; in short, they must be able to *communicate*. The regular and special education teacher must help ensure that technological aids and special training are available that will permit the gifted child with a disability not only to function "normally" in the regular class but to develop his or her superior abilities and gifts. A short list would include wheelchairs, hearing aids, lip reading, sign language, braille training, braille texts, magnifiers, tape recorders, artificial limbs and hands, paintbrush and pencil attachments for the head or arm, and computers.

Computers present growing possibilities for extending the communication potential of children with disabilities. For example, children who are learning disabled by reason of poor handwriting skills often do very poorly in written expression until they learn to use a word processing program. Using a computer for writing assignments has the dual advantages of encouraging both fluent expression and independence. Carnine (1989) pointed out how technology can free teachers from delivering drill instruction and can reduce performance differences between students with and without disabilities. He used videodisc, computer simulation, and computer-assisted instruction techniques to help students with disabilities learn earth science, chemistry, health, fractions, reasoning skills, and vocabulary. Gleason, Carnine, and Boriero (1990) compared problem-analyses learning for students with learning disabilities as taught by an expert teacher to computer-assisted instruction. The pre-post change with the teacher went from 51 percent to 93 percent, and for the computer group it went from 49 percent to 91 percent.

Vernon and LaFalce-Landers (1993) remind us

of some logistical problems that go with handicapped students' use of technology. Sometimes there is scarce space in the classroom for extra computers, and with secondary students who move from classroom to classroom, convenient computers may not be available. Finally, peers may envy the learning disabled student who may not appear so disabled but is permitted regular use of one of few computers in the classroom.

Another example of the use of computers is the computerized *Versa Braille,* which permits a child to type English letters and have them translated to braille, or to type braille letters and have them translated to English. (For information on Telesensory Systems and the nearest Versa Braille dealer, see www.telesensory.com.) *Digispeech* is a computer program that can be used to help students with learning disabilities recognize their spelling errors and increase their awareness of phrases. It reads back phonetically the stories that children have keyboarded into the computer. Errors become obvious to the children who are listening with headsets. (For DigiSpeech and many other aids for handicapped persons of all ages, contact Computers for Handicapped Independence Program, 914 E. Spruce Street, Suite 32, Yakima, WA 98901; http://polio.dyndns.org/chip/html/index.htm.) Recording for the Blind and Dyslexic (www.rfbd.org) is an organization that makes recordings of books, including many textbooks, available for a small fee to students who are legally blind or have reading disabilities. Also, many local libraries have books on tape available to all who are interested in listening.

James (1993) scolds educators for their failures in acquainting themselves with the growing new technologies for students with disabilities. She sees growing opportunities for creative computer applications, but finds a lack of communication between the universities where uses are often developed and public school systems where they are needed. For example, she cites the important work at Johns Hopkins University in computer applications to assisting persons with disabilities that has not been incorporated into many schools (Wagner, 1992).

In many cases, gifted and talented students with disabilities cannot be identified without aids that allow them to communicate. For example, in Wisconsin teachers in the Arts for the Handicapped Project (O'Connell, 1982) designed several devices that served to free physically disabled children from some limitations of their disabilities, permitting them to express themselves through art. The strategies allowed talented artists to be identified and they were taught advanced techniques and skills.

Some communication aids, incidentally, may have the initial effect of slowing down responding, learning, and cognitive functioning. However, once the communication skill is mastered, the child will have a vastly improved potential for in-depth development, achievement, and creative expression.

The gifted child with a disability clearly must be provided with all possible resources to become a skilled user of substitute means of communication. Without these aids, the expression of talent is impeded and locked within. Leaders of gifted programs not only must help obtain these resources but also must interpret to the community the beneficial effects of the aids and the potential talent that can be uncovered and developed when communication barriers are lifted.

## SELF-CONCEPT DEVELOPMENT

We noted earlier that rejection by others, labeling, lowered teacher expectations, and the sense of being different combine to make gifted children with disabilities feel less capable and of less worth than other children. Because a poor self-concept is a primary characteristic of underachievement, dealing with the extremely poor self-images of these children should be a primary underlying goal of a gifted program for students with disabilities.

In addition to feedback from others, the self-concept also is based upon a realistic appraisal of one's own skills and achievements. Therefore, program activities should be directed not only toward helping these children achieve but toward helping them appreciate the worth of their achievements. Nielsen and Mortorff-Albert (1989) found improved self-concepts for gifted students with learning disabilities who were involved in gifted or gifted/learning disability programs, compared with gifted students who were involved only in learning disability programs. Appropriate gifted programming can improve their sense of worth when they actually do qualify for these programs.

These achievements can be evaluated according to two sets of standards. The first set of standards would be the same as applied to nondisabled persons, which should make it clear to all that these contributions are valuable and even superior to the average. A second set of standards acknowledges the special talent and effort needed to overcome the disability. If gifted children with disabilities have high expectations placed upon them, and if communication barriers are removed, their academic and creative achievements can be as excellent as those of anyone else. And it is through the challenge of true high-level achievement that these children can realistically attain the positive self-concept they desperately need for their own personal growth.

## Social Skills

Nondisabled children use all of their senses and their mobility spontaneously to learn social skills that permit them to be accepted by their peers. Children with disabilities need to learn more concretely and specifically about the social life to which they, too, want and need to belong. This goal is indeed a challenge.

Gifted students with disabilities require social activities with other bright or creative children who have similar disabilities and similar goals and interests so they will not feel alone. Peer support and peer-support groups have been recommended throughout this text as an effective solution to many self-concept and social problems of gifted students. Also, due to lack of experience, gifted children with disabilities may require "social coaching" so they do not *guarantee* themselves rejection by, for example, trying to show off, forcing themselves on a group, or withdrawing completely. These are common, self-defeating coping strategies adopted unsuccessfully by many children and adolescents with disabilities who so strongly wish to be "part of the group" (Halverson & Victor, 1976).

The other children in the class, too, probably will require "sensitivity training" to help them empathize with the child who is disabled; that is, to help them understand the problems and feelings of individuals with disabilities so they will *think* before mistreating or excluding them. Group discussions, which encourage open and honest communication between disabled and nondisabled youth, can provide an important avenue for developing the social skills and social relationships of children with disabilities, while providing unique sensitivity insights for the nondisabled child. Inset 15.2 (Katt, 1988) includes sample activities that the Wyoming, Michigan, gifted and talented program used to increase their students' sensitivity to students with disabilities.

## Classroom Tactics

Several classroom strategies may increase contact and positive feelings between different student groups. For example, mixed learning teams, which require all members to work together, have been successful in improving between-group attitudes and friendships. In Aronson's (Aronson et al., 1975) *jigsaw* method mixed groups of six upper-elementary students are told that in one hour they will have a test to see how well they have learned, for example, about the life of newspaper publisher Joseph Pulitzer. Each of the six is given one paragraph covering a different aspect of Pulitzer's career. To do well, each student must read his or her own paragraph and then explain its contents to the others. Cooperation and interdependence are the only route to success. With mixed-race groups, teachers reported that changes in attitudes and self-concepts—and an improved classroom atmosphere—were very impressive.

Peer tutoring also has the effect of increasing "liking" between different students. Nondisabled gifted students may tutor gifted students with dis-

INSET 15.2 _____

## Activities for Encouraging Awareness of Handicaps

### PHYSICAL HANDICAPS

Rent or borrow a wheelchair. Ask nonhandicapped students to do one-hour activities in the wheelchair, including getting a drink from the water fountain, going out to recess, doing an assignment on the blackboard, changing classes, and so on.

### COMMUNICATIVE DISABILITY

Ask students to assume their speech and language abilities are interrupted. Have them attempt to tell the class something while mute.

### VISUAL IMPAIRMENT

Plan a sightless half day by use of blindfold and cane. Alert students to describing how their senses of hearing, touch, and smell can guide them through the day. Students will each need a buddy to guide them through the more difficult adventures such as recess games and equipment. Stop several times to discuss experiences and awareness.

Adapted from Katt (1988).

abilities or students with disabilities may tutor others. The disabled students also may tutor younger children. Gartner, Kohler, and Reissman (1971) stressed that when anxious, low-esteem, low-achieving students are placed in the important and prestigious role of *teacher,* they learn new skills, feel much better about themselves, and their attitudes toward school also improve. In addition, the younger children reap educational benefits and they learn that persons with disabilities are people too.

Coleman (1992) found gifted children with learning disabilities to be more planful in their use of problem-solving strategies than average children with learning disabilities. She thus recommended that direct teaching of coping strategies could be helpful to all children with learning disabilities. Montague (1991) found considerable differences among gifted students with learning disabilities in mathematical problem solving. She emphasized the importance of teaching effective math problem-solving strategies.

Although few school districts would consider a self-contained gifted learning-disabled class appropriate in the current era of degrouping, Wees (1993) reported outstanding success for ten elementary students in a two-year-program in Calgary. Emphasis was placed on kinesthetic learning and independent studies. The children, selected from regular and learning disability programs, made excellent progress with reading and writing skills. Work and organizational habits also improved. In junior high school these children were integrated into regular or learning disability programs, and the author reported continued success. Parents whose children attended a special school for gifted and learning disabled found their children achieved better in the private school than in public school special education programs (Hishinuma & Nishimura, 2000).

Self-assessment was found effective with preschool children with learning disabilities (Sainato et al., 1990) and with two school-aged gifted learning disabled children (Miller, 1991). The potential for combining self-assessment with the teaching of problem-solving strategies would seem appropriate for students who are gifted and learning disabled. Studies of successful gifted learning-disabled adults pointed out their skill in problem solving (Gerber, Ginsburg, & Reiff, 1991).

## Learning from the Past

Educators learn much about teaching children by studying the childhoods of successful adults. One such study sought to understand the characteristics and behaviors that permitted gifted learning disabled children to become highly successful (Gerber et al., 1991). This study identified crucial themes that could be adapted to assist students with disabilities.

With the successful adults, there seemed to be a conscious effort to gain control or take charge of their lives despite their disability. Adaptability that involved persistence, learning, creativity, and personal support systems made a difference. They set explicit goals for themselves and were able to reframe or reinterpret their learning disability experiences. They showed a capacity to confront their disabling challenges in order to live with or overcome them.

Teaching these characteristics sounds like a tall order for students and teachers alike. Yet by understanding that learning disabled gifted adults can be successful, students with disabilities can find inspiration and encouragement despite their own disabilities.

In an interesting study of 12 successful gifted college students who also were learning disabled, Reis, Neu, and McGuire (1995) found that the students' giftedness had masked their learning disabilities, and these disabilities were not discovered by others until later. Several of the students had not been included in gifted programs despite high IQ scores; three had been nominated for gifted programs but were not served because of low test scores.

These young adults with learning disabilities reported both positive and negative school experiences. The positive memories were of teachers who made accommodations for them such as providing extra time on tests and challenging them. The negative memories included social problems, difficulties with teachers, and frustrations with particular academic areas. Successful college students with learning disabilities advised that elementary and secondary school would have given

them better preparation if they had been taught learning strategies rather than just content (Reis, McGuire, & Neu, 2000). Positive experiences outside of school were part of what permitted learning disabled students to survive and eventually adapt to school. These students' memories provide useful tips to teachers of gifted children who are learning disabled.

Although mentorships are effective for most gifted children, mentorships for children with disabilities can be especially effective if the children are paired with talented adults who also have learning disabilities (Baum, 1990). This pairing not only provides good learning strategies for these students, but the student is more likely to identify with the adult because of their similarities (Hetherington & Frankie, 1967; Mussen & Rutherford, 1963).

## Encouraging Independent Learning

One-to-one attention is characteristic and often necessary for educational programs for students with disabilities. However, these children sometimes become too dependent upon the individual attention and the continuous positive feedback that supports their learning. Such dependence will limit the motivation and achievement of any child. Therefore, children with disabilities must be encouraged to develop both intrinsic motivation, with learning and success as their own rewards, and the ability to learn independently. Further, they need both independent, self-initiated learning experiences and cooperative small-group activities in which they can serve as leaders and as equal participants.

In selecting methods by which children can compensate for their disability, attention to independence is very important. For example, the child who has a writing disability could (1) tell his or her story to a teacher, (2) dictate the story into a tape recorder, or (3) compose the story with a word processor. The first increases dependence; the latter two permit independence. Blind children could (1) have material read to them, (2) they could read the material in braille, or (3) hear it on a tape recorder. Again, the first helps keep the children dependent while the last two aid independence. Dependent help certainly is appropriate occasionally, but too much dependency can further cripple the already disabled child.

Independent, self-initiated learning and learning as part of a class group are important for all children, especially gifted ones who will be faced with challenging college work and complex professions. We must be innovative in providing independent learning opportunities for gifted children with disabilities just as they are provided for gifted children who are nondisabled.

## HIGH-LEVEL, ABSTRACT THINKING SKILLS

We noted earlier that limited sensory input may have the effect of depressing the development of high-level, abstract-thinking skills. Compared to persons with unimpaired senses, experiences of sensory disabled students tend to be interpreted in a more concrete vocabulary. For children with disabilities a weakness in abstract and high-level thinking skills should not be viewed as "lack of ability," but as a deficiency that may require even more attention than with nondisabled gifted children.

More than for other gifted students, then, the gifted child with a disability must be exposed to programming methods that foster the development of skills such as *creativity, problem solving, critical thinking, classifying, generalizing, analysis, synthesis,* and *evaluation.* Encouraging such skill development is common in most gifted programs but is doubly important for the gifted child with a disability.

An example of introducing abstract thinking skills is provided by a creative problem solving (CPS) program for 16 emotionally disabled aggressive middle school students who were not identified as gifted (Mathew, 1984; see Chapter 9). The researcher taught the youths to apply CPS to real problems. The effect of CPS training on these children was increased creativity as measured by the Torrance Tests of Creative Thinking. The intervention also reduced aggression significantly.

Baum (1984) described the use of Renzulli's Enrichment Triad Model (Chapter 7) with gifted children who were learning disabled. Their gifted behavior was exhibited outside of the classroom and was definitely absent within the classroom. Baum emphasized that enrichment activities should be designed to develop strengths and interests and to challenge, not necessarily to provide remediation. Inset 15.3 describes the triad program that helped them feel more motivated, challenged, and confident. Baum's (1988) success with the Triad model for gifted/learning disabled students was again demonstrated with seven students who met $2\frac{1}{2}$ hours a week over a nine-month period. Gains in self-esteem, learning behavior, and creative productivity were found for six of the seven students. Huntley (1990) also reported a successful gifted learning disabilities program in the Norwich, Connecticut, public schools using the Triad model.

Daniels (1983) itemized the following as curriculum and remediation methods specifically for teaching gifted and talented children with learning disabilities. Note the emphasis on abstract and high-level learning objectives.

Classification
Levels of abstraction
Appreciating relevancy
Labeling
Abstracting
Generalizing
Learning concepts (not *words*)
Vocabulary, spelling
Writing, composition
Punctuation, proofreading

Hackney (1986) conducted a summer program for 15 gifted students with visual impairment at the Texas School for the Blind. The program included higher-level thinking skills, advanced problem solving, creative writing, mentorships, and most of the same elements included in many gifted programs. Outdoor risk taking, independent learning, and counseling were components that are more unique to programs for gifted children with disabilities. Ironically, this program

## Example of Enrichment Triad Model in Action for Learning Disabled Students

### TYPE I—EXPOSURE

The students were taken to see the Lego® Road Show. This is an elaborate display of Lego brick constructions of animals, buildings, and vehicles. These structures, built from thousands of Legos, were designed and built by Lego engineers. The students were overwhelmed by the exhibit and expressed a desire to become more elaborate in their own designs.

### TYPE II—TRAINING

We called Lego headquarters (fortunately located in our area) and arranged for consultation with an engineer. He explained to the group how designs evolved; how creative thinking skills, especially flexibility, are needed; and how principles of calculus and physics are part of the building process. Ideas basically come from experimenting with the bricks. Once the concrete structure is completed, the design is drawn. These students were delighted to hear this. So many school assignments reverse this process—"put your plan in writing before you begin."

### TYPE III—INVESTIGATION OF A REAL PROBLEM

The Lego executive in charge of marketing asked the students to design original structures for the museum display which the Lego Company was planning. The company agreed to furnish the bricks, offer technical advice, and display the product. Two boys, ages ten and twelve, eagerly accepted the challenge.

The ten-year-old designed and built an 18-wheeler truck, complete with separate tractor and trailer. The trailer was mounted on an appropriate platform and pivoted to allow a wide arc of movement. At the end of its two-foot-long trailer was a gate that opened and closed by means of a pulley. Concern was shown by the young engineer for streamlined design for maximum function and form.

The twelve-year-old created a motorized amusement park ride. Intersecting aerial arms supported four miniature planes suspended in mid-air that revolved around its three-foot-high base. Twenty-seven revolutions comprised the ride. When asked why there were 27 revolutions, the young designer replied, "Because I set up the gears that way."

Reprinted from "Meeting the needs of learning disabled students" by Susan Baum, *Roeper Review*, 1984, 7 (1), pp. 13–19. Reprinted by permission of the author and *Roeper Review*.

endured some of the same criticism that plagues all gifted programming: Some charged that the program was "elitist" and that there was no need to treat gifted children who are blind differently than other children who are blind.

### PARENTING

Parenting is a critical component of any program for children who are gifted. However, parents of gifted children with disabilities must deal with their child's special needs related to the disability as well as attend to his or her giftedness. Parents of children who are disabled often devote resources, time, energy, attention, and patience far beyond that given to a normal child, which can

result in advantages or, sometimes, disadvantages for the child. Consider these situations identified by Rimm in her psychology practice:

1. Intensive parental teaching of the child provided on a continuous one-to-one basis increases sensory awareness, knowledge, vocabulary, and skill development. The child will learn a great deal about his or her environment from this abundance of early teaching in the home. This obviously is an advantage.

2. Counteridentification, the parent's deriving of personal feelings of success and failure through the child's accomplishments, may cause a parent to do *too much* for the child. A too-helpful parent may rob the child of opportunities to learn skills

and build independence and self-confidence. In some cases a parent may even deny the existence of their child's disability (for example, dyslexia, partial hearing loss). In other cases parents may use the child's disability as an excuse for allowing the child to avoid responsibilities. Of course, the child soon learns to use the same kind of excuse to avoid unpleasant chores, for example, learning math facts. Thwarting independence and skill development is a disadvantage.

**3.** Manipulation by the child also can be an outcome of the parents' anxieties about the child. Because the parent is so anxious for their united success, the child, perhaps unconsciously, learns that he or she can easily control the parent ("I can't do it! You've got to help me!"). This manipulation skill may be extended to teachers and peers. Manipulative attention-getting behaviors may take the form of overly dependent behavior or a stubborn refusal to put forth effort in anything but the child's most preferred activities. This child and his or her parent will blame the school, the teacher, other children, and the remainder of the child's world for not helping the child to learn instead of encouraging the child to take responsibility for his or her own learning. Manipulation, dependence, and refusal to work also are disadvantages. Loving, caring parents and teachers can feel too sorry for a child who is disabled.

**4.** Involvement by one parent may be so intense that it precludes the other parent from participating. For example, special skills such as using braille, a sign language, or special teaching procedures may need to be learned by a parent. If the second parent (usually father) has not also learned these techniques, he may be omitted from the special relationship and may decide that he is not a very good parent. This is particularly a problem if the child is a boy and the close parent is a mother. The alienation of the father may deprive the boy of an important identification figure and impede his independence and growth. The boy, as he matures, will feel both grateful to his mother for her commitment but angry and impatient with her for his dependence on her. Neither mother nor son will understand the deterioration of what in childhood was such a strong positive relationship. Excluding one parent from close family relationships will always cause a serious problem. The movie *Mr. Holland's Opus* provided an excellent example of the problems caused by the father being excluded.

A parent involvement group should always be part of a gifted program that serves students with disabilities. Such a group can help parents avoid common problems. The group also can help parents focus on their children's strengths rather than dwell on their handicaps.

The *Retrieval and Acceleration of Promising Young Handicapped and Talented* (RAPYHT) project (Johnson, Karnes, & Carr, 1997; Karnes, Shwedel, & Lewis, 1983) is a program devoted to the early education of gifted children with disabilities. It includes an active and effective parent component. Noted Karnes et al., parent involvement helps maintain a consistent philosophy between home and school. In RAPYHT, parents participate in both identification and training. The latter involves parents in helping their children compensate for their disability and develop in their areas of giftedness. Parents are encouraged to help in the classroom and are given suggested activities to be carried out with their children at home. Large-group meetings, small-group discussion sessions, individual conferences, a newsletter, and a parent library all are part of the family involvement. The professional staff views family members as partners in the program (Karnes, 1984).

Although parents always should be involved in the education of their children, the special stresses and demands of parenting gifted students with disabilities requires an even closer partnership between the formal and informal educators—teachers and parents. Parents must be guided in setting appropriate high expectations for the gifted child despite his or her disability (Rimm, 1996a).

## SUMMARY

Gifted children with disabilities typically are recognized for their disability, not their gifts. There have been few G/T programs designed for the gifted who are disabled. Of the many varieties of physically and psychologically disabling conditions, perhaps only mental retardation precludes most forms of giftedness.

Too often schools fail to accommodate the gifted student who is disabled. If the gifted child can function reasonably well, special educational services may be withdrawn. Due largely to social rejection, students who are disabled frequently have poor self-concepts and some are disruptive in class.

Identification is difficult. Gifted students with disabilities tend to be unseen by teachers and even parents. Also, the disability may obscure the expression of gifts and talents or lead teachers to lower their expectations. While IQ scores can be extremely useful, they may be depressed by the tendency of sensory-impaired students to think less abstractly. In-service training dealing with characteristics of giftedness and identification methods is important.

Eisenberg and Epstein successfully used IQ and achievement scores, all Renzulli rating scales, peer nominations, and self-nominations for identification. Rimm emphasized the importance of discriminating between learning disabilities and underachievement. Maker and Silverman recommended comparing students who are disabled with other students who are disabled and to heavily weight skills used to compensate. The Renzulli Creativity Scale and the PRIDE, GIFT, and GIFFI inventories might be used for identifying creative giftedness.

Identifying gifted children with attention deficit disorders may be difficult because there is no biological test for ADHD, and some of the characteristics of giftedness overlap with the characteristics of ADHD. Teachers must be cautious in not over-recommending medication. However, gifted children with ADHD may require both medication and therapy.

G/T programs for gifted children with disabilities can include the same acceleration, enrichment, grouping, and counseling components as other programs.

Communication weaknesses must be compensated for via the use of mechanical aids and/or special training. James (1993) urged better communication between universities and school districts on computer use by students with disabilities.

Developing positive self-concepts should be a main program goal of teaching the gifted with disabilities. Learning to value their own superior achievements and talents should help their self-concepts. Helping other students to appreciate the achievements of gifted students with disabilities also may be valuable. Peer support groups may help gifted students with disabilities develop good self-concepts and social skills.

Other children probably will require sensitivity and values training to help them empathize with students who are disabled. Learning teams may help improve attitudes toward students with disabilities.

Teaching coping and problem-solving strategies and using self-assessments are appropriate for gifted students who are learning disabled. Understanding the characteristics and behaviors of gifted children who are learning disabled and who become successful adults can help teachers encourage and inspire learning disabled students. Mentorships, especially for children with disabilities, encourage identification with talented adults who are learning disabled.

Despite the necessity of one-to-one instruction for gifted students with disabilities, the teaching of independent learning and learning in small groups also is necessary. Even more than with other gifted students, high-level abstract thinking skills must be encouraged.

The great attention parents must pay to their child who is disabled may result in superior learning and cognitive development. However, it also can lead to the suppression of self-confidence and independence, learning to manipulate parents, teachers, and peers, and the elimination of one parent from the family relationship.

Parent involvement groups are a critical component of programs for gifted students with disabilities.

# CHAPTER 16

# PARENTING THE GIFTED CHILD

*I had a very special mom. . . . She brought me up to think I could be anybody I wanted to be. . . . She was great at finding cool programs for me to participate in. I was in gifted-learner programs starting in sixth grade. . . . My teachers made it really exciting to learn chemistry and physics.*

Cady Coleman, Ph.D., NASA Astronaut (from Rimm & Rimm-Kaufman, 2001, p. 159)

The "good parenting" any child needs is the main requirement for parenting the child who is gifted. However, there are some special obstacles, risks, errors, challenges, and joys that accompany being the parent of a child with unusual talents. Teachers should be sensitive to these issues in order to help guide parents of gifted children. For example: Contrary to popular belief, all parents everywhere do not believe their children are gifted. Some parents of gifted children will deny their children's special abilities in an attempt to keep them "normal" and "well-adjusted." Other parents, with the opposite attitude, seem to magnify their children's abilities and put excessive pressure on them for high achievement in all areas. This latter problem may include the tacit assumptions that (1) other children necessarily are inferior; and (2) by association, the parents also are superior. Either of these extremes, denying or magnifying giftedness, can cause problems for gifted children. As a matter of fact, avoiding extremes is an important key to parenting children who are gifted.

This chapter will emphasize some practical approaches to dealing with the special problems of parenting children who are gifted and talented. Although some concepts found here may apply to parenting all children, they are of special concern to parents—and therefore teachers—of gifted children.

## PARENTING BY POSITIVE EXPECTATIONS

Parenting by *positive expectations* can be extraordinarily successful in guiding gifted children both in school and out. If high achievement, positive attitudes, and constructive behavior are expected and reinforced by parents, they will become internalized by the child, and the need for punishment will usually be minimal. How do some parents guide their children so well without punishment while others seem to need and use it so frequently?

In questionnaires completed by successful women in nontraditional careers (Rimm, Rimm-Kaufman, & Rimm, 1999), most, with only a few exceptions, indicated that their parents had set high expectations for them.

Clear and consistent *messages,* agreed upon by both parents and transmitted to the child, are basic. In Bloom's (1985) study of talent development of concert pianists, sculptors, mathematicians, and neurologists, he found that all had in common some very clear early messages provided by parents.

> . . . parents placed great stress on achievement, on success and on doing one's best at all times . . . they were models of the "work ethic" in that they were regarded as hard workers. . . . To excel, to do one's best, to work hard, and to spend one's time constructively were emphasized over and over again (p. 510).

Rimm, Rimm-Kaufman, and Rimm (1999) found the same early messages of high expectations given to the successful women whose childhoods were researched. Mental health practitioners and educators might have considered those expectations too high, yet the successful women felt the stated expectations proved their parents believed in them. The author (Rimm) attributes the success of these messages to their being given in the voice of parents as *coaches* rather than judges, and the pairing of those high expectations with strong work ethics. For example, Catherine Burns (a pseudonym), civil engineer at MIT, recalls her dad's dual messages as "You can do anything you want if you work hard" and "Nothing comes for free" (Rimm et al., 1999, p. 204).

Csikszentmihalyi (described in Adler, 1991) studied 210 high school students who were exceptionally talented in math, science, music, sports, or art. He discovered that the most motivated ones came from families who provided both support and challenge. He compared these students to students from families that provided challenge but not support, support but not challenge, and neither challenge nor support. The students from the supportive and challenging families were more intrinsically interested in learning and were more alert while they were studying.

In a study of 394 gifted middle school students, the importance placed on mathematics and sciences by parents was the most powerful influence on the students' decisions to take math and science courses (Olszewski-Kubilius & Yasumoto, 1994). Parental support, even compared to that of friends and romantic partners, was found to be the most important factor in predicting college grades (Cole, Colangelo, Assouline, & Russell, 1994).

Parental agreement on such values as (1) the importance of study, learning, and school; (2) respect for individuality; and (3) recognition of the need for reasonable amounts of recreation and fun seem to underlie a positive and achievement-oriented atmosphere.

If the gifted child (or children) in the family are performing well, enjoying the expression of their talents, and growing positively in other ways, it is reasonable to assume that parents are doing their parenting job very well. Again, there is no one right way but many. However, if the children (1) appear to be under stress, (2) are not achieving well and responsibly, (3) have serious social problems, and/or (4) have unusually difficult family relationships, one should look for a possible family pattern causing the problem.

Parents certainly can be effective mentors for their children (McCollim, 1992; Roberts, 1992). A comment by one gifted person bears this out (Krueger, 1978):

> My family has valued education and has strong interests in art, literature, and music. Because we are close, I've tried to emulate my parents. It is by imitating them, rather than from their telling me what to do, that I've developed a passion for learning and a compulsion to work in an organized manner. But I strongly believe that because of their love and affection, my parents gave me the self-esteem which is an essential element in constructive thinking.

In studies of giftedness and eminence (Bloom, 1985; Walberg, Williams, & Zeiser, 2003; Rimm & Lowe, 1988); there were always themes of family organization and consistent and predictable expectations for conduct. High energy and an achievement orientation also were characteristic of almost all parents (Albert, 1980; Bloom, 1985; Goertzel & Goertzel, 1962).

## SOME SPECIAL PARENTING CONCERNS

Other issues related to gifted children in the family must be addressed. Teachers also can be helpful in advising parents in these areas.

### The "Who's in Charge?" Problem

> If gifted children were meant to run their homes, God would have created them bigger (Rimm, 1995d).

Children who show unusual verbal and abstract thinking ability appear to be wise and mature beyond their years, and to a degree they are. These deceptive characteristics may obscure the lack of experience and maturity that is typical of all children. It sometimes happens that devoted parents, intent on providing an ideal climate for their gifted children, fall into the trap of believing that these little beings, by virtue of their extensive vocabularies and impressive speech and logic, are capable very early of making complex decisions and setting their own goals and directions.

Bromfield (1994) reminds parents that accelerated language does not guarantee accelerated development. Language may enhance experiences, he points out, but it does not necessarily bring advanced emotional maturity.

Highly verbal children may carry additional burdens. Well-meaning parents often share their own psychological problems with such children, and highly verbal children are often expected to be especially well behaved or compliant, resulting in self-conscious or overly inhibited behavior.

The interests and concerns of these highly capable children should be considered, of course, but parents and teachers must not abdicate responsibility for guidance or protection. Parents of gifted children must constantly remind themselves to stay in charge. They have the maturity and responsibility for setting limits and guiding those unusual children despite the children's giftedness. The story in Inset 16.1 illustrates what can happen if parents do not take charge.

Hollingworth (1942) pointed out how critical it was to reach the "middle ground between arbitrary abolition of all argument and incessant argumentation." Finding that middle ground helps the child to accept the behavioral demands of adults while maintaining reasonable independence (Sebring, 1983). Ginsberg and Harrison (1977) made the following recommendation:

> Discipline your gifted child when he needs disciplining. Correct him when he needs correction. Give direction when he needs direction. He should not be granted special privileges nor should unacceptable behavior be tolerated because of his intellectual gifts (p. 7).

Regarding educational guidance, successful gifted achievers will usually agree that throughout their schooling they felt confident that (1) their parents and teachers were concerned and knowledgeable about an appropriate direction for

---

**INSET 16.1**

### A Sad Story of an Overempowered Gifted Child

Seven-year-old Jessica Dubroff intended to set a cross-country flying record—an ambitious quest that led to her death. Jessica's Cessna Cardinal had been modified so she could reach the pedals and see over the instrument panel. On this flight she was accompanied by her father and her flying instructor. Tragedy struck on the second leg, minutes after her takeoff from Cheyenne, Wyoming, into a driving thunderstorm. Her plane crashed, killing all three aboard. Mark Smith, a pilot who knew the child, anticipated accusations by proclaiming, "She wasn't forced to fly," and added, "She was seven going on twenty-five."

Jessica clearly was gifted. In her impressive childhood she played with tools instead of toys, and she even built some of her own furniture. By age four she earned money with a paper route and worked on a horse farm. She sounded like an adult when she talked to pilots about rpms and left and right rudders.

Jessica's parents claimed they did not push her. Others agreed that "she set her own goals." Her parents seemed to believe that Jessica should make most of her own choices, regardless of her obviously young age.

their education and that (2) following their lead was usually a wise decision.

Empowering children with adult decision-making provides power without wisdom. This can lead to formidable and continuing conflicts between gifted children and their parents as they compete for the power that parents give too early and try to recover too late. The resulting adversary mode may force adolescents to rebel too stubbornly, parents to respond too negatively, and both to lose the positive home atmosphere that is so valuable in educating a gifted child (Rimm, 1995d).

Baldwin (1988) described "Cornucopia Kids" as children who were given too much. He indicated that overindulged children acquire an inappropriate sense of power. Whatever the reasons for the overindulgence, it gives the children a sense of control over their parents and the belief that getting what they want is their right. He noted that it sets the stage for problems throughout life in both work and personal relationships.

### Competition and Pressure

Competition encourages and motivates gifted children to perform to the best of their high ability, and the recognition they receive for their successes provides the motivation for continued competition. The successful women in the Rimm report (Rimm, Rimm-Kaufman, & Rimm, 1999) indicated "winning in competition" as a positive experience in their childhood more frequently than any other. Winning was both motivating and exhilarating to many of the women. Furthermore, many of these women learned resilience from their competitive involvement. For example, environmental engineer Teresa Culver (Rimm & Rimm-Kaufman, 2001) was very competitive and even took the risk of competing in music, an area in which she did not excel although her sister did. She found that monitoring her personal progress and breaking difficult material into small manageable parts served her later in her challenging engineering courses.

Karnes and Riley (1996a, 1996b) suggested that entering competitions can enhance gifted children's process and presentation skills, including critical thinking, written and oral communication, group dynamics, and leadership. Expanding organizational and people skills also come with meeting deadlines, following rules, and interacting with sponsors and judges. Parents can find any number of competitions to match the strengths and interests of their gifted children in the compendium of competitions in Karnes and Riley's book, *Competitions: Maximizing Your Abilities* (see Chapter 6).

However, there are some negative side effects of extreme competitiveness. The too-competitive child may feel under continuous *stress*. Such children may exhibit symptoms of tension such as nail biting, enuresis (bed wetting), extreme sibling rivalry, loss of appetite, bullying, irritability, stomach pains, headaches, or nightmares. These problems can complicate children's lives; they also can be informative to parents who are aware of the potential meaning of such symptoms. Of course, every normal child exhibits these symptoms occasionally. However, continued or increased symptoms very often can be attributed to competitive stress; they are physical reactions to frustrations and anxieties.

Parents and teachers should try to help the child identify specific stressors and then restructure tasks and goals to diminish the stress. For example, the parents or teachers of a high school student can help the student decide upon a sensible academic load that challenges his or her abilities but is not overwhelming. Extracurricular activities must be made manageable. Younger children also can find themselves under too much pressure, with plenty of homework, music lessons, Little League soccer, and trying hard to excel in all subjects and interests while simultaneously burdened with too many friends who have plenty of ideas of their own.

A subtle source of competitive stress comes from repeated adult praise that comments on being "perfect" or the "best" or the "smartest" or the "most beautiful." Such superlatives may have the impact of creating unreasonable pressure to be perfect or the best or the smartest or the most beautiful. Adults do not intend to create pressure for children by such comments. To the contrary, their intent is to build confidence. However, if children receive too much attention based on "being first," it takes on a value that they may feel pressured to maintain. Exaggerated praise that uses such terms as *brilliance, genius, smartest, most creative,* or *most talented* leads to pressure, but with very gifted children these words are often hard to resist. Of course, occasional overpraise will not cause serious harm, and comments from adults that address effort, improvement, perseverance, good thinking, creative problem solving, kindness, sensitivity, talent, and intelligence—and which do not emphasize "best" and "first"—will encourage motivation without pressure.

Cornell and Grossberg (1989) found that all of the 83 families of children who were involved in gifted programs thought of their children as gifted. There were no significant differences between children in either achievement or adjustment regardless of how parents defined *giftedness* or whether they thought of their children as "usually" or "sometimes" gifted. However, among the 25 percent of the children who were verbally referred to as "gifted" by their parents, there were more who were likely to experience adjustment problems that included discipline and/or poor self-control plus anxiety and guilt. The authors suggest that direct reference to the child as "gifted" places excessive pressure on the child. Perhaps telling the child he or she is "gifted" operates in precisely the same way as does extreme praise.

In some cases children who appear not to get anything done may also be feeling stress. The tension may stem more from worries about inadequacy and from work undone than by the actual hard work. Here is an example:

*Bobby, a gifted fourth-grader, complained of stomachaches which he related to worrying about the difficulty of his mathematics. He said that even while he watched TV and tried not to think about his math, he felt sick to his stomach. It was recommended that Bobby change his study habits and do his math right after school, before watching TV and worrying. The stomachaches "miraculously" disappeared and Bobby found math to be much simpler than he thought.*

Rimm's Law (Rimm, 1995d) that covers this case states:

Children feel more tension when they are worrying about their work than when they are doing that work.

If parents or teachers cannot identify the source of the stress, professional help from a guidance counselor or a school or clinical psychologist may be required. It is much easier to identify and treat a stress problem early than after it leads to habitual maladaptive coping patterns for the child.

A helpful way to understand the relationship between stress and efficient performance is illustrated by the classic *Yerkes-Dodson law* (Hebb, 1972; Figure 16.1). This principle holds that under very low stress (or motivation, or "psychological arousal") people perform inefficiently. As the stress or arousal level increases, efficiency also increases. Performance and efficiency peak at an intermediate level, which will vary for different persons and different tasks. As stress continues to increase, efficiency decreases until, at extreme tension levels, performance is disorganized.

Competitive children—and many gifted children are competitive—are more vulnerable to stress. Parents and teachers cannot deliver them from stress, but they can model and teach stress reduction measures. Involvement in many different competitive activities may help children learn to cope with competition in a more routine way. Suggesting that they concentrate on the activity itself instead of their place in the competition encourages less stress and better quality performance.

Some other simple approaches to dealing with stress include regular physical exercise, recreational and "fun" activities, and especially the availability of a safe and empathic environment in which children can talk openly about their pressures and anxieties. A caution, however, is that in providing that safe environment, parents should not counteridentify so much with the child that their own felt anxiety actually increases the anxiety level of their child.

Webb, Meckstroth, and Tolan (1982) recommend using humor to help reduce stress. For example, parents can be melodramatic about their

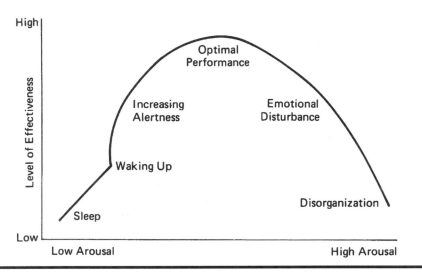

**FIGURE 16.1**  The Yerkes-Dodson Law Relating Stress (or Arousal) to Level of Effectiveness.

From D. O. Hebb, *Textbook of psychology,* 3rd ed. (1972). Copyright © 1972 by Saunders College Publishing, a division of Holt, Rinehart and Winston, reprinted by permission of the publisher.

own "intolerable" stresses and problems—making it clear that they are laughing at themselves. Internationally renowned violinist Pamela Frank was eight years old and performing a concert for none other than her own parents and grandparents. She recalls making a mistake and running off to her bedroom to pout in disappointment at her performance. Her father followed her, not to sympathize with her perceived disaster, but to humor her in her crisis and explained, "Who do you think you are, Itzak Perlman [who can't make a mistake]?" Pamela recalls her parents reminding her often that the "most important thing in life is a sense of humor." She considers her family's sense of humor a gift that always gave her perspective on her life (Rimm & Rimm-Kaufman, 2001).

Parents can also encourage the child to "think out loud" about stress by gently raising questions such as, "What is the worst thing that could happen in that situation?" and "How big a catastrophe would that be?"

In sum, parents and teachers can best help children deal with stress from competition by (1) identifying the source of the stress and then helping the student redefine priorities to reduce the stress, (2) recognizing that a moderate and manageable amount of stress is necessary for peak performance, (3) helping provide outlets or "therapy" in the form of physical and other enjoyable activities, and (4) lending an understanding, empathic, and perhaps humorous ear. These techniques can be very useful in preventing deterioration of performance due to high stress.

***Noncompetitive Intellectual Activities.***  Gifted high achievers and gifted underachievers both may be highly competitive and competition conscious. In the case of the high achievers, such competitiveness is functional. For underachievers it is dysfunctional, since they may perceive themselves as "losers" in the school game and withdraw from activities they perceive as competitive.

For both groups, however, involvement in intellectual activities that are noncompetitive can be extremely valuable. Some examples of noncompetitive intellectual activities might include individualized self-paced instruction (for example, with the computer, at learning centers, or with language-learning cassettes), after-school clubs or interest groups, home hobbies or interests such as computers or reading, small-group field trips, independent research projects, or creative arts, drama, or writing. For the highly competitive achiever, such activities broaden knowledge and interests, encourage the reflective pause necessary for creativity, and provide a comfortable respite from more highly competitive efforts. For underachievers, noncompetitive intellectual activities entice them into playing the learning/thinking game without fear of failure. To experience the joy of intellectual discovery is a critical goal for all gifted children, and noncompetitive intellectual activities are good routes to this goal.

### Sibling Pressures

Sibling rivalry seems inherent in Western civilization. It can be minimized and adjusted for, but it will not disappear. The underlying cause of sibling rivalry is competition for parents' attention and, sometimes, resources. With gifted children, particular sibling combinations seem to cause special complications and therefore require special handling by parents and teachers. Several of these will be described shortly.

First, however, it is important to recognize a vital underlying principal for the care and handling of all children: *Each and every child in a family should be provided the most ideal opportunity for intellectual and creative development for that particular child.* Opportunities for gifted children should not be avoided or ignored simply because less able and less interested siblings cannot participate in the same activity. Other children can be offered comparably attractive—but not necessarily identical—educational or recreational opportunities. For example, if one child strongly wishes to attend a Russian language camp or a Saturday computer class, then an alternative in music, art, swimming, or tennis could be offered to a sibling who might feel cheated. Children

have different abilities and different needs, and the most productive and most fair approach is to accommodate those differences. Treating siblings the same actually exacerbates competition as children vie for recognition of their own individuality.

A subtle source of sibling rivalry may stem from preferential treatment of one child over the other from significant others, for example, grandparents, aunts, uncles, or neighbors. Certainly, parents should ask those adults to be cautious and fair to all siblings. Sometimes this does not work and parents must take the responsibility of monitoring fair treatment. Grandparents and important adults may continue to provide individual children with special opportunities based on age or particular interests and abilities, but not based on a favored child relationship.

### The Gifted Child with Less Talented Siblings

The gifted child with very high intelligence or an extraordinary special talent provides impossible competition in his or her area of giftedness for other children. The unique ability often requires the investment of an inordinate amount of time and resources to provide the special educational opportunities necessary to develop the talent and meet this child's unconventional needs. In the process, the gifted child naturally receives a large amount of attention and recognition. His or her brothers and sisters need to be able to admire the gifted sibling's success but also recognize that a similar level of success probably is not attainable for them. They must use a different measuring stick to evaluate their own abilities, or they may fall into the trap of viewing their own real successes (and themselves) as failures. In the words of one successful and gifted "second sibling":

> Once I realized that there was nothing I could do to achieve as well as my sister, I decided to stop competing with her, to do the best I could, and to realize that what I was doing was really good too.

Although this youngster came to realize that he could be successful despite his being a "second place" student, that realization was not automatic. In addition to rewarding the victories of their most gifted child, parents also must recognize and reward the successes of other siblings—basing those rewards on each child's abilities and efforts.

Research on families in which one child is identified as gifted and others are not confirms that problems arise for the nonlabeled child. In one study, parents reported a negative and disruptive effect on the nongifted siblings, which disturbed the status quo of the family (Fisher, 1981). Cornell (1983) also found "nongifted" siblings of gifted children to be less well adjusted than a control group of other nongifted children. In a study by Cornell and Grossberg (1986), children who had been rated as "less gifted" than their siblings had higher anxiety and lower self-esteem than their sisters and brothers in gifted programs. Grenier (1985) also reported higher self-esteem for children labeled "gifted" compared with their siblings. Furthermore, there was increased friction when the age difference between siblings was less than three years. Pfouts (1980) similarly found that the closer the age spacing the more the siblings were affected negatively in family relationships and personal adjustment, and also that younger siblings were affected negatively in academic performance. Strangely, Ballering and Koch (1984) found that the gifted children perceived the sibling relationships as more negative than did their nongifted brothers and sisters.

Although all the above studies included gifted children and their nonlabeled siblings, the Pfouts (1980) study was based on siblings at all intelligence levels—suggesting that the results of gifted/nongifted comparing may be less related to the labeling than to sibling rivalry in general. Furthermore, Colangelo and Brower (1987a) concluded that there were no long-term effects (five years or more) from the differential labeling within the family, and that nongifted siblings eventually "came to terms" with the gifted label of their siblings.

A study by Chamrad, Robinson, and Janos (1995) referred to negative sibling relationships as a "myth" when one or more children in a family were gifted. They examined the sibling relationships of 366 triads that included mothers and children ages 7 to 14 in two-child families in which at least one child was gifted. They used a questionnaire and targeted school achievement, mental ability, adjustment, and sibling relationships. Contrary to the previous studies already mentioned, they found giftedness to be associated with more positive responses by mothers and siblings. The authors suggested that their unusual findings might be attributed to using a questionnaire rather than an interview, inferring that in an interview families might be more likely to complain about problems in light of having a sympathetic listener.

An analysis of the success of siblings of the successful women in the Rimm report (Rimm et al., 1999) suggested a differential effect on girl siblings compared to boy siblings. For example, in two-child families when the sibling of the successful women was a brother, 87 percent of the brothers had earned college degrees and had successful professional careers. When the sibling was a sister, 76 percent of the sisters had earned college degrees, but only 43 percent were using their degrees in professions outside the home. In many families, if one sister identified herself as a professional, the other saw herself as a homemaker. In interviews with the successful women, the women often described that difference from childhood. Here's an example:

Dr. Anne Caroles (a pseudonym) was referred to as the "brain" in her family. Her sister was called the "beauty." As a teenager, Anne viewed herself as "ugly" and believed she would never be attractive to anyone. Her studies became a hiding place for her. Now she looks back at her pictures and realizes she was quite normal looking. Although at the time Anne felt stigmatized by the label, she believes now that her label gave her an advantage. She was inspired to go on with her education, while her beautiful sister discontinued her education to marry after high school although she, too, had high intelligence.

As a psychologist who specializes in working with gifted children, this author (Rimm) finds continuous impact of giftedness on siblings. It is often difficult to ferret out the impact because children may prefer not to admit that they resent their siblings. They know they are supposed to get along well. Here are three case studies:

### Case 1

*Maria, a seven-year-old first grader, seemed happy in school but complained to her parents that she didn't like reading and was bored at school. She was in the highest reading group in her class and apparently was sufficiently challenged. Her IQ test scores were in the 130s, and her achievement test scores suggested she had been appropriately placed in the high reading group. Yet she maintained that she was not happy at school.*

*One sister, Beth, had been grade skipped the year before, had read spontaneously before entering school, and had an IQ test score in the 190s. When asked how she felt about her sister's grade skip, Maria, in a burst of emotion, confessed she "hated it" and it made her "feel dumb." The intense sibling rivalry she expressed is unlikely to have been apparent in any questionnaire. Her parents were shocked to realize the impact of Beth's giftedness and grade skip on her younger sister's confidence. With only a little assistance, Maria adjusted to and enjoyed school.*

*Maria's parents were encouraged to be sensitive to the sibling rivalry that was very intense between all the sisters in the family but particularly between the extremely gifted child and her less gifted sister. Beth, incidentally, did not express feelings of rivalry, but her efforts to keep her sister "in her place" were subtly, and sometimes not so subtly, apparent.*

### Case 2

*Roger, age 14, was the younger of two brothers. His older brother was adopted, and Roger was the "surprise" natural child that his parents believed they would never have. Both boys had IQ scores in the very superior range. Both were talented in music and sports. Roger, however, was an underachiever in all his talent areas. His words reflected the extreme sibling rivalry he felt: "How would you feel," he asked, "if everything you did your brother did better?" (Rimm, 1990b)*

### Case 3

*Sonya was a high-achieving talented junior in high school. She carried an all-A average except for a B in Honors Math, which she vowed to the psychologist to improve. Her brother, Alex, also intellectually talented, underachieved since fourth grade and had failing grades the first quarter of the seventh grade. Sonya helped him during the second quarter and his grades improved.*

*Sonya wanted to help her brother further and appealed to the psychologist, who was hoping to build Alex's independence but who also was aware that the sibling relationship could be maintaining Alex's underachievement. Sonya—bright, sophisticated, and open—had difficulty understanding that she could do any harm to Alex. When asked how she would feel if Alex suddenly reversed his underachievement and excelled in math, finding it to be so easy that he surpassed her math achievement, Sonya's instant response was, "That would be horrible!" She immediately grasped the competitive issue. Sonya did not appear to be competitive, but that would only hold true as long as she held her competitive edge.*

Of course, these three examples are only case studies, not research. However, they are a few samples of dozens or perhaps hundreds of sibling rivalry situations in which gifted students, whether achieving or underachieving, act out the sibling rivalry they feel. Many do not express these feelings openly, and only a minority of parents are aware of how competitive their children are with each other. Whether there is more sibling rivalry among families with gifted children than families with children of average intellect cannot be verified by case histories, but the existence of significant rivalry is clear. It is not a myth.

### The Gifted Child in a Family of Other Achieving Gifted Children

It is not unusual to find that all children in a family are gifted; this could be due to genetics, a favorable environment, positive parent and teacher expectations, or most likely all of the above. It is important to recognize that each child in the family will feel increased pressure to fulfill the expectations set by preceding siblings. The first day of school for "child two," "child three," or "child four" inevitably begins with, "Oh yes, I know your sister. She was such a good student!" If the child is gifted and confident, this identification may be pleasing because he or she recognizes that the teacher has expectations that can be fulfilled. Moreover, this early recognition may quickly produce privileges and trust that otherwise would take longer to earn.

On the other hand, a less confident child may see the early identification by the teacher as a threat, since the child may worry that his or her performance will be less impressive than that of the older sibling. A sensitive teacher will quickly learn to recognize differences between siblings. Nonetheless, parents still may need to explain, "Mrs. Jones had Carlos too, but she'll soon get to know that you're also a good worker, even though you're different than your brother."

Perhaps most important, parents of several gifted children may need to make a specific effort to ease the grade pressure for younger children. Parents should let them know that the parents understand the special pressures the children feel due to the inevitable comparisons with their siblings. The parent's "expectation message" should be that each child is expected to do the very best he or she can and that the child's performance will be individually evaluated, not compared with the record of the older brother or sister.

Regardless of differences in sibling ability, it usually is better to acknowledge achievements and to reward them, relative, as we noted before, to each child's capabilities. Democratically pretending that differences do not exist, withholding important opportunities from the gifted child, or else accepting less than the best efforts from less capable children are common but unproductive responses of parents of gifted children.

Generally, helping parents to deal with their children's competitive feelings is a difficult problem. However, the patterns described in this section are common and recurrent ones, and the recommended solutions have proven effective again and again. The teacher should be aware of

the patterns, set to recognize them, and prepared to make good recommendations to parents.

Suggestions teachers can make for raising a "whole smart family" are in Inset 16.2.

### Gender Issues

Parents should be sensitized to the gender issues and stereotypes that may prevent their gifted children from fulfilling their potential. Although Chapter 14 of this book is devoted to issues for gifted girls, and some issues for boys (e.g., underachievement, disabilities) have been discussed in other chapters, gender issues of concern to parents will be summarized here. Teachers can encourage and sensitize parents to problems that may relate to their children being either male or female.

### Raising Gifted Girls

From the time girls enter school, they are immediately presented with education-oriented role models in the form of primary teachers. Successful women often idolized their teachers early and were thus inspired to learn in school (Rimm et al., 1999). Motivation to learn often resulted in the women being excellent students; however, there are also some long-term achievement problems related to being "good little girls." Overcompliance, fear of being assertive, and fear of failure may cause "good little girls" to set their life goals below their abilities. Parents need to encourage girls' excellent performance, but also encourage them to accept challenges and think creatively. Girls also need to learn to cope with competition and to understand that they can continue to contribute even when they are not the best in their class or interest area.

Girls' underachievement often comes later in life or in adulthood when they fear becoming involved in enterprises where they can't be assured of success. For example, Charlotte Otto, vice president at Procter & Gamble, struggled for years with self-blame until she learned the risk-taking style and self-affirmation she needed for

INSET **16.2** _____

## What Parents Can Do to Create a Whole Smart Family

*Avoid Labeling.* Although it's obvious that all children in the family are not exactly alike and that some children may be different in intellectual, artistic, musical, or physical abilities, it is also obvious that family competition encourages each child to seek special attention that is different from that of the other children. When parents emphasize their children's differences, it seems to label them and limit their confidence in almost all other areas.

*Prioritize Education as First.* It's important for parents to consider all their children intelligent even if one seems a bit more intelligent than the others. When parents of the successful women in the Rimm study (Rimm et al., 1999) expected *all* their children to be smart and value challenge, the children were actually less competitive with each other.

*Consider Both Parents Intelligent.* When the parents of the successful women considered each other to be intelligent, their children had high regard for both. Even when their mothers were full-time homemakers, they were valued by the entire family as intelligent. Regardless of which parent the women identified with, they automatically considered themselves smart.

An example of raising a whole smart family:

Dr. Teresa Culver's (Rimm & Rimm-Kaufman, 2001) family provides an excellent prototype of how parents can raise a whole smart family. Although there were five children in the family, all went to college and all have careers. Teresa's parents considered all the kids to be smart, including Teresa's brother, who had a learning disability. Being smart and hardworking were emphasized. The children varied in their musical and athletic skills and activities, but all participated. The whole family was included whether they were going to a concert or a basketball game. Music, science, camping, and sports were part of growing up in their enriched family environment. It was assumed that all would continue their education beyond high school, and indeed, they all did.

Adapted from S. Rimm, *What Happens to Jack and Susan: How to Raise a Whole Smart Family,* 2000. Retrieved from World Wide Web: http://www.seejanewin.com/interesting.html.

her successful career (Rimm & Rimm-Kaufman, 2001).

The "girl-poisoning" culture, which emphasizes appearance and thinness, described by Mary Pipher (1995) in *Reviving Ophelia* also needs to be addressed by parents. Fathers who continually talk about their daughters' beauty will find that value backfire when the girls gain a few pounds during adolescence or don't look quite as attractive as they did at age four or eight. Their daughters will fear they are not beautiful enough to measure up to their fathers' expectations. Mothers who are themselves very beautiful or fashion conscious may also have difficulty understanding why their gifted daughters are distracted from learning by the need to be excruciatingly thin and fashionable. If parents make it clear to girls from the start that they are more than their appearance and put appearance in appropriate perspective, they may be able to help them counter the media and peer pressure they feel during adolescence. Recent research by Girl Scouts of the U.S.A. (2000) suggests these sexual and appearance pressures are being felt by girls earlier than ever, and that they are indeed behaving like "teens before their times."

Involvement in activities that help girls to establish their personal identities is important during early adolescence and the teen years (Rimm et al., 1999). Encouraging girls to think ahead to career plans also discourages their getting distracted into early parenthood before they have developed their own identities. Many of the obstacles faced by females occur during their early adulthood. Parents who are good role models for how careers and families can be balanced are automatically teaching girls to form their own identities. For example, said NBC television correspondent Soledad O'Brien (2001):

> When my daughter was born last October, I never felt like I had to choose between child and career. I knew I could do both; I'd watched my own mother raise six kids while working full-time as a high school French and Spanish teacher.
>
> Mom wasn't Superwoman, she just knew how to prioritize. Family came first, but it was important to her to have a life outside that. Her job wasn't just a paycheck, but a source of self-esteem and accomplishment. I've always used Mom as a guide when making decisions in my life. She told me to love both my job and my child and not to feel guilty about it; she never did. Now, I hope my daughter will see me the same way I see my mother: as someone who's successful and happy at work and at home. (p. 43)

### Raising Gifted Boys

Although women certainly seem to have disadvantages in lifetime careers, men seem to have their share of disadvantages in childhood. Durden-Smith and DeSimone (1982) itemized some apparently biological differences between the sexes that, on balance, make females look noticeably superior physically, psychologically, and socially. Consider these differences:

Girls are stronger in verbal and communication abilities.

There are more boys at both ends of the intellectual spectrum—retardates and geniuses.

Girls develop faster.

More boys have major birth defects and are born less sturdy.

Boys are four or five times more likely to be autistic (being mute or having bizarre speech) or aphasic (unable to produce or comprehend speech; aphasia also includes emotional and thinking disorders).

Boys are much more likely to be unable to read (dyslexia), unable to do arithmetic (dyscalculia), or to have other learning disabilities.

Boys are five times more likely to stutter.

Some traditional observations might also be mentioned: Boys are more likely to be hyperactive, disruptive, and aggressive in class. Girls have better handwriting.

Important issues for boys need to be brought to the attention of parents early, for example, that of male role models in education. There are very few male teachers in most elementary schools, and boys may easily see school as a female enterprise if fathers and other males don't make it clear to boys how important they believe education to be. Yet fathers often opt out of the getting-ready-for-school routine.

Furthermore, boys often have handwriting problems. Perhaps some of these could be prevented. If parents of preschool boys encourage them to color, write, cut, and paste, they might not find those pencil tasks so difficult.

With so many boys being diagnosed with attention deficit disorder, teaching boys concentration skills is a priority. Reading to boys and encouraging them to work on puzzles and listen to CDs and tapes—instead of watching television—also might improve their concentration and early success in school.

Sibling issues for boys seem also to be more competitive, with one child establishing himself as the achiever and the other the underachiever

(Rimm, 1995d). Being sensitive to that possibility and helping boys through their competitive feelings with their "perfect" sister or older brother could prevent the problem.

The issue of manliness or machismo is an important issue for gifted boys. Boys who are not athletic or are very sensitive are often shamed and alienated by other boys, and sometimes not even accepted by their own fathers because they are not masculine enough (Pollock, 1998). Although it's healthy for all children to be physically fit and sports should be encouraged for both genders, parents need to make it clear that being "manly" includes sensitive expression of one's feelings through verbal, written, or artistic modalities. Too many gifted boys have been taunted and teased for their sensitivity instead of being supported in its valuable expression.

Finally the issue of violence must be dealt with, especially since gifted boys have, indeed, been involved in some of the recent episodes of violence in schools. Although isolation and being taunted should never be an excuse for violence, problems of exclusion need to be dealt with so that they never lead to violence. The social and emotional needs of gifted children who feel isolated need to be addressed by counseling staffs within the schools, and not only by referrals outside of school, with which parents may never follow through.

## Peer Pressure

During early childhood, virtually all children are motivated by a desire to please parents and teachers and to be "good" children. Kohlberg (1974, 1976; Kuhmerker, 1991), in fact, titled this period the "good boy, good girl" stage in children's moral development. During these years, there is little peer pressure to distract the child from parental and school goals. Beginning usually in the preadolescent period, grades 4 or 5, however, the normal tendency to conform to peer norms and expectancies begins to exert its influence. Peer pressures become strongest and most influ-

ential in the adolescent years. This is a time when gifted adolescents often describe feelings of being different from their peers (Rimm et al. 1999; Swiatek & Dorr, 1998).

Adolescence marks the beginning of a crucial development phenomenon, the formation of a perhaps permanent *identity*—a personal knowledge of who and what one is and where one is going in life (Erikson, 1968). The youth, who is changing rapidly both physically and mentally, may have a difficult time during this "identity crisis" period. It is the structured standards of adolescent peers that often provide the needed direction, support, and strength. Close family relationships and good parent models will help to diffuse some of the ambiguity, but the necessary chore of establishing an identity separate from the family reduces parental influence during this period—and strengthens peer influence.

While positive relationships with parents typically are not harmful to peer relationships (Montemayer, 1984), reliance on peers for advice and acceptance can be negatively associated with closeness to parents (Kandel & Lesser, 1972). Continuous bickering with parents seems to propel adolescents to more dependence on and acceptance of peer norms, with rejection of parent norms (e.g., Hill, 1980). The gifted child who previously had taken pride in earning high grades now faces a difficult personal contradiction. The greatest tragedy occurs when the gifted young person mentally drops out of school, accepting literally the peer mandate that "studying is not cool." Maintaining a positive family environment helps gifted children deal with the anti-gifted peer pressure they may feel during adolescence. A case study:

*Jon came to the psychological clinic of his own volition. He felt desperately in need of help. As a junior in a highly academic high school, he had little confidence that he could do anything about his problem. Although Jon's IQ score was 147, his grades were mainly Cs with the exception of one D. He was no longer in accelerated courses. He wanted to go to the University of Wisconsin-Madison but no longer ranked in the top third of his class, an absolute requirement for entrance. He had been a straight A student until sixth grade. When he entered junior high school he decided that he no longer wanted to be known as a "nerd." He looked at his older brothers who were underachievers and decided that they were much more "casual." His two sisters were excellent students, but they were known as nerds. He embarked on his new "casual" approach to school. His grades went down to Bs at first, and then to Cs. He never failed a course and was not worried until he heard about the new college entrance requirements. He then felt it might be too late to again open opportunities for the college of his choice.*

Uncomfortable peer pressures will be reduced for scholarly adolescent boys if they can dissipate their brainy image with excellence in sports and for girls if they have the good fortune to be pretty (Coleman, 1961). Recent surveys of high school students (Schroeder-Davis, 1998, 1999) showed that 66 percent of high school students felt that high school athletes received more recognition than student scholars.

Another important qualification for peer acceptance is skill in playing down one's academic ability and excellence, for example, by not using a sophisticated vocabulary, not showing high enthusiasm for high achievement, not carrying too many books at one time, and not mentioning one's large quantity of reading and studying or one's enjoyment of intellectual matters. A gifted student may continue to achieve, however.

Most gifted students agree that continued achievement exacts a social price (Rimm et al., 1999; Rimm, 2001b). When over 3500 Minnesota secondary students were asked in a survey conducted by Schroeder-Davis (1999; see also Gross, 2001) if they would rather be best looking, most athletic, or smartest in their class, over half (53.8 percent) indicated "most intelligent," 37.3 percent, "most athletic," and 8.9 percent, "best looking." While on first examination the results seem to favor giftedness, further review of these students' essays revealed an anti-intellectual stigma that they perceived was expressed by their peers,

and almost none described any social benefit to being intelligent.

Swiatek and Dorr (1998) investigated the social coping strategies used by gifted adolescents and found five main approaches. They were (1) denial of giftedness (saying their ability isn't really that good), (2) emphasis on popularity (the extent to which they emphasize popularity), (3) peer acceptance (their perceived impact of giftedness on social integration), (4) social interaction (the extent to which students get involved in extracurricular activities), and (5) downplaying giftedness (not telling people test grades, etc.). They found that girls were more likely than boys to deny their abilities and report high levels of socialization.

The successful women in the Rimm report (Rimm et al., 1999) also seemed to become extremely involved in extracurricular activities to cope with their feelings of difference. The specific activities of their involvement were often predictive of skills they used in later careers; for example, attorneys were often involved in debate, and women in media were writers or in drama.

A survey conducted by Brown and Steinberg (1990) of 8000 high school students in California and Wisconsin found that less than 10 percent of the high achievers were willing to be identified as part of the "brain" crowd, and students often withdrew from debate, computer clubs, and honors classes to avoid being labeled a "geek" or "nerd." The percentage was lower for females than for males, higher for Asian American (14 percent), and lower for African American students. *None* of the high-achieving African Americans were willing to be considered part of the brain crowd. Luftig and Nichols (1989) also found evidence that gifted boys hide or mask their giftedness, for example, by being funny. In contrast, Luftig and Nichols (1990) found that gifted boys ranked as most popular, nongifted boys and nongifted girls as second most popular, and finally, gifted girls as least popular of the four groups. Rachel Seligman (1990) described peer pressure she experienced at the beginning of the ninth grade:

*The most foolish thing I have done this year is to compromise my intelligence. You may ask why, and the answer is simple: Love. I was dating a sophomore who has also been identified as gifted. At the beginning of the relationship I let him do all the talking. It finally got to the point where I would say nothing even though I knew I was right or I knew I was comprehending something a lot better than he was. He grew so accustomed to my saying inane things that I continued to act silly around him. Once in a while I would pop out with something intelligent, but he'd just look at me as if I were crazy. Isn't it awful what love can do to a person?*

Overall, these studies show peer pressures on gifted students to which parents should be alerted. Brown and Steinberg (1990) ask a critical question: "Are we supporting a peer system that trains students to harbor diminished aspirations so that, as adults, gifted individuals continue to underachieve in order to be socially acceptable?"

Many studies that have compared peer pressures of moderately gifted students to students with extremely high IQs have concluded that popularity is a much greater problem for students with unusually high intelligence (e.g., Feldman, 1986; Gallagher, 1958; Hollingworth, 1942). Gross (1993a, 1993b) found continuing ongoing stress for a group of students with IQs over 160. Eighty percent reported experiencing intense social isolation and continuous monitoring of their social behavior for peer acceptance.

As we have mentioned several times, probably the best way to stimulate gifted and talented students, particularly adolescents, is to help assemble a gifted cohort group. Such a group will encourage high achievement and reinforce the full use of one's talents. For example, youth symphony orchestras, high-level Saturday and summer programs, special classes, and gifted-peer discussion groups help young people to value their talent and build constructive self-concepts and identities.

It also is important for parents to value and support their children's talent during this precarious period in their development and not to add to the pressures the child already is feeling, for example, by sending messages stressing high popularity and

social success. Parents may have to counter peer messages of popularity by pointing out that the emphasis on popularity, as a competitive form of friendship, ends at high school graduation (Rimm, 1988b). They will need to point out, subtly if possible, that students who are conscientious about their studies will carry away the best scholarships and will be accepted to first-rate colleges, and that once college begins the stress on popularity is viewed as irrelevant and immature.

Finally, consider two thoughts pertaining to peer pressures and the stresses of adolescence: First, if the gifted child has been accelerated, there is a tendency to blame difficulties of the adolescent period on the acceleration practice—"Well, skipping sixth grade just didn't work!" Maybe the acceleration was working fine, and the child might have been worse off without it. Second, if a gifted child is not achieving up to capacity—due entirely to an unchallenging curriculum—it is not unusual to blame anti-academic peer pressures rather than educational deficiencies. Tips for guiding gifted children through peer pressure are discussed in the Gifted Modules of the *Parenting for Achievement* course (Rimm, 1994a).

## PRESCHOOL CHILDREN

Parents of very young gifted children frequently ask teachers how they can best help their children before they enter school. It is an important matter, because research clearly demonstrates the strong impact of early environment on language and cognitive development.

For example, White, Kaban, and Attanucci (1979) found in their Harvard Preschool Project that "live language" directed at the child during his or her first three years was the single most critical factor in the child's later competence in cognitive, linguistic, and social areas. Morrow (1983) compared the home environments of 58 kindergarten children showing high interest in reading with the homes of 58 children showing low interest. The high-interest children came from homes with supportive literary environments. That is, the family used the public library, parents did a great deal of reading, and parents read to children frequently; there were more books in the home and, specifically, in the children's bedroom. In a study of the parenting differences between a gifted and nongifted group of middle-class children (Karnes, Shwedel, & Lewis, 1984), the clearest difference was in the amount of time spent reading and engaging in academically related activities with the child.

The evidence provides a clear directive to parents regarding the need for early concentrated involvement with their child for the full development of both the child's language and nonlinguistic abilities.

Language experience is probably the most critical kind of involvement. Talking to children, reading and telling stories, rhyming and imitation, word games, children's records, and even simply listening to children all increase the children's opportunities to learn communication and attention skills. Being read to at home continues to be the best indicator of advanced reading ability in the preschool years (Teale, 1984). Puzzles, blocks, and construction toys help them develop small-muscle coordination, spatial abilities, and concentration skill. Large toys (tricycles, wagons, riding horses) help the development of large-muscle coordination. Many games help children learn to follow directions and cooperate. Questioning, curiosity, and independence should also be encouraged.

Moss (1983) compared the teaching strategies of 14 mothers with gifted preschoolers against those of 14 mothers with nongifted children of the same age. The first group of mothers tended to structure problems and then permit their children to derive their own solutions, learning to relate parts of the task to the goal. In the second group, mothers were more directive and actually tended to provide solutions to their children rather than permitting them to arrive at their own solutions. It seems important for gifted children to gain early experience in independent thinking and problem solving.

A quantitative and qualitative analysis of the parenting behaviors of 46 gifted preschoolers in nine states (Snowden & Christian, 1999) focused on important strategies of parents of gifted children. All but one of the families in the study included two working parents. Parents were dedicated to their children's learning and were authoritative in their parenting approaches. A quantitative analyses of the Parent as a Teacher Inventory (PAAT; Strom, 1984) showed that parents "fostered creativity, showed low levels of frustration, exerted an appropriate amount of flexible control, viewed play as a highly valuable activity, showed confidence in their abilities as teachers, and acted as facilitators of the teaching/learning process" (p. 215).

Unfortunately, this study had no control group. In a second study comparing parents of precocious and nonprecocious gifted preschoolers using the same PAAT (Snowden & Conway, 1996), there were no significant differences between the two sets of parents. This study also had some serious limitations. All families lived in a university community and were described as upper middle class and likely to be raising successful children. The mothers of these children were all stay-at-home mothers, and scores on the PAAT were above average for all dimensions. It seems that both studies found parents who were being good parents as teachers, but neither reveals the true extent to which good parenting contributes to giftedness.

The following are a few more preschool precautions, some do's and don't's in helping gifted children. First, television watching, which is basically a passive-receptive activity, should be monitored and limited (Jensen, 1995). Healy (1990) found the effect to be "neurologically addictive" and it may actually change the brain's electrical impulses. Furthermore, she indicates that "zombie" TV watching may impair listening, problem solving, and sustaining attention. This observation seems particularly important in a time when many gifted children are being identified with attention deficit disorders.

A Carnegie report (Carnegie Council on Adolescent Development, 1995) stated that adolescents watch television for an average of 22 hours per week and by age 18 have spent less time in the classroom than they have spent watching television. Television, the report asserts, may be more influential than peers. Abelman (1992a) emphasized that this can be either good news or bad news for gifted kids. The bad news is that the average child will watch, on television, about 1000 murders, rapes, or aggravated assaults during a one-year period (Carnegie Council on Adolescent Development, 1995). Bushman and Anderson (2001) argued that the magnitude of violence on TV is as toxic a relationship to violence in our society as cigarette smoking is to lung cancer, yet scientists have not successfully been able to argue their case. The good news is that in studies of gifted children of all ages, they are often attracted to programming that is more complex and intellectually stimulating and tend to be bored by more standardized program formats. A second piece of bad news for gifted youth is that they are rarely represented on TV. When they are, they are typically viewed as social misfits (Abelman, 1992b, 1986).

During the preschool years, gifted children watch significantly more television than other children. They also seem to be more actively involved while watching television (Ableman & Rogers, 1987). If the quality of children's television is good, it may contribute to their knowledge base that enhances their giftedness. It may also help to fulfill their thirst for learning.

In the Morrow (1983) study mentioned earlier, the high-interest kindergarten readers came from homes in which there were rules regarding television and in which mothers watched less television than mothers in the homes of low-interest readers. Educational programs should obviously be included within the limited watching.

Abelman (1987, 1991) found that parents rarely mediated the television watching of gifted children, but when mediation did occur, it was highly focused and purposeful. It seems wise not only for parents to mediate their children's TV watching but to become vocal to the networks about the importance of quality TV for their children. In 1990, the Children's Television Act was passed to emphasize service to children as part of broadcasters' obligations to the public.

Second, overstimulation, for example, from too many peers or too much adult talk, can confuse children and detract from active involvement, concentration, and learning. While parent communication to the child is desirable, continuous talk and long abstract lectures are virtually meaningless, certainly boring, and exceed children's limited attention span. For some children, endless chatter will cause them to become restless and "hyperactive"; they know they should pay attention, but they cannot. For other children, overwhelming talking by a parent has the opposite effect, preventing the child's contributions and encouraging him or her to slow down and become very quiet. They give up trying to communicate with this parent.

Third, if your child is reading spontaneously, teach the child some basic writing skills. A simple workbook purchased from a local department store can be used for teaching the child to copy printing. Exercising that fine motor coordination will help a gifted child feel more evenly skilled in the classroom. Teachers often suggest leaving writing until school, but this unevenness in abilities often causes children anxiety related to their writing skills. Be sure not to pressure the child. Five minutes a day will provide sufficient practice and will help the child feel more comfortable with pencils. This advice was followed by the mother of a gifted kindergartner. The subtest score that measured writing skills increased dramatically from below average to a score well above average in four months of brief daily practices (Rimm, 1996a).

Fourth, some daily "alone time" for a preschool child also is helpful. Interaction with peers and siblings is important to preschoolers, but some small amount of time each day for a child to play alone will encourage independent behavior and imagination. Creative persons of all ages seem to thrive on some amount of time alone.

Fifth, parents of the gifted require flexibility and tolerance of ambiguity. Orth (1988) found that parents who displayed flexible characteristics related to their child's questions, expressions of fear and anxieties, needs for attention, play behavior, getting dirty at play, and making noise had preschool children who scored higher on the Torrance (1982) creativity test for preschoolers, *Thinking Creatively in Action and Movement.*

These precautions can help children be active participants in their environments, to take initiative very early, and to think more creatively.

**Early Identification and Testing**

There is good evidence that parents can recognize their children's giftedness quite early. Table 16.1 (Gogul, McCumsey, & Hewett, 1985) summarizes the identification results of a national survey of 1039 parents of gifted children. Note that 70 percent of these children were identified accurately by parents by age three, most of those between ages one and three. Of the characteristics that caused parents to suspect giftedness, "early verbal expressions" was mentioned most frequently. Other observed characteristics included an unusually long attention span, a good memory, high level of curiosity, and an early demonstration of original and creative behavior.

The reliability of parents' recognition of preschool giftedness was also supported by a program at Towson State University in Baltimore, Maryland (Hanson, 1984). Parents were encouraged to enroll their children in a program for four-, five-, and six-year-old gifted children based on their own perceptions of the children's verbal

**TABLE 16.1** Percentage of Children Identified as Gifted at Various Ages by Parents

| Percentage | Age |
|---|---|
| 7 | 0–6 months |
| 15 | 6–12 months |
| 23 | 1–2 years |
| 25 | 2–3 years |
| 17 | 4–5 years |
| 13 | Later |
| 100 | |

From Gogul, McCumsey, & Hewett, 1985, reprinted by permission of the first author and *Gifted Child Today* magazine.

giftedness. After enrollment these children were given a battery of tests. Ninety percent of the children tested at least one year above grade level in reading and all of the five- and six-year-olds had high scores on the Fund of Knowledge subtests. Mathematics scores were not as consistently high, but parents had not been asked to consider math skill in their decision making. Louis and Lewis (1992) also found that parents' beliefs about their preschool children's giftedness squared well with the children's actual abilities.

Eighteen preschool children between the ages of 2 and 5 years, 11 months were brought to the author's (Rimm) Family Achievement Clinic for evaluation following a local newspaper article about Mensa's youngest member ever admitted, a child age 2 years, 4 months with an IQ score of 175 on the Stanford-Binet LM. Of the eighteen children brought to the clinic, three of the two-year-olds were found to be too young to test. The remaining children were evaluated with the WPPSI, Stanford-Binet LM, or the Stanford-Binet IV. IQ scores varied between 120 and 175, and PRIDE creativity scores were between the 47th percentile and 99th percentile. All children tested at least within the superior range of ability, and two-thirds of those tested scored 130 or above (Rimm, 1999).

Although we have no way of knowing the percentage of children who are missed by a parent identification procedure, the evidence suggests that parents do not overidentify to the extent that teachers often believe. Some studies indicate that parents usually underestimate rather than overestimate their children's giftedness (e.g., Chitwood, 1986).

In Inset 16.3 Silverman and Kearney (1989) summarize some of the impact and challenges that accompany the evaluation and identification of highly gifted children. Many parental and family adjustments clearly will be in order.

If parents believe their preschool children are gifted, they should ask to have them evaluated. Tests of preschool children are appropriate with the caution that such early tests are somewhat unreliable. Scores can be adversely affected by many

**INSET 16.3** _____

## Impact of Extraordinarily Gifted Children on Parents

The discovery of one or more exceptionally gifted children in a family brings with it some extraordinary challenges. Some of these challenges are unique to families of highly gifted children, and some are intensified issues that all families of the gifted face. Among these issues are:

- Gaining an accurate assessment of the child's abilities
- Coming to terms with the results of testing
- Determining appropriate educational provisions for their children
- Handling financial stress—even in upper-middle class families
- Dealing with society's lack of understanding of and responsiveness toward this group
- Coping with the heightened sensitivity, intensity, and perfectionism of these children
- Facing the possibility of an early empty nest because of the extreme acceleration of the children
- Discovering and coming to terms with one's own giftedness
- Developing one's own aspirations versus devoting oneself to nurturing the children's development

---

From Silverman and Kearney (1989). Reprinted by permission of the first author and *Advanced Development Journal*.

factors, including fatigue, stress, and diet (Perino & Perino, 1981). The scores should not be taken as an absolute measure of the child's ability and certainly not viewed as a limit to that ability. Tests of young children are likely to be conservative estimates of their ability since "test construction makes it virtually impossible to score at a level higher than his or her potential" (Chitwood, 1986).

A survey by Sankar-DeLeeuw (1999) of 91 parents who belonged to a gifted association in Edmonton, Alberta, and 44 preschool teachers found that only 74 percent of the parents and 50 percent of the teachers believed that preschool children should be assessed during those early years.

There are good reasons for early assessment (Rimm, 2001a):

- Children who are intellectually gifted may benefit from early entrance to kindergarten, special curriculum planning within kindergarten, or a uniquely enriched preschool environment.
- Test scores give quantitative data, which you may or may not choose to share with the school

when communicating about your child's special needs. These quantitative data are usually normative, which compares your child's development to that of a sample of average children of similar age.
- Weak areas may be discovered that may be masked by your child's intellectual giftedness. Preschool testing permits you to assist your child in practicing these skills.
- Test scores give you confidence in your personal observations or correct them appropriately. They can prevent you from placing too much pressure on your child.
- Early test scores provide baseline information for monitoring your child's intellectual growth and progress.

If parents have doubts about early entrance, then start the child at the regular age, with subject acceleration in the child's areas of greatest strength. Observation by the teacher in the accelerated subject will provide the required evidence for the next decision. Teachers will be good observers provided they, too, have knowledge about gifted children and acceleration research (Rimm & Lovance, 1992a, 1992b).

Recently there has been a trend to delay entrance to kindergarten in the belief that an older, more mature child will have an educational and confidence advantage. However, research consistently confirms that average children who are delayed entrants do not achieve better academically or socially than typical age entrants (e.g., Davis, Trimble, & Vincent, 1980; Langer, Kalk, & Searls, 1984). Ceci (1991), in analyzing 200 studies of the relationship between schooling and IQ, found that a child's IQ score falls behind that of others of the same age when formal classroom education is delayed, as when entrance to kindergarten is postponed. Perhaps that is not surprising because the child is less likely to be in an enriched learning environment, and IQ scores compare children's learning performance to their age rather than their grade level.

## Day Care and Preschools

Day care and preschools for young gifted children have become increasingly common as more women seek to combine careers with child rearing. The importance of language stimulation during early childhood seems to recommend a close parent-child relationship during this critical period. A day-care center on a full-time basis cannot substitute for that unique attentional experience, although part-time care may be satisfactory. A high-quality babysitter, who will talk to and interact with the child on a one-to-one basis, is a good alternative for a full-time working mother.

Attending preschool for two or three half-days per week for a year or two before kindergarten can provide excellent language training and other forms of skill development and educational enrichment for any three- to five-year-old child. Note, however, that (1) the quality of the nursery school, (2) its sensitivity to the needs of very bright children, and (3) its encouragement of language and creative expression would be important considerations in making a selection.

Creel and Karnes (1988) confirmed that parents of gifted preschool children were eager to have educational services for their young children. Forty-nine of 51 such parents surveyed indicated that they would support having a specialized gifted preschool program on at least a half-day basis. Strom et al. (1992) designed a curriculum for *parents* of 68 gifted minority and low-income preschool and primary children that was very helpful to them in developing a family/school partnership.

The decision as to whether to place the gifted child in day care or a preschool is not an easy *yes* or *no* one. It must be a careful decision based on an examination of the particular needs of the child and the alternatives available for that child.

However, quality of that environment does count. According to a study by the University of North Carolina (1999):

> Children in higher quality classrooms displayed more advanced cognitive skills in two areas: language development and pre-math skills. They scored higher on individual assessments of receptive language ability, indicating they had a better understanding of language than children in lower quality classrooms. Children's understanding of language showed the strongest relationship to quality of all the outcomes measured. Children in higher quality classrooms also evidenced better socio-emotional development.

A further study by the National Research Council (1998) found:

> The number of months that children spend in preschool has been found to be related to achievement test scores in second grade, behavior problems in third grade, and school retention in kindergarten through third grade. Children with more preschool experience had higher achievement scores and fewer behavior problems and were less likely to be required to repeat a grade.

Although none of these studies were of gifted children specifically, the findings are especially important for disadvantaged gifted children. Today, quality child care is important for all children because more are in early child care than ever before.

## NONTRADITIONAL PARENTING

According to a Census Bureau report, half of the children in the United States live in nontraditional families (Udansky, 1994). Rogers and Nielson (1993) assert that gifted children of divorced families may indeed be an underidentified and underserved population in gifted education. They base their concerns on the very few research studies that compare parents' marital status to the stereotypes laid down by the longitudinal study by Terman (1925) over 75 years ago. He concluded that fewer gifted children came from divorced homes than from the usual population. Among the 1036 women in the Rimm study (Rimm et al., 1999), there were also fewer who came from divorced homes than in the typical population; however, those who did often credited their single mothers for their effectiveness as role models. The authors call for new research on the families of gifted children and emphasize that almost no current research is available on children of divorce in the gifted population.

Nontraditional family settings can cause extra stress for parents and children. However, there are some precautions that can be followed to lessen that stress and enhance the child's adjustment.

### Single-Parent Families

One estimate is that as of 1990, a full 50 percent of today's children will have spent part of their childhood in a single-parent setting (Schreeve et al., 1986). More anxiety and emotional disturbance exist for children in single-parent homes compared to children in homes that have two parents (Henderson, 1981; Hetherington, Cox, & Cox, 1982). However, there also are some positive effects.

In research reported by Cornelius and Yawkey (1985), children in single-parent families tended to have higher imaginativeness scores, had more imaginary companions, used more imaginative talk with their fantasy friends, played more imaginative games alone, and engaged in more imaginative out-of-doors games than those in two-parent families. These results were based on a group of

50 preschoolers aged 4 and 5 who were administered a 28-item *Imaginative Predisposition Interview Scale* (Yawkey, 1983). Manosevitz, Prentice, and Wilson (1973) suggested that individual imaginativeness and single-parent families reciprocally nurture each other by reason of the amounts of "empty space" preschoolers have within single-parent families.

An example of the impact of increased attention and stimulation stemming from single parenting comes from a clinical case study.

*Elizabeth was born to a teenage mother of average ability. Her father left the area immediately after he discovered the pregnancy. There was no indication of his having above average ability. Elizabeth's mother felt a great deal of guilt about the out-of-wedlock pregnancy and promised herself she would compensate Elizabeth by almost total attention. Elizabeth received extraordinary amounts of time, attention, talk, and reading to during her preschool years. In third grade her measured IQ score was 155.*

Increased stimulation and attention, as well as valued time alone for the child in a single-parent family, can provide some advantages for giftedness and imagination. However, there also are risks for these children. Schreeve et al. (1986) found in a sample of normal ability children that those from single-parent homes ranked lower in achievement than peers from two-parent families. Gelbrich and Hare (1989) also found that gifted male and female students in single-parent families achieved at lower levels than students from traditional families; the underachievement problem was greater for males than for females.

Studies of gifted children in single-parent homes are based on female-led families. While there are many more single-parent families led by mothers, there are now an increasing number of single fathers who lead their homes. Very little research is available on the effects of single parenting on children, and none specifically on father-led families of gifted children. Research is needed. In Inset 16.4 Rimm (1995d, 1996a) summarizes some precautions for single parents.

## Suggestions for Single Parents

As a single parent, are you destined to have an underachieving child? Of course not, but your job is more difficult. Here are some simple rules to guide you—simple only in that they're few and straightforward. In reality, they're terribly difficult for single parents to negotiate. Pat yourself on the back for each successful day. You deserve it.

- Find a career direction for your life to give you a sense of purpose and to build your personal self-confidence. Making your children your only purpose gives them power and causes them pressure that will be too stressful for them to manage.
- Find some adult social outlets for yourself. Don't feel guilty about enjoying yourself as an adult away from your children.
- Find a reliable babysitter or daycare facility for your children. Consistency in caregivers and surroundings is important for young children.
- Treat your child as a child, not a toy to be played with nor an adult to be depended upon. *Do not* share your bed with your child (except during thunderstorms). That is an adult status that you should reserve for a spouse.
- Don't tell your children you will love them more than anyone else forever, or a new partner will cause them to believe you deceived them.
- If your children come home from a visitation and are unruly, don't blame that poor behavior on the other parent. Instead, tell them you're pleased they had a nice time, and if you can manage a nice comment about the other parent, they'll settle down more easily. They need to know they can love you both.
- Take time (you have little) to enjoy your children's achievements and encourage them to take responsibilities.

Below are three special rules for single mothers who are parenting boys:

- Boys should have an older male as a model. Find effective role models for your boys. Uncles, grandfathers, teachers, Boy Scout leaders, and Big Brothers may all be helpful to your sons in learning to be comfortable with their masculinity.
- If you don't view your children's natural father as an effective role model, absolutely don't tell your boys how much they look like and remind you of their father, especially when you are angry.
- Avoid power struggles with your children's father. If their father mistreats you and shows open disrespect toward you, your sons are likely to imitate this powerful but disrespectful behavior.

These rules will sound simplistic to some of you and impossible to others. They may be difficult for a single parent to live by, but they are effective for parenting your children in a single-parent household. Remember, many successful and happy children have been brought up in single-parent families.

From Sylvia B. Rimm, *How to Parent So Children Will Learn,* 1996. New York: Crown.

### Multiple Parent Families

When children have multiple parents living in different homes by reason of divorce or remarriage, the challenge of appropriate parenting certainly is extended. There are many books written specifically on the topic, so this brief summary will emphasize only some key risks related to giftedness. Since gifted children by reason of vocabulary and advanced reasoning appear so adultlike, the biggest problem is that during a divorce one or both parents will assign them adult roles. That is, they are often treated as confidant, partner, and counselor. Initially they may enjoy this new adult status because they feel empowered by it. However, the risks are great. These children feel torn by their loyalty to both parents who no longer seem to like each other. They feel insecure because of the adult responsibility given too early. They easily fall victims to manipulations and learn a manipulative style of relating to both parents. Often, the mother who confides in her adolescent gifted child in an adult manner during the immediate pre- and post-divorce period is likely to find herself with an unmanageable adolescent. It is as if the teenager who has been given adult status refuses to acknowledge the parent's right to parent him or her thereafter. Even during the trauma of divorce, gifted children must reserve the right to remain children, or their social-emotional health will suffer. Parents going through divorce should get professional counseling for support rather than depending on their children at this vulnerable time. Children also should have the opportunity to talk things through with a "safe" person who is not an involved member of the family strife.

## PARENT SUPPORT GROUPS

Since gifted children by definition are a minority, in many cases adequate educational opportunities will be provided for them only if there is a vocal and visible support group in the community. If adequate G/T programs are not available, joining or organizing a parent support group should be a top priority for concerned parents of gifted children and for teachers interested in gifted education. A fringe benefit of such visible membership is that parents make a clear statement to their children that education, cultural growth, and challenge are top priorities in family values.

The results of a survey of 1039 parents of gifted students (Gogul, McCumsey, & Hewitt, 1985) showed that "parental persistence was the key factor in success in working with schools." Perhaps positive persistence and school advocacy are the best ways to describe appropriate parents' roles.

Smutney (2001) recommended that parent advocates take a three-step approach when they need to "stand up" for their gifted child. The first step is to talk with their child so that they are confident of his or her feelings or needs. The second step is to talk to the child's teacher, and the third step, moving "up the ladder" of administration, should take place only after a good-faith effort

has been made to talk to the teacher. Hopefully, in most cases the third step will be unnecessary.

Incidentally, the Fresno (California) Parents for the Gifted organization had to ignore the positive "lukewarm" approaches advocated by most parent gifted organizations. They succeeded in getting a gifted specialty school by using an adversarial approach (Rowe, 1990). However, this "negative" strategy was adopted only after more positive approaches failed. Fortunately, most parent groups need not resort to an antagonistic approach, which risks alienating persons whose help is needed.

For parents who believe they may wish to explore legal remedies for their children's inadequate education, Karnes and Marquardt (1991a, 1991b, 2000, 2003; see Chapter 1) have assembled court case histories and guidelines for decision making in three comprehensive books: *Gifted Children and the Law, Gifted Children and Legal Issues in Education,* and *Gifted Children and Legal Issues: An Update.* Educators, too, would benefit by exploring this legal information to ascertain that, indeed, they are providing for the educational needs of the gifted children within their schools. Legal recourse is in order only when all positive efforts have failed, because the time-consuming nature of the legal process may not benefit their own child's immediate needs.

Names, addresses, and websites of three national organizations are listed at the end of this chapter. These organizations can direct parents and teachers to state and local groups. They are also a source of information and have publications on giftedness and gifted education.

It is critical that teachers of gifted children recognize the important role of parent groups and parent support. Teachers must not view these parents as threatening, even though they are certain to make their desires known. Parent groups can help educate individual parents regarding the problems and needs of gifted children and the educational opportunities that are—or should be—provided to them. Parent groups also can help organize enrichment activities for gifted children, such as Saturday, summer, or mentor programs. Individual parents themselves may teach special art, music, math, or computer mini-courses (e.g., Tkach, 1986, 1987). Parents can also serve as the important volunteer staff—tutoring, transporting, chaperoning—which will extend the opportunities that schools can provide to gifted and talented children.

Parents can bring attention to the needs of gifted students in the community through the use of the media. Local newspapers, radio, and television provide opportunities to focus on exemplary school programs for talented children. A caution in sharing these programs is that it should not appear that an unfair proportion of resources are being targeted for the gifted students. If you wish to feature a special activity or field trip, make sure it's one for which the participating students have earned the funds.

Rimm (1996b) found in her own work that the media is extremely effective in informing the public about the needs of gifted children. Here are some pointers based on the author's experience that may help parents and educators use the media in ways that benefit all children.

• *Personal interest helps.* Search out those people in the media who care and who share your goals. They are the most likely to invite you to their talk shows or interview you for the press.

• *Make their interest your interest.* Be sensitive to ways you can help with some of the media's other goals, for example, by volunteering for on-the-air fund-raisers. Your contributions will be appreciated, and you will likely be asked to return for more help and more publicity for your case and theirs.

• *Don't talk too much.* Time on the air and screen is precious. Viewers and listeners are accustomed to fast-moving programs, and normal conversation often takes too long for radio and television. Plan ahead and organize the main ideas you want to share. Be sure to focus the interview to include your points. Be succinct.

• *Make your host look good.* When on the air, do not show off your expertise by appearing to be smarter than your host. They are on regularly and need to maintain their credibility. You can present your message in a win-win conversation as long as your host agrees with your message at the start.

• *Consider your strengths.* Persons with very different personalities are successful in the media. If humor is not your strength, leave the jokes to someone else. Rimm found that if she forgets the audience and talks and laughs directly with Matt Lauer or Katie Couric, her conversations seem most genuine. A different style may work for you. Researchers need to present their data; parents their stories. Both affect change.

• *Prepare for persistence.* You may have to call back multiple times. You may feel like no one cares about your important message because they may not return your call. Don't feel hurt. You have a mission. You will eventually get your three minutes or your small column. Consider how many people will learn about gifted and talented educational needs if you *just don't quit!*

In summary, the media can help you multiply your mission messages by millions and can also provide some fun experiences.

## SUMMARY

Some parents will deny their child's giftedness; others may exaggerate it.

Parenting by positive expectations includes expectations of high achievement, good attitudes, and positive support.

With the "Who's in Charge" problem, children are given too much adultlike decision-making power, leading to later conflicts. This is especially true for highly verbal children.

Competitiveness motivates high achievement. However, feelings of competitiveness that are too strong cause stress, perhaps leading to loss of appetite, enuresis, nightmares, irritability, and so forth. Parents should help gifted children and adolescents to identify sources of stress and guide them in making the burdens more manageable. A subtle source of stress may come from too-frequent adult praise that emphasizes superlatives and perfection.

As demonstrated in the Yerkes-Dodson law, an intermediate level of stress (arousal) produces optimal performances; stress beyond that level becomes counterproductive. Recreation, exercise, an empathic environment, and humor can help reduce stress.

Noncompetitive intellectual activities, such as individualized learning, clubs, hobbies, field trips, or independent research projects, lead to enjoyable experiences of intellectual discovery without fear of failure.

Sibling rivalry is usually due to competition for parents' attention or resources, and giftedness can have a significant impact on sibling achievement.

One basic recommendation is that each child receive individualized opportunities for creative and intellectual development; a democratic attitude of treating all children alike is counterproductive. Each child should be evaluated and reinforced for accomplishments relative to his or her own abilities and efforts. Preferential treatment and labeling by significant others such as grandparents, aunts, and uncles may exacerbate sibling rivalry.

Parents should be sensitized to how gender issues affect achievement. In raising gifted girls, parents should avoid teaching overcompliance, since the resulting self-criticism and perfectionism can inhibit later risk taking and creativity. Countering the societal emphasis on appearance and thinness is a parental responsibility. Involvement in interests and activities can help girls form their identities. Parents who are good role models make an important difference.

Although girls may have achievement disadvantages later in life, boys seem to have more than their share in childhood. Boys are not exposed to many male teachers in their early school years and thus lack male role models in school. Boys tend to have more handwriting and concentration problems, which can be prevented. They also struggle with pressures of machismo, and sensitive boys are too often shamed for their sensitivity. The involvement of gifted boys in violence is an important social-emotional issue that may be related to the pressures for manliness.

Peer pressure, combined with adolescent identity formation, severely reduces parental influence. A disdain for academic accomplishment is a common form of peer influence that can lead to underachievement, that is, mentally dropping out. Popularity should be deemphasized by parents and explained as a competitive form of friendship that ends at high school graduation.

The gifted student can learn to downplay his or her "brainy image" but still be a high achiever, although surveys and research continue to show that gifted high achievers usually pay a social price. The best solution is to help assemble interest groups of gifted peers who support the gifted student's achievement orientation.

Preschool learning is critically important for language and cognitive development. Research indicates that habits of reading and skills of independent problem solving are acquired in the early home environment. Parents are very important early teachers for their children.

Precautions can be taken with preschool children to enhance their learning. Television watching should be moderated and monitored. Quality television watching may contribute to children's knowledge base that enhances giftedness. Violence on TV may have as much of a relationship to violence in our society as cigarette smoking does to lung cancer. Moderated parent chatter, teaching of basic writing skills, daily alone time, and flexibility also are recommended.

Studies show that parents are good identifiers of preschool giftedness. Parents who observe characteristics of giftedness in their preschool children may have them evaluated. The benefits of identification and testing are early entrance to kindergarten, comparison with other children, discovery of weak areas, confidence in personal observations, and baseline information.

Studies have found a decline in IQ when formal classroom education is delayed.

Quality of day care and preschools has been found to make a significant difference in children's cognitive abilities. It is especially important because more children than ever before are in early child care.

Nontraditional parenting and multiple parent families provide special problems for gifted children. New and updated research is needed to identify gifted children of divorce and of families led by single fathers.

Parent support groups can lead to the creation of G/T programs, teach children that parents value education, help educate individual parents, organize enrichment activities, teach mini-courses, and assist with the G/T program. Parents can also use the media to bring the needs of gifted children to the attention of the community.

Parents need to "stand up for their gifted kids." Although proactive approaches are always recommended, in some cases, legal remedies may need to be pursued.

## APPENDIX 16.1: NATIONAL GIFTED AND TALENTED EDUCATIONAL ORGANIZATIONS

Council for Exceptional Children—Talented and Gifted (CEC-TAG)
1920 Association Drive
Reston, VA 22091
www.cec.sped.org

National Association for Gifted Children (NAGC)
1707 L Street NW
Washington, DC 20036
www.nagc.org

Mensa
201 Main Street, Suite 1101
Fort Worth, TX 76102
www.mensa.org

# CHAPTER 17

# UNDERSTANDING AND COUNSELING GIFTED STUDENTS

*Gifted students by their very advanced cognitive abilities and intensity of
feelings deal with issues about self and others in ways that are unique from
the general population and therefore require specialized understanding.*
Nicholas Colangelo (2003, p. 373)

In contrast with the educational and career counseling needed by all students as they approach high school graduation, gifted students—from the lowest elementary grades through high school—need help with a variety of self-definition, social, and family issues, along with education- and career-related problems.

Many thoughtful specialists in gifted education continue to argue strongly that counseling and guidance are essential for the full development of gifted children, and that counseling should be an integral component of every gifted program (e.g., Bireley & Genshaft, 1991; Colangelo, 2003; Dai & Renzulli, 2000; Delisle, 1992; Gallagher, 1990, 1991a; Landrum, 1987; Perrone, 1997; Roeper, 1982; Silverman, 1997; VanTassel-Baska, 1983a; Webb, Meckstroth, & Tolan, 1982).

*As a general rule, the greater the gift, the greater the counseling need.*

As a preliminary sample of counseling needs, the common problem of feeling different and not fitting in with family and friends is a virtual given with highly gifted children and adolescents. Bright students usually become idealistic thinkers many years ahead of their peers. The average child's narrow personal concerns contrast sharply with the gifted child's deep and often upsetting concern for moral issues and justice, such as world hunger, high divorce rates, and the unequal distribution of wealth that jams prisons with the minority poor. Personal and home problems can

include conflicts with siblings, peers, and especially parents (Peterson, 2001); resistance to authority; depression and withdrawal; and sometimes alcoholism, drug addition, delinquency, and even suicide (e.g., Blakeley, 2000; Cross, 1996; Fleith, 2001). Many are bored with school learning, sometimes leading to apathy and underachievement. As mentioned in Chapter 13, one estimate is that 18 to 25 percent of all dropouts are gifted (Solorzano, 1983; Renzulli & Park, 2000). Sadowski (1987; described in Renzulli & Park, 2000) reported that gifted high school dropouts had "unstable" homes, consumed alcohol and drugs, had low school motivation, were rebellious toward school and authority, had poor peer relations and social adjustment—*and there was poor counseling in high school and inadequate communication with parents.*

While some gifted students drop out, others waste their talent by choosing not to attend college. In contrast, still other gifted students become overcommitted with school and outside activities, and need help coping with the pressures.

Nongifted family members and peers may not understand giftedness, leading in some cases to unrealistic expectations and in others to jealousy, resentment, or outright hostility about the high ability (e.g., Clasen & Clasen, 1992; Silverman, 1983b). As noted in Chapter 16, research by Brown and Steinberg (1990) showed that many teenagers express their resentment of high achievers by relating the label *brain,* meaning high achiever, to the label *nerd,* meaning loser in the peer social system. Underachievement and its seeming reverse, an irrational compulsion for perfectionism, are both common. Their high intelligence, self-analytic ability, and perfectionism lead many highly gifted youth to evaluate themselves critically, often harshly (e.g., Reis & Moon, 2002). As described by Piechowski (1997), highly gifted and creative students will experience self-judgment, self-doubt, self-criticism, and sometimes even self-loathing; they may desperately search for meaning in their lives and for their place in the world; they may feel weak, unbalanced, and irrational; and as we will explain later, many are intricately sensitive yet relentlessly intense. Because of their obvious uniqueness, many ask themselves "What's wrong with me?" and some look for themselves in descriptions of mental disorders (Piechowski, 1997; Tolan, 1987).

Some of the most frequently occurring problems are these (Dai & Renzulli, 2000; Delisle, 1992; Landrum, 1987; Niehart et al., 2002; Silverman, 1983a, 2002):

- Difficulty with social relationships; isolation from peers
- Conformity pressures; hiding talents in order to be accepted by peers
- Anxiety; depression
- Difficulty in accepting criticism
- Nonconformity and resistance to authority
- Lack of sufficient challenge in schoolwork
- Refusal to do routine, repetitive assignments
- Excessive competitiveness
- Poor study habits
- Difficulty with self-understanding and self-discovery
- Difficulty understanding the nature and significance of intellectual differences
- Intellectual frustration in day-to-day and life situations
- Difficulty in selecting a satisfying vocation from among a diversity of interests (multipotentiality)
- Developing a satisfying philosophy of life

Drawing from many sources, Landrum (1987) itemized goals of counseling programs in the categories of personal-social, career-vocational, and academic needs (Inset 17.1).

Counseling should be done by those who are sensitive to the unique emotional and cognitive characteristics of the gifted. Usually, persons in the best position to council are the gifted program teacher/coordinators as well as other teachers, counselors, and school psychologists who work with gifted children. There sometimes are important roles for gifted peers, mentors, and as we will see later, parents and school administrators.

A main goal of this chapter is *understanding* the unique personal and educational problems of gifted students. When teachers, counselors, parents, or gifted peers comprehend the problems, then they can aid and support the troubled gifted students, helping them realize they are not abnormal, they are not weird, and they are not alone. Many counseling activities are designed to assist gifted students in self-discovery—understanding themselves and their abilities, motives, interests, and values. A second goal is to suggest *counseling* functions, activities, and strategies that can be carried out by teachers, counselors, parents, or others.

As a further introduction to the topic of counseling the gifted, see the principles formulated by Joyce VanTassel-Baska (1983b) in Inset 17.2.

The remainder of this chapter will review the topics of:

Historical background
Personal and social issues
Perfectionism
Emotional sensitivity and overexcitability
Gifted and gay
Suicide
Career guidance and counseling
Personal essay writing and bibliotherapy
Stress management
Developing a counseling program for gifted students
Counseling functions of administrators, teachers, counselors, and parents

**INSET 17.1** _____

## Goals of Counseling Programs

Landrum (1987) collated information from several sources related to goals of counseling programs in personal-social, academic, and career-vocational areas. These suggest foci and activities for teachers and counselors of the gifted at the elementary school (E), middle school (M), and secondary (middle/high) school (S) level.

In the *personal-social* area, teachers and counselors can help students:

- Develop an appreciation for similarities and differences between themselves and others (E).
- Develop skills in social adaptation (E).
- Recognize and accept their abilities and limitations and learn that superiority may not permeate all activities (E).
- Participate with and get along with others (E).
- Develop and understand positive attitudes toward school and learning, community, and society (E).
- Clarify their values and resolve moral conflicts (E).
- Understand and learn to cope with intellectual, social-emotional, and physical changes occurring during adolescence (M).
- Explore interests (M).
- Analyze personal problems (S).
- Become self-directive and responsible for their behavior (S).

In the *academic* area students will:

- Experience educational and extracurricular activities that provide balance and satisfaction (E).
- Experience academic programs that are intellectually stimulating (E).
- Acquire effective problem-solving skills (E).
- Resolve problems that interrupt learning (E).
- Establish attainable and realistic goals (M).
- Locate resources that will help satisfy needs (S).
- Analyze academic problems (S).
- Develop study skills and test-taking skills (S).
- Enroll in classes that pursue identified interests (S).

In the *career/vocational* area, students can be helped to:

- Develop a sense of career opportunity based on their strengths and weaknesses (S).
- Explore implications of various careers through independent study and first-hand experience (S).
- Examine colleges and universities that are consistent with their career and academic needs and interests (S).
- Develop an understanding of the world of work and one's competence as a future worker (S).

Adapted from Landrum (1987). By permission of *Roeper Review*.

**INSET 17.2**

## Guiding Principles for Counseling the Gifted

In the introduction to her small but excellent book of readings entitled *A Practical Guide to Counseling the Gifted in a School Setting*, Joyce VanTassel-Baska (1983b) summarized some of the most important counseling principles as follows:

1. Persons who counsel the gifted should be conscious of differences in emotional as well as intellectual characteristics.
2. To prevent feelings of differentness, inferiority, or social alienation, counselors must help gifted students understand their special characteristics.
3. Academic, career, and psychosocial counseling programs should focus on both cognitive and affective (emotional) needs of gifted students.
4. Counselors should act as advocates for the gifted, assisting with their individual progress through appropriate school experiences.
5. Counselors should make available valuable outside resources, not only mentors and role models but libraries, universities, museums, and the like.
6. Because gifted students will have more educational and career choices than other students, and may make them earlier, counselors should aid them in decision-making and planning skills.
7. Counselors should encourage and help students to value self-initiated and independent learning.

8. Counselors should evaluate the strengths and weaknesses of gifted students and help students develop plans around them.
9. Counselors should encourage students to read about their particular problems or situations (bibliotherapy) and provide relevant reading lists and arrange follow-up discussions.
10. Counselors should be sensitive to value conflicts of low socioeconomic gifted students. These students require help clarifying and actualizing their goals.
11. Counselors should establish of special network of female students to promote high-level academic aspirations and taking more courses in math and science.
12. Counselors must communicate with other school staff regarding problems and needs of individual gifted students.
13. Counselors should initiate processes for identifying gifted students for G/T programs and for individual attention from other staff.
14. Counselors should work with parents, psychologists, and others to arrange in-service staff training related to severe problems such as underachievement, social adjustment, or personal crises. Outside specialists likely would be used.

Adaptation of counseling principles from the Introduction to *A Practical Guide to Counseling the Gifted in a School Setting*, by Joyce VanTassel-Baska, pp. 1–5. Copyright 1983 by the Council for Exceptional Children. Reprinted with permission.

### HISTORICAL BACKGROUND

In Chapters 1 and 2 we commented briefly on Terman's landmark longitudinal studies of high IQ gifted persons (Burks, Jensen, & Terman, 1930; Terman, 1925; Terman & Oden, 1947, 1959). One of the best-known findings of that research flew in the face of the folklore assumption that intellectually gifted people are physically and mentally inferior. In 1895, for example,

Cesare Lombroso tied genius to insanity and feebleness. The philosophy of the nineteenth century seemed to be that the "average man" is nature's ideal, and deviations toward better or worse are nature's mistakes (Boring, 1950; Silverman, 1983b). Kretschmer (1931) claimed that genius children were born of ill-matched parents, a type of bastardization. Silverman noted that in the past many parents were ashamed of and frightened by their child's "abnormal" precocity and sought to hide the gifts and teach the child to conform and be "normal."

Terman and associates found that, in fact, his IQ 140+ people were physically, psychologically, and socially superior. He thus erased one myth, but simultaneously created another—the idea that gifted children are clearly well adjusted and therefore do not need counseling.

Leta Hollingworth's (1926, 1942) early work helped correct Terman's conclusion. For example, she noted that because regular schooling fails to meet the needs of the gifted, many become apathetic. She also identified problems stemming from gaps between intellectual, emotional, and physical development. "To have the intellect of an adult and the emotions of a child combined in a childish body is to encounter certain difficulties" (Hollingworth, 1942, p. 282).

In the early 1930s, John Rothney and John Gowan studied at Harvard University under the direction of John Brewer and Truman Kelly, who were pioneers in educational guidance (Silverman, 1983a). Gowan, founder of the National Association for Gifted Children, argued the case for counseling services for the gifted throughout his career (see, e.g., Gowan, 1979).

In the 1950s, John Rothney founded the Guidance Laboratory for Superior Students at the University of Wisconsin in Madison. Later renamed the Guidance Institute for Talented Students (GIFTS), the lab conducted in-service training and workshops on counseling the gifted, helped establish guidance programs in schools, and provided direct counseling services to gifted high school students. Regrettably, GIFTS ended in 1984.

SENG—Supporting the Emotional Needs of the Gifted—was founded in 1981 by James T. Webb at Wright State University following the 1980 suicide of Dallas Egbert, a highly precocious 16-year-old student attending Michigan State University who wanted desperately to be "normal." Now based in Scottsdale, Arizona, SENG continues to focus on the counseling and psychological needs of the gifted.

In 1982, Barbara Kerr at the University of Nebraska established the Guidance Laboratory for Gifted and Talented, extending the work of both GIFTS and SENG (Colangelo, 1997). In 1988 the Connie Belin and Jacqueline N. Blank International Center for Gifted Education and Talent Development was created by Nicholas Colangelo and Barbara Kerr. The Belin-Blank Center retains a strong focus on personal counseling, career guidance, and family counseling, as well as offering four summer programs for the gifted (see Chapter 6) and biannual conferences.

As a final "historical" comment, Silverman (1983a) noted that in the first half-century of interest in counseling the gifted, the greatest strides had been made in understanding underachievement, describing characteristics of the creative, recognizing the special problems of the culturally diverse, addressing the plight of gifted women, and developing career counseling programs.

## PERSONAL AND SOCIAL ISSUES

### Self-Concept, Self-Esteem, Social Adjustment, and Identity

Problems and challenges associated with giftedness begin early. Silverman (1997) related that beginning at birth gifted children are active babies who may sleep less than their parents, respond intensely to their environment, and may exhaust parents with their need for stimulation.

Development may be uneven, for example, precocious verbal skills may accompany average small muscle coordination (Rimm, 1995d). Bright students may prefer to play with older children, sometimes "mother" younger children, and often relate well to adults. They have problems playing with average agemates.

Because regular classes group students according to chronological age, not mental age, gifted students find themselves in situations that meet neither their intellectual nor their social needs. Many experience feelings of isolation, social frustration, and even depression (e.g., Sands & Howard-Hamilton, 1995). They may develop poor social skills from their inability to find "true peers"—other gifted students with similar abilities, interests, problems, and needs. They may become social outcasts among agemates who do not appreciate peers who are more adult in their abilities and interests, who are labeled *gifted,* and who learn and excel with little apparent effort (Sanborn, 1979).

In Chapter 2, we summarized a few findings by Kunkel et al. (1995), indicating that, on the positive side, seventh- and ninth-grade gifted students felt skillful, self-satisfied, intellectually superior, and that other people trusted them and asked for their help. On the negative side, they felt social stress, different from others, often

bored, and that "people make fun of me and make me wish I wasn't smart." See the response of one 12-year-old girl to the question "What does it mean to be gifted?" in Inset 17.3.

The self-esteem of all school children is affected by their level of academic achievement. It follows that, typically, gifted children have higher self-esteem and self-confidence than regular students—at least regarding academic matters (Colangelo, 2003; Dixon, 1998). However, while *academic* self-concepts are strong, *social* self-concepts often are poor. Many believe that nongifted peers have negative opinions of them, which is often true, and even that some teachers

---

**INSET 17.3** _____

### What Does It Mean to Be Gifted?

James R. Delisle (1987) compiled delightful and insightful remarks from gifted children in a small book entitled *Gifted Kids Speak Out.* For example, when asked "What does it mean to be gifted?" a young girl from Germany replied, "Being gifted means having to stay in for kindergarten recess to do first-grade math." (With this school policy, chances are good that not many Deutsch kinder wanted to be "gifted.")

A 12-year-old Pennsylvania girl responded in writing to "What does it mean to be gifted?" with this thoughtful reaction:

**A**    Afraid, that at some point in time I'll slip and do something wrong and everyone will notice.

**G**    Guilty, when pressured into *not* doing my best.

**I**    Isolated, when others make me feel left out of "the group."

**F**    Frustrated, when I do something great and everyone laughs.

**T**    Terrified, when I don't know the answer and everyone stares at me.

**E**    Excited, when I create something that everyone appreciates.

**D**    Disgusted, that my special needs are neglected.

**P**    Privileged, when I get extra time during school to do something for myself.

**E**    Embarrassed, when the teacher announces my grades.

**R**    Relieved, when people don't laugh at me for getting less than 100 percent.

**S**    Satisfied, when I am able to help someone else with something they don't understand.

**O**    On top of the world, when somebody says they enjoyed my work.

**N**    Nervous, when pressured to always be the best.

share this negative view (e.g., Colangelo & Kelly, 1983; Kerr, Colangelo, & Gaeth, 1988; Dixon, 1998; Gross, 2003). Some will hide their giftedness to improve their friendships or to avoid being judged a "nerd" or a "geek."

It seems that the higher the IQ, the greater the chances of poor peer relations. Silverman, Chitwood, and Water (1986; Silverman, 1991), for example, found no discrepancy between intellectual and social self-concepts for nongifted students, small but insignificant differences with "mildly gifted" students (IQ = 120–131), but intellectual self-concepts were much stronger than social self-concepts with a more highly gifted group.

Over a half-century ago, Hollingworth (1942) noted that children with IQ scores between 120 and 145 are in an ideal range—they can achieve virtually whatever they wish, yet can have normal social relationships. Above that IQ level, the child may be too different, too alone, too impatient with slow-witted friends and teachers, and too aware of so many irrationalities and hypocrisies in the world.

Due to their social isolation, uniqueness, feelings of not being normal, and self-analytic ability, many gifted youth experience severe identity problems regarding who they are and what they wish to become. Colangelo (2003) recommended that counselors help gifted students clarify and understand self-perceptions and relationships with others. He suggested exploring these kinds of discussion questions with individuals or groups:

What does it mean to be gifted? (Variations: What do your parents think it means to be gifted? What do your teachers think it means to be gifted? What do other kids in school think it means?)

How is being gifted an advantage to you? How is it a disadvantage?

Have you ever deliberately hidden your giftedness? How?

How is your participation in this group different from your regular school day?

Would you rather be a gifted boy? Gifted girl?

What does it mean to be gifted and Latino?

Is there a time in school (elementary, middle, high school) when it is easiest to be gifted? More difficult? Why?

When bright students have the good fortune to be placed in special schools, classes, and programs where all students are gifted—and where intelligence and capability are valued—social relationships blossom, and both academic and social self-concepts become strong (Higham & Buescher, 1987; Silverman, 1997).

The downside of special schools and special classes is that highly gifted students profit from interacting with regular students, and regular students profit from high-achieving models.

In a study of 44 adolescent girls, ages 13 to 17, who were accelerated into a residential college program, Cornell, Callahan, and Lloyd (1991) found that individual social and personal maladjustment—for example, depression, suicide threats, lack of friends, rule breaking, or dropping out due to stress—was related to prior adjustment and family relationships. Specifically, these adolescents were more likely to have adjustment problems if they entered the program with a poor self-concept (social, academic, or physical), a weak sense of responsibility, or disharmonious family relationships, particularly a poor-quality relationship with their mothers.

### Adjustment Problems of Rural, Poor, and Culturally Different Students

In rural, economically disadvantaged, and many minority communities the absence of adult models—successful, gifted adults who understand and empathize with gifted students—adds to problems of isolation and identity. For gifted African American students, Exum (1983) recommended family counseling that addresses such parental concerns as loss of authority over the gifted child, worries about the student's loss of respect for family and culture, the student's emotional stability, and the student's ability to interact normally with other people. Exum warned that a gifted student might deliberately underachieve to preserve the integrity of a family that is threatened by the giftedness. There often are strong peer pressures on gifted minority students not to achieve—not to "act white."

The choice between personal development and growth versus group acceptance can be a deplorable problem for the gifted minority student—and a clear challenge for counselors.

## Labeling

Labeling is always a dilemma in gifted education as well as in special education designed for students with retardation, emotional disturbance, or learning disabilities. The classification and labeling are necessary for obtaining funding and providing programs. Nonetheless, when students are labeled "gifted" or as having "retardation," "emotional disturbance," or "a learning disability," these labels cause adults to make stereotyped and often false assumptions about individual children. The labels also cause the children to perceive themselves differently.

Although the *gifted* label strikes most of us as strongly positive, Colangelo and Davis (2003) and Weiss and Gallagher (1980) pointed out that *giftedness* and *gifted programs* run counter to the idea of a democratic, egalitarian society. The ambivalence has produced a "love-hate" relationship between society and the concept of giftedness: We value and admire talent and drive, especially in someone who rises from a humble beginning, but we also are deeply committed to the concept that "All people are created equal." As we noted in Chapter 1, the love-hate relationship peaked in the early 1990s, due largely to trends toward abolishing ability grouping. In 1992 Joseph Renzulli told an American Educational Research Association audience that "the word *gifted* has become the worst ethnic, gender slur word."

Most elementary school children are willing to be labeled *gifted* and to participate in school G/T programs; but when they become conformity-conscious teenagers, some may not want such a label and may drop out of gifted programs.

Having a gifted child in the family may increase sibling jealousy and competition (see Chapter 16). Further, siblings of children labeled *gifted* may be less well adjusted socially and emotionally than siblings of nongifted children (Cornell, 1983). Colangelo and Brower (1987a, 1987b) found that sibling difficulties appear to be most intense when the sibling is first labeled *gifted*; within five years the negative effects seem to wear off.

Inset 17.4 shows some responses Delisle (1987) elicited to the question of how students came to label themselves as *gifted*.

As we saw in Chapters 1 and 7, leaders Treffinger and Feldhusen (1996; Treffinger, 1995b) and Renzulli (1994) solve this and other problems by adopting the concept of *talent development,* instead of *giftedness*. The focus is on strengthening the talents of all students, including highly able ones. The strategy also circumvents social problems created by labeling a few students "gifted" and the rest, by exclusion, "not gifted."

## Risk-Taking

Some degree of risk taking is essential for academic and career success. According to Neihart (1999a), taking a risk means making an active choice toward one's own growth. If students are unable to take risks, they severely compromise their potential for high achievement or strong leadership. Neihart noted that students must examine their feelings about success and failure, and select a risk-taking route toward increased confidence, sense of control, and readiness to take on a new challenge. Of course, risk taking, she noted, inherently presents the possibility of failure—otherwise it would be called *sure-thing-taking.*

Five types of risk-taking itemized by Niehart (1999a) are intellectual risks (e.g., taking calculus), social risks (e.g., becoming best friends with a minority student or an unpopular boy or girl), emotional risks (e.g., telling someone you really

**INSET 17.4**

### How Did You Find Out You Were Gifted?

In Delisle's (1987) *Gifted Kids Speak Out* the question "How did you find out you were gifted?" provoked a variety of informative and entertaining responses:

> "In second grade; it was announced over the intercom" (girl, age 12).
> "When I was first born. My doctor told my mother and my mother told me" (girl, 13).
> "I learned I was gifted on September 12, 1982. I found out when I got a letter from my teacher" (boy, 10).
> "I learned I was gifted from my mother. (Intelligence is hereditary in our family)" (girl, 12).
> "In grade four, although I had the suspicion since grade two" (boy, 10).
> "In first grade in a first/second mixed class. I would use big words and even the second graders didn't know what I meant" (girl, 10).
> "When I passed the gifted test, my mommy told me" (girl, 7).
> "I found out in third grade. I always finished my work early and would disturb others because I had nothing to do" (girl, 12).
> "In third grade. I was in school on a Tuesday afternoon and my teacher called me into the hall and broke it to me easy" (boy, 11).

---

like them), physical risks (e.g., bungee jumping), and spiritual risks (e.g., questioning your religious beliefs). As a teacher of the gifted and a school counselor, Neihart included the topic of risk taking in classroom curricula and in individual, group, and family therapy. She acquainted persons with the dynamics of risk taking and required students to take one risk per quarter. She helped students and others understand the different types of risk taking, along with these six steps:

1. Understanding the benefits of risk taking
2. Self-assessment of risk-taking categories
3. Identifying personal needs
4. Selecting a risk to take
5. Taking the risk
6. Processing the risk-taking experience (the most important step)

With increased understanding and experience, said Neihart (1999a), risk taking increases. Are you, the reader, right now examining your own usual level of risk taking? What do you think? Is there room for a healthy change?

### Subtypes of Giftedness

Betts and Kercher (1999) suggested labels that help us understand six categories of gifted students, based on both cognitive and personality/motivational dimensions. Their profiles include what each type needs for better functioning.

**1.** The *successful* gifted are conforming, achieving, and perfectionistic. While admired and liked by peers and adults, they need to develop risk taking, assertiveness, and intrinsic motivation.

**2.** The *challenging* gifted are creative, but frustrated, bored, rebellious, and lean toward power struggles. They need greater self-awareness, self-control, flexibility, and sense of group belonging, as well as support for their creativeness.

**3.** The *underground* gifted are insecure, shy and quiet, and have poor self-concepts. They may be unrecognized as gifted, or else viewed as conformers and poor risk takers. They need more self-awareness, self-acceptance, interaction with gifted peers, and independence in making choices.

**4.** Gifted (potential) *dropouts* are resentful, angry, explosive, and burned out because the system has not met their needs for many years. Adults may see them as rebellious loners; their high school peers may see them as "airheads" or even "druggies." Self-esteem is low. They need a close working relationship with an adult they can trust, supplemented with individual and family counseling.

**5.** The *double-labeled* gifted may have a learning disability, a physical handicap, or an emotional disturbance. They have low self-esteem and feel frustrated, powerless, and angry. Adults and peers alike may see only the handicap and view them as of average ability or weird. Such gifted students require coping skills, emphases on strengths, skill development, and a support group of adults and peers who reinforce their giftedness.

**6.** Finally, the *autonomous* gifted have a good sense of self and accept both their strengths and weaknesses. They are enthusiastic, intrinsically motivated, and psychologically healthy. They are admired and viewed as responsible by adults and peers. They require support, advocacy, and facilitation and opportunities for developing their gifts and talents.

Several of the stated goals of the Betts and Kercher (1999) Autonomous Learner Model (Chapter 7) relate to counseling issues, for example, helping students understand giftedness, develop good self-concepts, and develop social skills.

## PERFECTIONISM

According to one estimate, half the population of America has perfectionist tendencies (Adderholdt-Elliot, 1987). For gifted students, the proportion is higher. One study of 112 gifted adolescents in grades 7 and 8 showed 87.5 percent to have strong tendencies toward perfectionism (Schuler, 1999).

The good news is that healthy (normal) perfectionism is a positive characteristic that drives high effort and accomplishment. Healthy perfectionists derive strong pleasure from their concentrated

effort, and they can adjust their work level as the situation requires. But perfectionism can be *normal* or *neurotic* in its emotional and interpersonal effects (Schuler, 1999, 2002). Baker (1996) confirmed that gifted students are stressed by perfectionism more than others, but that "Perfectionism becomes a clinical concern only when it prohibits gifted students from appreciating their competency or the adequacy of their work" (p. 365). Typically, when writers speak of "perfectionism" problems of the gifted, they always mean "neurotic perfectionism."

Neurotic perfectionism is born in gifted students' long history of outstanding school work and the perpetual glowing feedback from teachers and parents. Because of their advanced vocabulary and reasoning and outstanding schoolwork, parents may laughingly call them "genius," "Einstein," or "perfect." Many gifted children internalize the high praise and come to depend on it for their self-definition. They feel strong pressure to achieve at a level that matches the praise (Rimm, 1990a, 1990b). They work desperately—neurotically—to protect their identity. Some believe they are loved mainly for their high ability and scholastic performance, and do not allow mistakes or less-than-perfect performance. Yet they are rarely satisfied with their accomplishments because they set standards that are "high beyond reach or reason" (Siegle & Schuler, 2000, p. 39), and therefore outcomes are never good enough. When they do less than perfect in *all* areas, and regardless of their high level of performance, they feel guilty, frustrated, depressed, and of low self-worth.

There may be additional family and social pressures toward perfection. Parents of first-born children, especially, may overdo the Suzuki violin for tots, French for toddlers, early math and reading, and so on. TV role models appear perfectly thin, rich, successful, and nearly always good looking.

Some children have perfectionistic tendencies only in specific areas (Rimm, 2002). For example, different children may be perfectionistic about grades, clothes and appearance, room organization and cleanliness, athletic prowess, or their music or art talent. They may be perfectionistic in two or three areas, but not disturbed by imperfection in other areas. Such "specifically" or "partially" perfectionistic students "are more likely to be healthy perfectionistis" (Rimm, 2002, p. 2).

Focusing on both healthy and dysfunctional perfectionism, Schuler (1999) itemized suggestions for teachers and for counseling gifted students. For example, teachers can:

- Learn how perfectionism affects the social and emotional traits of gifted students.
- Recognize stressful perfectionism (e.g., inability to tolerate mistakes; impatience with others' lack of perfectionism; delays in starting work; refusal to turn in less-than-perfect work).
- Expect excellence, not perfectionism. Teachers can discuss the difference with students.
- Discuss how high standards motivate good work.
- Encourage the flexible and creative principle *dare to dream*. Reward creativity.
- Offer choices. Encourage perfectionist students to explore areas in which they are not guaranteed success and perfection.
- Provide an environment that is safe for trying new experiences, taking risks, and perhaps failing.
- Use humor to lighten the atmosphere. Create a "Humor Bulletin Board." Laugh at yourself.

Counselors and teachers can help students:

- Recognize strengths and weaknesses, and understand that no one is superior in everything.
- Appreciate similarities and differences among people.
- Accept mistakes; help them reduce their fear of failure.
- Analyze personal problems.
- Develop creative and problem-solving skills.
- Develop a good attitude toward learning, school, and society.

- Learn to help others and receive help from others.
- Develop a sense of humor in regard to accepting themselves and others.

Are you a perfectionist? See the traits and behavior patterns of maladaptive perfectionism in Table 17.1.

**TABLE 17.1**   Characteristics of Maladaptive Perfectionism

People with perfectionist tendencies:

- Stay up all night (or two nights) working on a paper and then turn it in late, because it had to be absolutely perfect.
- Make themselves sick trying to maintain straight A grades. They might even cheat.
- Argue about test scores, even when they don't affect final grades.
- Have sweaty palms and accelerated heart rate the morning of tests—because there is a chance of missing a couple of questions.
- Compulsively compare test scores with those of other good students.
- Procrastinate—they study and write papers at the last minute. While procrastination sounds inconsistent with perfectionism, it is not. Each new project contains the threat of failure, and so starting is put off. Procrastination also presents an ego-saving insurance policy—"If I don't have enough time, I can't do perfect work."
- Work alone, because no one is as good as they are.
- Are resentful of editorial changes of their work.
- Are critical of and refuse to associate with non-straight A students.
- Avoid new experiences, because they pose a threat of making mistakes or failing.
- Get upset if something started cannot be finished.
- Are overly precise.
- Often feel dissatisfied with or even guilty about good work.

Adapted from Adderholdt-Elliot (1987), by permission of Free Spirit Publishing Co.

Numerous famous, successful people were not perfect in every respect: Charles Dickens, Claude Monet, Isadora Duncan, and Mark Twain never finished grade school; George Gershwin, Will Rogers, both Wright Brothers, and newscaster Peter Jennings were high school dropouts (Adderholdt-Elliot, 1987). (What do you call the person who finishes at the bottom of the medical school class?*)

## EMOTIONAL SENSITIVITY AND OVEREXCITABILITY: THE EMOTIONALLY GIFTED

Many highly intellectually or creatively gifted young people possess a level of emotional sensitivity and "overexcitability" that is quite foreign to other children and adolescents, parents, and teachers. (Two good summary descriptions of this syndrome appear in Piechowski, 1997, and Silverman, 1983a.) As an example of "emotional giftedness" Silverman (1983a, p. 6) reproduced this essay, written for her by a high school valedictorian whose "cry of outrage against the emotionally barren school environment went unanswered. No one heard . . . no one responded to her despair. While other students were busy trying to master the course material, she was trying to grasp the purpose of her existence":

*What can I say about school? It was a way of life for twelve years, a lesson in accommodation and retreat, a pervasive and debilitating servility which the circumstances thrust upon all of us, even the very strongest. It was a few ephemeral brilliances— here a teacher deeply loved, and here another, years later. It was lessons in one's capacity to comfort and to care, the cries of a once-friend or a friend-to-be which went unanswered. But most of all it was silence, an illimitable silence which pressed me ever deeper into myself, so that I felt myself growing weaker day by day, growing less human because I was treated as a student, as a thing, not as "she who," but as "it that."*

*I was a good student. Indeed, a superb student. But not, after all, a model student, because there*

*were too many questions, too many rude hopes piercing the lost, desolate hours, too much rage in the face of fatuity and lies and cruel indifference, too wild a desperation in the attempt to discover what being human in this world could possibly mean for me.*

The essay reveals not only the young woman's intellect and creativity, but her perceptiveness of the nature of social institutions, sensitivity to an emotional void, and idealistic vision of the way the world ought to be (Silverman, 1983a). Note this dilemma: *It is precisely this high level of sensitivity and excitability that energizes the highly gifted to great accomplishments and interesting lives.* Yet the sensitivity and emotionality may be ignored or even repressed by others, not only peers but teachers and counselors. A predicament indeed.

Drawing from Dabrowski (1967, 1972; see also O'Connor, 2002), Piechowski (1997, 1999) described the effects of heightened emotional sensitivity and overexcitability in five areas: psychomotor, intellectual, imaginational, sensual, and emotional.

In the *psychomotor* area, such students show a surplus of energy, drive, enthusiasm, and restlessness, marked by compulsive talking and rapid speech. They feel pressure for action and often act impulsively. They may have nervous habits such as nail biting. They may be workaholics, like fast games and sports, and may get caught up in delinquent behavior. Note that these characteristics also typify attention deficit hyperactivity disorder (ADHD), creating a high risk of ADHD diagnosis (Rimm, 1997; see also Leroux & Levitt-Perlman, 2000; Kaufmann, Kalbfleisch, & Castellanos, 2000). Shaywitz et al. (2001) confirmed that, according to teacher and parent ratings, and compared with less gifted and learning disabled students, a group of boys IQ 140+ in grades four to seven showed comparatively high levels of activity, impulsivity, negative affect (depression, pessimism, peer rejection), and especially "tractability" (an early history of difficulty with baby-sitters, needing constant supervision, and "going wild in a crowd," p. 18). One teacher of

*Doctor.

the gifted advised Rimm that—incredibly—*half* of her students were receiving Ritalin, the calming drug prescribed for ADHD children.

In the *intellectual* area, these students enjoy questioning, discovery, the search for truth, and they love ideas and theoretical analysis. They are curious. Their learning is characterized by extensive reading, sustained concentration, probing questions, problem solving, conceptual integration, metathinking (thinking about thinking), and a preoccupation with certain problems. A concern for values and moral thinking leads to the development of strong universal values, values that are right and good based on effects upon others, independent of authority (Davis, 2003a).

The *imaginational* area includes typical characteristics and activities of highly creative people, and more. Sensitive, overexcitable students enjoy free play of their imaginations, with vivid imagery, fantasy, dreams, animistic thinking, magical (e.g., paranormal) thinking, metaphorical thought, inventions, and poetic and dramatic perceptions (see, e.g., Daniels-McGhee & Davis, 1994). There may be a mixing of truth and fiction, high visual recall, and despite their liking of the unusual, there may be fears of the unknown.

In the *sensual* area there is an aliveness of sensual experience. These students take pleasure in seeing, smelling, tasting, touching, and hearing. According to Piechowski (1997), sensual expression may include overeating, buying sprees, and frequent masturbation and other sexual activity.

Finally, the *emotional* area includes intensely positive and negative feelings, with soaring highs and dark lows. The "highs" include waves of joy, feeling fantastically alive and stimulated, and feeling incredibly energetic. Integrated with their strong sense of right and wrong, emotionally gifted students identify with others' feelings, show concern for others, and are sensitive to injustice.

The emotional area includes these troublesome "lows." The emotionally gifted may be shy, fearful, and anxious. They may show symptoms of a tense stomach, sinking heart, flushing, concern with death, feelings of guilt, depressive and suicidal moods, scrupulous self-evaluation and self-judgment, and feelings of inadequacy and inferiority (Piechowski, 1997). They examine themselves and their lives, sensing the discrepancy between the real and the ideal—the way one *is* versus the way one *should be*.

In her clinic, Silverman (1994) experienced dozens of gifted children who had been:

. . . fighting injustice, befriending and protecting handicapped children, conserving resources, becoming terribly upset if a classmate is humiliated, becoming vegetarian in meat-eating families, crying at the violence in cartoons, being perplexed at why classmates push in line, refusing to fight back because they considered all forms of violence morally wrong, writing letters to the president to try to end the Gulf War, and writing poems of anguish at the cruelty in the world. I have found that the higher the IQ, the earlier moral concerns develop and the more profound effect they have on the child. It usually takes maturity before the child can translate moral sensitivity into consistent moral action.

Children and adolescents characterized by the above traits—and who realize that others are not—feel different, embarrassed, and even guilty for their differentness. Others may tease or criticize. Because they cannot help their extraordinary level of sensitivity and excitability, they feel isolated and doubtful about themselves, and may come to believe there is something wrong with them. They might try to be more "normal" or emotionally withdraw, resulting in lost vitality, reduced achievement, and confusion about their identity (Piechowski, 1997).

What can counselors do? In the words of Piechowski (1991, p. 287):

When gifted people, and those who live and work with them, are introduced to these concepts, there is often an instant recognition and a sense of relief. It helps to find out that there is a theoretical model that makes sense out of a manner of feeling and acting that is so often at odds with normal behavior.

As we mentioned earlier, emotional giftedness, with its components of high energy and thirst for knowledge, powers the achievements and accomplishments of the gifted. Further, their sense of justice, sensitivity to others' feelings, and compassion present strong potential for moral leadership and inspiration to others. Unfortunately, it may be difficult for a gifted student to find a teacher or counselor who understands the dynamics of emotional sensitivity and overexcitability.

## GIFTED AND GAY

Imagine you are in high school, and you are not only gifted but gay (that is, gay, lesbian, bisexual [GLB], or "even just questioning"; Cohn, 2002, p. 145). Your double category of being gifted and gay almost guarantees social, emotional, and intellectual isolation. According to Cohn, about 1 to 3 per 1000 students are both gifted and gay. Almost no gifted gays, including you, will admit their sexual orientation until they are in college. (Average coming out age is 21.) Do you have *any* gifted and gay peers? What about gifted and gay role models? Who can you talk with about your sexual identity problems? The only gay subculture activities—bars and drinking—are for adults, not you.

GLB students often are depressed because of feelings of guilt, fears of rejection by peers and family, and rock-bottom self-esteem—perhaps even self-revulsion to the point of considering suicide (Peterson & Rischar, 2000). Both insults and physical violence from anti-gay peers—or even one's family—are possible, perhaps likely (Hetrick & Martin, 1987). According to Peterson and Rischar, the school climate for gifted gay students is "uncomfortable at best, dangerous at worst" (p. 232). GLB students are more likely than *all* other students to engage in self-destructive behaviors, namely, drug abuse, smoking, risky sex, or running away from home. They are more likely than other gifted students to channel their identity fears and self-labeling into extreme academic, athletic, or extracurricular accomplishment—a neurotic perfectionism.

Teachers typically know little about gay students, and do not address gay issues in supportive ways. Some thoughtless teachers and coaches even make homophobic comments, clearly announcing an absence of needed support.

Thoughts of coming out put fear of rejection by family and peers in direct conflict with "continuing to live a lie." According to Peterson and Rischar (2000), a common initial parent reaction to a gay child's coming out is *grief*, because of dashed hopes for their child's future. Usually, negative reactions are short-lived and soon become positive, particularly with mother rather than father, and particularly if family relationships have been positive.

In Peterson and Rischar's own survey, 18 gay, lesbian, and bisexual persons age 18 to 25 strongly agreed that GLB students need role models, and that there is virtually no support for coming out. The GLB persons made these recommendations for school support:

- Treat GLB students with compassion—they have rough lives.
- Let them know they are all right—not bad, nor evil, nor sick.
- Let them know they are not alone.
- Never dismiss or show disappointment in youths' sexual feelings.
- Raise teachers' awareness that every classroom can include GLB students—who are scared, confused, and lonely.
- Raise awareness that suicide attempts, drug abuse, or dropping out might stem from an upset student's sexual orientation problem.
- Raise awareness that compulsive perfectionism may be rooted in homosexuality.
- Insure that every classroom is safe and respectful. Name calling is intolerable.

Peterson and Rischar (2000) recommended these school support strategies:

- Train counselors to work with GLB students.
- Provide therapeutic interventions to address, for example, sexual identity, fears and emotional problems, social problems, daydreams, and attractions.

- Educate school staff about problems and issues—including a self-examination of homophobia.
- Implement policies to combat discrimination and violence against gay students.
- Provide health and other information.
- Include gay historical and literary figures in the curricula.
- Establish school, out-of-school, and distance [email, Internet] support groups.

There is an obvious danger to GLB-friendly educators. Their positive and therapeutic efforts may be received badly by parents, the general public, and the district office. Such persons may accuse gay-helpful counselors and teachers of "condoning" homosexuality (which is not entirely incorrect) or even "promoting" homosexuality (which is incorrect). One Salt Lake City high school made national news when it canceled *all* of its after-school clubs to stop a newly created gay-lesbian club.

As a consideration suggested by Cohn's (2002) "just questioning," Rimm verified in her clinical practice that some high school students have not yet confirmed their sexual identities. Many young people experiment with homosexuality and heterosexuality before settling on a sexual preference. Indeed, the average coming-out age of 21 may relate to a normal search for sexual identity as much as a fear of society's homophobia. Counselors and teachers should not assume "gay" teens are locked into their sexual identity; rather, they should support them and encourage patience in searching for their sexual identity. Many young people will continue to search into their 20s.

As examples, in the Rimm and Rimm-Kaufman (2001) research, publisher Annik LaFarge assumed she was heterosexual as a teenager—she had boyfriends and an active social life. She discovered her lesbianism in her late teens. Further, one of her homosexual partners later became happily married and had children. John Nash, whose life was detailed in the book and movie *A Beautiful Mind,* married a woman after several intimate relationships with men.

Nonetheless, as emphasized by Peterson and Rischar (2000), for many high-school GLB students, nonaction can be life-threatening.

## SUICIDE

According to Neihart and colleagues (2002; see also Kerr & Milliones, 1995), "suicide among adolescents has skyrocketed" (p. 94), up 300 percent for older adolescent males in the past 30 years. About 10 percent of adolescents make "one suicide attempt or gesture" (p. 94). While there is no evidence that suicide rates are higher or lower for gifted students (Gust-Brey & Cross, 1999; Neihart et al., 2002), many characteristics of gifted students are, in fact, suicide risk factors: high cognitive functioning (asynchronous development), social isolation, neurotic perfectionism, overexcitability, high sensitivity, and a heightened awareness of world problems, sometimes accompanied by feelings of frustration and powerlessness about their inability to improve matters (Fleith, 2001; Neihart et al., 2002; Schuler, 2002; see also Reis & Moon, 2002).

Fleith (2001) noted these warning signs that parents and teachers must recognize:

- Suicide threats ("I can't go on any longer," "I wish I were dead")
- Sudden changes in behavior (skipping school, no longer caring how they look, losing interest in formerly favorite things, weight changes, withdrawing from friends, giving away valued possessions)
- Low self-esteem ("I'm stupid")
- Lack of energy and enthusiasm
- Increased irritability and rebelliousness
- Overt self-destructive behavior (driving recklessly, carrying a gun, drinking heavily)

Suicide prevention must include family, school, and peers, said Fleith (2001). Parents must:

- Supply "quality time," communication, approval, and trust.
- Respond to their children's needs.
- Support their children's interests.

- Reconcile their own demands with their children's ambitions.
- Learn more about adolescent suicide.

The school can:

- Identify sources of stress on students.
- Schedule individual and group counseling.
- Train personnel in suicide prevention (e.g., student essays may contain suicidal thoughts).
- Teach suicide prevention to all adolescent students—who are in good position to identify suicidal classmates.
- Help gifted students accept themselves, understand their strengths (and weaknesses), and avoid overcommitment.
- Challenge the idea that suicide is an honorable solution to one's problems. (It is a foolish permanent solution to a temporary problem.)
- Use humor in tense situations; create an environment where students can talk about their problems.
- Implement activities that support student interests and abilities.

The problem is real, and all suicidal students must be helped.

## CAREER GUIDANCE AND COUNSELING

Career selection is significant for everyone, and it is rightly perceived by gifted students as crucial. Their future career will be their identity and means of self-expression. It will reflect their philosophy of life and values.

### Career Decision Making

Perrone (1997) noted that *social class, intelligence,* and *gender* are three main determiners of students' self-concepts and career selection. Drawing mainly from Gottfredson (1981), he described five stages of career perceptions and aspirations. A 3- to 5-year-old child values control over resources and gratifications—and may wish to eventually own a candy or toy store. At

age 6 to 8, the child becomes conscious of gender roles, and not many boys wish to be secretaries nor girls soldiers. Between 9 and 13, job prestige and social class affect career aspirations. Students realize that ability is crucial; and higher-ability students aspire to higher-level careers. Apart from ability, higher social class students also have higher aspirations. Students with high ability and high social class see most occupations as accessible; attending college is assumed.

Beginning at age 14 additional criteria are considered. According to Perrone (1997), gender-inappropriate careers are eliminated first, followed by occupations above or below one's "social class comfort range" (p. 402). For most students, careers that may demand excessive effort also are discarded, although "this thought may not enter the minds of many gifted students" (p. 402). For gifted students, in late adolescence and early adulthood a final stage reflects one's rich experiences, wisdom, and "reflective consideration of the human condition" (p. 402). Gifted students come to understand and accept their relationship to (and conflicts with) society. They trust their intuitions, and means become as valuable as ends. With values-based criteria, such persons may alter their earlier aspirations and select a career that squares better with their deeper world view.

Career decision making by gifted persons differs in many ways from such decision making by others (see Inset 17.5). Also, one's personality logically should match one's life career. With a view toward vocational guidance, Holland (1973) described six personality types and their relationships to career decisions (see Inset 17.6).

### Multipotentiality

The dilemma of multipotentiality has been described as an "embarrassment of riches," the ability to excel in many different areas (Colangelo, 2003; Delisle, 1997; Sanborn, 1979). The gifted student can find it confusing and difficult to make one or two choices from among the many possibilities.

In a case known to the authors, a gifted student who took the *Differential Aptitude Career Test*

INSET 17.5

## Features of Career Decision Making by Gifted Students

Based on his lengthy leadership at the Guidance Institute for Talented Students at the University of Wisconsin, Philip Perrone (1997) described unique features of career decision making by gifted persons that he placed in the categories of psychological, psychocreative, and social factors:

In the category of *psychological* factors:

- Sex-role stereotypes are less a factor for gifted students.
- Gifted persons are more likely to work at one job for life.
- The career is central to the identity of gifted persons; ego involvement in the career is high.
- Their achievement and mastery needs are strong.
- Gifted students have a strong urge to make an impact on society.
- They frequently feel exhilarated when pursuing a goal, which makes both means and ends satisfying.

*Psychocreative* factors include:

- Gifted persons habitually test personal and environmental limits, challenge the status quo, question themselves and others, and have less need for closure.
- They are capable of creating their own futures.
- They are risk takers.
- Gifted persons are likely to create and maintain dissonance in their lives as evidence to themselves that they are fully engaged in life.

In the category of *social* factors:

- Gifted persons have a more worldly view.
- They have a greater sense of social responsibility.

Adapted from Perrone (1997).

INSET 17.6

## Matching Personality Types with Career Decisions

Holland (1973) described six personality types that a counselor might consider when discussing career choices with students. An assumption is that there are six corresponding types of work environments, creating optimum compatibility between the person and the career.

Few individuals will fall exclusively into just one category. Rather, a counselor can help a person identify and explore occupations related to both "primary" and "secondary" personality types.

**1.** *Investigative.* The investigative or researcher type enjoys the opportunity to creatively design research, observe the outcomes, and interpret and communicate the information. The person may study social, biological, or physical phenomena, for example, in a university or commercial research setting.
**2.** *Artistic.* The artistic person prefers the freedom to design, manipulate, express, and create in one or more modes of art.
**3.** *Social.* The social personality type enjoys teaching, training, supporting, and working with others. They prefer to avoid routine, systematic, and fully predictable activities.

**4.** *Enterprising.* The enterprising person shows entrepreneurial and leadership traits in manipulating others to achieve goals. Again, there is an aversion to explicit, systematic routine.
**5.** *Conventional.* This and the next personality type do not fit most descriptions of gifted and creative individuals. The conventional type enjoys explicit and well-organized manipulation of data, with low tolerance for ambiguity or lack of order; bookkeeping, for example.
**6.** *Realistic.* The realistic type resembles the conventional type in enjoying explicit, ordered manipulations, but this time with tools, machines, or animals. Again, there is little tolerance for ambiguity or lack of structure.

scored above the 95th percentile in eight of the nine possible career areas. Such feedback hardly provides clear future direction.

Sanborn (1979) reproduced the following written concerns of a gifted 12th-grade male: "Nothing is so simple for me that I can do a perfect job without effort, but nothing is so hard that I cannot do it. This is why it is so difficult to decide my place in the future." From a female: "There are so many things I'd like to do and be, and I'd like to try them all; where to start is the problem . . . I'd like to be a physical therapist, a foreign correspondent, a psychiatrist, an anthropologist, a linguist, a folk singer, an espionage agent, and a social worker."

The following are two examples of the multipotentiality problem known to the authors. One extraordinary student took college courses in philosophy and computer science while in high school; both professors were rightly impressed and invited her to major in their subjects. When in college, professors in literature and science areas similarly encouraged her to major in their fields. Another college sophomore shared this confusion about college majors: He had earned a 3.9 grade-point average in engineering, political science, chemistry, math, history, and psychology and liked them all. How could he make a firm career decision?

One often-cited study, whose title proclaimed, "It was never there," argued that few gifted students actually possess multipotentiality. Achter, Lubinski, and Benbow (1996) found that only 5 percent of 1000 mathematically gifted adolescents showed multipotentiality (comparable ability in other areas). It seems unsurprising that 95 percent of gifted students carefully selected for their outstanding mathematical capability showed less remarkable talent in other domains. Even if only 5 percent—likely an underestimate—did show multipotentiality, it would remain a problem for 1 in 20 gifted students. Tannenbaum's (2003) thought-provoking response was that the "lesser advanced of two impressive aptitudes" (p. 52) probably is essential to support high creative achievement in the domain of the strongest aptitude.

Counselors should help students consider not only their innate capabilities, but their likes or loves for particular areas. Perhaps more important, counselors should help students consider open-ended vocations that permit long-term challenges and professional growth, not just jobs with glittering immediate appeal. Research, of course, perhaps tied to college teaching or industry, permits limitless creativity and opportunity. Also, many talented students pursue "mixed" college degrees that create unique career challenges and opportunities. For example, they might combine a law degree with training in business, medicine, or geology; combine history with photography; or create some combination of a technical field (e.g., engineering or biochemistry) with an art area.

### Expectations

The problem of *expectations* has many facets. For example, some parents expect great things—the highest test scores and grades, academic awards, enrollment in a prestigious university, and a high status profession (Zaffrann & Colangelo, 1979). Other parents may ignore their children's special abilities and expect them to enter the family business or work on the farm, with little or no support for a college education. Parents without a college education may have little knowledge, experience, or confidence related to setting expectations for their gifted children.

While parents and relatives, and even gifted students themselves, may expect high academic and career accomplishments, the students actually may prefer to live in a totally different way. From a high school girl's essay:

> I'd like to move to England and live in the fog with a house by the sea . . . I'd like to write books . . . [but] my future probably will be much different. I'll go to college for four years and major in something like math. Then I'll teach high school for a while and get married and have a bunch of kids. . . . I'm saying to myself that this is what you should do with your life, and if I keep saying it maybe I'll start believing it.

It is especially important that counselors help gifted students from economically deprived homes to aspire beyond the lifestyle familiar to them. In guiding these students, counselors must be innovative in searching out scholarship assistance that can make high career aspirations possible. One guidance counselor helped a high school student from a financially squeezed family discover enough scholarship aid to support her entire college education. This guidance counselor changed the girl's life, opening doors to a professional career. The girl's name is Sylvia Rimm.

## PERSONAL ESSAY WRITING AND BIBLIOTHERAPY

### Personal Essay Writing

Personal essay writing helps gifted students clarify their problems, feelings, perceptions, and aspirations without an anxious student-counselor discussion (Pulvino, Colangelo, & Zaffrann, 1976; Schuler, 1999). A variety of creative writing strategies clarify—for the counselor and student—areas of tension, stress, and anxiety related to self-concepts and peer-group relations.

Students may be asked to write about important personal, social, educational, or career problems and their impressions and emotions regarding those problems. One productive topic is "My Place in the Future." Other personal essays include: poetry; short stories; letters of the "Dear Abby" type addressed to "Dear Sigmund"; fictitious resumés based on personal, educational, and professional qualities the student hopes to possess; character self-sketches from the point of view of another person; autobiographies; takeoffs on "This Is Your Life"; and others. The writing can focus on such title-topics as "My Hidden Self," "Secret Dreams," "The Inside Story," "Let Me Out of Here!," "Who Am I?," "I Can't, But I Can," "I Am Mary's Angry Feelings," "What I Do and Don't Like About Myself," "Me, Myself, and I," "My Secret Hopes," and "My Future Plans."

### Bibliotherapy

Bibliotherapy is the use of reading material, usually young adult literature, to help students cope

with emotional and social problems (Delisle, 1992; Hébert & Kent, 2000). With gifted students, bibliotherapy is reading about the predicaments and benefits of being gifted as a route to self-understanding and reassurance. *The Bookfinder: When Kids Need Books* (Spredemann-Dryer, 1989) is a primary source for bibliotherapeutic literature. The volume provides synopses of books that address a list of social problems encountered by children ages 5 to 18, for example, sibling rivalry, friendship, obesity—and having intellectual talents. For busy educators, Delisle called the book "an inexpensive gold mine."

The value of bibliotherapy is reflected in this 12-year-old girl's response to the question "How did you find out you were gifted?" (Delisle, 1987, p. 11): "I've been in a gifted program since fourth grade but I didn't know I was 'gifted' until sixth grade when we were given these pamphlets on what being gifted really meant."

Rimm (1990a) published *Gifted Kids Have Feelings Too: And Other Not-So-Fictitious Stories for and About Teenagers* to help gifted teenagers grapple with such problems and topics as being a "nerd," hiding one's giftedness, popularity and social life, underachievement, emotional sensitivity, boredom and intolerance with school, drugs, abusive family relationships, teachers who do not support smart kids, sibling problems, peer pressures, competition, and being overweight. The stories are based on lives of gifted adolescents Rimm has known or treated in her family achievement clinic.

As a sample of the stories, "The Boy Who Wouldn't Go to School" begins:

"Brad, why won't you go to school?" Dr. Ann Ryan, the psychologist, queried pleasantly.

Brad hesitated, eyed the floor and responded briefly, "I can't. I'm just too bored. I can't learn like that."

"Like what, Brad?" she continued, puzzled. "Do you mean that there aren't any classes in your high school that you find appropriately interesting and challenging?"

"Not really. I absolutely hate Shakespeare and that boredom I won't ever tolerate. But I'd like the math, science and computers if only they'd let me learn it my way."

Rimm reproduced a poem entitled "The GIFT" written by Lisa, an 11-year-old girl:

*She was a wild flower*
*refusing to be bred*
*    Into a hybrid*
*just like the others.*
*    Didn't they know*
*she was perfect already?*
*    She may have been revolting*
*to others' eyes*
*    But to her the*
*shelves she saw*
*    With identical plants*
*were the most revolting sight.*
*    Zombie slaves to human monsters,*
*that she will not become.*
*    She will not be one of many,*
*but will keep her individuality.*
*    She refuses to bloom,*
*except on the wild forest floor*
*    Or will wait until the pressure builds*
*and crushes her velvety petals.*

A companion book, *Exploring Feelings: Discussion Book for Gifted Kids Have Feelings Too* (Rimm & Priest, 1990), includes discussion questions and projects and activities aimed at helping gifted students understand their feelings and problems. For example, some discussion questions to accompany *The Boy Who Wouldn't Go to School* include:

**1.** Have you ever felt so bored in a class that you believed you couldn't sit through it? If so, what did you do?

**2.** If Brad couldn't have left his school and you were Dr. Ryan, can you think of ways you might have helped him at his old school?

**3.** When Brad refused to go to school and did nothing but sit and watch TV, he was feeling depressed. What are the characteristics of depression? Have you ever felt depressed? What seems to help you get out of your depression?

For "The GIFT" three discussion questions were:

**1.** Do you think that Lisa felt lonely or good about her individuality? Have you had similar feelings? Describe feelings of pressure which you may feel to be either similar or different from others.

**2.** How do you feel about Lisa's use of the word *perfect*? What are the advantages and disadvantages of feeling "perfect" or never feeling "perfect" enough?

**3.** What are some of the difficulties associated with being an individual or being different?

Here's an example of a creative writing project that accompanied the poem: "Write a personal letter to Lisa to explain how you feel about the issues she presented to you in her poem."

Overall, the stories in Rimm's books, and bibliotherapy generally, help gifted students understand their problems and realize that they and their feelings are neither unique nor "wrong."

In addition to personal essay writing and bibliotherapy for helping gifted students understand and cope with their problems, Schuler (1999) suggested small group discussions of a problem; small group research projects aimed at clarifying a difficult issue; keeping a journal about a problem; self-expression in art, music, or film-making; and classroom simulations and role playing.

## STRESS MANAGEMENT

Everyone experiences stress. In part, it is related to innate differences in temperament and anxiety levels (e.g., Eysenck, 1967). Some people, gifted or not, therefore are more distraught and more easily upset than others. It also is true that people function best at a medium level of stress—enough challenge to raise interest and energy, but not so much as to devitalize or paralyze from anxiety and frustration.

Throughout this chapter we have noted that gifted children are subject to unique forms of stress. Particularly, problems of feeling "different" or "out of step" are common sources of stress that can be amplified by their emotional sensitivity and overexcitability.

Webb, Meckstroth, and Tolan (1982) itemized a number of stress-management strategies that counselors can help gifted students understand and use. All aim at raising students' awareness of personal values, priorities, and beliefs and strengthening confidence in their worth as people.

***Managing Yourself.*** Gifted students can be upset—stressed—by peers' jealous, resentful, or other insensitive behavior. However, while they cannot control others' thoughtless actions, they can learn to control their own reactions. They can be polite without accepting the stressors from others; they can tolerate and cope with stressful behavior from others. Gifted students can learn to conform when necessary, but without necessarily giving up their probably better ideas or attitudes.

***Self-talk.***   We all engage in self-talk—"Boy, did I do lousy that time" or "Hey, I was really good!" Gifted children may evaluate themselves in self-talk at the age of two or three (Webb, Meckstroth, & Tolan, 1982). *Negative* self-talk—self-criticisms and put-downs—happen when one's behavior falls short of personal goals, which for perfectionistic gifted children can be often.

Of course, negative self-talk is stressful. Gifted students can learn to recognize the negative self-talk that occurs when they think they are not meeting their own high standards or when there are conflicts with what others think they should be doing or thinking. They also can recognize *positive* self-talk and verbally reward themselves for doing a good job or just for having strong capabilities and values.

***Awareness of Irrational Beliefs.***   Some negative self-talk is rooted in irrational belief systems about what we "should" do, think, or believe about ourselves. Gifted students can be made aware of these traps and probably will laugh about some. The following list of irrational beliefs is adapted from Webb, Meckstroth, and Tolan (1982), Ellis and Harper (1975), Adderholdt-Elliot (1987), and Delisle, (1992):

- I must be perfect in all things.
- Everyone must like me.
- I must like everyone.
- I must not disappoint anyone.
- The majority is always right.
- The majority is always wrong.
- If I'm not popular, then I'm a social outcast.
- Boys are supposed to be smart, girls are supposed to be popular.
- I always have to finish what I start.
- Everything must be done precisely correct, right down to the last detail.
- When things do not go the way I want them, it is horrible, terrible, dreadful, beastly, shocking, and awful.
- If something unpleasant occurs, it is essential that I become upset about it.
- It is important for me to worry continually about "all-important" things in the past in order to limit my future possibilities.
- People and things should be better, and it is a terrible catastrophe if perfect solutions are not found immediately.
- If I happen to behave badly, I am therefore a bad person.
- My happiness is caused only by other people and events, not by how I think about myself.

***Other Suggestions for Reducing Stress.***   Webb, Meckstroth, and Tolan (1982) itemized other strategies for helping gifted students control their stress levels. For example, students can be helped to understand that covering up problems and denying difficulties usually increase stress, while talking about them reduces stress—even if that confrontation temporarily intensifies the discomfort.

As noted in Chapter 16, if a student shares a stress source with a G/T teacher or other counselor, the adult can ask, "What is the worst thing that could happen?" and then "And how disastrous would that be?" Such questions help the student gain a better, less stressful perspective.

Students also can be helped to understand that *"failures" provide feedback*—stepping stones toward success. When you fail, you know more than you did before. Failures should not just trigger depression or blame. Edison failed over 1500 times in creating a successful filament for his light bulb; he announced with pleasure that he now knew 1500 solutions that won't work. Other versions of this story put the number of failures at 2,000 or 3,000. Whatever the truth, he failed a lot and learned a lot.

Students can also understand that blaming someone else for their failure ("I can't get anything done because you won't do your part!") will only immobilize them. It puts them in the position of being a passive and helpless victim because the other person is perceived as having control. It is better to accept at least part responsibility for failure and view themselves as active, competent, and creative problem solvers.

Students can learn to *compartmentalize*. If one life area is stressful, for example, a theater production or trouble with one teacher, all other areas need not be affected.

*Calming* techniques can help students who overreact or who suffer acute stresses such as anger, fear, or excessive tension. Jogging or aerobics are known to be therapeutic. One also can learn to deliberately relax muscles, concentrate on breathing (thus clearing the mind), and count slowly to 10. Sleep also is a stress reducer.

Counselors can raise students' awareness of the HALT phenomena (Webb, Meckstroth, & Tolan, 1982). When we are *H*ungry, *A*ngry, *L*onely, or *T*ired, we tend to experience greater stress and to overreact irrationally. Some families use HALT as a code word to alert an upset child as to how feelings of stress and negative self-talk can be magnified due to hunger, anger, loneliness, or tiredness.

*Humor* typically is quite keen among gifted students, and it can be used therapeutically to reduce stress. Absurdities in situations can be pointed out. A counselor also can be humorously melodramatic about a problem, so long as the counselor does not appear cynical or to be laughing at the student. Some students use humor to handle stressful situations. Said one child, "When being smart is handy is when others try to put you down. You can turn it around and make it a joke" (Webb, Meckstroth, & Tolan, 1982, p. 119).

*Active ignoring* is another coping strategy. Students can deliberately think about something else and reduce the stewing by putting the stress source out of mind.

## DEVELOPING A COUNSELING PROGRAM FOR GIFTED STUDENTS

Colangelo (2003) described two possible approaches to developing counseling programs for the gifted, *remedial* and *developmental*. The remedial approach essentially is a therapeutic model. When gifted students have problems or difficulties, a counselor is "on call" to help.

The developmental approach is preferred. Although a counselor is available for short-term therapy, as with the remedial approach, the primary and ongoing goal is to create a school environment and home circumstances that support the educational growth of gifted students.

A developmental counseling plan would include the following components (Colangelo, 2003):

- Activities based on emotional and intellectual needs.
- Counselors who are knowledgeable about giftedness and attendant problems.
- A strong component of individual, family, and teacher consultations, along with rehabilitative/therapy services.
- Input and participation from teachers, parents, administrators, and students who are served.

### Counseling Roles for Administrators, Teachers, Counselors, and Parents

The following are some specific counseling-related roles and responsibilities for administrators, teachers, counselors, and parents (adapted from Landrum, 1987):

**Administrators will:**

- Learn what *gifted* is and what it means.
- Recognize that the needs and problems of gifted students can be best met if specialized individuals are given responsibility and time to coordinate the process.
- Ensure that the teachers and other personnel have received proper training.
- Coordinate cooperative efforts among teachers, counselors, and other student personnel workers.
- Provide school and district in-services on gifted education, including counseling-related concerns.
- Allow for regular meetings for G/T or talent development staff members.
- Know the educational options for gifted students.
- Listen and respond to concerned staff.
- Ensure that adequate monies are earmarked to finance the program.
- Provide suitable facilities for the program.

**Teachers will:**

- Listen to gifted and talented students.
- Know the children's talents and limits and not expect them to be gifted all the time in every subject.
- Make an effort to understand test data and other information in records.
- Intellectually challenge the students.
- Support and stimulate students' personal interests.
- Acquaint students with occupational information.
- Share information about students with members of the counseling/guidance staff.
- Establish a list of resource personnel and community mentors.

**Counselors will:**

- Listen to students.
- Orient young students to counseling.
- Help children make commitments to constructive values—character education.

- Arrange for students to make self-referrals to the guidance office.
- Provide individual and group conferences.
- Assist students in finding appropriate resources, for example, bibliotherapy, educational, or career information.
- Locate special services when necessary.
- Conduct classroom guidance activities and assist teachers in doing the same.
- Explore students' interests in relation to educational and career pursuits.
- Collect information about individual students as "unique persons."
- Work with teachers, principals, and other staff to foster a better school climate for gifted and talented students.
- Consult with parents.
- Coordinate the total guidance/counseling program.
- Evaluate strengths and weaknesses of the guidance program.

**Parents will:**

- Listen to the student.
- Keep open communications with the school.
- Get involved in the educational process.
- Form parent advocacy groups.
- Give children quality time.
- Help the child to learn time management.
- Guide their child in wise decision making.
- Allow creative thinking time.
- Promote reading.
- Model appropriate risk taking and leisure activities.
- Expect age-related behavior.
- Support the child's interests.
- Not expect the child to fill the parent's unfilled aspirations.

### Counseling Activities for Teachers and Counselors

To supplement the above, the following are samples of more specific intervention strategies and activities that can be conducted by teachers and counselors in the *personal-social, academic,* and *career-vocational* areas (Landrum, 1987).

These strategies meet personal-social goals of raising self-awareness, developing strong self-concepts, and working toward self-discovery, self-improvement, and self-actualization:

- Use group counseling to create a community of gifted peers and to provide gifted students with an opportunity to discuss problems and issues.
- Use simulations and role-playing activities to aid understanding of problems.
- Use bibliotherapy and personal writing to raise self-awareness.
- Encourage girls to take courses in math, science, and computers.

These strategies are directed toward academic goals such as improving studying, problem solving, and self-directed learning:

- Conduct units on note taking, summarizing, reviewing, memorizing, test taking, and reading for fun.
- Create activities in which problem-solving skills are practiced and developed, for example, analyzing and clarifying problems, clarifying solution needs, formulating solution strategies, and planning courses of action.
- Foster the development of independent learning and research skills, such as the use of library and Internet resources.
- Use questioning to promote higher-level thinking skills—such as Bloom's (1974) *applying, analyzing, synthesizing,* and *evaluating* and others (see Chapter 11)—such as those related to social issues.
- Expose children to art, music, science, and reading, particularly students with deprived backgrounds.
- Be alert to and support students' spontaneous areas of interest.
- Hold Saturday seminars taught by community resource persons.

These strategies can help meet career-vocational goals:

- Take pictures of career people; create collages.
- Have students interview and prepare class reports about people in various careers.
- Accompany PTA members on a "day on the job."
- On birthdays of famous people, discuss their careers.
- Use parents and members of the community as mentors.
- Visit universities.
- Review college application procedures with students (contact college admissions staff for information).
- Have graduates return to the classroom to discuss their education, careers, and related problems and challenges.

## COMMENT

Many students who are highly intelligent, creative, and/or artistic will have special kinds of problems and conflicts. These require special—and individual—understanding and guidance by regular teachers, G/T teacher-coordinators, counselors, parents, and sometimes specialty teachers or mentors (e.g., artists, researchers, business persons). An overriding strategy noted throughout this text is to bring gifted students together; they need friends and peers with whom they can share feelings, problems, and aspirations.

While gifted students may indeed "make it on their own," knowledgeable counseling and guidance will make the task less painful and more sensible. It also will help those gifted and talented youth who will not "make it on their own."

Finally, many, if not all, chapters in this book are filled with characteristics, problems, and suggestions related to counseling the gifted. Especially, Chapter 2 summarized characteristics of gifted students; Chapter 8 focused on self-concept development, moral development, and leadership; Chapter 12 described problems of economically and culturally disadvantaged gifted students; Chapter 13 reviewed underachievement; Chapter 14 discussed problems of female gifted students; Chapter 15 covered unique problems of gifted students with disabilities; and Chapter 16 reviewed recurrent parent and sibling problems. Often, a need for counseling was recommended or implied.

## SUMMARY

Gifted students need help with personal problems, social and family problems, and educational/career guidance problems. Some common difficulties include social isolation, stressful concern for moral issues, depression, and lack of challenge in school. A major counseling goal is fostering self-understanding. Eighteen to 25 percent of dropouts may be gifted.

Historically, Terman's conclusions about the superior physical and mental health of his gifted subjects created the illusion that gifted children do not need counseling. Hollingworth noted that gifted children's mental, emotional, and physical development is uneven, and some become apathetic about school. Rothney founded the Guidance Laboratory for Superior Students at Wisconsin in the 1950s. Webb created SENG following the 1980 suicide of Dallas Egbert. Kerr in 1982 created a guidance laboratory at the University of Nebraska; Colangelo and Kerr in 1988 created the Connie Belin and Jacqueline N. Blank International Center for Gifted Education and Talent Development at the University of Iowa.

The high activity levels of gifted children often appear at birth.

Regular school programs may meet neither academic nor social needs. Gifted students may be rejected due to differentness.

High achievement leads to good academic self-concepts; but poor peer relations lead to poor social self-concepts. Hollingworth noted that IQs between 120 and 145 are ideal for both success and social adjustment. Both academic and social self-concepts are usually strong when students are placed in programs for the gifted.

Research on unpopular, average, and popular gifted students showed no differences in academic achievement or ability but differences in self-concept and father's occupation.

Success in an acceleration program can depend upon prior adjustment and harmonious family relationships, especially with the mother.

Counseling problems with minority students include the absence of role models, strained family relationships, and peer pressures.

Labeling leads adults to make stereotyped assumptions about individual students, causes students to perceive themselves differently, and may increase sibling jealousy. The label *gifted* elicits a "love-hate" reaction. The negative effect of labeling on siblings wears off in about five years. Some leaders embrace the *talent development* concept, which reduces the labeling problem while emphasizing the inclusion of all students.

Neihart recommended that gifted students be trained in risk taking because it is essential for educational and career success.

Betts and Kercher identified six categories of gifted students: successful (conforming), challenging (creative), underground (poor self-concepts), dropouts, double-labeled (e.g., disabled), and autonomous learners (psychologically healthy).

Perfectionism may be healthy or neurotic. Neurotic perfectionism stems from continual success, feedback from parents and teachers, and even "perfect" TV role models. The syndrome includes, for example, compulsive work to produce "perfect" papers, compulsively studying for exams, worrying about grades, procrastination, avoiding new experiences, dissatisfaction with good work. Schuler itemized ways teachers and counselors can help (neurotic) perfectionists.

Heightened emotional sensitivity and overexcitability are common among highly intellectually gifted children and adolescents. The syndrome includes high energy, curiosity, compassion, idealism, an active imagination, high sensuality, and intensely positive and negative feelings, as well as anxiety, feelings of inadequacy, and other negatives. An awareness of their (normal) heightened sensitivity is therapeutic, according to Piechowski.

Students who are gay and gifted have virtually no peer group or role models. Depression, fear of rejection, and even self-contempt are common, as are self-destructive behaviors (e.g., drugs) and physical violence from anti-gay students. Peterson and Rischar recommended training counselors, educating staff, combating discrimination and violence, and other measures. While nonaction is life-threatening, helping gay students is often criticized.

Many gifted students show suicide risk factors: social isolation, perfectionism, and (moral) supersensitivity. Suicide prevention steps for parents include responding to children's needs and understanding adolescent suicide. Schools can identify stress sources, schedule counseling, teach suicide prevention, and help gifted students understand themselves.

Career guidance aims at clarifying personal and educational requirements for various careers. Perrone summarized five age-related stages of occupational aspirations that evolve around social class, intelligence, and gender. He also itemized characteristics of the gifted that influence career decision making in the areas of psychological, psychocreative, and social factors.

Holland described six personality-career types: investigative, artistic, social, enterprising, conventional, and realistic.

Multipotentiality is the dilemma of having too many abilities and interests to make an easy educational and career choice. Counselors should encourage open-ended careers that offer continual creative challenge.

The problem of expectations includes both family and self-expectations. Parents may expect high or low career achievement. Students may prefer a life other than what the family expects. Socioeconomic level influences self-expectations.

Personal essay writing helps counselors and students clarify areas of stress.

Bibliotherapy promotes self-understanding by having students read about other gifted students with similar problems.

Stress management strategies include helping gifted students manage their reactions to stress, recognize negative self-talk, become aware of irrational beliefs, accept failures as feedback, compartmentalize different life areas, learn calming techniques such as HALT, put the stress source out of mind, and use humor to reduce the exaggerated seriousness of a problem.

Counseling programs can be remedial or developmental. The preferred developmental approach provides coherent services directed toward emotional and intellectual needs.

Landrum described counseling roles for administrators, teachers, counselors, and parents. For example, administrators will learn about giftedness and coordinate counseling and other services for gifted students. Teachers listen to and challenge students and supply occupational and community resource information. Counselors have many functions, for example, orienting students to counseling, holding individual and group conferences, assisting students with bibliotherapy and career information, and consulting with parents. Parents can get involved with schooling and promote decision making, creativity, reading, and time management.

Intervention strategies, like all of counseling, focus on personal-social, academic, and career-vocational interests and problems.

Gifted students have special kinds of problems and conflicts that require special understanding and guidance by regular teachers, G/T coordinators, counselors, and parents.

### RECOMMENDED READING

Adderholdt-Elliott, M. (1987). *Perfectionism: What's bad about being too good?* Minneapolis, MN: Free Spirit Publishing.

Bireley, M., and Genshaft, J. (Eds.). (1991). *Understanding the gifted adolescent: Educational, developmental, and multicultural issues.* New York: Teachers College Press.

Colangelo, N. (2003). Counseling gifted students. In N. Colangelo & G. A. Davis (Eds.), *Handbook of gifted education* (3rd ed., pp. 373–387). Boston: Allyn & Bacon.

Delisle, J. R. (1992). *Guiding the social and emotional development of gifted youth.* New York: Longman.

Neihart, M., Reis, S. M., Robinson, N. M., & Moon, S. M. (Eds.) (2002). *Social and emotional development of gifted children: What do we know?* Waco, TX: Prufrock.

Perrone, P. (1997). Gifted individuals' career development. In N. Colangelo & G. A. Davis (Eds.), *Handbook of gifted education* (2nd ed., pp. 398–407). Boston: Allyn & Bacon.

Piechowski, M. M. (1997). Emotional giftedness: The measure of intrapersonal intelligence. In N. Colangelo & G. A. Davis (Eds.), *Handbook of gifted education* (2nd ed., pp. 366–381). Boston: Allyn & Bacon.

Rimm, S. B. (1990). *Gifted kids have feelings too.* Watertown, WI: Apple.

Rimm, S. B. (1995). *Why bright kids get poor grades— and what you can do about it.* New York: Crown.

Rimm, S. B. (2003). *See Jane win for girls: A smart girl's guide to success.* Minneapolis, MN: Free Spirit Press.

Rimm, S. B., & Rimm-Kaufman, S. (2001). *How Jane won: 55 successful women share how they grew from ordinary girls to extraordinary women.* New York: Crown.

Rimm, S. B., Rimm-Kaufman, S., & Rimm, I. (1999). *See Jane win: The Rimm Report on how 1000 girls became successful women.* New York: Crown.

VanTassel-Baska, J. (Ed.). (1983). *A practical guide to counseling the gifted in a school setting.* Reston, VA: Council for Exceptional Children.

Webb, J. T. (n.d.). *Do gifted children need special help?* (Video). Scottsdale, AZ: Great Potential Press.

Webb, J. T., Meckstroth, E. A., & Tolan, S. S. (1982). *Guiding the gifted child.* Scottsdale, AZ: Great Potential Press.

# CHAPTER 18

# PROGRAM EVALUATION

*There are two ways in which evaluation information might be used: To prove or to improve.*

(C. M. Callahan and M. Caldwell, 1995)

## WHY MUST PROGRAMS BE EVALUATED?

Developers of programs for the gifted tend not to evaluate the success of their programs or the effectiveness of program components. There seem to be several reasons for this reluctance. First, they typically feel that because they created their program in good faith it necessarily is "successful." Second, they prefer to invest their time in planning and teaching. A third reason is that "success" in teaching gifted and talented students is difficult to assess, compared with using achievement test data to evaluate basic skills programs. A fourth reason for hesitancy is that the evaluation results could threaten the program itself. For example, if the creativity tests, thinking skills tests, self-concept inventories, or other measures of complex constructs fail to show an improvement—perhaps because the instruments were unreliable or unrelated to what was taught— the data might be taken as evidence of program failure.

Traxler (1987) surveyed 192 school districts having gifted programs. She found that half of the programs were not evaluated at all, and of those evaluated most did not employ trained evaluators. Observations by teachers and evaluations of student products were the most common types of assessments. Very few states provide a plan for ongoing gifted program evaluation (Olenchak & Castle, 1995; Schwartz & Taylor, 1995).

Although gifted programs are more difficult to evaluate than other programs, this evaluation is vital. Gifted programs come and go; the record of continuity is dismal. Therefore, if teachers and program directors hope to maintain or expand their programs, they must be able to demonstrate the success of the program to their administration, to school board members, to parents, and to state or federal funding sources. This is *accountability*. These publics will want to know who is being served by the program, how they are being served, and the beneficial effects of the program. They also will want to know if the program is cost-effective. Equally important, teachers and program directors need information that will allow them to revise and improve the program. Beyond creating classroom quizzes or evaluating student papers and projects, teachers and coordinators usually have little training or experience in educational evaluation. This chapter is intended to simplify and clarify the evaluation of G/T programs and guide the teacher or coordinator in the evaluation process.

## EVALUATION DESIGN: BEGIN AT THE BEGINNING

Although evaluation is the topic of the last chapter in this book, evaluation of a gifted program belongs at the *beginning* of program planning. At the outset, when setting goals and objectives for a G/T program, one should design a methodology for measuring whether or not those objectives are reached (e.g., Tomlinson & Callahan, 1994). Not only should evaluation begin at the beginning, but it should be ongoing throughout the school year, and not just an end-of-the-year assessment of progress.

## "Difficult" and "Easy" Evaluations

Callahan (1986; see also Callahan, 1993b) set forth some of the difficulties that are unique to evaluations of gifted programs. She pointed out that (1) "no agreed upon standards of good programming exist within the field of gifted education and (2) many of the objectives in programs for the gifted are very complex and not easily defined."

Some examples of *difficult* objectives for evaluation are improvements in leadership, self-awareness, self-concept, decision making, reasoning, analyzing, synthesizing, evaluating, social responsibility, intrinsic motivation, critical thinking, and creative thinking. Other objectives are comparatively *easy* to evaluate. Acceleration programs, for example, provide almost self-evident evaluation data. Did students succeed in the advanced classes, the college courses, or the correspondence courses? Did the grade-skipping or the early admission to kindergarten work well for the students involved? Enrichment plans that result in a bona fide product—a school newspaper, a report of a research project, a poetry book, a dramatic production, artwork, a movie—also provide relatively easy evaluation data. Such products reflect a clear change in student skills and performances that, most likely, would not have occurred without the G/T program (Renzulli & Smith, 1979). Smith, LeRose, & Clasen (1991) used easily obtained statistics to show a profound effect of the Racine, Wisconsin, Lighthouse Project (LeRose, 1977, 1978): None of the minority students who participated in the program dropped out of high school and 76 percent planned to attend college. Among comparably talented minority students in the Racine district, 45 percent dropped out.

Whether objectives are difficult or easy to evaluate, we nonetheless must try to evaluate every planned objective.

## EVALUATION MODELS

There are many models for structuring the evaluation of education programs. Several will be summarized here in an admittedly oversimplified fashion. In all cases, the intrigued reader will need to explore the more complete, original statements.

Provus's (1972) *discrepancy* model assumes five stages in the creation of a program. At each stage the reality of the program is compared with a standard, and any discrepancy is corrected. In Stage 1, *Design,* the initial program plan is compared with a set of theory-based design criteria, perhaps as defined by an outside consultant. If there is a discrepancy, the program plan is modified accordingly. In Stage 2, *Installation,* the reality of the program as it is implemented is compared with the design adopted in Stage 1. Again, any discrepancies between program design and installation will guide changes. These changes could be in the installation or in the Stage 1 design criteria. In Stage 3, *Process,* the actual program activities are compared with the proposed program activities, and any discrepancies will result in corrective alternatives. Stage 3 is especially important for creating an effective, successful program. In Stage 4, *Product,* actual student products are compared with the planned ones. This may be the main evaluation of program objectives. Stage 5, *Product Comparison,* involves a comparison of students' products and learning outcomes with those of other programs to determine program efficiency in the cost-benefit sense.

Part of Eash's (1972; see also Renzulli, 1975) *differential evaluation* model involves three considerations in the evaluation process: (1) *Effort*—how time is spent (that is, the program activities); (2) *Effect*—products and outcomes; and (3) *Efficiency*—the relationship of effort and resources to the quality of effects realized. As the program evolves from a newly planned, innovative program (initiatory stage), through the implementation and field testing of the program (developmental stage), to the established and stable level (integrated stage), more emphasis is placed on evaluating effects and efficiency (2 and 3).

The Renzulli and Ward (1969) DESDEG (*Diagnostic and Evaluative Scales for Differential Education for the Gifted*) model was designed specifically for evaluating programs for gifted and talented students. It also may be used for program planning and development (Renzulli, 1975). DESDEG includes a set of five published documents corresponding to the five parts of the model. Part I is the Manual, which explains everything you ever wanted to know about DESDEG. Part II, Evaluative Scales, includes scales for evaluating each of 15 "ideally conceived educational practices" or Program Requirements, which subdivide into the five Key Features (general areas) in Table 18.1. Part III consists of Basic Information Forms, "a comprehensive inventory of factual information about all aspects of a program . . . organized and keyed . . . to each of the five Key Features." These aid in the objective collection of data. Part IV is the Evaluator's Workbook, designed to aid the evaluator in handling the information derived from the Basic Information Forms and from observations. Part V is the Summary Report, which (1) permits the evaluator to transfer numerical data to statistical and graphic summary sheets, and (2) aids in the creation of a summary narrative related to each Program Requirement.

In contrast with other recommendations, Borland (2003) recommended that we take a broader view of evaluating gifted programs. Specifically, he proposed that we consider the social, political, and moral and ethical impact on other persons in the school and community. What are the effects on other students? Other teachers? The school district? The community? For example, Borland described a case in which only students in a gifted program were given expensive three-day trips to Washington, DC, and Boston, which (1) consumed funds at the expense of other programs and (2) would have benefitted all students.

Borland's (2003) own five-step evaluation model is designed for teachers and G/T coordinators and requires no psychometric training. Briefly, step one is clarifying goals and "making certain they refer to benefits that will accrue to students as a result of program intervention" (p.

**TABLE 18.1** The DESDEG Model

Key Feature A: Philosophy and Objectives
    Program Requirement  1:         Existence and Adequacy of a Document
    Program Requirement  2:         Application of the Document
Key Feature B: Student Identification and Placement
    Program Requirement  3:         Validity of Conception and Adequacy of Procedures
    Program Requirement  4:         Appropriateness of Relationship Between Capacity and Curriculum
Key Feature C: The Curriculum
    Program Requirement  5:         Relevance of Conception
    Program Requirement  6:         Comprehensiveness
    Program Requirement  7:         Articulation
    Program Requirement  8:         Adequacy of Instructional Facilities
Key Feature D: The Teacher
    Program Requirement  9:         Selection
    Program Requirement 10:         Training
Key Feature E: Program Organization and Operation
    Program Requirement 11:         General Staff Orientation
    Program Requirement 12:         Administrative Responsibility and Leadership
    Program Requirement 13:         Functional Adequacy of the Organization
    Program Requirement 14:         Financial Allocation
    Program Requirement 15:         Provision for Evaluation

302). Step two is selecting just a few of these goals (three or four) for an annual evaluation. Not all goals need to be evaluated every year. Step three is identifying "those activities in which student behavior can be observed that will shed light on progress toward each goal" (p. 304). The criteria (desired level of performance) should be specified, for example, "a certain percentage of students completing projects" (p. 304) might be one criterion for a goal. Step four is recording students' actual performance. Step five is writing the evaluation report. This report should include the effects of the program on the broader context, including "the moral and ethical consequences of the program's existence and activities" (p. 304).

It can be seen even in these sketchy outlines that the evaluation of education programs, including G/T programs, can be approached from many different viewpoints, use different strategies, and focus on a variety of dimensions and considerations.

## THE RIMM MODEL

Rimm's (1977) model both (1) structures program evaluation in a relatively easy-to-follow fashion and (2) ties it to the initial program plan. Summarizing a program in one picture is very helpful for conceptualizing program components and therefore for relating evaluation needs to those components. Figure 18.1 demonstrates how the different parts of a program fit together and, importantly, how evaluation can help one monitor all educational *Inputs (resources),* all *Processes (activities),* and all *Outcomes (goals and objectives).* Using the model has many advantages. First, it helps us understand the relationships among educational resources, processes, and outcomes. Second, using the model helps prevent the implementation of any activity without considering its eventual *evaluation.* Third, the model helps us become more sensitive to the close relationship

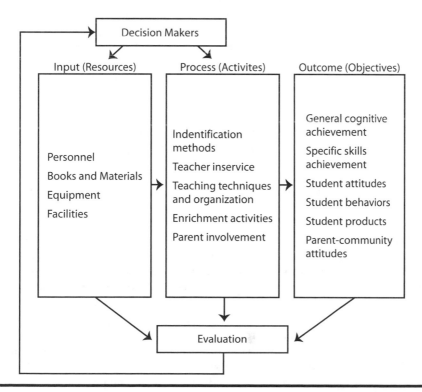

**FIGURE 18.1**    Framework for the Evaluation and Monitoring of a Gifted Program.

of program decisions to the many student outcomes. Finally, and most importantly, the model itemizes on one page the program components that should be evaluated in regard to both (1) how well the component was implemented and/or (2) how successfully that component helped achieve program goals.

The components within each of the three steps of the model reflect specific areas that should be evaluated. That is, each of the various types of input/resources (Step I), processes/activities (Step II), and outcomes/objectives (Step III) should be evaluated. Evaluation data (Step IV) from the components will present a comprehensive picture of the success and impact of a gifted program. This information is brought together and fed back to the decision makers who will use it for further planning—for modifying the input and process steps, which may include program expansion. Without the crucial evaluation step, there would be little clear basis for good decisions.

The reader may wish to draw a blank framework to outline his or her own program and evaluation model and complete the diagram as this chapter is read.

Step I: *Input* represents resources. Resources typically include such program ingredients as teaching and support personnel, books, materials, equipment, and facilities. Resources also may include more specific categories such as community resource persons, specific student populations, or funding sources. Resources are the investments in the program and they usually are relatively easy to identify and list.

Step II: *Process* includes the activities of the program—everything that is planned to make the program effective. Typical categories of activities include identification procedures, teaching techniques, educational groupings, enrichment experiences, acceleration plans, teacher in-service training, and parent involvement activities. One may wish to itemize more specific curriculum activity components of the program, for example, creative-thinking instruction, creative writing, a computer mini-course, accelerated mathematics, Renzulli's (1977) Enrichment Triad model, and so on.

Step III: *Outcome* represents the goals and objectives of the gifted program. It actually may be easier to complete the list for Step III *before* completing Steps I and II. What do you expect to accomplish? What are the purposes of the program? Ideas for program goals were listed in Chapter 3.

Note that increased academic achievement is not necessarily a central outcome of a gifted program, although it may be an objective for gifted underachievers or, for example, for an accelerated math, biology, or reading program. More frequently, increases in specific *skills* are the intended outcomes of a program, for example, creative, critical, or evaluative thinking and independent study and research skills. Positive student *attitudes,* including self-concepts, attitudes toward education, and high career aspirations, also are frequently stated goals. In addition, scientific, literary, and artistic *products* are important and potentially measurable objectives. Parent and community attitudes toward the program and toward the needs of gifted children are further important outcomes to monitor.

Completing the model by inserting program components into each of the four steps should provide the reader with an overview of the entire program and assist with planning the necessary evaluations.

## COMPLEXITY OF EVALUATION AND AUDIENCE: A HIERARCHY

The sophistication of an evaluation will be related to the intended audience—the persons who are the decision makers for a particular program. These decision makers can be placed in a *hierarchy* in terms of the quantity and the quality (statistical complexity) of the information they must have to carry out their own responsibilities. The goal should be to provide the appropriate information to match the information needs of these decision makers. Callahan and Caldwell (1995) refer to audiences as *stakeholders*. A suggested form for identifying relevant stakeholders can be found in Appendix 18.1.

Briefly, (1) students and parents will need less information than (2) teachers and program directors, who in turn need less information than (3) administrators and school board members. (4) The state department of education will require still more technical information, and (5) the federal government, with its highly experienced grant reviewers, will require the greatest amount and the highest technical level of information.

Table 18.2 summarizes the relationship between levels of the decision-making hierarchy, components of the program emphasized, and the persons primarily responsible for the evaluation.

The hierarchy of decision makers is based on the different purposes or uses of the program evaluation information. A student or his or her parents may need to know only if the activity is generally interesting, challenging, motivating, and beneficial in very personal terms in order to decide if the student should continue in the program. A relatively small amount of information is needed for a decision that may have an important impact upon just one student. The student and his or her parents, with the help of the program teacher and/or coordinator, can assess the value of the program for that student.

The teacher or program director requires quite a bit more information in order to modify, improve, and perhaps expand the program. This function of evaluation is called *formative evaluation.* Conducted throughout the school year, it is intended to provide immediate and continuous feedback to the staff regarding program strengths and weaknesses. The main focus of formative evaluation will be on *process* (Figure 18.1); that is, on the value of various activities and experiences. House and Lapan (1994) recommend that more formative evaluation be done because it requires less formalistic design and serves to improve the program. Formative evaluation usually is conducted quite effectively by program staff, although observations of an independent (outside) evaluator usually add objectivity, insights, and ideas to the evaluation.

The school principal, district administrators, and members of the elected school board must decide whether to continue, change, or expand the gifted program, and hopefully not to fold it up. To make these kinds of decisions, a *summative evaluation* must be conducted. The emphasis is on *outcomes,* and so a summative evaluation is conducted at the end of a unit, project, or most often, the school year. It "sums up" program success. Administrators and school board members may expect the staff to relate program *input* and *process* to outcomes in order to estimate some kind of cost effectiveness. A teacher or program director with training in evaluation and statistics sometimes can successfully conduct such an evaluation. Board of education members primarily will want to know if a program has been "effective," and so the *hows* and *whys* of its effectiveness must be clearly and simply communicated.

**TABLE 18.2**   Summary of the Relationship between Hierarchy of Decision Making and Evaluation Plan

| Hierarchy of Decision Making | Model Component Emphasized | Staff Responsibility |
|---|---|---|
| Individual Student or Parent | Individual Process and Outcome | Student, Teacher, and/or Parent |
| Teacher or Program Director | Process and Outcomes | Teacher, Program Director, or Administrator with some background in evaluation or Independent Evaluator |
| State or Federal Government | Input, Process, and Outcomes | Independent Evaluator with support of Program Staff |

Generally, local school people will feel their accountability obligation is met if they can prove that (1) the program was conducted as planned, (2) the students learned what was taught, and (3) the process of learning was a positive one.

However, if a program is state or federally funded, a professional summative evaluation conducted by an experienced outside evaluator probably will be necessary. This evaluation typically includes a more technical, experimentally oriented evaluation and provides an "objective eye" (Fetterman, 1993; Olenchak & Castle, 1995). The teacher's role then becomes one of *cooperator*. The teacher need only inform the evaluator of the resources, activities, and objectives, and provide him or her with the needed data. Some test administration may be involved. Clear communication with the evaluator and full cooperation in gathering the necessary data will facilitate an accurate evaluation of the program. The outside evaluator should not be considered an adversary who is anxious to pounce on weaknesses. His or her role is to provide constructive feedback to the staff for program improvement, and to objectively report the reasonableness and effectiveness of the program plans, methods, activities, and so forth. Although the objectivity of outside evaluators may appear threatening during early program development, that same objectivity will be extraordinarily reinforcing when a program is stabilized and functioning well.

The outside evaluation may require the use of a *control group* of subjects (for example, students of similar ability in another school district where there is no program). Test scores from such a control group, when compared with scores of students in the program, would help determine if any improvements (for instance, in creativity scores, self-concept development, or achievement) are due to the program and not due simply to maturation, the passage of time, or other educational experiences. Teacher-coordinators likely will drown in a sea of statistics if they attempt this type of evaluation on their own.

As emphasized earlier, an important first consideration for effective evaluation is outlining the evaluation design at the same time the rest of the program is planned, namely, before the program begins. Even an expert evaluator will be less able to do his or her job if the program begins without coordinating the program objectives with their eventual evaluation. Beginning a G/T program without an evaluation design is comparable to beginning one's classroom teaching without a curriculum plan. In both cases, the preplanning helps outline where you are going, how to get there, and what to do when you arrive.

In summary, no program for the gifted should be conducted without some evaluation. Whether the decision makers are students, parents, teachers, administrators, school board members, or state or federal agencies, they will want to know about the "success" and the particular "effects" of the program.

## INSTRUMENT SELECTION

Some form of measurement is almost always necessary to determine the degree to which program objectives have been achieved (e.g., those in the *outcome* rectangle of Figure 18.1). Ideally, in order to reach sound conclusions one should try to obtain *two* measurements of each objective, particularly the most important ones. Also, whenever possible one should use instruments—tests, questionnaires, rating forms—already available. To do a proper job of developing one's own instruments requires a considerable amount of time and usually requires training and experience in test construction.

Besides, with a little digging a teacher-coordinator most likely will discover that the test-building work already has been done. Many instruments for assessing innumerable aspects of G/T programs are available, for example, in Renzulli (1975), Renzulli and Reis (1985, 1997), Renzulli, Reis, and Smith (1981), Sjogren, Hopkins, and Gooler (1975), and the Association for the Gifted Evaluation Committee (1979). If the same or similar program plans are used in several schools or districts, evaluation questionnaires may be shared.

A parent questionnaire for an Enrichment Triad Model, Revolving Door Identification

Model, or Schoolwide Enrichment Model program appears in Appendix 18.2 (Renzulli and Reis, 1985). Teacher, student, and parent questionnaires are available for the evaluation of many components of the Renzulli program models, for example, a *Student Product Assessment Form, Type I Enrichment Evaluation Form, Scale for Evaluating Creativity Teaching Materials,* and others (see Renzulli and Reis, 1985, 1997).

For new evaluation ideas, check current journals on gifted education and creativity and documents of the National Research Center on the Gifted and Talented (e.g., Delcourt et al., 1994); they frequently describe instruments that have been recently developed and validated. Some sample instruments appear at the end of this chapter.

Although there are indeed many different tests for review, it can happen that an instrument exactly right for a specific purpose will not be found. Do not make the mistake of using an instrument—no matter how carefully designed—that measures something other than what the program plans to teach. It is essential that the *objectives* of the program activities, on one hand, be matched with the *purposes* and the *contents* of the tests and inventories, on the other. If test purposes or contents do not match program objectives and activities, one is not very likely to find a measurable effect of the program. This simple point may seem self-evident to the sensible reader. However, it is a common error for G/T teachers and coordinators to teach one set of contents and skills (for example, creativity), yet evaluate others (for example, advanced reading)—and then be surprised and disappointed to find "no effects" or "no transfer" of the training experience. Standardized tests may be especially inappropriate in evaluating disadvantaged gifted programs. Test scores for these programs may reflect socioeconomic status, linguistic abilities, or cultural factors rather than the varied dimensions of the actual gifted program (House & Lapan, 1994). As mentioned earlier, negative evaluation findings can easily be misused: They can readily and logically be interpreted as evidence that the program was ineffective.

## Pilot Testing

A program evaluator may need to *pilot* a test, that is, try it out with a few children to help decide if it is appropriate for the desired purpose. For example, suppose a program included accelerated reading or math and the evaluator wanted to determine if a particular norm-referenced test could be used to evaluate student achievement. (A *norm-referenced* test is one of moderate difficulty that is designed to produce a normal, bell-curve distribution of scores, for example, a standardized achievement test.) If the test is administered to two or three students and they "top out" near the maximum possible score, this would immediately signal that the test does not assess the high achievement level of the gifted students. It may be necessary to pilot three or four tests to find an appropriate one. One strategy is to pilot several tests simultaneously with several small groups of students. This quickly provides plenty of information for test comparison and selection.

## Topping Out, Regression Toward the Mean, and Reliability

As discussed earlier in this book, the topping-out phenomenon is a frequent occurrence when gifted students take standardized, norm-referenced achievement tests. The tests often are not difficult enough to discriminate among or evaluate the learning of high-achieving gifted children. If we measure improvements from pretests to post-tests but students already have achieved ceiling scores on the pretests, it will appear that the students showed no measurable improvement. In fact, there simply was no place for the scores to go. Actual progress could not be measured.

A potentially more serious problem related to using too-easy achievement tests comes from the *regression toward the mean* effect. This simply means that given a first score that is extreme (either very high or very low), by chance alone the next score is likely to "regress" toward the mean. Now if some gifted students score near the very top of a pretest, their scores on the post-test by chance alone are likely to be lower—incorrectly suggesting that participation in the special G/T activities damaged their learning. With regressed scores on a basic skills test, an audience could conclude that the gifted program is having a negative effect on the basic skills of students. Because pulling students out of the regular classroom often is a controversial issue in the first place, such an interpretation could be devastating to an excellent program.

Tests should be precise enough to measure changes from pretest to post-test. Therefore, tests should have good test-retest and/or alternate forms reliability. Rating scales must have a sufficiently wide scoring range to detect pre- to post-test differences (Beggs, Mouw, and Barton, 1989).

Divergent thinking tests can produce different results depending on variations in instructions, differences in motivational levels, or other reasons. In one evaluation by the second author, post-test scores on the *Torrance Tests of Creative Thinking* (TTCT) were significantly *lower* than pretest scores, despite an excellent creative thinking program. Perhaps the lower scores were due to a less motivating classroom climate toward the end of the year, compared with the more stimulating "new opportunity" at the beginning of the program. It also was possible that the two TTCT test forms are not equivalent (i.e., the more difficult form was given as a post-test); or that these divergent thinking tests simply did not measure the kinds of creative dispositions and abilities that were learned (Davis, 1998). Whatever the reason(s), such findings can be damaging to a good program.

## TEST CONSTRUCTION

There are times when a state or federal agency will require evidence for the effectiveness of a program, but the exactly appropriate tests and measures simply do not exist. It therefore may be necessary to construct original tests or questionnaires in order to evaluate specific student skills, information, attitudes, or abilities; the effectiveness of specific program components; or even the overall quality of the total program. Technical help from an evaluation expert at a university or private consulting firm, someone experienced in evaluating G/T programs and in constructing tests, probably will be needed.

To select a consultant, contact directors of other G/T programs and state or even national leaders in gifted education to find who in the area is available and qualified. When a consultant is recommended, one can elicit opinions of his or her work from teachers and program directors for whom the consultant has provided services. One also can ask to review tests and reports the consultant has prepared for other clients.

Remember, a poor instrument or evaluation is worse than none at all, even if the cost is low. Test construction may be expensive, which is one good reason to use established tests, as recommended earlier.

## Rating Students' Products

Artistic, literary, scientific, or other types of student products may be outcomes of a program, and although they are difficult to evaluate reliably, their quality is measurable. Product evaluation usually involves either of two approaches. With the first *gain score* approach, samples of students' work obtained at the outset of the program (pretest products) are compared with students' products at the end of the educational experience (post-test products). Gain scores may be used to evaluate products that reflect the development of skills and abilities in art, creative writing, divergent thinking, technical skills, or other areas.

With the second *absolute* approach, individual students' products are evaluated according to their excellence without an objective comparison with earlier products. The absolute approach would be used if science or other major projects (for example, of the Renzulli Type III variety) are evaluated for which earlier comparison products are not available.

With either the gain score or the absolute method, rating scales may be used to quantify the judgments. As two examples, Renzulli (1975) recommended the scale in Appendix 18.3, developed by the Warwick, Rhode Island, Public Schools, for evaluating the quality of visual arts products. The scale in Appendix 4.5 may be used to evaluate the excellence of virtually any type of student product.

The rating scales in Appendices 18.3 and 4.5 could serve as models for creating one's own product-rating scales. Alternatively, the following steps could be used to develop and apply original rating scales:

***Step 1. Determine the evaluation criteria (for example, creativeness, technical skill) and the specific scales for rating those criteria.*** The criteria should come from the teaching objectives. Note the objectives reflected in each scale in Appendices 18.3 and 4.5. As for the rating scales themselves, while Appendix 18.3 uses six-point scales, a five-point scale as in Appendix 4.5 usually is most comfortable. It is best to describe the meaning of each point on the scale. The "low," "moderate," and "high" descriptions of Appendix 18.3 and the "To a great extent," "Somewhat," and "To a limited extent" of Appendix 4.5 are very minimal descriptions. For example, a scale for evaluating the use of *humor* in creative writing might be based on the following descriptors:

"1": No use of humor.
"2": One humorous comment, which does not appear original.
"3": Two or three humorous statements or paragraphs, which do not appear original.
"4": Two or three statements or paragraphs that do appear original.
"5": Original humorous themes skillfully integrated into the entire story.

Such scale-point descriptions will improve the accuracy (reliability) of the ratings.

***Step 2. Collect pretest products from each child in the program.*** All products should be identified with code numbers so that the students' names and the date of collection will not be obvious to the raters.

***Step 3. Select at least two raters.*** They may be teachers or community members. Train them to use the particular scales with extra products that will not be used as evaluation data. After rating several products together, use a few more extra products for individual raters each to rate separately.

***Step 4. Calculate the percentage of rater agreement.*** With five-point scales, two raters should agree on at least 80 percent of the practice ratings before they begin rating the pretest and post-test products. If the raters do not agree at an 80 percent level, they need more training, including a discussion of the reasons for their disagreements.

***Step 5. After interrater reliability is established, to minimize bias, raters should rate all products.*** This should be done without knowing the names of the children and without knowing which are pretest products and which are post-test products.

***Step 6. Calculate the average pretest ratings for the group and compare them with the average post-test ratings.*** If a program is effective, the average post-test rating should be higher, indicating that skill development increased since the pretest products were created. Statistics may be necessary in order to conclude that the overall increase is not due to chance. Also, as noted earlier, a control group may be necessary to prove that the improvement of the trained students was not due to the passage of time or to other educational experiences.

For information regarding the gains (or losses) of individual students, one would examine the differences between pretest and post-test ratings for each student.

***Step 7. In reporting the findings, the means (and other statistics, if any) must be meaningful, reliable, and valid.*** If possible, include a few sample products (for example, samples of creative writing, scientific reports, or photos of artwork) to illustrate the student gains. These sample products will help any audience understand the meaning of the ratings.

Hennessey and Amabile (1988) used a much more informal system for rating the creativeness of children's stories given orally in response to pictures. Three teachers, experienced in children's creative writing, were simply asked to rate the creativeness of each story "using your own, subjective definition of creativity." They were given no training and made their assessments independently. Despite the lack of training and simplicity of the rating task, interjudge reliability was a high 0.91. These results are sufficiently impressive and surprising that your authors would recommend a replication before using teacher ratings of creative stories, for example, as a prudent measure of the success of a creative writing program.

## Classroom Observation Data

Parents, administrators, school board members, and government agencies usually like to know what happens in a gifted program, and so classroom observation data are good data to collect. A structured observation form can be developed for a program and used to describe "who is doing what with whom and when" in a very specific way. As one example, Appendix 18.4 (from Rimm, 1981) shows a structured observation form used for monitoring a reading program. The letters at the top of each column represent each of the ten students observed. Filling in a circle indicates that a student is involved in one of the activities listed in the rows. An objective observer would enter the classroom at random times of the day and observe ten randomly selected students, recording their activities on the checklist. Descriptive comment may be added to each observation to provide a richer description of the class environment.

A form such as the one in Appendix 18.4 could be adapted for use with any particular G/T program. Category headings could be modified or new ones created; each would have specific subcategories. For example, one might wish to record student's interest level, student's behavior, student's interactions, teacher's instructional activities, materials and equipment in use, or activities of other adults. Additional headings, each with specific subcategories, could be included depending upon the special activities of the program.

If desirable, at the end of the year summary forms can be tabulated and percentages calculated to describe the specific *type* and *extent* of the activities engaged in during that year. This summary provides objective documentation of the year's program activities. Thus if a school board member wanted to know how much time microcomputers were in use, how many students participated in the *Junior Great Books* discussions, or what proportion of the G/T program time was spent in independent projects, numbers and percentages would be available to support personal observations and impressions. Nothing is quite so convincing as hard data.

## Questionnaires

Activities in both the *process* and *outcomes* components of Rimm's model may be evaluated with questionnaires. The best way to find answers is to ask questions. Decision makers at all levels will want to know (and have a right to know) the effectiveness and special strengths of a program as well as its weaknesses as perceived by others. They also are interested in others' constructive suggestions for improving the program. If questionnaires are brief and require only that a few numbers be circled and/or a few questions be answered, most persons will respond. You can bet that those who are strongly enthusiastic and those who are most disappointed or critical will be certain to respond.

Questionnaires use various types of items. Objective items include *checklists, rating scales, rankings,* and *multiple-choice* statements. The advantages of objective items include ease of development, efficiency of administration, clear response options, easy and objective scoring, and ready quantifiability for statistical purposes. Some disadvantages include the limited nature of the response options, along with little or no information about the *reasons* for the judgments.

Because of these disadvantages, many objective questionnaires also include open-ended items. Open-ended items provide an opportunity for students, teachers, parents, principals, and/or school board members to voice reasons for their opinions, as well as to contribute suggestions and potential solutions to problems. Information can indeed be rich and valuable. For formative evaluation purposes, open-ended items usually are more valuable than objective items. In the negative column, open-ended items are more time-consuming for both respondents and scorers, interpretations may be ambiguous, and the answers are not easily quantified.

As examples of combining objective with open-ended questionnaires, Appendix 18.5 presents a brief questionnaire that could be used by teacher participants in an in-service program. Appendix 18.6 shows a questionnaire that allows school board members to evaluate G/T services of a high school. Appendix 18.7 presents a nonobjective open-ended form that students can use to evaluate a learning center.

Generally, it is wise to set aside a few minutes in every program for teachers and students to complete the evaluation forms. If you create the time, persons will fill out the questionnaires on the spot; questionnaires taken home or mailed often are not returned.

### Interviews

Interviews can be used to gather information about input, process, or outcomes. Fetterman (1993) described several kinds of interviews. Formally structured and semistructured interviews are similar to questionnaires in that they use specific formats and questions, and so data can be compared. Informal interviews are easiest to conduct and often are spontaneous, almost as if they were extensions of conversation. Fetterman points out that informal interviews may answer some important questions that would not be answered by more formal interviews.

Retrospective interviews involve reconstructing the past. Although not the most accurate, they not only are useful but sometimes are the only type of interview that can provide insight into difficulties. Retrospective interviews can be either formal or informal.

### DAILY LOGS

As a general principle, *log everything*. Each staff member should keep a notebook handy in which to make brief notes on daily activities. The value

of the entries will far outweigh the few minutes invested each day. The kinds of information that could be logged include:

A description of activities
Preparation for the activities
Number of participants
Perceived effectiveness of the activities
Modifications for the future
Any data collected
Any anecdotal material

A personal log kept by each staff member can provide important program documentation serving at least three purposes. First and foremost, it can provide a description of the activities and accomplishments of the students and, therefore, of the value of the specific learning activities and projects. Second, it can assure administration and board members that the staff member has indeed made critical contributions to the program. Third, it will serve to remind the teacher of the quantity and quality of his or her own contributions and accomplishments.

### INDICATORS

Measures including high-school dropout rates, increased attendance, and percentages of students going to college are recommended by House and Lapan (1994) to evaluate gifted programs for disadvantaged students. Other indicators, such as number of students taking advanced courses or classes in which they will continue after programming, could be helpful for some gifted programs.

Indicators should be tied specifically to the objectives of the gifted program. For example, a program targeted toward encouraging gifted girls to achieve should compare indicators of female success to past female performance rather than to male performance. Hopefully, the gender gap in performance will eventually close, but female success should not become a contest between the sexes. Improvement of female performance is the most important indicator of an effective program for females.

Although it is difficult for schools to do follow-up studies of high school graduates, data on academic adjustment to college, percentage of high school students who complete college, attendance at graduate school, and career choices all could be valuable indicators of successful gifted programs. House and Lapan (1994) point out that studies typically are funded for short periods of time, and demands for accountability tend to be short term. Nevertheless, whenever longitudinal studies are possible, they provide important evaluation information.

## STUDENT SELF-EVALUATIONS

Student self-evaluations are important in G/T programs. Primarily, they provide individual students with a clear measure of accomplishment relative to their own goals and objectives. Positive feedback reinforces student motivation and commitment, while objectively documenting their personal progress. For program evaluators, when individual self-evaluations are combined they become important measures of student outcomes, some of which could not be obtained in any other way.

Independent self-monitoring usually can be conducted quite handily by students in junior and senior high school. Younger children also can take responsibility for self-evaluation, with a little help from their teachers. One example of a summative, end-of-the-year student self-evaluation form appears in Appendix 18.8.

## PERFORMANCE CONTRACTING

Student *performance contracting* is another vehicle for individual student evaluation. Within the student contract, the teacher and the student spell out:

1. Specific *objectives,* including skills to be learned and final projects and papers to be completed.
2. The *activities* in which the student plans to engage to achieve the objectives.
3. The *deadline* by which the objectives will be completed.

4. The *materials* the student will produce (or collect) in support of his or her attainment of the objectives.
5. The *methods* and *criteria* by which the attainment of the objectives will be evaluated.

The student contract is a "study guide" for both the student and the teacher, as well as the basis for an evaluation and documentation of the student's personal performance. Performance contracts are a type of learning activity that encourages the independence and creativity that most gifted students thrive on. Thus individual student needs are served while also providing program evaluation and accountability data.

## QUALITATIVE AND QUANTITATIVE EVALUATION

Although some evaluation techniques have already been described, Linnemeyer's (1994) list of evaluation techniques in Table 18.3 can help program coordinators remember some of the many qualitative and quantitative techniques that are available.

## COMMITMENT TO EVALUATION

Teachers and coordinators in gifted programs are likely to view evaluation as burdensome. Their time always is scarce, and time used for evaluation will be at the expense of time for students. It thus is very tempting simply to avoid evaluation altogether. However, skipping the evaluation process is a short-sighted decision for gifted programs—which, we repeat, have a history of being quickly cut from district, state, and federal budgets. Good evaluation is the only way to determine the most effective way to enhance the education of gifted learners. It also is the only way to prove to sponsors and decision makers that the program is indeed accomplishing its objectives.

As a final note, Table 18.4 summarizes guidelines proposed by House and Lapan (1994) for evaluating programs for gifted disadvantaged students. These same guidelines seem very appropriate for evaluating other gifted programs.

**TABLE 18.3**   Qualitative and Quantitative Techniques

*Qualitative Evaluation*

| | |
|---|---|
| Case Studies | Logs |
| Inventories | Autobiographies |
| Questionnaires | Portfolios |
| Scrapbooks | Videos |
| Recordings | Tape Recordings |
| Report Cards | Diaries |
| (Descriptive) | Activity Records |
| Behavior Journals | Anecdotal Records |
| Collections | Profiles |
| Samples of Work | Scope and Sequence |
| Writing Samples | Charts |
| Sociograms | Student Interest Surveys |
| Self-Concept Scales | Essays |

*Quantitative Evaluation*

| | |
|---|---|
| Achievement Tests | Mental Ability Tests |
| Checklists | Creativity Tests |
| Criterion Referenced | Auditions |
| Tests | Grades |
| Pupil Graphs | Music Tests |
| Critical Thinking tests | Teacher-Made Tests |
| Report Cards | Classroom Climate Tests |
| (Numerical) | Art Tests |
| Charts | Psychomotor Ability |
| Sociometric Tests | Tests |
| Leadership Tests | |

From Linnemeyer (1994), by permission of the Illinois Association for Gifted Children.

## SUMMARY

Evaluation in gifted education has been minimal. However, it is important both for demonstrating success to outsiders and for improving the program. Evaluation plans should be made at the outset of program planning.

Some objectives are difficult to evaluate, such as improvements in self-awareness, creativity, analyzing, and social responsibility. Other outcomes are comparatively easy to assess, such as the success of acceleration or the improved quality of student products.

**TABLE 18.4**   Guidelines for Conducting an Evaluation of Programs for the Gifted Disadvantaged

- Students are identified by (nontraditional) procedures that are appropriate to the particular types of students and the program.
- Critical components of the program have been adequately described in the evaluation, including descriptions of the actual classroom teaching.
- Higher level thought processes, creativity, and other particularly appropriate outcomes for gifted students, depending on the particular program, have been examined by appropriate means other than standardized tests.
- Multiple measures have been employed.
- Possible negative side-effects of the program have been examined.
- Other unanticipated effects on students, teachers, parents, the community have been examined.
- The program contains culturally relevant material for culturally different students and recognizes and respects their particular cultural identity.
- The program displays sensitivity to females and includes materials with female role models, etc.

From House and Lapan (1994), by permission of the Association for the Gifted.

Provus' discrepancy model includes five steps: Design, Installation, Process (activities), Product, and Product Comparison. At each step one compares the program reality with a standard and then corrects the discrepancy. Eash's differential evaluation model focuses on three considerations, Effort (activities), Effect (products and outcomes), and Efficiency (the relationships of effort and resources to the quality of the Effects).

Renzulli's DESDEQ model included five steps corresponding to five documents: the Manual, Evaluation Scales, Basic Information Forms, Evaluator's Workbook, and the Summary Report.

Borland recommended evaluating the social and ethical impact on others in the school and community. His five-step model comprised clarifying program goals, selecting a few goals for evaluation, identifying student activities that reflect progress toward a goal, recording students' performance, and writing the evaluation report, which will include effects on others.

Rimm's model structures the program evaluation and ties it to the initial program plan. The three steps of Input (resources), Process (activities), and Outcome (objectives), each with specific subcategories, all may be evaluated.

Increased academic achievement may or may not be a central outcome. Rather, improvements in process skills and attitudes are usual goals of G/T programs.

Audiences form a hierarchy in the quality and quantity of needed evaluation information. Students and parents need relatively little information to decide whether to continue in the program. Teachers and program directors require more information, particularly continuous, formative evaluation for program improvement. Administrators and school board members will require summative information to decide whether to continue or expand the program. State or federal funding sources will need considerable detailed information, including, for example, test scores and statistical comparisons with control groups.

One should try to obtain two measurements of each important objective. It usually is easier and cheaper to locate already validated tests than to construct your own. It is important to be certain that the test measures the objectives that were the basis of the teaching. Using the wrong tests will produce negative results, creating a bad impression. Standardized tests may be inappropriate for evaluating gifted programs for the disadvantaged.

Pilot testing is advisable, for example, to cope with the topping-out problem common with gifted students. On a second testing, very high scores may regress toward the mean, creating the appearance that the program damaged, for example, basic skill development. Tests should be sufficiently precise (reliable, wide scoring range) to measure pre- to post-test changes.

With a gain-score approach, ratings of preprogram projects are compared with ratings of post-program projects. With the absolute approach, complex projects are evaluated without comparison to earlier projects.

In creating original rating scales, one would determine the evaluation criteria, collect pretest products, select and train at least two raters, determine rater agreement, use "blind" ratings, and compare average pretest ratings with average post-test ratings. It is desirable to include sample projects in final reports.

Classroom observation data present objective information regarding "what happens" in a gifted program.

The process (activities) and outcome (objectives) sections of Rimm's model may be evaluated with questionnaires.

Objective questionnaire items (for example, checklists, rating scales, multiple-choice questions) are easily administered and scored. They may be combined with less objective and more time-consuming—but highly informative—open-ended questions.

Interviews are useful for gathering information about input, process, and outcomes. Informal interviews are easier to conduct and may yield more information than formal interviews. Retrospective interviews, which reconstruct the past, can provide insights.

Daily logs provide valuable records of activities, preparation, participants, perceived effectiveness, ideas for modifications, and anecdotal information.

The use of indicators (e.g., dropout rates) are recommended for the evaluation of gifted programs. Indicators should be tied to the objectives of specific programs, such as those for disadvantaged and female gifted students. Follow-up studies, although difficult to conduct, also provide valuable indicators of a program's success.

Self-evaluations provide positive, motivating feedback to students as well as unique program evaluation data.

Performance contracting can be used to individualize instruction and to document student accomplishments.

There are many qualitative and quantitative evaluation techniques available to gifted program coordinators.

Good evaluation is absolutely essential for the continuity and improvement of any gifted program.

## APPENDIX 18.1   IDENTIFYING RELEVANT STAKEHOLDERS

We have started a list of relevant stakeholders for you, but this list is *only a beginning.*

1. Read over this list and *eliminate* any individuals or groups who are not important to your program.
2. Read over the list and *add* any individuals or groups who are significant to your program.

*School Administrators*
Superintendent
Associate Superintendent for Instruction
Principals
Supervisors or Directors of Instruction

*Program Staff*
Program Coordinator/Director
Teachers in the Program
Mentors

*Other Decision-Makers*
School Board Members

*Other School Staff*
Regular Classroom Teachers (if they are not program staff)
Librarians
School Psychologists
Counselors

*Other Community Members*
President of the PTA

*Parents of Gifted Students*

*Parents of Students not in the Program*

*Students in the Program*

*Funding Agents*

From: C. M. Callahan and M. S. Caldwell, *A Practitioner's Guide to Evaluating Programs for the Gifted,* a service publication of the National Association for Gifted Children. University of Virginia, 1995.

**APPENDIX 18.2  SAMPLE PAGE FROM A PARENT QUESTIONNAIRE**

## Revolving Door TAG Program Parent Questionnaire

### *Directions:*

Please do not sign your name to this questionnaire. No attempt will be made to identify persons completing these forms. Please return the questionnaire in the enclosed envelope within the next two or three days.

You can help to make our program better by giving careful thought to each of the questions that follow. Because of the relatively small number of persons involved in the project, each person's opinion will weigh heavily in analyzing the results. We appreciate your cooperation and assistance in helping us to evaluate this program. We suggest that you read through the entire questionnaire before you begin to answer the questions.

|  | YES | NO |
|---|---|---|
| 1. Did you attend the meeting held earlier this year at which we explained the Revolving Door TAG Program? | ___ | ___ |
| 2. Do you feel that you have been provided with enough information about the Revolving Door Identification Model in general? | ___ | ___ |
| 3. Are you familiar with the procedures for revolving a student into the resource room? | ___ | ___ |
| 4. Has your child been revolved into the resource room this year? | ___ | ___ |
| 5. If the answer to Question No. 4 is yes, are you familiar with the project or topic that your child worked on while in the resource room? | ___ | ___ |
| 6. Are you familiar with the procedures for revolving a student out of the resource room? | ___ | ___ |
| 7. Are you familiar with a procedure we use in the TAG Program called "Curriculum Compacting"? | ___ | ___ |
| 8. Have you been invited to visit the resource room? | ___ | ___ |
| 9. Do you feel that you have been offered sufficient opportunity to contact the school or make an appointment to discuss your child's work in the TAG Program? | ___ | ___ |
| 10. Has your child encountered any problems with his/her friends as a result of being involved in the TAG Program? If yes, please explain. | ___ | ___ |
| 11. Has your child encountered any problems as a result of leaving the regular classroom to participate in the TAG resource room? If yes, please explain. | ___ | ___ |
| 12. Has your child expressed a concern about missing work in the regular classroom or making up assignments because he or she is out of the classroom to attend the TAG resource room? | ___ | ___ |
| 13. Have you had any communication with your child's classroom teacher about his/her participation in the TAG Program? If yes, please describe. | ___ | ___ |

From Renzulli and Reis (1985), reprinted by permission.

## APPENDIX 18.3   PROJECT GIFTED: EVALUATION SCALE FOR VISUAL ARTS

Code No. _____   Age _____   Boy/Girl _____   TOTAL SCORE _____

Evaluator _____ Position _____ Date _____

| Elements | Low 1 | 2 | Moderate 3 | 4 | High 5 | 6 |
|---|---|---|---|---|---|---|
| 1.  Creative Expression, Imagination, Uniqueness | | | | | | |
| 2.  Flexibility, Appreciation, and Adaptability to Various Media | | | | | | |
| 3.  Fluency, Variety or Number of Ideas | | | | | | |
| 4.  Sensitivity-Composition-Design | | | | | | |
| 5.  Manipulative Skills: Construction, Weaving, etc. | | | | | | |
| 6.  Growth | | | | | | |
| Column Total | | | | | | |
| Weight | 1 | 2 | 3 | 4 | 5 | 6 |
| Weighted Column Total | | | | | | |
| TOTAL SCORE | | | | | | |

From J. S. Renzulli, *An Evaluation of Project Gifted.* Storrs, University of Connecticut, 1973. Reprinted by permission.

## APPENDIX 18.4 EXAMPLE OF A STRUCTURED OBSERVATION FORM

Date _____  a.m. _____  p.m. _____  Observer _____

**a.m.**

| 1. Pupil's Location | abc | def | ghij |
|---|---|---|---|
| Desk or table | 000 | 000 | 0000 |
| Carrel | 000 | 000 | 0000 |
| Open area | 000 | 000 | 0000 |
| Materials center | 000 | 000 | 0000 |
| Other (specify): | 000 | 000 | 0000 |

| 2. Instructional Content | abc | def | ghij |
|---|---|---|---|
| Readiness | 000 | 000 | 0000 |
| Decoding skills | 000 | 000 | 0000 |
| Comprehension | 000 | 000 | 0000 |
| Enjoyment or appreciation | 000 | 000 | 0000 |
| Vocabulary | 000 | 000 | 0000 |
| Spelling | 000 | 000 | 0000 |
| Grammar | 000 | 000 | 0000 |
| Composition | 000 | 000 | 0000 |
| Oral expression | 000 | 000 | 0000 |
| School library usage | 000 | 000 | 0000 |
| Speed reading | 000 | 000 | 0000 |
| Dictionary skills | 000 | 000 | 0000 |
| Other (specify): | 000 | 000 | 0000 |

**p.m.**

| 3. Pupil's Instructional Grouping | abc | def | ghij |
|---|---|---|---|
| Whole-class group instruction | 000 | 000 | 0000 |
| Partial-class group instruction | 000 | 000 | 0000 |
| Tutorial (one to one) instruction | 000 | 000 | 0000 |
| Independent work on individually-assigned activity | 000 | 000 | 0000 |
| Independent work on a group-assigned activity | 000 | 000 | 0000 |
| Shared work on group-assigned activity | 000 | 000 | 0000 |
| Shifting group patterns | 000 | 000 | 0000 |

4. Instructional and Audiovisual Materials and Equipment in Use

5. Pupil's Behavior

6. Person Relating to Pupil

7. Person's Instructional Role

From S. Rimm, "Evaluation of gifted programs—as easy as ABC." In R. E. Clasen et al. (eds.), *Programming for the Gifted, Talented, and Creative.* Madison, University of Wisconsin, 1981.

## APPENDIX 18.5   EVALUATION FORM FOR IN-SERVICE WORKSHOPS

Workshop Title: _____ CREATIVITY IN THE CLASSROOM _____

Circle the appropriate numbers below.

1. I found this program to be . . .

| 1 | 2 | 3 | 4 | 5 |
|---|---|---|---|---|
| Dull | | Of average Interest | | Very Interesting |

2. I think that what I learned today will be . . .

| 1 | 2 | 3 | 4 | 5 |
|---|---|---|---|---|
| Useless | | Somewhat Useful | | Very Useful |

3. I would like to have more inservice programs on this topic.

| 1 | 2 | 3 | 4 |
|---|---|---|---|
| No, not at all | Yes, but not for a while | Yes, more this year | Other (Explain Below): |

Explanation: _____

_____

_____

4. The things I liked most about this in-service were: _____

_____

_____

_____

5. The things I liked least about this in-service were: _____

_____

_____

_____

## APPENDIX 18.6   SCHOOL BOARD QUESTIONNAIRE

We suggest you read the questionnaire before you start to answer.

Please indicate the extent to which you agree or disagree with each of the following statements by circling the appropriate letter. The letters mean the following:

SA — Strongly agree
A — Generally agree
U — Undecided
D — Generally disagree
SD — Strongly disagree

Please use the comment line if you want to explain your answer. Answer question 9 only if you have children in the high school.

1.  School E High School provides a well-        SA   A   U   D   SD
    balanced educational program.

    Comment_____

2.  This school has a good program for           SA   A   U   D   SD
    able students.

    Comment_____

3.  Most parents feel School E is a good         SA   A   U   D   SD
    school.

    Comment_____

4.  The School E program is mainly for the       SA   A   U   D   SD
    college-bound student.

    Comment_____

5.  Students at School E are receiving a good    SA   A   U   D   SD
    education in the basics like math, English,
    history, science.

    Comment_____

6.  There are too many frills in the School E    SA   A   U   D   SD
    program.

    Comment_____

7.  School E has a good extracurricular program, SA   A   U   D   SD
    i.e., athletics, music, school paper, drama,
    clubs, etc.

    Comment_____

8.  School E should have more vocational courses. SA  A   U   D   SD

    Comment_____

9.  Most of the teachers our child has had at    SA   A   U   D   SD
    School E have done a good job.

    Comment_____

From D. Sjogren, T. Hopkins, and D. Gooler, *Evaluation Plans and Instruments: Illustrative Cases of Gifted Program Evaluation Techniques.* Center for Instructional Research and Curriculum Evaluation, Champaign-Urbana, University of Illinois, 1975. Reprinted by permission.

**APPENDIX 18.7   STUDENT EVALUATION: LEARNING CENTER PROGRAM**

```
                    STUDENT EVALUATION
                  LEARNING CENTER PROGRAM

For the past sixteen weeks you have been attending sessions at the
_____ County Learning Center.  We would like to know some
of your feelings about the program.  By answering questions and
completing the following sentences, you can help us in improving
the program.


 1.  Which class did you like best?  _____

 2.  Why?  _____

 3.  Of the classes I was not in, I wish I could have taken  _____

     _____

 4.  Why?  _____

 5.  I wish my classes at the Learning Center were longer _____,

     shorter _____, the same _____ (check one).

 6.  The Learning Center needs more _____

 7.  The class in which I learned or accomplished most was _____

     _____

 8.  If I could change three things about the Learning Center, I would

     a.  _____

     b.  _____

     c.  _____

 9.  Has the Learning Center helped you in any way with things you do

     at school?  _____

10.  How?  _____

11.  Has the Learning Center helped you in any way with things you do

     at home?  _____

12.  How?  _____

13.  Has the Learning Center helped in any way with the way you get

     along with or feel about people?  _____.  If so, how? ___

     _____
```

From Florida's *State Resource Manual for gifted Child Education.* State of Florida Department of Education, 1973. Reprinted by permission.

## APPENDIX 18.8   PUPIL SELF-EVALUATION

---

PUPIL SELF-EVALUATION

Pupil's Name _____

Think of yourself at the present time in comparison to last year.  As a result of <u>this year's</u> work, please rate yourself on the following items. Place the <u>letters a, b, c, d,</u> and <u>e</u> on the line following each item according to the scale below.

(a)  Much less                    (d)  More
(b)  Less                         (e)  Much more
(c)  About the same

1.  Ability to think things through for yourself         _____

2.  Knowledge of subject matter areas (science, social
    studies, and others I have taken)                    _____

3.  Interest in school                                   _____

4.  Ability to see how things go together in a situation
    (see relationships)                                  _____

5.  Ability to find information                          _____

6.  Ability to work well by myself                       _____

7.  The liking and respect of other pupils for me        _____

8.  Ability to judge the usefulness of facts             _____

9.  Ability to get along with my teacher(s)              _____

10.  Enjoyment of learning                               _____

11.  Knowledge of arithmetic, spelling, and other basic
     skills                                              _____

12.  Curiosity about learning new things                 _____

13.  Ability to accept responsibility                    _____

14.  Opportunity to make things, experiment, and use ideas  _____

15.  Knowledge of my strengths and weaknesses            _____

16.  Willingness to do work as a leader                  _____


Please answer the following questions:

17.  Has the school year been helpful to you?  Yes _____    No _____
     Please explain.

     _____

     _____


18.  Has any part of the school work this year created any problems for
     you?                              Yes _____    No _____
     Please explain.

     _____

     _____

---

From R. E. Simpson & R. A. Martinson, *Educational Program for Gifted Pupils*. Sacramento, California State Department of Education, 1961. Reprinted by permission.

Abelman, R. (1986). Television and the exceptional child. *G/C/T, 9*(4), 26–28.

Abelman, R. (1987). Parental mediation of television viewing. *Roeper Review, 9,* 217–220, 246.

Abelman, R. (1991). Parental communication style and its influence on exceptional children's television viewing. *Roeper Review, 14,* 23–27.

Abelman, R. (1992a). *Some children under some conditions: TV and the high potential kid.* Storrs, CT: National Research Center on the Gifted and Talented.

Abelman, R. (1992b). Television and gifted children: What the research says. *Roeper Review, 15,* 80–84.

Abraham, W. (1976). The early years: Prologue to tomorrow. *Exceptional Child, 42,* 330–335.

Accorinti, S. (2002). *Philosophy for children.* Retrieved April 22, 2002, from www.rescognitans.it/ita/scenari/scuola/contrieduc2.htm.

Achter, J. A., Lubinski, D., & Benbow, C. P. (1996). Multipotentiality among the intellectually gifted: It was never there and already it's vanishing. *Journal of Counseling Psychology, 43,* 65–76.

Adams, A. A. (1989). Prospective minority scientists. *Gifted Child Today, 12*(4), 40.

Adams, C. M. (1996, Summer). Gifted girls and science: revisiting the issues. *Journal of Secondary Gifted Education, 7,* 447–458.

Adams, M. (1981, December). *Attribution theory and gifted females.* Paper presented at the meeting of the CEC-TAG National Topical Conference on the Gifted and Talented Child, Orlando, FL.

Adderholdt-Elliott, M. (1987). *Perfectionism: What's bad about being too good?* Minneapolis, MN: Free Spirit.

Adderholdt-Elliott, M. (1989). Perfectionism and underachievement. *Gifted Child Today, 12*(1), 19–21.

Addison, L. (1981, December). Attribution theory and gifted females. Paper presented at the meeting of the CEC-TAG National Topical Conference on the Gifted and Talented Child, Orlando, FL.

Adler, T. (1991, September). Support and challenge: Both key for smart kids. *Science Monitor,* 10.

Alamprese, J. A., & Erlanger, R. (1988). *No gift wasted: Effective strategies for educating highly able, disadvantaged students in mathematics and science. Vol. I: Findings.* Washington: COSMOS Corporation.

Albert, R. S. (1980). Family positions and the attainment of eminence: A study of special family positions and special family experiences. *Gifted Child Quarterly, 24,* 87–95.

Allen, R. R., Kauffeld, F. J., & O'Brien, W. R. A. (1968). *Semiprogrammed introduction to verbal argument,* Parts 1–4. Madison: Wisconsin Research and Development Center for Cognitive Learning.

Allen, R. R., & Rott, R. K. (1969). *The nature of critical thinking* (Theoretical Paper No. 20). Madison: Wisconsin Research and Development Center for Cognitive Learning.

Allen, M. S. (1962). *Morphological creativity.* Englewood Cliffs, NJ: Prentice-Hall.

Almquist, E. M., & Angrist, S. (1971). Role model influences in college women's career aspirations. *Merrill-Palmer Quarterly, 17,* 263–279.

Alvino, J. (1990, February). Building better thinkers. *Learning 90,* 40–41.

American Association of University Women. (1991). *Shortchanging girls, shortchanging America.* Washington, DC: Author.

American Association of University Women. (1992). *Shortchanging girls, shortchanging America: A call to action.* (ERIC Document Reproduction Service No. ED 340658).

American Association of University Women. (2001, Fall). Equity watch. *Outlook, 95*(2), 10–12.

American Psychiatric Association (1994). *Diagnostic and statistical manual for mental disorders* (4th ed.). Washington, DC: Author.

Anastopoulos, A. D., & Barkley, R. A. (1991). Biological factors in attention deficit-hyperactivity disorder. *CH.A.D.D.ER, 5*(1), 15–16, 27–28.

Anderson, R. S. (1975). *Education in Japan: A century of modern development.* Washington, DC: U.S. Government Printing Office.

Archambault, F. X., & Hallmark, B. W. (1992, April). Regular classroom practices: Results of a national survey. In J. S. Renzulli (Chair), *Regular classroom practices with gifted students. Findings from the National Research Center on the Gifted and Talented.* Symposium conducted at the meeting of the American Educational Research Association, San Francisco.

Archambault, F. X., Westberg, K. L., Brown, S., Hallmark, B. W., Zhang, W., & Emmons, C. (1993). Regular classroom practices with gifted students: Findings from the classroom practices survey. *Journal for the Education of the Gifted, 16,* 103–119.

Armstrong, J. M. (1980). *Achievement and participation of women in mathematics: An overview.* Denver, CO: Education Commission of the States. (ERIC Document Reproduction Service No. Ed 184878).

Arnold, K., & Denny, T. (1985, April). *The lives of academic achievers: The career aspirations of male and female valedictorians and salutatorians.* Paper presented at the meeting of the American Educational Research Association, Chicago.

Arnold, K., & Subotnik, R. (1995). Mentoring the gifted: A differentiated model. *Educational Horizons, 73,* 118–123.

Aronson, E., Blaney, N., Sikes, J., Stephan, C., & Snapp, M. (1975). Busing and racial tension: The jigsaw route to learning and liking. *Psychology Today, 8*(9), 43–50.

Arthur, G. (1950). *The Arthur adaptation of the Leiter International Performance Scale.* Chicago: Stoelting.

Associated Press. (2002, February 18). High schoolers' college classes hit. *Capital Times,* p. 2A.

Association of American Medical Colleges. (2000). *Women in U.S. medicine, statistics 1999–2000.* [Interpretive Summary.] Washington, DC. Retrieved June 18, 2001, from http://www.aamc.org/about/prgemph/wommed/stats00/summary.html.

Association for the Gifted Evaluation Committee. (1979). *Sample instruments for the evaluation of programs for the gifted and talented.* Storrs: University of Connecticut.

Association for Supervision and Curriculum Development. (1988). *Dimensions of thinking.* Reston, VA: Author.

Assouline, S. G., & Lupkowski-Shoplik, A. E. (1997). Talent search: A model for the discovery and development of academic talent. In N. Colangelo & G. A. Davis (Eds.), *Handbook of gifted education* (2nd ed.; pp. 170–179). Boston: Allyn & Bacon.

Assouline, S. G., & Lupkowski-Shoplik, A. (In press). *Developing mathematical talent: A guide for teachers and parents of gifted students.* Waco, TX: Prufrock Press.

Atkinson, J. W. (1958). *Motives in fantasy, action, and society: A method of assessment and study.* New York: Van Nostrand.

Atkinson, J. W. (1974). The mainsprings of achievement-oriented activity. In G. A. Davis & T. F. Warren (Eds.), *Psychology of education: New looks* (pp. 220–226). Lexington, MA: D. C. Heath.

Bagley, M. T., & Hess, K. K. (1984). *200 ways of using imagery in the classroom.* New York: Trillium.

Baker, J. A. (1996). Everyday stressors of academically gifted adolescents. *Journal of Secondary Gifted Education, 7,* 356–368.

Baker, J. A., Bridger, R., & Evans, K. (1998). Models of underachievement among gifted preadolescents: The role of personal, family, and school factors. *Gifted Child Quarterly, 42,* 5–13.

Baldwin, A. Y. (1985). *Baldwin identification matrix 2.* New York: Trillium.

Baldwin, A. Y. (1987). I'm Black, but look at me, I am also gifted. *Gifted Child Quarterly, 31,* 180–185.

Baldwin, A. Y. (1991). Gifted black adolescents: Beyond racism to pride. In M. Bireley & J. Genshaft (Eds.). *Understanding the gifted adolescent: Educational, developmental, and multicultural issues* (pp. 231–239). New York: Teachers College Press.

Baldwin, A. Y. (1993). Teachers of the gifted. In K. A. Heller, F. J. Mönks, & A. H. Passow (Eds.), *International handbook of research and development of giftedness and talent* (pp. 621–629). New York: Pergamon.

Baldwin, A. Y., & Vialle, W. (1999). *The many faces of giftedness: Lifting the masks.* Belmont, CA: Wadsworth Publishing Co.

Baldwin, B. A. (1988). *Beyond the cornucopia kids: How to raise healthy achieving children.* Wilmington, NC: Directions Dynamics.

Ballering, L. D., & Koch, A. (1984). Family relations when a child is gifted. *Gifted Child Quarterly, 28,* 140–143.

Banbury, M. M., & Wellington, B. (1989). Designing and using peer nomination forms. *Gifted Child Quarterly, 33,* 161–164.

Bandura, A. (1986). *Social learning theory.* Englewood Cliffs, NJ: Prentice-Hall.

Banks, J. A. (1991). Multicultural literacy and curriculum reform. *Educational Horizons, 69*(3), 135–140.

Banks, J. A. (1993). Multicultural education: Historical development, dimensions, and practice. In L. Darling-Hammond (Ed.), *Review of Research in Education* (pp. 3–49). Washington, DC: American Educational Research Association.

Banks, W. (1979). *Teaching strategies for ethnic studies* (2nd ed.). Boston: Allyn & Bacon.

Barbie's remarks don't quite add up. (1992, October 21). *New York Times,* p. 142.

Bardwick, J. M. (1971). *Psychology of women.* New York: Harper & Row.

Barell, J. (1984). Reflective thinking and education for the gifted. *Roeper Review, 6,* 194–196.

Barell, J. (1991). *Teaching for thoughtfulness.* White Plains, NY: Longman.

Barron, B. (2000). Problem solving in video-based micro-world: Collaborative and individual outcomes of high-achieving sixth-grade students. *Journal of Educational Psychology, 92,* 391–398.

Barron, F. (1969). *Creative person and creative process.* New York: Holt.

Barron, F. (1988). Putting creativity to work. In R. J. Sternberg (Ed.), *The nature of creativity* (pp. 76–98). New York: Cambridge University Press.

Baum, S. (1984). Meeting the needs of learning disabled gifted students. *Roeper Review, 7,* 16–19.

Baum, S. (1988). An enrichment program for gifted learning disabled students. *Gifted Child Quarterly, 32,* 226–230.

Baum, S. (1990). *Gifted but learning disabled: A puzzling paradox.* Reston, VA: Council for Exceptional Children. (ERIC Digest E479)

Baum, S. M., Olenchak, F. R., & Owen, S. V. (1998). Gifted students with attention deficits: Fact and/or fiction? Or, can we see the forest for the trees? *Gifted Child Quarterly, 42,* 96–104.

Baum, S., & Owen, S. V. (1988). High ability/learning disabled students: How are they different? *Gifted Child Quarterly, 32,* 321–326.

Bauman, M. K., & Kropf, C. A. (1979). Psychological tests used with blind and visually handicapped persons. *School Psychology Digest, 8,* 257–270.

Baytops, J. L. (1994). At-risk African-American gifted learners: Enhancing their education. *Research in Social Policy, 3,* 1–32.

Becker, D., & Forsyth, R. (1990, April). *Gender differences in grades 3 through 12: A longitudinal analysis.* Paper presented at the meeting of the American Educational Research Association, Boston.

Beggs, D. L., Mouw, J. T., & Barton, J. A. (1989). Evaluating gifted programs: Documenting individual and programmatic outcomes. *Roeper Review, 12,* 73–76.

Begley, S. (1995, March 27). Gray matters. *Newsweek,* pp. 48, 50–54.

Beisser, S. R. (2000, Spring). Females and technology: Lack of equity for gifted adolescent girls. *Iowa Talented and Gifted News,* 1–4.

Belin-Blank Center (n.d.). *National Scholars Academy.* Retrieved March 27, 2002, from http://www.uiowa.edu/~belinctr/programs/summer/index.html.

Belton, B. (1996, March 27). More workers owe employment to women. *USA Today,* p. B6.

Bem, S. L. (1974). The measurement of psychological androgyny. *Journal of Consulting and Clinical Psychology, 42,* 155–162.

Benbow, C. P. (1986). SMPY's model for teaching mathematically precocious students. In J. S. Renzulli (Ed.), *Systems and models for developing programs for the gifted and talented* (pp. 2–25). Mansfield Center, CT: Creative Learning Press.

Benbow, C. P. (1992a). Academic achievement in mathematics and science between ages 13 and 23: Are there differences among students in the top one percent of mathematical ability? *Journal of Educational Psychology, 84,* 51–61.

Benbow, C. P. (1992b). Mathematical talent: Its origins and consequences. In N. Colangelo, S. G. Assouline, & D. L. Ambroson (Eds.), *Talent development: Proceedings from the 1991 Henry B. and Jocelyn Wallace National Research Symposium on Talent Development* (pp. 95–123). Unionville, NY: Trillium Press.

Benbow, C. P., & Arjmand, O. (1990). Predictors of high academic achievement in mathematics and science by mathematically talented students: A longitudinal study. *Journal of Educational Psychology, 82,* 430–441.

Benbow, C. P., & Lubinski, D. (1994). Individual differences amongst the mathematically gifted: Their educational and vocational implications. In N. Colangelo, S. Assouline, & D. Ambroson (Eds.), *Talent development: Proceedings from the 1993 Henry B. and Jocelyn Wallace National Research Symposium on Talent Development* (pp. 83–100). Dayton: Ohio Psychology Press.

Benbow, C. P., & Lubinski, D. (1997). Intellectually talented children: How can we best meet their needs? In N. Colangelo & G. A. Davis (Eds.), *Handbook of gifted education* (2nd ed.; pp. 155–169). Boston: Allyn & Bacon.

Benbow, C. P., & Stanley, J. C. (1980). Sex differences in mathematical ability: Fact or artifact? *Science, 210,* 1262–1264.

Benbow, C. P., & Stanley, J. C. (1981). Mathematical ability: Is sex a factor? *Science, 212,* 118–121.

Benbow, C. P., & Stanley, J. C. (1982). Consequences in high school and college of sex differences in mathematical reasoning ability: A longitudinal perspective. *American Educational Research Journal, 19,* 598–622.

Benbow, C. P., & Stanley, J. C. (1983). Sex differences in mathematical reasoning ability: More facts. *Science, 222,* 1029–1031.

Berger, S. L., & McIntyre, J. (1998). Technology-based instruction for young gifted children. In J. F. Smutney (Ed.), *The young gifted child: Potential and promise* (pp. 535–546). Cresskill, NJ: Hampton Press.

Bernal, E. M. (1979). The education of the culturally different gifted. In A. H. Passow (Ed.), *The gifted and the talented* (pp. 395–400). Chicago: National Society for the Study of Education.

Bernard, J. (1972). *The future of marriage.* New York: Bantam.

Bestor, A. E. (1953). *Educational wastelands.* Urbana: University of Illinois Press.

Betts, G. T. (1985). *Autonomous learner model: For the gifted and talented.* Greeley, CO: Autonomous Learning Publications and Specialists.

Betts, G. T. (1991). The autonomous learner for the gifted and talented. In N. Colangelo & G. A. Davis (Eds.), *Handbook of gifted education* (pp. 142–153). Boston: Allyn & Bacon.

Betts, G. T., & Kercher, J. K. (1999). *Autonomous learner model: Optimizing ability.* Greeley, CO: Alps Publishing.

Beyer, B. K. (1988). *Developing a thinking skills program.* Boston: Allyn & Bacon.

Binet, A., & Simon, T. (1905a). Methodes nouvelles pour le diagnostic du niveau intellectuel des anormaux. *L'Année Psychologique, 11,* 191–244.

Binet, A., & Simon, T. (1905b). Sur la necessité d'établir un diagnostic scientific des états inférieurs de l'intelligence. *L'Année Psychologique, 11,* 163–190.

Bireley, M. (1991). The paradoxical needs of the disabled gifted. In M. Bireley & J. Genshaft (Eds.), *Understanding the gifted adolescent: Educational, developmental, and multicultural issues* (pp. 163–175). New York: Teachers College Press.

Bireley, M., & Genshaft, J. (1991). Adolescence and giftedness: A look at the issues. In M. Bireley & J. Genshaft (Eds.), *Understanding the gifted adolescent: Educational, developmental, and multicultural issues* (pp. 1–17). New York: Teachers College Press.

Birnbaum, J. A. (1975). Life patterns and self-esteem in gifted family-oriented and career-committed women. In M. T. Mednick, S. S. Tangri, & L. W. Hoffman (Eds.), *Women and achievement: Social and motivational analyses.* New York: Halsted Press.

Black, H., & Black, S. (1984). *Building thinking skills, book 1—verbal.* Pacific Grove, CA: Critical Thinking Books and Software.

Black, H., & Black, S. (1988). *Lesson plans and teacher's manual: Building thinking skills, book 3—verbal.* Pacific Grove, CA: Critical Thinking Books and Software.

Blakeley, S. (2001, Spring). *The emotional journey of the gifted and talented adolescent female.* Storrs, CT: National Research Center on the Gifted and Talented.

Blanton, M. (1982, September/October). Blooms' taxonomy revisited. *G/C/T, 22.*

Bloom, B. S. (Ed.). (1974). *Taxonomy of educational objectives.* New York: McKay.

Bloom, B. S. (Ed.). (1985). *Developing talent in young people.* New York: Ballantine Books.

Bloom, B. S., Englehart, M. D., Furst, E. J., Hill, W. H., & Krathwohl, D. R. (1956). *Taxonomy of educational objectives, handbook I: Cognitive domain.* New York: Longmans Green.

Bloom, B. S., & Sosniak, L A. (1981). Talent development vs. schooling. *Educational Leadership, 39,* 86–94.

Boodoo, G. M., Bradley, C. L., Frontera, R. L., Pitts, J. R., & Wright, L. B. (1989). A survey of procedures used for identifying gifted learning disabled children. *Gifted Child Quarterly, 33,* 110–114.

Boring, E. G. (1950). *History of psychology.* New York: Appleton-Century-Crofts.

Borland, J. H. (2003). Evaluating gifted programs: A broader perspective. In N. Colangelo & G. A. Davis (Eds.), *Handbook of gifted education* (3rd ed., pp. 293–307). Boston: Allyn & Bacon.

Brandon, P. R., Newton, B. J., & Hammond, O. W. (1987). Children's mathematics achievement in Hawaii: Sex differences favoring girls. *American Educational Research Journal, 24,* 437–461.

Breggin, P. R. (1991). *Toxic psychiatry.* New York: St. Martin's Press.

Bridgemen, B., & Burbach, H. (1976). Effects of black and white peer models on academic expectations and actual performance of fifth-grade students. *Journal of Experimental Education, 45,* 9–12.

British Columbia Ministry of Education Special Education Services. (1995). A manual of policies, procedures, and guidelines. Retrieved from http://www.bced.gov.bc.ca/specialed/ppandg/planning_5.htm.

Brody, L. E., & Benbow, C. P. (1987). Accelerative strategies: How effective are they for the gifted? *Gifted Child Quarterly, 31,* 105–110.

Brody, L. E., & Fox, L. H. (1980). An accelerative intervention program for mathematically gifted girls. In L. H. Fox, L. Brody, & D. Tobin (Eds.), *Women and the mathematical mystique.* Baltimore, MD: Johns Hopkins University Press.

Brody, L. E., & Mills, C. J. (1997). Gifted children with learning disabilities: A review of the issues. *Journal of Learning Disabilities, 30,* 282–286.

Brody, L. E., & Stanley, J. C. (1991). Young college students: Assessing factors that contribute to success. In W. T. Southern & E. D. Jones (Eds.), *The academic acceleration of gifted children* (pp. 102–132). New York: Teachers College Press.

Bromfield, R. (1994). Fast talkers: Verbally precocious youth present challenges for parents and teachers. *Gifted Child Today, 17*(6), 32–33.

Brophy, J. E. (1982, April). *Research on the self-fulfilling prophecy and teacher expectations.* Presented at the meeting of the American Educational Research Association, New York.

Brown, B. B., & Steinberg, L. (1989). How bright students save face among peers. *National Center for Effective Secondary Schools Newsletter, 4*(2), 2–8.

Brown, B. B., & Steinberg, L. (1990). Academic achievement and social acceptance: Skirting the "brain-nerd" connection. *Education Digest, 55*(7), 55–60.

Brown, S. W. (1984). The use of WISC-R subtest scatter in the identification of intellectually gifted handicapped children: An inappropriate task? *Roeper Review, 7*(1), 1–3.

Bruch, C. B., & Curry, J. A. (1978). Personal Learnings: A current synthesis on the culturally different gifted. *Gifted Child Quarterly, 22,* 313–321.

Budmen, K. O. (1967). What do you think, Teacher? Critical Thinking, a partnership in learning. *Peabody Journal of Education, 45,* 2–5.

Buffery, A. W. H., & Gray, J. A. (1972). Sex differences in the development of spatial and linguistic skills. In C. Ounsted & D. C. Taylor (Eds.), *General differences: Their ontogeny and significance.* Baltimore: Williams & Wilkins.

Burk, E. A. (1980). *Relationship of temperamental traits to achievement and adjustment in gifted children.* Ann Arbor, MI: University Microfilms International.

Burks, B. S., Jensen, D. W., & Terman, L. M. (1930). *Genetic studies of genius: Vol. 3. The promise of youth: Follow-up studies of a thousand gifted children.* Stanford, CA: Stanford University Press.

Burns, J. M., Mathews, F. N., & Mason, A. (1990). Essential steps in screening and identifying preschool gifted children. *Gifted Child Quarterly, 34,* 102–107.

Bushman, B. J., & Anderson, C. A. (2001). Media violence and the American public: Scientific facts versus media misinformation. *American Psychologist, 56,* 477–489.

Butler, O. (1988). *Kindred.* Boston: Beacon.

Callahan, C. M. (1986). Asking the right questions: The central issue in evaluating programs for the gifted and talented. *Gifted Child Quarterly, 30,* 38–42.

Callahan, C. M. (1991). An update on gifted females. *Journal for the Education of the Gifted, 14,* 284–311.

Callahan, C. M. (1993a). *Contexts for promises: Noteworthy practices and innovations in the identification of gifted students.* Storrs, CT: National Research Center on the Gifted and Talented (ERIC Document Reproduction Service No. ED 372 592).

Callahan, C. M. (1993b). Evaluation programs and procedures for gifted education: International problems and solutions. In K. A. Heller, F. J. Mönks, & A. H. Passow (Eds.), *International handbook of research and development of giftedness and talent* (pp. 605–618). New York: Pergamon.

Callahan, C. M., Adams, C. M., Bland, L. C., Moon, T. R., Moore, S. D., Peri, M., & McIntire, J. A. (1996). Factors influencing recruitment, enrollment, and retention of students in special schools of mathematics, science, and technology. In K. Arnold, K. D. Noble, & R. F. Subotnik (Eds.), *Remarkable women: Perspectives on female talent development* (pp. 243–260). Cresskill, NJ: Hampton Press.

Callahan, C. M., & Caldwell, M. S. (1995). *A practitioner's guide to evaluating programs for the gifted.* Washington, DC: National Association for Gifted Children.

Callahan, C. M., Cornell, D. G., & Loyd, B. (1990). Perceived competence and parent-adolescent communication in high ability adolescent females. *Journal for the Education of the Gifted, 13,* 256–269.

Callahan, C. M., Cunningham, C. M., & Plucker, J. A. (1994). Foundations for the future: The socio-emotional development of gifted, adolescent women. *Roeper Review, 17,* 99–105.

Callahan, C. M., Hunsaker, S. L., Adams, C. M., Moore, S. D., & Bland, L. C. (1995a). *Instruments used in the identification of gifted and talented students.* Storrs, CT: National Research Center on the Gifted and Talented.

Callahan, C. M., Tomlinsin, C. A., Moon, T. R., Tomchin, E. M., & Plucker, J. A. (1995b). Project START: Using a multiple intelligences model in identifying and promoting talent in high-risk students. (Research Monograph No. 95316). Charlottesville: University of Virginia.

Campbell, J. R., & Verna, M. A. (n.d.). *American TAG teachers assessment of what works and what does not work.* Unpublished manuscript, St. John's University, Jamaica, NY.

Carelli, A. O. (1981). Creative dramatics for the gifted: A multi-disciplinary approach. *Roeper Review, 5*(2), 29–31.

Carlsmith, L. (1964). Effect of early father absence on scholastic aptitude. *Harvard Educational Review, 34,* 3–21.

Carnegie Corporation of New York. (1996). *Years of promise: A comprehensive learning strategy for America's children.* Executive Summary. New York: Carnegie Task Force of Learning.

Carnegie Council on Adolescent Development. (1995). *Great transitions: Preparing adolescents for a new century.* New York: Carnegie Corporation of New York.

Carnine, D. (1989). Teaching complex content to learning disabled students: The role of technology. *Exceptional Children, 55*(6), 524–533.

Carroll, J. B. (1993). *Human cognitive abilities: A survey of factor analytic studies.* Cambridge, UK: Cambridge University Press.

Casey, K. M. A., & Shore, B. M. (2000). Mentors' contributions to gifted adolescents affective, social, and vocational development. *Roeper Review, 22,* 227–230.

Cash, A. B. (1999). A profile of gifted individuals with autism: The twice-exceptional learner. *Roeper Review, 22,* 22–27.

Casserly, P. L. (1979). Helping able young women take math and science seriously in school. In N. Colangelo & R. T. Zaffrann (Eds.), *New voices in counseling the gifted.* Dubuque, IA: Kendall/Hunt.

Cassidy, J., & Hossler, A. (1992). State and federal definitions of the gifted: An update. *Gifted Child Today, 15*(1), 46–53.

Cassidy, J., & Johnson, N. (1986). Federal and state definitions of giftedness: Then and now. *Gifted Child Today, 9*(6), 15–21.

Catalyst. (2001, April 18). *Number of women chief executives in Fortune 500 doubles in 2001.* [Press Release.] New York. Retrieved May 9, 2001, from http://www.catalystwomen.org/press/releases/release041901.html.

Ceci, S. J. (1991). How much does schooling influence general intelligence and its cognitive components: A reassessment of the evidence. *Developmental Psychology, 27,* 703.

Chamrad, D. L., Robinson, N. M., & Janos, P. M. (1995). Consequences of having a gifted sibling: Myths and realities, *Gifted Child Quarterly, 39,* 135–145.

Character Education Partnership. (2002). *CEP 9th National Forum: Cultivating citizens for a changing world.* Washington, DC: Author.

Chisholm, S. (1978, November/December). Address at the National Forum on the Culturally Disadvantaged Gifted Youth. *G/C/T, 2–4,* 40–41.

Chitwood, D. G. (1986). Guiding parents seeking testing. *Roeper Review, 8,* 177–179.

Cielak-Golonka, M., & Morten, B. (2000). The women scientists of Bologna. *American Scientist, 88,* 68–73.

Clark, B. (1983). *Growing up gifted* (2nd ed.). Columbus, OH: Merrill.

Clark, M. L. (1991). Social identity, peer relations, and academic competence of African-American adolescents. *Education and Urban Society, 24*(1), 41–52.

Clasen, D. R. (1982). *Meeting the rage to know: College for kids, an innovative enrichment program for gifted elementary children.* Unpublished manuscript, University of Wisconsin, Department of Educational Psychology, Madison.

Clasen, D. R., & Clasen, R. E. (1989). Using telecommunications to meet the staff development and networking needs of educators of the gifted in small or rural school districts. *Roeper Review, 11,* 202–205.

Clasen, D. R., & Clasen, R. E. (1992). The acceptance-rejection model (ARM): Adolescent responses to the gift vs. group conflict. In N. Colangelo, S. G. Assouline, & D. L. Ambroson (Eds.), *Talent development: Proceedings from the 1991 Henry B. and Jocelyn Wallace National Research Symposium on Talent Development* (pp. 353–356). Unionville, NY: Trillium Press.

Clasen, D. R., & Clasen, R. E. (1995). Underachievement of highly able students and the peer society. *Gifted and Talented International, 10*(2), 67–76.

Clasen, D. R., & Clasen, R. E. (1997). *Handbook of gifted education* (2nd ed.; pp. 218–229). Boston: Allyn & Bacon.

Clasen, D. R., & Clasen, R. E. (2003). Mentoring the gifted and talented. In N. Colangelo & G. A. Davis (Eds.), *Handbook of gifted education* (3rd ed., pp. 254–267). Boston: Allyn & Bacon.

Clasen, D. R., Middleton, J. A., & Connel, T. J. (1994). Assessing artistic and problem-solving performance in minority and nonminority students using a nontraditional multidimensional approach. *Gifted Child Quarterly, 38,* 27–37.

Cohen, R., Duncan, M., & Cohen, S. L. (1994). Classroom peer relationships of children participating in a pull-out enrichment program. *Gifted Child Quarterly, 38,* 33–37.

Cohn, S. J. (2002). Gifted students who are gay, lesbian, or bisexual. In M. Neihart, S. M. Reis, N. M. Robinson, & S. M. Moon (Eds.), *Social and emotional development of gifted children: What do we know?* (pp. 145–153). Washington, DC: National Association for Gifted Children.

Colangelo, N. (1997). Counseling gifted students: Issues and practices. In N. Colangelo & G. A. Davis (Eds.), *Handbook of gifted education* (2nd ed.; pp. 353–365). Boston: Allyn & Bacon.

Colangelo, N. (1999). *Gifted education in rural schools.* Iowa City: Connie Belin & Jackqueline N. Blank International Center for Gifted Education and Talent Development, University of Iowa.

Colangelo, N. (2003). Counseling gifted students. In N. Colangelo & G. A. Davis (Eds.), *Handbook of gifted education* (3rd ed., pp. 373–387). Boston: Allyn & Bacon.

Colangelo, N., & Assouline, S. G. (2000). Counseling gifted students. In K. A. Heller, F. J. Mönks, R. J. Sternberg, & R. F. Subotnik (Eds.), *International handbook of giftedness and talent* (2nd ed., pp. 595–607). New York: Elsevier.

Colangelo, N., Assouline, S. G., Baldus, C. M., & New, J. K. (2003). Gifted education in rural schools. In N. Colangelo & G. A. Davis (Eds.), *Handbook of gifted education* (3rd ed., pp. 572–581). Boston: Allyn & Bacon.

Colangelo, N., Assouline, S. G., Cole, V., Cutrona, C., & Maxey, J. E. (1996). Exceptional academic performance:

Perfect scores on the PLAN. *Gifted Child Quarterly, 40,* 102–109.

Colangelo, N., & Brower, P. (1987a). Gifted youngsters and their siblings: Long-term impact of labeling on their academic and social self-concepts. *Roeper Review, 10,* 101–103.

Colangelo, N., & Brower, P. (1987b). Labeling gifted youngsters: Long-term impact on families. *Gifted Child Quarterly, 31,* 75–78.

Colangelo, N., & Davis, G. A. (2003) Introduction and overview. In N. Colangelo & G. A. Davis (Eds.), *Handbook of gifted education* (3rd ed.). Boston: Allyn & Bacon.

Colangelo, N., & Kelly, K. R. (1983). A study of student, parent, and teacher attitudes toward gifted programs and gifted students. *Gifted Child Quarterly, 27,* 107–110.

Cole, J. R., & Zuckerman, H. (1987, June). Motherhood and science do mix. *Psychology Today, 57.*

Cole, V., Colangelo, N., Assouline, S., & Russell, D. (1994). Parental social support as a predictor of college grades. In N. Colangelo, S. G. Assouline, & D. L. Ambroson (Eds.), *Talent development: Proceedings from the 1993 Henry B. and Jocelyn Wallace National Research Symposium on Talent Development* (pp. 299–303). Dayton: Ohio Psychology Press.

Coleman, J. S. (1961). *The adolescent society.* New York: Free Press.

Coleman, L. J., & Cross, T. L. (2000). Social-emotional development and the personal experience of giftedness. In K. A. Heller, F. J. Mönks, R. J. Sternberg, & R. F. Subotnik (Eds.), *International handbook of giftedness and talent* (2nd ed., pp. 203–212). New York: Elsevier.

Coleman, M. R. (1992). A comparison of how gifted/LD and average/LD boys cope with school frustration. *Journal for the Education of the Gifted, 15,* 239–265.

Comer, J. P. (1988). Educating poor minority children. *Scientific American, 259*(5), 42–48.

Connor, E. W. (1991). Gifted all the time. *Gifted Child Today, 14*(5), 14–17.

Cooley, M. R., Cornell, D. G., & Lee, C. (1991). Peer acceptance and self-concept of black students in a summer gifted program. *Journal for the Education of the Gifted, 14,* 166–177.

Cornelius, G. M., & Yawkey, T. D. (1985). Imaginativeness in preschoolers and single parent families. *Journal of Creative Behavior, 19,* 56–66.

Cornell, D. G. (1983). Gifted children: The impact of positive labeling on the family system. *American Journal of Orthopsychiatry, 53*(2), 322–355.

Cornell, D. G., Callahan, C. M., & Lloyd, B. H. (1991). Socioemotional adjustment of adolescent girls enrolled in a residential acceleration program. *Gifted Child Quarterly, 35,* 58–66.

Cornell, D. G., & Grossberg, I. N. (1986). Siblings of children in gifted programs. *Journal for the Education of the Gifted, 9,* 253–264.

Cornell, D. G., & Grossberg, I. N. (1989). Parent use of the term "gifted": Correlates with family environment and child adjustment. *Journal for the Education of the Gifted, 12,* 218–230.

Costa, A. L. (1986). Teaching for, of, and about thinking. In A. L. Costa (Ed.), *Developing minds: A resource book for teaching thinking.* Washington, DC: National Assessment of Educational Progress.

Costa, A. L. (2003). In the habit of skillful thinking. In N. Colangelo & G. A. Davis (Eds.), *Handbook of gifted education* (3rd ed., pp. 325–334). Boston: Allyn & Bacon.

Costa, A. L., & Lowery, L. E. (1989). *Techniques for teaching thinking.* Pacific Grove, CA: Critical Thinking Books and Software.

Covington, M. V., & Beery, R. G. (1976). *Self-worth and school learning.* New York: Holt.

Covington, M. V., & Omelich, C. L. (1979). It's best to be able and virtuous too: Student and teacher evaluative responses to successful effort. *Journal of Educational Psychology, 71,* 688–700.

Cox, C. M. (1926). *Genetic studies of genius: Vol. 2. The early mental traits of three hundred geniuses.* Stanford, CA: Stanford University Press.

Cox, J. (1986). The Richardson Study: Results and recommendations. In J. VanTassel-Baska (Ed.), *The Richardson Study: A catalyst for policy change in gifted education.* Evanston, IL: Northwestern University.

Cox, J., & Daniel, N. (1983, September/October) The role of the mentor. *G/C/T,* 54–61.

Cox, J., & Daniel, N. (1988). The Richardson study concludes. *Gifted Child Today, 11*(1), 45–47.

Cox, J., & Daniel, N. (1991). The International Baccalaureate. In R. E. Clasen (Ed.), *Educating able learners* (pp. 157–166). Madison: Madison Education Extension Programs, University of Wisconsin-Madison.

Cox, J., Daniel, N., & Boston, B. A. (1985). *Educating able learners: Programs and promising practices.* Austin: University of Texas Press.

Crabbe, A. B. (1982). Creating a brighter future: An update on the Future Problem Solving program. *Journal for the Education of the Gifted, 5,* 2–9.

Cramer, J., & Oshima, T. C. (1992). Do gifted females attribute their math performance differently than other students? *Journal for the Education of the Gifted, 16,* 18–35.

Cramer, R. H. (1991). The education of gifted children in the United States: A Delphi study. *Gifted Child Quarterly, 35,* 84–91.

Cramond, B. (1994) Attention-deficit hyperactivity disorder and creativity—what is the connection? *Journal of Creative Behavior, 28,* 193–210.

Cramond, B. (1997). The use of multiple criteria for identifying gifted students. *Roeper Review, 20,* A-2.

Crawford, R. P. (1978). The techniques of creative thinking. In G. A. Davis & J. A. Scott (Eds.), *Training creative thinking* (pp. 52–57). Melbourne, FL: Krieger.

Creel, C. S., & Karnes, F. A. (1988). Parental expectancies and young gifted children. *Roeper Review, 11,* 48–50.

Cresci, M. M. (1989). *Creative dramatics for children.* Glenview, IL: Scott, Foresman.

Croft, L. J. (2003). Teachers of the gifted: Gifted teachers. In N. Colangelo & G. A. Davis (Eds.), *Handbook of gifted education* (3rd ed., pp. 558–571). Boston: Allyn & Bacon.

Cropley, A. J. (1997). Fostering creativity in the classroom. In

M. Runco (Ed.), *Handbook of creativity* (pp. 81–112). Cresskill, NJ: Hampton Press.

Cropley, A. J., & Urban, K. K. (2000). Programs and strategies for nurturing creativity. In K. A. Heller, F. J. Mönks, R. J. Sternberg, & R. F. Subotnik (Eds.), *International handbook of giftedness and talent* (2nd ed.). New York: Elsevier.

Cross, T. L. (1996). Psychological autopsy provides insight into gifted adolescent suicide. *Gifted Child Today, 19*(3), 22–23, 50.

Cross, T. L., Hernandez, N. R., & Coleman, L. (1991). Governor's schools: An idea whose time has come. *Gifted Child Today, 14*(3), 29–30.

Csikszentmihalyi, M., & Wolfe, R. (2000). New concepts and research approaches to creativity: Implications of a systems perspective for creativity in education. In K. A. Heller, F. J. Mönks, R. J. Sternberg, & R. F. Subotnik (Eds.), *International handbook of giftedness and talent* (2nd ed., pp. 81–93). New York: Elsevier.

Dabney, M. (1983, July). *Perspectives and directive in assessment of the black child.* Paper presented at the meeting of the Council for Exceptional Children, Atlanta, GA.

Dabrowski, K. (1967). *Personality shaping through positive disintegration.* Boston: Little, Brown.

Dabrowski, K. (1972). *Psychoneurosis is not all an illness.* London: Gryf.

Dai, D. Y., & Feldhusen, J. F. (1999). A validation study of the thinking styles inventory: Implications for gifted education. *Roeper Review, 21,* 302–307.

Dai, D. Y., & Renzulli, J. S. (2000). Dissociation and integration of talent development and personal growth: Comments and suggestions. *Gifted Child Quarterly, 44,* 247–251.

Dalzell, H. J. (1998). Giftedness: Infancy to adolescence: A developmental perspective. *Roeper Review, 20,* 259–264.

Daniels, P. R. (1983). *Teaching the gifted/learning disabled child.* Rockville, MD: Aspen.

Daniels-McGhee, S., & Davis, G. A. (1994). The imagery-creativity connection. *Journal of Creative Behavior, 28,* 151–176.

Davalos, R., & Griffin, G. (1999). The impact of teachers' individualized practices on gifted students in rural heterogeneous classrooms. *Roeper Review, 4,* 308–314.

Davidson, K. (1986). The case against formal identification. *Gifted Child Today, 9*(6), 7–11.

Davis, B. G., Trimble, C. S., & Vincent, D. R. (1980). Does age of entrance affect school achievement? *Elementary School Journal, 80*(3), 133–143.

Davis, G. A. (in preparation). Thinking skills model for character education.

Davis, G. A. (1975). In frumious pursuit of the creative person. *Journal of Creative Behavior, 9,* 75–87.

Davis, G. A. (1981a). Personal creative thinking techniques. *Gifted Child Quarterly, 25,* 99–101.

Davis, G. A. (1981b). Review of the Revolving Door Identification Model. *Gifted Child Quarterly, 25,* 185–186.

Davis, G. A. (1987). How to get a hippo out of the bathtub: What to teach when you teach creativity. *Gifted Child Today, 10*(1), 7–19.

Davis, G. A. (1989a). Gary Davis speaks to teachers: Objectives and activities for teaching creative thinking. *Gifted Child Quarterly, 33,* 81–84.

Davis, G. A. (1989b). Testing for creative potential. *Contemporary Educational Psychology, 14,* 157–174.

Davis, G. A. (1993). Identifying the creatively gifted. In J. Genshaft, M. Bireley, & C. L. Hollinger (Eds.), *A guidebook for serving the gifted and talented.* Washington, DC: National Association of School Psychologists.

Davis, G. A. (1998). *Creativity is forever* (4th ed.). Dubuque, IA: Kendall/Hunt.

Davis, G. A. (1999). Barriers to creativity and creative attitudes. In M. A. Runco and S. R. Pritzker (Eds.), *Encyclopedia of creativity* (Vol. 1, pp. 165–174). New York: Academic Press.

Davis, G. A. (2003a). *Character education: Activities and exercises for developing positive attitudes and behavior* (2nd ed.). Unionville, NY: Royal Fireworks.

Davis, G. A. (2003b). Identifying creative students, teaching for creative growth. In N. Colangelo & G. A. Davis (Eds.), *Handbook of gifted education* (3rd ed., pp. 311–324). Boston: Allyn & Bacon.

Davis, G. A. (2003c). *Values are forever: Self-guided activities in character education* (2nd ed.). Unionville, NY: Royal Fireworks.

Davis, G. A., & DiPego, G. (1973). *Imagination express: Saturday subway ride.* Buffalo, NY: DOK.

Davis, G. A., Helfert, C. J., & Shapiro, G. R. (1992). Let's be an ice cream machine! Creative Dramatics. In S. J. Parnes (Ed.), *Source book for creative problem solving* (pp. 384–392). Buffalo, NY: Creative Education Foundation.

Davis, G. A., & Rimm, S. B. (1980). *GIFFI II: Group inventory for finding interests.* Watertown, WI: Educational Assessment Service.

Davis, G. A., & Rimm, S. B. (1982). Group inventory for finding interests (GIFFI) I and II: Instruments for identifying creative potential in junior and senior high school. *Journal of Creative Behavior, 16,* 50–57.

Davis, G. A., & Rimm, S. B. (1985). *Education of the gifted and talented.* Englewood Cliffs, NJ: Prentice-Hall.

Deaux, K. (1976). Ahhh, she was just lucky. *Psychology Today, 10,* 70.

de Bono, E. (1973). *CoRT Thinking.* Elmsford, NY: Pergamon.

de Bono, E. (1983). The direct teaching of thinking as a skill. *Phi Delta Kappan, 64,* 703–708.

de Bono, E. (1985, September). Partnerships of the mind: Teaching society to think. *ProEducation,* 56–58.

de Bono, E. (1986). *CoRT thinking skills program.* Oxford, England: Pergamon Press.

Delcourt, M., Lloyd, B. H., Cornell, D. G., & Goldberg, M. D. (1994). *Evaluation of the effects of programming arrangements on student learning outcomes.* Storrs, CT: National Research Center on the Gifted and Talented.

Delcourt, M. (1994, Spring). Exemplary elementary school programs in gifted education. *NRC/GT Newsletter,* 6–9.

DeLeon, P. H. (1989, February). *Why we must attend to minority gifted: A national perspective.* Paper presented at the Johnson Foundation Wingspread Conference, Racine, WI.

Delisle, J. R. (1987). *Gifted kids speak out.* Minneapolis: Free Spirit Publishing.

Delisle, J. R. (1992). *Guiding the social and emotional development of gifted youth.* New York: Longman.

Delisle, J. R. (1996). Multiple intelligences: Convenient, simple, wrong. *Gifted Child Today, 19*(6), 12–13.

Delisle, J. R. (1997). Gifted adolescents: Five steps toward understanding and acceptance. In N. Colangelo & G. A. Davis (Eds.), *Handbook of gifted education* (2nd ed.; pp. 475–482). Boston: Allyn & Bacon.

DeMille, R. (1973). *Put your mother on the ceiling.* New York: Viking/Compass.

Dickens, M. N. (1990). *Parental influences on the mathematics self-concept of high achieving adolescent girls.* Unpublished doctoral dissertation, University of Virginia, Charlottesville.

Dickens, M. N., & Cornell, D. G. (1993). Parent influences on the mathematics self-concept of high ability adolescent girls. *Journal for the Education of the Gifted, 17,* 53–73.

Dixon, J. A. (1998). Social and academic self-concepts of gifted adolescents. *Journal for the Education of the Gifted, 22,* 80–94.

Dobrzynski, J. H. (1995a, September 12). Women less optimistic about work, poll says. *New York Times,* p. D5.

Dobrzynski, J. H. (1995b, October 29). How to succeed? Go to Wellesley: Its graduates scoff at glass ceilings. *New York Times,* pp. C1, C9.

Dole, S. (2000). The implications of the risk and resilience literature for gifted students with learning disabilities. *Roeper Review, 23,* 91–96.

Donnelly, J. A., & Altman, R. (1994). The autistic savant: Recognizing and serving the gifted student with autism. *Roeper Review, 16,* 252–256.

Doyle, R. (2000, April). Women and the professions. *Scientific American,* 30.

Dressel, P. L., & Mayhew, L. B. (1954). *General education: Explorations in evaluation.* Washington, DC: American Council on Education.

Drews, E., & Teahan, J. (1957). Parental attitudes and academic achievement. *Journal of Clinical Psychology, 13,* 328–332.

Drzewiecki, L. A., & Westberg, K. L. (1997, Spring). Gender differences in high school students' attitudes toward mathematics in traditional versus cooperative groups. *National Research Center on Gifted and Talented Newsletter,* 13–14.

Duff, C. (2000, October). Online mentoring. *Educational Leadership,* 49-52.

Dunn, M. M. (1995, March 3). The performance of women's colleges. *Chronicle of Higher Education,* p. 3.

Dunn, R., Dunn, K., & Price, G. E. (1981). *Learning style inventory.* Lawrence, KS: Price Systems.

Dunn, R., & Griggs, S. A. (1985, November/December). Teaching and counseling gifted students with their learning styles preferences: Two case studies. *G/C/T,* 40–43.

Dunn, R., & Griggs, S. A. (1988). *Learning styles: Quiet revolution in American secondary schools.* Reston, VA: National Association of Secondary Principals.

Duran, B., & Weffer, R. (1992). Immigrants' aspirations, high school process, and academic outcomes. *American Educational Research Journal, 29,* 165–168.

Durden-Smith, J., & DeSimone, D. (1982, November). Is there is superior sex? *Readers Digest,* 263–270.

Dweck, C. S., & Bush, E. S. (1976). Sex differences in learned helplessness: I. Differential debilitation with peer and adult evaluators. *Developmental Psychology, 12,* 147–156.

Eash, M. (1972). *Issues in evaluation and accountability in special programs for gifted and talented children.* Chicago: University of Illinois-Chicago Circle.

Eberle, B. (1995). *Scamper.* Waco, TX: Prufrock.

Eberle, B., & Hall, R. (1975). *Affective education guidebook: Classroom activities in the realm of feelings.* Buffalo, NY: DOK.

Eberle, B., & Stanish, B. (1985). *CPS for kids.* Carthage, IL: Good Apple.

Eccles, J., Wigfield, A., Harold, R. D., & Blumenfeld, P. (1993). Age and gender differences in children's self- and task perceptions during elementary school. *Child Development, 64,* 830–847.

Educational Research Service. (2000, May). Superintendents: Status and views. *ERS Bulletin, 27*(9). Retrieved May 8, 2001, from http://www.ers.org/ERSBulletins/0500e.htm.

Educational Testing Service (1989a). *1989 profile of SAT and achievement test takers.* Princeton, NJ: Author.

Educational Testing Service (1989b). *What Americans study.* Princeton, NJ: Author.

Eisenberg, D., & Epstein, E. (1981, December). The *discovery and development of giftedness in handicapped children.* Paper presented at the meeting of the CEC-TAG National Topical Conference on the Gifted and Talented Child, Orlando, FL.

Eisenberg, D., & Epstein, E. (1982). *The special gifted student.* New York: Special Education Training and Resource Center.

Elkind, D. (1981). *The hurried child: Growing up too fast too soon.* Reading, MA: Addison-Wesley.

Ellingson, M., Haeger, W., & Feldhusen, J. F. (1986, March/April). The Purdue mentor program. *G/C/T,* 2–53.

Ellis, A., & Harper, R. A. (1975). *A new guide to rational living.* New York: Institute for Rational Living.

Emerick, L. J. (1989, November). *The gifted underachiever: Classroom strategies for reversing the pattern.* Paper presented at the meeting of the National Association for Gifted Children Conference, Cincinnati.

Emerick, L. J. (1992). Academic underachievement among the gifted: Students' perception of factors that reverse the pattern. *Gifted Child Quarterly, 36,* 140–146.

Ennis, R. H. (1962). A concept of critical thinking: A proposed basis for research in the teaching and evaluation of critical thinking ability. *Harvard Educational Review, 32,* 83.

Ennis, R. H. (1964). *Critical thinking readiness in grades 1-12: Phase I. Deductive reasoning in adolescence.* Ithaca, NY: Cornell University, School of Education.

Enrico, D. (1995, October 23). Computer use declines as girls age. *USA Today,* p. A1.

Erickson, D. P., & Ellett, F. S. (1990). Taking student responsibility seriously. *Educational Researcher, 19*(9), 3–9.

Erikson, E. H. (1959). *Identity and the life cycle: Selected papers by Erik H. Erikson.* New York: International Universities Press.

Erikson, E. H. (1968). *Identity: Youth and crisis.* New York: Norton.

Ernest, J. (1976). Mathematics and sex. *American Mathematical Monthly, 83,* 595–614.

Evered, L. J., & Nayer, S. (2000). Novosibirsk's school for the gifted–changing emphases in the new Russia. *Roeper Review, 23,* 22–24.

Ewing, N. J., & Yong, F. L. (1992). A comparative study of the learning style preferences among gifted African-American, Mexican-American, and American-born Chinese middle grade students. *Roeper Review, 14,* 120–123.

Exum, H. (1983). Key issues in family counseling with gifted and talented black students. *Roeper Review, 5*(3), 28–31.

Eysenck, H. J. (1967). *The biological bases of personality.* Springfield, IL: Charles C. Thomas.

Fantini, M. D. (1981). A caring curriculum for gifted children. *Roeper Review, 3*(4), 3–4.

Farley, F. H. (1986, May). The big T in personality. *Psychology Today,* 47–52.

Farnham, P. (1988, February). Women in science: Numbers have improved, but problems remain. *FASEB,* 171.

Fasko, D. (2001). An analysis of multiple intelligences theory and its use with the gifted and talented. *Roeper Review, 23,* 126–130.

Fedler, F. (1973). The mass media and minority groups. *Journalism Quarterly, 50,* 109–117.

Feingold, A. (1988). Cognitive gender differences are disappearing. *American Psychologist, 43,* 95–103.

Feldhusen, H. J. (1981). Teaching gifted, creative, and talented students in an individualized classroom. *Gifted Child Quarterly, 25,* 108–111.

Feldhusen, H. J. (1986). *Individualized teaching of gifted children in regular classrooms.* East Aurora, NY: DOK.

Feldhusen, J. F. (1989a). Synthesis of research on gifted youth. *Educational Leadership, 46*(6), 6–11.

Feldhusen, J. F. (1989b). Why the public schools will continue to neglect the gifted. *Gifted Child Today, 12*(2), 55–59.

Feldhusen, J. F. (1991). Saturday and summer programs. In N. Colangelo & G. A. Davis (Eds.), *Handbook of gifted education* (pp. 197–208). Boston: Allyn & Bacon.

Feldhusen, J. F. (1992). Talent identification and development in education. *Gifted Child Quarterly, 36,* 123.

Feldhusen, J. F. (1997). Secondary services, opportunities, and activities for talented youth. In N. Colangelo & G. A. Davis (Eds.), *Handbook of gifted education* (2nd ed.; pp. 189-197). Boston: Allyn & Bacon.

Feldhusen, J. F., & Clinkenbeard, P. R. (1982). Summer programs for the gifted: Purdue's residential programs for high achievers. *Journal for the Education of the Gifted, 5,* 178–184.

Feldhusen, J. F., Dai, D. Y, & Clinkenbeard, P. R. (2000). Dimensions of competitive and cooperative learning among gifted learners. *Journal for the Education of the Gifted, 23,* 328–342.

Feldhusen, J. F., Enersen, D. L., & Sayler, M. F. (1992). Challenging the gifted through problem solving experiences—design and evaluation of the COMET program. *Gifted Child Today, 15*(4), 49–54.

Feldhusen, J. F., Hansen, J. B., & Kennedy, D. M. (1989).

Curriculum development for GCT teachers. *Gifted Child Today, 12*(6), 12–19.

Feldhusen, J. F., Hoover, S. M., & Sayler, M. F. (1990). *Identifying and educating gifted students at the secondary level.* Unionville, NY: Royal Fireworks.

Feldhusen, J. F., & Kolloff, P. B. (1978, January/February). A three-stage model of gifted education. *G/C/T,* 3–5, 53–57.

Feldhusen, J. F., & Kolloff, P. B. (1981). A three-stage model for gifted education. In R. E. Clasen, B. Robinson, D. R. Clasen, & G. Libster (Eds.), *Programming for the gifted, talented and creative: Models and methods.* Madison: University of Wisconsin-Extension.

Feldhusen, J. F., & Kolloff, P. B. (1986). The Purdue three-stage enrichment model for gifted education at the elementary level. In J. S. Renzulli (Ed.), *Systems and models for developing programs for the gifted and talented* (pp. 126–152). Mansfield Center, CT: Creative Learning Press.

Feldhusen, J. F., Proctor, T. B., & Black, K. N. (1986). Guidelines for grade advancement of precocious children. *Roeper Review, 9,* 25–27.

Feldhusen, J. F., & Ruckman, D. R. (1988). A guide to the development of Saturday programs for gifted and talented youths. *Gifted Child Today, 11*(5), 56–61.

Feldhusen, J. F., & Sayler, M. F. (1990). Special classes for academically gifted youth. *Roeper Review, 12,* 244–249.

Feldman, D. H. (1986). Giftedness as a developmentalist sees it. In R. J. Sternberg & J. E. Davidson (Eds.), *Conceptions of giftedness* (pp. 285–305). Cambridge, MA: Cambridge University Press.

Feldman, D. H. (with Goldsmith, L. T.). (1991). *Nature's gambit: Child prodigies and the development of human potential.* New York: Teachers College Press.

Feldman, D. H. (1994). *Beyond universals in cognitive development* (2nd ed.). Norwood, NJ: Ablex.

Felton, G. S., & Biggs, B. E. (1977). *Up from underachievement.* Springfield, IL: Charles C. Thomas.

Fennema, E. (1980). Sex-related differences in mathematics achievement: Where and why. In L. H. Fox, L. Brody, & D. Tobin (Eds.), *Women and the mathematical mystique.* Baltimore, MD: Johns Hopkins University Press.

Fennema, E., & Carpenter, T. P. (1998). New perspectives on gender differences in mathematics: An introduction. *Educational Researcher, 27*(5), 4–21.

Fennema, E., Carpenter, T. P., Jacobs, V. R., Franke, M. L., & Levi, L. W. (1998a). A longitudinal study of gender differences in young children's mathematical thinking. *Educational Researcher, 27*(5), 6–11.

Fennema, E., Carpenter, T. P., Jacobs, V. R., Franke, M. L., & Levi, L. W. (1998b). New perspectives on gender differences in mathematics: A reprise. *Educational Researcher, 27*(5), 19–21.

Fennema, E., & Sherman, J. A. (1978). Sex-related differences in mathematics achievement and related factors: A further study. *Journal for Research in Mathematics Education, 9,* 189–203.

Fernandez, A. T., Gay, L. R., Lucky, L. F., & Gavilan, M. R. (1998). Teacher perceptions of gifted Hispanic limited English proficient students. *Journal for the Education of the Gifted, 21,* 335–351.

Fetterman, D. M. (1993). *Evaluate yourself.* Storrs, CT: National Research Center on the Gifted and Talented.

Feuerstein, R. (1980a). *Instrumental enrichment: An intervention program for cognitive modifiability.* Baltimore: University Park Press.

Feuerstein, R. (1980b). *Instrumental enrichment* (thinking skills materials). Washington, DC: Curriculum Development Associates.

Feuerstein, R., Rand, Y., & Hoffman, M. (1979). *The dynamic assessment of retarded individuals: The learning potential assessment device, theory, instruments, and techniques.* Glenview, IL: Scott, Foresman.

Fiedler, E. D., Lange, R. E., & Winebrenner, S. (1993). In search of reality: Unraveling the myths about tracking, ability grouping and the gifted. *Roeper Review, 16,* 4–7.

Fine, M. J., & Pitts, R. (1980). Intervention with underachieving gifted children: Rationale and strategies. *Gifted Child Quarterly, 24,* 51–55.

First Official U.S. Education Mission to the USSR. (1959). *Soviet commitment to education, Bulletin 1959, No. 16.* Washington, DC: Department Education.

Fisher, E. (1981). The effect of labeling on gifted children and their families. *Roeper Review, 3*(2), 49–51.

Fleith, D. (2000). Teacher and students' perceptions of creativity in the classroom environment. *Roeper Review, 22,* 148–157.

Fleith, D. (2001, Spring). Suicide among gifted adolescents: How to prevent it. *National Research Center on the Gifted and Talented Newsletter,* 6–8.

Flint, L. J. (2001). Challenges of identifying and serving gifted children with ADHD. *Teaching Exceptional Children, 33*(4), 62–69.

Ford, D. Y. (1993). Support for the achievement ideology and determinants of underachievement as perceived by gifted, above-average, and average black students. *Journal for the Education of the Gifted, 16,* 280–298.

Ford, D. Y. (1994a). Nurturing resilience in gifted black youth. *Roeper Review, 17,* 80–85.

Ford, D. Y. (1994b). *Recruitment and retention of African-American students in gifted education programs: Implications and recommendations.* Storrs, CT: National Research Center on the Gifted and Talented.

Ford, D. Y. (1996). *Reversing underachievement among gifted black students.* New York: Teachers College Press.

Ford, D. Y. (2003). Equity and excellence: Culturally diverse students in gifted education. In N. Colangelo & G. A. Davis (Eds.), *Handbook of gifted education* (3rd ed., pp. 506–520). Boston: Allyn & Bacon.

Ford, D. Y., Grantham, T. C., & Harris, J. J. (1997). The recruitment and retention of minority teachers in gifted education. *Roeper Review, 19,* 213–220.

Ford, D. Y., & Harris, J. J. (1997). A study of the racial identity and achievement of black males and females. *Roeper Review, 20,* 105–110.

Ford, D. Y., & Harris, J. J. (1999). *Multicultural gifted education.* New York: Teachers College Press.

Ford, D. Y., Howard, T. C., Harris, J. J., & Tyson, C. A. (2000). Creating culturally responsive classrooms for gifted African-American students. *Journal for the Education of the Gifted, 23,* 397–427.

Ford, D. Y., & Trotman, M. F. (2001). Teachers of gifted students: Suggested multicultural characteristics and competencies. *Roeper Review, 23,* 235–239.

Fox, L. H. (1974). *Facilitating the development of mathematical talent in young women.* Unpublished Ph.D. thesis, Johns Hopkins University, Baltimore.

Fox, L. H. (1977). Sex differences: Implications for program planning for the academically gifted. In J. C. Stanley, W. C. George, & C. H. Solano (Eds.), *The gifted and the creative: A fifty-year perspective.* Baltimore: Johns Hopkins University Press.

Fox, L. H. (1979). Programs for the gifted and talented: An overview. In A. H. Passow (Ed.), *The gifted and talented* (pp. 104–126). Chicago: National Society for the Study of Education.

Fox, L. H. (1981, February). Mathematically able girls: A special challenge. *Arithmetic Teacher,* 22–23.

Fox, L. H., & Brody, L. (1983). Models for identifying giftedness: Issues related to the learning-disabled child. In L. H. Fox, L. Brody, & D. Tobin (Eds.), *Learning disabled gifted children* (pp. 101–116). Boston: University Park Press.

Fox, L. H., Sadker, D., & Engle, J. L. (1999, Fall). Sexism in the schools: Implications for the education of gifted girls. *Gifted and Talented International, 14*(2), 66–79.

Fox, M. A. (1999, April 30). High-level groups study barriers women face. *Science, 284,* p. 727.

Frasier, M. M. (1990, April). *The equitable identification of gifted and talented children.* Paper presented at the meeting of the American Educational Research Association, Boston.

Frasier, M. M. (1991a). Disadvantaged and culturally diverse gifted students. *Journal for the Education of the Gifted, 14,* 234–245.

Frasier, M. M. (1991b). Response to Kitano: The sharing of giftedness between culturally diverse and non-diverse gifted students. *Journal for the Education of the Gifted, 15,* 20–30.

Frasier, M. M. (1993). Issues, problems and programs in nurturing the disadvantaged and culturally different talented. In K. A. Heller, F. J. Mönks, & A. H. Passow (Eds.), *International handbook of research and development of giftedness and talent* (pp. 685–692). New York: Pergamon.

Frasier, M. M. (1994). *A manual for implementing the Frasier Talent Assessment Profile* (F-TAP). Athens: Georgia Southern Press.

Frasier, M. M. (1997). Multiple criteria: The mandate and the challenge. *Roeper Review, 20,* A4–A6.

Frasier, M. M., Garcia, J. H., & Passow, A. H. (1995). *A review of assessment issues in gifted education and their implications for identifying gifted minority students.* Storrs, CT: National Research Center on the Gifted and Talented.

Frasier, M. M., & Passow, A. H. (1994). *Toward a new paradigm for identifying talent potential.* Storrs, CT: National Research Center on the Gifted and Talented.

Frazier, A., Passow, A. H., & Goldberg, M. L. (1958). Curriculum research: Study of underachieving gifted. *Educational Leadership, 16,* 121–125.

French, J. L. (1959). *Educating the gifted: A book of readings.* New York: Holt.

French, J. I. (1964). *Pictorial test of intelligence.* Boston: Houghton Mifflin.

Freud, S. (1949). *An outline of psychoanalysis.* New York: Norton.

Friedman, J. M., & Master, D. (1980). School and museum: A partnership for learning. *Gifted Child Quarterly, 25,* 42–48.

Frierson, H. T., Jr. (1990). The situation of black educational researchers: Continuation of a crisis. *Educational Researcher, 19*(2), 12–17.

Frieze, I. H. (1975). Women's expectations for and causal attributions of success and failure. In M. T. Mednick, S. S. Tangri, & L. W. Hoffman (Eds.), *Women and achievement: Social and motivational analyses.* New York: Halsted.

Fuchs, L. S., Fuchs, D., Hamlett, C. L., & Karns, K. (1998). High-achieving students' interactions and performance on complex mathematical tasks as a function of homogeneous and heterogeneous pairings. *American Educational Research Journal, 35,* 227–268.

Fuchs, L. S., Fuchs, D., Kazdan, S., Karns, K., Calhoon, M. B., Hamlett, C. L., & Hewlett, S. (2000). Effects of work-group structure and size on student productivity during collaborative work on complex tasks. *Elementary School Journal, 100*(3), 183–212.

Gabor, A. (1996). *Einstein's wife: Work and marriage in the lives of five great twentieth century women.* New York: Penguin.

Gagné, F. (2000). Understanding the complex choreography of talent development through DMGT-based analysis. In K. A. Heller, F. J. Mönks, R. J. Sternberg, & R. F. Subotnik (Eds.), *International handbook of giftedness and talent* (2nd ed., pp. 67–79). New York: Elsevier.

Gagné, F. (2003). Transforming gifts into talents: The DMGT as a developmental theory. In N. Colangelo & G. A. Davis (Eds.), *Handbook of gifted education* (3rd ed., pp. 60–74). Boston: Allyn & Bacon.

Gallagher, J. J. (1958). Peer acceptance of highly gifted children in elementary school. *Elementary School Journal, 58,* 465–470.

Gallagher, J. J. (1990). Editorial: The public and professional perception of the emotional status of gifted children. *Journal for the Education of the Gifted, 13,* 202–211.

Gallagher, J. J. (1991a). Educational reform, values, and gifted students. *Gifted Child Quarterly, 35,* 12–19.

Gallagher, J. J. (1991b). Issues in the education of gifted students. In N. Colangelo & G. A. Davis (Eds.), *Handbook of gifted education* (pp. 14–23). Boston: Allyn & Bacon.

Gallagher, J. J. (1997). Issues in the education of gifted students. In N. Colangelo & G. A. Davis (Eds.), *Handbook of gifted education* (2nd ed.; pp. 10–23). Boston: Allyn & Bacon.

Gallagher, J. J. (2000). Unthinkable thoughts: Education of gifted students. *Gifted Child Quarterly, 44,* 5–12.

Gallagher, J. J. (2003). Issues and challenges in the education of gifted students. In N. Colangelo & G. A. Davis (Eds.), *Handbook of gifted education* (3rd ed., pp. 11–24). Boston: Allyn & Bacon.

Gallagher, J. J., & Coleman, M. R. (1992). *State policies on the identification of gifted students from special populations: Three states in profile* (Final Report). Chapel Hill, NC: Gifted Education Policy Studies Program.

Gallucci, N. T., Middleton, G., & Kline, A. (1999a). The independence of creative potential and behavior disorders in gifted children. *Gifted Child Quarterly, 43,* 194–203.

Gallucci, N. T., Middleton, G., & Kline, A. (1999b). Intellectually superior children and behavioral problems and competence. *Roeper Review, 22,* 18–21.

Galton, F. (1869). *Hereditary genius.* London: Macmillan.

Gamoran, A., & Weinstein, M. (1998). Differentiation and opportunity in restructured schools. *American Journal of Education, 106*(3), 385–415.

Ganapole, S. J. (1989). Designing an integrated curriculum for gifted learners: An organizational framework. *Roeper Review, 12,* 81–86.

Gardner, H. (1983). *Frames of mind: The theory of multiple intelligences.* New York: Basic Books.

Gardner, H. (1993). *Multiple intelligences.* New York: Basic Books.

Gardner, H. (1997). Six afterthoughts: Comments on "Varieties of Intellectual Talents." *Journal of Creative Behavior, 31,* 120–124.

Gardner, H. (1999). *Intelligence reframed: Multiple intelligences for the 21st century.* New York: Basic Books.

Gardner, H. (2000, October). *Multiple intelligences.* Paper presented at the meeting of the National Association for Gifted Children, Atlanta, GA.

Garland, A. F., & Zigler, E. (1999). Emotional and behavioral problems among highly intellectually gifted youth. *Roeper Review, 22,* 41–47.

Garmezy, M. (1991). Resiliency and vulnerability to adverse developmental outcomes associated with poverty. *American Behavioral Scientist, 34,* 416–430.

Gartner, A., Kohler, M., & Reissman, F. (1971). *Children teach children.* New York: Harper & Row.

Gavin, M. K. (1996). The development of math talent: Influences on students at a women's college. *Journal of Secondary Gifted Education, 7,* 476–485.

Gay, J. E. (1978). A proposed plan for identifying black gifted children. *Gifted Child Quarterly, 22,* 353–357.

Gelbrich, J. A., & Hare, E. K. (1989). The effects of single parenthood on school achievement in a gifted population. *Gifted Child Quarterly, 33,* 115–117.

Gentry, M. L. (1999). *Promoting student achievement and exemplary classroom practices through cluster grouping: A research-based alternative to heterogeneous elementary classrooms.* Storrs, CT: National Research Center on the Gifted and Talented.

Gentry, M. L., & Ferriss, S. (1999). A model of collaboration to develop science talent among rural middle school students. *Roeper Review, 21,* 316–320.

Gerber, P. J., Ginsburg, R. J., & Reiff, H. B. (1991). *Identifying alterable patterns in employment success for highly successful adults with learning disabilities* (Project

133G80500). Washington, DC: U.S. Department of Education, Office of Special Education and Rehabilitation Services.

Getzels, J. W. (1977). General discussion immediately after the Terman memorial symposium. In J. C. Stanley, W. C. George, & C. H. Solano (Eds.), *The gifted and the creative: A fifty-year perspective.* Baltimore, MD: Johns Hopkins University Press.

Getzels, J. W., & Jackson, P. W. (1962). *Creativity and intelligence.* New York: Wiley.

Giele, J. Z. (1978). *Women and the future: Changing sex roles in modern America.* New York: Free Press.

Gifted Child Society. (1990). *The Saturday workshop: Activities for gifted children and their parents.* Glen Rock, NJ: Author.

Ginsberg, G., & Harrison, C. H. (1977). *How to help your gifted child.* New York: Monarch Press.

Girl Scouts of the U.S.A. (1991). *Girl scouts: Its role in the lives of American women of distinction.* New York: Louis Harris & Associates.

Girl Scouts of the U.S.A. (2000). *Teens before their time.* New York: Louis Harris & Associates.

Glasneen, L. K., & Crowley, S. L. (1999, November). More women in the driver's seat. *AARP Bulletin, 3,* 24–26.

Gleason, M., Carnine, D., & Boriero, D. (1990). A comparison of CAI with teacher instruction in teaching math story problems to mildly handicapped students. *Journal of Special Education Technology, 10,* 129–136.

Goertzel, V., & Goertzel, M. G. (1962). *Cradles of eminence.* Boston: Little, Brown.

Goertzel, M. G., Goertzel, V., & Goertzel, T. G. (1978). *300 eminent personalities.* San Francisco: Jossey-Bass.

Goff, K., & Torrance, E. P. (1999). Discovering and developing giftedness through mentoring. *Gifted Child Today, 22*(3), 14–15, 52–53.

Gogul, E. M., McCumsey, J., & Hewett, G. (1985, November/December). What parents are saying. *G/C/T, 7*–9.

Goldberg, M. D., & Cornell, D. G. (1998). The influence of intrinsic motivation and self-concept on academic achievement in second- and third-grade students. *Journal for the Education of the Gifted, 21,* 179–205.

Goleman, D. (1995). *Emotional intelligence.* New York: Bantam.

Good, T. L., & Weinstein, R. S. (1986). Teacher expectations: A framework for exploring classrooms. In K. K. Zumwalt (Ed.), *Improving teaching: 1986 ASCD yearbook.* Alexandria, VA: Association for Supervision and Curriculum Development.

Goodlad, J., & Oakes, J. (1988). We must offer equal access to knowledge. *Educational Leadership, 45,* 16–22.

Gordon, W. J. J. (1961). *Synectics.* New York: Harper & Row.

Gordon, W. J. J. (1974). *Making it strange.* Books 1–4. New York: Harper & Row.

Gordon, W. J. J., & Poze, T. (1972a). *Teaching is listening.* Cambridge, MA: SES Associates.

Gordon, W. J. J., & Poze, T. (1972b). *Strange and familiar.* Cambridge, MA: SES Associates.

Gordon, W. J. J., & Poze, T. (1980). *The new art of the possible.* Cambridge, MA: Porpoise.

Gottfredson, L. S. (1981). Circumspection and compromise: A developmental theory of occupation aspirations. *Journal of Counseling Psychology, 28,* 545–579.

Gottfredson, L. S. (1997a). Mainstream science on intelligence: An editorial with 52 signatories, history, and bibliography. *Intelligence, 24*(1), 13–23.

Gottfredson, L. S. (1997b). Why g matters: The complexity of everyday life. *Intelligence, 24*(1), 79–132.

Gottfredson, L. S. (2003). The science and politics of intelligence in gifted education. In N. Colangelo & G. A. Davis (Eds.), *Handbook of gifted education* (3rd ed., pp. 24–40). Boston: Allyn & Bacon.

Gottfredson, L. S. (in press). g, jobs, and life. In H. Nyborg (Ed.), *The scientific study of mental ability: Tribute to Authur R. Jensen.* New York: Pergamon.

Gourley, T. J. (1981). Adapting the varsity sports model to nonpsychomotor gifted students. *Gifted Child Quarterly, 25,* 164–166.

Gowan, J. C. (1979). Differentiated guidance for the gifted: A developmental view. In J. C. Gowan, J. Khatena, & E. P. Torrance (Eds.), *Educating the ablest: A book of readings* (2nd ed.; pp. 190–199). Itasca, IL: Peacock.

Grandin, T. (1995). *Thinking in pictures.* New York: Doubleday.

Grant, D. F., Battle, D. A., & Heggoy, S. J. (2000). The journey through college of seven gifted females: Influences on their career-related decisions. *Roeper Review, 22,* 251–260.

Gray, H. A., & Hollingworth, L. S. (1931). The achievement of gifted students enrolled and not enrolled in special opportunity classes. *Journal of Educational Research, 24,* 255–261.

Green, M. H. (1992). Remanent monasticism. *Science, 258,* 829–830.

Greenlaw, M. J., & McIntosh, M. E. (1988). *Educating the gifted: A source book.* Chicago: American Library Association.

Gregory, E. H. (1984). Search for exceptional academic achievement at California State University, Los Angeles. *Gifted Child Quarterly, 28,* 21–24.

Gregory, E. H., & March, E. (1985). Early entrance program at California State University, Los Angeles. *Gifted Child Quarterly, 29,* 83–86.

Grenier, M. E. (1985). Gifted children and other siblings. *Gifted Child Quarterly, 29,* 164–167.

Griffin, J. B. (1992). Catching the dream for gifted children of color. *Gifted Child Quarterly, 36,* 126–130.

Griffith, S. (1999, September 9). *More doctors are marrying doctors.* CWRU Campus News.

Griggs, S. (1984). Counseling the gifted and talented based on learning style. *Exceptional Children, 50,* 429–432.

Griggs, S., & Dunn, R. (1984). Selected case studies of the learning style preferences of gifted students. *Gifted Child Quarterly, 24,* 115–129.

Grigorenko, E. L., & Sternberg, R. J. (1997). Styles of thinking, abilities, and academic performance. *Exceptional Children, 63,* 295–312.

Grimm, J. (1995). *A study of gifted program services in Minnesota for gifted students with disabilities.* Unpublished doctoral dissertation, University of Minnesota, Minneapolis.

Grimm, J. (1998). The participation of gifted students with disabilities in gifted programs. *Roeper Review, 20,* 285–286.

Gross, M. U. M. (1992a). The early development of three profoundly gifted children of IQ 200. In P. Klein & A. J. Tannenbaum (Eds.), *To be young and gifted* (pp. 94–140). Norwood, NJ: Ablex.

Gross, M. U. M. (1992b). The use of radical acceleration in cases of extreme intellectual precocity. *Gifted Child Quarterly, 36,* 91–99.

Gross, M. U. M. (1993a). *Exceptionally gifted children.* New York: Routledge.

Gross, M. U. M. (1993b). Nurturing the talents of exceptional gifted individuals. In K. A. Heller, F. J. Mönks, & A. H. Passow (Eds.), *International handbook of research and development of giftedness and talent* (pp. 473–490). New York: Pergamon.

Gross, M. U. M. (1999). Small poppies: Highly gifted children in the early years. *Roeper Review, 21,* 207–214.

Gross, M. U. M. (2000). Issues in the cognitive development of exceptionally and profoundly gifted individuals. In K. A. Heller, F. J. Mönks, R. J. Sternberg, & R. F. Subotnik (Eds.), *International handbook of giftedness and talent* (2nd ed., pp. 179–192). New York: Elsevier.

Gross, M. U. M. (2001). Social and emotional issues for exceptionally intellectually gifted students. In M. Neihart, S. M. Reis, N. M. Robinson, & S. M. Moon (Eds.), *Social and emotional development of gifted children: What do we know?* (pp. 19–29). Washington, DC: National Association for Gifted Children.

Gross, M. U. M. (2003). International perspectives. In N. Colangelo & G. A. Davis (Eds.), *Handbook of gifted education* (3rd ed., pp. 547–557). Boston: Allyn & Bacon.

Gubbins, E. J. (1998, Spring). NRC/GT's suggestions: Evaluating your programs and services. *National Research Center on the Gifted and Talented Newsletter,* 1–3. Storrs, CT: University of Connecticut.

Gubbins, E. J. (1999, Winter). Planning gifted programs. *National Research Center on the Gifted and Talented Newsletter,* 1–4. Storrs, CT: University of Connecticut.

Gubbins, E. J. (2000, Fall). NRC/GT: Professional development–not an event. *NRC/GT Newsletter,* 1–3.

Guilford, J. P. (1967). *The nature of human intelligence.* New York: McGraw-Hill.

Guilford, J. P. (1977). *Way beyond the IQ.* Buffalo, NY: Creative Education Foundation.

Guilford, J. P. (1979). Some incubated thoughts on incubation. *Journal of Creative Behavior, 13,* 1–8.

Guilford, J. P. (1988). Some changes in the structure of intellect model. *Educational and Psychological Measurement, 48,* 1–4.

Gurin, P., & Epps, E. (1966). Some characteristics of students from poverty backgrounds attending predominantly Negro colleges in the deep south. *Social Forces, 45,* 27–39.

Gust-Brey, K., & Cross, T. (1999). An examination of the literature base on the suicidal behaviors of gifted students. *Roeper Review, 22,* 28–35.

Gutbezahl, J. (1995). *How negative expectancies and attitudes undermine female's math confidence and performance: A review of the literature.* Amherst: University of Massachu-

setts. (ERIC Document Reproduction Service No. ED 380 279)

Hackney, P. W. (1986). Education of the visually handicapped-gifted: A program description. *Education of the Visually Handicapped, 18*(2), 85–95.

Hadary, D., Cohen, S., & Haushalter, R. (1979). Out of darkness and silence. *Science and Children, 16,* 40–41.

Hall, E. G. (1980). Sex differences in IQ development for intellectual gifted students. *Roeper Review, 2*(3), 25–28.

Hall, E. G. (1982, November/December). Accelerating gifted girls. *G/C/T,* 49–50.

Hall, E. G. (1983). Recognizing gifted underachievers. *Roeper Review, 5*(4), 23–25.

Hallinan, M., & Sorensen, A. (1987). Ability grouping and sex differences in mathematics achievement. *Sociology of Education, 60,* 63–72.

Hallowell, K. (1991). Recruitment and selection procedures of governors' schools: A national survey. *Gifted Child Today, 14*(3), 24–27.

Halverson, C., & Victor, J. (1976). Minor physical anomalies and problem behavior in elementary school children. *Child Development, 47,* 281–285.

Han, K.-S., Marvin, C. (2000). A five year follow-up study of the Nebraska Project: Still a long way to go. *Roeper Review, 23,* 25–33.

Hansen, S., Walker, J., & Flom, B. (1995). *Growing smart: What's working for girls in school.* Washington, DC: American Association of University Women Educational Foundation.

Hanson, I. (1984). A comparison between parent identification of young bright children and subsequent testing. *Roeper Review, 7*(1), 44–45.

Harnadek, A. (1979). *Inference-B: Inductive thinking skills.* Pacific Grove, CA: Critical Thinking Books and Software.

Harris, C. R. (1991, Summer). Identifying and serving the gifted new immigrant. *Teaching Exceptional Children,* 26–30.

Harris, J. J., & Ford, D. Y. (1991). Identifying and nurturing the promise of gifted Black American children. *Journal of Negro Education, 60,* 42–28.

Hartman, M. S. (1994). Leadership: The agenda for women in the 1990s. *Douglass Alumnae Bulletin, 67*(4), 11–13.

Hauser, S. T., Vieyra, M. A. B., Jacobson, A. M., & Wertlieb, D. (1989). Family aspects of vulnerability and resilience in adolescence: A theoretical perspective. In T. Dugan & R. Coles (Eds.), *The child in our times: Studies in the development of resiliency* (pp. 109–133). New York: Brunner-Mazel.

Hayes, P. A., Norris, J., & Flaitz, J. R. (1998, July). A comparison of the oral narrative abilities of underachieving and high-achieving gifted adolescents: A preliminary investigation. *Language, Speech, and Hearing Services in Schools, 29,* 158–171.

Haynes, V. D. (1999, September 30). Boys and girls in a class apart. *Chicago Tribune,* pp. 1, 17.

Healy, B. (1992). Women in Science: From panes to ceilings. *Science, 255,* 1333.

Healy, J. (1990). *Endangered minds: Why our children can't think.* New York: Simon and Schuster.

Hebb, D. O. (1972). *Textbook of psychology* (3rd Ed.). Philadelphia, PA: Saunders.

Hébert, T. P. (1996). Portraits of resilience: The urban life experience of gifted Latino young men. *Roeper Review, 19,* 81–90.

Hébert, T. P. (2001). "If I had a new notebook, I know things would change": Bright underachieving young men in urban classrooms. *Gifted Child Quarterly, 45,* 174–193.

Hébert, T. P., Cramond, B., Neumeister, K. L. S., Millar, G., & Silvian, A. F. (2002). *E. Paul Torrance: His life, accomplishments, and legacy.* Storrs, CT: National Research Center on the Gifted and Talented.

Hébert, T. P., & Kent, R. (2000). Nurturing social and emotional development in gifted teenagers through young adult literature. *Roeper Review, 22,* 167–171.

Hébert, T. P., & Olenchak, F. R. (2000). Mentors for gifted underachieving males: Developing potential and realizing promise. *Gifted Child Quarterly, 44,* 196–207.

Heck, A. O. (1953). *Education of exceptional children* (2nd ed.). New York: McGraw-Hill.

Heilbrun, A. B. (1973). *Aversive maternal control.* New York: Wiley.

Heller, K. A., & Ziegler, A. (1996). Gender differences in mathematics and the sciences: Can attributional retraining improve the performance of gifted females? *Gifted Child Quarterly, 40,* 200–208.

Helman, I. B., & Larson, S. G. (1980). *Now what do I do?* Buffalo, NY: DOK.

Helms, J. E. (1992). Why is there no study of cultural equivalence in standardized cognitive ability testing? *American Psychologist, 47,* 1083–1101.

Helson, R. (1971). Women mathematicians and the creative personality. *Journal of Consulting and Clinical Psychology, 36,* 210–211, 217–220.

Henderson, R. W. (1981). *Parent-child interaction: Theory, research and prospects.* New York: Academic Press.

Hennessey, B. A., & Amabile, T. M. (1988). Story-telling: A method for assessing children's creativity. *Journal of Creative Behavior, 22,* 235–246.

Hermann, K. E., & Stanley, J. C. (1983, November/December). An exchange: Thoughts on nonrational precocity. *G/C/T,* 30–36.

Herrnstein, R. J., & Murray, C. (1994). *The bell curve.* New York: Simon & Schuster.

Hershey, M., & Crowe, B. (1989). When independent study doesn't work. *Gifted Child Today, 12*(1), 31–33.

Hess, R. J. (1975). *Hess school readiness scale.* Johnstown, PA: Mafex.

Hetherington, E. M., Cox, J., & Cox, R. (1982). Effects of divorce on parents and children. In M. E. Lamb (Ed.), *Nontraditional families: Parenting and child development* (pp. 233–288). Hillsdale, NJ: Erlbaum.

Hetherington, E. M., & Frankie, G. (1967). Effects of parental dominance, warmth and conflict on imitation in children. *Journal of Personality and Social Psychology, 6,* 119–125.

Hetrick, E. S., & Martin, A. D. (1987). Development issues and their resulting for gay and lesbian adolescents. *Journal of Homosexuality, 14,* 25–42.

Heward, W. L., & Orlansky, M. D. (1992). *Exceptional children* (4th ed.). Columbus, OH: Merrill.

Hickey, M. G. (1990). Classroom teachers' concerns and recommendations for improvement of gifted programs. *Roeper Review, 12,* 265–267.

Higham, S. J., & Buescher, T. M. (1987). What young gifted adolescents understand about feeling different. In T. M. Buescher (Ed.), *Understanding gifted and talented adolescents: A resource guide for counselors, educators, and parents* (pp. 26–30). Evanston, IL: Center for Talent Development, Northwestern University.

Hill, J. P. (1980). The family. In M. Johnson (Ed.), *Toward adolescence: The middle school years.* Chicago: National Society for the Study of Education.

Hine, C. Y. (1994). *Helping your child find success at school: A guide for Hispanic parents.* Storrs: CT: National Research Center on the Gifted and Talented.

Hishinuma, E. S., & Nishimura, S. T. (2000). Parent attitudes on the importance and success of integrated self-contained services for students who are gifted, learning disabled, and gifted/learning disabled. *Roeper Review, 22,* 241–250.

Hiskey, M. (1966). *Hiskey-Nebraska test of learning aptitude.* Lincoln, NE: Union College Press.

Hobbs, N. (1980). Feuerstein's instrumental enrichment: Teaching intelligence to adolescents. *Educational Leadership, 38,* 566–568.

Hobson, J. R., (1979). High school performance of underage pupils initially admitted to kindergarten on the basis of physical and psychological examinations. In W. C. George, S. J. Cohn, & J. C. Stanley (Eds.), *Educating the gifted: Acceleration and enrichment* (pp. 162–171). Baltimore: Johns Hopkins University Press.

Hoffman, B. (1964). *The tyranny of testing.* New York: Collier Books.

Hoffman, J. L, Wasson, F. R., & Christianson, B. P. (1985, May/June). Personal development for the gifted underachiever. *G/C/T,* 12–14.

Holahan, C. K. (1981). Lifetime achievement patterns, retirement and life satisfaction of gifted aged women. *Journal of Gerontology, 36,* 741–749.

Holden, C. (1998, March 6). Boys + girls + math. *Science, 279,* p. 1459.

Holland, J. L. (1961). Creative and academic performance among talented adolescents. *Journal of Educational Psychology, 52,* 136–147.

Holland, J. L. (1973). *Making vocational choices: A theory of careers.* Englewood Cliffs, NJ: Prentice-Hall.

Holland, S. H. (1991). Positive role models for primary-grade black inner-city males. *Equity and Excellence, 25*(1), 40–44.

Hollinger, C. L. (1985). The stability of self perceptions of instrumental and expressive traits and social self esteem among gifted and talented female adolescents. *Journal for the Education of the Gifted, 8,* 107–126.

Hollinger, C. L., & Kosek, S. (1986). Beyond the use of full scale IQ scores. *Gifted Child Quarterly, 30,* 74–77.

Hollingsworth, P. L. (1991). Parts of the whole: Private schools, public schools, and the community. *Gifted Child Today, 14*(5), 54–56.

Hollingworth, L. S. (1926). *Gifted children: Their nature and nurture.* New York: Macmillan.

Hollingworth, L. S. (1929). Facts about bright children. *Babyhood, 54,* 359, 361, 372.

Hollingworth, L. S. (1938). An enrichment curriculum for rapid learners at Public School 500, Speyer School. *Teachers College Record, 39,* 296–306.

Hollingworth, L. S. (1939). What we know about the early selection and training of leaders. *Teachers College Record, 40,* 575–592.

Hollingworth, L. S. (1942). *Children above 180 IQ Stanford-Binet: Origin and development.* New York: World Book.

Hong, E. (1999). Studying the mind of the gifted. *Roeper Review, 21,* 244–252.

Horner, M. S. (1972). Toward an understanding of achievement related conflicts in women. *Journal of Social Issues, 28,* 155–175.

Hostetler, S. (1989). *Honors for underachievers: The class that never was.* Chico, CA: Chico Unified School District.

House, E. R., & Lapan, S. (1994). Evaluation of programs for disadvantaged gifted students. *Journal for the Education of the Gifted, 17,* 441–446.

Howard-Hamilton, M. (1994). An assessment of moral development in gifted adolescents. *Roeper Review, 17,* 57–59.

Howard-Hamilton, M., & Franks, B. A. (1995). Gifted adolescents: Psychological behaviors, values, and developmental implications. *Roeper Review, 17,* 186–191.

Hultgren, H. W., & Seeley, K. R. (1982). *Training teachers of the gifted: A research monograph on teacher competencies.* Denver: University of Denver, School of Education.

Hunkins, F. P. (1976). *Involving students in questioning.* Boston: Allyn & Bacon.

Huntley, L. B. (1990). Setting up shop: A program for gifted learning disabled students. *Gifted Child Today, 13*(4), 52–56.

Hyde, J., & Fennema, E. (1990, April). *Gender differences in mathematics performance and affect: Results of two meta-analyses.* Paper presented at the meeting of the American Educational Research Association, Boston.

Hyland, C. R. (1989). What we know about the fastest growing minority population: Hispanic Americans. *Educational Horizons, 67*(4), 131–135.

International Baccalaureate Organization (n.d.). Retrieved March 26, 2002, from http://www.ibo.org.

Jackson, N. E. (1988). Precocious reading ability: What does it mean? *Gifted Child Quarterly, 32,* 196–199.

Jackson, N. E. (2003). Young gifted children. In N. Colangelo & G. A. Davis (Eds.), *Handbook of gifted education* (3rd ed., pp. 470–482). Boston: Allyn & Bacon.

Jackson, R. M., Cleveland, J. C., & Mirenda, P. F. (1975). The longitudinal effects of early identification and counseling of underachievers. *Journal of School Psychology, 13,* 119–128.

Jacobs, J. E., & Eccles, J. S. (1985). Gender differences in math ability: The impact of media reports on parents. *Educational Researcher, 14*(3), 20–25.

Jacobs, J. E., Finken, L. L., Griffin, N. L., Wright, J. D. (1998). The career plans of science-talented rural adolescent girls. *American Educational Research Journal, 35,* 681–704.

Jacobs, J. E., & Weisz, V. (1994). Gender stereotypes: Implications for gifted education. *Roeper Review, 16,* 152–155.

James, J. E. (1993). The gifted-handicapped: Metaphor for humanity. *Gifted International, 8*(1), 38–42.

Jenkins, R. C. (1979). The identification of gifted and talented students through peer nomination (Doctoral dissertation, University of Connecticut, 1978). *Dissertation Abstracts International, 40,* 167A.

Jensen, A. R. (1976). Test bias and construct validity. *Phi Delta Kappan, 58,* 340–346.

Jensen, A. R. (1980). *Bias in mental testing.* New York: Free Press.

Jensen, E. (1995). *The learning brain.* San Diego: Turning Point.

John-Steiner, V. (2000). *Creative collaboration.* New York: Oxford University Press.

Johnson, L. J., Karnes, M. B., & Carr, V. W. (1997). Providing services to children with gifts and disabilities: A critical need. In N. Colangelo & G. A. Davis (Eds.), *Handbook of gifted education* (2nd ed.; pp. 516–527). Boston: Allyn & Bacon.

Johnson, S. K., Haensley, P. A., Ryser, G. R., & Ford, R. F. (2002). Changing general education classroom practices to adapt for gifted students. *Gifted Child Quarterly, 46,* 45–63.

Johnson, S., Starnes, W., Gregory, D., & Blaylock, A. (1985). Program of assessment, diagnosis, and instruction (PADA): Identifying and nurturing potentially gifted and talented minority students. *Journal of Negro Education, 54*(3), 416–430.

Juntune, J. E. (1981). *Successful programs for the gifted and talented.* Washington, DC: National Association for the Gifted and Talented.

Kandel, D. B., & Lesser, G. S. (1972). *Youth in two worlds.* San Francisco: Jossey-Bass.

Kaplan, S. N. (1974). *Providing programs for the gifted and talented.* Ventura, CA: Office of the Ventura County Superintendent of Schools.

Kaplan, S. N. (1986). The grid: A model to construct differentiated curriculum for the gifted. In J. S. Renzulli (Ed.), *Systems and models for developing programs for the gifted and talented* (pp. 180–193). Mansfield Center, CT: Creative Learning Press.

Kaplan, S. N. (2001). Synchronizing gifted education with general education. *Gifted Education Communicator, 2001, 32*(1), 30–32.

Kaplan, S. H., Sullivan, L. M., Dukes, K. A., Phillips, C. F., Kelch, R. P., & Schaller, J. G. (1996, October 24). Sex differences in academic advancement. *New England Journal of Medicine,* 1282–1289.

Karnes, F. A., & Brown, K. E. (1981). Moral development and the gifted: An initial investigation. *Roeper Review, 3*(4), 8–10.

Karnes, F. A., & Chauvin, J. C. (1982, September/October). Almost everything that parents and teachers of gifted secondary school students should know about early college enrollment and college credit by examination. *G/C/T,* 39–42.

Karnes, F. A., & Chauvin, J. C. (2000). Leadership development program (rev. ed.). Scottsdale, AZ: Great Potential Press.

Karnes, F. A., & D'Ilio, V. R. (1989). Leadership positions and sex role stereotyping among gifted children. *Gifted Child Quarterly, 33,* 76–78.

Karnes, F. A., & Marquardt, R. G. (1991a). *Gifted Children and Legal Issues in Education: Parents' Stories of Hope.* Dayton: Ohio Psychology Press.

Karnes, F. A., & Marquardt, R. G. (1991b). *Gifted Children and the Law: Mediation, Due Process, and Court Cases.* Dayton: Ohio Psychology Press.

Karnes, F. A., & Marquardt, R. G. (2000). *Gifted children and legal issues: An update.* Scottsdale, AZ: Gifted Psychology Press.

Karnes, F. A., & Marquardt, R. G. (2003). Gifted education and legal issues: Procedures and recent decisions. In N. Colangelo & G. A. Davis (Eds.), *Handbook of gifted education* (3rd ed.; pp. 590–603). Boston: Allyn & Bacon.

Karnes, F. A., & Riley, T. L. (1996a) *Competition: Maximizing your abilities.* Waco, TX: Prufrock Press.

Karnes, F. A, & Riley, T. L. (1996b, December). Parenting Q & A: Expert answers to your questions. *Parenting for High Potential,* 13–14.

Karnes, F. A., Troxclair, D. A., & Marquardt, R. G. (1997). The Office of Civil Rights and the gifted: An update. *Roeper Review, 19,* 162–165.

Karnes, M. B. (1979). Young handicapped children can be gifted and talented. *Journal for the Education of the Gifted, 2,* 157–172.

Karnes, M. B. (1984). A demonstration/outreach model for young gifted/talented handicapped. *Roeper Review, 7*(1), 23–26.

Karnes, M. B., Shwedel, A. M., & Lewis, G. F. (1983). Short-term effects of early programming for the young gifted handicapped child. *Journal for the Education of the Gifted, 6,* 266–278.

Katt, T. (1988). Gifted students develop handicap awareness. *Gifted Child Today, 11*(5), 26–27.

Kaufman, A. S. (1976a). A new approach to the interpretation of test scatter on the WISC-R. *Journal of Learning Disabilities, 9,* 160–168.

Kaufman, A. S. (1976b). Verbal-performance IQ discrepancies on the WISC-R. *Journal of Consulting and Clinical Psychology, 44,* 739–744.

Kaufman, A. S. (1979a). WISC-R research: Implications for interpretation. *School Psychology Digest, 15,* 176–179.

Kaufman, A. S. (1979b). *Intelligence testing with the WISC-R.* New York. Wiley-Interscience.

Kaufmann, F. (1986). *Helping the muskrat guard his musk: A new look at underachievement.* Bossier City, LA: Bossier Parish School Board.

Kaufmann, F., Kalbfleisch, M. L., & Castellanos, F. X. (2000). *Attention deficit disorders and gifted students: What do we really know?* Storrs, CT: National Research Center on the Gifted and Talented, University of Connecticut.

Kaufmann, F. A., Harnel, G., Milam, C. P., Woolverton, N., & Miller, J. (1986). The nature, role, and influence of mentors in the lives of gifted adults. *Journal of Counseling and Development, 64,* 576–578.

Kay, S. I. (2001). A talent profile for facilitating talent development in schools. *Gifted Child Quarterly, 45,* 45–53.

Kelble, E. S. (1991). Overview of private schools for the gifted. *Gifted Child Today, 14*(5), 2–4.

Kelly, K. R., & Colangelo, N. (1984). Academic and social self-concepts of gifted, general, and special students. *Exceptional Children, 50,* 551–554.

Kelly-Benjamin, K. (1990, April). *Performance differences on SAT math questions.* Paper presented at the meeting of the American Educational Research Association, Boston.

Keneal, P. (1991). Teacher expectations as predictors of academic success. *Journal of Social Psychology, 31,* 305–306.

Kerr, B. A. (1985). *Smart girls, gifted women.* Dayton: Ohio Psychology Press.

Kerr, B. A. (1995). *Smart Girls Two.* Dayton: Ohio Psychology Press.

Kerr, B. A. (1997). *Smart girls two: A new psychology of girls, women and giftedness* (rev. ed.). Scottsdale, AZ: Gifted Psychology Press.

Kerr, B. A., & Colangelo, N. (1994). Something to prove: Academically talented minority students. In N. Colangelo, S. G. Assouline, & D. L. Ambroson (Eds.), *Talent development: Proceedings from the 1993 Henry B. and Jocelyn Wallace National Research Symposium on Talent Development* (pp. 299–303). Dayton: Ohio Psychology Press.

Kerr, B. A., Colangelo, N., & Gaeth, J. (1988). Gifted adolescents' attitudes toward their giftedness. *Gifted Child Quarterly, 32,* 245–247.

Kerr, B. A., & Nicpon, M. F. (2003). Gender and giftedness. In N. Colangelo & G. A. Davis (Eds.), *Handbook of gifted education* (3rd ed.; pp. 493–505). Boston: Allyn & Bacon.

Kerr, M. M., & Milliones, J. (1995). Suicide and suicidal behavior. In V. B. Van Hasselt & M. Hersen (Eds.), *Handbook of adolescent psychopathology* (pp. 653–664). New York: Lexington Books.

Kerr, N. L. (1983). Motivation losses in small groups: A social dilemma analysis. *Journal of Personality and Social Psychology, 45,* 819–828.

Kimura, D. (1985, November). Male brain, female brain: The hidden difference. *Psychology Today,* 50–58.

King, A. R. (1998). Family environment scale predictors of academic performance. *Psychological Reports, 83,* 1319–1327.

Kinney, D. A. (1993). From nerds to normals: The recovery of identity among adolescents from middle school to high school. *Sociology of Education, 66,* 21–40.

Kirschenbaum, R. J. (1998). Dynamic assessment and its use with underserved gifted and talented populations. *Gifted Child Quarterly, 42,* 140–147.

Kirton, M. J. (1976). Adaptors and innovators: A description and measure. *Journal of Applied Psychology, 61,* 622–219.

Kitano, M. K. (1991). A multicultural educational perspective on serving the culturally diverse gifted. *Journal for the Education of the Gifted, 15,* 4–19.

Kleiman, C. (2000, Sept. 12). Household chore division slow to change. *Chicago Tribune.* Retrieved June 20, 2001 from http://www.chicagotribune.com/business/smallbusiness/article/0,2669,2-46878,00.html.

Klein, A. G. (2000). Fitting the school to the child: The mission of Leta Stetter Hollingworth, founder of gifted education. *Roeper Review, 23,* 97–103.

Klein, A. G., & Zehms, D. (1996). Self-concept and gifted

girls: A cross sectional study of intellectually gifted females in grades 3, 5, 8. *Roeper Review, 19,* 30–34.

Kluever, R. C., & Green, K. E. (1990). Identification of gifted children: A comparison of the scores on Stanford-Binet 4th Edition and Form LM. *Roeper Review, 13,* 16–20.

Kohlberg, L. (1974). The child as moral philosopher. In G. A. Davis & T. F. Warren (Eds.), *Psychology of education: New looks* (pp. 144–154). Lexington, MA: D. C. Heath.

Kohlberg, L. (1976). Moral states and moralization: The cognitive developmental approach. In T. Lockona (Ed.), *Moral development and behavior.* New York: Holt, Rinehart, & Winston.

Kolata, G. B. (1980). Math and sex: Are girls born with less ability? *Science, 210,* 1234–1235.

Kolata, G. B. (1983). Math genius may have hormonal basis. *Science, 222,* 1312.

Kolb, K. J., & Jussim, L. (1994). Teacher expectations and underachieving gifted children. *Roeper Review, 17,* 26–30.

Kolloff, P. B. (2003). State-supported residential high schools. In N. Colangelo & G. A. Davis (Eds.), *Handbook of gifted education* (3rd ed.; pp. 238–246). Boston: Allyn & Bacon.

Kolo, I. A. (1999). The effectiveness of Nigerian vs. United States teacher checklists and inventories for nominating potentially gifted Nigerian preschoolers. *Roeper Review, 21,* 179–183.

Krauss, M. W. (1990). New precedent in family policy: Individualized family service plan. *Exceptional Children, 56*(5), 388–395.

Krechevsky, M., & Scidcl, S. (1998). Minds at work: Applying multiple intelligences in the classroom. In R. J. Sternberg & W. M. Williams (Eds.), *Intelligence, instruction, and assessment: Theory into practice* (pp. 17–42). Mahwah, NJ: Erlbaum.

Kretschmer, E. (1931). *The psychology of men of genius* (R. B. Cattell, Trans.). New York: Harcourt, Brace.

Krisel, S. C. (1997). Georgia's journey toward multiple-criteria identification of gifted students. *Roeper Review, 20,* A1–A3.

Krueger, M. L. (1978). *On being gifted.* New York: Walker.

Kryaniuk, L. W., & Das, J. P. (1976). Cognitive strategies in native children: Analysis and intervention. *Alberta Journal of Educational Research, 22,* 271–280.

Kuhlthau, A. A. (1994). Supervising independent projects. *Understanding Our Gifted, 6,* 11–14.

Kuhmerker, L. (1991). *The Kohlberg legacy for the helping professions.* Birmingham, AL: R.E.P. Books.

Kulik, J. A. (1992a). Ability grouping and gifted students. In N. Colangelo, S. G. Assouline, & D. L. Ambroson (Eds.), *Talent development: Proceedings from the 1991 Henry B. and Jocelyn Wallace National Research Symposium on Talent Development* (pp. 261–266). Unionville, NY: Trillium.

Kulik, J. A. (1992b). *An analysis of the research on ability grouping: Historical and contemporary perspectives.* Storrs, CT: National Research Center on the Gifted and Talented.

Kulik, J. A. (2003). Grouping and tracking. In N. Colangelo & G. A. Davis (Eds.), *Handbook of gifted education* (3rd ed., pp. 268–281). Boston: Allyn & Bacon.

Kulik, J. A., & Kulik, C.-L. (1984). Effects of accelerated instruction on students. *Review of Educational Research, 54,* 409–425.

Kulik, J. A., & Kulik, C.-L. C. (1997). Ability grouping. In N. Colangelo & G. A. Davis (Eds.), *Handbook of gifted education* (2nd ed.; pp. 230–242). Boston: Allyn & Bacon.

Kunde, D. (1995, December 3). Women MBA grads outpace men in pay. *New Haven Register,* pp. D1, D8.

Kunkel, M. A., Chapa, B., Patterson, G., & Walling, D. D. (1995). The experience of giftedness: A concept map. *Gifted Child Quarterly, 39,* 126–134.

Kutner, L. (1991, November 18). The new family. *Newsweek,* pp. 18–19.

Laffoon, K. S., Jenkins-Friedman, R., & Tollefson, N. (1989). Causal attributions of underachieving gifted, achieving gifted, and nongifted students. *Journal for the Education of the Gifted, 13,* 4–21.

LaFrance, E. B. (1995). Creative thinking differences in three groups of exceptional children as expressed through completion of figural forms. *Roeper Review, 17,* 248–252.

Lamb, M. E. (1976). *The role of the father in child development.* New York: Wiley.

Landrum, M. S. (1987). Guidelines for implementing a guidance/counseling program for gifted and talented students. *Roeper Review, 10,* 103–107.

Langer, P., Kalk, J. V., & Searls, D. T. (1984). Age of admission and trends in achievement: A comparison of blacks and caucasians. *American Educational Research Journal, 21,* 61–78.

Lazear, D. (1991). *Seven ways of teaching: The artistry of teaching with multiple intelligences.* Palatine. IL: Skylight.

Leader, W. (1995, November). *How and why to encourage metacognition in learners.* Paper presented at the meeting of the National Association for Gifted Children, Tampa, FL.

Learning Network (2001). *Women in the house.* San Francisco: Author. Retrieved May 4, 2001, from http://www.factmonster.com/ipka/A0768502.html.

Lee, E. L. (1995, May 1). A lesson in confidence; Virginia middle school tries all-girl classes. *Washington Post,* p. A1.

Lee, J. C., & Cynn, V. E. H. (1991). Issues in counseling 1.5 generation Korean Americans. In C. C. Lee & B. L. Richardson (Eds.), *Multicultural issues in counseling: New approaches to diversity* (pp. 127–140). Alexandria, VA: American Association for Counseling and Development.

Lee, V. E., & Smith, J. B. (1999). Social support and achievement for young adolescents in Chicago: The role of school academic press. *American Educational Research Journal, 36,* 907–945.

Lefkowitz, W. (1975). Communication grows in a "Magic Circle." In D. A. Read & S. B. Simon (Eds.), *Humanistic education sourcebook.* Englewood Cliffs, NJ: Prentice-Hall.

Leifer, A., Neal, G., & Graves, S. (1974). Children's television: More than more entertainment. *Harvard Educational Revue, 44,* 1213–1245.

Lemley, D. (1994). Motivating underachieving gifted secondary students. *Gifted Child Today, 17*(4), 40–41.

Leppien, J. H. (1995). *The paradox of academic achievement of high ability African-American female students in an urban elementary school.* Storrs, CT: National Research Center on the Gifted and Talented.

LeRose, B. (1977). *The lighthouse design: A model for educating children.* Racine, WI: Racine Unified School District.

LeRose, B. (1978). A quota system for gifted minority children: A viable solution. *Gifted Child Quarterly, 22,* 394–403.

Leroux, J. A., & Levitt-Perlman, M. (2000). The gifted child with attention deficit disorder: An identification and intervention challenge. *Roeper Review, 22,* 171–176.

LeTendre, J. J. (1991). Improving Chapter 1 programs: We can do better. *Phi Delta Kappa, 72,* 576–580.

Levy-Agresti, J., & Sperry, R. W. (1968). Differential perceptual capacities in major and minor hemispheres. *Proceedings of the National Academy of Sciences* (p. 61). Washington, DC: National Academy of Sciences.

Lewin, T. (1999, April 11). Amid equity concerns, girls' schools thrive. *New York Times.*

Lewis, G. (1989). Telelearning: Making maximum use of the medium. *Roeper Review, 11,* 195–198.

Lewis, J. D., & Knight, H. V. (2000). Self-concept in gifted youth: An investigation employing the Piers-Harris subscales. *Gifted Child Quarterly, 44,* 45–53.

Lewis, J. F. (1982). Bulldozers or chairs? Gifted students describe their ideal teacher. *Gifted Child Today, 23,* 16–19.

Li, A. K. F., & Adamson, G. (1992). Gifted secondary students' preferred learning style: Cooperative, competitive, or individualistic. *Journal for the Education of the Gifted, 16,* 46–54.

Limburg-Weber, L. (1999/2000). Send then packing: study abroad as an option for gifted students. *Journal of Secondary Gifted Education, 11*(2), 43–51.

Linn, M., & Hyde, J. (1989). Gender, mathematics, and science. *Educational Researcher, 14,* 51–71.

Linnemeyer, S. A. (1994). Evaluation: A key to defensible programming for the gifted. In J. Smutney (Ed.)., *The Journal Portfolio.* Springville: Illinois Association for Gifted Children.

Lipman, M. (1981). What is different about the education of the gifted? *Roeper Review, 4*(1), 19–20.

Lipman, M. (1988). *Philosophy goes to school.* Philadelphia: Temple University Press.

Lipman, M. (1991). *Thinking in education.* New York: Cambridge University Press.

Lipman, M., Sharp, A. M., & Oscanyan, F. S. (1980). *Philosophy in the classroom* (2nd ed.). Philadelphia: Temple University Press.

Lipson, J. (2001, Fall). Equity: Fact or fiction? *Outlook, American Association of University Women, 95*(2), 14–19.

Loeb, R. C., & Jay, G. (1987). Self-concept in gifted children: Differential impact in boys and girls. *Gifted Child Quarterly, 31,* 9–14.

Lombroso, C. (1895). *The man of genius.* London: Scribners.

Long, R. (1981, April). *An approach to a defensible non-discriminatory identification model for the gifted.* Paper presented at the meeting of the Council for Exceptional Children, New York.

Louis, B., & Lewis, M. (1992). Parental beliefs about giftedness in young children and their relationship to actual ability level. *Gifted Child Quarterly, 36,* 27–31.

Loveless, T. (1999). *The tracking wars: State reform meets school policy.* Washington, DC: Brookings Institution.

Lucas, S. R. (1999). *Tracking inequality: Stratification and mobility in American high schools.* New York: Teachers College Press.

Luftig, R. L., & Nichols, M. L. (1989). Assessing the perceived loneliness and self-concept functioning of gifted students in self-contained and integrated settings. Unpublished manuscript, Miami University, Department of Educational Psychology, Oxford, OH.

Luftig, R. L., & Nichols, M. L. (1990). Assessing the social status of gifted students by their age peers. *Gifted Child Quarterly, 34,* 111–115.

Lupkowski-Shoplik, A., Benbow, C. P., Assouline, S. G., & Brody, L. E. (2003). Talent searches: Meeting the needs of academically talented youth. In N. Colangelo & G. A. Davis (Eds.), *Handbook of gifted education* (3rd ed., pp. 204–218). Boston: Allyn & Bacon.

Lupkowski-Shoplik, A., & Swiatek, M. A. (1999). Elementary student talent searches: Establishing appropriate guidelines for qualifying test scores. *Gifted Child Quarterly, 43,* 265–272.

Lutey, C. (1977). *Individual intelligence testing: A manual and sourcebook* (2nd ed.). Greeley, CO: Carol J. Lutey.

Lynch, S., & Mills, C. J. (1990). The skills reinforcement project (SRP): An academic program for high potential minority youth. *Journal for the Education of the Gifted, 13,* 364–379.

Lynn, D. B. (1974). *The father: His role in child development.* Monterey, CA: Brooks/Cole.

Lyon, G. R., Alexander, D., & Yaffe, S. (1997). Progress and promise in research in learning disabilities. *Learning Disabilities: A Multidisciplinary Journal, 8*(1), 1–6.

Maccoby, E. E., & Jacklin, C. (1974). *Psychology of sex differences.* Stanford, CA: Stanford University Press.

Mackin, J., Macaroglu, E., & Russell, K. (1996). Providing opportunities to go beyond traditional curriculum. *Gifted Child Today, 19*(3), 16–20, 49.

MacKinnon, D. W. (1962). The nature and nurture of creative talent. *American Psychologist, 17,* 484–495.

MacKinnon, D. W. (1978). Educating for creativity: A modern myth? In G. A. Davis & J. A. Scott (Eds.), *Training creative thinking* (pp. 194–207). Melbourne, FL: Krieger.

Magoon, R. A. (1980, March/April). Developing leadership skills in the gifted, creative, and talented. *G/C/T,* 40–43.

Magoon, R. A. (1981). A proposed model for leadership development. *Roeper Review, 3*(3), 7–9.

Maker, C. J. (1977). *Providing programs for the handicapped gifted.* Reston, VA: Council for Exceptional Children.

Maker, C. J. (1982). *Curriculum development for the gifted.* Rockville, MD: Aspen.

Maker, C. J. (1993). Creativity, intelligence, problem solving: A definition and design for cross-cultural research and measurement related to giftedness. *Gifted Education International, 9,* 68–77.

Maker, C. J. (1996). Identification of gifted minority students: A national problem, needed changes and a promising solution. *Gifted Child Quarterly, 40,* 41–50.

Maker, C. J., & Nielson, A. B. (1996). *Curriculum develop-*

*ment and teaching strategies for gifted learners.* Austin, TX: Pro-Ed.

Maker, C. J., Nielsen, A. B., & Rogers, J. A. (1994). Giftedness, diversity, and problem solving. *Teaching Exceptional Children, 27,* 4–19.

Maker, C. J., & Schiever, S. (Eds.). (1989). *Critical issues in gifted education: Defensible programs for cultural and ethnic minorities* (Vol. 2). Austin, TX: Pro-Ed.

Maker, C. J., & Udall, A. (1983). A pilot program for elementary-age learning disabled/gifted students. In L. Fox, L. Brody & D. Tobin (Eds.), *Learning disabled gifted children* (pp. 141–152). Baltimore: University Park Press.

Makler, S. J. (1980). On instrumental enrichment: A conversation with Frances Link. *Educational Leadership, 38,* 569–571, 582.

Mann, J. (1994). *The difference: Growing up female in America.* New York: Warner Books.

Manosevitz, M., Prentice, N. M., & Wilson, F. (1973). Individual and family correlates of imaginary play companions in preschool children. *Developmental Psychology, 8,* 72–79.

Marini, M. M. (1978). Sex differences in the determination of adolescent aspirations: A review of Research. *Sex Roles: A Journal of Research, 4,* 723–754.

Marland, S. P., Jr. (1972). *Education of the gifted and talented, Volume 1. Report to the Congress of the United States by the U. S. Commissioner of Education.* Washington, DC: U.S. Government Printing Office.

Marone, N. (1988). *How to father a successful daughter.* New York: Ballantine Books.

Marshall, E. (2001, May 18). Shirley Tilghman: Princeton's unconventional new chief. *Science, 292,* 1288–1289.

Martin, S. C., Parker, R. M., & Arnold, R. M. (1988). Careers of women physicians: Choices and constraints. *Western Journal of Medicine, 149,* 758–760.

Martinson, R. A. (1974). *The identification of the gifted and talented.* Ventura, CA: Office of the Ventura County Superintendent of Schools.

Marx, J. L. (1982). Autoimmunity in left-handers. *Science, 217,* 141–142, 144.

Masten, W. G., Plata, M., Wenglar, K., & Thedford, J. (1999). Acculturation and Teacher Ratings of Hispanic and Anglo-American Students. *Roeper Review, 22,* 64–65.

Math Theory Gains Ground: Girls' Classes Help Them Learn (1994, November 6). *Charleston Newspapers: Sunday Gazette Mail,* p. A3.

Mathew, S. T. (1984). A creative problem-solving (CPS) program for emotionally handicapped children to reduce aggression. *Journal of Creative Behavior, 18,* 278.

Mathews, J. (2001). IB or not IB?: Many colleges decline credit for some advanced courses. *Washington Post,* August 7.

Matthews, M. (1995). Successful practices at Home schools–respect for all individuals. In K. L. Westberg & F. S. Archambault, (Eds.), *Profiles for successful practices for high ability students in elementary classrooms* (pp. 71–84). Storrs, CT: National Research Center on the Gifted and Talented.

Mayer, J. D., Perkins, D. M., Caruso, D. R., & Salovey, P. (2001). Emotional intelligence and giftedness. *Roeper Review, 23,* 131–137.

McBeath, M., Blackshear, P., & Smart, L. (1981, August). *Identifying low income, minority gifted and talented youngsters.* Paper presented at the meeting of the American Psychological Association, Los Angeles, CA.

McCarney, S. B., & Anderson, P. D. (n.d.). *Gifted evaluation Scale (GES).* Retrieved February 18, 2002, from www.psychpress.com.

McCaslin, N. (1974). *Creative dramatics in the classroom.* New York: McKay.

McClelland, D. C. (1976). *The achieving society.* New York: Irvington.

McClusky, K. W., Baker, P. A., & Massey, K. J. (1996). A twenty-four year longitudinal look at early entrance to kindergarten. *Gifted and Talented International, 11,* 72–75.

McCoach, D. B. (1999, Spring). Free summer programs for talented teens. *NRC/GT Newsletter, 3*–8.

McCollim, L. (1992). Mentors at home: Empowering parents. *Gifted Child Today, 15*(3), 15–17.

McCormick, M. (1997, April 3). *Math and science-related career choice: Sociocognitive career theory and academically gifted adolescent girls.* Paper presented at the meeting of the National Association of School Psychologists, Anaheim, CA.

McEvoy, V. (1993, May/June). "Mommy track"—track or trick? *Journal of the American Women's Association, 48*(3).

McKay, D. (1994). The AAUW report: How schools shortchange girls. *Douglass Alumnae Bulletin, 67*(4), 3–6.

McLoyd, V. C. (1990). The impact of economic hardship on black families and children: Psychological distress, parenting, and socioeconomic development. *Child Development, 61,* 311–346.

McManus, S. M., & Gettinger, M. (1996). Teacher and students' evaluations of cooperative learning and observed interactive behaviors. *Journal of Educational Research, 90*(1), 13–31.

Meckstroth, E. (1989, November). Parenting. *Understanding Our Gifted,* p. 4.

Meeker, M. N. (1969). *The structure of intellect: Its interpretation and uses.* Columbus, OH: Merrill.

Meeker, M. N. (1978). Nondiscriminatory testing procedures to assess giftedness in black, Chicano, Navajo and Anglo children. In A. Baldwin, G. Gear, & L. Lucito (Eds.), *Educational planning for the gifted.* Reston, VA: Council for Exceptional Children.

Meeker, M. N., & Meeker, R. (1986). The SOI system for gifted education. In J. S. Renzulli (Ed.), *Systems and models for developing programs for the gifted and talented* (pp. 194–215). Mansfield Center, CT: Creative Learning Press.

Meichenbaum, D. H. (1977). *Cognitive-behavior modification.* New York: Plenum.

Metfessel, N. S., Michael, W. B., & Kirsner, D. A. (1969). Instrumentation of Bloom's and Krathwohl's taxonomies for the writing of educational objectives. *Psychology in the Schools, 6,* 227–231.

Meyer, A. E. (1965). *An educational history of the Western world.* New York: McGraw-Hill.

Millar, G. W. (1995). *The creativity man: An authorized biography.* Norwood, NJ: Ablex.

Miller, M. (1991). Self-assessment as a specific strategy for teaching the gifted learning disabled. *Journal for the Education of the Gifted, 14,* 178–188.

Mills, C. (1980). Sex-role-related personality correlates of intellectual abilities in adolescents. *Roeper Review, 2*(3), 29–31.

Minner, S. (1990). Teacher evaluations of case descriptions of LD gifted children. *Gifted Child Quarterly, 34,* 37–39.

Money, J. (1987). Sin, sickness, or status? Homosexual gender identity and psychoneuroendrocrinology. *American Psychologist, 42,* 384–399.

Montague, M. (1991). Gifted and learning-disabled gifted students' knowledge and use of mathematical problem-solving strategies. *Journal for the Education of the Gifted, 14,* 393–411.

Montemayer, R. (1984). Changes in parent and peer relationships between childhood and adolescence: A research agenda for gifted adolescents. *Journal for the Education of the Gifted, 8,* 9–23.

Moon, S. M. (1995). The effects of an enrichment program on the families of participants: A multiple-case study. *Gifted Child Quarterly, 39,* 198–208.

Moon, S. M. (1996). Using the Purdue three-stage model to facilitate local program evaluations. *Gifted Child Quarterly, 40,* 121–128.

Moon, S. M., & Rosselli, H. C. (2000). Developing gifted programs. In K. A. Heller, F. J. Mönks, R. J. Sternberg, & R. F. Subotnik (Eds.), *International handbook of giftedness and talent* (2nd ed., pp. 499–521). New York: Elsevier.

Moore, B. A. (1979). A model career education program for gifted disadvantaged students. *Roeper Review, 2*(2), 20–22.

Morelock, M. J. (1995). *The profoundly gifted child in family context.* Unpublished doctoral dissertation, Tufts University, Medford, Massachusetts.

Morelock, M. J. (1996). On the nature of giftedness and talent: Imposing order on chaos. *Roeper Review, 19,* 4–12.

Morelock, M. J. (1997). Imagination, logic, and the exceptionally gifted child. *Roeper Review, 19,* A-1.

Morelock, M. J. (2000). A sociohistorical perspective on exceptionally high-IQ children. In R. C. Friedman & B. Shore (Eds.), *Talents unfolding: Cognition and development* (pp. 55–75). Washington, DC: American Psychological Association.

Morelock, M. J., & Feldman, D. H. (1993). Prodigies and savants: What they have to tell us about giftedness and human cognition. In K. A. Heller, F. J. Mönks, & A. H. Passow (Eds.), *International handbook of research and development of giftedness and talent* (pp. 161–181). New York: Pergamon.

Morelock, M. J., & Feldman, D. H. (1997). High IQ children, extreme precocity, and savant syndrome. In N. Colangelo & G. A. Davis (Eds.), *Handbook of gifted education* (2nd ed.; pp. 439–459). Boston: Allyn & Bacon.

Morelock, M. J., & Feldman, D. H. (2003). Extreme precocity: Prodigies, savants, and children of extraordinarily high IQ. In N. Colangelo & G. A. Davis (Eds.), *Handbook of gifted education* (3rd ed., pp. 455–469). Boston: Allyn & Bacon.

Morelock, M. J., & Morrison, K. (1999). Differentiating "developmentally appropriate": The multidimensional curriculum model for young gifted children. *Roeper Review, 21,* 195–200.

Morrow, L. (1983, April). *Home and school correlates of early interest in literature.* Paper presented at the meeting of the American Educational Research Association, Montreal.

Moses, S. (1991, July). Ties that bind can limit minority valedictorians. *Education Monitor,* p. 47.

Mosley, J. H. (1982, November/December). Ten suggestions to insure the brevity of your gifted program. *G/C/T,* 46.

Moss, E. (1983, April). *Mothers and gifted preschoolers-teaching and learning strategies.* Paper presented at the meeting of the American Educational Research Association, Montreal.

Moss, E. (1990). Social interaction and metacognitive development in gifted preschoolers. *Gifted Child Quarterly, 34,* 16–20.

Mussen, P. H., & Rutherford, E. (1963). Parent-child relations and parental personality in relation to young children's sex-role preferences. *Child Development, 34,* 589–607.

Nadelson, T., & Eisenberg, L. (1977). On being married to a professional woman. *American Journal of Psychiatry, 134,* 1071–1076.

National Association for Gifted Children. (2000). Web sites to help teachers create more challenging curriculum for gifted students. *Teaching for high potential, 2*(2), 1–4. [This newsletter appears inside the National Association for Gifted Children *Communique 2000, 13*(1).]

National Commission on Excellence in Education. (1983). *A nation at risk: The imperative for educational reform.* Washington, DC: U.S. Government Printing Office.

National Committee on Pay Equity. (2000). *Wage gap widens in 1999. Women make 72 percent of men's earnings.* Hyattsville, MD: Author.

National Research Council. (1998). *Preventing reading difficulties in young children.* Author. Washington, DC.

National Science Foundation. (2000). *Women, minorities and persons with disabilities in science and engineering: 2000.* Arlington, VA: Author.

Neihart, M. (1999a). Systematic risk-taking. *Roeper Review, 21,* 289–292.

Neihart, M. (1999b). The impact of giftedness on psychological well-being: What does the empirical literature say? *Roeper Review, 22,* 10–17.

Neihart, M. (2002). Gifted children and depression. In M. Neihart, S. M. Reis, N. M. Robinson, & S. M. Moon (Eds.), *Social and emotional development of gifted children: What do we know?* (pp. 93–101). Washington, DC: National Association for Gifted Children.

Neihart, M., Reis, S. M., Robinson, N. M., & Moon, S. M. (Eds.) (2002). *Social and emotional development of gifted children: What do we know?* Washington, DC: National Association for Gifted Children.

Nelson, K. C., & Prindle, N. (1992). Gifted teacher competencies: Ratings by rural principals and teachers compared. *Journal for the Education of the Gifted, 15,* 357–369.

Nelson-Jones, R. (1990). *Managing and preventing personal problems.* Pacific Grove, CA: Brooks-Cole.

Newland, T. E. (1969). *Manual for the blind learning aptitude test: Experimental edition.* Urbana, IL: Newland.

Newland, T. E. (1976). *The gifted in socioeducational perspective.* Englewood Cliffs, NJ: Prentice-Hall.

Nichols, J. G. (1979). Development of perception of own attainment and causal attribution for success and failure in reading. *Journal of Educational Psychology, 71,* 94–99.

Nichols, T. M. (1992). The Junior Great Books program. *Gifted Child Today, 15*(5), 50–51.

Nielsen, M. E, & Mortorff-Albert, S. (1989). The effects of special education service on the self-concept and school attitude of learning disabled/gifted students. *Roeper Review, 12,* 29–36.

Noble, D. F. (1992). *A world without women.* New York: Knopf.

Noble, K. D. (1989). Counseling gifted women: Becoming the hcrocs of our own storics. *Journal for the Education of the Gifted, 12,* 131–141.

Norman, A. D., Ramsay, S. G., Roberts, J. L., & Martray, C. R. (2000). Effect of social setting, self-concept, and relative age on the social status of moderately and highly gifted students. *Roeper Review, 23,* 35–39.

Norman, C. (1988). Math education: A mixed picture. *Science, 241,* 408–409.

Oakes, J. (1985). *Keeping track.* New Haven: Yale University Press.

O'Brien, J. S. (n.d.). *Character education partnerships.* Washington, DC: U.S. Department of Education.

O'Connell, B. (1982). *Arts for the handicapped* (ESEA Title IV-C Model Sites Project). Sheboygan: Wisconsin Department of Public Instruction.

O'Connell, P. (1993). *National excellence: A case for developing America's talent.* Washington, DC: U.S. Department of Education.

O'Connell, P. (1997). Federal policy on gifted and talented education. In N. Colangelo & G. A. Davis (Eds.), *Handbook of gifted education* (2nd ed., pp. 553–559). Boston: Allyn & Bacon.

O'Connell P. (2003). Federal involvement in gifted and talented education. In N. Colangelo & G. A. Davis (Eds.), *Handbook of gifted education* (3rd ed., pp. 604–608). Boston: Allyn & Bacon.

O'Connor, K. J. (2002). The application of Dabrowski's theory to the gifted. In M. Neihart, S. M. Reis, N. M. Robinson, & S. M. Moon (Eds.), *Social and emotional development of gifted children: What do we know?* (pp. 51–60). Washington, DC: National Association for Gifted Children.

Oden, M. (1968). The fulfillment of promise: 40-year follow-up of the Terman gifted group. *Genetic Psychology Monographs, 77,* 3–93.

Office of Special Education Programs (1994). *Implementation of the Individuals with Disabilities Education Act* (Sixteenth Annual Report to Congress). Washington, DC: U.S. Department of Education.

Office of Special Education Programs (1995). *Implementation of the Individuals with Disabilities Education Act* (Seventeenth Annual Report to Congress). Washington, DC: U.S. Department of Education.

Ogbu, J. U. (1992). Understanding cultural diversity and learning. *Educational Researcher, 21*(8), 5–14.

Ogbu, J. U. (1994). Understanding cultural diversity and learning. *Journal for the Education of the Gifted, 17,* 355–383.

Okagaki, L., & Frensch, P. A. (1998, Spring). Parenting and children's school achievement: A multiethnic perspective. *American Educational Research Journal, 35*(1), 123–144.

Olenchak, F. R. (1999). Affective development of gifted students with nontraditional talents. *Roeper Review, 21,* 302–307.

Olenchak, F. R., & Castle, C. (1995, November). *Reliable and valid attitude assessment in gifted education.* Paper presented at the meeting of the National Association for Gifted Children, Tampa, FL.

Olenchak, F. R., & Reis, S. M. (2001). Gifted students with learning disabilities. In M. Neihart, S. M. Reis, N. M. Robinson, & S. M. Moon (Eds.), *Social and emotional development of gifted children: What do we know?* (pp. 177–191). Washington, DC: National Association for Gifted Children.

Olsen, H. (1970). A comparison of academic self-concept, significant others of black and black precollege students. *Child Study Journal, 1,* 28–32.

Olshen, S. R. (1987). The disappearance of giftedness in girls: An intervention strategy. *Roeper Review, 9,* 251–254.

Olszewski-Kubilius, P. (1995). A summary of research regarding early entrance to college. *Roeper Review, 18,* 121–126.

Olszewski-Kubilius, P. (1997). Special summer and Saturday programs for gifted students. In N. Colangelo & G. A. Davis (Eds.), *Handbook of gifted education* (2nd ed.; pp. 180–188). Boston: Allyn & Bacon.

Olszewski-Kubilius, P. (2003). Special summer and Saturday programs for gifted students. In N. Colangelo & G. A. Davis (Eds.), *Handbook of gifted education* (3rd ed., pp. 219–228). Boston: Allyn & Bacon.

Olszewski-Kubilius, P., Grant, B., & Seibert, C. (1994). Social support systems and the disadvantaged gifted: A framework for developing programs and services. *Roeper Review, 17,* 20–25.

Olszewski-Kubilius, P., & Laubscher, L. (1996). The impact of a college counseling program on economically disadvantaged gifted students and their subsequent college adjustment. *Roeper Review, 18,* 202–208.

Olszewski-Kubilius, P., & Limburg-Weber, L. (1999). *Designs for excellence: A guide to educational program options for academically talented middle & secondary students.* Evanston, IL: Center for Talent Development, Northwestern University.

Olszewski-Kubilius, P., Shaw, B., Kulieke, M. J., & Willis, G. B. (1990). Predictors of achievement in mathematics for gifted males and females. *Gifted Child Quarterly, 34,* 64–71.

Olszewski-Kubilius, P., & Yasumoto, J. (1994). Factors affecting the academic choices of academically talented adolescents. In N. Colangelo, S. G. Assouline, & D. L. Ambroson (Eds.), *Talent development: Proceedings from the 1993 Henry B. and Jocelyn Wallace National Research Symposium on Talent Development* (pp. 393–398). Dayton: Ohio Psychology Press.

Ondo, E., & Session, E. (1989). Update: The pyramid project. *Gifted Child Today, 12*(3), 46–49.

Orange County Department of Education. (1981). *Project IMPACT.* Costa Mesa, CA: Author.

Orth, L. C. (1988). The relationship of parental child-rearing attitudes to creativity in gifted preschool children (abstract). *Journal of Creative Behavior, 22,* 70.

Ortiz, V. Z., & Gonzalez, A. (1989). A validation study of a WISC-R short form with accelerated and gifted Hispanic students. *Gifted Child Quarterly, 33,* 152–155.

Ortiz, V. Z., & Gonzalez, A. (1991). Gifted Hispanic adolescents. In M. Bireley & J. Genshaft (Eds.), *Understanding the gifted adolescent: Educational, developmental, and multicultural issues* (pp. 240–247). New York: Teachers College Press.

Orum, L. (1986). *Education of Hispanics: Status and implications.* Washington, DC: National Council of La Raza.

Osborn, A. F. (1963). *Applied imagination* (3rd ed.). New York: Scribners.

Ovando, C. J. (2001, April). Beyond blaming the victims: Successful schools for Latino students. Book Reviews. *Educational Researcher, 30*(3), 29–31.

Oxygen/Markle Pulse. (2000, November). *Survey on life balance.* New York: Author.

Pallas, A. M., & Alexander, K. L. (1983). Sex differences in quantitative SAT performance: New evidence on the differential coursework hypothesis. *American Educational Research Journal, 20,* 165–182.

Pallone, N., Richard, F., & Hurley, R. (1973). Further data on key influencers of occupational expectations of minority youth. *Journal of Counseling Psychology, 20,* 484–486.

Parish, T. S., & Nunn, G. D. (1983, April). *Locus of control as a function of family type and age at onset of father absence.* Paper presented at the meeting of the American Educational Research Association, Montreal.

Parker, J. (1983, September/October). The leadership training Model. *G/C/T,* 8–13.

Parnes, S. J. (1981). *Magic of your mind.* Buffalo, NY: Creative Education Foundation.

Parsons, J. E., Adler, T., & Kaczala, C. (1982). Socialization of achievement attitudes and beliefs: Parental influences. *Child Development, 53,* 310–321.

Passow, A. H. (1981). The nature of giftedness and talent. *Gifted Child Quarterly, 25,* 5–10.

Passow, A. H. (1997). International perspectives on gifted education. In N. Colangelo & G. A. Davis (Eds.), *Handbook of gifted education* (2nd ed.; pp. 528–535). Boston: Allyn & Bacon.

Patton, J. M. (1992). Assessment and identification of African-American learners with gifts and talents. *Exceptional Children, 59*(2), 150–159.

Patton, J. M., Prillaman, D., & VanTassel-Baska, J. (1990). The nature and extent of programs for the disadvantaged gifted in the United States and territories. *Gifted Child Quarterly, 34,* 94–96.

Patton, J. M., & Townsend, B. L. (1997). Creating inclusive environments for African-American children and youth with gifts and talents. *Roeper Review, 20,* 13–17.

Paul, R., Binker, A. J. A., Martin, D., Vetrano, C., & Kreklau, H. (1989). *Critical thinking handbook: A guide for remodelling lesson plans in language arts, social studies, and science* (6th–9th grades). Rohnert Park, CA: Sonoma State University, Center for Critical Thinking and Moral Critique.

Perino, S. C., & Perino, J. (1981). *Parenting the gifted—developing the promise.* New York: Bowker.

Perkins, E. (1975). *Home is a dirty street: The social oppression of black children.* Chicago: Third World Press.

Perleth, C., Lehwald, G., & Browder, C. S. (1993). Indicators of high ability in young children. In K. A. Heller, F. J. Mönks, & A. H. Passow (Eds.), *International handbook of research and development of giftedness and talent* (pp. 283–310). New York: Pergamon.

Perrone, P. (1997). Gifted individuals' career development. In N. Colangelo & G. A. Davis (Eds.), *Handbook of gifted education* (2nd ed.; pp. 398–407). Boston: Allyn & Bacon.

Persson, R. S., Joswig, H., & Balogh, L. (2000). Gifted education in Europe: Programs, practices, and current research. In K. A. Heller, F. J. Mönks, R. J. Sternberg, & R. F. Subotnik (Eds.), *International handbook of giftedness and talent* (pp. 703–734). New York: Elsevier.

Peterson, J. S. (1993). What we learned from Genna. *Gifted Child Today, 16*(1), 15–16.

Peterson, J. S. (1999). Gifted through whose cultural lens? An application of the post-positivistic mode of inquiry. *Journal for the Education of the Gifted, 22,* 354–383.

Peterson, J. S. (2001). Gifted and at risk: Four longitudinal case studies of post-high school development. *Roeper Review, 24,* 31–39.

Peterson, J. S., & Margolin, L. (1997). Naming gifted children: An example of unintended reproduction. *Journal for the Education of the Gifted, 21,* 82–100.

Peterson, J. S., & Rischar, H. (2000). Gifted and gay: A study of the adolescent experience. *Gifted Child Quarterly, 44,* 231–246.

Pfeiffer, S. I. (2000). *Talent identification program: Celebrating 20 bright years.* Durham, NC: Duke University.

Pfeil, M. P. (1978, March). Fourth Street School's new claim to fame. *American Education,* 10–13.

Pfouts, J. H. (1980). Birth order, age spacing, IQ differences and family relations. *Journal of Marriage and the Family, 42,* 517–521.

Piaget, J., & Inhelder, B. (1969). *The psychology of the child* (H. Weaver trans.). New York: Basic Books.

Piechowski, M. M. (1991). Emotional development and emotional giftedness. In N. Colangelo & G. A. Davis (Eds.), *Handbook of gifted education* (pp. 285–306). Boston: Allyn & Bacon.

Piechowski, M. M. (1997). Emotional giftedness: The measure of intrapersonal intelligence. In N. Colangelo & G. A. Davis (Eds.), *Handbook of gifted education* (2nd ed.; pp. 366–381). Boston: Allyn & Bacon.

Piechowski, M. M. (1999). Overexcitabilities. In M. A. Runco & S. R. Pritzker (Eds.), *Encyclopedia of Creativity* (Vol. 2, pp. 325–334). New York: Academic Press.

Piechowski, M. M. (2003). Emotional and spiritual giftedness. In N. Colangelo & G. A. Davis (Eds.), *Handbook of gifted education* (3rd ed., pp. 403–416). Boston: Allyn & Bacon.

Pierce, J. W., & Bowman, P. (1960). Motivation patterns of superior high school students. *Cooperative Research Monograph No. 2,* 33–36.

Piers, E. V. (1984). *Manual for the Piers-Harris Children's Self-Concept Scale.* Los Angeles: Western Psychological Services.

Pine, G. J., & Boy, A. V. (1977). *Learner-centered teaching: A humanistic view.* Denver: Love.

Pipher, M. (1995). *Reviving Ophelia: Saving the selves of adolescent girls.* New York: Ballantine Books.

Plomin, R., DeFries, J. C., McClearn, G. E., & McGuffin, P. (2001). *Behavioral genetics* (4th ed.). New York: Worth.

Plomin, R., & Price, T. S. (2003). The relationship between genetics and intelligence. In N. Colangelo & G. A. Davis (Eds.), *Handbook of gifted education* (3rd ed., pp. 113–123). Boston: Allyn & Bacon.

Plowman, P. D. (1981). Training extraordinary leaders. *Roeper Review, 3*(3), 13–16.

Plucker, J. A. (1996). Gifted Asian-American students: Identification, curricular, and counseling concerns. *Journal for the Education of the Gifted, 19,* 315–343.

Plucker, J. A. (1999). Reanalysis of student responses to creativity checklists: Evidence of content generality. *Journal of Creative Behavior, 33,* 126–137.

Plucker, J. A., Callahan, C. M., & Tomchin, E. M. (1996). Wherefore art thou, multiple intelligences? Alternative assessments for identifying talent in ethnically diverse and low income students. *Gifted Child Quarterly, 40,* 81–90.

Plucker, J. A., & Stocking, V. B. (2001). Looking outside and inside: self-concept development of gifted adolescents. *Exceptional Children, 67,* 535–548.

Pollina, A. (1995). Gender balance: Lessons from girls in science and mathematics. *Educational Leadership, 53,* 30–33.

Pollock, W. (1998). *Real boys: Rescuing your sons from the myths of boyhood.* New York: Henry Holt.

Poloma, M. M. (1972). Role conflict and the married professional woman. In C. Safilios-Rothschild (Ed.), *Toward a sociology of women.* Lexington, MA: Xerox College.

Pool, R. (1990). A lost generation? *Science, 248,* 435.

Poelzer, G. H., & Feldhusen, J. F. (1997). The International Baccalaureate: A program for gifted secondary students. *Roeper Review, 19,* 168–171.

Post, R. D. (1981). Causal explanations of male and female academic performance as a function of sex-role biases. *Sex Roles, 7,* 691–698.

Potee, R. A., Gerber, A. J., & Ickovics, J. R. (1999). Medicine and motherhood: Shifting trends among female physicians from 1922 to 1999. *Academic Medicine, 74,* 911–919.

Power, F. C., Higgins, A., & Kohlberg, L. (1989). *Lawrence Kohlberg's approach to moral education.* New York: Columbia University Press.

Prillaman, D., & Richardson, R. (1989). The William and Mary mentorship model: College students as a resource for the gifted. *Roeper Review, 12,* 114–118.

Proctor, T. B., Black, K. N., & Feldhusen, J. F. (1986). Early admission of selected children to elementary school: A review of the research literature. *Journal of Educational Research, 80*(2), 70–76.

Provus, M. M. (1972). *Discrepancy evaluation.* Berkeley, CA: McCutchan.

Pufal-Struzik, I. (1999). Self-actualization and other personality dimensions as predictors of mental health of intellectually gifted students. *Roeper Review, 22,* 44–47.

Pulvino, C. J., Colangelo, N., & Zaffrann, R. T. (1976). *Laboratory counseling programs.* Madison, WI: University of Wisconsin, Department of Counseling and Guidance.

Purcell, J. H. (1995). Gifted education at a crossroads: The program status study. *Gifted Child Quarterly, 39,* 57–65.

Pyryt, M. C. (2003). Technology and the gifted. In N. Colangelo & G. A. Davis (Eds.), *Handbook of gifted education* (3rd ed., pp. 582–589). Boston: Allyn & Bacon.

Radin, N. (1971). Observed maternal behavior with four-year-old boys and girls in lower-class families. *Child Development, 45,* 1126–1131.

Radin, N. (1976). The role of the father in cognitive, affective and intellectual development. In M. E. Lamb (Ed.), *The role of the father in child development.* New York: Wiley.

Radin, N., & Epstein, A. (1975). *Observed paternal behavior and the intellectual functioning of preschool boys and girls.* Paper presented at the meeting of the Society for Research in Child Development, Denver.

Ramos-Ford, V., & Gardner, H. (1997). Giftedness from a multiple intelligences perspective. In N. Colangelo & G. A. Davis (Eds.), *Handbook of gifted education* (2nd ed.; pp. 54–66). Boston: Allyn & Bacon.

Raymond, C. L., & Benbow, C. P. (1989). Educational encouragement by parents: Its relationship to precocity and gender. *Gifted Child Quarterly, 33,* 144–151.

Rea, D. W. (2000). Optimal motivation for talent development. *Journal for the Education of the Gifted, 23,* 187–216.

Redding, R. E. (1990). Learning preferences and skills patterns among underachieving gifted adolescents. *Gifted Child Quarterly, 34,* 72–75.

Rees, D., Argys, L. M., & Brewer, D. J. (1996). Tracking in the United States: Descriptive statistics from NELS. *Economics of Education Review, 15*(1), 83–89.

Reid, C., & Romanoff, B. (1997). Using multiple intelligence theory to identify gifted children. *Educational Leadership, 55*(1), 71–74.

Reid, C., Romanoff, B., Algozzine, B., & Udall, A. (2000). An evaluation of alternative screening procedures. *Journal for the Education of the Gifted, 23,* 378–396.

Reif, S. F. (1993). *How to reach and teach ADD/ADHD children.* West Nyack, NY: Center for Applied Research in Education.

Reis, S. M. (1987). We can't change what we don't recognize: Understanding the special needs of gifted females. *Gifted Child Quarterly, 31,* 83–89.

Reis, S. M. (1990a, February). Teaching techniques. *Learning90,* 46–47.

Reis, S. M. (1990b, February). What to teach, when to teach it. *Learning90,* 44–45.

Reis, S. M. (1995). Talent ignored, talent diverted: The cultural contest underlying giftedness in females. *Gifted Child Quarterly, 39,* 162–170.

Reis, S. M. (1998a, Spring). Underachievement for some, dropping out with dignity for others. *ITAG News, Iowa Talented and Gifted Association Newsletter, 23*(4), 12–15.

Reis, S. M. (1998b). *Work left undone. Choices and compromises of talented females.* Mansfield Center, CT: Creative Learning Press.

Reis, S. M., & Burns, D. E. (1987). A schoolwide enrichment team invites you to read about methods for promoting community and faculty involvement in a gifted education program. *Gifted Child Today, 49*(2), 27–32.

Reis, S. M., & Callahan, C. M. (1989). Gifted females: They've come a long way—or have they? *Journal for the Education of the Gifted, 12,* 99–117.

Reis, S. M., & Callahan, C. M. (1996). My boyfriend, my girlfriend, or me: The dilemma of talented teenaged girls. *Journal of Secondary Gifted Education, 7,* 434–446.

Reis, S. M., & Dobyns, S. M. (1991). An annotated bibliography of non-fictional books and curricular materials to encourage gifted females. *Roeper Review, 13,* 129–130.

Reis, S. M., Gentry, M., & Maxfield, L. R. (1998). The application of enrichment clusters to teachers' classroom practices. *Journal for the Education of the Gifted, 21,* 310–334.

Reis, S. M., Hébert, T. P., Díaz, E. I., Maxfield, L. R., & Ratley, M. E. (1995). *Case studies of talented students who achieve and underachieve in an urban high school.* Storrs, CT: National Research Center on the Gifted and Talented.

Reis, S. M., McGuire, J., Neu, T. W. (2000, Spring). Compensation strategies used by high-ability students with learning disabilities who succeed in college. *Gifted Child Quarterly, 44,* 123–134.

Reis, S. M., & Moon, S. M. (2002). Models and strategies for counseling, guidance, and social and emotional support of gifted and talented students. In M. Neihart, S. M. Reis, N. M. Robinson, & S. M. Moon (Eds.), *Social and emotional development of gifted children: What do we know?* (pp. 251–265). Washington, DC: National Association for Gifted Children.

Reis, S. M., Neu, T. W., & McGuire, J. M. (1995). *Talents in two places: Case studies of high ability students with learning disabilities who have achieved.* Storrs, CT: National Research Center on the Gifted and Talented.

Reis, S. M., & Renzulli, J. S. (1986). The secondary triad model. In J. S. Renzulli (Ed.), *Systems and models for developing programs for the gifted and talented* (pp. 267–304). Mansfield Center, CT: Creative Learning Press.

Reis, S. M., & Renzulli, J. S. (1991). The assessment of creative products in programs for gifted and talented students. *Gifted Child Quarterly, 35,* 128–134.

Reis, S. M., Westberg, K., Kulikovich, J., Caillard, F., Hébert, T., Purcell, J., Rogers, J., & Smist, J. (1992, April). Modifying regular classroom instruction with curriculum compacting. In J. S. Renzulli (Chair), *Regular classroom practices with gifted students: Findings from the National Research Center on the Gifted and Talented.* Symposium conducted at the meeting of the American Educational Research Association, San Francisco.

Reis, S. M., Westberg, K. L., Kulikovich, J. M., & Purcell, J. H. (1998). Curriculum compacting and achievement test scores: What does the research say? *Gifted Child Quarterly, 42,* 123–129.

Rejskind, G. (2000). TAG teachers: Only the creative need apply. *Roeper Review, 22,* 153–157.

Renzulli, J. S. (1975). *A guidebook for evaluating programs for the gifted and talented.* Ventura, CA: Office of the Ventura County Superintendent of Schools.

Renzulli, J. S. (1977). *Enrichment triad model: A guide for developing defensible programs for the gifted and talented.* Mansfield, CT: Creative Learning Press.

Renzulli, J. S. (1986). The three-ring conception of giftedness: A developmental model for creative productivity. In R. J. Sternberg & J. E. Davidson (Eds.), *Conceptions of Giftedness* (pp. 53–92). Cambridge, MA: Cambridge University Press.

Renzulli, J. S. (1987, April). *The triad/revolving door model.* Workshop presented in Madison, WI.

Renzulli, J. S. (1988). The Multiple Menu Model for developing differentiated curriculum for the gifted and talented. *Gifted Child Quarterly, 32,* 298–309.

Renzulli, J. S. (1991). The National Research Center on the Gifted and Talented: The dream, the design, and the destination. *Gifted Child Quarterly, 35,* 73–80.

Renzulli, J. S. (1992, April). Chair/discussant comments. In J. S. Renzulli (Chair), *Regular classroom practices with gifted students: Findings from the National Research Center on the Gifted and Talented.* Symposium conducted at the meeting of the American Educational Research Association, San Francisco.

Renzulli, J. S. (1994). *Schools for talent development: A practical plan for total school improvement.* Mansfield Center, CT: Creative Learning Press.

Renzulli, J. S. (1995, November). *Past reflections—future directions.* Address presented at the meeting of the National Association for Gifted Children, Tampa, FL.

Renzulli, J. S. (2003). Conception of giftedness and its relationship to the development of social capital. In N. Colangelo & G. A. Davis (Eds.), *Handbook of gifted education* (3rd ed., pp. 75–87). Boston: Allyn & Bacon.

Renzulli, J. S., Callahan, C. M., Smith, L. H., Renzulli, M. J., & Ford, B. G. (2000). *New directions in creativity* (2nd ed.). Mansfield Center, CT: Creative Learning Press.

Renzulli, J. S., & Park, S. (2000). Gifted Dropouts: The who and the why. *Gifted Child Quarterly, 44,* 261–271.

Renzulli, J. S., & Reis, S. M. (1985). *The schoolwide enrichment model: A comprehensive plan for educational excellence.* Mansfield Center, CT: Creative Learning Press.

Renzulli, J. S., & Reis, S. M. (1991). The reform movement and the quiet crisis in gifted education. *Gifted Child Quarterly, 35,* 26–35.

Renzulli, J. S., & Reis, S. M. (1994). Research related to the Schoolwide Enrichment Triad Model. *Gifted Child Quarterly, 38,* 7–20.

Renzulli, J. S., & Reis, S. M. (1997). *The schoolwide enrichment model: A how-to-guide for educational excellence* (2nd ed.). Mansfield Center, CT: Creative Learning Press.

Renzulli, J. S., & Reis, S. M. (2003). The schoolwide enrichment model: Developing creative and productive giftedness. In N. Colangelo & G. A. Davis (Eds.), *Handbook of gifted education* (3rd ed., pp. 184–203). Boston: Allyn & Bacon.

Renzulli, J. S., Reis, S. M., & Smith, L. H. (1981). *Revolving door identification model.* Mansfield, CT: Creative Learning Press.

Renzulli, J. S., & Smith, L. H. (1978a). Developing defensible programs for the gifted and talented. *Journal of Creative Behavior, 12,* 21–29, 51.

Renzulli, J. S., & Smith, L. H. (1978b). *Learning styles inventory.* Mansfield Center, CT: Creative Learning Press.

Renzulli, J. S., & Smith, L. H. (1979). Issues and procedures in evaluating gifted programs. In A. H. Passow (Ed.), *The gifted and the talented* (pp. 289–307). Chicago: National Society for the Study of Education.

Renzulli, J. S., Smith, L., White, A., Callahan, C., & Hartman, R. (2001). *Scales for rating the behavioral characteristics of superior students* (rev. ed.). Manual and nine rating scales. Mansfield Center, CT: Creative Learning Press.

Renzulli, J. S., & Ward, V. S. (1969). *Diagnostic and evaluative scales for differential education for the gifted.* Storrs: University of Connecticut, Department of Educational Psychology.

Rest, J. R. (1988). *Test manual for the Defining Issues Test* (3rd ed.). Minneapolis: University of Minnesota Center for the Study of Ethical Development.

Restak, R. (1979). *The brain: The last frontier.* New York: Doubleday.

Reyes, E. I., Fletcher, R., & Paez, D. (1996). Developing local multidimensional screening procedures for identifying giftedness among a Mexican American border population. *Roeper Review, 18,* 208–211.

Reynolds, M. C. (Ed.). (1962). *Early admission for mentally advanced children.* Washington, DC: Council for Exceptional Children.

Richards, R. L. (1990). Everyday creativity, eminent creativity, and health. *Creativity Research Journal, 3,* 300–326.

Richards, R. L. (1999). Affective disorders. In M. A. Runco & Stephen R. Pritzker (Eds.), *Encyclopedia of creativity* (Vol. 1, pp. 31–43). New York: Academic Press.

Richardson, T. M., & Benbow, C. (1990). Long-term effects of acceleration on the social-emotional adjustment of mathematically precocious youths. *Journal of Educational Psychology, 82,* 464–470.

Richardson, W. B., & Feldhusen, J. F. (1986). *Leadership education: Developing skills for youth.* New York: Trillium Press.

Ritchart, R. (2001). From IQ to IC: A Dispositional View of Intelligence. *Roeper Review, 23,* 143–150.

Richert, E. S. (1985). Identification of gifted students: An update. *Roeper Review, 8,* 68–72.

Richert, E. S. (1987). Rampant problems and promising practices in the identification of disadvantaged gifted students. *Gifted Child Quarterly, 31,* 149–154.

Richert, E. S. (1991a). Patterns of underachievement among gifted students. In M. Bireley & J. Genshaft (Eds.), *Understanding the gifted adolescent: Educational, developmental, and multicultural issues* (pp. 139–162). New York: Teachers College Press.

Richert, E. S. (1991b). Rampant problems and promising practices in identification. In N. Colangelo & G. A. Davis (Eds.), *Handbook of gifted education* (pp. 81–96). Boston: Allyn & Bacon.

Richert, E. S. (1997). Excellence with equity in identification and programming. In N. Colangelo & G. A. Davis (Eds.), *Handbook of gifted education* (2nd ed.; pp. 75–88). Boston: Allyn & Bacon.

Richert, E. S. (2003). Excellence with justice in identification and programming. In N. Colangelo & G. A. Davis (Eds.), *Handbook of gifted education* (3rd ed., pp. 146–158). Boston: Allyn & Bacon.

Richert, E. S., Alvino, J. J., & McDonnel, R. C. (1982). *National report on identification: Assessment and recommendations for comprehensive identification of gifted and talented youth.* Washington, DC: U.S. Department of Education, Educational Information Resource Center.

Rimland, B. (1995). Reaching the gifted student with autism. *Autism Research Review International, 9*(2), 2.

Rimm, S. B. (1976). *GIFT: Group inventory for finding creative talent.* Watertown, WI: Educational Assessment Service.

Rimm, S. B. (1977, Fall). Foreword: A comprehensive framework for total educational evaluation. *Journal of the Wisconsin Association for Supervision and Curriculum Development,* 9–18.

Rimm, S. B. (1981). Evaluation of gifted programs—as easy as ABC. In R. E. Clasen, B. Robinson, D. R. Clasen, & G. Libster (Eds.), *Programming for the gifted, talented and creative: Models and methods.* Madison: University of Wisconsin-Extension.

Rimm, S. B. (1982). *PRIDE: Preschool interest descriptor.* Watertown, WI: Educational Assessment Service.

Rimm, S. B. (1983, March/April). Identifying creativity (Part 1). *G/C/T,* 34–37.

Rimm, S. B. (1984, January/February). If God had meant gifted children to run our homes, she would have created them bigger. *G/C/T,* 26–29.

Rimm, S. B. (1986). *AIM: Achievement identification measure.* Watertown, WI: Educational Assessment Service.

Rimm, S. B. (1987a). *GAIM: Group achievement identification measure.* Watertown, WI: Educational Assessment Service.

Rimm, S. B. (1987b). Marching to the beat of a different drummer. *Gifted Child Today, 10*(1), 2–6.

Rimm, S. B. (1987c). Why do bright children underachieve? The pressures they feel. *Gifted Child Today, 10*(6), 30–36.

Rimm, S. B. (1988a). *AIM-TO: Achievement identification measure—teacher observation.* Watertown, WI: Apple.

Rimm, S. B. (1988b). Popularity ends at grade twelve. *Gifted Child Today, 11*(3), 42–44.

Rimm, S. B. (1990a). A theory of relativity. *Gifted Child Today, 13*(3), 32–36.

Rimm, S. B. (1990b). *Gifted kids have feelings too.* Watertown, WI: Apple.

Rimm, S. B. (1990c). *How to parent so children will learn.* Watertown, WI: Apple.

Rimm, S. B. (1991a). The attention deficit-hyperactivity disorder epidemic. *How to Stop Underachievement Newsletter, 1*(4), pp. 7–8. Educational Assessment Service, Watertown, WI.

Rimm, S. B. (1991b). What's the hurry. *How to Stop Underachievement Newsletter, 1*(4), 1–3. Educational Assessment Service, Watertown, WI.

Rimm, S. B. (1992a). A response on competition from Kansas. *How to Stop Underachievement Newsletter, 2*(4), 6–7. Educational Assessment Service, Watertown, WI.

Rimm, S. B. (1992b). *On raising kids.* Watertown, WI: Apple.

Rimm, S. B. (1992c). A bicycle ride: Why we need grouping. *How to Stop Underachievement Newsletter, 1*(3), 1–3. Educational Assessment Service, Watertown, WI.

Rimm, S. B. (1994a). *Gifted module: Parenting for achievement.* Watertown, WI: Apple.

Rimm, S. B. (1994b). *Keys to parenting the gifted child.* Hauppauge, NY: Barron's Educational Series.

Rimm, S. B. (1995a). Gender effects on achievement. *How to Stop Underachievement Newsletter*, 6(2), 1–5. Educational Assessment Service, Watertown, WI.

Rimm, S. B. (1995b). How sports can help your children achieve. *How to Stop Underachievement Newsletter*, 5(4), 1–3. Educational Assessment Service, Watertown, WI.

Rimm, S. B. (1995c). Will we now drug those troublesome gifted children? *IAGC Journal Portfolio,* Article 17, 1–3.

Rimm, S. B. (1995d). *Why bright kids get poor grades—and what you can do about it.* New York: Crown.

Rimm, S. B. (1996a). *Dr. Sylvia Rimm's smart parenting: How to raise a happy, achieving child.* New York: Crown.

Rimm, S. B. (1996b, Fall). Using the media to advocate for gifted and talented education. *NAGC Parent-Community Newsletter.* National Association for Gifted Children, Washington, DC.

Rimm, S. B. (1997). Underachievement syndrome: A national epidemic. In N. Colangelo & G. A. Davis (Eds.), *Handbook of gifted education* (2nd ed.; pp. 416–434). Boston: Allyn & Bacon.

Rimm, S. B. (1998). Creativity and underachievement. In J. F. Smutney (Ed.), *The young gifted child: Potential and praise, an anthology.* Cresskill, NJ: Hampton.

Rimm, S. (1999, Fall). The assessment of preschool gifted children. *Perspectives in Gifted Education: Young Gifted Children, 1,* 3–14. Institute for the Development of Gifted Education, University of Denver.

Rimm, S. (2001a). *Keys to parenting the gifted child* (2nd ed.). Hauppauge, NY: Barron's Educational Series.

Rimm, S. (2001b). Peer pressures and social acceptance of gifted students. In National Association for Gifted Children (Ed.), *The Social and Emotional Development of Gifted Children: What Do We Know?* (pp. 13–18). Waco, TX: Prufrock Press.

Rimm, S. B. (2002). What's wrong with being perfect? *Sylvia Rimm on Raising Kids Newsletter, 12*(4), 1–41

Rimm, S. B. (2003a). *See Jane win for girls: A smart girl's guide to success.* Minneapolis, MN: Free Spirit Publications.

Rimm, S. B. (2003b). Underachievement: A national epidemic. In N. Colangelo & G. A. Davis (Eds.), *Handbook of*

*gifted education* (3rd ed., pp. 424–443). Boston: Allyn & Bacon.

Rimm, S. B., Cornale, M., Manos, R., & Behrend, J. (1989). *Guidebook for implementing the TRIFOCAL underachievement program in schools.* Watertown, WI: Apple.

Rimm, S. B., & Davis, G. A. (1976). GIFT: An instrument for the identification of creativity. *Journal of Creative Behavior, 10,* 178–182.

Rimm, S. B., & Davis, G. A. (1980). Five years of international research with GIFT: An instrument for the identification of creativity. *Journal of Creative Behavior, 14,* 35–36.

Rimm, S. B., & Davis, G. A. (1983, September/October). Identifying creativity (Part 2). *G/C/T,* 19–23.

Rimm, S. B., & Lovance, K. J. (1992a). How acceleration may prevent underachievement syndrome. *Gifted Child Today, 15*(2), 9–14.

Rimm, S. B., & Lovance, K. J. (1992b). The use of subject and grade skipping for the prevention and reversal of underachievement. *Gifted Child Quarterly, 36,* 100–105.

Rimm, S. B., & Lowe, B. (1988). Family environments of underachieving gifted students. *Gifted Child Quarterly, 32,* 353–359.

Rimm, S. B., & Olenchak, F. R. (1991). How FPS helps underachieving gifted students. *Gifted Child Today, 14*(2), 19–22.

Rimm, S. B., & Priest, C. (1990). *Exploring feelings.* Watertown, WI: Apple.

Rimm, S., & Rimm-Kaufman, S. (2001). *How Jane won: 55 successful women share how they grew from ordinary girls to extraordinary women.* New York: Crown.

Rimm, S., Rimm-Kaufman, S., & Rimm, I. (1999). *See Jane win: The Rimm report on how 1,000 girls became successful women.* New York: Crown Publishers

Rimm-Kaufman, S. (1996). *Infant predictors of kindergarten behavior: The contribution of inhibited and uninhibited temperament types.* Unpublished doctoral dissertation, Harvard University.

Riordan, C. (1990). *Girls and boys in school: Together or separate?* New York: Teachers College Press.

Ritchart, R. (2001). From IQ to IC: A Dispositional View of Intelligence. *Roeper Review, 23,* 143–150.

Roberts, J. L. (1992). Parents can be mentors, too. *Gifted Child Today, 15*(3), 36–38.

Robinson, A. (1991). *Cooperative learning and the academically talented student.* Storrs, CT: National Research Center on the Gifted and Talented.

Robinson, A. (1997). Cooperative learning for talented students: Emergent Issues and Implications. In N. Colangelo & G. A. Davis (Eds.), *Handbook of gifted education* (2nd ed.; pp. 243–252). Boston: Allyn & Bacon.

Robinson, A. (2003). Cooperative learning and high ability students. In N. Colangelo & G. A. Davis (Eds.), *Handbook of gifted education* (3rd ed., pp. 282–292). Boston: Allyn & Bacon.

Robinson, A. & Clinkenbeard, P. R. (1993). *Cooperative learning and theories of motivation.* Paper presented at the Henry B. and Jocelyn Wallace National Research Symposium on Talent Development, Iowa City, Iowa.

Robinson, N. M., & Noble, K. D. (1992). Acceleration: Valuable high school to college options. *Gifted Child Today, 15*(2), 20–23.

Robinson, N. M., Reis, S. M., Neihart, M., & Moon, S. M. (2001). Emotional issues facing gifted and talented students: What have we learned and what should we do now? In M. Neihart, S. M. Reis, N. M. Robinson, & S. M. Moon (Eds.), *Social and emotional development of gifted children: What do we know?* (pp. 267–289). Washington, DC: National Association for Gifted Children.

Robinson, N. M., & Weimer, L. J. (1991). Selection of candidates for early admission to kindergarten and first grade. In W. T. Southern & E. D. Jones (Eds.), *Academic acceleration of gifted children* (pp. 29–50). New York: Teachers College Press.

Rodenstein, J. M., & Glickauf-Hughes, C. (1979). Career and lifestyle determinants of gifted women. In N. Colangelo & R. T. Zaffrann (Eds.), *New voices in counseling the gifted.* Dubuque, IA: Kendall/Hunt.

Roeper, A. (1982, November) How the gifted cope with their emotions. *Roeper Review, 5*(2), 21–24.

Roeper, A. (1995). *Educating children for life.* Monroe, NY: Trillium.

Rogers, C. R. (1949). A coordinated research in psychotherapy: A non-objective introduction. *Journal of Consulting Psychology, 13,* 49–51.

Rogers, C. R. (1962). Toward a theory of creativity. In S. J. Parnes & H. F. Harding (Eds.), *A source book for creative thinking.* New York: Scribners.

Rogers, J. A., & Nielson, A. B. (1993). Gifted children and divorce: A study of the literature on the incidence of divorce in families with gifted children. *Journal for the Education of the Gifted, 16,* 251–267.

Rogers, K. B. (1991). *The relationship of grouping practices to the education of the gifted and talented learner.* Storrs, CT: National Research Center on the Gifted and Talented.

Rogers, K. B. (1992, November). *Using effect size to make good decisions about acceleration.* Paper presented at the meeting of the National Association for Gifted Children, Little Rock, Arkansas.

Rogers, K. B. (1996). What *The Bell Curve* says and doesn't say: Is a balanced view possible? *Roeper Review, 18,* 252–255.

Roper Starch Worldwide. (1998, May). *Report card on the new providers: Kids and moms speak.* New York: Author.

Rosenthal, R. J., & Jacobson, L. (1968). *Pygmalion in the classroom.* New York: Holt.

Rossiter, M. (1995). *Women scientists in America: Before affirmative action, 1940–1972.* Baltimore: John Hopkins University Press.

Rowe, I. H. (1990). The power of parent persuasion. In S. Baily, E. Braggett, & M. Robinson (Eds.), *The challenge of excellence: A vision splendid* (pp. 358–361). Australia: Australian Association for the Education of the Gifted and Talented.

Rubenstein, E. (1997, October 13). Right data. *National Review,* p. 16.

Ruckman, D. R., & Feldhusen, J. F. (1988). Evaluation of a university/school district consortium for gifted education. *Roeper Review, 11,* 79–85.

Runco, M. A. (1993). *Creativity as an educational objective for disadvantaged students.* Fullerton: California State University.

Russo, C. J., Harris, J. J., & Ford, D. Y. (1996). Gifted education and the law: A right, privilege, or superfluous? *Roeper Review, 18,* 179–182.

Sadker, D., & Sadker, M. (1994, February 4). Why schools must tell girls: You're smart, you can do it. *USA Weekend,* 4–6.

Sadker, M. P., Sadker, D. M., & Hicks, T. (1980). The one-percent solution? Sexism in teacher education texts. *Phi Delta Kappan, 61,* 550–553.

Sadowski, A. J. (1987). A case study of the experiences of and influences upon gifted high school dropouts. *Dissertation Abstracts International, 48*(04), 893 (University Microfilms International No. AAC87-16185).

Safer, D. J., & Krager, J. M (1988). A survey of medication treatments for hyperactive/inattentive students. *Journal of the American Medical Association, 260,* 2256–2258.

Sainato, D. M., Strain, P. S., Lefevre, D., & Rapp, N. (1990). Effects of self-evaluation on the independent work skills of preschool children with disabilities. *Exceptional Children, 56*(6), 540–549.

Salovey, P., & Sluyter, D. J. (Eds.). (1997). *Emotional development and emotional intelligence.* New York: Basic Books.

Salter, J., & Tozier, L. (1971). A review of intelligence test modifications used with the cerebral palsied and other handicapped groups. *Journal of Special Education, 4,* 391–398.

Sanborn, M. (1979). Career development: Problems of gifted and talented students. In N. Colangelo & R. T. Zaffrann (Eds.), *New voices in counseling the gifted.* Dubuque, IA: Kendall/Hunt.

Sands, T., & Howard-Hamilton, M. (1995). Understanding depression among gifted adolescent females: Feminist therapy strategies. *Roeper Review, 17,* 192–195.

Sankar-DeLeeuw, N. (1999). Gifted preschoolers: Parent and teacher views on identification, early admission and programming. *Roeper Review, 21,* 174–179.

Sapon-Shevin, M. (1994). *Playing favorites: Gifted education and the disruption of community.* Albany: State University of New York Press.

Sarouphim, K. M. (1999). DISCOVER: A promising alternative assessment for the identification of gifted minorities. *Gifted Child Quarterly, 43,* 244–251.

Sarouphim, K. M. (2000). Internal structure of DISCOVER: A performance-based assessment. *Journal for the Education of the Gifted, 23,* 314–327.

Sarouphim, K. M. (2001). DISCOVER: Concurrent validity, gender differences, and identification of minority students. *Gifted Child Quarterly, 45,* 130–138.

Satler, M. (1982). *Assessment of children's intelligence and special abilities* (2nd ed.). Boston: Allyn & Bacon.

Sayler, M. R., & Brookshire, W. K. (1996). Social, emotional, and behavioral adjustment of accelerated students in gifted classes and regular students in eighth grade. *Gifted Child Quarterly, 37,* 150–254.

Schack, G. D. (1996). All aboard or standing on the shore? Gifted educators and the educational reform movement. *Roeper Review, 18,* 190–197.

Schatz, E. (1990, May/June). Ability grouping for gifted learners. *Educating Able Learners, 3–5, 15.*

Schiff, M. M., Kaufman, A. S., & Kaufman, N. L. (1981). Scatter analysis of WISC-R profiles for learning disabled children with superior intelligence. *Journal of Learning Disabilities, 14,* 400–404.

Schlichter, C. L. (1986). Talents Unlimited: An inservice education model for teaching thinking skills. *Gifted Child Quarterly, 30,* 119–123.

Schlichter, C. L. (1997). Talents unlimited model in programs for gifted students. In N. Colangelo & G. A. Davis (Eds.), *Handbook of gifted education* (2nd ed.; pp. 318–327). Boston: Allyn & Bacon.

Schlichter, C. L., & Palmer, W. R. (1993). *Thinking smart: A primer of the Talents Unlimited model.* Mansfield Center, CT: Creative Learning Press.

Schnur, J. O., & Stefanich, G. P. (1979). Science for the handicapped gifted child. *Roeper Review, 2*(2), 26–28.

Schreeve, W., Goetter, W. G. J., Bunn, A., Norby, J. R., Stueckle, A. F., Midgley, T. K., & de Michele, B. (1986). Single parents and students' achievements—a national tragedy. *Early Child Development and Care, 23,* 175–184.

Schroeder-Davis, S. J. (1998). Swimming upstream against the cultural current. *Parenting for High Potential, National Association for Gifted Children.* Washington, D.C.

Schroeder-Davis, S. J. (1999). Brains, brawn, or beauty: Adolescent attitudes toward three superlatives. *Journal of Secondary Gifted Education, 10,* 134–147.

Schuler, P. A. (1999). *Voices of perfectionism: Perfectionistic gifted adolescents in a rural middle school.* Storrs, CT: National Research Center on the Gifted and Talented.

Schuler, P. A. (2002). Perfectionism in gifted children and adolescents. In M. Neihart, S. M. Reis, N. M. Robinson, & S. M. Moon (Eds.), *Social and emotional development of gifted children: What do we know?* (pp. 71–79). Washington, DC: National Association for Gifted Children.

Schwartz, J., & Taylor, E. L. (1995, November). *Accountability in gifted education: Indicators of success.* Paper presented at the meeting of the National Association for Gifted Children, Tampa FL.

Scott, M. S., Perou, R., Urbano, R., Hogan, A., & Gold, S. (1992). The identification of giftedness: A comparison of white, Hispanic, and black families. *Gifted Child Quarterly, 36,* 131–139.

Scruggs, T. E., & Cohn, S. J. (1983). A university-based summer program for a highly able but poorly achieving Indian child. *Gifted Child Quarterly, 27,* 90–93.

Sears, P. S. (1979). The Terman genetic studies of genius, 1922–1972. In A. H. Passow (Ed.), *The gifted and the talented* (pp. 75–96). Chicago: National Society for the Study of Education.

Sebrechts, J. S. (1992). The cultivation of scientists at women's colleges. *Journal of NIH Research, 4,* 22–26.

Sebring, A. D. (1983). Parental factors on the social and emotional *adjustment of the gifted. Roeper Review, 6*(2), 97–99.

Seligman, M. E. P. (1975). *Helplessness: On depression, development and death.* San Francisco: Freeman.

Seligman, R. (1990). A gifted ninth grader tells it like it is. *Gifted Child Today, 13*(4), 9–11.

Serbin, L., & O'Leary, D. K. (1975). How nursery schools teach girls to shut up. *Psychology Today, 9*(12), 56–58.

Shade, B. J. (1978, April). Social-psychological characteristics of achieving black children. *Negro Educational Review, 29*(2), 80–86.

Shade, B. J. (1983, December). The social success of black youth: The impact of significant others. *Journal of Black Studies, 14*(2), 137–150.

Shallcross, D. J. (1981). *Teaching creative behavior.* Englewood Cliffs, NJ: Prentice-Hall.

Sharan, Y., & Sharan, S. (1990). Group investigation expands cooperative learning. *Educational Leadership, 47*(4), 17–21.

Sharp, A. M., & Reed, R. F. (1992). *Studies in philosophy for children: Harry Stottlemeier's discovery.* Philadelphia: Temple University Press.

Shaw, M. C. & McCuen, J. T. (1960). The onset of academic underachievement in bright children. *Journal of Educational Psychology, 51,* 103–108.

Shaywitz, S. E., Holahan, J. M., Freudenheim, D. A., Fletcher, J. M., Makuch, R. W., & Shaywitz, B. A. (2001). Heterogeneity within the gifted: Higher IQ boys exhibit behaviors resembling boys with learning disabilities. *Gifted Child Quarterly, 45,* 16–23.

Shaywitz, B. A., Shaywitz, S. E., Fletcher, J. M., Pugh, K. R., Gore, J. C., Constable, R. T., et al. (1997). The Yale Center for the study of learning and attention: Longitudinal and neurobiological studies. *Learning Disabilities: A Multidisciplinary Journal, 8*(1), 21–29.

Sheppard, S. & Kanevsky, L. (1999). Nurturing gifted students' metacognitive awareness: Effects of training in homogeneous and heterogeneous classes. *Roeper Review, 21,* 266–272.

Shore, B. M., & Kanevsky, L. (1993). Thinking processes: Being and becoming. In K. A. Heller, F. J. Mönks, & A. H. Passow (Eds.), *International handbook of research and development of giftedness and talent* (pp. 133–147). Oxford, England: Pergamon.

Shurkin, J. (1992). *Terman's kids: The groundbreaking study of how the gifted grow up.* Boston: Little-Brown.

Siegle, D., & Reis, S. M. (1994, Winter). Gender differences in teacher and student perceptions of student ability and effort. *Journal of Secondary Gifted Education, 86–92.*

Siegle, D., & Reis, S. M. (1998). Gender differences in Teacher and student perceptions of gifted students' ability and effort. *Gifted Child Quarterly, 42,* 39–47.

Siegle, D., & Schuler, P. A. (2000). Perfectionism differences in gifted middle school students. *Roeper Review, 23,* 39–44.

Silverman, L. K. (1983a). Issues in affective development of the gifted. In J. Van Tassel-Baska (Ed.), *A practical guide to counseling the gifted in a school setting* (pp. 2–10). Reston, VA: Council for Exceptional Children.

Silverman, L. K. (1983b). Personality development: The pursuit of excellence. *Journal for the Education of the Gifted, 6,* 5–19.

Silverman, L. K. (1989). Invisible gifts, invisible handicaps. *Roeper Review, 12,* 37–42.

Silverman, L. K. (1991). Helping gifted girls reach their potential. *Roeper Review, 13,* 122–123.

Silverman, L. K. (1993a). *Counseling the gifted and talented.* Denver: Love.

Silverman, L. K. (1993b). Counseling needs and programs for the gifted. In K. A. Heller, F. J. Mönks, & A. H. Passow (Eds.), *International handbook of research and development of giftedness and talent* (pp. 631–647). New York: Pergamon.

Silverman, L. K. (1994). The moral sensitivity of gifted children and the evolution of society. *Roper Review, 17,* 110–116.

Silverman, L. K. (1997). Family counseling with the gifted. In N. Colangelo & G. A. Davis (Eds.), *Handbook of gifted education* (2nd ed.; pp. 382–397). Boston: Allyn & Bacon.

Silverman, L. K. (1998). Through the lens of giftedness. *Roeper Review, 20,* 204–210.

Silverman, L. K. (2002). Asynchronous development. In M. Neihart, S. M. Reis, N. M. Robinson, & S. M. Moon (Eds.), *Social and emotional development of gifted children: What do we know?* (pp. 145–153). Washington, DC: National Association for Gifted Children.

Silverman, L. K. (2003). Gifted children with learning disabilities. In N. Colangelo & G. A. Davis (Eds.), *Handbook of gifted education* (3rd ed.; pp. 533–543). Boston: Allyn & Bacon.

Silverman, L. K., Chitwood, D. G., & Water, J. L. (1986). Young gifted children: Can parents identify giftedness? *Topics in Early Childhood Special Education, 6,* 23–38.

Silverman, L. K., & Kearney, K. (1989). Parents of the extraordinarily gifted. *Advanced Development Journal, 1,* 41–56.

Simberg, A. L. (1964). *Creativity at work.* Boston: Industrial Education Institute.

Simon, S. B., Howe, L., & Kirschenbaum, H. (1978). *Value clarification: A handbook of practical strategies for teachers and students* (rev. ed.). New York: Hart.

Simon, S. B., & Massey, S. (1973). Value clarification. *Educational Leadership, 5,* 738–739.

Simonton, D. K. (1985). Intelligence and personal influence in groups: Four nonlinear models. *Psychological Review, 92,* 532–547.

Simonton, D. K. (1988). Creativity, leadership, and chance. In R. J. Sternberg (Ed.), *The nature of creativity* (pp. 386–426). New York: Cambridge University Press.

Simonton, D. K. (1996). Creative expertise: A life-span developmental perspective. In K. A. Ericsson (Ed.), *The road to excellence: The acquisition of expert performance in the arts, sciences, sports, and games* (pp. 227–253). Mahwah, NJ: Lawrence Erlbaum Associates.

Simonton, D. K. (2003). When does giftedness become genius? And when not? In N. Colangelo & G. A. Davis (Eds.), *Handbook of gifted education* (3rd ed., pp. 358–370). Boston: Allyn & Bacon.

Sisk, D. A. (1990). Expanding worldwide awareness of gifted and talented children and youth. *Gifted Child Today, 13*(5), 19–25.

Sisk, D. A. (1993). Leadership education for the gifted. In K. A. Heller, F. J. Mönks, & A. H. Passow (Eds.), *International handbook of research and development of giftedness and talent* (pp. 491–505). New York: Pergamon.

Sisk, D. A., Gilbert, P., & Gosch, R. (1991). Developing leadership in a multi-cultural society. *Gifted Child Today, 14*(4), 60–61.

Sjogren, D., Hopkins, T., & Gooler, D. (1975). *Evaluation plans and instruments: Illustrative cases of gifted program evaluation techniques.* Champaign: University of Illinois, Center for Instructional Research and Curriculum Evaluation.

Slavin, R. E. (1992). When and why does cooperative learning increase achievement? Theoretical and empirical perspectives. In R. Hertz-Lazarowitz & N. Miller (Eds.), *Interaction in cooperative groups: The theoretical anatomy of group learning* (pp. 145–173). New York: Cambridge University Press.

Slavin, R. E., Madden, N. A., & Stevens, R. J. (1990). Cooperative learning models for the 3 R's. *Educational Leadership, 47*(4), 22–28.

Smith, J., LeRose, B., & Clasen, R. E. (1991). Underrepresentation of minority students in gifted programs: Yes! It matters. *Gifted Child Quarterly, 35,* 81–83.

Smith, J. M. (1966). *Setting conditions for creative teaching in the elementary school.* Boston: Allyn & Bacon.

Smith, L. G. (1981). Centuries of educational inequities. *Educational Horizons, 60,* 4–10.

Smith, S. J. (1990). What are you counting as service to gifted and talented students? *Gifted Child Today, 13*(4), 23–24.

Smutney, J. F. (2001). *Stand Up for Your Gifted Child.* Minneapolis: Free Spirit.

Snowden, P. L., & Christian, L. G. (1999). Parenting the young gifted child: Supportive behaviors. *Roeper Review, 21,* 215–221.

Snowden, P. L., & Conway, K. D. (1996). A comparison of self-reported parenting behaviors and attitudes of parents of academically precocious and nonprecocious preschool children. *Roeper Review, 19,* 97–101.

SOI Systems. (n.d.). Retrieved March 21, 2002, from http://www.soisystems.com.

Solomon, A. O. (1974). Analysis of creative thinking of disadvantaged children. *Journal of Creative Behavior, 8,* 293–295.

Solorzano, L. (1983, August). Now, gifted children get some breaks. *U.S. News & World Report, 8,* 32.

Somers, J. V., & Yawkey, T. D. (1984). Imaginary play companions: Contributions to creativity and intellectual abilities of young children. *Journal of Creative Behavior, 18,* 77–89.

Sonnert, G., & Holton, G. (1996). Career patterns of women and men in the sciences. *American Scientist, 84,* 63–71.

Sosniak, L. (1997). The tortoise, the hare, and the development of talent. In N. Colangelo & G. A. Davis (Eds.), *Handbook of gifted education* (2nd ed.; pp. 207–217). Boston: Allyn & Bacon.

Sosniak, L. A. (2001). The development of talent: Welcoming youth into communities of practice. In N. Colangelo and S. G. Assouline (Eds.), *Talent development IV* (pp. 281–291). Scottsdale, AZ: Great Potential Press.

Sosniak, L. (2003). Developing talent: Time, task, and context. In N. Colangelo & G. A. Davis (Eds.), *Handbook of gifted education* (3rd ed., pp. 247–253). Boston: Allyn & Bacon.

Southern, W. T., & Jones, E. D. (1991). Objections to early entrance and grade skipping. In W. T. Southern & E. D. Jones (Eds.), *Academic acceleration of gifted children* (pp. 51–73). New York: Teachers College Press.

Southern, W. T., & Jones, E. D. (1992). The real problems with academic acceleration. *Gifted Child Today, 15*(2), 34–38.

Southern, W. T., Jones, E. D., & Fiscus, E. D. (1989). Practitioner objections to the academic acceleration of gifted students. *Gifted Child Quarterly, 33,* 29–35.

Southern, W. T., & Spicker, H. H. (1989). The rural gifted on line: Bulletin boards and electronic curriculum. *Roeper Review, 11,* 199–202.

Spicker, H. H., Southern, W. T., & Davis, B. I. (1987). The rural gifted child. *Gifted Child Quarterly, 31,* 155–157.

Spredemann-Dryer, S. (1989). *The bookfinder: When kids need books.* Circle Pines, MN: American Guidance Services.

Springer, S. P., & Deutsch, G. (1985). *Left brain, right brain* (rev. ed.). New York: Freeman.

Stake, J. E. (1981). The educator's role in fostering female career aspirations. *Journal of NAWDAC, 43,* 3–10.

Stanish, B. (1977). *Sunflowering.* Carthage, IL: Good Apple.

Stanish, B. (1979). *I believe in unicorns.* Carthage, IL: Good Apple.

Stanish, B. (1981). *Hippogriff feathers.* Carthage, IL: Good Apple.

Stanish, B. (1986). *Mindglow.* Carthage, IL: Good Apple.

Stanish, B. (1988). *Lessons from the hearthstone traveler: An instructional guide to the creative thinking process.* Carthage, IL: Good Apple.

Stankowski, W. M. (1978). Definition. In R. E. Clasen & B. Robinson (Eds.), *Simple gifts.* Madison, WI: University of Wisconsin-Extension.

Stanley, J. C. (1976). Test better finder of great math talent than teachers are. *American Psychologist, 31,* 313–314.

Stanley, J. C. (1978a). Concern for intellectually talented youths: How it originated and fluctuated. In R. E. Clasen & B. Robinson (Eds.), *Simple gifts.* Madison, WI: University of Wisconsin-Extension.

Stanley, J. C. (1978b). Identifying and nurturing the intellectually gifted. In R. E. Clasen & B. Robinson (Eds.), *Simple gifts.* Madison, WI: University of Wisconsin-Extension.

Stanley, J. C. (1979). The study and facilitation of talent for mathematics. In A. H. Passow (Ed.), *The gifted and the talented* (pp. 169–185). Chicago: National Society for the Study of Education.

Stanley, J. C. (1982, October). *Finding intellectually talented youths and helping them greatly via educational acceleration.* Address presented at the meeting of the Wisconsin Council on Gifted and Talented, Madison.

Stanley, J. C. (1985, August). *Fostering use of mathematical talent in the USA: SMPY's rationale.* Address presented at the Sixth World Conference on Gifted and Talented Children, Hamburg, Germany.

Stanley, J. C. (1987). State residential high schools for mathematically talented youth. *Phi Delta Kappan, 68,* 770–772.

Stanley, J. C. (1988). Some characteristics of SMPY's "700–800 on SAT-M before age 13 group": Youths who reason *extremely* well mathematically. *Gifted Child Quarterly, 32,* 205–209.

Stanley, J. C. (1989). A look back at educational non-acceleration: An international tragedy. *Gifted Child Today, 12*(4), 60–61.

Stanley, J. C. (1991a). An academic model for educating the mathematically talented. *Gifted Child Quarterly, 35,* 36–42.

Stanley, J. C. (1991b). Critique of "Socioemotional adjustment of adolescent girls enrolled in a residential acceleration program." *Gifted Child Quarterly, 35,* 67–70.

Stanley, J. C. (1992). The future of research and theory construction in talent development. In N. Colangelo, S. G. Assouline, & D. L. Ambroson (Eds.), *Talent development: Proceedings from the 1991 Henry B. and Jocelyn Wallace National Research Symposium on Talent Development.* New York: Trillium.

Stanley, J. C. (1994). Gender differences for able elementary school students on above-grade-level ability and achievement tests. In N. Colangelo, S. G. Assouline, & D. L. Ambroson (Eds.), *Talent development: Proceedings from the 1993 Henry B. and Jocelyn Wallace National Research Symposium on Talent Development* (pp. 141–148). Dayton: Ohio Psychology Press.

Stanley, J. C., & Benbow, C. P. (1983). Educating mathematically precocious youths: Twelve policy recommendations. *Educational Researcher, 11*(5), 4–9.

Stanley, J. C., & Benbow, C. P. (1986). Youths who reason exceptionally well mathematically. In R. J. Sternberg & J. E. Davidson (Eds.), *Conceptions of giftedness* (pp. 361–387). New York: Cambridge University Press.

Stanley, J. C., & McGill, A. M. (1986). More about "young entrants to college: How did they fare?" *Gifted Child Quarterly, 30,* 70–73.

Starko, A. J. (1990). Life and death of a gifted program: Lessons not yet learned. *Roeper Review, 13,* 33–38.

Steinberg, L., Dornbusch, S. M., & Brown, B. B. (1992). Ethnic differences in adolescent achievement: An ecological perspective. *American Psychologist, 47,* 723–729.

Sternberg, R. J. (1983). Criteria for intellectual skills training. *Educational Researcher, 12*(1), 6–13.

Sternberg, R. J. (1984a). Fighting butter battles. *Phi Delta Kappan, 65,* 700.

Sternberg, R. J. (1984b). How can we teach intelligence? *Educational Leadership, 42,* 38–48.

Sternberg, R. J. (1988a). Beyond IQ testing. *National Forum, 68*(2), 8–11.

Sternberg, R. J. (Ed.). (1988b). *The nature of creativity.* New York: Cambridge University Press.

Sternberg, R. J. (1988c). Three-facet model of creativity. In R. J. Sternberg (Ed.), *The nature of creativity* (pp. 125–147). New York: Cambridge University Press.

Sternberg, R. J. (1990). *Robert Sternberg's ten tips to enhance creativity* (poster). Minneapolis, MN: Free Spirit.

Sternberg, R. J. (1995). What do we mean by giftedness? A pentagonal implicit theory. *Gifted Child Quarterly, 39,* 88–94.

Sternberg, R. J. (1996). The sound of silence: A nation responds to its gifted. *Roeper Review, 18,* 168–172.

Sternberg, R. J. (1997a). *Successful intelligence.* New York: Plume.

Sternberg, R. J. (1997b). *Thinking styles.* New York: Cambridge University Press.

Sternberg, R. S. (2000a). Identifying and developing creative giftedness. *Roeper Review, 23,* 60–64.

Sternberg, R. S. (2000b). Wisdom as a form of giftedness. *Gifted Child Quarterly, 44,* 252–260).

Sternberg, R. E. (2003). Giftedness according to the theory of successful intelligence. In N. Colangelo & G. A. Davis (Eds.), *Handbook of gifted education* (3rd ed., pp. 88–99). Boston: Allyn & Bacon.

Sternberg, R. J., Callahan, C., Burns, D., Gubbins, E. J., Purcell, J., Reis, S. M., Renzulli, J. S., & Westberg, K. (1995). Return gift to sender: A review of *The Bell Curve,* by Richard Herrnstein & Charles Murray. *Gifted Child Quarterly, 39,* 177–179.

Sternberg, R. J., & Clinkenbeard, P. R. (1995). The Triarchic Model applied to identifying, teaching, and assessing gifted children. *Roeper Review, 17,* 255–260.

Sternberg, R. J., & Grigorenko, E. L. (1993). Thinking styles and the gifted. *Roeper Review, 16,* 122–130.

Sternglanz, S. H., & Serbin, L. A. (1974). Sex-role stereotyping in children's television programs. *Developmental Psychology, 10,* 710–715.

Stevens, K. R., & Karnes, F. A. (2000). State definitions for the gifted and talented revisited. *Exceptional Children, 66,* 219–238.

Strom, R. (1984). *Parent as a teacher.* Inventory and manual. Bensenville, IL: Scholastic Testing Service.

Strom, R., Johnson, A., Strom, S., & Strom, P. (1992). Designing curriculum for parents of gifted children. *Journal for the Education of the Gifted, 15,* 182–200.

Striker, F. (n.d.). *Creative writing workbook and the morphological approach to plotting.* Unpublished manuscript, University of Buffalo.

Subotnik, R. (1998). The academic road to capitol hill: Personal experiences of schooling and the making of educational policy. In N. Colangelo & S. G. Assouline (Eds.), *Talent development IV: Proceedings from the 1998 Henry B. and Jocelyn Wallace national research symposium on talent development.* Scottsdale, AZ: Great Potential Press.

Subotnik, R. F., & Strauss, S. (1990, April). *Gender differences in achievement and classroom participation: An experiment involving advanced placement calculus classes.* Paper presented at the meeting of the American Educational Research Association, Boston.

Sullivan, P. M., & Vernon, M. (1979). Psychological assessment of hearing impaired children. *School Psychology Digest, 8,* 271–290.

Suter, D. P., & Wolf, J. S. (1987). Issues in the identification and programming of the gifted/learning disabled child. *Journal for the Education of the Gifted, 10,* 227–237.

Sutherland, S. L. (1978). The unambitious female: Women's low professional aspirations. *Signs: Journal of Women in Culture and Society, 3,* 774–794.

Sutton-Smith, B., Rosenberg, B. G., & Landy, F. (1968). Father-absence effects in families of different sibling compositions. *Child Development, 39,* 1213–1221.

Swartz, R. J., & Perkins, D. N. (1990). *Teaching thinking: Issues and approaches.* Pacific Grove, CA: Critical Thinking Books and Software.

Swenson, J. E. (1978). Teacher assessment of creative behavior in disadvantaged children. *Gifted Child Quarterly, 22,* 338–343.

Swesson, K. (1994). Helping the gifted/learning disabled: Understanding the special needs of the "twice exceptional." *Gifted Child Today, 17*(5), 24–26.

Swiatek, M. A., & Benbow, C. P. (1992). *A ten-year longitudinal followup of participants in a fast-paced mathematics course.* Unpublished manuscript, Iowa State University, Department of Psychology.

Swiatek, M. A., & Dorr, R. M. (1998). Revision of the social coping questionnaire: Replication and extension of previous findings. *Journal of Secondary Gifted Education, 10,* 252–59.

Tallent-Runnels, M. K., & Sigler, E. A. (1995). The status of the selection of gifted students with learning disabilities for gifted programs. *Roeper Review, 17,* 246–248.

Tannen, D. (1990). *You just don't understand: Women and men in conversation.* New York: Ballantine Books.

Tannenbaum, A. J. (1979). Pre-Sputnik to post-Watergate concern about the gifted. In A. H. Passow (Ed.), *The gifted and the talented* (pp. 5–27). Chicago: National Society for the Study of Education.

Tannenbaum, A. J. (2000). A history of giftedness in school and society. In K. A. Heller, F. J. Mönks, R. J. Sternberg, & R. F. Subotnik (Eds.), *International handbook of giftedness and talent* (2nd ed., pp. 23–53). New York: Elsevier.

Tannenbaum, A. J. (2003). Nature and nurture of giftedness. In N. Colangelo & G. A. Davis (Eds.), *Handbook of gifted education* (3rd ed., pp. 45–59). Boston: Allyn & Bacon.

Tardif, T. Z., & Sternberg, R. J. (1988). What do we know about creativity? In R. J. Sternberg (Ed.), *The nature of creativity* (pp. 429–440). New York: Cambridge University Press.

Taylor, A. R. (1991). Social competence and the early school transition: Risk and protective factors for African-American children. *Education and Urban Society, 24*(1), 15–26.

Taylor, C. W. (1978). How many types of giftedness can your program tolerate? *Journal of Creative Behavior, 12,* 39–51.

Taylor, C. W. (1986). Cultivating simultaneous student growth in both multiple creative talents and knowledge. In J. S. Renzulli (Ed.), *Systems and models for developing programs for the gifted and talented* (pp. 306–351). Mansfield Center, CT: Creative Learning Press.

Taylor, C. W. (1988). Various approaches to and definitions of creativity. In R. J. Sternberg (Ed.), *The nature of creativity* (pp. 99–121). New York: Cambridge University Press.

Teale, W. (1984). Reading to young children: Its significance for literacy development. In H. Goelman, A. Oberg, & T. Smith (Eds.), *Awakening to Literacy* (pp. 110–121). Portsmouth, NH: Heinemann.

Teiso, C. L. (2002). *Effects of grouping and curricular practices on intermediate students' math achievement.* Storrs, CT: National Research Center on the Gifted and Talented.

Terman, L. M. (1925). *Genetic studies of genius: Vol. 1. Mental and physical traits of a thousand gifted children.* Stanford, CA: Stanford University Press.

Terman, L. M. (1954). The discovery and encouragement of exceptional talent. *American Psychologist, 9,* 221–230.

Terman, L. M., & Oden, M. H. (1947). *Genetic studies of genius: Vol. 4. The gifted child grows up.* Stanford, CA: Stanford University Press.

Terman, L. M., & Oden, M. H. (1951). The Stanford studies of the gifted. In P. A. Witty (Ed.), *The gifted child.* Lexington, MA: Heath.

Terman, L. M., & Oden, M. H. (1959). *Genetic studies of genius: Vol. 5. The gifted group at midlife: Thirty-five years' follow-up of a superior group.* Stanford, CA: Stanford University Press.

Tesch, B. J., Wood, H. M., Helwig, A. L., & Nattinger, A. B. (1995). Promotion of women physicians in academic medicine: Glass ceiling or sticky floor? *Journal of the American Medical Association, 273,* 1022–1025.

Thomson, R. A. (1989). Operation adventure in Wisconsin. *Gifted Child Today, 12*(5), 58–59.

Thorndike, R. L., & Hagen, E. P. (1977). *Management and evaluation in psychology and education.* New York: Wiley.

Thorndike, R. L., Hagen, E. P., & Sattler, J. M. (1986). *Stanford-Binet intelligence scale* (4th ed.). Chicago: Riverside.

Tidball, E. (1986). Baccalaureate origins of recent natural science doctorates. *Journal of Higher Education, 57,* 606–620.

Tieso, C. L. (2002). *The effects of grouping and curricular practices on intermediate students' math achievement.* Storrs, CT: National Research Center on the Gifted and Talented.

Tkach, J. R. (1986, March/April). What to do with a gifted kid this summer. *G/C/T,* 24–25.

Tkach, J. R. (1987, May/June). Perennial problem for parents: What to do with a gifted kid this summer II. *G/C/T,* 6–8.

Tolan, S. S. (1987). Parents and "professionals," a question of priorities. *Roeper Review, 9,* 184–187.

Tomlinson, C. A., & Callahan, C. M. (1994). Planning effective evaluations for programs for the gifted. *Roeper Review, 17,* 46–51.

Tonemah, S. (1987). Assessing American Indian gifted and talented students' abilities. *Journal for the Education of the Gifted, 10,* 181–194.

Tonemah, S. (1991). *Gifted and talented American Indian and Alaska Native students.* Indian Nations at Risk Task Force Commission Papers. Washington, DC: U.S. Department of Education.

Tongue, C., & Sperling, C. (1976). *Parent nomination form.* Raleigh: North Carolina Department of Public Instruction.

Torrance, E. P. (1962). *Guiding creative talent.* Englewood Cliffs, NJ: Prentice-Hall.

Torrance, E. P. (1965). *Rewarding creative behavior.* Englewood Cliffs, NJ: Prentice-Hall.

Torrance, E. P. (1966). *Torrance tests of creative thinking.* Bensenville, IL: Scholastic Testing Service.

Torrance, E. P. (1971). Are the Torrance tests of creative thinking biased against or in favor of disadvantaged groups? *Gifted Child Quarterly, 15,* 75–81.

Torrance, E. P. (1977). *Creativity in the classroom.* Washington, DC: National Educational Association.

Torrance, E. P. (1979). *The search for satori and creativity.* Buffalo, NY: Creative Education Foundation.

Torrance, E. P. (1980). Assessing the further reaches of creative potential. *Journal of Creative Behavior, 14,* 1–19.

Torrance, E. P. (1981a). Creative teaching makes a difference. In J. C. Gowan, J. Khatena, & E. P. Torrance (Eds.), *Creativity: Its educational implications* (2nd ed.; pp. 99–108). Dubuque, IA: Kendall/Hunt.

Torrance, E. P. (1981b). Non-test ways of identifying the creatively gifted. In J. C. Gowan, J. Khatena, & E. P. Torrance (Eds.), *Creativity: Its educational implications* (2nd ed.; pp. 165–170). Dubuque, IA: Kendall/Hunt.

Torrance, E. P. (1981c). Sociodrama as a creative problem-solving approach to studying the future. In J. C. Gowan, J. Khatena, & E. P. Torrance (Eds.), *Creativity: Its educational implications* (2nd ed.; pp. 294–303). Dubuque, IA: Kendall/Hunt.

Torrance, E. P. (1982). *Thinking creatively in action and movement.* Bensenville, IL: Scholastic Testing Service.

Torrance, E. P. (1984). Teaching gifted and creative learners. In M. Wittrock (Ed.), *Handbook of research on teaching* (3rd ed.). Chicago: Rand-McNally.

Torrance, E. P. (1987). *The blazing drive: The creative personality.* Buffalo, NY: Bearly Limited.

Torrance, E. P. (1988). The nature of creativity as manifest in its testing. In R. J. Sternberg (Ed.), *The nature of creativity* (pp. 43–75). New York: Cambridge University Press.

Torrance, E. P. (1995). *Why fly?: A philosophy of creativity.* Norwood, NJ: Ablex.

Torrance, E. P., & Ball, O. E. (1984). *Torrance tests of creative thinking: Streamlined (revised) manual, figural A and B.* Bensenville, IL: Scholastic Testing Service.

Torrance, E. P., & Torrance, J. P. (1978). The 1977–78 future problem-solving program: Interscholastic competition and curriculum project. *Journal of Creative Behavior, 12,* 87–89.

Towers, E., & Porath, M. (2001). Gifted teaching: Thought and action. *Roeper Review, 23,* 202–206.

Traxler, M. A. (1987). Gifted education program evaluation: A national review. *Journal for the Education of the Gifted, 10,* 107–113.

Treffert, D. A. (1989). *Extraordinary people: Understanding "idiot savants."* New York: Harper & Row.

Treffinger, D. J. (1982). Gifted students, regular students: Sixty ingredients for a better blend. *Elementary School Journal, 82,* 267–273.

Treffinger, D. J. (1986). Fostering effective, independent learning through individualized programming. In J. S. Renzulli (Ed.), *Systems and models for developing programs for the gifted and talented* (pp. 429–460). Mansfield Center, CT: Creative Learning Press.

Treffinger, D. J. (1995a). Creative problem solving: Overview and educational implications. *Educational Psychology Review, 7,* 301–312.

Treffinger, D. J. (1995b). Talent development: An emerging view. *Understanding Our Gifted, 7*(4), 3.

Treffinger, D. J., & Feldhusen, J. F. (1996). Talent recognition and development: Successor to gifted education. *Journal for the Education of the Gifted, 19,* 181–193.

Treffinger, D. J., Isaksen, S. G., & Dorval, K. B. (1994a). *Creative problem solving: An introduction* (rev. ed.). Sarasota, FL: Center for Creative Learning.

Treffinger, D. J., Isaksen, S. G., & Dorval, K. B. (1994b). Creative problem solving: An overview. In M. A. Runco (Ed.), *Problem finding, problem solving, and creativity* (pp. 223–236). Norwood, NJ: Ablex.

Treffinger, D. J., Isaksen, S. G., & McEwen, P. (1987). *Checklist for preparing for evaluating thinking skills instructional programs.* Sarasota, FL: Center for Creative Learning.

Treffinger, D. J., & Sortore, M. R. (1992a). *The programming for giftedness series. Volume l: Programming for giftedness—A contemporary view.* Sarasota, FL: Center for Creative Learning.

Treffinger, D. J., & Sortore, M. R. (1992b). *Programming for giftedness series. Vol. II: A process approach to planning for contemporary programming.* Sarasota, FL: Center for Creative Learning.

Treffinger, D. J., & Sortore, M. R. (1992c). *Programming for giftedness series. Vol. III: Leadership guide for contemporary programming.* Sarasota, FL: Center for Creative Learning.

Treffinger, D. J., Sortore, M. R., & Cross, J. A. (1993). Programs and strategies for nurturing creativity. In K. A. Heller, F. J. Mönks, &. A. H. Passow (Eds.), *International handbook of research and development of giftedness and talent* (pp. 555–567). New York: Pergamon.

Trigg, L. J., & Perlman, D. (1976). Social influences on women's pursuit of a nontraditional career. *Psychology of Women Quarterly, 1*(2), 138–150.

Tsuin-chen, O. (1961). Some facts and ideas about talent and genius in Chinese history. In G. Z. F. Bereday & J. A. Lauwerys (Eds.), *Concepts of excellence in education: The yearbook of education.* New York: Harcourt, Brace & World.

Turner, S. E., & Bowen, W. G. (1990, October). The flight from the arts and sciences: Trends in degrees conferred. *Science,* 517–520.

Udall, A. J. (1987). *Peer referral as a process for locating Hispanic students who may be gifted.* Unpublished doctoral dissertation, University of Arizona, Tucson.

Udall, A. J., & Passe, M. (1993). *Gardner-based/performance-based assessment notebook.* Charlotte, NC: Charlotte-Mecklenburg Schools.

Udansky, M. L. (1994, August 30). More kids live in changing family. *USA Today,* A1.

University of North Carolina. (1999). *Cost, quality and child outcomes in child care centers.* Chapel Hill, NC: Author.

University of Wisconsin-Eau Claire. (1992). *The distance learning pilot project for gifted and talented students.* Eau Claire: University of Wisconsin-Eau Claire Education Outreach and CESA 11.

Urban, K. K. (1993). *Test for creative thinking-drawing production (TCT-DP): Design and empirical studies.* Hannover, Germany: University of Hannover.

Urban, K. K., & Jellen, H. G. (1993). *Manual for the Test for Creative Thinking: Drawing Production.* Hannover, Germany: University of Hannover.

U.S. Congress. (1975). *The education for all handicapped children act of 1975.* Washington, DC: Government Printing Office.

Vahidi, S. (1998, Winter). I learn, therefore I am: Descartes ideology in cyberage. *NRC/GT Newsletter,* 5–8.

Vail, P. L. (1990, February). Obstacles to thinking. *Learning90,* 48–50.

VanTassel-Baska, J. (1981, December). *The great debates: For acceleration.* Paper presented at the meeting of the CEC/TAG National Topical Conference on the Gifted and Talented Child, Orlando, FL.

VanTassel-Baska, J. (1983a). Introduction. In J. VanTassel-Baska (Ed.), *A practical guide to counseling the gifted in a school setting* (pp. 1–5). Reston, VA: Council for Exceptional Children.

VanTassel-Baska, J. (1983b). School counseling needs and successful strategies to meet them. In J. VanTassel-Baska (Ed.), *A practical guide to counseling the gifted in a school setting* (pp. 40–46). Reston, VA: Council for Exceptional Children.

VanTassel-Baska, J. (1986). Acceleration. In C. J. Maker (Ed.), *Critical issues in gifted education* (pp. 179–196). Rockville, MD: Aspen Publishers.

VanTassel-Baska, J. (1988). Developing scope and sequence in curriculum for the gifted learner: A comprehensive approach (Part 1). *Gifted Child Today, 11*(2), 2–7.

VanTassel-Baska, J. (1989). The role of the Family in the success of disadvantaged gifted learners. *Journal for the Education of the Gifted, 13,* 22–36.

VanTassel-Baska, J. (1991). Identification of candidates for acceleration: Issues and concerns. In W. T. Southern & E. D. Jones (Eds.), *Academic acceleration of gifted children* (pp. 148–161). New York: Teachers College Press.

VanTassel-Baska, J. (1994). *Comprehensive curriculum for gifted learners* (2nd ed.). Boston: Allyn & Bacon.

VanTassel-Baska, J. (1995). The development of talent through curriculum. *Roeper Review, 18,* 98–102.

VanTassel-Baska, J. (2000). Theory and research on curriculum development for the gifted. In K. A. Heller, F. J. Mönks, R. J. Sternberg, & R. F. Subotnik (Eds.), *International handbook on giftedness and talent* (2nd ed., pp. 345–365). London: Pergamon Press.

VanTassel-Baska, J. (2003). What matters in curriculum for gifted learners: Reflections on theory, research, and practice. In N. Colangelo & G. A. Davis (Eds.), *Handbook of gifted education* (3rd ed., pp. 174–183). Boston: Allyn & Bacon.

VanTassel-Baska, J., Bass, G., Ries, R., Poland, D., & Avery, L. D. (1998). A national study of science curriculum effectiveness with high ability students. *Gifted Child Quarterly, 42,* 200–211.

VanTassel-Baska, J., & Little, C. A. (in press). *Reform-based content curriculum for high-ability learners.* Waco, TX: Prufrock Press.

VanTassel-Baska, J., Olszewski-Kubilius, P., & Kulieke, M. (1994). A study of self-concept and social support in advantaged and disadvantaged seventh and eighth grade gifted students. *Roeper Review, 16,* 186–191.

VanTassel-Baska, J., Patton, J., & Prillaman, D. (1989). Disadvantaged gifted learners: At risk for educational attention. *Focus on Exceptional Children, 22*(3), 1–15.

VanTassel-Baska, J., Zuo, L., Avery, L. D., & Little, C. A. (in press). A curriculum study of gifted student learning in the language arts. *Gifted Child Quarterly.*

Velle, W. (1982). Sex hormones and behavior in animals and man. *Perspectives in Biology and Medicine, 25,* 295–315.

Vernon, M., & LaFalce-Landers, E. (1993). A longitudinal study of intellectually gifted deaf and hard of hearing people. *American Annals of the Deaf, 138,* 427–434.

Vespi, L., & Yewchuk, C. (1992). A phenomenological study of the social/emotional characteristics of gifted learning disabled children. *Journal for the Education of the Gifted, 16,* 55–72.

von Károlyi, C., Ramos-Ford, V., & Gardner, H. (2003). Multiple intelligences: A perspective on giftedness. In N. Colangelo & G. A. Davis (Eds.), *Handbook of gifted education* (3rd ed., pp. 100–112). Boston: Allyn & Bacon.

von Oech, R. (1983). *A whack in the side of the head.* New York: Warner Communications.

Wagner, C. G. (1992). Enabling the disabled: Technologies for people with handicaps. *The Futurist, 26,* 29–32.

Walberg, H. J. (1982). Child traits and environmental conditions of highly eminent adults. *Gifted Child Quarterly, 25,* 103–107.

Walberg, H. J. (1988). Creativity and talent as learning. In R. J. Sternberg (Ed.), *The nature of creativity* (pp. 340–361). New York: Cambridge University Press.

Walberg, H. J., Tsai, S., Weinstein, T., Gabriel, C. L., Rasher, S. P., Rosecrans, T., Rovai, E., Ide, J., Truijillo, M., & Vukosavich, P. (1981). Childhood traits and environmental conditions of highly eminent adults. *Gifted Child Quarterly, 25,* 103–107.

Walberg, H. J., Williams, D. B., & Zeiser, S (2003). Talent, accomplishment, and eminence. In N. Colangelo & G. A. Davis (Eds.), *Handbook of gifted education* (3rd ed., pp. 350–357). Boston: Allyn & Bacon.

Walker, B. A., Reis, S. M., & Leonard, J. S. (1992). A developmental investigation of the lives of gifted women. *Gifted Child Quarterly, 36,* 201–206.

Wallach, M. A., & Kogan, N. (1965). *Modes of thinking in young children.* New York: Holt.

Wallas, G. (1926). *The art of thought.* New York: Harcourt, Brace, & World.

Wallich, P. (1996, March). The analytical economist: Having it all. *Scientific American, 274,* 253–256.

Warren, J. (2002). Iowa Governor's Institute focuses on leadership. *Vision, 9*(1), 1–3. (Published by the Belin/Blank International Center for Gifted Education and Talent Development, University of Iowa, Iowa City, IA 52242.

Warren, T. F. (1974). How to squelch ideas. In G. A. Davis & T. F. Warren (Eds.), *Psychology of education: New looks* (pp. 428–430). Lexington, MA: Heath.

Way, B. (1967). *Development through drama.* London: Longman.

Webb, J. T. (n.d.). *Do gifted children need special help?* (Video). Scottsdale, AZ: Great Potential Press.

Webb, J. T. (1993, August). *Gifted intensity or attention deficit-hyperactivity disorder.* Paper presented at the Seventh National Rimm Underachievement Institute, Milwaukee.

Webb, J. T., Meckstroth, E. A., & Tolan, S. S. (1982). *Guiding the gifted child.* Scottsdale, AZ: Great Potential Press.

Webb, N. M., Nemer, K. M., Chizhik, A. W., & Sugrue, B. (1998). Equity issues in collaborative group assessment: Group composition and performance. *American Educational Research Journal, 35,* 607–651.

Webb, N. M., & Palincsar, A. S. (1996). Group processes in the classroom. In D. Berliner & R. Calfee (Eds.), *Handbook of educational psychology* (3rd ed., pp. 841–873). New York: Macmillan.

Weber, J. (1981). Moral dilemmas in the classroom. *Roeper Review, 3*(4), 11–13.

Wechsler, D. (1991). *WISC-III: Wechsler intelligence scale for children* (3rd ed.). New York: Psychological Corporation.

Wees, J. (1993). Gifted/learning disabled: Yes, they exist and here are some successful ways to teach them. *Gifted International, 8*(1), 48–51.

Weiner, B. (1985). *Human motivation* (2nd ed.). New York: Holt.

Weinstein, J., & Laufman, L. (1981). The fourth R: Reasoning. *Roeper Review, 4*(1), 20–22.

Weiss, P., & Gallagher, J. J. (1980). The effects of personal experience on attitudes toward gifted children. *Journal for the Education of the Gifted, 3,* 194–206.

Werner, E. (1989). Children of the garden island. *Scientific American, 261,* 106–111.

Westberg, K. L., & Archambault, F. X. (1995). Profiles of successful practices for high ability students in elementary classrooms. Storrs, CT: National Research Center on the Gifted and Talented.

Westberg, K. L., Burns, D. E., Gunnins, E. J., Reis, S. M., Park, S., & Maxfield, L. R. (1998, Spring). Professional development practices in gifted education: Results of a national survey. *NRC/GT Newsletter,* 3–4.

Westberg, K. L., Dobyns, S., & Salvin, T. (1992). Regular classroom practices observation results. In J. S. Renzulli (Chair), *Regular classroom practices with gifted students: Findings from the National Research Center on the Gifted and Talented.* Symposium conducted at the meeting of the American Educational Research Association, San Francisco.

White, D. A., & Breen, M. (1998). Edutainment: Gifted education and the perils of misusing multiple intelligences. *Gifted Child Today, 4*(2), 12–14, 16–17.

White, B. L., Kaban, B. T., & Attanucci, J. S. (1979). *The origins of human competence: Final report of the Harvard Preschool Project.* Lexington, MA: Heath.

Whitmore, J. R. (1980). *Giftedness, conflict, and underachievement.* Boston: Allyn & Bacon.

Whitmore, J. R., (1986). Understanding a lack of motivation to excel. *Gifted Child Quarterly, 30,* 66–69.

Wiley, J., & Goldstein, D. (1991). Sex, handedness and allergy: Are they related to academic giftedness? *Journal for the Education of the Gifted, 14,* 412–422.

Willard-Holt, C. (1994). *Recognizing talent: Cross-case study of two high potential students with cerebral palsy.* Storrs, CT: National Research Center on the Gifted and Talented.

Willard-Holt, C., & Holt, D. G. (1997). Multiple intelligences and gifted education. *Gifted Education Press Quarterly, 99*(2), 6–9.

Williams, A. T. (1986, January/February). Academic game bowls as a teaching/learning tool. *G/C/T,* 2–5.

Winebrenner, S. (2001). *Teaching gifted kids in the regular classroom.* Minneapolis: Free Spirit.

Winner, E., & Martino, G. (2000). Giftedness in non-academic domains: The case of the visual arts and music. In K. A. Heller, F. J. Mönks, R. J. Sternberg, & R. F. Subotnik (Eds.), *International handbook of giftedness and talent* (2nd ed., pp. 95–110). New York: Elsevier.

Winner, E., & Martino, G. (2003). Artistic giftedness. In N. Colangelo & G. A. Davis (Eds.), *Handbook of gifted education* (3rd ed., pp. 335–349). Boston: Allyn & Bacon.

Winocur, S. L., & Maurer, P. A. (1997). Critical thinking and gifted students: Using IMPACT to improve teaching and learning. In N. Colangelo & G. A. Davis (Eds.), *Handbook of gifted education* (2nd ed.; pp. 308–317). Boston: Allyn & Bacon.

Witham, J. (1991). A full-time solution to part-time problems. *Gifted Child Today, 14*(6), 10–12.

Witters, L. A., & Vasa, S. F. (1981). Programming alternatives for educating the gifted in rural schools. *Roeper Review, 3*(4), 22–24.

Witty, P. A. (1967). Twenty years in education of the gifted. *Education, 88*(1), 4–10.

Witty, P. A. (1971). The education of the gifted and the creative in the U.S.A. *Gifted Child Quarterly, 15,* 109–116.

Woliver, R., & Woliver, G. M. (1991). Gifted adolescents in the emerging minorities: Asians and Pacific Islanders. In M. Bireley & J. Genshaft (Eds.). *Understanding the gifted adolescent: Educational, developmental, and multicultural issues* (pp. 248–257). New York: Teachers College Press.

Wood, B., & Feldhusen, J. F. (1996, July/August). Creative special interest programs for gifted youth: Purdue's Super Saturday serves as successful model. *Gifted Child Today,* 22–25, 28–29, 40–42.

Woods, S. B., & Achey, V. H. (1990). Successful identification of gifted racial/ethnic group students without changing classification requirements. *Roeper Review, 13,* 21–26.

Working Mother. (2001, May). An ode to working moms. *Working Mother,* 41–44.

Wright, L., & Borland, J. H. (1992). A special friend: Adolescent mentors for young, economically disadvantaged, potentially gifted students. *Roeper Review, 14,* 124–129.

Yawkey, T. D. (1983). *Imaginative predisposition interview scale: Test and administration manual.* Unpublished manuscript, Pennsylvania State University, University Park.

Yell, M. L., & Espin, C. A. (1990). The handicapped children's protection act of 1986: Time to pay the piper? *Exceptional Children, 56*(5), 396–407.

Yewchuk, C., & Lupart, J. L. (1993). Gifted handicapped: A desultory duality. In K. A. Heller, F. J. Mönks, & A. H. Passow (Eds.), *International handbook of research and development of giftedness and talent* (pp. 709–725). New York: Pergamon.

Yoder, J. (1985, September). Gifted education is for rural students too. *NASSP Bulletin,* 68–74.

Yong, F. L. (1992). Mathematics and science attitudes of African-American middle school students identified as gifted: Gender and grade differences. *Roeper Review, 14,* 137–140.

Yong, F. L. (1994). Self-concepts, locus of control, and Machiavellianism of ethnically diverse middle school students who are gifted. *Roeper Review, 16,* 192–194.

Zaffrann, R. T., & Colangelo, N. (1979). Counseling with gifted and talented students. In N. Colangelo and R. T. Zaffrann (Eds.), *New voices in counseling the gifted* (pp. 142–153). Dubuque, IA: Kendall/Hunt.

Zametkin, A. (1991). The neurobiology of attention-deficit hyperactivity disorder. *CH.A.D.D.E.R, 5*(1), 10–11.

Zeldin, A. L., & Pajares, F. (2000). Against the odds: Self-Efficacy beliefs of women in mathematical, scientific, and technological careers. *American Educational Research Journal, 37,* 215–246.

Zentall, S. S., Moon, S. M., Hall, A. M., & Grskovic, J. A. (2001). Learning and motivational characteristics of boys with AD/HD and/or giftedness. *Exceptional Children, 67,* 499–519.

Ziegler, A. & Heller, K. A. (2000). Attribution retraining with gifted girls. *Roeper Review, 23,* 217–248.

Zilli, M. G. (1971). Reasons why the gifted adolescent underachieves and some of the implications of guidance and counseling for this problem. *Gifted Child Quarterly, 15,* 279–292.

Zimmerman, W. E., & Brody, L. E. (1986, March/April). Part-time college for gifted high school students. *G/C/T,* 32–33.

Zinner, J. (1985, June). Thinking makes an IMPACT. *Thrust,* 30–32.

# SUBJECT INDEX